THE MODEL RAILWAY NEWS

CLOCKWORK, STEAM AND ELECTRIC

Volume 1.

THE

THE MODEL RAILWAY NEWS

CLOCKWORK, STEAM AND ELECTRIC

Volume 1.

JANUARY—DECEMBER,
1925.

London :

PERCIVAL MARSHALL & Co.

66, FARRINGDON STREET, E.C.4

Model and Allied Publications,
Argus Books Ltd,
14 St James Road,
Watford, Herts,
England

First published by Percival Marshall Ltd, 1925
This facsimile reprint, 1977

ISBN 0 85242 518 X

Reproduced and printed in Great Britain for the publishers, Argus Books Ltd, by Clarke, Doble and Brendon Ltd, The Oakfield Press, Burrington Way, Plymouth, and bound by Garden City Press Limited, Letchworth, Herts.

Note to this Facsimile Edition

MODEL RAILWAY NEWS was not the first journal to be devoted to model railways, but it lays claim to being the first to deal exclusively with the smaller scales which are now thought of as true 'miniatures' for indoor operation. 'MRN', as it soon became known, first appeared in 1925, as the latest venture of the enterprising Percival Marshall whose publishing house already included *Model Engineer* and many related books. The big growth of scale model railways has kept pace with the progress of 'MRN' ever since, and 'MRN', now under the more abbreviated title of MODEL RAILWAYS, continues to flourish for the benefit of the model railway enthusiast. Back in 1925, 0 gauge was the most common of the small scales and the story of today's most common miniature gauges, 00 and H0, was just beginning. Some of the early controversy which has accompanied the side-by-side growth of the 00 and H0 gauges can be gleaned from this facsimile reprint of the first ever bound volume of MODEL RAILWAY NEWS. For the modern railway modeller, this book gives a fascinating glimpse of the early ideas and development in miniature railway modelling but at the same time it offers a good selection of valuable reference material and information which is still useful today. Here are the first twelve issues of 'MRN' just as they would have been returned to you if you had sent in your copies for binding over half a century ago.

Wonderful Offer of Sundry Track
and Points at "Knock-Out" Prices.

In order to make room for our Christmas supplies, we are clearing out the undermentioned oddments at prices practically below the cost of raw material.

A Unique Opportunity for Model Railway Owners to secure replacements for the coming season.

"SIMPULL" TRACK AND POINTS.

"Simpull" Track is well-known to most model railway users, and consists of wooden sleepers, stained black, and tinned sheet steel rail pressed into shape and sliding into grooves formed in the sleepers. We have now ceased manufacturing this line, and therefore, only what is in stock can be supplied.

60 "SIMPULL" POINTS, Gauge 1, either Right or Left-Hand Turnout. **PRICE, 1/6 each.**
50 "SIMPULL" ELECTRIC STRAIGHT RAILS, Gauge 1. **PRICE, 2d. per length.**
50 "SIMPULL" ELECTRIC CURVED RAILS, Gauge 1, 3 ft. radius. **PRICE, 2d. per length.**
16 "SIMPULL" ELECTRIC POINTS, Right and Left-hand Turnout. Gauge 1. **PRICE, 2/3 each.**

ELECTRIC RAILS (Tinplate).

72 LENGTHS TINPLATE ELECTRIC STRAIGHT RAILS. Gauge 1. These are similar to those we are now manufacturing, but have the centre rail in *tinned steel* instead of brass. **PRICE, 2d. per length**
30 LENGTHS CURVED TINPLATE ELECTRIC RAILS, with terminals. Gauge 1. Continental make. **PRICE, 1d. per length.**

RAILS AND POINTS (Tinplate).

200 LENGTHS CURVED RAILS, 2″ gauge. **PRICE, 1d. per length.**
150 LENGTHS CURVED RAILS, 2½″ gauge. **PRICE, 1d. per length.**
25 RIGHT AND LEFT-HAND TINPLATE POINTS, for straight run; 2½″ gauge. **PRICE, 1/- each.**
15 RIGHT AND LEFT-HAND TINPLATE POINTS, for curves; 2½″ gauge. **PRICE, 1/- each.**
52 SCISSORS CROSSINGS, old radius, tinplate. Gauges 2″ & 3″. **PRICE, 2/6 each.**
32 CROSSOVER ROADS, large radius, tinplate, gauge 2. **PRICE, 3/- each.**
34 DOUBLE LINE JUNCTIONS, gauges 1¾″ & 2″, tinplate. **PRICE, 4/- each.**
15 THREE-WAY POINTS, gauge 1, tinplate. **PRICE, 1/6 each.**
72 RIGHT AND LEFT-HAND POINTS, 2″ & 2½″ gauge, for curves. Tinplate; from large to small radius. **PRICE, 1/- each.**
11 RIGHT AND LEFT-HAND POINTS, 2½″ gauge, for curves. Tinplate; from large to small radius. **PRICE, 1/3 each.**
28 LENGTHS HALF-RAILS, 2″ gauge, tinplate. **PRICE, 2/- the lot.**
32 LENGTHS HALF-RAILS, 2½″ gauge, tinplate. **PRICE, 2/6 the lot.**
300 LENGTHS CURVED HALF-RAILS, 2″ gauge, tinplate. **PRICE, 1/3 per doz.**
150 LENGTHS CURVED HALF-RAILS, 2½″ gauge, tinplate. **PRICE, 1/6 per doz.**

BRASS "LOWKO" TRACK.

30 POINTS, RIGHT AND LEFT-HAND, 2″ gauge, brass "Lowko" track, 7 ft. 6 in. radius. **PRICE, 1/9 each.**
35 ACUTE ANGLE CROSSINGS, 2″ gauge, brass "Lowko" track. **PRICE, 1/- each.**
24 ACUTE ANGLE CROSSINGS, 2½″ gauge, large section brass "Lowko" track. **PRICE, 1/6 each.**

The prices of the above items are so low that it would be worth while for the model maker to buy them and take them to pieces, just for the material.

Final Offer of L.N.W.R. BRAKE-THIRD COACHES.

We have now only 53 Gauge O L.N.W.R. Brake Thirds left in stock, and are prepared to sell these at the low price of **7/6 each,** carriage paid. They are the standard vehicle as per our catalogue, 13 in. long, and originally sold at 15/–.

N.B.—*All the above items—with the exception of the coaches—are Carriage Forward, but they can be delivered free to our London Branch, 112 High Holborn, for those purchasers living in London who could arrange to call for them.*

BASSETT-LOWKE LTD.

LONDON BRANCH
112. HIGH HOLBORN. W.C.1

NORTHAMPTON

EDINBURGH BRANCH
1. FREDERICK STREET.

BING ELECTRIC TRAINS

Look for this Brand Mark on all Metal Toys.

are correct in every detail

Every part of the Bing Miniature Railway systems is a working model, exact to the smallest detail. There are Electric, Steam, and Clockwork Engines, Rolling Stock, Tracks, Points, Sidings, Buffers, Signals, Signal Boxes, Stations, Bridges, Tunnels, etc. At a moderate cost you can purchase a whole table railway service, or build one up from sep rate parts. Whichever you do, you will find Bing is the most absorbing hobby and the most interesting method of imparting accurate mechanical instruction. See them at your nearest dealers to-day and ask for the FREE Bing Catalogue; it is packed with illustrations of the complete range of these fascinating models. In case you cannot get your copy write to address below.

Send now for the complete Catalogue of Bing Models

NG ADVERTISING DEPT. 2, LINCOLN HOUSE, HIGH HOLBORN, W.C.1.

A SPECIAL OFFER

TO GAUGE 1 ENTHUSIASTS.

SCALE MODEL 4-4-0 EXPRESS ENGINE AND TENDER (Clockwork—Gauge 1).

SPECIFICATION:

Frames. Planished steel, with footplates and super-structures of pressed steel.

Wheels. Scale pattern. Cast iron, with nickelled treads and standard flanges.

Movement. Best quality four-coupled spring-mechanism, fitted with latest pattern governor, two-speed gear, brake and reverse.

Handsomely finished, hand enamelled and lined; can be supplied in the colours of the old L.N.W. Railway, also G.W. Railway. Price, post free - - **70/-**

Our profusely Illustrated Catalogue of Scale Models (R.N.4) will be sent post free on request.

Hamleys

Estd. 1760.

HAMLEY BROS. LTD.

Pay us a visit and inspect our stocks for yourself.

200/202, REGENT STREET, W. 1.

Branches throughout London.

GAMAGES

THE MODEL ENGINEER'S SHOP

Wonderful display for Model
:: Enthusiasts of all Ages ::

SEND FOR MODEL ENGINEER ILLUSTRATED CATALOGUE FREE

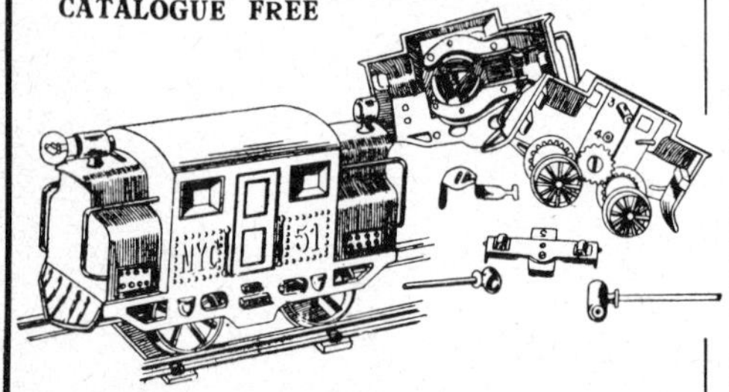

The DORFAN Loco-Builder,

O GAUGE MODEL. There are only nine major parts to this new Loco-Builder, and we have tried to make it as easy as possible for you to put them together; the only tool you need is a screwdriver. The parts are all numbered, and full instructions and diagram go with each set, As Illustration, **18/6.** Also set No. 2, which makes a Motor as well as a Loco. Price **25/-**

The "Gamage" Rustless Steel Scale Model Permanent Way. **The finest and most realistic Track on the market.**

Rail is made from finest Rustless Steel.
Chairs and Fish Plates are of Oxydized Spring Steel.
Sleepers and Battens are made from selected and seasoned wood, of the same thickness and width throughout

	Per Length.
Gauge 0. Curves, 12 to circle of 4 ft. diam ...	**1/3**
Gauge 1, ,, 16 ,, ,, 6 ft. ,, ..	**1/6**
Gauge 0. Straight, 12 in. long	**1/3**
Gauge 1. ,, 12 in. ,, ...	**1/6**
Gauge 0. Crossings, ... Each.	**7/6**
Gauge 1. ,, ...	**8/6**
Switches with Lever, as used on the L.N.W.R. to-day	
Gauge 0. Right or left .. .. .. Each.	**11/6**
Gauge 1. ,, ,, ...	**12/6**
Rail only, in lengths of 3 ft. .. **5/-** doz. lengths.	
Chairs, spring steel	**2/6** per 100
Slip Chairs, fitted with brass angle-plates	**1/3** per doz.
Check-Rail Chairs, spring steel ...	**8**d. per doz.
(The last two are for use only on Points).	
Cast Check-Rail Chairs	**1/6** per doz.
Gauge 0 Sleepers	**3/6** per 100.
Gauge 1 ,, ...	**3/9** per 100.
Battens, in 3 ft. lengths	**4**d. per pair.
Holding-down Spikes	**6**d. per pkt.

Postage extra under 20/-

A. W. GAMAGE, LTD., HOLBORN, LONDON, E.C. 1

City Branch: BENETFINKS, CHEAPSIDE, E.C. 2

Index

GENERAL INDEX TO VOLUME 1

The asterick (*) *denotes that the subject is illustrated with photographs. The dagger* (†) *denotes that the subject is illustrated with drawings.*

A. C. Shaw & Co., Ltd., 7, St. John's Lane, Clerkenwell, E.C.

The MODEL RAILWAY NEWS

Editorial and Publishing Offices :
66, FARRINGDON STREET, LONDON, E.C. 4.

Single Copies, post free, 7½d. Annual Subscription, 7s. 6d.

Vol. I. No. 1. JANUARY, 1925. Price, 6d.

Notes of the Month.

CORDIAL GREETINGS to all model railway enthusiasts! We hope that No. 1 of the MODEL RAILWAY NEWS will please you and that you will rally round and give your whole-hearted support to the new little journal.

* * *

We do not pretend that our first issue is perfect—first issues never are. It will, however, give you a good idea of the lines on which we intend to proceed, and if you respond, as we hope you will do, with photographs and descriptions of your models, with interesting correspondence, and with questions for our experts to answer, our pages will become more helpful to you every month. Please remember that we want this to be *your* paper, and we look to every one of you to regard himself as the special correspondent for his own particular model railway. Tell us about your new developments and extensions; of your new locomotives and rolling stock; of your new tunnels, stations, bridges, and signalling arrangements; of any constructive work you have carried out; and of all the little gadgets and improvements you have devised and made. Help us to make this a real *news* paper for the model railway world.

* * *

We want you to keep an eye on the big railways, too. As you travel about you will notice some change in real practice that your model railway friends ought to know about. It may be a new type of engine or a new station or bridge, or it may be only an alteration in the pattern of a ventilator or a door handle. A snapshot, if you have a camera, or a sketch, or even only a few lines of description will be an item of news which the model railway world will be glad to have. Your recompense will be the knowledge that you are helping fellow model railwaymen; they in turn will be glad to help you in a similar way through our pages. Remember always when you are travelling that you are a correspondent of the M. R. NEWS, and look out for items of interest for the next number.

* * *

There is a point about real railway photographs worth noting. We do not need photographs which are merely picturesque views of real railway scenes, or which show an express train at full speed. The model railwayman wants something of a different kind. He wants constructive detail, and a clear picture of the end-on view of a new coach, or a "close-up" of a tunnel-mouth or a signal gantry is more helpful to him in making the detail of his own railway accurate than any number of merely pretty pictures.

* * *

This paper gives you one advantage which you may not at first sight realize. The fact that you are a reader immediately makes you a member of the model railway family the world over. You are no longer an isolated enthusiast ploughing a lonely furrow; in your fellow-readers you have friends everywhere, anxious to know what you are doing and willing to help you when you are in a technical difficulty. It will give you a new interest in your own model railway, and you will feel encouraged to improve and develop your installation so that yours may become as good as the other fellow's.

* * *

We want to make it quite clear that in inviting contributions from our readers, we are asking for them on a voluntary basis for the general good of the model railway hobby. It is only by very economical management that such a specialized paper as this can make ends meet, and there is no margin for the payment of general contributors. We believe, however, that model railway men in general are sufficiently interested in their hobby to give for the benefit of their fellow-readers as much useful information as possible as some slight acknowledgment of the information and assistance they receive in return. Co-operation must be the key-note of the MODEL RAILWAY NEWS, and only by co-operative effort on all sides can it be produced successfully. We are glad to say that the leading firms in the trade have promised their help very willingly. While we shall not lend ourselves to any unjustifiable "boosting" of trade products, we shall regard it as part of our duty to keep our readers regularly informed as to the doings of the trade, and as to interesting new goods which are placed on the market from time to time.

* * *

How many model railway clubs are there in this country? We only know of three—the Model Railway Club of London, the Wimbledon Model Railway Club, and the new club at Mill Hill School. If any others have been formed we should be glad to hear about them. Now that the M. R. NEWS provides model railway men in any district with the means of getting acquainted, we have no doubt that the club movement will develop rapidly. Mr. A. W. H. Pealling, of 108, Forest Road, Dalston, would like to get into touch with model railway enthusiasts in his district with a view to forming a local club. Later on we shall publish the rules of the Model Railway Club of London, which will serve as a useful basis for the constitution of any new local club.

* * *

While on the subject of clubs, we should like to give Wimbledon members a well-deserved pat on the back. They are chock full of enthusiasm, and their first exhibition, which is fully reported elsewhere in this issue, went with a swing. Excellent competition work and good track running showed how capable the members are, and we shall look for big developments to come. It was obvious that some good staff work had been put in by the officers and committee, and we offer them our sincere congratulations on their *debut* as exhibition organizers.

* * *

Interest in model railway construction is steadily growing in the U.S.A. and Canada. Several visitors from across the Atlantic last summer took home British-made models and drawings of locomotives and rolling stock. We expect soon to hear of model railway clubs in New York and in Chicago.

* * *

Model railway engineers will much regret to hear that Mr. James C. Crebbin has been very ill. Latest reports indicate an improvement in his condition, but it will be some little time before he is completely fit again. Meanwhile, we are glad to report that he has been unanimously re-elected chairman of the Society of Model and Experimental Engineers. Mr. Crebbin's famous model locomotive, "*Cosmo Bonsor*," recently celebrated its twenty-first birthday, and achieved a world's record for a model by reaching a total of 70,000 passengers hauled on the track.

Model Railway Engineering as a Hobby.

Special Interview with Mr. G. P. Keen

(*President of the Model Railway Club*)

EVERY model railwayman in London knows Mr. G. P. Keen, the popular president of the Model Railway Club. At least, everybody ought to know him, for there is no member of the model railway world who is a greater enthusiast in his hobby, or who has a greater desire to see model railway interest develop and to help fellow-enthusiasts along the road to success. Mr. Keen is the life and soul of the Model Railway Club; he has a cheery greeting for every member, he is full of helpful advice and practical suggestions, and he is always bringing some example of his own work to the meetings to shew that good and original construction can be done, and how it was done. When we told Mr. Keen about our plans for The MODEL RAILWAY NEWS, he said, "Splendid! Come along and have a chat about it."

Mr. G. P. Keen.

We took an early advantage of this invitation, and fired off a pretty big question for a start.

"What do you think of model railway engineering as a hobby?"

"Well, you know what I think—I love it. I have been at it from my boyhood's days. My father, who was a great yachtsman, was a splendid mechanic, and I think I inherited my fondness for engines and making things from him. It is a great relief for me to get away from the worries of business to the restfulness of my model railway. I am just starting on a new railway which is going to take me about three years to complete. Model railway building has a peculiar advantage over other mechanical hobbies in this respect, it is not all precision work. If you are tired and do not feel fit enough to tackle the very accurate details, there is always some less exacting work to be done which you can carry on comfortably. You can keep the precision work for those hours when hand and eye and brain are all working well together."

"What about the expense?" we asked.

Here Mr. Keen rather surprised us. "Well," he said, "I call it a poor man's hobby—so much can be done with so little in the way of equipment. I know men who do some first-rate work with only a few tools—a few files, a hand-drill, a soldering outfit, and so on. All sorts of scrap material can be worked into models, and some of the cheaper kinds of rolling stock can be improved out of all knowledge by the addition of realistic details here and there."

"But surely," we replied, "it needs a good deal of mechanical skill to do this."

"Yes and no," said Mr. Keen. "It does need care and patience, I admit, but almost anybody can do it. Too many model railway people are afraid of tackling their jobs—they are beaten before they start. Over and over

First stage—before Ballasting.

again I have persuaded the doubtful ones to try something they have been afraid of. They have surprised themselves with the results and, encouraged by their first success they have gone on to better and bigger things. Some people spoil their work by lack of finish. Blobs of solder here and there, and bad paint work ruin the appearance of an otherwise very creditable production. I have taken a model locomotive suffering from these defects and by removing the old paint, scraping away all the superfluous solder, and re-painting it with a nice dead-black, have converted it into a really good-looking job.

"Now, Mr. Keen, please tell us something about your new railway, What is your general scheme ?"

"I am glad you ask me about my general scheme. I think every model railway ought to be thoughtfully planned ; it ought to be something more than a mere collection of tracks and stations, and rolling stock. It ought to have an idea behind it. In my own case I have imagined that my house and garden are a country which requires a railway system. It is a manufacturing country producing manufactured iron and steel, importing ore for these industries, and also exporting coal. By reason of my track being planned to finish on a higher floor level than the starting point there will be steep gradients corresponding to a hilly country. The locomotives will, therefore, be of a type suitable for hauling heavy freight over these gradients, and my rolling stock will be specially designed to deal with the ore and the heavy steel castings and forgings for which transportation is desired. I have rather a fancy for designing and building wagons for carrying out-of-gauge loads, and my new railway will give me plenty of scope in this direction. I shall not follow any existing type of rolling stock very closely. It will be an entirely free-lance system, except that it will all be designed to conform to accepted good engineering practice, and possibly I may show some leaning towards North-Eastern types of wagons. Every country needs a food supply and passenger service, and, of course, provision for fish and meat traffic and for excursion trains will be made on my model system. In the small section of track I have already put down, there are over 4,000 sleepers, to carry four main lines, and ten sidings. The sleepers are correctly laid to one-inch centres, and are ballasted with granite chips passed through a one-eighth-inch sieve."

"What motive power do you propose to use ?" we asked.

Second stage—Ballasting complete.

Model G.C. Tank Locomotive built by Mr. Beeson, Junr., for Mr. Keen.

" Electricity. I am convinced that there is a big future for electrically operated model railways. Clockwork and steam both have their merits, but electrical power and electrical control have a very great fascination, as well as affording cleanliness and convenience. It is quite possible to employ electrical lighting and signalling on a clockwork or steam railway, while even a steam locomotive may be electrically controlled. In fact, I think that the application of electricity to model railway working offers far more scope for interesting experiment than does the reception of wireless broadcasting, which has temporarily stolen the affections of so many model makers."

" And the colours for your stock ? "

" I am adopting my own colour scheme, holly green with gold lining for coaches and dead black for locomotives. Here is a sample. I am enlisting the aid of my wife for the lettering on the rolling stock. See, this is the last wagon she lettered for me."

We examined a very nicely lettered truck, and casually asked if Mrs. Keen ventured on any more mechanical work. " Oh, yes ! " said Mr. Keen with a smile. " She is becoming quite a skilled turner on a small precision lathe, and has already turned up some of the clack-boxes and other details for my new locos."

" How long will it be before your railway is finished ? "

" Never," said Mr. Keen, mysteriously. " I think a model railway should always be complete, but never finished. It should always be complete enough to run its contemplated service, but it can never be finished, because there will always be alterations, additions and renovations to be carried out. If you are a real model railwayman you have a never-ending source of interest in your model railway. I think, however, I have about three years' work in front of m before my general lay-out is completed, and the whole scheme is in running order."

" How long will the completed system be ? "

" I estimate that there will be an end-to-end run of about 600 feet. I have a complete indoor loop, with deep and shallow water quays, warehouses, cranes, sidings, a repair shop, and an excursion terminus. This also serves as a testing loop, and for indoor running during the winter months. The main line will branch off through an opening in the wall into the garden, where, after a complete detour, it will

An 0—8—4 Tank Model for banking trains to main line.

mount a stiff incline into the conservatory to the other terminus. You can see that I am planning a pretty extensive system, and it will take quite a long time to construct."

" Just a final question, Mr. Keen—how is the Model Railway Club getting along ? "

" Fine—the members are a splendid lot of fellows, there are no cliques; everybody is willing to help everybody else and we have some rattling good evenings together. Sometimes we need a " stunt " of sorts to quicken the enthusiasm, or someone has to be prodded to get up and talk at a discussion, but the material is all there, and perhaps it is just a little natural modesty which keeps it back. We always give new members or visitors a cordial welcome, and are glad for them to join us. The MODEL RAILWAY NEWS is just what we want to bring all model railwaymen together: I think it is splendid of you to take the trouble to produce it, and we, of the Model Railway Club, will back you up all we possibly can."

Some Beginners' Questions.

When anyone first gets the happy idea of putting down a model railway of his own, he is confronted with several important questions. He is not like the expert who knows exactly what he wants to do and how to set about it. The beginner has only got the idea that he would like to have a model railway; he is probably not sure what kind of a railway will best suit his pocket, or the space at his disposal, and if he starts on the wrong lines, he may become very disappointed with the results.

Here are some of the questions which many beginners would like to have answered :—

(1) What are the respective advantages of steam, electric and clockwork systems ?

(2) What space is necessary for a reasonably good system ?

(3) How do steam, electric and clockwork systems compare in cost of installation and upkeep ?

(4) What is a convenient form of initial lay-out which can be gradually extended and developed ?

(5) What are the relative merits of the various gauges ?

(6) What is the minimum outlay on which a decent start can be made ?

(7) What are the relative advantages of indoor and outdoor systems ?

Perhaps some of our more experienced readers may like to reply to one or more of these questions for the benefit of newcomers into the model railway world.

A Scale Model 0 Gauge Solid Fuel Tank Engine.

By C. L. Bennett.

Mr. C. L. Bennett's Model L.B.S.C. Solid Fuel Tank Engine.

I THINK I am right in saying that I believe this to be the first scale model 0 gauge solid fuel loco to be built. By this I mean of an existing prototype and not a free-lance design. The prototype is one of the smallest at that, working on the Brighton section of the Southern Railway, viz.: the D 1 class tank 0—4—2 designed by William Stroudley.

As originally sketched out (scale dimensions were to be rigidly adhered to), it was to be driven by an oscillating cylinder in the cab and spirit firing; but before I started it the merits of fire-tube and water-tube boilers were discussed at some length in the *Model Engineer*, and then I wondered if it were possible to make a successful solid fuel loco in 0 gauge. As I had not heard of one, I thought it was worth trying, so with this object in view I set to and designed boiler and motion to work as near as possible to the real thing. Many were the interesting and tricky problems encountered, especially in designing the two cylinders with slip eccentric reversing gear to fit in the limited space between main frames ($\frac{27}{32}$ in.), and from the photo it will be seen that the scale appearance has not suffered; in fact, from the end view at first glance it is hard to believe that it is not the prototype itself.

When first tested the only item requiring attention was the blast pipe, which was a trifle high. When this was altered the engine more than came up to my greatest expectations; then to minimize stoking I scrapped the trailing axle and fitted wheels on studs and fixed a false firebox bottom in place of ash-pan.

The only parts purchased were one dozen $\frac{1}{16}$-in. nuts and four white-metal driving wheels (these are to be replaced with built-up steel wheels), everything else being made from raw material, including screws, the two trailing wheels being built up.

The chassis measures $8\frac{11}{16}$ in. and is built of brass with chief joints riveted and screwed. Slots are cut in the frames to accommodate the cylinders, which are machined from a block of gun metal and are $\frac{5}{16}$-in. bore by $\frac{1}{2}$-in. stroke. These have phosphor-bronze faced valves working underneath. Covers are fitted to each cylinder, by four $\frac{1}{16}$-in. screws. The piston-rod glands are of the screw-in type $\frac{3}{16}$ in. by 40 T.P.I., the valve spindles being of the studded type. Each crosshead has two slide bars, and the little end of connecting rod is fixed to the inner face of crosshead, the big ends being fitted with brasses. The slip eccentrics are connected to the valve spindles by rockers to enable motion to clear front coupled wheels axle. Driving pins for eccentrics are fixed to the semi-built-up crank shaft, and all steel wearing parts are casehardened.

The boiler is a piece of $1\frac{1}{4}$-in. by $5\frac{5}{8}$-in. by 26 gauge S.D. copper tube, one end of which is opened out for $2\frac{1}{4}$ in. to form the outside shell of the firebox, which has water on all sides, and throat plate, front tube plate and dome are silver soldered in. The inner firebox is built up of 26 gauge copper with tube plate, two $\frac{5}{16}$-in. tubes and firehole ring all silver soldered so as to form a single unit; the back plate is flanged and screwed. The fittings are :—Water gauge ($\frac{5}{32}$-in. glass) pressure gauge, blower valve, regulator (steam from dome) and check valve.

The cab, bunker, side tanks, splashers, lamp brackets and coal rails are all made from "cocoa tin," with water holes which are made to open, built up and silver soldered. The casing for the dome is made in two pieces.

The smokebox is built up of brass and silver soldered throughout, the door being a press-in fit, and is equipped with petticoat, ring blower and a modified type of steam union. The model is painted umber with letters cut from gilded tin-foil.

Below I give a few results I have so far obtained :—

Starting from "all cold" the length of run is about five minutes, by which time the water is exhausted, as the hand-feed pump is not yet finished. With firebox full of charcoal and a sprinkling of anthracite on top the loco has pulled a load of $10\frac{1}{4}$ lb. at 40 lb. per square inch, on a six-foot length of track, and this with valves leaking owing to grit. It has run light on 15 lb. per square inch and maintained this pressure with fire nearly burnt out. Also when running light with firebox full and water $\frac{1}{4}$ in. above firebox crown—and pressure at 15 lb. per square inch—the gauge needle has risen to 45 lb. per square inch, at which pressure the safety valve is at present set to blow off.

The cylinder lubricator, hand pump, scale steel wheels and $\frac{1}{2}$-in. pressure gauge have yet to be completed, details of which I hope will be given in the near future.

Signal Cabin Names in America.

In America, where train despatching was performed by telegraph messages, the signal "towers" or cabins were generally designated by one or two initial letters, for convenience and brevity in transmitting orders. With the widespread adoption of the telephone for this purpose, specific names have been found of greater utility than call letters. Most of the towers of the Pennsylvania railroad system have therefore been renamed, with place names as a general rule. In one case, where a geographical name was not applicable, the tower has been named after a retiring servant, Conductor Ragan, who has been with the company over 51 years.

A. W. LINE.

A Good Story.

An Irish locomotive driver in America was reprimanded by the superintendent for making out his report at too great a length. He was told not to waste the time of the head office, but to send in something short and to the point. A few days later he had a derailment, so he sent in this report to the chief—"Off agin, on agin, away agin—Finnigan." One of his mates had a similar inspiration when a tube burst. He wired—"On number two, a busted flue, what shall I do? O'Donnohue." If you know any good model railway stories, send them along, a smile is good for us all.

The Possibilities of 00 Gauge.

By A. Stewart-Reidpath.

A Southern Railway combined Kitchen and Dining Saloon in 00 Gauge.

THERE can be no doubt that 00 gauge has an enormous number of advantages over larger-gauge model railways, among which are its small size and portability. In this latter respect it should be the means of making the model railway hobbyist a much more sociable person. Imagine one's fellow model "railwayac" arriving one evening for an hour or two's time table running with a miniature Feltham yard in an attaché case. One could become a veritable perambulating Swindon with a small Gladstone bag or a suit case. A friend of mine arrived to see me a few days ago with, apparently, nothing, but he eventually produced quite a respectable goods train from his various pockets.

Perhaps a few words on the subject may prove helpful to some of the readers of this Journal and if the following suggestions and observations help to settle some doubts and dispel some fancies my object in thus appearing in print will have been achieved. If at the same time I happen to tread on anyone's "pet corn" please do not regard it as personal, as I am not criticizing. A querist in the *Model Engineer* asked "Why make it 3½-mm. scale." Well, it was originally decided to experiment with half-0 gauge, and the experience gained during these experiments decided the scale. A scale of ⅛" proved to be just too small for efficient tractive power and 4-mm. or $\frac{3}{16}$" scale revealed that the saving in space required for a layout (which is one of the main objects in the introduction of this new gauge) would have been considerably less in proportion, as the ratio of square to linear measure is an important item often overlooked when discussions on scale arise. Halve the scale and you quarter the area. For instance, I have a plan for a most elaborate layout in 00 gauge which is accommodated very comfortably in 10 ft. by 7 ft., *i.e.*, 70 square feet. The same layout in 0 gauge, which is only twice the scale, would require 20 ft. by 14 ft., which is 280 square feet. The $3\frac{1}{2}$-mm. scale has proved to be the happy medium for this small gauge and is not by any means as awkward as it sounds, also it is mathematically more convenient than fractions of an inch.

Quite a number of correspondents have asked for locomotives of G.W.

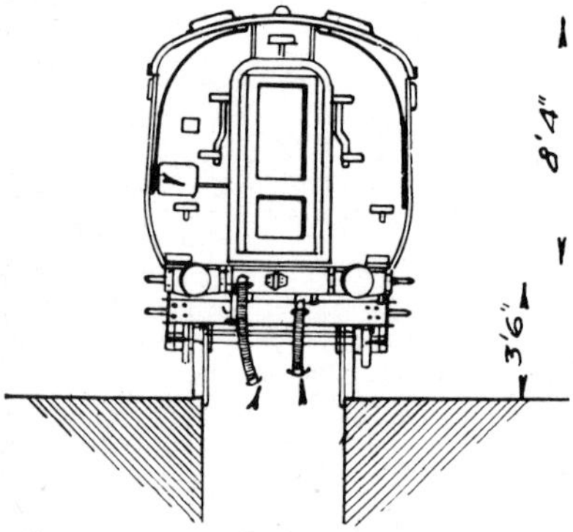

End view of Dining Saloon.

type—very nice! But much as I personally admire the G.W. and all that appertains thereto, their tapered boiler does not take kindly to the new patent spring-driven mechanism which is at present the only really powerful clockwork drive evolved. This mechanism uses the whole of the boiler space, and the G.W. engines have boilers which at the smoke box end are really very small in diameter.

With the Editor's kind permission I will deal with this mechanism in detail in a subsequent issue. At present I can only state that a loco fitted with it is now undergoing tests and has, up to date, pulled two pounds and will run over one hundred feet with one wind. It is fitted with reverse from cab or track, self-releasing treadle brake, combined variable speed and hand brake in cab, also free-wheel action.

Blue Prints.

A blue print of standard measurements based on $3\frac{1}{2}$-mm. scale can now be obtained (Marshall, Stewart & Co., price 1*s.* 3*d.*, post 2*d.*), which shows clearly all the necessary clearances for use with the new all-brass permanent way now on the market.

Wheels.

A word about wheels. I cannot see the necessity or advantages of wheels having treads 5-mm. wide even for the German made tin-plate sets. A wheel of this size could quite well be used for 0 gauge tinplate track without any risk. It is not only unsightly, it is bordering on the ridiculous. It means that if such a wheel were used it would be impossible to build a model having scale outlines or even approaching scale. By using built-up permanent way, wheels having treads $1\frac{1}{2}$-mm. wide and flanges 1-mm. deep can be used with confidence, the only important point being that track must be well and truly laid. My experience has proved that in almost every case of complaint about wheels being bad and causing derailments it is nothing to do with the wheels, it is purely bad track and point work. A model railwayite of my acquaintance,

Internal view of Southern Railway Dining Saloon in 00 Gauge.

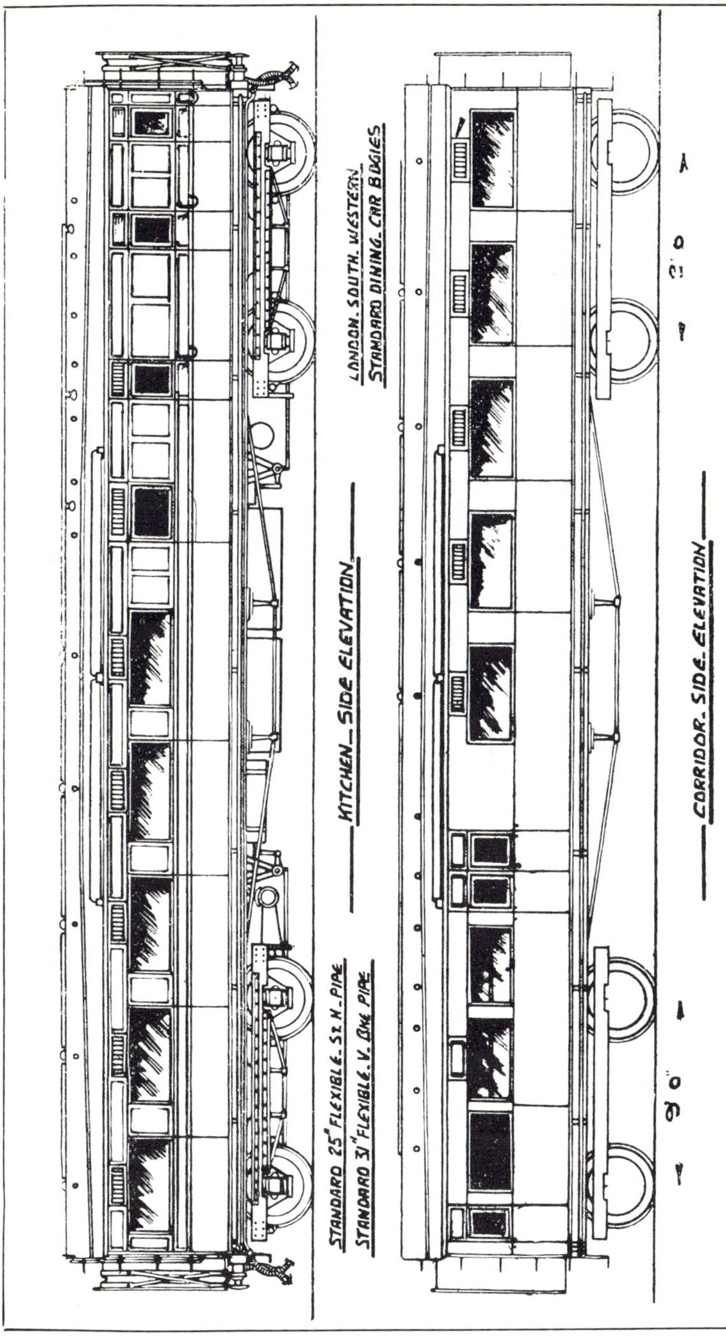

Drawing of Southern Railway Combined Kitchen and Dining Saloon, in 00 Gauge.

(From Marshall, Stewart & Co.'s Blueprint).

who is a prolific builder of very good locos and rolling stock, told me that he was "fed up" with the positively awful wheels now being turned out and "what could I suggest." I went and had a look at his line with the result that the said line has been entirely relaid. A tramline after a very late company meeting is straight compared with what that line was.

Again, certain critics have said that detail work is impossible in this scale. I beg to differ. An examination of the accompanying photograph reproduced will reveal the fact that practically every detail can be included, as the dining saloon illustrated is complete with properly laid tables, upholstered seats, photographs on the walls and other internal detail, working vestibules are also included, whilst the underframes and bogies are complete with all brake gear, dynamo, truss rods, steam and vacuum pipes, etc. The coach is strictly to scale length and will negotiate a two-feet radius curve with ease. A drawing of this coach is also reproduced approximately three-quarter full size, but the reproduction does not include the table of principal measurements and colour details as shown on the original drawing which, together with those for other coaches, locos, points, cross-overs, etc., are obtainable as blue prints (full size).

In conclusion, I hope that these few notes will encourage those amateurs who have been in doubt to produce some high-grade model locos and rolling stock. A few points I should like to emphasize are :—

Scale is a thing that matters and it is possible to work to it. Detail is worth the trouble and time it takes, even if it is only for the sake of saying "it's all there"

Lay your track carefully and accurately, although it may be a tedious job, you will save yourself much nervous strain when you eventually get to the running of trains. (This applies to other gauges as well as to 00.)

Always work to drawings and see that they are good ones, a few more pence spent on a good drawing is money well spent.

And, for the love of Mike, never say "That's near enough."

A Model 0 Gauge Bogie Property Truck.

By Henry Greenly.

FOR carrying theatrical scenery and other effects the L.N.W.R. some years ago produced at their Wolverton works some excellent bogie "property" trucks fitted up for working on passenger trains and built with coach bogie frames and wheels. These trucks are over 50 feet long, and are arranged in the same style as the standard four-wheel carriage trucks. They can, therefore, be employed for carrying road vehicles as well as theatrical properties. The trucks are perhaps a little long for the average model railway, but there is no reason why this should not be curtailed to suit the exigencies of any particular line, without spoiling the general effect of the model.

The under frame is of simple construction. A floor board about $\frac{5}{32}$-in. thick and 53 mm. wide, the whole length of the coach, forms the basis of the framing. This should be stiffened by the headstocks, solebars and five transomes. The bogie-pin transomes should be a little deeper than the others, being made flush with the lower surface of the solebar members. The projection of the bogie transomes will depend on the "brand" of bogie employed—that is, if the frames

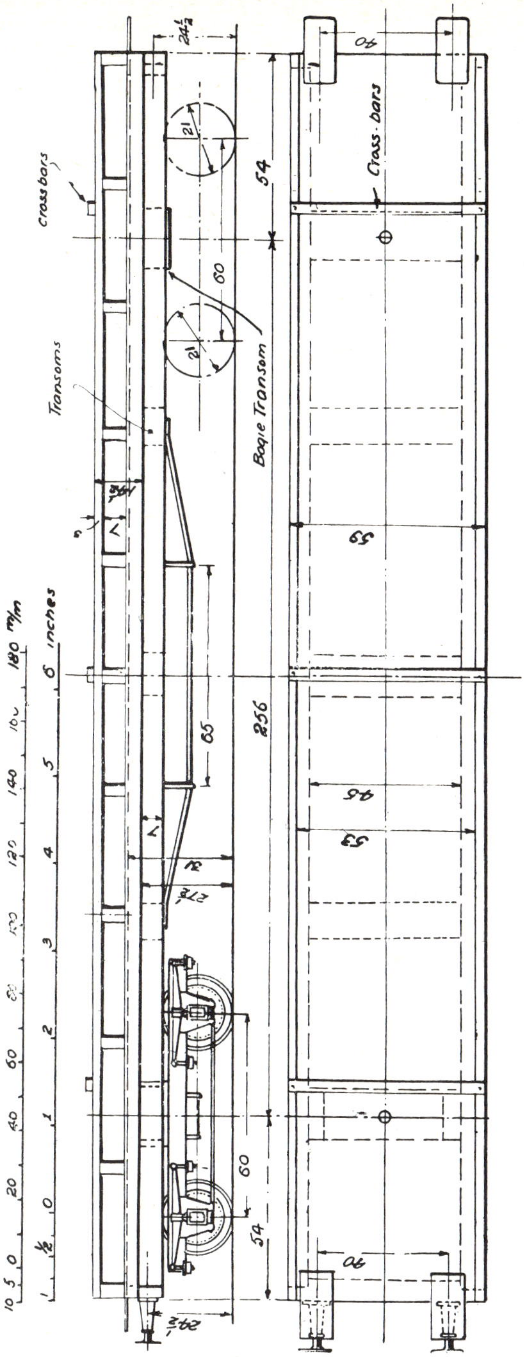

Design for a Model 0 Gauge Bogie Scenic Property Truck.

By Henry Greenly.

are not made by the builder of the wagon. The details of these should be available at the outset, as the wheel bases of various model carriage bogies in No. 0 gauge differ and it may be necessary to modify the drawings to suit the bogies. The end (leading and trailing) wheels should not be more than 24 mm. away from the faces of the headstocks. The sides of the truck are an open post and rail scheme. These should be made from the main body of the vehicle and, when completed, planted on to the sides of the underframes. In full-size carriage trucks the cross-bars are loose fittings and are adjustable for position. In the model they may be fixed and form a firm support to the side rails. Tread plates made o thin sheet tin or brass are necessary over each of the buffers. These are used for loading cars and carriages from platform carriage-docks. Oval buffers and pivoted (side-swinging) couplings are, of course, recommended, as in other examples of bogie passenger vehicles. The painting, lettering and lining may be made to suit the owner's requirements, but a very pleasing effect is produced by painting the outside of the body a chocolate or dark lake colour with a buff interior and black for the iron work and fittings.

Hints on Starting a Model Railway.

"MAKE haste slowly" is a good motto when beginning to put down a model railway. Otherwise you may change your mind when the railway is half-built, and you will then want to pull it up and start all over again.

First consider well the space at your disposal. It may be in an attic, or a sitting-room, or a basement. There may be doors, cupboards, or windows to be taken into account. Survey the space well and decide how much of the room you will ultimately be able to use. Then, having decided upon your guage, take a sheet of paper and plan out a really good system; not the system you are going to complete at once, but the one to which you will eventually attain. Put down a portion of the system first, enough track to give you some decent running, but only a portion of the entire system. Then build gradually up to your original ideal. Experience may cause you to modify your ideas as you go along, but it is better to be adding constantly and wisely to a small system in the light of experience, than to have to undo work on which many hours have been spent.

If your available cash is limited, start with a modest equipment, but let it be the best you can afford to buy. There is so much you can build yourself. If you purchase only one locomotive and a few feet of track, that is a start. You can add more track by degrees; you can add a second running road to give you an up and a down line; you can add a few sidings or a loop. You can build a station, an engine shed, some signals, a bridge. You can always be adding something for the cost of a few simple materials and an extra tool or two. There is always something to do in building or improving your rolling-stock. The pleasure of model railway engineering comes as much from the planning and constructing as it does from the running of the trains, and there is no other hobby so varied in the pleasurable jobs it affords for clever fingers. Wood working, metal working, painting, glazing, upholstering, bridge building, landscape modelling, electric lighting, and dozens of other jobs have to be tackled, and they are all very interesting and instructive too. Additional locomotive and rolling stock can be purchased or built from time to time. If you have bought a good model locomotive at starting, you will have set yourself a good standard to work up to.

Make a friend of your model railway ; let its construction be a labour of love, doing a little bit at a time and doing it well. Don't hurry to get it done ; let it be always growing and always improving. Keep your eyes open when you are travelling on real railways. Here and there you will see some bridge or tunnel-mouth, or station building, or some small fitting, which pleases your eye. It may be a big job or only a tiny detail, but it pleases you, and you go home and reproduce it in miniature on your own line.

If you start a model railway in the right way, you are creating a friend and companion for yourself, not for the duration of a few hours, but for many years, perhaps for a life time.

A 2½-in. Scale L.N.E.R. Electric Locomotive.

A model 2½-in. Scale L.N.E.R. Electric Locomotive.

THIS locomotive is a scale reproduction, as far as the principal outer details are concerned, of a standard 4—6—2 Pacific, and was built by Messrs. Bassett Lowke, Ltd., to the order of Mr. Brunner.

It is equipped with a standard " A " size Lowko-type motor, with an eight-pole drum armature, exactly as sold to the public in the ordinary way. The motor is wound to run on 16 volts A.C. and takes 2 amps. It is fitted in the boiler barrel, but is not attached to the boiler, being actually supported by brackets built into the framing, and the whole is so arranged that by removing two screws in the smoke box the complete boiler barrel may be slipped forward, leaving the motor, reverser, and the driving gear open for inspection and adjustment.

The motor is geared on to the middle axle through a correctly proportioned and properly hobbed bronzed worm wheel and steel worm. The latter is ·625 diameter, four threads, ·166 pitch, ratio of the gearing 9—1. The drive is so arranged that the worm shaft has a bearing at each end of the worm, thus supporting the worm close to its work.

The locomotive is built to take a minimum radius of eight feet, this being accomplished by widening the main frames at the rear and permitting of increased pony-truck play, and further by slightly reducing the diameter of the bogie wheels.

On the track under test the locomotive, running on 16 volts, starts easily, and pulls a dead weight behind the tender of 114 lb. Any increase of the load above this weight produces wheel slip at starting. On loading-up the locomotive itself with lead wieghts up to 30 lb., a dead weight of 160 lb. behind the tender was started and pulled easily at a good speed without any sign of wheel slip, the total dead weight thus being 190 lb.

A Model Express Electric Motor Coach.

By Henry Greenly.

THE accompanying design illustrates a type of vehicle which is already, in a measure, a feature of our electrified railways. True, coupling rods are not employed, as it is usual to fit motor bogies with a separate motor for each axle. However, single-motor bogies are used in several continental electric vehicles, and for a model is the most efficient arrangement that can be adopted.

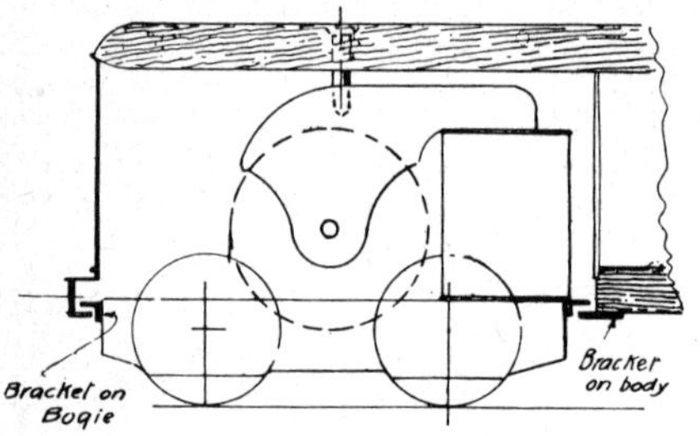

Retaining lugs for Motor Bogie.

In the drawing herewith a specially made large single field-coil motor is suggested. The magnet for this could be built up of wrought iron or mild steel, the maximum width over field-coil and armature being about 19 mm. (¾-in.), with armature of 45 mm. (1¾-in.) diameter. This should make an extremely efficient power unit and allow a simple single reduction gear to be used. On one side of the motor the brass bearing plate would form the side frame F1. The other side frame of the motor (F) would be made of the same material, but would only extend to footplate level. Above this would be arranged the armature-shaft bearing on the commutator side of the motor. This would be bent outwards, as shown, to accommodate the block of insulating material (B) carrying the brushes. The frame F1 supports the pinion, idler-wheel, and, of course, embraces the driving and coupled axles. The former passes through one of the limbs of the field magnet and thereby secures the whole mechanism into a self-contained unit.

The front portion of the motor coach is made of metal, to provide the maximum space for the motive mechanism to swing in. The roof, however, is made of wood, and is a continuation of the roof of the coach.

As the electro-motor occupies the whole of the centre of the bogie, the best method of pivoting this to the coach, is undoubtedly through the roof. A stout screw can be fixed into the roof timber and engage a hole drilled in the iron field magnet, to retain the bogie in position—but, at the same time, allowing it a perfect free movement on curves and over a rough track. A pair of clips, one at each end of the motor bogie, may be arranged, similar lugs on the buffer plank and coach floor when the vehicle is lifted. The motor end of the coach may be painted and lined to represent the driver's and rheostat compartments of the coach.

Ready-made motor mechanisms complete with wheels and coupling rods can of course, be obtained, and

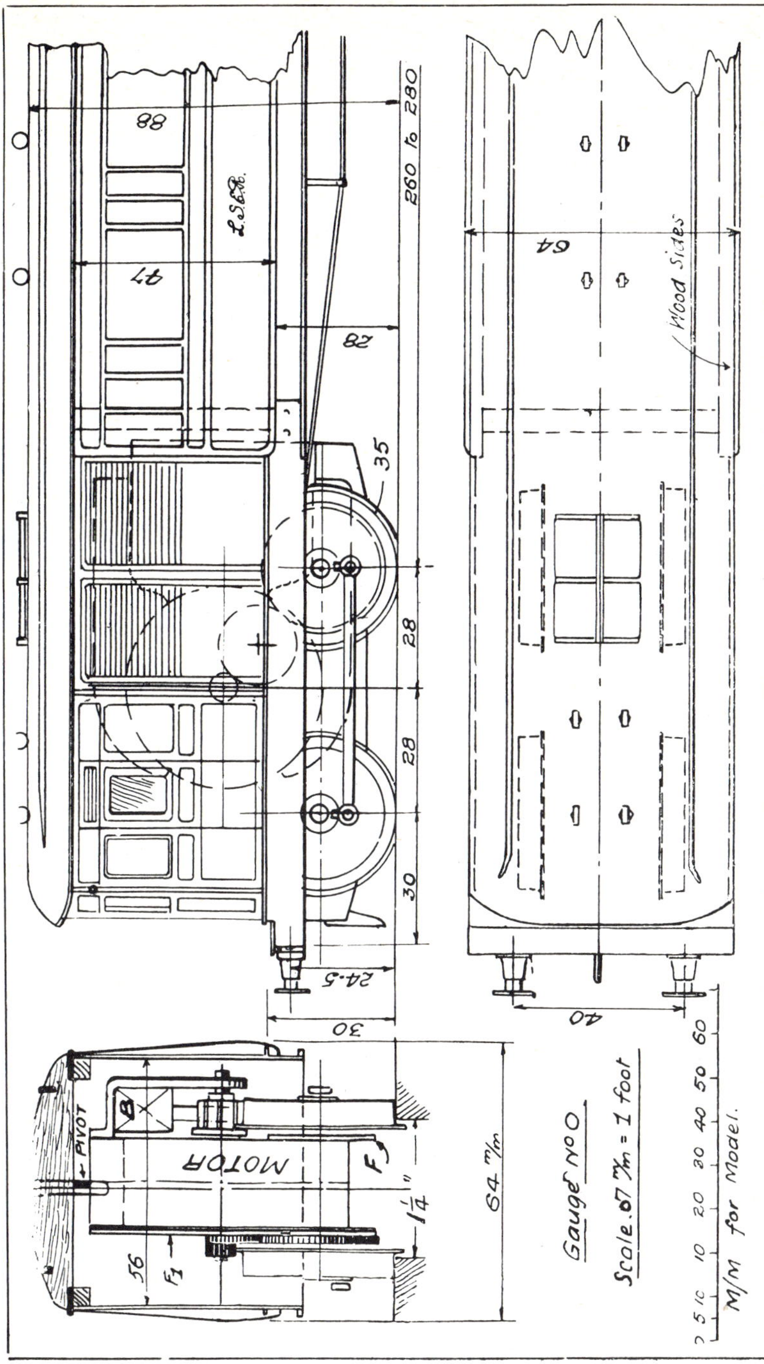

A design for a Model Express Electric Motor Coach for 0 Gauge.

By Henry Greenly.

could be fitted into a motor coach in much the same way as the motor indicated in the accompanying drawing. These mechanisms are usually of the permanent magnet type and can, therefore, be reversed by changing over the direction of the current in the usual way. Where a wound field magnet motor is employed, a separate polarized reverser is necessary. This can be housed inside the coach, in any convenient position, the "contractor" compartment being increased in length if necessary.

A Successful Exhibition at Wimbledon.

THE first competition and social evening of the Wimbledon Model Railway Club was held on Monday, December 1st, at the Red Cross Hall, Church Road, Wimbledon. After a strenuous half-hour of arrangement by a small "working party," the doors opened at 7.30 p.m., and visitors, members and models began to arrive. By 7.45 the entries for the "Shephard Cup" and competition were all arranged on the club track and the loan section and trade models suitably disposed in other parts of the hall. A large number of members, with their relatives and friends, had by this time arrived, and everyone was pleased to see that Mr. Percival Marshall, the Editor of the *Model Engineer* and founder of the M.R. NEWS was present.

There was an excellent show of models, and the competition entries are as follows :—

Mr. A. Knock. (1) 7-mm. scale, 0 gauge U.S. Great Northern, 4—6—2 locomotive, electric drive; (2) 7-mm. scale, 0 gauge electric L.S.W.R., 4—6—2 tank loco, No. 516, and goods stock; (3) "Humane pattern" American stock car, 0 gauge, 7-mm. scale; (4) L.S.W.R. restaurant car, with all interior fittings, 7-mm. scale, 0 gauge. All these are "super-detail" models.

Mr. A. E. Lilley. Southern Ry., Pullman car, 0 gauge, internally fitted.

Mr. H. E. Doe. (1) 0 gauge L.M.S.R. 4—4—0 rebuilt loco "Lord Glenarthur," electric drive; (2) 0 gauge, breakdown crane, electric drive.

Mr. S. Warren. ½-in. scale, 0—4—4 tank loco, steam.

Mr. A. R. Walkley. 00 gauge, 3½-mm. scale, 2-road level-crossing lay-out (signalled).

The following models were in the loan section :—L.Y.R. 4.40 express, L.S.W.R. 0—4—4 F class tank and L.S.W.R. rail motor coach, all 0 gauge, clockwork. By Mr. Thomson Clark. 3½-mm. scale, electric wharf crane, harbour lighthouse, and 00 gauge, railway components. By Messrs. F. D. and A. R. Walkley.

The trade section :—Messrs. Marshall Stewart, 209, Balham High Road, S.W. 17, were showing some wonderful 00 gauge models, including an internally fitted Southern (L.S.W.R.) restaurant car with all table fittings, etc., a standard 4—6—2 tank loco with ingenious clockwork mechanism, signal box, track, etc., all demonstrating the possibilities of accurate scale work in this small gauge.

Mr. L. A. Richards, 23D, Merton Road, Wimbledon (near theatre), was showing a selection of the Leeds Model Co.'s 0 gauge components, including locos, rolling stock, track, blue-prints, etc. Literature was available on both stands.

At 7.45 p.m. ballot papers were distributed to members, who then recorded their votes in connection with the competition. Mr. Marshall and Mr. Braen kindly consented to take charge of the counting and shortly after 8 o'clock the president, Mr. T. B. Stoakley, announced the results and in a few well-chosen remarks introduced Mr. Marshall, who presented the prizes. Mr. Marshall said that it gave him great pleasure,

Mr. Percival Marshall hands the Cup to Mr. Knock.

as a former resident in Wimbledon, to take part in the proceedings and he congratulated the club on the excellent quality of the exhibits, and thought Wimbledon had set a very good example to other districts. As far as he knew, this was the only model railway club outside Central London—at any rate in the South of England.

The prizes were then presented as follows :—

(1) Mr. W. H. Shephard's cup for best work—0 gauge American loco. By Mr. A. Knock.

(2) One guinea presented by Mr. H. H. Hudson for second best work —0 gauge L.S.W.R. loco. By Mr. A. Knock.

(3) Half-guinea presented by Mr. C. F. Cook for signal work—00 guage level crossing lay-out. By Mr. A. R. Walkley.

(4) Half-guinea presented by Mr. C. F. Cook for coach work—0 guage L.S.W.R. restaurant car. By Mr. A. Knock.

(5) Half-guinea presented by Mr. C. G. T. Plume for goods rolling stock—0 gauge American stock car. By Mr. A. Knock.

The hearty applause during the presentations clearly showed that Mr. Knock's somewhat wholesale appropriation of the prizes was fully deserved, and his subsequent announcement that he wished to present one of the prizes for competition among the junior members was much appreciated. Mr. Marshall then said that he was much impressed by the sporting spirit shown, both by the way the results had been received and by Mr. Knock's generous proposal. He felt sure that the other members were not discouraged and would put all their energies into work for the next competition. (Applause.) He concluded by wishing the club all success in the future.

Mr. T. B. Stoakley, seconded by Mr. R. Shephard, then proposed a vote of thanks to Mr. Marshall, which was enthusiastically accorded. Mr. Stoakley said they were indeed pleased to see the large number of visitors present, and he wished to thank Mr. Marshall and all those who had taken part in the evening's proceedings. Also he would like to take the opportunity of thanking Mr. and Mrs. Shephard for their efforts on behalf of the club, particularly in connection with the recent successful whist drive. Mr. R. Shephard said he was sure that all members were grateful to Mr. Marshall for his kind remarks and interest in the club. He mentioned that several members had taken positions in the railway world and had no doubt that recent improvements in services, etc., on certain lines was a direct result of this. (Laughter and applause.) He felt that competitions of this kind did much to stimulate interest in model railway work.

The press photographers then "got busy," and photos of the visitors and members, the prize winners and models were duly taken. A move was then made to the "refreshment department," where Mrs. Knock and Mrs. Ashmole, who had kindly consented to officiate, were kept extremely busy. During this time the test track was cleared, steam was raised, keys produced and, shortly afterwards the track was in full operation. The following members were running locos. during the evening:—Mr. H. Cook was in charge of the track. Mr. Lamb, half-inch scale coal-fired 4—4—2 free lance loco. Mr. Lilley, gauge 0 clockwork. Mr. Knock, gauge 0 American and L.S.W.R. 4—6—2 tank locos. (prize winners), towed by Mr. Shephard's 4—4—0 clockwork. Mr. Clark, L.S.W.R. loco. 0 gauge clockwork. Mr. Walkley, 00 gauge 2—4—0 tank, clockwork.

These, in particular Mr. Lamb's half-inch scale steam loco., aroused great interest.

The Wimbledon and District Model Railway Club hold their meetings the first and third Mondays each month at the Red Cross Hall, Church Road, Wimbledon, at 7.30 p.m. The Hon. Secretary, Mr. R. Shephard, 27, Bernard Gardens, S.W. 19, is always pleased to give full particulars to prospective members.

A. R. W.

An Indoor 1¾-in. Gauge Model Railway.

By P. Ransome-Wallis.

THIS model railway first started in 1913 in the form of a dozen German-made tinplate rails and a German-built 0—4—0 steam engine. After the war steps were taken to build a model railway with some attempt at realism, so the tinplate rails were scrapped and a large amount of "Lowko" track bought in parts. When assembled this made a very good and serviceable track. The acquisition of a top room (too good to be called an attic), about 15 feet square, made it possible gradually to build up the line as it is to-day. The track is laid out on trestle tables at a height of about three feet from the floor.

The accompanying plan is, I think, sufficiently clear to show the principle on which the line is worked. The main line is, at present, only a single road, and consists of rustless steel permanent way. With some difficulty the "Lowko" track was made to fit in for some of the sidings, while the goods yard is laid out in "Simpull" track. The curves leading to this yard are severe, but since it is never used for fast trains it answers quite well. The line is ballasted with marble chippings; these are, however, too large, and are being replaced by coarse grit, of the kind given to poultry.

There are two stations, " Braintree " and " Saffron "—both termini. Both stations have booking offices, waiting-rooms, bookstalls, automatic machines, lavatories, advertisements, etc. The booking-offices and waiting-rooms are made out of an old set of " Dometo " bricks and look very well indeed.

The line has to pass through a half-demolished cupboard, the shelves of which are indispensable; in order to keep a realistic appearance this part of the line was covered in. A good strong piece of canvas, arranged in an irregular shape, glued and painted, made an ideal tunnel, and the tunnel-mouths were once the entrances to a tin-plate bridge.

The present "Braintree" Station.

The Signal.

The signals, with two exceptions, are home-made, on the principle of Bassett-Lowke's scale models, and are all worked, as are the points, from signal cabins, of which there are four. At the entrance to the tunnel is an experimental colour-light signal. The current is supplied from a dry battery in " B " signal cabin, and the two bulbs are lit alternately by means of a two-way switch, which also has an " all-off " position. I am making two more of these signals for inside the tunnel; the present one works very satisfactorily. My locomotives are four in number, two steam and two clockwork. The former are an M.R. 0—4—0 tender engine and an L.N.W. 2—2—2 tender engine. The clockwork models are an M.R. 4—4—0, No. 483 (Bassett-Lowke), and an M.R. 0—6—0 shunting tank engine I have recently wired the track with an electric circuit so that when a train enters a section it causes a red light to show in the signal cabin controlling that section.

The large photograph of Braintree Station shows it in its original condition. It has since been much improved by the addition of a roof and a new platform. A new five-arm signal has been introduced, controlling the three-way junction leading to

"Braintree" Station before being completed.

A portion of the Main Line.

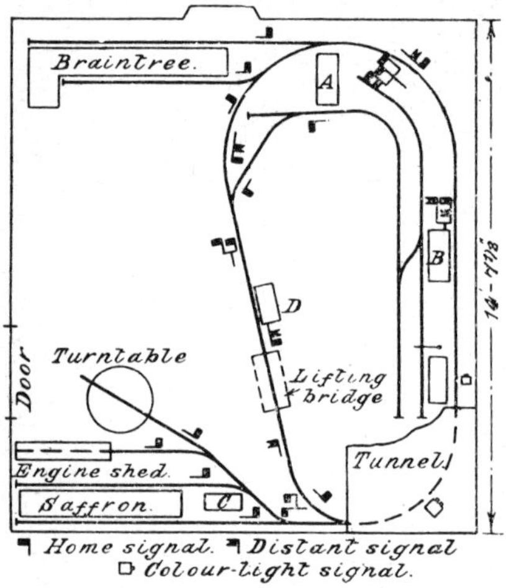

Plan of the System.

Braintree Station, and the junction signal cabin has been changed from a six to a 12-lever frame.

In conclusion, I should like to say how very pleased I shall be to have visits from any model railway enthusiasts and to show them the working of the line.

You can only make sure of getting the MODEL RAILWAY NEWS by ordering it in advance from your newsagent, or sending a subscription direct to our office. No surplus copies will be printed.

Model Railway Terminal Station Plan.

By J. A. DEAN.

WITH regard to the No. 0 gauge terminal station plan on page 45 of the August issue of *Junior Mechanics*, I enclose a drawing of a scheme which I consider eliminates certain faults it contains. These may be enumerated as below :—The arrival trains are unable to enter platforms 1 and 2 without running on No. 3 and then shunting on to departure line, and then going to Nos. 1 or 2 platforms. This means great delay in dealing with a number of trains quickly.

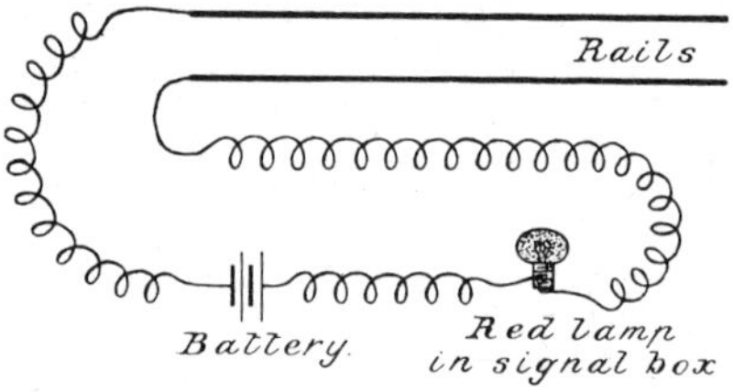

Electric Circuit for Signal Lamp.

No siding for spare locomotive to take out arrival trains when ready for departure. A siding for holding at least one large passenger express loco or two tank locos should be provided.

The Lifting Bridge.

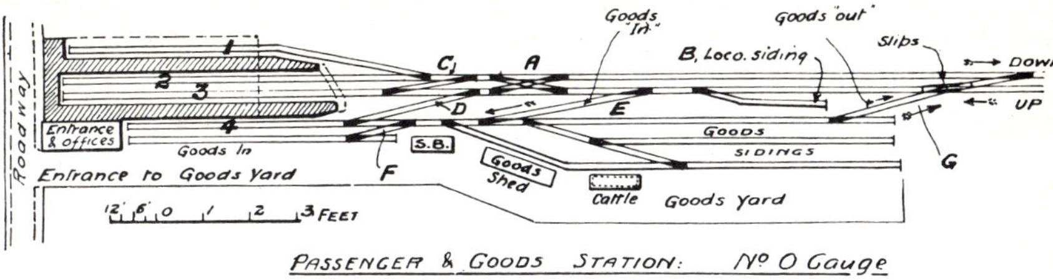

Scheme for a Model Railway Terminal.

Goods road from crossover to goods shed. This portion is too long relative to the portion from crossover to stop blocks nearest station building. From the scale the short portion is only 18 inches. The portion from crossover to shed is 36 inches. If the goods wagons are shunted over by a loco then the wagons would have to be brought up to goods shed by hand or capstan. My improved design has a passenger station comprising four platforms, and arrival trains can be run to platforms 1, 2, 3 or 4, or depart from any platform without any shunting.

A. Scissor crossing. Trains for platforms 1 and 2 use this crossing.

B. Locomotive siding. Locomotives can back on to any passenger train from this siding.

C. If desired, this crossover can be left in. Train can leave No. 3 platform whilst one is entering No. 4 platform.

D. Road to No. 4 platform.

The departures may be made as follows :—

From platform 1.—By point near crossover at C direct on to down line.

From platform 2.—Train already on down line.

From platform 3.—By crossover C or scissor crossing at A.

From platform 4.—Over crossover D and crossing A.

When a train departs, the remaining locomotive is run out of the station to the siding at B. This method always ensures having an engine ready for every train.

Goods trains enter the depot by the crossover at E, proceeding to crossover at F. A long goods train can be held between the station offices and the signal box. The train can then be shunted into the goods sidings without taking the engine off.

For the lighter goods and cattle a special loop is provided. Wagons can be loaded or unloaded without interfering with the mineral portion of goods yard. The crossover at F is an optional connection with platform road No. 4, for which there is no real need. When ready, a departing goods train is shunted on to the goods departure road. The engine is then run on to the proper end, by means of crossover E, to the down line by the single slips near G road, and backed on the goods train, clear of the catch points. With the exception of putting engines on to the departing goods trains, the goods traffic does not interfere with the working of passenger trains. The sidings for coaches could be placed off the down line.

[The plan referred to in the reply to query was not intended to be the last word in terminal-station design, but was a suggested improvement to a plan sent to us. We, however, welcome your excellent further development of the scheme, but it must be noted that it requires a space 16 feet in length.—
Editor, M. R. News.]

Track and Wheel Standards for 0 Gauge.

By Geo. Winteringham.

AS this size model railway has now become the most popular for indoor use, probably a few words regarding the track and wheel standards will not be altogether out of place. The writer has always taken great interest in model railways, the permanent way in particular, and was the originator of the first real scale model-track that was ever turned out as a commercial article. Perhaps a short account of how this came about may be of interest, more especially to some of the older readers of the *Model Engineer*.

At one time the writer and his family were living on board a yacht of about 250 tons, lying in the Hamble River, near Southampton.—a somewhat curious place to have a workshop and be making a model railway, but here it was that the first permanent-way was designed and manufactured.

A large deckhouse had been converted into a workshop, and in it a small railway to a scale of five-sixteenths of an inch to the foot, and one and a half inches gauge was being constructed for the amusement of the youngsters. A photograph of some of the rolling stock for this railway appeared in Vol. IV, page 135, of the *Model Engineer*.

Early Experiments.

Of course, the question of what sort of track should be used was an important one. Several experiments were carried out and all sorts of things considered and discarded. A good many feet were laid of one-eighth round tinned iron wire, soldered into little flat tin chairs and nailed down on to wooden sleepers. (*See* Fig. I.) This was not very successful; the points and crossings proved anything but satisfactory and gave a great deal of trouble in fitting up. This experiment convinced the writer that round rails are the very worst possible shape for model railways, and so the whole thing was scrapped, and one-eighth square iron substituted. These square section rails were fixed down in the same way as the round ones, and were a perfect success in every way, the points and crossings gave no trouble whatever, and although the wheels of the rolling stock had only little flanges of about one-thirty-second of an inch deep, they would run at a tremendous pace over the points and round curves without derailment.

Twenty-five Years ago.

It was some remarks which appeared on the Editor's page of the *Model Engineer* of November 15th, 1900, Vol. III, page 307, and again in Vol. IV, page 41, which attracted the writer's attention and caused him to consider the track question more seriously. Here an enthusiast from Newcastle was complaining that he was unable to obtain any suitable railway lines in England, but had to get them from Germany. This was replied to on page 89 of the same volume by some English manufacturers, who stated that they made large quantities of these goods and would be pleased to supply samples to interested persons. The writer, being a particularly interested person, obtained the said samples. They consisted of ordinary tin-plate rails, a piece of bar iron about five-sixteenths by three-thirty-seconds of an inch, as far as can be remembered, and a piece of drawn brass, the section of which was a very poor resemblance of a flat-bottomed or flanged rail.

There was no suggestion of chairs, fishplates or sleepers, or any means of fixing the rails down, making points and crossings or anything of that sort.

This settled matters, and after a little further consideration it was decided to get out drawings of a proper track to a scale of three-quarters of an inch to the foot, the standard adopted by The Society of Model Engineers.

The rails were to be of hard-drawn brass of bull-head section, the chairs and fishplates cast in a special hard white-metal alloy, the sleepers of good quality red deal, the keys of mahogany, and the spikes of hard brass. The particulars of design were

Fig. 1.—The unsatisfactory round rod track.

taken from standards adopted by the big railway companies.

Having finished the drawings, moulds were made for the chairs and fishplates. These proved entirely satisfactory, but it very soon became evident that if there was anything like a big demand for the track it would be quite impossible to keep up the supply by ordinary hand-casting methods; therefore, a machine worked by hand and treadle was designed and built. This worked well after a little adjustment and produced chairs as fast as the metal would set, the rate being about fifty a minute. This machine is still intact and used when required.

It was decided to trade as George and Co., of Hamble, Hants, and under this name a sample piece of track three and a half inches gauge was laid and sent to the Editor of the *Model Engineer* for inspection, and on February 1st, 1902, Vol. III, page 72, he very kindly gave it a favourable notice.

About this time orders commenced to come in, the notice just referred to in the *Model Engineer* undoubtedly being the chief reason, and a good and steady demand for the track continued.

In 1903, negotiations were opened with a well-known firm of model engineers and it was arranged for them to take over the sole agency. At the same time the workshop on the yacht was given up and the manufacturing transferred to new premises close to the agents. Here, a year or two later, the smaller size permanent way was brought out, the scale of this being about half an inch to the foot, and this track proved in every way to be as good as the larger one.

About 1912 the writer realized that this track, although small, was absurdly large for 0 gauge models and commenced to get out a smaller one. of about 7 mm. to the foot. This got as far as the production of the rails, but owing chiefly to opposition of interested persons on the ground that it was much too small and that the wheel flanges and treads would also have to be so small that there would be nothing but derailments, and the whole thing would be a failure both mechanically and commercially, its

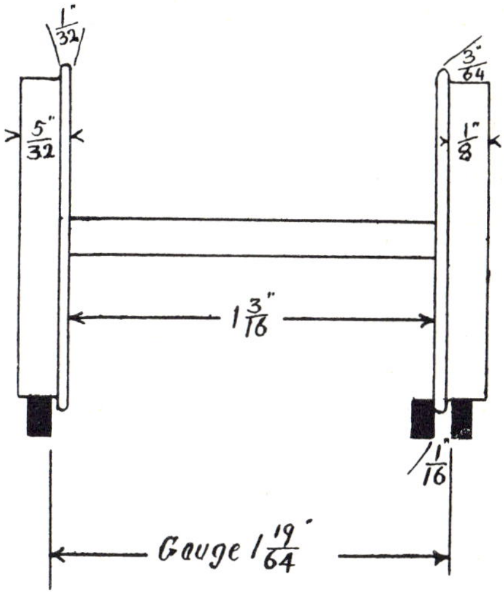

Fig. 2.—Wheel dimensions for 7mm. track

production was, therefore, abandoned.

Soon after that came the war, and the writer forgot all about models and got interested in high explosives, shells, etc., but the old love is returning: hence this article.

To make new standards and get them adopted is not usually an easy matter, but unless alterations are made from time to time it is practically impossible to go ahead and improve things, whether it be model railways or anything else.

Wheel standards for 0 gauge railways have been more or less fixed by manufacturers for some time past, these no doubt being very suitable for the purpose for which they were intended, namely, for the ordinary commercial engines and rolling stock of the tin-plate variety, and intended in most cases to run on the standard tin-plate rails, or something similar. These standards, however, are totally unsuitable for anything pertaining to a working scale model; they provide the wheels with treads and flanges very much larger than necessary, which completely spoil the whole appearance of both engines and rolling stock; in fact 0 gauge locomotives often look more like road rollers than railway engines. Generally speaking, the average model 0 gauge track is such a poor affair and so badly laid that the wheel flanges have to be of abnormal proportions to make the vehicles keep the track at all.

Wheel Standards.

The writer has proved to his own satisfaction over and over again that small model rolling stock and locomotives fitted with wheels having flanges of not more than three sixty-fourths of an inch deep will keep the track over points and round curves at high speeds, provided that the rails are of suitable section and properly laid, that the wheels are true and correct to dimensions, and the vehicles are provided with springs or other arrangements to keep the wheels down on the rails, and this proviso is the crux of the whole thing.

The scale used for 0 gauge, as most people are aware, is 7 mm. to the foot, therefore $1\frac{1}{4}$-in. gauge does not really represent the English standard of 4 ft. $8\frac{1}{2}$ in. It should be $1\frac{19}{64}$-in., and this is not absolutely correct, but the error is so small as to be negligible.

The dimensions, Fig. 2, were those fixed in 1912, by the writer, when preparing the 7-mm. scale track already referred to and were only arrived at after giving the matter considerable thought and making numerous experiments; they are obviously not absolutely to scale, but are considered near enough for any really well-made model railway. Probably any further reduction in the flanges, etc., would only give derailment trouble and perhaps complete failure of the whole model railway. The adoption of these standards is confidently recommended to any one making a proper model railway to a scale of 7 mm. to the foot, and it will not only be the general appearance of the engines and rolling stock that has been improved, but the whole working and running will be found incomparably superior in every way to models made to larger standard wheel and track measurements.

Home-made Tracks.

For a home-made track the type to be described is very suitable for any amateurs to make and lay down, as it does not require a great deal of skill, and only a very few tools will be found necessary. It will look well and when complete give excellent results.

It is merely an improvement upon the track laid with $\frac{1}{8}$-in. square rails referred to in the earlier part of this article, the only difference being that the rails are $\frac{1}{8}$ in. by $\frac{1}{16}$ in.

Either brass or mild steel may be used; both can be purchased in straight lengths from some of the firms whose advertisements appear from time to time in the *Model Engineer*.

As to which is the best metal to use for model railway lines is a somewhat difficult question to answer. As far as the actual running of the models is concerned, there is absolutely no difference whatever; they will run equally as well on one as the other. But one thing is certain: brass rails and fittings are much the best to use out of doors or in damp rooms. Where iron or steel is used, in spite of rust-proofing and all that sort of thing, rust will set in, particularly where it is most harmful, and that is wherever the rails have been cut at the joints or filed and fitted up for the points and crossings, etc.

It is often said that steel looks so much more realistic than brass, but does it ? When a real railway is laid the rails, fish-plates and chairs, etc., are generally a reddish-brown rust colour all over and get more so as time goes on, with the exception, of course, on the top and edge, which become brightened by friction of the wheels passing over them.

Models laid with steel rails never look like this, but are usually more or less bright all over, or a kind of zinc colour, excepting where rust sets in, and then that frequently attacks them on the running surface, just where it is not wanted, as well as where they have been cut or filed.

Brass rails certainly do not look in the least realistic when new, but after a time they tone down and become a dull colour and do not look at all bad. However, the choice of material may be left to individual taste.

A Model Railway at Mill Hill School.

THE boys of Mill Hill School, that is to say, some 30 of them, one day last term, formed the Mill Hill School Model Railway Society, and a few days ago a representative of the MODEL RAILWAY NEWS paid a visit of inspection. There is no doubt about it—the Society is a very ambitious undertaking. Apart from the fact that Mill Hill is the first public school in the world, as far as is known, to inaugurate and maintain its own model railway club, the plan of the system, with its lay-out of sidings and junctions, embankments, tunnels, cuttings, viaducts and bridges, is extremely well thought out, and the work has been most ably executed.

The society was formed quite recently—the first bit of track was laid on Midsummer day. Since then the institution has prospered exceedingly. The idea having been mooted, a fewof the boys approached the Head with a proposition that a society of model railway engineers should be formed in the school and the idea was most favourably received. A large room, a one-time physics laboratory, was allocated to the work and the task of bringing the society into being began right away. A committee composed of boys and *one* master met and definitely laid down the principles which were to govern the scheme and the lay-out of the track. This lay-out was divided up into sections on the "block" system, and six members of the society are responsible for each section.

A glance at the plan of the lay-out shows exactly how the system works. The room in which the track is laid, and which is the envy of all non-members, measures some 28 ft. by 14 ft., and is exceedingly well lighted. In the top right-hand corner is "Weymouth Station." This has three platforms, into which run four roads. It is a terminus and has wonderful electrically lit booking halls, parcels offices, and bookstalls, with garden seats dotted about in the most approved fashion, while the walls are covered with the most natural advertising posters it is possible to imagine. A loop-line encircles the station for goods traffic purposes and this opens out on to an up and down road which converge just outside the departure platform to pass over a viaduct in the top centre of the plan shown as a single track. From this viaduct, trains may be switched into "Winterstoke Station," on the left of the main roads, or, if desired, continue straight ahead, in which case they have to pass through

The cantilever Swing-bridge.

"Burton Bank Tunnel," which, again, is operated by a single line of track. As the train leaves the tunnel the road again opens up into two tracks which pass over a semi-cantilever swing bridge. This bridge is a real necessity, for it has to be opened every time any member of the society wishes to enter the room. Before passing over the bridge, however, a junction with two roads leads to a very fine piece of work in the shape of a model of a modern engine shed. Once over the swing bridge, trains may be passed on to "Burton Bank Station" or turned off into "Port Ridgeway," a splendid piece of sidings work which occupies quite a fifth of the whole railway scheme.

Main line sidings continue along through "Collinson Junction," shown in the bottom right-hand corner of the lay-out, until the line runs abreast of "Weymouth Station," where it debouches to the left to cross a viaduct, where it is proposed to construct a big suspension bridge modelled on the lines of the Tower Bridge, with bascules that may be raised and lowered, and by means of a second viaduct, "Burton Bank Station" is again reached and the tour of the system has been completed. With the exception of the viaducts and the suspension bridge, the track is finished and in running order. An interesting feature of the railway is its complete system of signalling. All lamps, both in the stations and in the signals themselves, are lit electrically from the current supplying the school, the current, of course, having first passed through a transformer. All posts are enamelled white with suitable colourings for the semaphores, and each signal is correct in every detail.

It might be mentioned in this connection that in some sections of the line an ingenious piece of mechanism in the shape of an automatic electric signal stop prevents a train approaching the swing bridge while it is open. All danger of collision in "Burton Bank Tunnel," too, is averted by an electrical signalling device which prevents two trains being in the tunnel at the same time, where, as has been noted, there is only a single track.

Altogether, there are about 30 vehicles and engines in service, all of the latter, so far, being propelled by clockwork. Ultimately it is hoped to introduce steam and electricity. So far, nearly all the engines and rolling stock have been lent by members, until such time as the society has sufficient funds in hand to purchase its own.

Burton Bank Tunnel entrance.

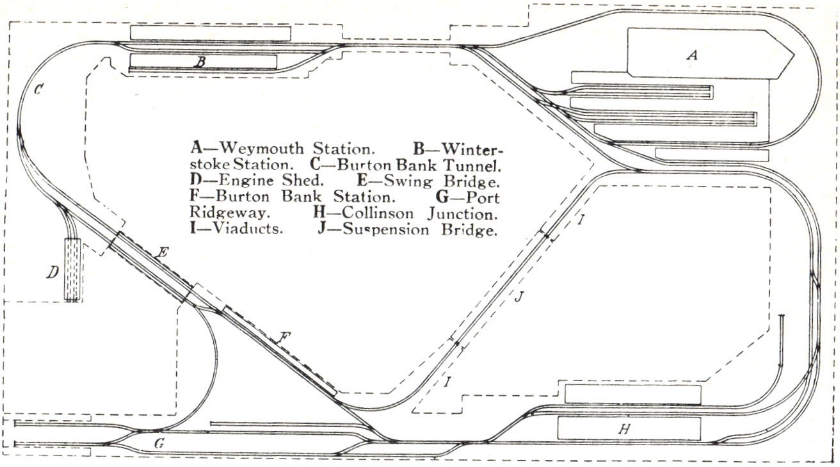

Plan of the Model Railway at Mill Hill School.

Up to the present nothing has been said about the permanent way, which in itself is a clever piece of work, about 250 feet of gauge 0 track being laid on chairs with sleepers one inch apart, the interstices being filled with granite chippings. There are about 30 sets of points, all of which are operated by hand.

It is difficult to over-estimate the enthusiasm with which Millhillians have entered into the scheme. Although a total of 30 has been fixed as the membership of the society, there is already a large waiting list. The subscription is 5*s.* per term, with an entrance fee of 2*s.* 6*d.*

Gradients on Model Clockwork Railways.

By H. Greenly.

A CORRESPONDENT, Mr. T. Horn, of Manchester, writing on the subject of the value of gradients on small gauge indoor lines using clockwork locomotives, says that he does not quite agree with the remarks in the book "Model Railways." He says that "a branch line or even a main line with gradients enormously increases the interest of working, and the large reserve of power in modern clockwork models makes the climbing reasonably easy with light loads. Most scale models in 0 gauge will now take six or seven bogies (180—200 tons) on the level, and should manage four (120 tons) up to 1 in 50/60. A year or two ago I had a railway which involved 30 feet at 1 in 60, including 8 feet on 24-in. radius curves (tin plate). A Bassett-Lowke 2—4—2 G.W. tank used regularly to start at the foot of this with 116 tons and climb steadily to the top. With a better track, better results should be obtained, though I imagine that 1 in 40 is about the limit. I agree that the lack of control in descending is a difficulty : but this can be mitigated (1) by heavy loads, possibly even with a braked vehicle next to the engine, (2) by large radius curves and good track, (3) by only winding low, sufficient to travel to foot of gradient, (4) by applying brake at top of gradient automatically. My latest loco, a 0—4—4 T, L.M.C. mechanism is so powerful that when fully wound it overcomes brake-resistance on the level, unless hauling at least 90 tons. It would therefore, easily travel to the foot of a long gradient at a moderate speed."

While admitting that under certain conditions an undulating railway could be made to work well as a general rule, I still think that a level line is to be desired, but here again the planning of the line has a bearing on the subject. The ideal arrangement for a line using clockwork locomotive is, I think, a terminal to terminal railway—a non-continuous line. The distance between the terminals should be less than the maximum distance the least powerful engine employed can travel with its usual train at one winding. There should be enough power in reserve to allow the engine of an arrival train to shunt into its siding or depot, after the train has been disposed of by another engine.

The laying of a line with gradients down to each terminus should under these conditions help the locomotive and make it possible to lengthen the distance between terminals quite considerably—or at least allow an engine to be loaded with a train heavier than that which could be negotiated on a perfectly level line.

The power of a clockwork locomotive falls rapidly as the spring unwinds and is greatest at the beginning of the journey. At the start of the run after the train has been accelerated to its normal speed, it is only kept in check by the action of the automatic governor. This is really a spring-governed brake and absorbs energy in friction. Such energy is entirely lost. By having an up gradient about a train's length out of the terminus an excess of speed will be checked and the energy stored in lifting the train will to a certain extent be available at the end of the run, when the train runs down the complementary gradient into the second terminus. On the return journey the same thing happens. If there is an intermediate stopping station this could be placed at the summit of the line somewhere about the middle of the system. Other readers' ideas and experiences on this subject would be welcomed by both myself and Mr. Horn.

Queries and Replies

Model G.N. (L.N.E.R.) 5-ton Fish Van.

(1) R. P. (Newcastle) writes:—"Can you publish a drawing of a model G.N.R. fish van in No. 0 gauge."

The accompanying sketch is reproduced half full size for a No. 0 gauge model and has a scale attached to enable it to be used for a No. 1 gauge vehicle. The width of the model in No. 0 gauge should be 60 mm. and in No. 1 gauge 82 mm. Standard solid wheels and coach axleguards can be used.

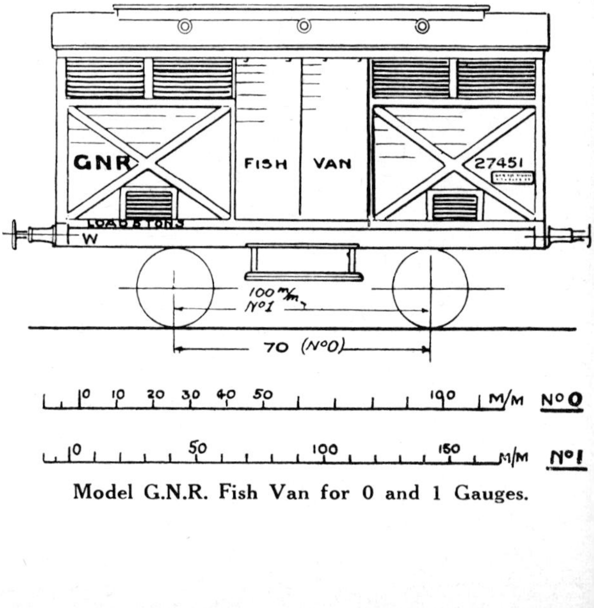

Model G.N.R. Fish Van for 0 and 1 Gauges.

Our Mail Bag.

From Sir Aubrey Brocklebank, Bt.

Dear Mr. Marshall,

I am delighted to hear you are about to start a new monthly paper specially devoted to model railways, and I sincerely hope the new venture will be a success.

All engineering and all forms of model-making are interesting, but there is a peculiar fascination about railways that appeals to perhaps a wider circle than does any other form of engineering.

My experience of model railways began with a 4-inch gauge line in the late eighties, which were the days of soft solder and hard language, to say nothing of the scoffing of that Victorian age which had not then realized that while any hobby is a godsend, a hobby which teaches one how and why the wheels go round, and which is always presenting a fresh difficulty to be overcome, is still more to be encouraged.

I well remember the modest beginnings of the *Model Engineer*, and I think I can appreciate what an educational force it has been. If the new paper is carried on with the same skill and with the same sympathy, as I am sure it will, there should be no doubt as to its success.

Yours truly,
AUBREY BROCKLEBANK.

Liverpool.

From Mr. W. J. Bassett-Lowke.

December 13th, 1924.

DEAR MR. MARSHALL,

I was very delighted to hear that you have decided to publish a monthly magazine devoted entirely to model railways and locomotives.

The MODEL RAILWAY NEWS will just fill that want, because I have always felt that so important a hobby as ours should possess a journal of its own and a magazine which will concern itself mostly with model railways, their development and possibilities, and, of course, their relation to their prototypes.

In the year 1909 I ambitiously endeavoured, with the co-operation of Mr. H. Greenly, to run a monthly magazine, *Model Railways*, in the form of a house journal, and the idea was hailed with enthusiasm, but it was not, alas, a financial success.

But times have changed since those early days of model railway work, and I am certain that the tremendous interest the younger generations take in model railway engineering now-a-days will not only ensure a tremendous reception for your venture but will render certain an ever-increasing support and an ever-growing circulation.

It will give me the very greatest pleasure to help you in every possible way, and I feel sure that in saying this, I am voicing not only my own sentiments, but also those of thousands of model railway enthusiasts who have the future of our fascinating model railway hobby at heart.

Yours sincerely,
W. J. BASSETT-LOWKE.

Northampton.

From Col. Henvey.

Dear Mr. Marshall,

With reference to your letter of the 3rd inst., I will certainly do all I can to help your new paper.

I enclose a copy of the rules of the Model Railway Club, and will send you a list of the members in the course of a few days.

I think it a good idea for the new paper to be the official organ of the club, and shall get the suggestion brought up at the annual general meeting, which is early in January.

Wishing MODEL RAILWAY NEWS every success.

Yours very truly,
R. HENVEY,
Hon. Sec. Model Railway Club

Shirley.

Model Wagons and Carriages.

To the Editor MODEL RAILWAY NEWS.

DEAR SIR,

With reference to the method of fixing axleguards shown in Figs. 381 and 382 of Mr. Greenly's new book "Model Railways," this scheme seems to be very sound. It not only permits of easy fixing, but also of easy removal—an important matter, I find; there is nothing like being able to take working parts down for cleaning, repairing or repainting. I found recently, in fixing some L.M.C. axleguards, that in No. 0 gauge, 48 mm. were required between solebars: this might be due to use of the Mansel wheels instead of the ordinary wagon wheels.

I have never seen coach parts for 0 gauge advertised for building up on the method Figs. 390 in the book mentioned. Are they obtainable?

For combined solebars and footboards on gauge 0 coaches, why not use $\frac{1}{4}$-in. or even $\frac{3}{16}$-in. angle brass, drilled and screwed to cross transoms? I have not tried this yet, but I think it would make a sound, strong fixture.

Yours faithfully,

T. HORN.

Manchester.

[The dimensions for the standard distance between the solebars of model wagon stock were fixed to suit the Leeds Model Co's cast white-metal axleguards and as far as we have experienced are quite satisfactory. Naturally, the 46 mm. given is the minimum, but it allows a certain amount of sideplay. The coach-body parts with the interlocking grooves and tenons and sunk panels, were taken up by Messrs. Mills Bros., 89, Ellesmere Road, Sheffield, and at the last "M.E." exhibition some No. 0 gauge "Pullman" cars were shown made up in this way.—*Editor*, MODEL RAILWAY NEWS.]

We have to thank many other correspondents for letters containing good wishes.

The Wimbledon Model Railway Club.

On Monday, December 15th, the Junior Competition for the prizes presented by Messrs. A. Knock and W. H. Shephard took place—the result being decided by ballot. Mr. H. E. Doe obtained first prize for an electric breakdown crane, L.M.S. 0 gauge, and Mr. A. E. Lilley obtained second prize for a S.R. 3rd class Pullman coach and "Zeebrugge-Harwich" covered van. 0 gauge.

IMPORTANT:—Annual General Meeting, January 5th, 7.30 p.m., Red Cross Hall, Church Road. *Every* member is requested to attend.

Hon. Secretary:—R. Shephard, 27, Bernard Gardens, Wimbledon.

Scale Models at Hamley's.

The extensive scope of Messrs. Hamley's model department at 200–202, Regent Street, London, W. 1, is well exemplified in their excellent 52-page catalogue. This covers a good range of model steam, electric, and clockwork locomotives, rolling stock, permanent way, railway accessories, boats, stationary engines, boiler fittings and tools. A particularly good line is the "Henley" steam launch, 24 inches over all, which is light, strong, and fast. A sample which we have examined shows it to be a really well-made boat which should give very satisfactory running results. A full description appears in the catalogue, which will be sent post free on application.

Bassett-Lowke's Model Railway Catalogue.

We have received a copy of the new model railway section of this well-known firm's catalogue. It is a veritable encyclopaedia of every model railway requisite, containing over 160 pages, and is splendidly illustrated and produced. Copies may be had post free, 1s. each, from Messrs. Bassett-Lowke, Ltd., 112, High Holborn, London, W.C., or 1, Frederick Street, Edinburgh, or Northampton.

The MODEL RAILWAY NEWS

Editorial and Publishing Offices:
66, FARRINGDON STREET, LONDON, E.C. 4.

Single Copies, post free, 7½d. Annual Subscription, 7s. 6d.

Vol. I. No. 2. FEBRUARY, 1925. Price, 6d.

Notes of the Month.

THE following General Order is hereby issued from the Superintendent's office of the MODEL RAILWAY NEWS:—"The Editor desires to thank very sincerely all ranks of the model railway world for their messages of approval of No. 1. The good wishes contained in many letters are much appreciated, and are most cordially reciprocated."

* * *

We should like to issue another General Order to read something like this:—"All model railways are to be inspected by their owners forthwith, and all work necessary to put them into up-to-date condition, and good running order is to be executed without delay." There must be many model railways up and down the country which have suffered from the effects of time, or which for various reasons have been allowed to fall into disuse and possibly into bad repair. Now is the time to get busy and put them into good going order again. With some it will only be a matter of dusting, a little repainting, and perhaps some minor repairs. In other cases, a re-laying of track, and perhaps a complete re-planning of the system is desirable. Engines and rolling-stock generally, need bringing up to date; there is new signalling to be done, and the long-thought-of bridge or tunnel to be built. So now, model railwaymen, get busy, and make your system into one of which you can be proud.

Many model railwaymen have doubtless become interested in wireless, and, in the course of their investigations of the properties of aerials, valves, and crystals, have become expert electricians. Why not electrify that clock-work model railway? The problems of loco-running and train control, of signalling, and of lighting, on an electrical model railway are very fascinating, and the advantages of control from a fixed point are very great. The model railway of the future will be the electrical railway. Steam and clockwork will always have their adherents, but the great expansion of the model railway hobby will come through the enormous interest which arises from electrical operation.

* * *

In modernizing your railway, or in converting it to electrical control, you will doubtless find yourself with some discarded engines, rolling stock, and other accessories. There is always some other reader looking out for additions to his own equipment at a tempting price, and you will find a ready market for anything you wish to sell in our Sale and Exchange Column. We want this feature to develop along useful lines, and we hope, therefore, that whenever there is anything that you want to buy, sell, or exchange with a fellow-reader, you will send along a small advertisement for that column.

Keep your eye on 00 gauge developments. There are signs that this small gauge is going to be very popular, and with several trade firms giving it their close attention, some interesting productions will be forthcoming in the near future. We think that 00 gauge is going to bring a new class of model railway enthusiast into being, viz., those who have hitherto been precluded from having a complete railway for want of space, and those service men and others who have from time to time to move their quarters, and, therefore, need a system which is reasonably portable.

* * *

Curiously enough, there is also evidence of a considerable activity in the building of the larger models of locomotives up and down the country. Independently of the late Count Zborowski's 15-in. gauge "Pacific" locomotives, which will be completed by the contractors, Messrs. Davey, Paxman & Co., Ltd., Colchester, a Worcester enthusiast is making a 7¼-in. gauge model American "Pacific" engine of maximum dimensions. Other 1½-in. scale engines are being started including a redesigned George V L.M.S.R. (L.N.W.), 4—4—0 engine by Messrs. Bassett-Lowke, Ltd., and a 0—4—2 type mixed-traffic tender locomotive by a Surrey reader. A design for a 3¼-in. gauge George V has recently been made for Major Simpson, of Carlisle, and the work of building will be started in the near future. We think this renewed interest in model locomotives in all its phases to be very largely due to the last Model Engineer Exhibition, where so many excellent examples of working model locomotives were shown under running conditions. At the recent Reading Society's Exhibition, Mr. Steadman Jackson had a partly finished 2½-in. gauge American "Pacific" on view which he is making for himself from his firm's "JR" standard locomotive parts. We hope to illustrate this and the other engines referred to as soon as opportunity permits.

For the Munich Transport Exhibition next year Herr Roland Martens, the well-known model engineer, who before the war had the three first half-inch scale coal-fired engines made in England, is designing three 15-in. gauge Pacific engines of approximately the same size as those being built for Count Zborowski. Messrs. The Krauss Locomotive Co., have secured the contract, and Mr. Henry Greenly is in collaboration with Herr Martens on various details. The "pop" safety valves similar to those used on the R.R. Railway "River Esk" are being made by Messrs. Jackson, Rigby & Co., Shalford, for these engines and the vacuum apparatus for working the brakes will most likely be made by the same firm.

" " "

The 15-in. gauge locomotive put into service last year on the Eskdale Railway has just been put into the shops with a view of the patentees effecting certain improvements in their valve motion. The engine has been in steam continuously since last March with the exception of about four days.

* * *

The Model Railway News is making its way abroad. Subscriptions have already been received from France, Switzerland, Holland, Portugal, Sweden, Germany, Austria, Czecho-Slovakia, Canada, and the U.S.A.

* * *

We are sorry that some of our readers experienced a little delay in getting No. 1 through their newsagents, although it was published promptly on January 1st There is no reason for any similar delay with future issues, which will be ready on the 1st of each month, if a regular order is placed with the bookstall clerk or newsagent.

* * *

Have any of our readers yet experimented in model railway control by wireless? Major Raymond Phillips gave demonstrations at the 1923 *Model Engineer* Exhibition, to show that it can be done.

NOTABLE MODEL RAILWAYS

The Downs School Railways.

By "Pedagogue."

THE Downs School Railway Company owns at present nine locomotives ranging in size from gauge 0 to a 1-in. scale Atlantic. The $1\frac{1}{4}$-in. and 2-in. gauge tracks are of a portable nature and are laid down when required in a large room; the smaller of these systems is worked entirely by electricity and calls for no special comment. The 2-in. gauge line is used by "Belinda," shown in the accompanying photographs, and is a much more exciting affair to work, as the lady in question is very fierce indeed when "roused," and thinks nothing of whisking a 30-foot train round her track at a speed which would make the entire Board of Trade turn pale.

"Belinda"—2-in. gauge.

The larger locomotives (with the exception of a $\frac{3}{4}$-in. scale G.N.R. Atlantic, which is too beautifully painted and finished to be run, and reposes in a glass case) have had, or are having, tracks laid for them in the garden. Work is at present proceeding on a line for the N.E.R. Atlantic, and it is hoped that by the Summer (if we ever have another) a hundred yards or more may be available for real passenger traffic, and extensions have been planned which will give a total length of over 300 yards if all goes well. It is, however, too early to speak of this railway at present; when it is in working order perhaps the Editor will allow room for some notes about it if there is anything of interest to report

The veterans of the collection are two $3\frac{1}{4}$-in. gauge locomotives; "Lizzie," a G.W.R. tank, and "Mary," a a Midland compound. Both engines are over 20 years old, being among the first ever fitted with the Smithies type of water-tube boiler, and both have cylinders $\frac{5}{8}$-in. bore by $1\frac{1}{4}$-in. stroke with slip-eccentric reversing gear. "Lizzie" is shown in the illustration in her present rejuvenated condition, but "Mary" is far too disreputable to be photographed, though she is still more or less in running order.

Three years ago an effort was made to provide these engines with a track, and after much strenuous labour at embankment-raising, a rough road was laid down providing some 200 feet of continuous run. For the rails we used the iron strips on which the sliding doors of cupboards are made to run. This is cheap and easy to fix, as lugs are stamped out of the rail itself every six or seven inches, with holes ready drilled for the spikes. The sleepers were made of inch-square stuff nailed down to longitudinal strips of the same section, and the whole well ballasted with granite chips.

At first all went well. The line looked realistic and various features were added to lend enchantment to the view. A hill was erected on purpose to accommodate a tunnel six feet long, and there was a real girder bridge over a pond, the abode of several frogs and even occasionally, in very wet weather, of a little water. "Lizzie" and "Mary" were both originally spirit-fired, but after the first budget the Chancellor of the Exchequer ordered petrol burners, and these were forthwith fitted. The line was an out-and-home arrangement, pear-shaped on plan, with one set of points where the two tracks diverged just beyond the terminus. Unfortunately, the surveying was scamped, and although the line looked level enough to the eye, "Lizzie" and "Mary" thought otherwise; moreover, the curves were the very minimum that these sorely tried sisters would negotiate at even a moderate speed, and moderation was a virtue neither possessed in matters of fuel, water, or velocity.

"Belinda" with an easy load.

The programme was usually as follows:—While the engine was being tuned up at the terminus and the final dose pumped into her boiler from a tank at the side of the line, a couple of privileged engineers would be loading the two trucks with bricks, and three score "gangers" posting themselves round the track, on the outside, to "catch her." Steam would be turned on with 60 lb. in the gauge, and "Lizzie" would puff demurely out of the terminus and take the points at a gentle trot. Over the bridge a stiff gradient would threaten a tota stop and there would be cries for more steam. A ganger having obliged by pushing the regulator full open "Lizzie" would awaken to life and plunge into the tunnel with a snort. After that it was only a question of "how long." Rolling like an Atlantic liner in a gale, she would make for the big curve at fully 100 miles an hour amid shrieks of excitement and a general run for cover, and a second or two later we should be bending over her kicking corpse and tenderly straightening out guard-irons, hand-rails and steps. Sometimes, however, she got round, and then we knew we were "for it"; after the curve came a long, straight run to the points, with a slightly falling gradient, and here "Lizzie" showed what was in her. She would take the points like a bird and enter the terminus under full steam at something over 200 miles an hour, having successfully dodged the frantic efforts of half a dozen gangers to shut off steam. Over the scene at the buffer-stops we will draw a veil: it is sufficient tribute to "Lizzie" to record that she was usually ready five minutes later for another trip.

"Lizzie"—3½-in. gauge.

"Mary" was as speedy as her sister, but not so reliable at cornering, though she has one or two record runs to her credit. Finally the line began to warp so badly that we had to abandon it to its fate. The rails were pulled up and the tunnel let to a local rabbit, while weeds soon covered the embankments and hid the wooden substructure from sight. "Mary" retired to a cupboard in a very battered condition, but "Lizzie" was sent away to be cleaned up and painted, and now is enjoying a "green" (literally) old age as an ornament. She is still in excellent going order and may some day renew her youth on a better track.

Our experiences with this railway have taught us some valuable lessons which are of use to us in laying the larger 5-in. gauge line we are now planning. They may be summarized as follows:—

(1) 3¼-in. gauge is a bad size for a railway, however good it may be from a purely model-making point of view. The engines are very powerful and difficult to control unless one is a born sprinter; they are too small to ride behind unless one gives up the idea of a real model railway and goes in for an elevated track on either side of which one can dangle one's legs.

(2) Gradients are an unmixed nuisance, and everything possible should be done to avoid them. The whole line should be most carefully surveyed before work is begun, and when the track comes to be laid everything should be tested and re-tested with a spirit level till all is dead true. An hour or two spent on this will save days of labour later on.

A side view of "Belinda."

(3) Spirit-firing is no good for anything over 2-in. gauge unless one is a millionaire, or content to run the engine once a month. Petrol burners give a good heat, but are variable and unreliable and are apt to go out at any moment. Moreover, they

take a deal of attention to keep them up to scratch.

(4) Curves should be laid with the greatest care and should be of ample radius. It is a mistake to try to squeeze a circular track into a small space by using minimum-radius curves, anyhow for large-size models which cannot be derailed with impunity.

This account is already too long, and nothing has yet been said about "Belinda" and her performances; if the Editor is willing we may perhaps deal with her in a future issue.

A Word to Correspondents.

In view of the many kind promises of contributions to our pages from our readers, we think a word or two on the subject of the suitability of contributions may be useful at this stage. There are two tests which should be applied by any intending contributor before he sets to work to photograph something, or to write something for us. (1) Is it going to help some other reader? and (2) does it show something of outstanding merit or interest? Our space is too valuable to be used merely for illustrating or describing things which, although creditable to the sender, are ordinary in character, or uninstructive. Half-a-dozen lines giving a practical hint in making or doing something, or a small drawing and a few notes showing how some neat accessory was made, are far more useful than a photograph and a page of description of an ordinary coach or wagon of which the chief merit is that some reader made it. Photographs are, of course, acceptable when they show something of special interest. For instance, a reader might describe a bridge that he had built. Bridges vary very much in design and appearance, and a photograph would be useful. But photographs of locomotives or rolling-stock of standard types do not convey very much that is new to the average reader. What he wants to know is—were any special dodges used in the construction, or were any difficulties got over in a simple way? If so, how?

While on the subject of photographs may we ask our readers to send us as good prints as possible, and of a size sufficient to enable the work illustrated to be clearly followed. We frequently get tiny snap-shots of model railways, often badly taken, but the sender apologizes for his pictures and "hopes we can make something of them." It is a waste of good money and useful space to attempt to reproduce such pictures, and it would be better that we should publish an issue without any photographs at all, rather than use some of the very amateurish snap-shots we receive. We are sure that they are sent with the best of intentions, but if a model railway is worth photographing, it is worth photographing well. So next time, please get a good camera on the job.

So far as sketches or drawings are concerned, correspondents need not be timid. While we like to receive a nicely made scale drawing, we can always re-draw any crude sketches provided they are sufficiently clear to show the sender's meaning. Do not hesitate, therefore, to illustrate your correspondence with rough sketches, if you are not a skilled draughtsman. Articles and correspondence should be written on one side of the paper only, and sketches or drawings should be on separate sheets, each bearing the sender's name and address.

A final point is that we should like contributors to mention in their articles the names of the firms from whom they obtained the equipment or material mentioned. Other readers may like to know where to obtain similar goods.

Everything submitted to the Editor will be welcomed, and will receive sympathetic consideration. It may not be published in the next issue, but it will be used as early as space permits, if it is really suitable. If it is not used, the friendly thought which prompted it will at least be appreciated.

A High Capacity Bogie Wagon.

By J. A. Dean.

MANY readers, no doubt, have some of the light-weight pattern of tinplate wagons on their railway and been annoyed by the behaviour of this type of wagon which, when being shunted, buckles up and comes off the track. However, by means of such wagons a very satisfactory and serviceable high-capacity bogie-wagon can be constructed easily and cheaply.

Commence operations by carefully taking the wagon body off each truck. Each body will be found to have a flange which rested on the truck. Drill two small holes through each flange. Now cut off one end only of each wagon body. This must be carefully and accurately done. The bodies are now screwed on to the strip of wood, being placed one at each

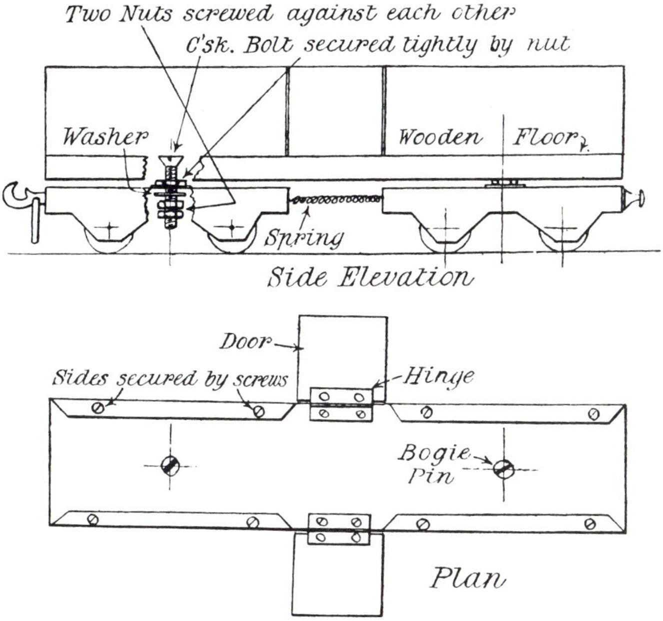

A High-capacity Bogie Wagon converted from tin-plate stock.

The materials required are:—Two light-weight pattern four-wheel wagons one strip of wood ($\frac{1}{4}$ in. thick) twice the length of a wagon side, plus the width of a wagon end. The width of this piece of wood is the same as the width of the wagon body. Two 4 B.A. bolts $1\frac{1}{4}$ in. long, six nuts 4 B.A., four washers, two small brass hinges, four small rivets, one dozen small wood screws, and a small piece of spring belt, about $1\frac{1}{2}$ in. to 2 in. long.

end, leaving a space in the centre on each side for the drop doors to be fitted. The drop doors consist of a wagon body end and are fitted one on each side of the bogie wagon. Each drop door is attached to a small hinge by small rivets and the hinge then screwed to the wagon base so that the doors will fall outwards. The bogie-wagon body should now appear a as shewn in the plan. The doors are kept up in position by means of a piece of strong wire pivoted on the wagon side and bent to clip over the top of a door, a clip being fitted on each side.

Now fasten, by means of small brads, the plates off each wagon truck to the side of the bogie body. When attached there is a space left under the doors. This space can be stained to take away the look of blankness.

The mounting of the bogies now takes place. Remove two buffers and one coupling hook from each truck, then drill a hole carefully through each truck-frame centre. Now take the bogie body, place upside down and lay each truck on upside down allowing the buffers and couplings to project over each end. Mark off holes for bogie pins, then, after accurately centreing the mark, drill a hole at each end. This hole must be a good snug fit for the bolts which are to form the bogie pins. Countersink the holes from the interior of the body, then screw each bolt through tight and secure rigidly by a nut screwed on and holding tight against the underside of the base. It is important that these bogie pins are absolutely rigid. Each bogie is now secured to the bogie pins in the following manner. A washer is placed on the bogie pin, then the bogie (formerly a four-wheel truck), another washer and finally two nuts which, after allowing the bogie sufficient play, are screwed up tight against each other. In order to prevent the bogies turning a complete circle the piece of spring belt is fastened to the inner ends of each bogie. The bogie wagon is now complete and will look much better than the sketch of the elevation can convey.

The principal feature about this type of bogie wagon is that the couplings are attached to the bogies, not to the body which is usually done. This method of coupling enables the wagons to take sharp curves quite easily and, as the buffers are also on the bogies, such a thing as buffer-locking, in shunting operations, is almost unknown, owing to the fact that the wheel base of each bogie is short and aligns itself to the track. Where couplings and buffers are placed on the bogie-truck bodies the amount of overhang at curves is too much and when shunting on reverse curves buffer locking takes place, with its consequent derailments.

The writer had a number of old wagons lying idle, in fact not used, as they would not keep to the metals. Therefore a bogie wagon was built in the manner described. The result was so gratifying that the rest of the old wagons were converted into bogie wagons. In the writer's case all the wagons are fitted with solid brass buffers.

In conclusion, these wagons run exceedingly well and smoothly and are very well worth the trouble of constructing, keeping on the rails either forward or backword or over points and crossings so well that they are a pleasure to use.

A Suggestion for Controlling Clockwork Trains.

While the average model railway man considers the auto-brakes fitted to clockwork locomotive as susceptible to improvement and the track-reversing gear as anathema, very little has been done by amateurs in the matter of improving the means of control. The writer suggests that electricity offers the best solution of controlling the engines from the track. The spring brakes could be easily modified into magnetic devices and collectors could be fitted to the engines to pick up current and apply the brakes at all points where trains may require to stop. Restarting is also simplified by such a device, and quite easily made electric brakes are applicable to coaches. One scheme which was tried by the writer in pre-war days was to fit coaches which have turned iron wheels with steel or iron brake shoes fitted on a connecting bar of iron rod. This rod has a coil of wire on it and the current energizes it and applies the brake by magnet attraction through the wheels and axle. H. G.

Walschaerts' Type Valve Gear for No. 0 and 1 Gauge Steam Locomotives.

Model L.S.W.R. 4—6—0 Loco with imitation Walschaerts' Valve Gear.

MODEL RAILWAY enthusiasts of less than a generation's experience will remember that when first brought out the low-pressure piston valve cylinder used on pressed tin-plate model locomotives was operated by a fixed eccentric which was placed outside the wheels. Later on, to hide it from view, it was put behind the wheels, an arrangement which was in every way satisfactory. The recent general adoption of Walschaerts' gear needed something different. Valve gears with slotted links, on the score of expense alone, had to be ruled out, as the method of changing over from one direction to the other by the usual reversing block had proved so successful from every point of view. To provide a reasonable imitation of the standard Walschaerts gear and to retain the use of the steam block at the same time, Mr. Henry Greenly designed and patented the gear illustrated in the accompanying photograph of one of Messrs. Bassett-Lowke's new No. 1 gauge steam models of the well-known L.S.W.R., 4—6—0 type engines. The primary motion, as in Walschaerts' valve-gear, is obtained from a return crank. This actuates a long vibrating lever slung from the footplate, and approximately midway between the fulcrum and the joint of the eccentric rod, the valve rod is attached. It is claimed that the gear has great merits for a small engine because the valve motion is reduced in amplitude from the primary motion. This reduces errors in distribution and allows a comparatively long valve travel to be obtained without trouble. The gear is, of course, applicable only to piston-valve cylinders, or their equivalent, which have attached or combined with them the usual change-over steam block which effects the reversing. Messrs. Bassett-Lowke are adopting the valve motion on all their new low-pressure models of Walschaerts' gear steam locomotives of the above type.

Making 0 Gauge Track.

By Geo. Winteringham.

HAVING decided on the question of material and made the necessary purchase, the first thing to do is to cut the rails up into equal lengths. A good standard length is 18 in.; if they are much longer they become somewhat awkward to handle and are liable to get bent or damaged in some way. 12 in. would be even more convenient, but it increases the number of joints in the track, which is not to be recommended. The ends of the rails should be filed off nice and square so as to ensure making good joints, and before putting them on one side as finished, care should be taken to see that each one is perfectly straight; if they are not, endless trouble will ensue later on.

Chair-Making.

The next job will be making the chairs. If the track is to be laid in a dry place indoors, tinplate will answer the purpose very well, but for out-of-doors it will not do, and brass or copper should be used. The size for the finished chairs is $\frac{3}{8}$ in. by $\frac{3}{16}$ in., and a little less than $\frac{1}{32}$ in. thick, each having two holes for fixing down on the sleepers. The best way to make them is to cut the sheets into strips $\frac{3}{16}$ in. wide and then cut these strips into $\frac{3}{8}$-in. lengths. If the sheets of metal are large it will be found much easier to cut them into smaller pieces of about 6 in. square than to cut the strips from the large sheet—a piece 6 in. square will make approximately 500 chairs. Two holes must now be made in each chair for the spikes or pins, and it will be better if these are only just large enough to allow the pins to pass through; if they are too large and the pins a very slack fit it will be found more difficult to keep the track straight while nailing it down to the sleepers. Obviously, however, it cannot be expected that every pin will be a perfect fit. It will not be found necessary to mark the position of the holes; this can be fixed quite near enough by eyesight.

The punch for making the holes can be made out of a piece of $\frac{1}{8}$-in. round silver steel, ground or filed down at one end to a sharp point, and will last longer if made slightly hard, but almost anything in the way of a sharp pointed tool will answer for making the holes.

A good block on which to punch the holes may be made by filling the lid of a tin box with lead—a flat one about $2\frac{1}{2}$ in. to 3 in. diameter will be found a convenient size. When the surface becomes too rough for further use owing to the numerous indentations caused by the punching, all that is necessary is to remelt the lead and it will then be as good as it was when new.

The chairs may be left rough, or if required for any special purpose, such as a show-stand, they should be trimmed up a little with a file to remove any unevenness on the edges, and the ends may be rounded off a trifle, which will very much improve their appearance. Punching the holes will cause them to curl up sometimes, but they can be easily be flattened again. The burrs left from punching the holes need not be removed.

All this sounds like a lot of work, but it will be surprising what a large number of chairs can be made in an hour after a little practice.

Fixing Chairs to Rails.

The chairs must now be soldered on to the rails and, in order to do this nicely and without difficulty, a rough jig should be made. The first point, however, to decide upon before making the jig will be the distance which the chairs are to be spaced apart. About 2 ft. 6 in. is a correct centre to centre measurement for spacing sleepers, and this scales out to just over $\frac{11}{16}$ in., but it will be sufficiently near to scale if $\frac{3}{4}$-in. spacing is adopted. Fig. 1 is a full-size drawing and gives some idea what the finished track will look like. No doubt many model railway engineers will say that considerably wider spacing would answer the

Making 0 Gauge Track.

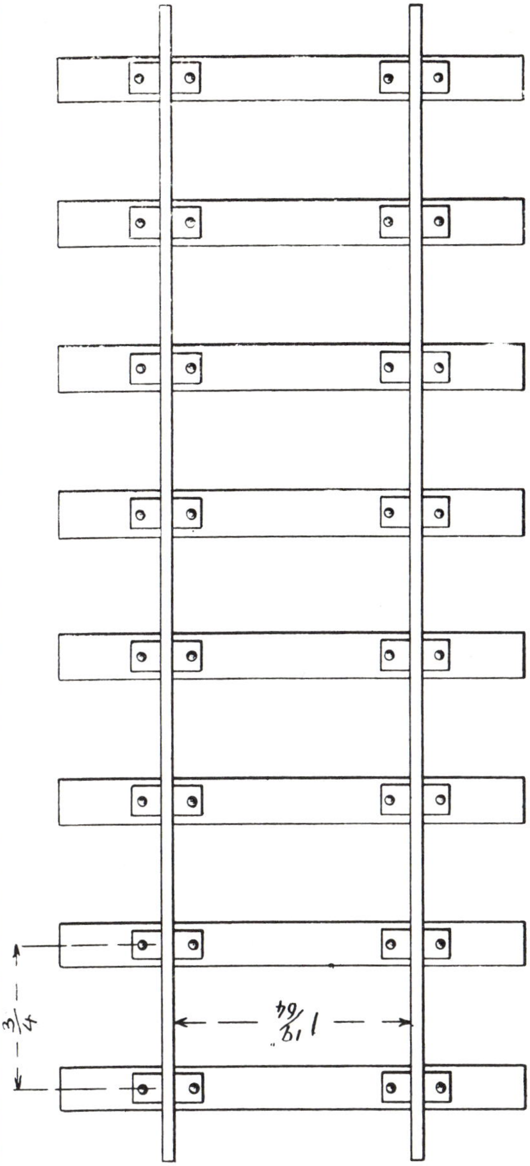

Fig. 1.—Full size drawing of 0 Gauge Track.

Fig. 2—Detail of Fish-plate.

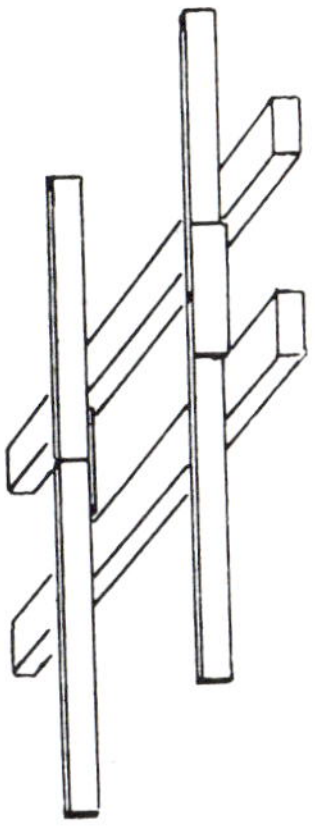

Fig. 3—Showing Fish-plates soldered in position.

purpose equally well. Possibly that may be so, but we are considering the general appearance of the model as well as its actual efficiency. The best way is to make a sort of compromise by using the proper number of chairs on the most important parts of the railway—at the stations, for example—and say half the number where it is not so much seen. This gives 1½ in. between each chair, a spacing which should be considered the maximum.

Joining the Rails.

Another job which must be decided on before going any further—and a most important one—is the joining of the rails. There are two ways, either of which will answer the purpose. The easiest perhaps is to simply butt the ends of the rails together and solder down on to a chair which has already been nailed down on to a sleeper. These joint chairs should be rather wider than the standard size of $\frac{3}{16}$ in.

A more realistic and much better method is to make fish-plates of thin tin or brass and solder them on to the rail-joints during the process of laying the track. These fish-plates are very simple, merely consisting of little pieces of metal ½ in. by $\frac{3}{16}$ in., one of the long edges being bent at right angles (*see* Fig. 2). They just fit against the outside of the rails at the joints, the narrow, turned-over edge being underneath and all soldered in position as shown in Fig. 3.

Having decided which method is to be adopted for securing the rail joints, the jig already referred to for soldering on the chairs may be taken in hand. It is quite a simple affair and will save a very great deal of time in the soldering-on process. Fig. 4 shows the finished jig and the metal parts required. The base should be made of a hard piece of wood, beech for preference, about 20 in. by 1½ in. by ½ in. thick. The fittings for spacing the chairs and holding the rail in position while being soldered are made of plate the same thickness as the chairs, and to prevent the solder from adhering to them they may be made of aluminium.

If fish-plate joints are to be adopted, 27 of these pieces will be required: two as shown at *a* Fig. 4, seven as *b* and 7 as *c*, but if joints are made by soldering-down on to chairs only 16 of *c* are necessary. The metal pieces must be screwed down into the base,

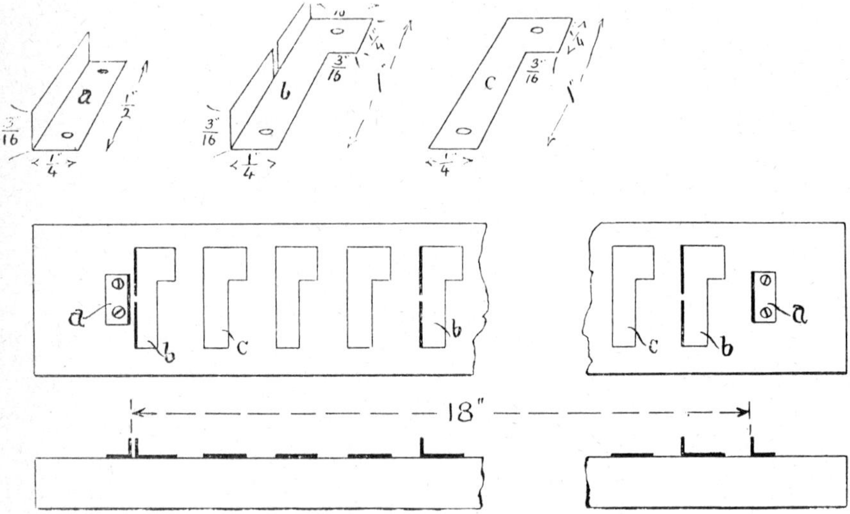

Fig. 4—Details of Jig for soldering on Chairs.

as is clearly shown in Fig. 4. Great care must be taken to get them all properly spaced so that the two end chairs each come $\frac{3}{8}$ in. from the ends of the rails, and the remainder $\frac{3}{4}$ in. apart. If the first method of soldering the ends to chairs is adopted, the two end chairs will each come $\frac{3}{4}$ in. from the rail ends. The seven parts *b*, for holding the rail in position, must be carefully screwed down so as to hold the rails perfectly straight; one of these should be as near to each end as possible, and the remaining five spaced as equally apart as they will come. The slots for holding the rails in part *b* should be nicely cut so as to hold the rail at right angles to the chair and without any slackness.

Soldering-on will be done quicker and better if the bottom edge of the rail is tinned and, if fish-plates are to be used, a quarter of an inch at each end may also be tinned. All the tinning should be done before commencing soldering-down.

Soldering-on the chairs hardly requires any explanation. Put the chairs on the jig in the recesses provided, keeping the burrs around the holes uppermost, then put in the rail and apply a small lump of solder to the side of each one, at the same time keeping the rail firmly pressed down.

The jig just described will only do for straight track and the outside rail of curves, as the inner rail on curves will be a trifle shorter than the outer one and consequently the chairs will come a little closer together, but curves will be dealt with later on.

A Model "Challenger" 2—8—2 Engine Type for an Indian Model Railway.

READERS interested in recent developments in model locomotive construction will remember that for the last "M.E." Exhibition a weight-pulling three-cylinder 2—8—2 type engine was made by Messrs. Bassett-Lowke, to demonstrate the possibilities of spirit firing. The general success of this model and the record that it holds has led an Indian prince to adopt the same prototype as the basis for a specially built $3\frac{1}{2}$-in. gauge locomotive, burning spirit not coal. The engine has only two cylinders 1 in. by $1\frac{1}{2}$ in. stroke, with an inside valve gear of the slip-eccentric type. This is connected to the outside in the same manner as used on the standard two-cylinder Great Western Railway locomotives, by a rocking shaft with two drop arms, one inside and one out, both on approximately the same centre. In arranging a gear of this kind it is not necessary to place the eccentrics and stop collars any differently to an engine with an ordinary directly connected valve gear, as the rocking levers moving the same

Model $3\frac{1}{2}$in. Gauge 2—8—2 Type Locomotive built for an Indian Prince.

Fig. 2—The ramp-operated Regulator.

way do not alter the motions relatively to the position of the cranks and pistons. With the ordinary rocker the eccentrics work in positions 180° from the usual.

The cylinders and steam chests are of the new type fitted with slide valves, but from the outside imitate piston-valve cylinders of the most modern type.

The following are the leading dimensions of the engine :—

- Cylinders (two outside)—1 in. by $1\frac{1}{2}$ in. stroke.
- Coupled wheels—$3\frac{3}{8}$ in. diameter on tread.
- Pony truck wheels—$2\frac{1}{4}$ in. diameter.
- Tender wheels—$2\frac{1}{2}$ in. diameter.
- Coupled wheelbase—$10\frac{7}{8}$ in.
- Total loco wheelbase—$23\frac{1}{2}$ in.
- Tender bogie wheelbase—$4\frac{1}{4}$ in.
- Tender total wheelbase—13 in.
- Length over loco frames—28 in.
- Length over tender frames—$18\frac{3}{8}$ in.
- Height of boiler centre—$6\frac{7}{8}$ in.
- Diameter at smoke box—$4\frac{1}{2}$ in.
- Diameter at firebox—5 in.
- Inner boiler — 3 in. diameter by 21 in. long.
- Width over foot-plates—$6\frac{5}{8}$ in.

The boiler is of the water-tube type and is especially interesting in that it can be fired by either spirit or paraffin by simply changing the burner. The tender is divided into four compartments. At the front end, the tank is fitted up to receive oil under pressure and has the usual pressure gauge, hand pump, filler and release valve to supply the " Primus " type burners. Behind this there is a space for methylated spirit, which supplies fuel to a wick lamp through a float feed tank fixed below the foot-plates, and between the two bogies. Next to this is the water tank, which has the usual lever force pump, and at the rear end a narrow compartment contains a battery supplying the electric head and tail lights of the engine.

The weight of the engine and tender loaded and empty is as follows :—

- Loco empty, 48 lb., equals 87·75 tons scale.
- Tender empty, 24·1 lb., equals 44·0 tons scale.
- Total empty, 72·1 lb., equals 131·75 tons scale.
- Loco (loaded), 52·5 lb., equals 95·5 scale tons.
- Tender (loaded), 38·0 lb., equals 69·1 scale tons.
- Total in working order, 90·5 lb., equals 154·6 scale tons.

These figures show that the engine is about correct scale weight. It should pull continuously a train of at least 1,000 scale tons, viz. :—nearly 550 lb., on a level track.

The engine was built by Messrs. Bassett-Lowke, Ltd., at Northampton.

Fig. 3—Arrangement of the Tender Tanks.

Realism in Model Railways.

By "The Looker-on."

Every model railway owner wants his railway to be as realistic in appearance as possible. The question arises—what are the qualities which make for realism ? I suppose most people would say "correctness of scale and completeness of detail." but I do not think that covers the while story.

I quite agree that correctness of scale is a very important feature, for there is nothing that offends the trained eye more than clumsy or disproportionate detail. When the locomotives. and rolling-stock are purchased from a good firm, correcness of scale in this department is usually well-assured, but, however good this feature may be, the realism of the whole system will be lost if the stations, bridges, signals and other details are not in close keeping with the scale. One of the details where scale is frequently departed from, is in the length of station platforms. This, I admit, is a real difficulty on many model systems. The total length of track is necessarily very short from a scale point of view, and if station platforms were extended to full scale length, two or three stations would fill up the whole system. On the other hand, a short, stubby station does not look realistic. Small country stations are easier to model in this respect, than the more extensive structures in populous centres. A point to be careful about is the naming of stations. There is nothing against the adoption of a fancy name, or a local name, but the name of any well-known big station should not be given to something which obviously is not representative of the real thing. I could not help a smile as I observed in a shop window recently a toy station labelled "Clapham Junction." It was quite a good model of a simple double-track platform, but, of course, absurdly unrepresentative of the real Clapham Junction.

Completeness of detail is a help to realism up to a point, but I think there is such a thing as overloading a model railway system with detail. Many of the details, to be true to scale, have to be very small and fragile, and, in view of frequent breakages, they become quite a nuisance. The real art of securing realism, to my mind, lies in knowing what to put in and what to leave out. in the way of detail, and in securing representative finish.

The features necessary for the operation of the railway *must* go in ; the non-essentials should be added with judgment and care.

The question of representative finish is, I think, a very important one, and it does not always receive the attention it deserves. Take, for instance, a brick wall. This is probably a piece of painted wood, with all the bricks carefully marked out in black or white lines. Compare the average "brick wall" on a model railway with the real thing and notice how glaring and hard and formal it usually is. It is probably too bright a red to start with, and the marking of the bricks is much too mechanlcally perfect. When an artist paints a tree or a field of grass, he does not paint in every leaf or blade. By a suitable use of masses of colour and light and shade he conveys to the mind of the observer the idea "that is a tree." He can even paint so deftly that you can tell the exact kind of tree, even from a few casual splashes of colour. Just in the same way, a brick wall, or a slate roof, or a paved platform can be indicated by a broad colouring, without the over-introduction of minute detail. A model railway builder may not be an artist, but I am sure he would do well to study real station buildings, bridges, embankments, and other features from the point of view of "general effect," as well as for their details of construction.

A Design for a Model No. 0 Gauge Electric Locomotive.

By Henry Greenly.

JUDGING by correspondence, the writer thinks that at the present time the interest in the development of model electric railways and the building of locomotives propelled by this power has almost reached the stage in popularity so long held by the steam engine. Certainly a greater proportion of model electric engines have "steam outlines" but there still is a strong feeling that a model electric locomotive should be a model of an electric locomotive. As will be seen by the historical section of the writer's book, "Model Electric Locomotives and Railways," although the electric engine came into being in the later days of railways and had the benefit of previous experience in rail vehicles, finality in design has not yet been reached. Irrespective of purely electrical problems, the disposition and number of motors to be used in a design of locomotive, the best method of transmitting the power to the wheels and other mechanical details, are still experimental when large powers have to be dealt with. Therefore, the types of electric locomotives to choose from, when it comes to making a working model, are legion. This, of course, makes the electric model locomotive all the more interesting. There is plenty of scope for free-lance efforts, and the accompanying design is only one of many possibilities.

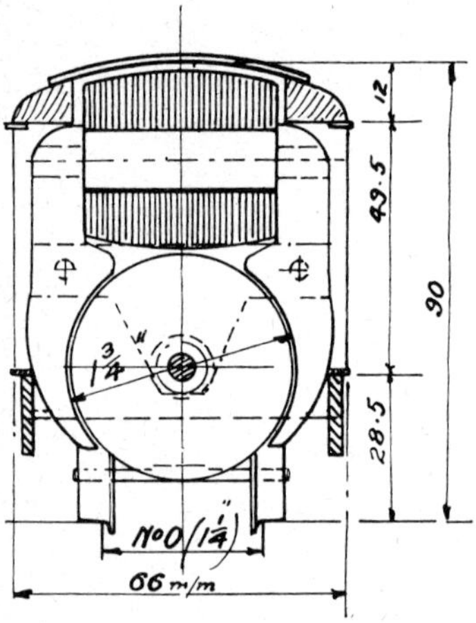

Fig. 2.—Cross-section through centre of loco showing motor.

The aims in this scheme are as follows :—

(1) Use of one motor with a very large diameter armature.

(2) Simple one-piece underframe and body structure carried on centre-pin bogies like an ordinary railway coach.

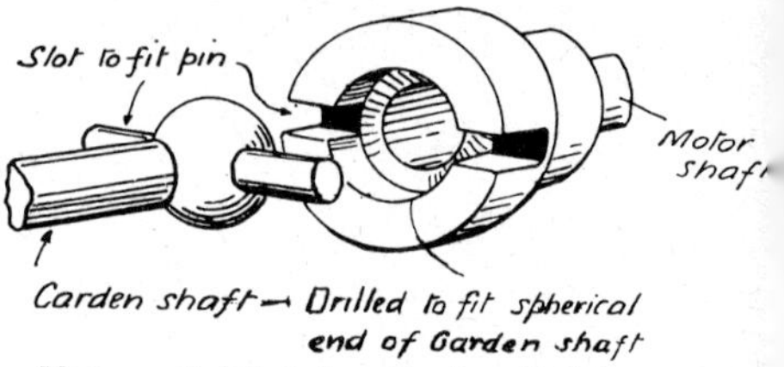

Universal joint for Carden Drivin; Shafts.

(3) Motor to be series wound.

(4) Maximum adhesion weight possible.

(5) Simple transmission gear.

(6) Spring-borne axleboxes.

(7) Consumption of under half an ampere on normal load on the level.

(8) Normal load of 350 scale tons, at 1¾ miles per hour (77 scale miles per hour).

The full width of the locomotive has been employed in housing the motor, and to keep it clear of all wheels and bogie frames it is placed exactly in the centre of the locomotive, with the motor shaft extending fore and aft longitudinally. The armature is about twice the normal diameter, and at the expense of a slight lengthening of the engine could be extended in width. The motor-bearing brackets should be of brass and are overhung. The field magnet is of the simplex type with the windings over the armature. To make

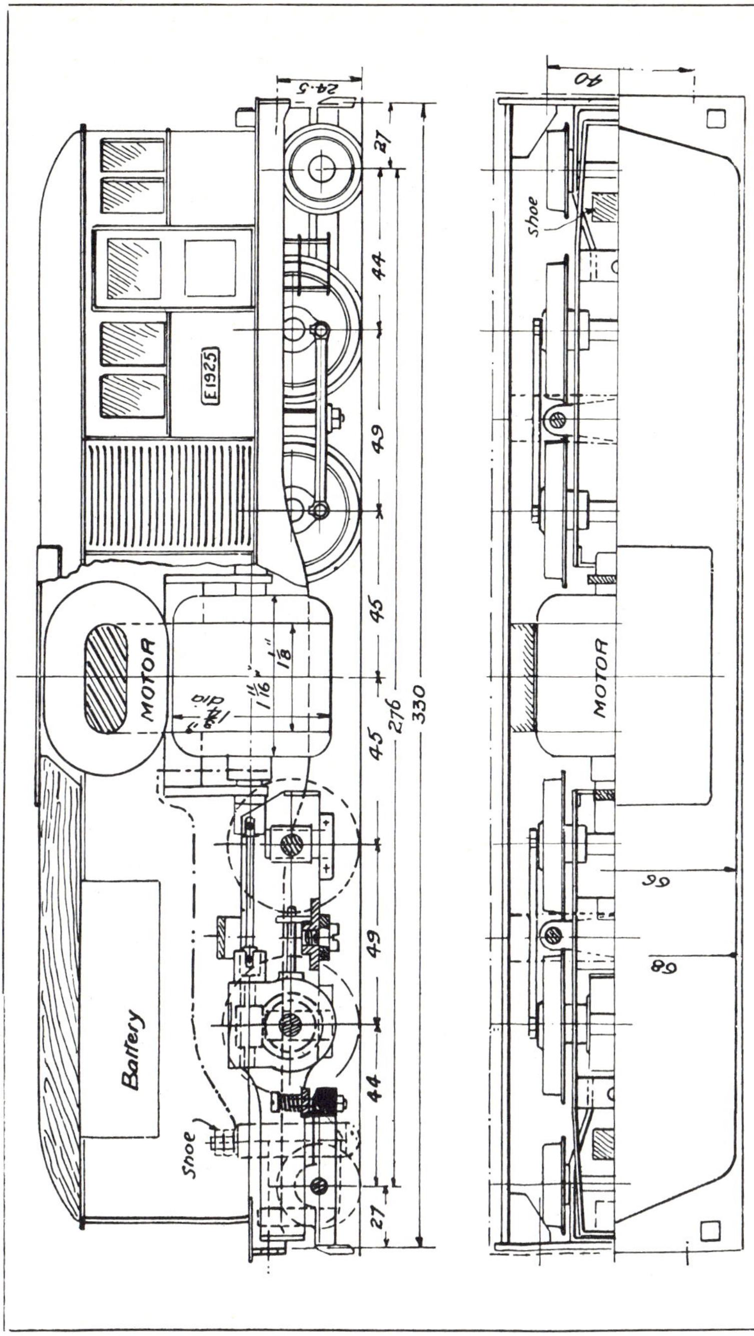

Design for a Model O Gauge Electric Locomotive.

Fig. 1—General arrangement—Elevation and Plan.

room for these, the wooden roof is cut away and the opening covered by a plate. This plate may be elaborated in design, if the extra work involved is not objected to, and made to represent a raised roof with ventilated sides.

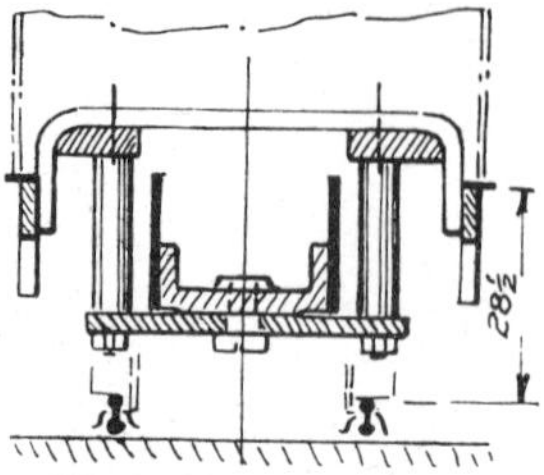

Fig. 3.—Method of Pivoting the Bogie.

The electrical scheme may take various forms. It would be possible to fit dry batteries and separately excite the fields. This is not a very economical scheme. A polarized reverser can, of course, be used, operating either on the single-field winding or double-winding system, as described in the above-mentioned book. A further alternative is also suggested. It is not always easy to obtain a permanent magnet of suitable size to make a polarized auto-reversing switch and therefore, a wound magnet energized by a small current supplied from a pocket battery would get over the trouble. A hand-switch could be fitted to cut out this battery when the engine is not being used.

The motor is fitted rigidly to the frames and the bogies are of the underslung type. The carden shafts may be made as illustrated in the detail Fig 4, herewith, or a spiral spring connection as employed in model boats, may be used to connect the motor to the worm gear box on the driving axle. The universal joint at the driven end is practically over the bogie centre in each case and, therefore, the amount of lateral movement will be very small.

A pony truck has been introduced at each end of the locomotive, more or less for appearances' sake, and on the frames of these are mounted heavily weighted copper collecting shoes.

Clayton Tunnel, North End, Southern Railway.

Photograph by G. H. Lake.

A Simple Model Water Tower.

By Lieut. E. A. O. Hutchinson, R.A.

THE accompanying sketch, which is dimensioned in millimetres for No. 1 gauge, shows a simple method of making a model water tower of the vertical-pipe pattern, which has been adopted by the writer. Such a tower is extremely simple to make and most effective when completed, while at the same time it takes up very little valuable space on the model railway. It should be noted that this water tower is merely a dummy and does not supply water.

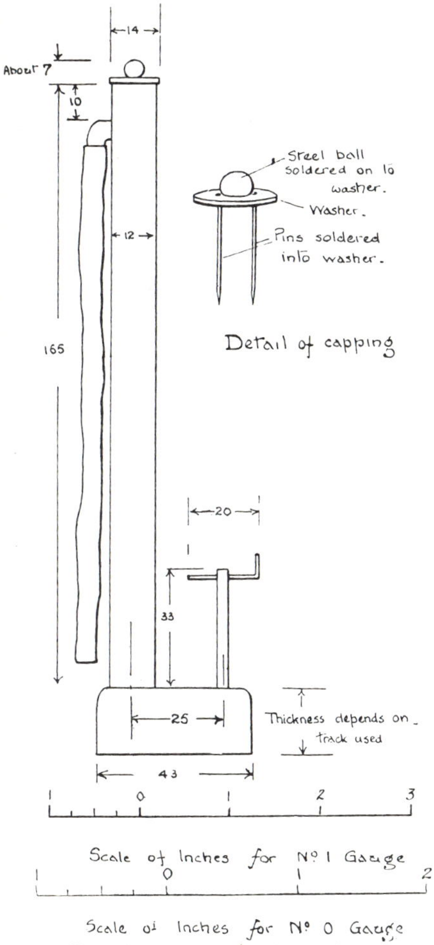

Details of Model Water Tower.

The vertical pipe of the tower is made of $\frac{1}{2}$-in. round dowel-pin wood and is $7\frac{1}{4}$ in. long. The bottom end is glued and panel-pinned into a hardwood base $1\frac{3}{4}$ in. by $1\frac{1}{2}$ in. The thickness of the base depends upon the type of track used, but with small-scale permanent way laid on battens $\frac{3}{4}$ in. is about right. The top edges and corners of this base are sand-papered off and it is painted to represent concrete.

A piece of $\frac{3}{16}$-in. round iron is bent to a right angle, each leg is cut off about $\frac{3}{8}$ in. long, and one is threaded up $\frac{1}{4}$ in. from the end. This leg is well coated with glue and screwed into a hole previously drilled to receive it half-way through the vertical pipe at $\frac{1}{2}$ in. from the top. If this hole is made a fairly tight fit and the iron is screwed in so that none of the thread shows, this method of fixing will be found to be neat and quite secure. Over the projecting leg of the iron, which is turned so as to point downwards, is slipped a suitable length of rubber tubing.

The tower is finished off at the top by a capping made from a $\frac{1}{4}$-in. ball (a steel ball from an old ball race will do), a washer slightly larger in diameter than the vertical pipe, and two pins. Two holes are drilled in the washer for the pins, as close as possible to the central hole and diametrically opposite. The steel ball is soldered to the washer with its bottom resting in the hole of the washer, the pins being soldered in place simultaneously. Any portion of the pins projecting above the washer are filed off flush, and the capping is secured by the pins being pushed down into the top of the vertical pipe. A dab of glue on top of the vertical pipe before the capping is pushed right home will further secure it.

The water-cock handle is made from a $2\frac{1}{2}$-in. wire nail driven through the base from underneath, $\frac{1}{2}$ in. then being cut off the pointed end. Care must be taken that the nail is vertical, for if it is not the appearance of the model will be spoilt. When the end is cut off, a $\frac{3}{64}$-in. hole is drilled through the top and a short length of wire bent to form a handle soldered in position. A length of $\frac{1}{8}$-in. rod can be used in place of the $2\frac{1}{2}$-in. nail if the latter is not available.

The vertical pipe and water-cock handle are painted either black or red oxide, the base being, as indicated above, painted to represent concrete.

If desired, additional details can be incorporated. The base can be enlarged and a dummy drain grating fitted below the rubber tubing, and a dummy stove, as is often fitted to water towers of this type to prevent freezing in winter, can be added. A suitable grating can be made by soldering parallel lengths of wire over the end of a short piece of $\frac{5}{8}$-in. tube, which is fitted into a hole drilled in the base to receive it. If it is desired to add a miniature stove, this can be cut out of wood and glued in position on the side of the vertical pipe at a scale height of about 2 ft. 6 in. or 3 ft. above the base. A length of fine-bore tube or a piece of $\frac{1}{8}$-in. rod, fitted into the top, will represent the chimney.

The Model Railway Club.

Prize Competitions, Season 1924—1925.

1. *Six-Coupled Clockwork Loco Hauling Competition.*—£1 1*s.*, presented by Mr. W. R. S. Smart. Conditions:—Loco to be within club 0 gauge loading gauge (14ft. by 10ft.); one single-spring mechanism. Marks awarded on basis of distance run by scale tons hauled.

2. *Mechanical Drawing Competition.*—£1 1*s.* and 10*s.* 6*d.*, presented by Mr. J. C. Cosgrave for the best mechanical drawings.

3. *Photographic Competition.*—Prizes presented by Mr. H. R. Norman. Conditions:—(*a*) £1 1*s.* for the best set of six photos of a member's model railway; (*b*) 10*s.* 6*d.* for the best set of three photos of any articles or article connected with model railways or locomotives constructed by a member.

4. *Silver Cup for the Most Efficient 0 Gauge Steam Loco.* — Presented by Col. R. Henvey. Conditions:—Loco to haul a minimum of 100 scale tons for at least five minutes. To be within the club loading gauge. To be the work of the member competing, but commercial cylinders, parts, etc., may be used. Marks awarded on the basis of scale tons hauled × time run. The cup will be won outright.

5. *Prize for the Best 0 Gauge Model of a Special Wagon.* £1 1*s.*, presented by Mr. G. P. Keen.

6. *Prize for the Best 0 Gauge Model of a Loco built not later than* 1870.—£1 1*s.*, presented by Mr. H. G. Kerr.

7. *Electric 0 Gauge Loco Hauling Competition.*—£1 1*s.*, presented by Mr. A. R. Annoot. Conditions:—Model to be within club loading gauge, to be of electric, not steam, outlines, and may be a "free-lance" design, or a model of an existing type. The model must haul its own source of energy. Marks awarded on the basis of scale tons hauled × distance × time.

8. Prize of 10*s.* 6*d.* for the best piece of 0 gauge coaching stock. Presented by Captain E. C. Ball.

9. *Robinson Cup.*—Silver challenge cup for 1 gauge locos; engine to be finished except painting; privately owned, but not necessarily privately built; to haul a minimum load of 100 scale tons for not more than 10 minutes, loading gauge, scale equivalent of 15 ft. × 10 ft. Marks awarded on basis of distance run × load hauled.

All entries to be made to the Hon. Sec. by a date to be notified later, about three weeks before Easter, 1925. Full particulars of all the competitions may be obtained from R. Henvey, Hon. Sec., Model Railway Club, White Cottage, Shirley, near Croydon.

Model Hydraulic Buffer Stops.

By Henry Greenly.

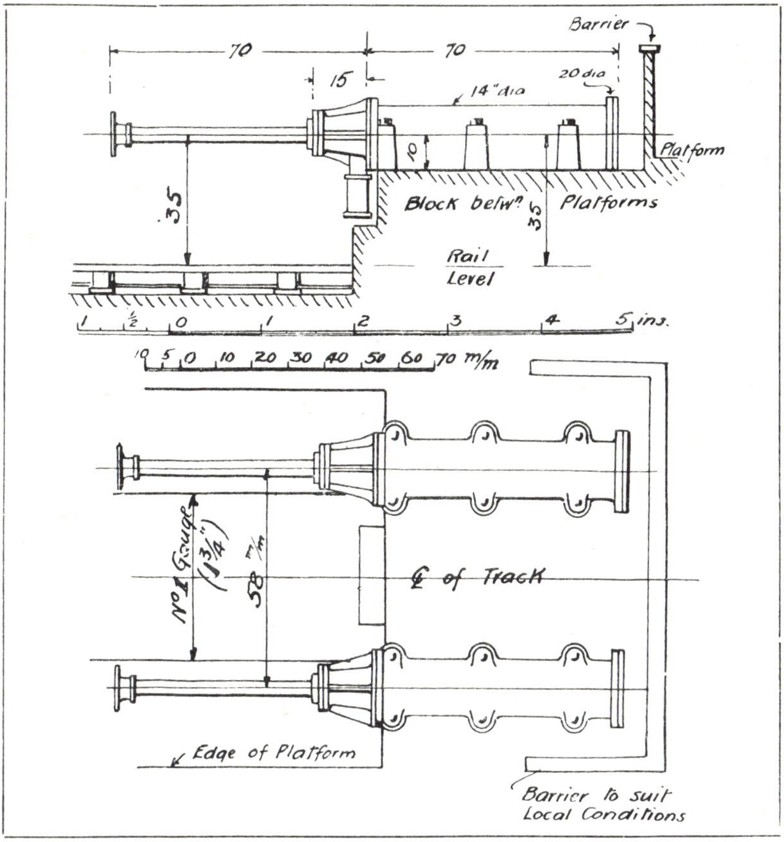

Elevation and Plan of Model Hydraulic Buffer Stops.

SINCE the evening 20 years ago the writer went to Euston to see the hydraulic buffers just installed there and subsequently made a sketch for the well-known models which have been on the market ever since, considerable improvements have been made in the details and capacity of these useful fittings. Just recently one of the leading makers has issued a catalogue illustrating the latest examples of buffer stops and from this the accompanying drawings have been prepared. It was noticed that the cylinders are now placed on substantial concrete or brickwork blocks built up approximately level with the adjacent platforms. The Marylebone (G.C.R.) stops have a stroke of five feet and will safely stop a 200-ton train travelling at six miles per hour, the overall length of the buffers being 14 ft. A set lately installed on the Paris-Orleans line in France are 19 ft. 9 in. long and have a stroke of seven feet. These will stop a train of 400 tons at ten miles per hour. The working cylinder is in this case 17 in. diameter.

In preparing the accompanying drawing for a No. 1 gauge model, the smaller G.C.R. dimensions have been adopted—there is often none too much room to spare in a model terminus. For a No. 0 gauge the stops would, of course, be only seven-tenths the size of the No. 1 gauge model and the centres of the buffers would be 40 mm. between and 24·5 mm. above rail-level.

Queries and Replies.

(2) S. R. Clockwork Locomotive Design.—S. K. West (West Croydon) requires a drawing for a No. 1 gauge model (clockwork) S.R. locomotive of the 2—6—0 type, South Eastern type.

We herewith reproduce an outline drawing of the No. 810 engine. The later No. 822, the three-cylinder engine, has been modified slightly. The chimney has a straight stalk and the cab windows are made to follow the outline of the cab and Belpaire firebox. The valve gear and the front end of this particular locomotive, of course, differs, because of the third cylinder.

In making a model of this prototype it is possible to reduce the coupled wheel-base 10 or even 15 mm. should the curves of the railway require it. In doing this the overhang at the trailing engine could be increased to 65 mm. at least without impairing the appearance. The tender should have a wheel-base of 130 mm., equally spaced with an overhang of 40 mm. at each end.

(3) Springs for Coupled Wheels for ¾ in. Scale Model Loco. — F. W. Baker (Liverpool) asks for the size of springs required for driving and coupled wheels of a ¾-in. scale model steam locomotive of a heavy type.

We would recommend springs designed for a maximum average load of 24 scale tons, viz., 13 lb. actual per axle. With four springs the load on each could be reckoned at 3½ lb. The convenient outside diameter is ¼ in. and the loaded length would be $\frac{9}{16}$ in. The unloaded length, with a deflection of $\frac{3}{16}$ in., would, therefore, be $\frac{9}{16} + \frac{3}{16} = \frac{3}{4}$ in. The spring should be able to close to $\frac{7}{16}$ in. With No. 2 gauge wire, 10 coils can be accommodated, and we find that, theoretically, a No. 21 gauge spring will deflect ·18 inches with a load of 3½ lb. This is near enough to the desired conditions for all practical purposes. The specification of the springs is therefore, as follows:—

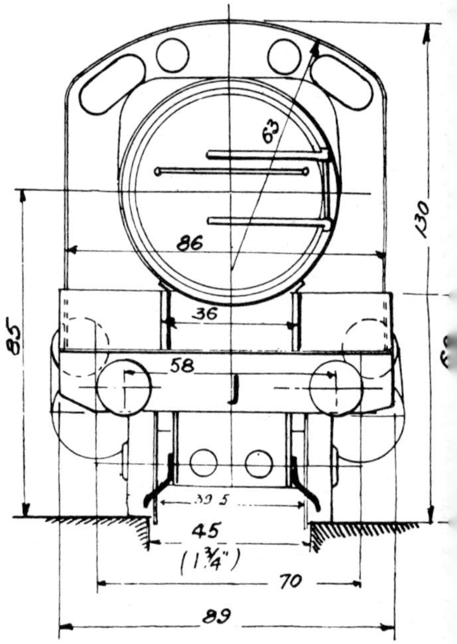

End Elevation of S.R. Clockwork Locomotive.

Compression springs, ¼ in: outside diameter; 10 coils; wire, No. 21 S.W.G. diameter; ¾ in. long, unloaded.

You can get springs from Terry's, of Redditch, if you are unable to obtain the right thing from a cycle dealer.

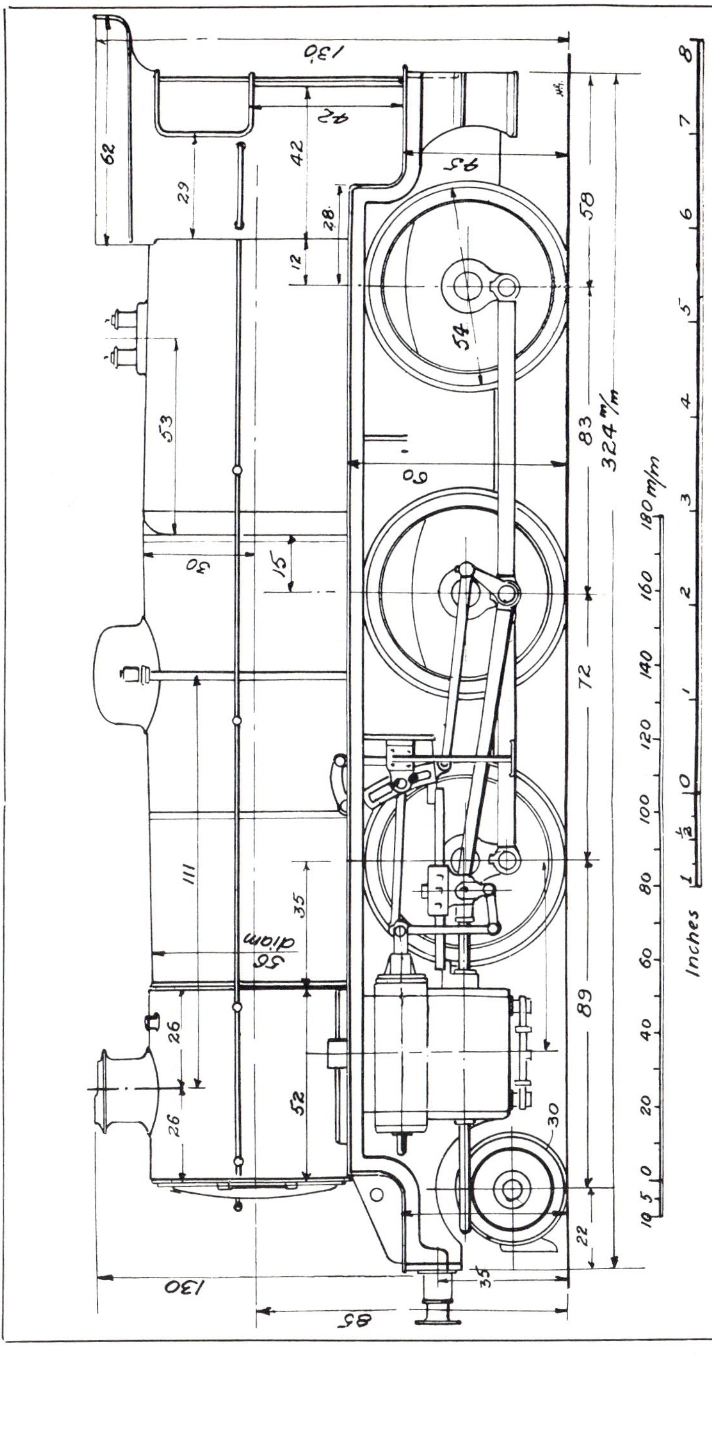

Design for S.R. Clockwork Locomotive in No. 1 Gauge. (Query No. 2).

(4) Model Locomotive Steam-Pipe Sizes — J. M. (Plymouth) asks us to elucidate the rule on page 128—129 of the *Model Steam Locomotive* (Marshall & Co., 1904), for steam and exhaust pipes and exhaust nozzle, and also what would be considered as the effective area of the piston where four cylinders (simple) are employed.

The above rule gives steam-pipe size as one-quarter diameter of piston and exhaust pipes, with a bore area of one-tenth that of the piston area, in the medium size of model, and still holds good. For a four-cylinder engine of the pistons-opposed type, as two cylinders are taking steam at one time, the effective piston area is twice that of an individual piston. Four $1\frac{1}{4}$ cylinders will require a steam pipe of twice the area of a two-cylinder ($1\frac{1}{4}$-in. bore) engine and while $\frac{1}{4}$-in. bore would suffice for the latter, $\frac{11}{32}$-in. bore will be required for the four cylinders. The same applies to the exhaust pipe. However, considerable latitude is allowable in the steam-pipe sizes, in smaller models owing to the relatively low piston speeds. With reference to blast nozzle our correspondent has chosen the $\frac{1}{25}$ piston-area rule. For a four-cylinder engine this works out as follows :—

Blast-nozzle area = $\frac{1}{25}$ effective piston area

$$\text{Do.} \quad \frac{1\frac{1}{4}\text{-in. area} \times 2}{25}$$

$$\text{Do.} \quad \frac{1{\cdot}227 \times 2}{25}$$

say, ·09 square inches = $\frac{11}{32}$ diameter.

The nozzle should be removable and a size smaller, say, $\frac{5}{16}$ in., should be made to allow for final experiment.

(5) Painting a Model Locomotive.— T. A. (Todmorden) writes asking for information on painting a No. 1 Gauge Locomotive.

It is presumed that the locomotive is a steam model, and in that case you will have to stove-enamel it. The model should be made quite clean and free from grease. This can be eliminated by rubbing down with a petrol-dipped rag, or with turpentine. All parts that can be taken down for separate painting should be removed. You can get enamel in the correct colours from Messrs. Bassett-Lowke, Ltd., Northampton, asking for the L.M.S. new colour and smokebox black. For brushes you can select some at any local colourman's shop, and it will pay to get about three good quality brushes of suitable size. Don't, however, attempt lining with a coach-painter's lining-out brush. You will be able to do this best with a draughtsman's pen. About three coats, applied very thinly, will be required and it will repay the time and trouble to allow each coat to harden thoroughly and to rub the surfaces of the model down after each of the first two coats, using pumice powder and water. The domestic gas oven may be used for stoving, the final temperature being about 140° Fahr. Don't allow the temperature to rise above this, as you may have trouble with soldered parts. Experiment on some of the smaller components first and then tackle the main job.

Answers to Correspondents.

A. W. L. (Dunkirk, N.Y., U.S.A.) :— We thank you for the Pennsylvania R.R. booklet illustrating the Broad Street station fire and the subsequent renovation.

Rev. S. Windsor (Bodmin) :—It is presumed that it is not intended that the model weigh-bridge should actually weigh railway vehicles. This would be difficult to accomplish without very delicate mechanism, but an approximation could very likely be obtained on a weigh-table which would embrace a complete vehicle, say a four-wheeled wagon, or its equivalent. The matter will be considered.

Readers sending in queries should read the conditions printed elsewhere in this issue. We want to be helpful, but would ask readers to assist us by presenting their queries in a form which can be easily dealt with.

Combined Passing and Terminal Stations.

To the Editor, MODEL RAILWAY NEWS.

DEAR SIR,

The design for a combined passing and terminal station on the lines of Rugby, published in *Junior Mechanics,* is interesting; but I have on the lines of York (simplified, of course), is a better scheme. My own idea for a large through terminal station is modelled on York. This has several advantages: York is on a curve, and in the main each platform can be used for up or down trains. I append a sketch (omitting bays)—all of which except one, I think, can be entered or left from the main lines.

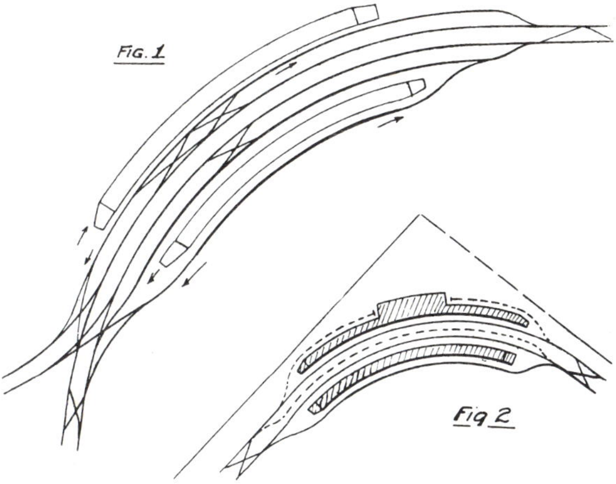

The various points at either end are not actually correct but only in general effect. I should simplify the plan as shown in Fig 2, and in this form each of three lines could be used for up or down trains, and one line would probably always be free for running round. If necessary a centre line could be added as indicated on dotted lines. Similarly, these show possible bays, if desired,

Fig. 1. Through terminal station, modelled on York.

Fig. 2. A simplified plan of Fig. 1.

Fig. 3. A still simpler plan

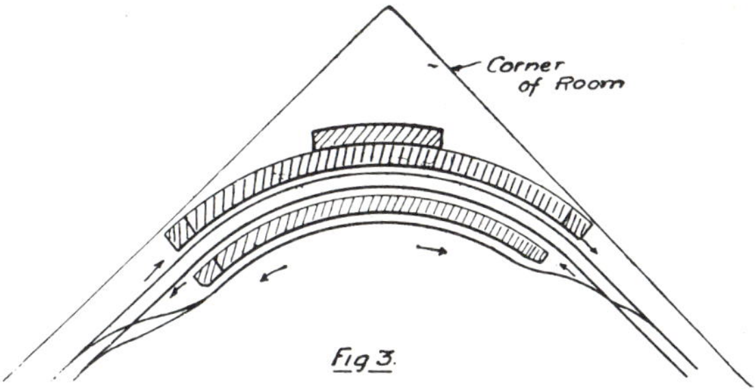

and the whole being on a curve, station buildings could be put out of the way in the corner. An even simpler plan would be as illustrated in fig. 3.

The inner line would then be used by trains requiring to reverse. I intend that the whole should be on a

one objection. A No. 0 gauge branch-line train of three coaches and a loco require four feet. This gives a good main platform length, but branch trains are severely limited, and where the station is the only important one on the line, any reversal of main-line trains would have to be done at a main-line platform. I think a station curve of 4 ft. 6 in. radius at least, and with a complete quarter circle, would give platform lengths of seven or eight feet.

Yours faithfully,
T. Horn.

Manchester.

Scale Wheels.

To the Editor Model Railway News.

Dear Sir,

I feel I must write and congratulate you on the first issue of the new magazine. If it keeps up to that standard it should do well.

The thing that strikes me most in the whole paper is that people want models as correct to scale in every detail as possible. I quite agree. Enough has been done to prove that exact scale working is possible to those who will, and when all is said and done, how much more interesting it is!

Just before Model Railway News appeared, my brother and I were trying a few experiments with wheel flanges on our 1 gauge line, consequently, Mr. Winteringham's article was of great interest and value to us; so also was the paragraph on page 10 concerning wheels and track.

Now that the model railway world is more united, as a result of your magazine, would it not be possible to adopt standard dimensions for wheels and rails, points, etc., more nearly, if not actually, to scale?

One quite realizes, of course, that for the commercial models, the existing sizes are advisable owing to crude tracks, but it seems a pity that these locos and vehicles should not also be supplied with scale flanges and wheels.

To make my meaning clearer, I had better state my own case. My line started about 16 years ago with standard Bassett-Lowke models and tinplate track. Ever since then it has been added to, and now we are building permanent way with which to replace all the old track gradually. Being a "true-to-scale" advocate, I want scale wheels (or nearly so) because it makes far more detail possible. Now the present rolling-stock is unsprung, but it seems to me that with scale-flanged and a very carefully erected line, they should not give trouble (my curves will be all over 5 ft. to 6 ft. radius). All new stock will be sprung.

I have not got the dimensions of 4 ft. $8\frac{1}{2}$ in. gauge tyres, but imagine they are about 5 in. wide, with 1 in 32 taper tread, and flanges about 1 in. × 1 in. In $1\frac{3}{4}$-in. gauge this would be approximately $\frac{5}{32}$ in. wide, and flanges $\frac{1}{32}$ in. × $\frac{1}{32}$ in.

It would be very interesting and helpful to have the whole question discussed and something settled.

Yours faithfully,
J. Francis Parker.

London, S.W. 1

---

0 Gauge Track.

To the Editor Model Railway News.

Dear Sir,

Referring to Mr. Winteringham's remarks about 0 gauge scale permanent way, we are prepared to supply a track in accordance with his suggestions, if we can find that there is a demand for it. We enclose herewith a sample of what we propose to produce at 1*s.* 9*d.* per 18-in. length and shall be pleased to have your comments thereon.

This track could be used equally for in or outdoor railways, as it is weatherproof, but one, of course, loses the realism of chairs, keys and the section of the running rail.

We are,
Yours faithfully,
Marshall, Stewart & Co.

London, S.W. 17

[The sample submitted is made up of rectangular rails of bright brass, soldered to brass sleepers spaced at 1-in. centres. The sleepers are finished in dead black, and the track looks very neat, but as our correspondent points out, is not entirely realistic.—

Editor, M.R.N.]

Mr. Clarke's 0 Gauge Clockwork Loco.

To the Editor MODEL RAILWAY NEWS.
66, Farringdon St., London.

January 1st, 1925.

DEAR SIR,

May I offer you my warmest congratulations on the splendid character of the MODEL RAILWAY NEWS, No. 1 of which I have just finished reading. Needless to say, I was delighted with it! At the last meeting of the Model Railway Club, our chairman, Mr. Keen, in speaking of the new magazine, and commending it to our members, laid emphasis on the fact that it was enthusiastic support that was wanted for the success of the new magazine.

I am, therefore, sending one or two photos with a short note, in the hope that they may be helpful, in a small way, towards the success of the MODEL RAILWAY NEWS, in which I notice you express the hope that model railwaymen will respond with photographs and descriptions of their models. I might mention that I work under somewhat restricted conditions, as my room measures only 9 ft. by 6½ ft.—hence the cramped appearance of the track in the view of Waterloo.

The first photo is of a 0 gauge L.S.W.R. "F" class mixed-traffic loco, which I have built recently for my model 0 gauge L.S.W. Railway. This engine is my first serious attempt at loco building and it is a great success, as it hauls four bogie coaches (120 tons) up the bank referred to, with ease. A L.M.C. mechanism is fitted. It was constructed with especially small wheels (1¼ in. diameter), to work traffic between "Salisbury" and "Exeter," as between these points there is a bank which averages 1 in 30 for about 14 feet. The summit of this bank can be seen in the second picture on the extreme right. The abrupt ending of the track is caused by the absence of a lifting bridge across the door of the room. The low-level tracks on the left are the "Waterloo" arrival and departure roads which, when photographed some months ago, were only just being laid. At the time of writing, however, the station is complete apart from signals. At a later date, with the Editor's permission, I will give a description of the line with some more photos.

Yours truly,
THOMPSON CLARKE.

Clapham Park.

[Readers will note the flat station buildings on right wall, giving pictorial effect in a minimum of space.]

Summit of bank between "Salisbury" and "Exeter."

Is Your Model Railway a Help to Others?

To the Editor MODEL RAILWAY NEWS.

DEAR SIR,

At first sight this may appear rather an unusual question, but if you are a model railway owner who has hitherto preferred to "keep yourself to yourself," as the saying goes, it is hoped these few lines may cause you to reconsider your position.

There are many model lines, complete systems, simply bristling with gadgets, ingenious signalling arrangements, realistic landscape effects and so forth, which, beyond being exhibited to occasional visitors (who invariably remark "How wonderful!"), never see the light of day—by which is meant that the owners never realize what real pleasure visits from fellow enthusiasts would afford.

How much more interesting would be the comments and questions of others as keen as oneself, others capable of viewing the line intelligently and perhaps making a few criticisms—compared with the "how wonderful" type of visitor, however kindly disposed.

On the other hand, it might well be termed a form of selfishness not to give the benefit of your experience (every model railway engineer gets plenty of experience and "experiences," too, sometimes) to others who may be requiring assistance. Who knows, someone may be patiently trying-out an idea that you have proved a "wash-out" long ago—or isn't *your* way of making-up points perhaps worth handing on? By now the reader may well be wondering what this is leading up to. It is simply that now there is a live paper catering solely for the model railway engineer, every owner of a line, however simple or elaborate it may be, should make a point of taking up his part in the model railway world—either by sending in a description and photos of the railway as a whole, accounts of how unusual jobs were tackled or taking part in the discussions in the correspondence columns of the MODEL RAILWAY NEWS.

Model engineers are a cheery band the world over, correspondence leads to visits, and visits sometimes to firm friendships—the moral being "Don't plough a lonely furrow."

In addition, the Model Railway Club movement is now coming to the fore and should be greatly fostered by the advent of the MODEL RAILWAY NEWS. The writer has the privilege of belonging to the Wimbledon and District Model Railway Club, the first to be formed outside Central London and in view of the benefits and enjoyment he has derived from membership, together with the pleasant friendships formed, would strongly urge all really keen model railway owners to join a club. If there is not one in your district, why not inaugurate it yourself?

Yours truly,

A. R. WALKLEY.

Wimbledon, S.W.

Model Electric Tramways.

To the Editor MODEL RAILWAY NEWS.

DEAR SIR,

Will the scope of your journal extend to model electric tramways? I think electric tramways have been rather neglected from the model maker's point of view, and I am wondering if any of your readers have done any work of this kind. Possibly a model tramway is not so picturesque as a model railway: it has none of the bridges, stations, signals, and other accessories which add so much to the interest of a railway. Still the electrification and control problems are very interesting, and as the whole system is somewhat simpler than a railway it might appeal to some of your readers in cases where space is a consideration. I might also suggest that owners of some of the more elaborate model railway systems should put down an electric tramway at some jünction on the line, as an auxiliary service.

Yours truly,

"CONTROLLER."

London, W.

Terminus Planning.

To the Editor MODEL RAILWAY NEWS.

DEAR SIR,

Let me congratulate you on the first issue of the MODEL RAILWAY NEWS. I noticed therein a scheme for a model railway terminus in gauge 0. This is, in my opinion, unnecessarily elaborate. Few model railwayists will have such a large volume of traffic to cope with as Mr. Dean allows for. I therefore enclose a simplified plan which will be found to give almost all the advantages of the plan mentioned.

Trains may use all four platforms for arrival or departure; the loco siding gives immediate access to all platforms. If space permitted it could be fitted with a turntable. The goods yard can be entered from either end, and this saves the reversal necessary in Mr. Dean's plan when leaving. Also I have reduced the overall length of the station by 4 ft.

Wishing success to the MODEL RAILWAY NEWS.

I am, yours truly,
H. D. PINNINGTON.

Liverpool.

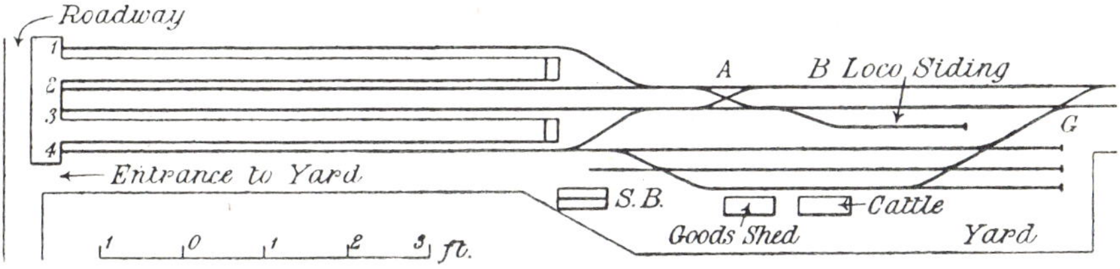

Mr. H. D. Pinnington's suggestion for a simple terminus lay-out.

Indoor *v.* Outdoor Systems.

To the Editor MODEL RAILWAY NEWS.

DEAR SIR,

First let me congratulate you upon No. 1; it is simply splendid. Though it is early yet to speak of bindings, I do hope when the time comes you will consider binding covers for the volumes, for I am sure everyone will want to keep their volumes in permanent form, as a work of reference.

You ask on page 6 for replies to certain questions which may be of use to beginners, so I will try and give you my experiences of No. 7. The respective merits of indoor *versus* outdoor systems. I shall be speaking throughout from the point of view of 0 gauge, as this is the only scale of which I have any experience.

When I first started seriously in 1910, my railway was out of doors, raised on a wooden substructure. It was in use for about three years, when a change of residence necessitated taking it up. At the new house I decided to lay it in a room in the basement. Hence I can compare the merits of the two systems as they affected me.

OUTDOORS.—Advantages are:—(1) Space. It is possible to get long straight runs, and the curves can be laid to a very large radius. (2) Any future extensions or additions can be laid in as desired, there are no room walls to get in the way. (3) Realism, scenery, etc., is easily obtained, although of course, wall-paper backgrounds are out of the question.

INDOORS. — Advantages are:—(1) Absence of "climatic troubles." Possibility of very minute details. Buildings, etc., can be "delicate," whereas outdoors they have to be made of much thicker materials, and hence suffer from a scale appearance. (2) Point rodding does not "clog up" in the guides and joints, an occasional oiling is all that is needed to keep them working freely. (3) Signals can be worked with strong thread instead of wire, which gives a much better result, as wire is inclined to have a certain amount of spring in it, and also is "heavier" in drawing back the slack. Outdoors thread is impossible; apart from its short life, it is seldom in adjustment, as a slightly damp atmosphere shrinks it and pulls all the signals "off." (4) Lever frames are free from the rapid deterioration evinced outdoors. (5) The system can be used in all weathers. Outdoors not only a fine day is needed, but also a comparatively warm one! (5) Reduction of maintenance work to the minimum. (In passing, the novice will do well to remember that a certain amount of maintenance is *always* needed, and that if he neglects this he will be laying up trouble for himself.)

The chief—indeed, I might say *only*—disadvantage of indoors is space limitation, for all the restrictions can be reduced to terms of this one. The beginner would do well in planning his system to make up his mind as to his minimum radius of curve beforehand, remembering that a sharp curve will limit him to short rolling stock. Always use the largest radius possible, even if this necessitates a limit to the scope of the railway. In my own case I have 4-ft, radius as a minimum for points and crossings on the main line, in station "yards," etc., while open curves on the main lines are to 6-ft. radius, or as near it as is possible. (Although a few points in the coach sidings, and even on the "*slow*" lines in the principal terminus "yard," are only 3 ft. 6 in. radius; but this is only done where necessary, and *where only the smaller stock will have to run, and then only at slow speeds.*) In this way I am not restricted as to length of stock, and find scale-length coaches, dining cars, etc., and long express locos quite at home on the system, nor am I troubled with buffer locking with "scale" couplings, except perhaps with the very longest stock, which has to have non-locking buffers *or* rigid-link, swivelling couplings.

To sum up, my idea of the ideal is an outdoor main line, with the principal stations—and their "yards"—in large sheds. But apart from this (which must in many cases be an impossible ideal), I think I should always "plump" for an indoor line. Of course, assuming one is considering gauge 0. In the case, for instance, of $2\frac{1}{2}$-in. gauge, most of the disadvantages of outdoors would vanish, or at least be modified, while those indoors would increase, as in an ordinary-sized room, not much more than a testing track could be obtained in this gauge.

Yours faithfully,

J. C. D. French.

Putney, S.W.

A War-time Locomotive.

To the Editor Model Railway News.

Dear Sir,

During some months of the war my spare time was given to making shell bases. As the equipment of big factories improved and their output increased it ceased to be worth while to collect work done by isolated amateurs and I thought I might get back to some sort of model work. Needless to say, anything to do with model work was, at the time, almost unobtainable. One day I happened to go into Messrs. Bond's, and on the counter was a box of odds and ends to do with models. If I remember rightly, everything they had left for model-making. I reduced their small stock by picking out six small loco wheels and two larger ones, with which I thought I could build a tank loco. When work was put in hand on these wheels most of the small ones were so chilled on the surface that no tool would touch them. However, they were mounted in the lathe and ground with a small carborundum wheel held in the slide rest and driven from the overhead. This quickly made a good job of them. In the scrap box were two cylinder castings originally intended for $\frac{1}{2}$-in. bore, but the patterns for them had been made slightly too small and they had been abandoned. They made up quite well as $\frac{3}{8}$-in. bore, 1-in. stroke. The tops and bottoms were made from bits of round rod. Out of odd bits of $\frac{1}{16}$-in. steel plate were cut the frames, connecting rods and a few other details. The curved top and bottom of the chimney were cut from what had once been the brass handle of a domestic poker. The smoke-box door was a disc, slightly dished of sheet steel; what it was originally used for or where it came from I know not, but every gadget ever likely to be useful goes to the scrap box. The boiler was a 6-in. length of copper tube, the ends were cut from odd bits of thick brass plate, and it was fitted with three $\frac{3}{16}$-in. water tubes. The outer casing, dummy tanks and bunker were made from tin boxes. The result was quite a presentable little 4—2—2 engine. Its chief fault is that the boiler is rather too small for the cylinders, but it runs.

Yours faithfully,
Ingatestone. H. G. A. CONYBEARE.

Miniature Steamship Posters.

To the Editor MODEL RAILWAY NEWS.

DEAR SIR,

An idea which recently occurred to me may interest your readers. Messrs. W. D. & H. O. Wills' cigarette cards now consist of ships. These cards, with Indian ink or a touch of paint, make up into very fair steamship posters which help to swell the comparatively small range which are, so far, commercially marketed, and as regards size are not so far out of scale.

Yours faithfully,
Birkenhead. F. W. SHAW.

No. 00 Gauge Dimensions.

To the Editor MODEL RAILWAY NEWS.

DEAR SIR,

As I submit that the gauge is not the correct method of arriving at the scale, I should like the designer to give me exact measurements of width from the actual model coach shown in your first issue on page 9, in the following particulars, viz.:—total width over the outside faces of the wheel-tyres, centres of buffers, and width over body at the waist.

The photograph to my eye evidences a slight "underbodied" appearance and I should like, as a matter of general interest, to study the proportions with reference to the figures requested.

Yours faithfully,
HENRY GREENLY.
Farnborough, Hants.

The Model Railway Club.

The Model Railway Club held their Annual Social Meeting at St. John's Schools, Tottenham Court Road, on the 8th January, nearly a hundred members and friends being present.

Although not a competitive exhibition in the full sense, a fine collection of locomotives, rolling stock, and railway appliances was on view, among the principal being Messrs. A. Adamson's 0 gauge locomotive superstructures; A. R. Annoot's group of clockwork and electric locomotives, 0 gauge; S. J. Beeson's two locomotives and two wagons, also in 0 gauge; L. E. Brewer's two 1 gauge L. & N. W. R. locomotives, one a Webb compound 4–6—0 goods engine; H. Chase's two cardboard locomotives, one a very fine 0 gauge model of a Stirling 4—4—0 (S.E.R.) express engine; H. T. Clarke's 0 gauge L. & S. W. R. locomotive; A. C. Davies' steam locomotive and coach, 1 gauge; E. A. Eldridge's goods wagon, coaches, and engine shed, 00 gauge; L. Forest's two 0 gauge coaches; S. M. H. Fish's three S. R. locomotives (Brighton Section); G. P. Keen's two free-lance 0 gauge locomotives, a G. W. R. "Macaw" wagon, and a water crane; H. D. Kerr's three 0 gauge Caledonian locomotives (clockwork), two Caledonian goods wagons, a 2—4—0 G.E.R. tender locomotive, and a 0—4—0 contractor's engine, both the latter in 00 gauge; Col. R. Henvey's 0—6—4 clockwork tank locomotive, 0 gauge; F. N. Lance's 0 gauge

L.B. & S.C.R. motor coach; C. T. Pond's two 0 gauge electric locomotives; W. R. S. Smart's comprehensive exhibit of S. R. locomotives and wagon stock; and W. H. Smart's G.C.R. wagons, 0 gauge.

Messrs. Percival Marshall and A. W. Bond kindly acted as judges and awarded the four certificates allotted as follows:—Mr. A. Adamson, for his unfinished superstructures, which, as Mr. Marshall pointed out, were especially interesting as showing a model locomotive in process of construction; Mr. H. G. Kerr, for his excellent pioneer work in 00 gauge locomotives with home-made mechanisms; Colonel R. Henvey, for his 0—6—4 tank locomotive with Stirling reversing gear, Westinghouse pump, and other fittings; Mr. F. N. Lance, for his motor coach, a particularly neatly finished piece of woodworking.

The certificates were presented by Mr. Percival Marshall, who said he was glad to be able to address them for a few moments, because it gave him the opportunity firstly of congratulating the members on their very excellent show of work that evening, and secondly of thanking them for the support and good wishes so many of them had given to the MODEL RAILWAY NEWS. In co-operation with Mr. A. W. Bond, it had given him much pleasure to examine the various exhibits, and both the judges felt that, in addition to the recipients of the four certificates awarded, there were several other exhibitors whose work was worthy of high commendation. At the same time the winning of an award was not the chief incentive to exhibit on these occasions. By placing a model on view members were contributing to interest and information of their fellow-members, and therefore, everyone who exhibited could find his reward in the fact that he was helping to promote the objects of the Club and the success of the evening generally. Mr. Marshall added that he was pleased to see that the Club encouraged the exhibition of unfinished work. Partly completed models were very instructive, especially to beginners who were able to see the stages through which work had to pass before completion was arrived at. He concluded by wishing the Model Railway Club continued and increasing success.

A hearty vote of thanks to Messrs. Marshall and Bond was then proposed by the chairman, Mr. G. P. Keen, seconded by the vice-chairman, Mr. W. R. S. Smart, and carried by acclamation.

The passenger-carrying track was in operatiou during the evening, the traffic being worked very successfully by Mr. Beeson's 0—6—0 tank locomotive and Mr. W. H. Irwin's 4—2—2 G.N. express engine, both of $2\frac{1}{2}$-in. gauge.

The Wimbledon and District Model Railway Club.

The fixtures for February are as follows:—February 2nd, Lecture by Mr. Henry Greenly, A.I.Loco.E., on "Ravenglass and Eskdale Railway." 7.30 p.m., February 16th, Test Track Night, 7.30 p.m. February 28th, Visit to the Croydon School of Signalling, Southern Railway. Members should make a point of attending on February 2nd, and visitors will be welcomed—a lecture by such a well-known authority as Mr. Greenly is sure to be unusually interesting.

The Hon. Treasurer reminds you that all subscriptions are due by the end of the month. Hon. Secretary, R. Shephard, 27, Bernard Gardens, Wimbledon.

Half-inch Scale Cylinders.

Messrs. Stuart, Turner & Walden, 42, North Street, Prittlewell, Southend, on-Sea, have sent us a sample pair of cylinders for $\frac{1}{2}$-in. scale model locos. These are in gunmetal, and are fitted with pistons, glands, slide-valves, rods, and steam inlet. They make a thoroughly sound job, well machined and finished, and are supplied at 35*s*. per pair.

The MODEL RAILWAY NEWS

Editorial and Publishing Offices :
66, FARRINGDON STREET, LONDON, E.C. 4.

Single Copies, post free, 7½d. Annual Subscription, 7s. 6d.

Vol. I. No. 3. MARCH, 1925. Price, 6d.

Notes of the Month.

"MODEL RAILWAY NEWS calling the model railway world. Here is the first news bulletin." Just as you are accustomed to hear a similar call on the wireless every evening at seven o'clock, so each month you will get the news bulletin of the model railway world in our pages. So make a habit of picking up the MODEL RAILWAY NEWS on the first of every month and listening-in.

* * *

Here, for instance, is a news item. St. Paul's, the famous London public school, has just started a model railway club. It will be a section of the Smee Society, the school society which deals with science, and thirty boys have already enrolled themselves as members. We hope before long to be able to give some details of the track and equipment about to be installed.

* * *

Another school also is installing a model railway. This is St. George's School, Harpenden, Herts, where the initial equipment includes 10 coaches, a mail-van, a 12-wheeled dining car, about 20 goods wagons, and nine locomotives, two of which are steam models. This is an excellent start, and the stock will no doubt be increased as time goes on. As with other schools, St. George's is unable to give a permanent home to the track at present, but two rooms are available during term-time, and a temporary track has been installed, having terminals and sidings in one room and a complete loop in the other.

Many public schools have a strong engineering or science side. Why should not the elements of railway engineering be included as a set subject in the school curriculum ? Transport plays a big part in the national life ; railway engineers will always be needed. So why not give them some preliminary training while at school ? There is much scope for the application of both mechanical and electrical knowledge in the planning, building and operation of a good model railway, and it may be made of real educational value if rightly used. Other schools, forward, please.

* * *

How many of our readers know the origin of the 4-ft. 8½-in. gauge ? What settled the choice of this precise figure ? Colonel Kitson Clark, of Leeds, in a speech the other day at Huddersfield, said that the first locomotives were substitutes for horses at the collieries. What would be the width of the carts the early engines had to draw ? These would be the width of the horse, then the two shafts outside, and then the two wheels outside that. Thus they got 4 ft. 8½ in., the gauge which Stephenson adopted, and which had continued to be adopted since. Were we able to use the same chimney height as the Americans employed, the difference in power would be incalculable, but we were using the same height as used by Stephenson, and bridges and tunnels were adapted to that height.

Model railway work, like every other good hobby, is very absorbing, and whether he be father, husband, or son, the model railway enginner of the family disappears for long periods of the day or night, to pursue in the basement or back-room or attic, the fascinating problems of his beloved model railway. What does the wife or the mother think about this? What is the woman's point of view? This is discussed by a correspondent elsewhere in this issue. The ideal state, of course, is when the women-folk of the family are also model railway enthusiasts, and come too, if not to work, at least to show a sympathetic interest. But even if *Madame* has other interests and other occupations in the home, there is at least a great deal to be said in favour of the model railway. There is no need for us to state the case for the defence—our readers know it quite as well as we do.

* * *

When we founded the *Model Engineer* more than a quarter of a century ago, one of our earliest correspondents was Col. William Hamilton, of Glenties, co. Donegal. It is a delightful coincidence to find that, despite the passing of the years, Col. Hamilton is again to the fore, sending us the cheeriest of letters to welcome the MODEL RAILWAY NEWS. He makes this interesting comment:—"I have tried all sorts of hobbies in a long life, but the only one that I did not tire of was model railways." How well that bears out the experience of every real enthusiast.

* * *

But Col. Hamilton has a friendly dig at us, too. He says that in No. I we gave too much prominence to electricity. He writes:—"I am well aware that electricity must have its place in the sun as well as steam and clockwork, but I noted that all but one of the splendid engines whose photos were given in No. 1 were electric! I was delighted with the interview with Mr. Keen, but I trust that gentleman will yet be a conver to steam, and that the 'honk-honk' of the good old blast may yet be heard on his splendid railway." We do not think the steam engine will ever die out completely, at least, not in this generation, for it undoubtedly has a fascination of its own, especially if it is large enough to sit behind and drive. Yet in spite of that, for indoor model railways, electricity is the coming motive power. Steam enthusiasts, however, need have no fear that we shall neglect their interests.

* * *

There is ample scope for the employment of both steam and electricity on the one railway. We remember many years ago, visiting the late Mr. Henry Lea, of Birmingham, who had a steam model railway in his garden, with electrical control. He could stop and start his beautifully made Midland steam model at the signals on his track, by means of electrical control from a fixed point. A correspondent elsewhere in this issue advances other ideas for steam-electric model locos. Steam and electricity will not necessarily always be competing for the favour of the model railway engineer; sometimes he will extend a friendly hand to both and make them co-operate.

* * *

The standard 15-in. gauge ($4\frac{1}{8}$-in. by $6\frac{3}{4}$-in. cylinders, 20-in. wheels) Atlantic locomotive built from H. Greenly's designs last year for the late Count Zborowski, and in use on his "Highams Railway" at Canterbury, has been sent to the Fairbourne Railway (Barmouth, North Wales), for service during the forthcoming summer. In honour of its late owner, who was so well known in motor car and model railway circles, it is, at the designer's suggestion, to be named "Count Louis."

* * *

Readers in Manchester and district who would be interested in forming a local model railway club are asked to communicate with Mr. J. A. Dean, 29, Gorse Lane, Stretford, Manchester.

NOTABLE MODEL RAILWAYS

Mr. W. A. Gosheron's Gauge 1 Model Railway.

AN interesting example of a very complete indoor model railway has lately been installed in South London in the house of Mr. W. A. Gosheron, who resides at Streatham Hill. What it lacks in size (and most London residences will not permit of very extensive lay-outs) it makes up for in attention to detail, which enables the system to be operated in almost all cases in accordance with approved railway practice. One room at the top of the house has been devoted entirely to the railway which is in itself a permanent fixture. The room measures some 16 ft. by 20 ft., of which the railway system occupies about 120 square feet.

Like most ambitious enterprises, the system under review began in a very humble way—tin-plate rails forming a circular track on the floor upon which ran a small German-made electric engine. To-day the system embraces about 100 feet of double track, which has been electrified and upon which both steam and electrically propelled engines are run. The lay-out is oval in form and stands upon a permanent base three feet in height and this, enamelled white, has a very pleasing appearance. Wherever possible, it is desirable for convenience sake, to operate a model railway from the centre; in this case, however, owing to exigencies of space, the system has to be controlled from the outer edge. A compensating advantage is that it is possible to give full play to sidings and cross-overs, and a scheme of sylvan

Mr. Gosheron's Model Railway and its Chief Engineer.

scenery as pleasing to the eye as it is realistic.

In the middle of the first photograph is the station complete with almost everything usually found there in real life. The buildings are to scale and correct in detail. The houses are of wood and the windows properly glazed: the features include a booking office, waiting room, lavatory, an awning, fencing, platforms, ramps and destination boards. In front of the station is a most realistic field in which are cattle grazing and across which runs a road upon which is the ordinary traffic peculiar to a wayside railway station. In the foreground will be noticed a circular water tank. This is by no means a dummy, for it is used regularly to water the engine. On the extreme right are two large engine sheds in front of which is a coal-tip and a number of sidings. In the left foreground is part of the signalling system, the semaphores of which are worked by the points to which the signal lines are attached, instead of being extended right through to and being operated from the cabin seen in the background. This, of course, is where the system deviates for a moment from railway practice proper.

The track itself is really a wonderful tribute to the art of the model railway engineer. The sleepers, all to scale, are creosoted, and on them are fixed the chairs securely fastened with metal holding-down spikes. The rails of solid hard-rolled brass, bull-head in section, are keyed down with miniature regulation wooden keys, so that the track itself is as immovable as if held in a vice. To complete the job, the sides of the tracks and the spaces between the sleepers are covered with ballast largely composed of tiny granite chippings, which gives the finishing touch to the scheme.

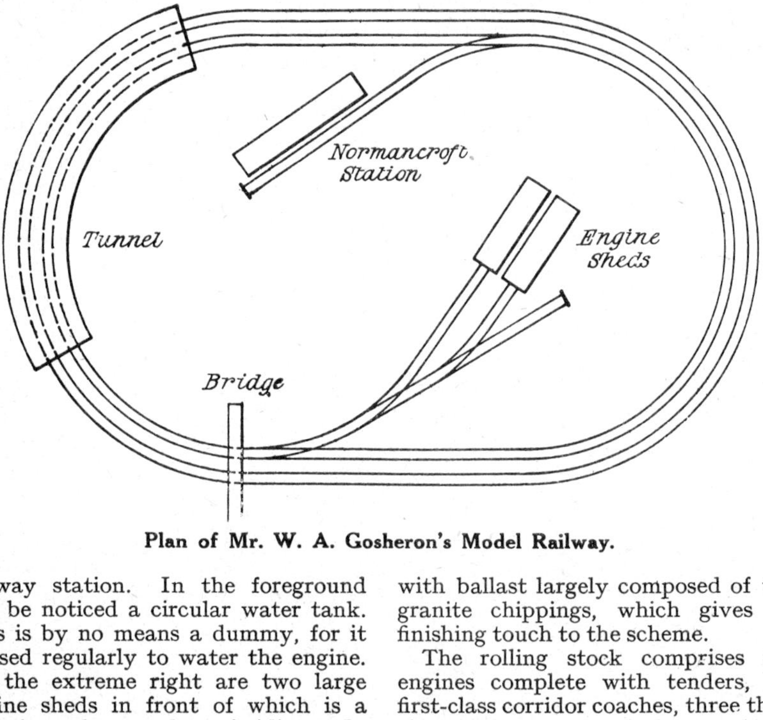

Plan of Mr. W. A. Gosheron's Model Railway.

The rolling stock comprises four engines complete with tenders, two first-class corridor coaches, three third-class brake coaches, and a number of vehicles, including goods brake vans, a refrigerator van, also several open and box wagons. The system throughout is Gauge 1.

In dealing with the engines, pride of place must be given to the Southern 4—6—0 express locomotive No. 736,

View showing Tunnel entrance.

in which four cylinders have been abandoned in favour of two of larger dimensions. The boiler, which is externally fired, is of the water-tube type and in the cab, among other fittings, are regulator, pressure gauge, water gauge, steam blower, check valve, safety valve and reversing gear for the Walschaerts valve motion. This engine is easily operated, and a full head of steam is raised in under five minutes. With the exception of a little slip in starting, owing to the fact that a long train is bound to occupy a curve somewhere, the engine hauls as many vehicles as can be attached, at quite a good speed.

The next engine in importance is the electrically driven 4—6—0 G.C.R. express locomotive, "Sir Sam Fay." In this engine the use of inside cylinders has been reverted to, these, incidentally, being the largest pair of cylinders ever arranged between frames for this gauge in this country. The flanges have been turned off the centre coupled wheels which, while not affecting their adhesive qualities, permits the locomotive to negotiate a smaller radius than would otherwise be the case. The motor is of the permanent magnet type, automatically reversing from track and fitted with a special form of current collector, with two shoes. Current to track and lamps is supplied from a very neat eight-volt accumulator wired up to the switchboard, as shown in the photograph.

Another loco. is a G.N.R. Atlantic-type express 4—4—2. The motor in this model is compound geared with spur wheels only, with ratio one to six. Another engine in working is a standard tank loco. of a type very familiar to contractors and others owning large works, being of 0—4—0 design, modelled on the London and South Western type (now Southern Railway). Curiously enough, these little engines were originally designed for working motor trains in which the engine is coupled permanently to one or two coaches and driven from either end of the train.

Taken altogether, Mr. Gosheron's miniature railway system is a splendid example of a well-designed model railway, largely due, no doubt, to the fact that Messrs. Bassett-Lowke were responsible for the whole of the work, and that from first to last its cost ran somewhere in the neighbourhood of £250.

Buffer Brown's Trial Run.

By "The Inspector."

"YES," said our Mutual Friend, "I went to see a very interesting model railway the other evening."

"Where was that?" we asked, immediately scenting a good article for the M. R. News.

"Oh! it belongs to Brown—Buffer Brown we call him because he is railway mad. It is *some* model railway too!"

"Tell us all about it" we asked with scarcely concealed eagerness, as we got out our note book and pencil.

"Well" said our Mutual Friend, "You usually start with the name, don't you? This was the Great Clatterton and Much Wobling Model Railway."

"Oh! indeed," said we, slightly raising an eyebrow.

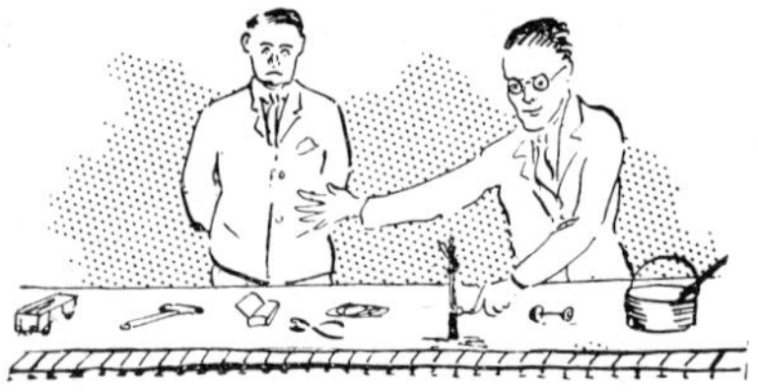

"Yes," he said, "it always does stick."

"Yes, sir, it is the best-named model railway in the kingdom, for there is a great clatter and much wobbling with every train that runs. You see, it was built in rather a hurry. In fact, Buffer Brown prides himself that he put down the whole system inside a week. He was dead keen on getting it running, and he stayed up till past midnight every evening, hammering down chairs and sleepers as fast as he could go. He's a worker; points and crossovers don't worry him much, and he's not one of these high-brow sticklers for dead-true-to-gauge track all through. Of course, his station buildings, and bridges are not quite completed yet, in fact, I brought some of the paint away with me on my clothes. But he's got his signals up, and they work. At least some of them were up, and some were down. He explained to me that there was a little slackness in some of the cords, but he's going to put that right. I tried to operate

Just in time to grab her.

a distance signal from the station box. It refused to budge. 'Yes,' he said, 'I put too much paint on that, it always does stick.'

"Then he said he'd show me a run. He proceeded to collect a train from various parts of the system. 'Why don't you run your engine out and pick up the coaches in the sidings and back into the station like they do on real railways?' I asked. 'Oh! well,' he said, with a smile, 'I could do that, but it's a beastly fag, and my crossovers are not fixed quite right yet. You wait till I let her

He went headlong to the floor!

rip—you'll see something.' Arranging his train at the 'main-line departure' platform, he wound up his clockwork loco, and said 'Now watch.' A touch of the starting lever and she was off. 'There, my boy,' he chortled, with beaming face, 'you don't often see them go like that, do you ? ' ' No,' I replied, 'not often,' for she was tearing away along the track with an amazing banging and clatter as she hit the joints in the rails, and her twistings and turnings as she wobbled over the uneven track would have done credit to a first-class contortionist. He darted across the room just in time to grab her as she reached the other terminal. ' I'll just run her back again,' he said, seizing the engine with one hand, and lifting it over to the other end of the train. ' They don't do that at Euston,' I commented. ' Perhaps not,' he said, ' but it simplifies things so much.' Re-winding the engine, and giving a shrill blast on a small whistle he produced from his pocket, he shouted ' Right away.' Off she went, full pelt. He stood for a moment in rapt admiration of the run. Suddenly—biff !—bang !—' She's off the rails,' he cried, as he leaped to save her. He was just in time to catch the loco, but, unfortunately, his foot caught a trestle and his sleeve hooked-up a pot of paint which he had left beside the track. He went headlong to the floor, dragging engine and coaches with him, and as he lay there, panting, a stream of bright signal-red paint dripped over his ruffled head and made him look like the ghastly victim of a real railway smash.

" He rose very solemnly. I was taken with a sudden fit of coughing, to hide my laughter, and mumbled as best I could ' bad luck, Buffer, old boy. By jove, I did not know it was so late, I must be going. So long ! I've enjoyed myself immensely." I left.

" Well," we asked at the end of this recital, " what's Buffer Brown doing now ? "

" Oh ! He's pulling it all up again ! He's got a new idea for a top-hole lay-out with one starting and finishing terminal, and umpteen loops on the way. He says it's safer to operate it all from one fixed point."

G.W.R. Models and Steam-Electric Locos.

By " Sparks."

MANY congratulations and all good wishes to your most interesting new venture.

May I make a few remarks and ask a few questions in your columns ? I am, like many others, I feel sure, a keen admirer of the G.W.R., and wish to have an all-G.W. model railway, but either like me, have not yet started, or will not enlarge an existing model railway, because of the scarcity of selection of G.W. models in 0 and 1 gauge on the market. I hate a " mixed " railway.

I am quite aware that I can get G.W. " Castle " and " County " class clockwork and electric engines in 0 gauge, but no brown and cream 60 or 70-ft. model corridor rolling stock with eliptical roofs in tin-plate or cheap wooden models, to make a realistic " Cornish Riviera " or " Fishguard Boat Express." The same applies to gauge 1 where, as far as I know, there is only a solitary " Court " class steam loco to be purchased.

While I fully understand the taper boiler offers difficulties to model well and accurately, still, the G.W. is by far the most " standardized " of all the new groups, and apparently will stay true to type in its locomotives and rolling stock and colouring. Consequently, model railway manufacturers can get on with the job, to use slang, knowing there is a less likelihood of any change of prototype, and to judge by results of G.W. advertising its engines by puzzles, books and post cards, there should be a good demand and sale.

Again, I have yet to see as good models of G.W.R. put on the market as there are of late L.N.W.R. and Midland. Somehow, G.W.R. models don't look so realistic as those of other railways. And surely clockwork mechanisms can be made to take kindly, to quote your columns, even to the taper boilers in 00 gauge.

Well, I look forward to your influence to try and work the oracle with the Swindons in miniature, or to get model Crewe, Derby, Doncaster and Gorton to take the broad hint.

Has anyone tried "steam-electric" models?

1. A steam engine whose boiler is heated electrically like the electric kettle, picking up current from the third rail? If so, what voltage and amperage would be required in gauge 1 and what boiler design would be required to fit in the "elements"? I have heard of a model railway like that in U.S.A.

2. Is it possible to have an ordinary steam locomotive in, say 1 gauge, with the tender fitted with an electric motor driving a small air compressor which would fill the boiler with compressed air, and so drive the engine?

In this way the engine could have two tenders and be used either "all steam" or "steam-electric" simply by attaching one or other tender.

These queries are prompted by remarks in your columns on the future of electric traction on model railways, and on the fact that one unfortunate may be struggling to solve a problem which has been proved hopeless or unsolvable by others.

In query 1, the result would be far less mess on the lines, more safety as far as fires go, but danger of damaging the boiler if the water was exhausted, as there would be no "fire" to burn out before the water evaporated.

In query 2, the engine could run continuously, picking up the current from the third rail, and of course be safe.

Cab for Electric Locomotive.

J. R. H. (Oundle), who is delighted with our first issue wants a sketch to make a cab for a four-wheeled electric locomotive.

We append a sketch showing the type of superstructure we would recommend for a four-wheeled engine. The vehicle is so short that with a sloping-end style of cab there is no room for side windows.

No, do not use ply wood, it is so bad to finish satisfactorily at the edge, and these are bound to be shown in a structure such as you are to make. Use any fine-grained wood—satin walnut for example. The design does not involve any piercing for windows and doorways. The sides may be in two pieces with a space between them for the doorway. An inside strip A may be added to join them together, this making a raised footplate. The cab ends are formed by a single central piece B, the sides bounding the other edge of the window opening.

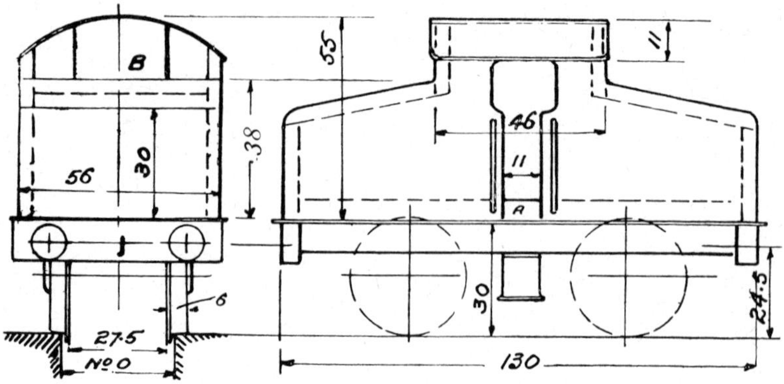

Simple Cab Design for Electric Locomotive.

Making a Gauge 1 Bogie Coach for 8s. 6d.

By F. Spade.

Mr. F. Spade's Model Bogie Coach.

I DON'T know whether I shall interest any of your readers in this, my first attempt at coach-building, but I have had hours of pleasure from it. My only plan was a blue print of gauge 1 dimensions which can be obtained from any of your model loco advertisers.

I used walnut 2·5 mm. thick for the sides, ends, partitions, roof, floor, sole-bars and footboards. For the buffer beams and bogies I used harder wood 3 mm. thick. Each side has two thicknesses of wood and one piece of glass, as in Fig. 1, the upright panels and window frames being glued a tight fit. Care must be taken to get glass the same thickness as the wood. My sides and glass are 465 mm. long. The ends are built up as Fig. 2, the bottoms of both ends and sides being planed away to give the necessary roundness. The end section before the end piece is fixed on is shown in Fig. 3.

The ventilators over the doors are made from the wood of match boxes and glued into position. I made the brake pipes with a piece of stout wire binding thread round tightly to represent the flexible part. The steps were cut out of an old cocoa tin and the dynamo is the handle of a baby's "dummy."

We now come to the most important part with regard to careful fitting—the bogies. My bogie frames are made of hard wood, faced with tin from the above-mentioned cocoa tin. When boring the frames for the wheels it is as well to do both sides at once to ensure accuracy. For the bogie-wheel springs I have used gauge 0 axle-guards, van type, cutting the tops off as will be seen in the photograph, and enlarging the holes to act as bearings for the wheels. Great care must be taken to cut everything square, otherwise you might find three wheels touching the rail and one not. Fig. 4 shows plan of my bogie. When mounting the bogies, care must be taken to get the centre of the buffers 35 mm. from top of rail.

I have upholstered each compartment in red velvet, using thin cardboard for the seats, and window straps are made of leatherette. Doors are not made to open. My coach weighs about two pounds and runs very easy, my wooden bogies answering very well. Length over buffers, 500 mm.

The enamelling and lining are done in the latest L.M.S. colours and finished off with a coat of varnish. I have made four coaches since my

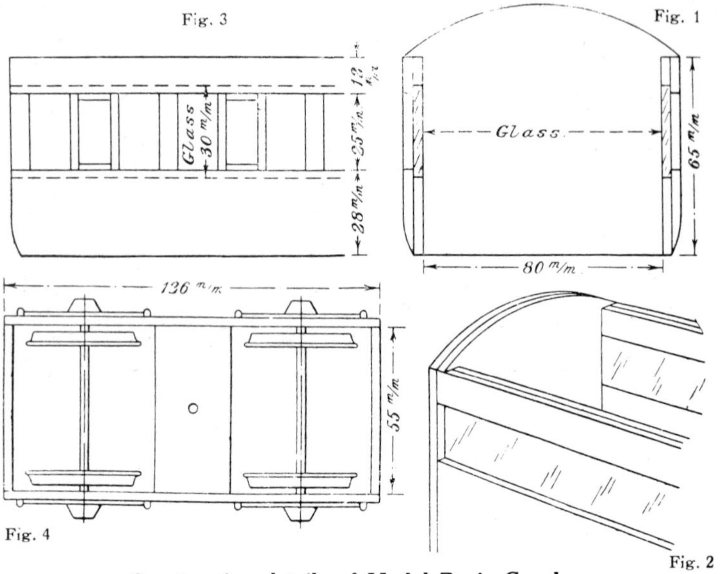

Construction details of Model Bogie Coach.

visit to the last M.E. Exhibition. A first-class coach, a third brake, a third-class coach and a brake van. Being a shopkeeper I do not get a lot of spare time, so most of my coach-building is done after 8 p.m., and on wet half-holidays. Cost of material for third-class coach as follows :—

	s.	*d.*
8 Ventilators at $1\frac{1}{2}d.$ each ...	1	0
16 Door handles at $\frac{1}{2}d.$ each ...	0	8
4 pair wheels at 6*d.* pair ...	2	0
8 gauge 0 axleguards, van type, at $2\frac{1}{2}d.$	1	8
4 brass buffers at 4*d.* each ...	1	4
Couplings	0	6
Glass	0	4
Wood, about	1	0
	8	6

I am now engaged on a 12-wheel composite dining car, 655 mm. over buffers, of my own detign. My track is an outdoor one with 6 ft. 6 in. radius curves, so that I can run the longest type of coach.

Finishing Models.

One of our readers asks for information in the following note. Will someone send us some hints for him ?

"I should be glad if some of your expert readers would give their methods of finishing models, particularly in regard to painting, lining, and lettering. What is the best way to do fine lining on curved surfaces, such as round the barrel of a locomotive boiler ? What is the best way of finishing the wood-work of coaches and wagons ? I find the grain of the wood has a tendency to swell and show through. How can this be avoided and a really good finish be obtained ? What is a good recipe for finishing metal parts dead black, so that the colour will not rub off easily ? What are the best kinds of brushes to use for fine-lining and lettering ?

Any hints on these points would, I am sure, be welcome to other readers as well."

A Chat about Model Electric Railway Motors.

By "ELECTROSCOPE."

THE subject of electric motors for model traction purposes is dealt with at considerable length by Mr. Henry Greenley in his book, "Model Electric Locomotives and Railways." Some brief information on using model railway motors will, however, probably be helpful to novices and even to experienced model railway engineers who are concerned more with the working of a railway than with design and construction of the locomotives. But I advise all model electric railway users to read Mr. Greenley's book, there is a wealth of useful matter in it. Maybe you already have a model electric railway or are about to start one and are eager to get along with the pleasure and interest of working it rather than study an extensive book.

How a Motor Works.

I assume that you know little or nothing about electrical technology. An electric motor consists of two principal parts, termed respectively, the field magnet and the armature. Usually, but not necessarily, the armature is the part which rotates and is connected by gearing to the axles of the driving wheels. In general practice the armature is wound with insulated wire through which current flows. The current magnetizes the core of the armature and enables it to exert a turning force by magnetic attraction or repulsion, or both of these together, in combined action with the magnetism of the field magnet. Turning effort, or torque, as it is termed, depends upon current; speed of rotation depends upon voltage. The greater the amount of current flowing through the armature the more powerful will be the turning effort. The higher the voltage applied to the armature the higher will be the speed of rotation. For pulling heavy loads the motor must have plenty of current, for running at high speed it must have plenty of voltage. But flow of current is dependent upon voltage, the windings of the motor offer resistance to the flow and you must apply enough voltage to send the current through the windings. The product of current and voltage gives the energy developed by the motor, that is, the rate at which it is doing work, in fact, the horse-power it is giving at any moment.

The Starting Effort.

At starting, the motor requires to exert a powerful turning effort; it has to overcome the "sticktion," that is, the stickiness of the axles of the coaches and locomotive and gearing; it has to impart motion to the standing weight and give acceleration, that is, increasing speed to this weight. Therefore, the battery or other supply of electricity must be capable of giving ample current. If you are working with a battery it should be of low internal-resistance type, such as an accumulator or a bichromate battery. When the train has been set in motion the "sticktion" disappears; the turning effort of the motor is then chiefly expended in accelerating the motion, that is, increasing the speed of the train, provided there is no undue friction in the bearings, gearing and brushes. When full running speed is attained the motor may not require so much current as at starting, but higher voltage may be required.

Current and Pressure.

An electric motor is a self-regulating machine; it will take current in proportion to the turning effort which it is exerting at any moment. A motor rated to take 8 volts and 2 amperes will not necessarily take 2 amperes. When starting a train it may take 3 amperes, when running speed is attained it may take less than 2 amperes. A pressure of 8 volts may not be required at starting; it may send too much current through the motor and acceleration will be excessive, the train will rush into speed and perhaps become derailed, but at full speed 8 volts may be required. The armature winding itself generates voltage when rotating, and this voltage is in opposition to the voltage applied to the railway. The greater the speed of rotation the higher will be the opposing voltage; therefore, if you desire high speed the voltage must be raised accordingly. The broad rule for working is: vary the amount of current according to the turning effort required, vary the applied voltage according to the speed desired.

Electricity Supply.

The battery or supply should be capable of giving more than the normal working current, the voltage should admit of regulation below the normal working voltage. If a speed higher than normal may be required, extra voltage should be available. If the battery is of a type which cannot give sufficient current, there will not be any gain in adding more cells in series. The voltage on the railway will be increased, but the internal resistance of the entire battery will be increased; this will nullify the increase of voltage.

The first essential in working an electric railway is current. If you are working with a battery and the motors will not run, refer the trouble to the battery first unless you are sure it is in order and has sufficient capacity for giving current. If you are taking current from supply mains through a resistance, whether lamps or wire, refer the trouble to the resistance; it may be of too high a value to permit sufficient current to flow. If the trouble is not in the resistance it may be due to the kind of current.

Direct and Alternating Current.

There are two kinds of supply current, direct and alternating. The latter current is not suitable for working a motor which has a steel permanent field magnet; it must be changed to a uni-directional current. To effect this, special apparatus is necessary. Motors which have wound field magnets can be worked by alternating current, but the results are not so good as with direct current; the starting effort will be small and there will be liability of excessive sparking at the brushes.

Reversing.

The rule for reversing the direction of rotation is to change the direction of flow of current either through the armature or the field-magnet winding, but not in both simultaneously. If the motor has a wound field magnet, changing the direction of current through both windings of armature and field magnet does not alter the direction of rotation. If the motor has a steel permanent field magnet, changing the direction of current through the armature winding alters the direction of rotation.

Model Station Overbridges for Gauge No. 0.

STATION overbridges have rather troubled model railway men in the past. Owing to the common methods of building these light structures in steel, it has been difficult to reproduce them in wood with a sufficient fineness of detail. Time has, therefore, been given to other more interesting and necessary items of railway construction, and overbridges have either been left out of the scheme altogether or modelled in a rather coarse manner. The writer did suggest in one of his articles on the subject that the Caledonian type of overbridge should be modelled by making a frame in small metal scantlings, fitting a wooden floor and covering in the sides of the bridge with a wire mesh.

The recent use of precast ferro-concrete units by Mr. W. H. Short, A.M.I.C.E., a district engineer (Exeter) on the Southern Railway, for platform footbridges, will allow the model maker to use thin ($\frac{1}{8}$-in.) wood for the bridge girders, strips which are a part of the re-inforcing scheme in

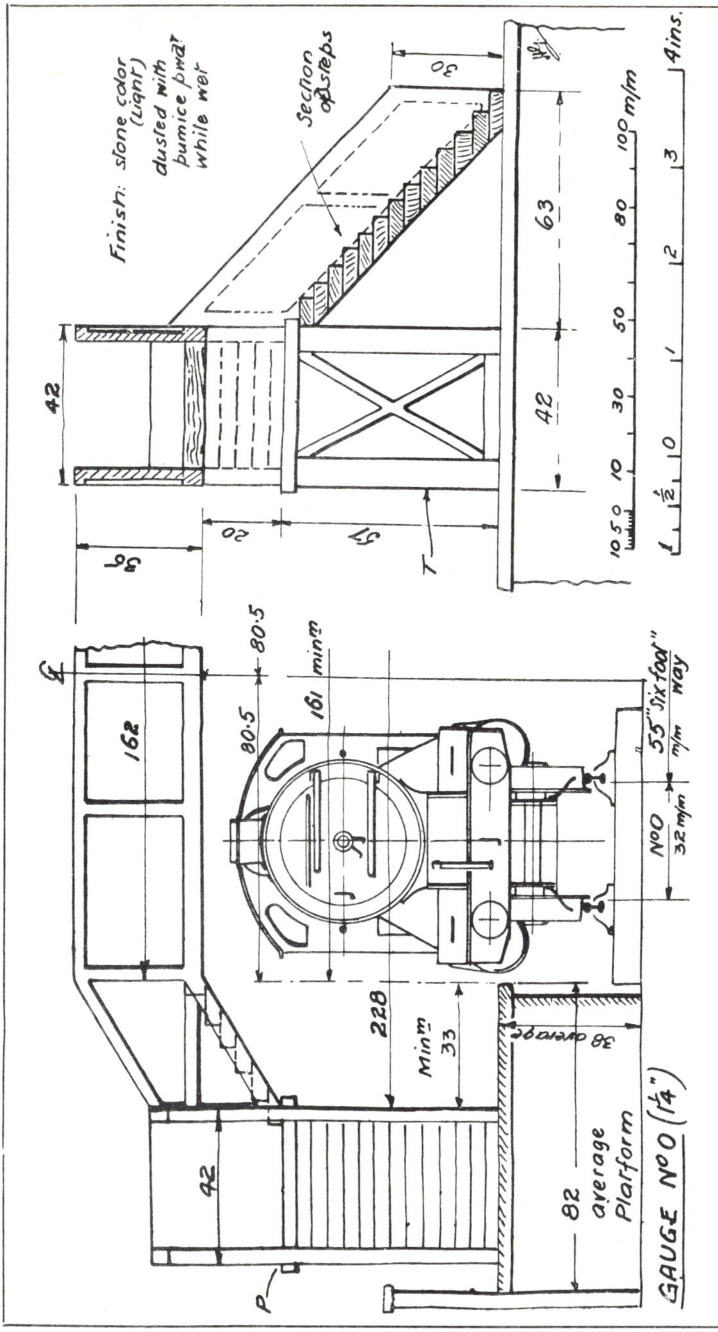

Design for a Model Station Overbridge, Gauge 0.

By Henry Greenly.

the prototype being glued on outside as illustrated in the drawing herewith. This sketch is arranged to suit the writer's No. 0 gauge loading-gauge standards.

The steps may be made out of rectangular strips of wood, 4 mm. by 12 mm. section, glued together to form the treads. This method will necessitate some form of notched jig to hold the pieces in place until the adhesive has become set and to allow the back (the underside) of the treads to be planed off smoothly.

The bridge portion with the short flights of steps at each end can be made up into a complete unit. As in the prototype, this can rest on the square platform or landing P, which is, in turn, supported on the four braced pillars T built up from the station platform level. The overbridge can be painted to represent concrete, a roughness being given to the surface by dusting it with pumice powder while the paint is still wet. For No 1. gauge the minor dimensions can be divided by seven and multiplied by ten, the main dimensions being arranged to accord with the standard loading-gauge dimensions for this scale. (*See* full-size blue-print drawing P 91.)

Power Signalling for Model Railways.

THE field, as in full-size practice, lies between compressed air and electricity. Undoubtedly, electricity is a very simple method of working a model signal but quite a low voltage and a small amperage is all that is necessary to move a model semaphore arm so long as the mechanism is fairly well made. The troubles in the earlier examples were largely due to the use of too large a power. The amperage passing through the energizing coils was, relatively to the work done, enormous, and as a result the solenoid coils became hot if the signal was maintained at danger for any length of time. All that is necessary for the largest installation is a voltage of under 2 volts—that of a single Leclanché or other cell. If a number of signals are to be worked, then the power of the battery may be amplified by one or two extra cells placed in parallel and not in series. A small solenoid magnet should not be allowed to take more than a twentieth of an ampere. This means that the solenoid coil should have a resistance of at least 40 ohms. This means that a long length of wire is required and that the coil may become rather bulky. However, it can usually be hidden under the base board of the track or in an adjacent hut.

With the series system, adopted by Mr. H. L. Stevens on his electric railway, the current flowing through the signals is governed by that taken by the train and quite a short coil of thick wire is all that is necessary. This scheme is fully described in "Model Electric Railways and Locomotives."

The pneumatic scheme is quite a satisfactory arrangement in that it requires no extraneous power. However, greater skill in manufacture is necessary. It is essential that perfectly round tube should be obtained to make the various cylinders employed and that the plungers should fit nicely. Having done this signals can be worked at a distance without wires or rodding—only ⅛-in. tube—and the only attention required will be the periodic oiling of the pistons. Points are a more difficult problem, but this applies to both power systems, and at the outset the mechanical operation of points through suitable rods and bellcranks may prove the most satisfactory arrangement.

A Model 0 Gauge L.N.W. Railway System.

By F. W. Shaw.

THE following particulars of a 0 gauge model railway, every component of which has been home made, with the exception of the locos and track, may be of interest to your readers. The original description was intended for the *M.E.*, and like many other MSS. was never forwarded. However, to lend a hand to our own journal, here it is, rewritten and up to date. Raised on trestles to a height of about 32 inches, the main line gives a run of 120 feet from terminus to terminus, there being in all about 400 feet of track, principally Lowke tin, spiked direct with panel pins to sleepers cut from trellis lathe and painted dead black. The principal station, Euston, has four platform faces varying from 4½ to 6 feet long. Just outside Euston a four-road to four-road crossover gives access to or from any line to any platform. This took about three months spare time to construct, and a new crossover with easier curves is at present building.

Passing the next station, Rugby, which calls for no special comment, the two pairs of track divide and by one Crewe is reached. This is a busy junction with accommodation at five platform faces, and the lay-out of the track lends itself well to traffic working especially to time tables. A reproduction on a very small scale of Runcorn Bridge originally stood just past Crewe but this had to go to make room for further improvements. Passing the Edgehill loco sheds the line reaches Liverpool, which was originally the second terminus, as in reality on the old North Western system. Now, however, the line continues, over a lifting bridge of ordinary plate girder type, round a horseshoe through Rugby and back into Euston again. This is hardly according to full-size practice but this can't be helped as the general scheme of the railway was, and is still, to make the most of available space.

The loco stud (all spring driven), consists of three "Georges," two "Precursor" tanks, a "Charles Dickens," two Midland Peckett tanks, a Midland 990 class and a Caley 4—4—0 in process of construction. The Midland 990 and "Charles Dickens" were also home made.

Rugby Station, from the South.

Rugby Station, from the North.

The scenery consists of railway posters, mostly "middle-distance" views. These make a frieze about a yard deep. Life and bustle is given to the stations by the usual porters and civilians and also milk churns, seats, lamps, auto machines and platform ticket issuers, all the latter being obtained at Hamley's. The line is fully equipped with platelayers' huts, cattle docks, water towers (2-oz. tobacco tins on pencils, painted), telegraph poles (meat skewers and beads), gradient posts and advertisement hoardings.

Ever since the line began as a six-piece circular track about 1904, it has always been a very keen source of interest and amusement not only to the builder and owner, but also to visitors, who average about two per day all the year round. Unfortunately, the photographs are not quite up to date, but they give a general idea of the line. The next job on hand is rebuilding Liverpool and Rugby stations.

The passenger stock consists of two four-coach corridor trains each with diner and mail van and two three-coach local train sets. The goods rolling stock consists of about 60

Home-made Great Northern Brake and Banana Vans.

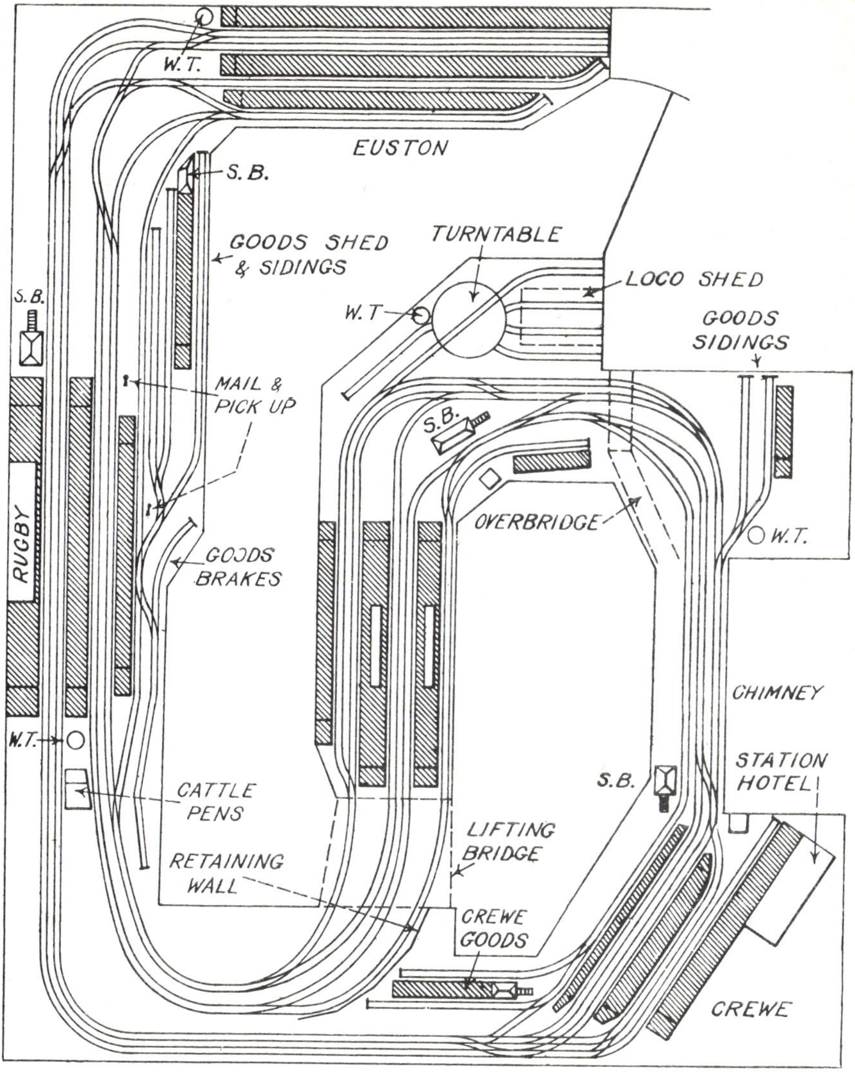

Lay-out of Mr. F. W. Shaw's Model L.N.W. Railway.

wagons of various types, some 30 odd of which are home made, including motor-car, fruit, banana, gunpowder, refrigerator and cattle wagons. All the stock, with few exceptions, is in the old North Western colours, although several pieces have been painted in L.M.S. livery, including a George V loco. Some wagon stock is lettered for two companies, that is, say, Great Western on one side and Midland on the other. As only one side of any train can be seen at one time this dodge has the effect of doubling the variety of wagons on the line without being noticeably absurd. In fact, several local owners have adopted the scheme.

All the points on the line were constructed with a little patience, a little file and a little hacksaw at home, and the signals are Hobbies strip wood with either tin or brass arms. The balance weights used are lead shot hammered flat. Signals and points work up to distances as far away from the cabins as six feet, the point rodding being strong thin galvanized iron wire held down at

M.R. 990 Class loco. and train at Rugby. The sidings in foreground have been dismantled and re-arranged.

three-inch intervals with pins made of the same materials. The levers in the signal cabins were made from the punched bars used in bird cages. These can be bought quite cheaply at most live-stock dealers and are useful in a variety of ways. The turntable began life as a biscuit tin, although that fact cannot be recognized now. Station platforms are stiff cardboard covered with "tile paper," tacked on trellis laths, faced with "brick paper" and painted white at the edges.

The Model Railway Club.

The fourteenth Annual General Meeting of the Model Railway Club was held at St. John's Schools, Tottenham Court Road, on January 22nd, 1925. After hearing the Committee's report upon the year's activities, and passing the accounts, which showed a very satisfactory balance, the meeting proceeded to the election of the new executive. Messrs. G. P. Keen and W. R. S. Smart were unanimously re-elected Chairman and Vice-Chairman respectively. Colonel R. Henvey was re-elected Honorary Secretary, and the following gentlemen were elected to the Committee: Messrs. J. C. Cosgrave (Librarian), C. T. Pond (in charge of Club Tracks), S. H. M. Fish, W. B. Hart, H. G. Kerr, T. W. Pitt, W. H. Smart, C. R. Straker, and J. A. Hines (Junior Member).

The Club's Exhibition willl be held a week after Easter—at Kingsway Hall on Friday and Saturday, April 17th and 18th.

Particulars of the Club can be obtained from the Hon. Secretary, R. Henvey, White Cottage, Shirley, near Croydon.

The Wimbledon and District Model Railway Club.

Events for March:—March 2nd—Lecture by Mr. G. Leaton on Railway Signalling. March 7th—Third Whist Drive to be held at Seymour's, The Broadway, Wimbledon. March 16th—Test Track and Demonstration by Mr. F. A. Evans, with "Torrid" oil-fuel burners. March 28th—Visit to Battersea (Brighton Section) Southern Railway Locomotive Depot. Members only. Meet at Battersea Station, 2.45 p.m.

Our membership list now stands at 40-in comparison with 15 in February, 1924. We hope to see a further increase this year.

Prospective members should communicate with the Hon. Secretary, R. Shephard, 27 Bernard Gardens, Wimbledon, who is always pleased to give full particulars of the Club's activities.

Making Sleepers for 0 Gauge Track.

By Geo. Winteringham.

SLEEPERS are the next consideration. They should be made of some nice, clean, straight-grained wood, such as good red deal, American white wood or Kauri pine, either of which will answer the purpose, but red deal is perhaps the best if it is clean and fairly free from knots. A harder wood is better in some respects, but gives a great deal more trouble in nailing down the chairs, as the very fine spikes or pins which it is necessary to use are much more difficult to drive in without bending.

The standard size for sleepers is $2\frac{1}{2}$ in. by $\frac{15}{64}$ in. by $\frac{1}{8}$ in. The most important dimensions to keep correct being the thickness, as varying thicknesses means an uneven and lumpy track.

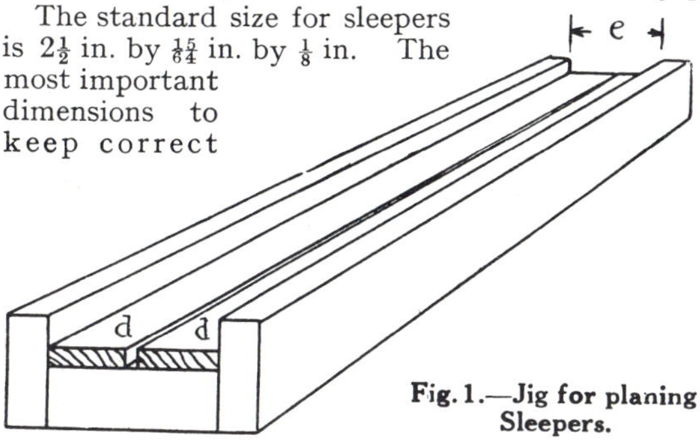

Fig. 1.—Jig for planing Sleepers.

The best way to make sleepers is to buy the wood ready planed to exact thickness. Almost any timber merchant who possesses a panel planer will do this, or some of the firms who advertise in The Model Railway News would no doubt supply what is required.

With $\frac{3}{4}$-in. spacing there will be 16 sleepers to the foot, so that 50 feet of track requires 800 sleepers. Allowing for waste caused by knots and saw cuts, etc., about six feet of board 9 in. wide will be required for every 50 feet of track.

The boards should be cut into 18-in. lengths for convenience and then cut into strips $\frac{1}{4}$ in. wide with a carpenter's cutting gauge, and should the edge of the board get out of straight after cutting a few strips it must be planed straight again before proceeding. It will be found that the edges of the strips are not quite square with the tops owing to the action of the blade of the cutting gauge and should therefore be planed. The most satisfactory way of doing this is to make a rough jig to hold the strips edge up. Fig. 1 shows how this can be made. The two pieces of wood *d* must be exactly $\frac{1}{4}$ in. thick and the gap between them $\frac{1}{8}$ in. wide, so that the strips will fit in the narrow way. The width at *e* should be such that it will just allow the plane to fit in and work easily. The plane should be nice and sharp and set to take a fine cut. The first stroke or two will remove a thin shaving from the middle portion of the two pieces *d*. The plane will then slide on its edges without cutting. Obviously if the sleeper strips are put in the groove and planed on both edges until the plane refuses to cut, they will be nice and square and all the same width.

A cutting-off box (*see* Fig. 2), should be made, as it will do the job much better and save a lot of time in cutting up the strips into correct lengths for sleepers. A fine-tooth tenon is the best kind of saw for cutting off. The stop at the end of the box should be $2\frac{1}{2}$ in. from the saw when in the slot in which it works.

The box should be $2\frac{7}{8}$ in. inside; it will then take 12 strips side by side and about eight layers may be put in at a time so that every cut with the saw produces 96 sleepers. The stop shown at the end of the box may be made of any pieces of scrap metal about $\frac{1}{16}$ in. thick. It is fixed to the

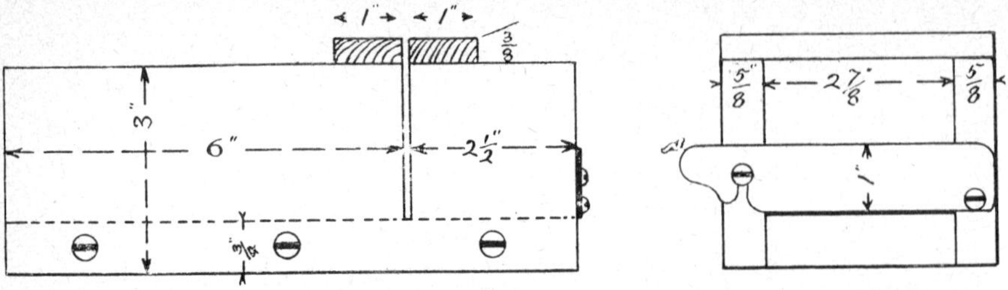

Fig. 2.—Cutting-off Box, for making Sleepers.

box by two round-head wood screws, one acting as a pivot for it to hinge upon and the other as a stud upon which it hooks when closed. After each cut is made with the saw, this metal stop is lifted up and the cut-off sleepers pushed out by advancing the strips. Both the jigs, Figs. 1 and 2, should be either screwed down or held in the vice while being used. The next job is to colour the sleepers, either black or nearly so. Common tar, thinned out with coal-tar naphtha, is a very good mixture to use, but is somewhat messy; the naphtha, being highly inflammable, must be kept away from naked lights. If the mixture is made fairly thin, the sleepers may be put into it in quantities and then picked out to drain and dry. This can be done by laying some of the strips of sleeper wood on a sheet of paper and resting the sleepers on them.

Design for a simple Model 2-in. Gauge Steam Locomotive.

COL. W. HAMILTON (Co. Donegal), requires a design for a model 2-in. gauge 4—4—0 tank locomotive of simple construction for 3½-ft. radius curves. The engine is intended for shunting and, as Col. Hamilton puts it, the "model is not for racing madly round a circle or to draw a man like the Tichborne Claimant." He mentioned that it could be outside fired.

The accompanying drawing shows a 4—4—0 of short-wheel base, using $\frac{7}{16}$ in. × $\frac{3}{4}$ in. standard cylinders and slip eccentrics. With regard to the boiler it has not been thought advisable to fit a 2¾-in. boiler. The loco is so short that it would impair the general appearance to use a boiler barrel larger than 2½ in. While the drawing shows a water-tube boiler, an outside-fired boiler could be used. In that case the water tubes could be a little shorter and the lamp-wick tube at the rear of the trailing axle would have to be omitted. The front of the cab would form the back end of the flame guard. The side tanks would, of course, be open at the top, and this flame guard (made of tinplate) would extend nearly to the top of the tanks. A lever hand-pump could be fitted in the back bunker. This pump would lie transversely and the bunker would have an open top, so that the feed water could be easily poured in and submerge the pump. The spirit tank, however, holds about six cubic inches, the plain outside-fired boiler containing about 25 cubic inches of water when two-thirds full. The water would, therefore, outlast the spirit. A pump is only necessary in the case of the water-tube boiler, which has a small working range of about 13 cubic inches of water. If a plain boiler is used, it is essential that the tube should not exceed 24 S.W.G. in thickness of metal. The maximum pressure would, therefore, be about 50 lb. per square inch if solid-drawn tube is employed, with a test pressure of 75 lb. maximum.

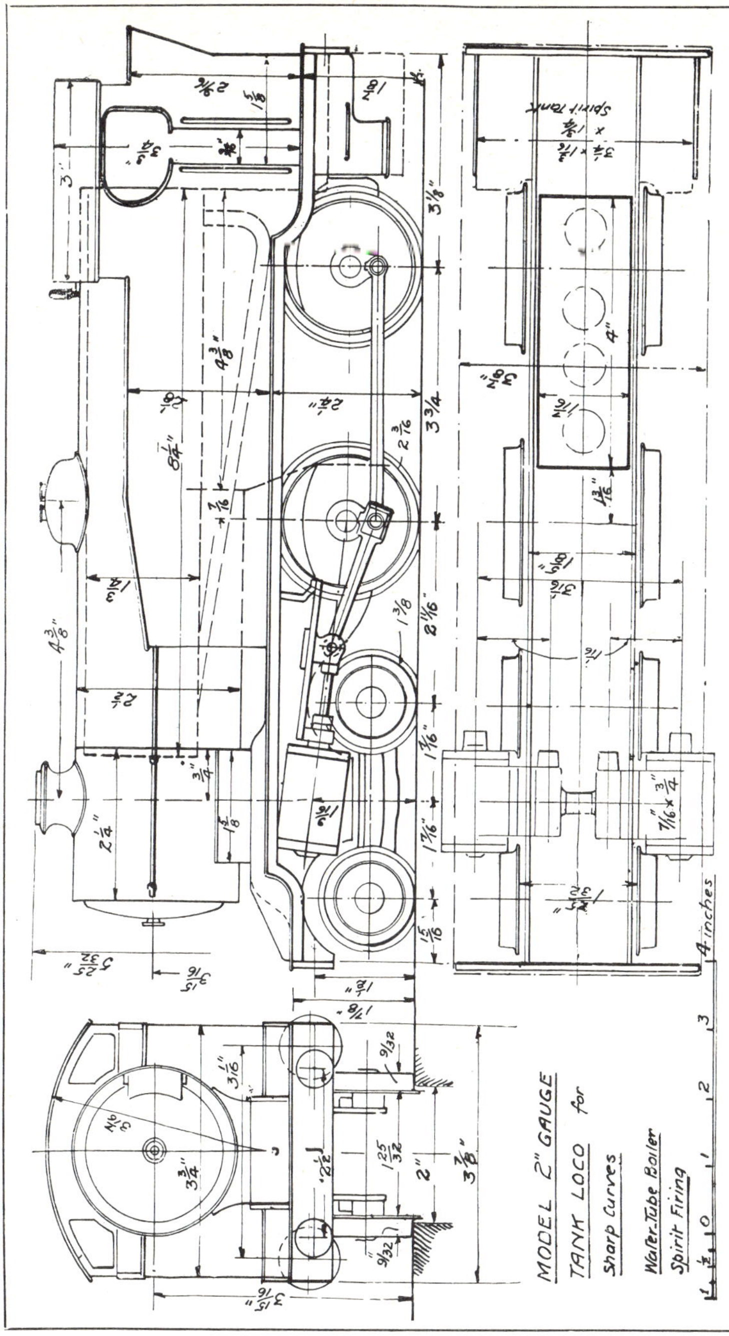

Design for a simple Model 2-in. Gauge Steam Locomotive.

By HENRY GREENLY

Notes on Model Wagon Building.

By Lt. E. A. O. Hutchinson, R.A.

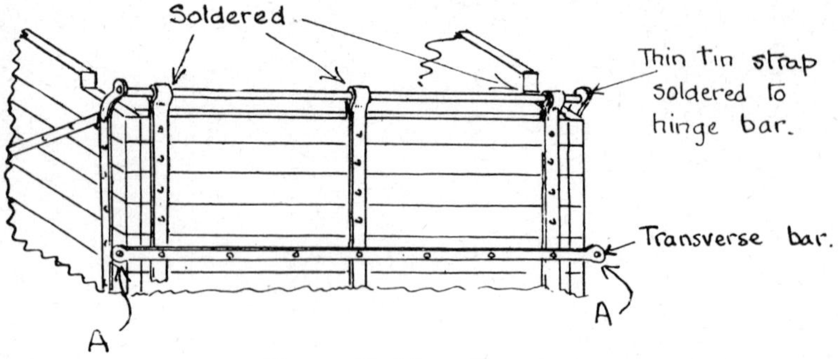

Fig. 1.—End-door Strapping.

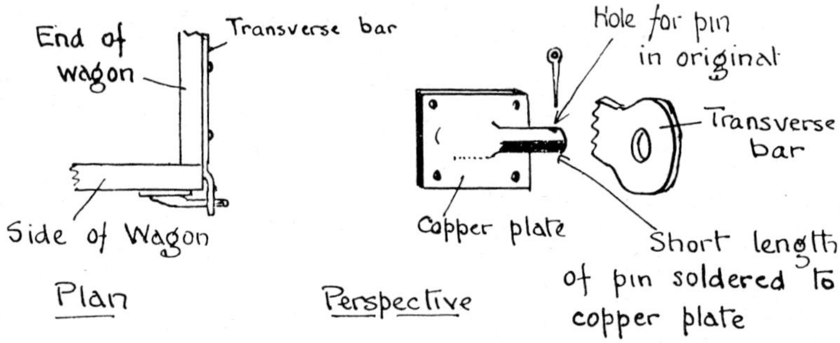

Fig. 2.—Details of Securing Pin.

THE following notes are based on experience gained in building gauge 1 goods stock, and are written in the hope that they will be of assistance to the younger school of model railwaymen whose inclination favours the building of their own rolling stock.

Preliminary.—In building wagons, it has been my aim to make each one as exact a model of its original as possible. Each of my wagons, therefore, is a model of a particular vehicle. The prototypes can be measured up in any docks or shunting yard, but before starting to measure wagons up in a yard, it will be as well to ask the yard foreman for permission. This is rarely refused, and when given prevents the interference of shunters. When measuring up, do not forget to note all the details required—the width of the straps, the position of isolated bolt-heads in the floor or solebar, and whether there any handles or ring-plates. It is also useful to note the numbers and tare weights of other wagons of the same pattern in case it is desired to make more than one. Side and end elevations are next prepared, and the work of building begun.

Strapping and Ironwork.—I find that for corner-plates and strappings the most suitable material is thin card, such as old visiting cards cut into strips of scale width and glued in position. The position of all bolts is marked on the straps, floor, solebars, etc., and the "bolts" themselves tapped in. These "bolts" are the very small type of pin known as Lilliputian pins, cut off close below the head. These pins are invaluable to model makers for representing bolt and rivet heads, and are obtainable from most drapers at small cost.

The only departure I have made from my general principle of using visiting cards for strapping is in the case of end-door mineral wagons. In these, as is shown in Fig. 1, the end is hung by three straps from a crossbar which is supported at each end by the side straps. It did not seem worth while to me to make these end-doors to open, but in order to give the necessary rigidity and support to the hinge-bar, I made the straps on the body sides of thin tin and soldered the bar into them. The hinge straps are also made of thin tin and are turned over the hinge-bar and secured by a touch of solder before being pinned to the end of the wagon.

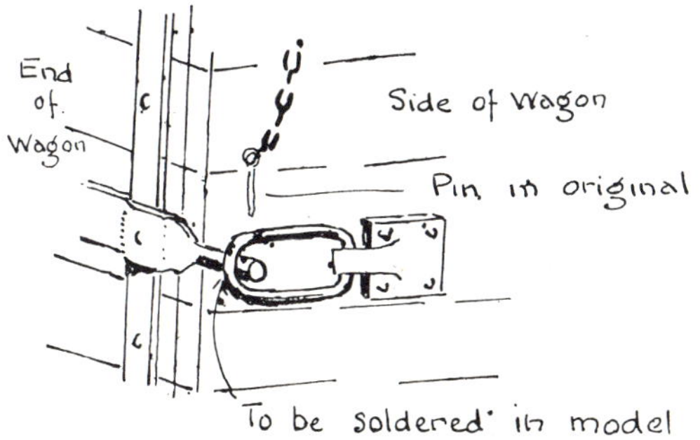

Fig. 3.—Link type of fastening.

The securing pin on the side of the wagon, over which the transverse strap on the wagon end fits, is made of a short piece of pin soldered to a small piece of very thin copper obtained from an old cylinder-head gasket. Such a gasket can often be begged from the local garage, if there is no other way of obtaining it, save by purchase. The split pin in the full-sized wagon is, of course, omitted. (*See* Fig. 2.)

Frequently this securing pin does not form part of a plate fixed to the wagon side, but projects from the end of one of the side-planks. In these cases there is no need to make the plate, a short length of pin being merely pushed through the card transverse strap into the end of the wagon side.

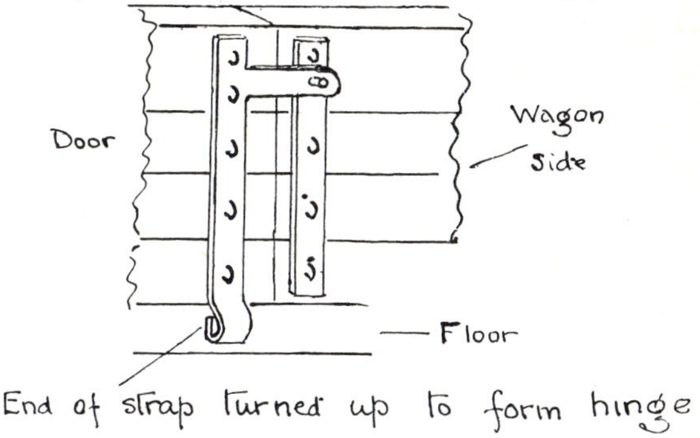

Fig. 4.—Door Strapping Hinge.

An alternative type of fastening for end-door coal wagons is the link type shown in Fig. 3. The construction of this is so obvious that it needs no description. It is, however, as well to remark that, owing to the absence of a split pin through the end of the transverse strap, the link will probably come off the strap unless secured by solder.

It should be unnecessary to say that all such soldering must be done before the various parts are fitted to the wagon, or else the woodwork will be burned. If a support for the work is required, use an old piece of wood of the size of the end of the wagon, fix all straps, etc., to it temporarily, and solder up. When the job is completed, remove straps and all complete, and fix to the wagon. Do not forget to drill the necessary bolt-holes for the pins before soldering up, for if these have to be drilled afterwards, the work will almost certainly be bent.

HINGES on door-strappings are easily made by cutting the strap rather long and turning up as small a piece as possible inwards, as shown in Fig. 4. When fixing hinge-strapping, do not forget the strip of wood which covers the hinge-bar on the original (Fig. 5). I glue these in position and further secure them by a couple of lengths of Lilliputian pins left over, after the heads have been cut off for bolts. Being headless, these do not show when pushed into the strip and floor and tapped home.

RING-PLATES.—Having occasion to use a large number of these recently on a L.M.S. (C.R. section) bogie well wagon, I obtained an old chain purse with links about 4-inch scale diameter, and used the links of this as rings. These rings were fixed by Lilliputian pin staples, the plate portion of the fitting being a small square of card (Fig. 6).

HANDLES, which are frequently required on solebars and end-doors, are simply elongated staples made of ordinary pins or fine wire.

TIE-RODS, such as are fitted to many L.Y. section wagons, are made of wire hooked into the W-irons below the axle-box, and bent over. This is shown in Fig. 7. Do not attempt to solder these to the W-iron, for the latter, being made of white metal, will melt as readily as the solder.

BRAKE GEAR is troublesome to make, but is well worth the time spent on it. I make mine of tin, with lead shoes and brass or aluminimum V-hangers. There is no point, to my mind, in having a working brake on a model wagon, so I do not hesitate to

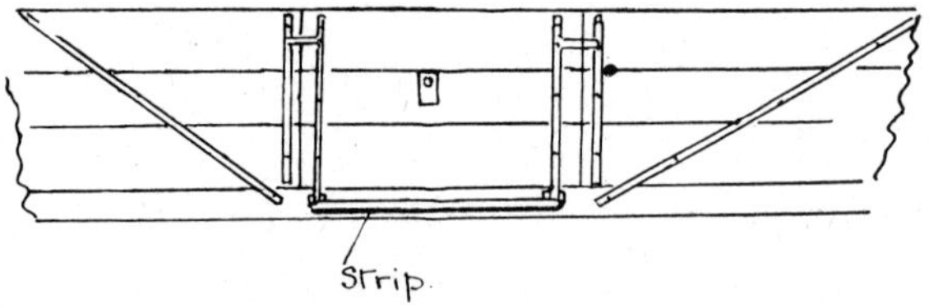

Fig. 5.—Hinge-bar covering strip.

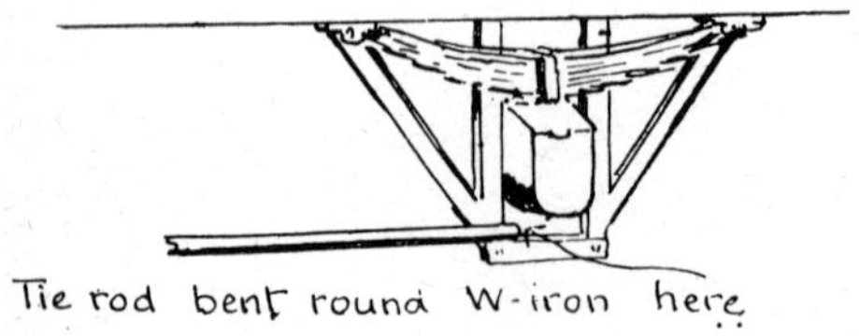

Fig. 7.—Method of making tie-rods.

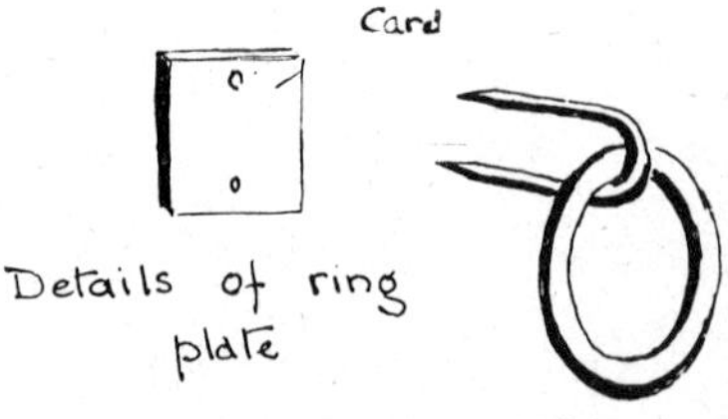

Fig. 6.—A simple ring plate.

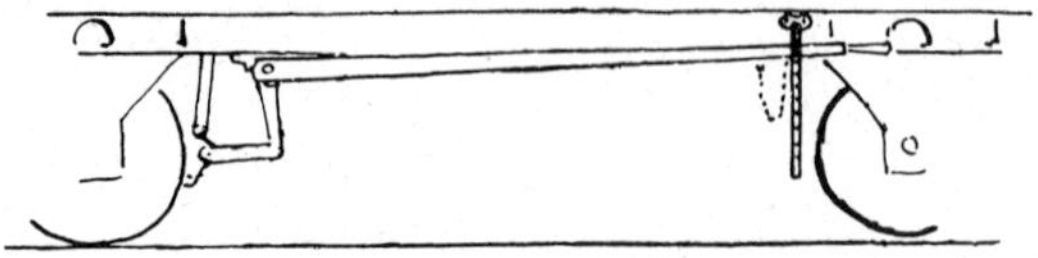

Fig. 8.—A simple type of brake.

solder all joints, the customary pin being passed through as an axis-pin from the outside before soldering, and being cut off short afterwards. This soldering makes a much stiffer job than if joints were left unsoldered.

A considerably simpler type of brake is that shown in Fig. 8, and is a common type on the Scottish railways, particularly on the G.N.S. and H.R. sections of the L.N.E. and L.M.S. Railways.

When fitting V-hangers to solebars, do not forget to fit the guard spring which prevents the door from swinging so far back as to foul the hanger, and do not forget the corresponding guard plate on the door. Such a plate is shown in Fig. 5.

BRAKE VAN DETAILS.—Footboards are best made of tin, with wire hangers soldered on. The hangers should be flattened at the top end and drilled for the bolts securing them to the solebars, the part immediately above the footboard being left circular in section.

Red glass-headed pins are most useful for the permanent type of taillight as used on the old pattern of L.N.W.R. brake van. The end of the van should be counter-sunk to receive the head of the pin, which is fixed in position with glue. Do not forget the brackets above each buffer, in cases where these are fitted.

Another use for glass-headed pins, both red and green, is for the lenses of ground signals.

These notes are not intended to cover the entire scope of model-wagon building, but rather to assist the younger railwayman who wants super-detail models, but has not the necessary wherewithal to purchase the very excellent small fittings now on the market. I shall be glad at any time to hear from readers who can supplement these notes as regards the construction of other fittings with which I have not dealt.

The Woman's Point of View.

A CORRESPONDENT sends us the following observations on what the wife thinks of her husband's model railway hobby. He does not indicate whether it is merely what he thinks she thinks, or whether she wrote it herself, and dared him to send it to the MODEL RAILWAY NEWS. Anyway, here it is :—

"Many a woman looks upon her husband's hobby with a certain amount of suspicion, and when that poor, deluded creature commences to exhibit signs of mental deterioration by an attack of 'Model Railwayitis' she is not only worried about but sorry for him. In the first place, it is so childish of him; fancy playing with a lot of toy trains and pretending to be a signalman or a shunter! Why, little Willie, who is only two years old, can do that and doesn't take up as much room.

"That wretched toy railway occupies the only spare room in the house which could be used so much more advantageously to store a lot of useless lumber in, and, although it is not needed for ordinary use, there is no reason why he should monopolize it. Sometimes the deluded creature, if he isn't an obstinate brute, gets talked out of his mania and switches off to become a wireless fiend. This, of course, is much more sensible from the feminine point of view, as she can sit and listen in to all sorts of things, good, bad and mostly indifferent. But—when the wireless set is definitely finished what becomes of poor hubby's hobby? There is nothing more to be made. He can't profitably construct more than one set for the household use, therefore he is at a loose end and quite possibly seeks recreation from home.

"Now, in going in for a model railway a man follows his natural inclination to make something. Some men have a mechanical instinct born in them; others have practically none, but no man will admit openly that he cannot 'make' things if he tries. A model railway may be finished, but it is never complete. A system which has been worked out most carefully and elaborately is suddenly discovered to be lacking in a necessary shunting bay that would clear the terminus more quickly and facilitate the running of more trains out and in. Up comes that section of the line and the work is forthwith carried out. This occupies every spare evening for some considerable time, and the mere wrecking of all his hard work gives him infinite pleasure as he contemplates how vast the improvement will be.

"Now, think of the advantages of your husband's hobby. It keeps him at home, expands his mind, improves his knowledge of mechanics and makes him a really useful thing to have about the house, because he is always handy and can do any running repairs without incurring the expense of getting a workman in every time a small job comes along."

Queries and Replies.

(6) Model Electric Railway Power Supply.—W. F. D. (Enfield) writes asking where he can get a motor rewound and also the resistance required to run a 12-volt loco. off a 240-volt D. C. supply.

We can recommend you to Messrs. Bond's, Ltd., 254, Euston Road, London, N.W. 1, for electric-motor repairs. The writer is not enamoured of this scheme of running a model electric railway. You will find details of this system on page 302 of "Model Electric Locos and Railways." Difficulties arise when it is attempted to run several locomotives over a line which is fully sectionalized and separate controls are employed for each section. These troubles are discussed in the above book. It is much better to arrange to work the railway from accumulator of, say, 40 to 60 ampere-hour capacity, and to charge the accumulator from a circuit taken through one of the most used house lights, as shown in Fig. 319, page 297, of the same book.

(7) L.N.W.R. (L.M.S.R.) North London Electric Coaches.—F. J. F. (Dollis Hill) writes :—Where can I get a drawing to ½-in. scale of the L.M.S. electric coaches working between Broad Street and Richmond. It is mainly the motor coach that I want.

We have no knowledge of published designs, but the accompanying diagram has been compiled from photographs and standard L.N.W.R. coach drawings. There are some slight differences in various coaches, but the drawing herewith is fairly representative. The trailing end of a motor coach finishes with a large vestibule door. The colouring and letterings are, of course, being modified from the L.N.W.R. to L.M.S.R. style. The drawing has been made to the No. 1 gauge standard; therefore, the scale appended for this gauge can be used as a scale of feet for the original.

The following are a list of dimensions in the various gauges as lettered on the drawing :—

	Gauge No. 0 mm.	*Gauge No. 1* mm.	*Gauge* 2½ in. in.
A	25	35	1⅞
B	56	80	4¼
C	238	340	16¼
D	400	570	29½
E	63	90	4 13/16
F	40	58	2 15/16
G	32	45	2½
H	24·5	35	1 13/16
N	27·5	39·5	29/32
T	6 or 6·5	7	5/16

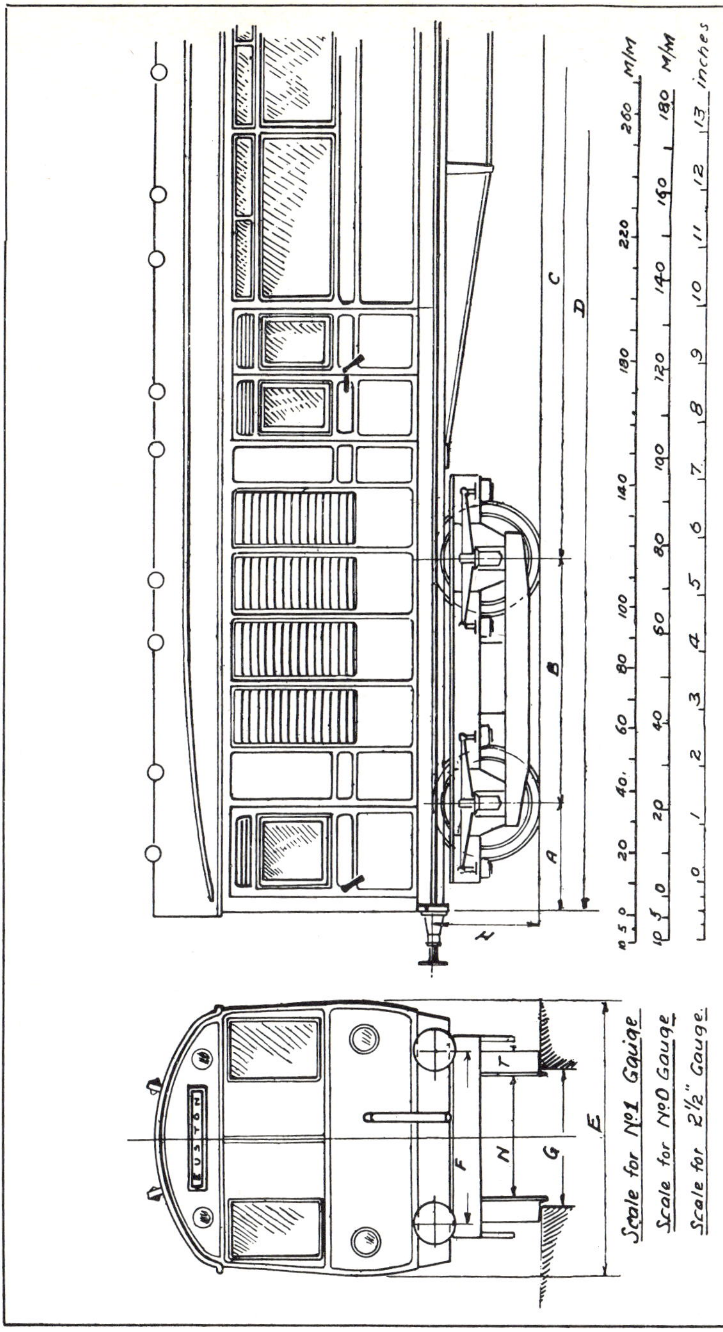

Drawing of L.M.S. (North London) Electric Coach. (*See* Query No. 7).

(9) Model Sleepers and Boiler Fittings.—R. P. (Folkestone): Are not the sleepers used in model railway work much out of scale? What is a ring blower and a check valve?

Yes, we know that gauge No. 0 ($1\frac{1}{4}$) is $\frac{1}{45}$th full size, but it would be absurd to make the sleepers exactly to scale except where they are firmly laid down on a sound sub-structure. The present standards have been settled with an eye to all-round practicability. For instance, on 15-in. gauge railways a full-size sleeper 10 in. × 5 in. × 3 ft. 6 in. long has been found to give the most satisfactory results. In all *working* models "scale" should be subservient to the dictates of a sound serviceable engineering job. Please see "Model Steam Locomotives" by Greenly, for particulars of steam "ring" blowers and other boiler fittings used in the larger examples of model steam engines.

(10) Model No. 0 Gauge Rail Plan.—C. B. W. (Bromley), writes:—"I am setting up my model railway in a loft, but owing to the shape I have difficulty in arriving at a suitable plan. The room is 14 ft. 7 in. long by 12 ft. wide, but nothing can be done on one side."

You omit to state the gauge of the line, but we have presumed it is No. 0 gauge. We append a suggestion which is a modification of the well-known combination of a terminal-to-terminal system and a continuous line illustrated in Fig. 22 of "Model Railways." The terminal branches are outside the circle, and instead of making the South side of the continuous road straight, an elliptical line is to be preferred. The lay-out of the terminals A and B may be as shown or be modified to suit the requirements of the proposed service. The length of line between the junctions at each end of the country station C may be doubled but this may be arranged as a later development. From your letter it would appear that you have not much time to get your line into working order, and that you will be obliged to leave some of the work until you return home again. The line, as planned, can be worked by a *personnel* of two or three train operators.

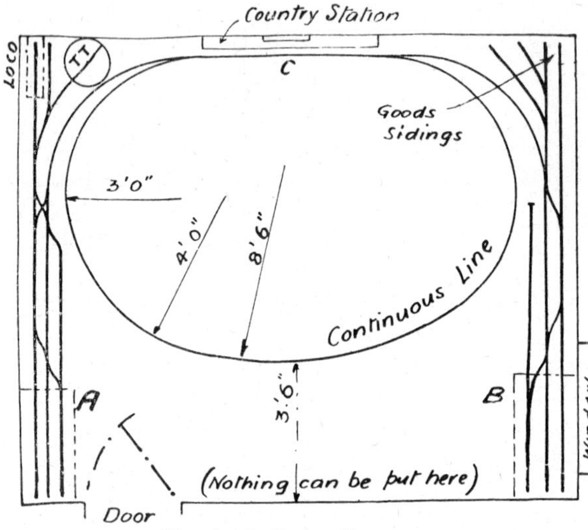

Simple 0 Gauge Lay-out.

Answers to Correspondents.

M. J. G. (London, N.).—The arrangement you have seen on G.E.R. (L.N.E.R.) locomotives is a part of the exhaust steam injectors.

S.A. (London, S.W.).—You should have sent a sketch of the room with detailed dimensions. The space 12 × 10 is just large enough for a No. 0 gauge railway if the chimney breast mentioned is not in too awkward a position. We cannot recommend an outdoor scheme in this gauge—in Britain at any rate.

Small Gauge Standards.

To the Editor MODEL RAILWAY NEWS.

DEAR SIR,

Please accept my congratulations on the first issue of the NEWS.

May I, however, raise a point in connection with two of the articles in this issue which appear to me to tend to cause confusion among model railway engineers?

Mr. Winteringham is suggesting the gauge 0 shall no longer be $1\frac{1}{4}$-in. (as it has been since its inception) but shall be increased by $\frac{3}{64}$-in. and the clearance between rail and check-rail reduced to $\frac{1}{64}$-in. This would mean a distance of $1\frac{11}{64}$-in. across two check-rails, and so render our present stock (built to the original standard of $1\frac{1}{64}$-in. between the wheels) almost useless.

Again, Mr. Stewart-Reidpath has insisted that the correct scale for 00 gauge is $3\frac{1}{2}$ mm.; whereas the original standards fixed by Mr. Greenly (as used for the tinplate models now on the market) is 4 mm.; this scale being also used by some of our English manufacturers.

From my own experience of some years of model railway work, I do not consider that the perfect track-laying (admitted to be necessary for the minute treads and flanges advocated) is possible with the usual conditions of amateur work, as not only the track itself is involved, but also the sub-structure; and unless one can go to a large expense for specially prepared and seasoned wood, etc., warping is bound to occur in time, with the result that derailments would be almost certain to happen.

Also, the smallness of the $3\frac{1}{2}$-mm. scale is apparent by the statement in the article that only particularly large-boilered engines can be built (the G.W.R. being barred), whereas in 4-mm. scale I have just completed a model G.E.R. 2—4—0 (T19 class rebuilt) loco with a reversing clock-work motor. This is not by any means a large prototype, and I should hesitate to attempt a similar model in $3\frac{1}{2}$-mm. scale.

I hope to forward to you photos. and drawings of the locomotive and its mechanism in the near future, as they may be of interest to others.

In making these remarks I am guided by the fact that there have been several cases of members of the Model Railway Club using particular scales to suit their own requirements, but it has been afterwards found that George Stephenson's advice about using the same gauges applies with equal force to model work, both as regards the gauges themselves and also the scales.

Yours truly,
H. G. KERR.

Eltham.

Track-Circuiting in 0 Gauge.

To the Editor MODEL RAILWAY NEWS.

DEAR SIR,

Previous to the dissolution of my "company," I had obtained some excellent results with track-circuiting, and I feel that I should like to pass on the idea to some of my railway confreres.

The section of track to be circuited must, first of all

(1) Be *completely* insulated from the track at either end of it.

(2) Have each rail insulated from the other.

To obtain the first condition I made a break between the rails (as shewn) about $\frac{3}{32}$ in. long, and connected the section *rigidly* to the remaining track by steel strip, screwed in the form shewn. These four strips now held the section in alignment.

Ah! No. 2 is where my tin-plate

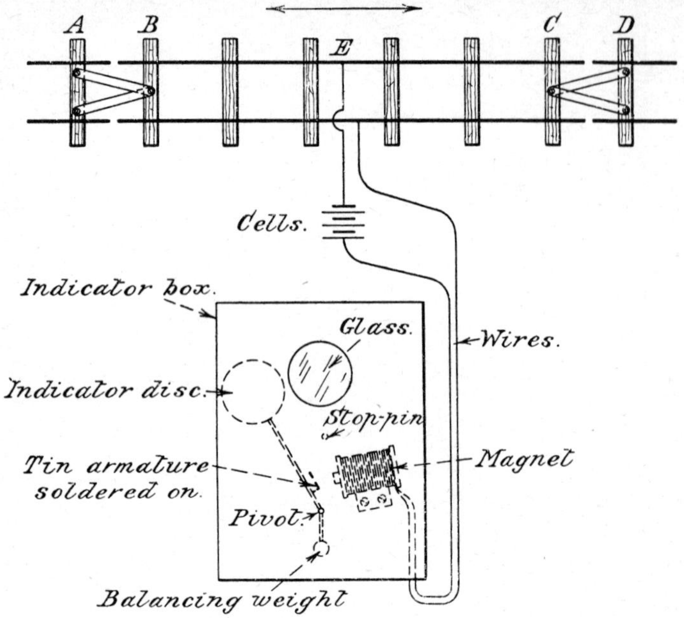

Diagram illustrating 0-Gauge Track Circuiting.

friends scratch their heads! *The two rails must also be insulated.* This brings the matter to sleepers. These must be non-conductors, as in "Lowko" track, scale-permanent way, etc.

I then soldered an electric wire on to the underside of each rail, and brought them away towards the signal-box. Into one wire I fitted the batteries, and then brought the wires to the indicator.

This can be made quite easily out of a small cigar box. A circular hole about 1½-in. diameter is cut in the lid of the box, in the position shewn, whilst the other fittings are fixed to the back of the box. I think the diagram explains itself. More realistic results are obtained if the back of box shewing in the hole is painted white, and the actual indicator disc red.

For good results, the following points should be noted :—

(1) The balancing weight should be *only just* heavy enough to swing disc out of sight when current is off.

(2) The weight should be so placed that when current is off, no vestige of the disc can be seen.

(3) Magnet should *not* be far from tin armature.

(4) Armature should be prevented from actually *touching* magnet when current is on by correctly placed stop pin.

(5) When on, the disc should just fill the space behind the hole in lid.

To put a finishing touch to the box, a piece of glass may be put over the hole, and the indicator "labelled" to say which section it indicates (*e.g.* Up Section, No. 3).

As will be seen, the whole thing may be quickly made out of scrap; the magnet out of an old bell being quite suitable.

As regards the track, the best results are forthcoming if the wires are connected to the "arrival" end of the section, *i.e.*, the end the train reaches first. If, however, the section is used on single-line railway, the wires should be attached to the middle of the section. I hope these notes may be of use to some "brother railway-men."

Yours truly,
T. WATSON.

A Simple Safety-Valve.

To the Editor MODEL RAILWAY NEWS.

DEAR SIR,

I am enclosing an enlarged drawing for a safety-valve for small-scale locomotives. The design should be

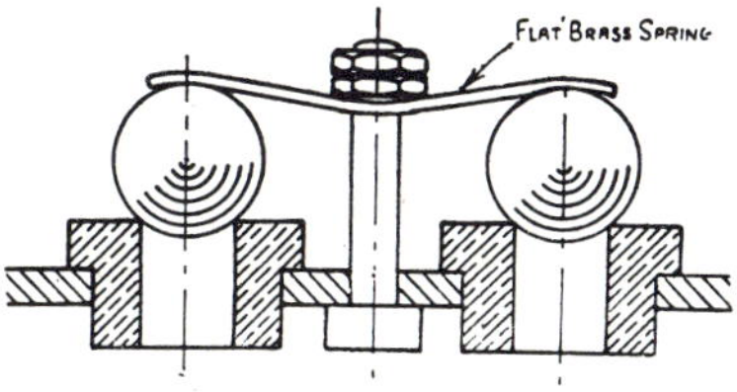

A Simple Safety-Valve.

useful for large-boilered locos where the head-room is limited. No dimensions are given, so experimenters can make these to suit their own locos.

Yours truly,
GEOFFERY B. DENTY.

Bristol.

No. 00 Gauge Dimensions.

To the Editor MODEL RAILWAY NEWS.

DEAR SIR,

In reply to Mr. Greenly's letter on page 63 of the February issue, I herewith give the measurements asked for :—

Total width over faces of wheel tyres	19 mm.
Buffer centres	20 mm.
Width of body at waist ...	31.5 mm.

As regards the "slightly under-bodied appearance" referred to, I would point out that South Western coaches are slightly narrower than most others, also the model shown is fitted with the S.W. Co.'s extra wide double-framed dining-car bogies, which make the body look narrower than it actually is. This appearance in the photo is accentuated by the angle from which the photo was taken, *i.e.*, below footboard level and pointing upwards. The proportions are those of the prototype.

My firm's blue print No. 3 M/P 3 will give Mr. Greenly all the information he needs for comparisons.

Yours faithfully,
A. STEWART REIDPATH.

Balham, S.W.

A Co-operative Model Railway.

To the Editor, MODEL RAILWAY NEWS.

DEAR SIR,

I was extremely pleased to know of a new magazine devoted entirely to model railway matters.

Although I have the *M.E. and E.* from No. 1 to date and the magazine *Model Railways* from 1909, my model interest is only 12 years old.

All through this interest the complete model railway has had first place.

Two or three years ago we revived the Coventry Model Engineering Society, and like all other societies it started splendidly, only to become divided by the many divisions of the hobby. This, I think, is the biggest problem in a provincial society of small membership A few members are interested in ships, a few others in locomotives, and so on, whereas, could a society consist only of people all interested in one definite form of model work then I feel inclined to believe that such a society could not help being immensely useful and of distinct advantage to every member.

My suggestions may not be original, and may have been tried by others, still, I would like to test the feeling in Coventry for a model railway club, not based on quite the same lines as existing clubs.

The greatest handicaps to most model railway enthusiasts are the lack of suitable space for a permanent lay-out, and the very considerable amount of money required to commence a comprehensive system.

If a small number, say 20, of real model railwayites could band themselves together to permanently rent cheaply a room about 50 ft. × 25 ft. and build in it a comprehensive system in 0 gauge, the members would realize their hobby in its highest form.

Such a model railway would be very ambitious, too much for one person.

At the commencement, planning committees would have to be appointed for the purpose of preparing the general scheme and the work of the different departments, as in the real thing.

Electrical control would have to be considered and automatic-block section control arranged after the permanent way had been planned.

Construction would then commence with its numerous sections of work, and to be a real electric system a miniature power station would be installed and lighting put in all buildings and trains, etc.

Time-table working of trains would be arranged for and on such a system six trains might be run simultaneously.

All the locomotives, rolling stock, buildings, in fact, everything, might be built to scale by the members.

Scenic effects would be thought of and installed, and really there would seem no end to the perfecting of a most complete system in the 0 gauge, on a similar grade to the one built by Mr. H. Foster, of Reading, also the system outlined by Mr. Keen in the first number of MODEL RAILWAY NEWS.

Of course, such a club could not be carried on for a subscription of 5*s*. a year, but I think it could be arranged if 20 members gave a nominal entrance fee of 5*s*. and put in 1*s*. a week *for which* they could have access to their railway in being on every week-day evening, if desired.

It might be interesting if other readers would give their views on the practicability of successfully managing a club on the lines suggested.

Wishing the magazine all success.

I remain,

Yours faithfully,

S. SHARP.

Coventry.

New Passenger Coaches.

We show in the photo herewith one of the new L.N.E.R. short-type bogie passenger vehicles in tin-plate. These are 9½ in. long over all for gauge 0 vehicles, and are supplied either as first-class, third-class, or passenger-brake coaches. The price is 8*s*. 6*d*. each. They are entirely made at the Northampton works of Messrs. Bassett-Lowke, Ltd., and a sample submitted for our inspection enables us to speak very highly of the appearance, finish, and general construction.

New short-type Bogie Coach.

Model Loco. Drawings.

We have received from Mr. A. W. H. Pealling, 108, Forest Road, Dalston, London, E. 8, some samples of outline drawings of locomotives in various gauges, which he is prepared to supply at very modest prices. The samples sent are very neatly done, and include G.N.R. and N.E.R. Pacifics, and L.M.S.R. No. 1670 in 0 gauge, and a G.N.R. tank, No. 1560 in 00 gauge. The 00 gauge drawings are priced at 8*d*. each, for both tank and tender locos, and there are now over a dozen types available.

The MODEL RAILWAY NEWS

Editorial and Publishing Offices :
66, FARRINGDON STREET, LONDON, E.C. 4.

Single Copies, post free, 7½d. Annual Subscription, 7s. 6d.

Vol. I. No. 4. APRIL, 1925. Price, 6d.

Notes of the Month.

THE Victoria Model Steamboat Club is a very well-known organization in the model engineering world and has just celebrated its 21st birthday. Being now quite grown up, it has decided to expand its scope by adding a model locomotive and stationary engine section to its membership. It has a nice Club House on the banks of the Bathing Lake in Victoria Park, London, E., and there is some adjoining ground available for the building of an outdoor model railway track, if the necessary permission can be obtained from the London County Council. The members of the V.M.S.C. are a very cheery crowd, and have a fine fleet of over 70 boats of all kinds. If they get really busy on model railway matters, they have plenty of ability in their ranks for producing good models, and we shall look to them to become the pioneers of model railways in the London Parks. The honorary secretary of the new section is Mr. G. Kennion, 744, Old Ford Road, Bow, E. 3, and he extends a cordial invitation to all model railway and stationary engine men to write to him, or to come and see him on any Sunday morning at the Club House in Victoria Park.

* * *

The event of the year, for London model railway men at any rate, is the forthcoming exhibition by the members of the Model Railway Club at Kingsway Hall, Kingsway, on Friday and Saturday, April 17th and 18th. The Exhibition will be open on the Friday from 2 till 10 p.m., and on the Saturday from 10 a.m. till 10 p.m. The prices of admission will be 1*s*. 3*d*. for adults, and 6*d*. for children under 12. We hear that there will be a splendid show of model railway work of all kinds, and there will be plenty of opportunity for visitors to meet members of the Club and discuss model railway matters to their heart's content. Now then, readers of ours, book the dates, and roll up in your thousands ; the Model Railway Club will be very glad to see you and make you feel at home.

* * *

We find that quite a number of our readers who send in letters to our Queries Department, expect us to supply them with a drawing of some particular engine or piece of rolling stock free of charge, or in return for the nominal query fee of 1*s*. While we may be able occasionally to prepare a special drawing where the subject is one likely to be of interest to other readers, and, therefore, worth publishing in our pages, it must be understood that we cannot undertake assistance of this kind as part of our regular query service. There are several people advertising in our pages who supply a wide range of model railway drawings at very reasonable prices, and we strongly recommend those in need of such drawings to fill their requirements as far as is possible from the stock held by these firms.

Points from Recent Letters.

We give below some extracts from letters recently received :—

A. A. (Leeds) writes :—" On all good clockwork mechanisms there are efficient brakes and governors, although it is not wise to reverse the loco from track. I once tried shunting this way, by a system of stop-catches and reverse levers. The result was far from pleasing from a financial point of view, as I broke a cog tooth. Clockwork locos can be run safely down a hill of 1 in 50, even if it has a curve at the botton, without fear of losing paint or varnish, and there are some devices to bring the train to a gradual stop, instead of the rude way in which stop - catches effect it. The chief advantage of a clockwork system is that there are no accumulators to keep up and no "meths," which are the despair of beginners."

Mr. F. T. Walker (Norton Lees) writes :—" I think you may be interested in the "Oolite" stone which I am advertising. This is Ketton stone, put through a crusher, which separates the little balls of stone from the carbonate of lime. The stone is composed of little balls of stone and carbonate of lime. For the embankments, etc., mix a little cement with the "Oolite" and then put it in position and mould it. I have a railway of my own and I have been experimenting with this and I have made a bridge, a road, embankments, wall, a lake, a platform, a tunnel and tunnel mouths. The embankments can only be painted with water-paint, on account of the cement, but I don't think this matters much."

R. S. H. (Norton) writes :—" I do not agree with you that the model railway of the future will be the electrical railway. No doubt small gauge railways, up to say 2-inch gauge, are better controlled by electricity, but in 2½-in. gauge and upwards, where one can be the actual driver, what is to beat steam ? What is there in electricity to equal handling the steam controls, where one is the actual 'man on the foot-plate ?' Also the sight of the fast-moving rods on outside cylinder locomotives is enough to stir the heart of any model railwayite."

G. S. D. (Bradford) writes :—" Here is a railway story for you. The usual guard had enlisted with the colours, and the Irish porter had been engaged. Outside the station was a steep gradient. The loco had a great deal of trouble to get up, and at the top she stopped. The driver came behind, saying that he had never had so much trouble in ascending. 'Shure !' replied Pat, 'she'd ha' slipped back often enough if Oi hadn't kept the brakes on toight all the time !' "

J. A. D. (Manchester) writes :—" One of the latest locomotives of the Great Western Railway is the 'Viscount Churchill,' and is a six-coupled leading bogie type, *i.e.*, 4—6—0, fitted with six-wheeled tender. In days gone by this locomotive was the famous one known as 'The Great Bear' No 111, and was of the 'Pacific' type, *i.e.*, 4—6—2, and had an eight-wheel bogie tender. In its new state the locomotive has had the boiler shortened and the firebox put further forward. In accordance with the new G.W.R. fashion, the steam pipes to the valve chests are brought outside the boiler. The old No. 111 is still retained. One of the reasons for converting from a 4—6—2 to a 4—6—0 was that considerable trouble was given by the trailing wheels at the firebox end. As now altered, the locomotive weighs 73 tons 15 cwt. empty, and the tender 18 tons 5 cwt. empty, a total of 92 tons. In running order, the weights are, 79 tons 17 cwt. for the loco, and 40 tons for the tender, total 119 tons 17 cwt."

NOTABLE MODEL RAILWAYS

Major Hugh Simpson's Model L.N.W. Railway.

HAVING always been a railway enthusiast, it was not until recent years that I made a serious start with a model railway. Being in the army, which means constant moving about, is somewhat of a deterrent to the indulgence of this fascinating hobby, but while still on the active list, I could no longer refrain from " falling." I first purchased about 150 ft. of scale model permanent way, and a "Brunel" 3½-in. gauge 0—6—0 tank locomotive (steam, fired internally by spirit), with three goods waggons, the parts of which I put together at home, from Bassett-Lowke.

I laid down the track as an " end - to - end " run, with a slight curve in the middle and two cross - overs at each end, to provide a loop for engine to run round. This was as much as the small dimensions of the garden would permit.

The next acquisition was a L. N. W. " Precursor " tank, 4—4—2, also spirit-fired, which I obtained second-hand from Bassett-Lowke. She had been specially fitted for the late owner with a real water-tank, and had a hand pump on the engine, which was a great advantage over " Brunel," whose boiler has to be replenished from a separate tank and pump at the side of the line, which has to be connected up to the check-valve of the boiler each time.

An Express passing a Station.

The " Precursor " also has a " Greenly-Joy " valve-gear, while " Brunel " has gear of the slip-eccentric type.

In a few months a fresh appointment entailed a move of abode, and the line had to be pulled up. The track had been laid on 6-ft. boards, which were taken up with the sleepers still nailed down, and chairs and rails in position, and was put together in the new site in much the same formation. By th's time the War had broken out, and there was little time for hobbies.

When ordered on active service, I dismantled the track, which was packed away and stored with the furniture.

My first settled job after the War afforded an opportunity for making a start again. In 1920 I had a small square-shaped garden, and decided to

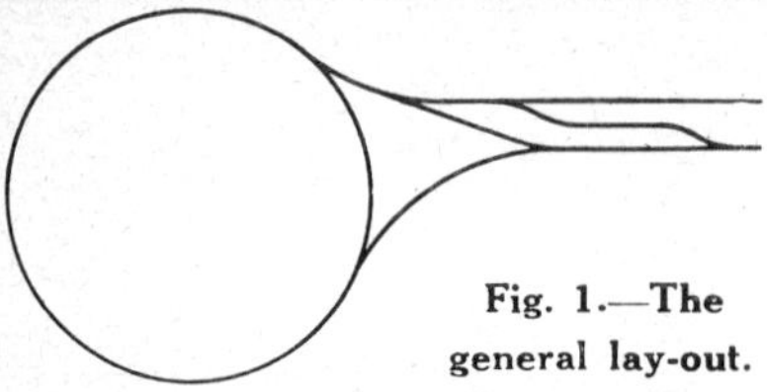

Fig. 1.—The general lay-out.

adopt a continuous track, to give the engines a better chance of displaying their powers. The accompanying sketch (Fig. 1, not to scale) shows the general lay-out. The circle was only 35 ft. in diameter, which is about the limit for the "Precursor."

The track was nailed to 4-ft. boards, somewhat thicker than before, and, as before, well tarred, but again much trouble was experienced with the warping of boards due to changing weather conditions. The boards turned up at the ends, making "peaks" on the rails at the point of junction, and causing many derailments. Another serious difficulty, which has not yet been entirely got over, has been the tendency of the rails to "cant" inwards in the chairs, beyond the standard inclination, reducing the gauge, and making the wheel flanges liable to mount the rails. This difficulty has to a large extent been counteracted by the employment of keys cut from $\frac{5}{32}$ in. square-section brass wire. These keys are slit half-way down the middle with a hack-saw, and the halves pinched together to form a wedge, as in Fig. 2.

Having retired from the Service two years ago, I am now settled in a country house in Cumberland, with a good-sized orchard. This has of course, provided the longed-for opportunity of laying down a longer and more interesting line, which it will be possible to develop indefinitely. 400 ft. of extra track has been acquired, still adhering to scale-model permanent way. This time I was able to come by a quantity of sleepers, 9ft. × 5in × 10 in., from Government surplus stock. The track, laid on these baulks, is of very solid nature, and all trouble arising from warping is obviated.

Fig. 2.

I have kept to the continuous-track lay-out, laid in a rough oblong, the main line being 470 ft. long. The land is on a slope of about 1 in 50,

A "Pick-up" Goods Train shunting.

so a cutting, about 1 ft. deep, was made through the high ground, the spoil being used to construct an embankment, about 1 ft. high at the lower end ; the earthworks were thus nicely "balanced." In this way the gradients have been much reduced, but there is still a short length of 1 in 51, and much at 1 in 60 and 90. Nevertheless, both engines haul heavy loads over the line at great speeds, and do not have to be flogged. The line is now ballasted with sand, not shown in the photographs, which were taken last summer, before also the engine-shed, water-tank, and tunnel were constructed. Fig. 3, not to scale, shows the present lay-out.

L.N.W. Brake, third corridor side.

About five years ago, through an advertisement in the *Model Engineer*, I was able to acquire a quantity of passenger and goods rolling stock, converted from 3½-in. gauge, from the late Col. Harvey, of Norwich. This stock had large brass centre buffers, with couplings attached above, which obviated all chance of interlocking when shunting, but the appearance was not good, and I found it very difficult to couple them with the engines, which had ordinary double buffers, and couplings in the centre of buffer-beam.

Eventually I had to adjust all the buffer-beams to correspond with those of the engines, which are to true $\frac{11}{16}$-in. scale. The shorter goods vehicles I provided with solid brass cupboard-door knobs from a local ironmonger. I made oval buffers for the long passenger coaches by cutting the original large round buffers with

Fig. 4.

a hack-saw and then filing them down to form 1½ in. × 1 in. ovals, as in Fig. 4.

Interlocking is now a thing of the past. The above stock was originally varnished, but I have now painted it to look as "North-Western" as possible. The stock includes mail van, two dining-cars, and a large oil-tank.

The line is being equipped as far as possible in affectionate memory of England's Premier Railway, murdered by Act of Parliament, December 31st, 1922—hence the name. As I was anxious for some real scale-model passenger stock, that would really "look the part," and I could not run across any suitable drawings, I applied to the authorities at Wolverton, who very kindly lent me official working drawings of a 3rd brake composite, 1st and 3rd composite, dining saloon, and sleeping saloon. These drawings were copied by Mr. R. W. Wright, of Norwich, who has already built the brake, using wood for the

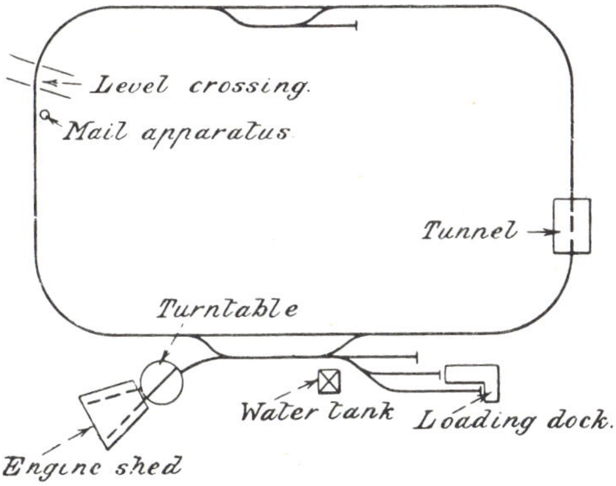

Fig. 3—The present lay-out.

frames and aluminium for the panels and roof. It has a most realistic appearance, as will be seen from the photographs, and the wonderful workmanship which Mr. Wright has put into the bogies makes the coach a marvel of easy running. Mr. Wright was much handicapped in the painting and lining, having no opportunity of observing L.N.W. stock at Norwich, so I was lucky in finding an enterprising firm of sign painters in Carlisle, who undertook the job with great interest, sending their painter to the station where he could make notes of panels and lining of the alas! fast disappearing chocolate and white coaches. The result is excellent. The photographs show the coach before repainting.

The Goods Loading Dock.

I must place on record the very great amount of valuable advice and assistance I have received from Mr. Wright, who has done great work for me besides in alterations, repairs, etc. Among other things he has made point-levers which gave a greater "throw" than those I could purchase from the trade, and has made fittings for my turn-table which have rendered it a satisfactory apparatus.

Mr. Wright has now (January, 1925) the sleeper in hand, which will shortly be finished.

I have been fully occupied in my spare time during the last two years in laying the track, constructing turn-table, tunnel, engine-shed, water-tank, etc. The water-tank consists of an old petrol can laid on its side and supported on a wooden erection representing a pumping engine-house. I have had to spend much time on alterations and adjustments of the track, but now we can run a train round the 470 ft. of main line in 57$\frac{4}{5}$ secs. and carry out complicated shunting movements without fear of derailments.

A good deal of trouble is experienced with spirit fires, and I have not yet been able to get over the difficulty. One opens the valve leading from tank to lamp a little too far, the spirit overflows on to the line and catches fire under the engine, causing a terrifying conflagration, then one closes the valve tightly to avert disaster, and the lamp runs dry while one is attending to other matters. On the "Precursor" I have tried the principle of the poultry drinking fountain, which has improved matters, but has not entirely obviated overflows. A float control in the lamp reservoir only proved a snare and a delusion.

As my chief interest lies in locomotive management, I have decided to try solid fuel. Mr. Greenly has prepared me drawings of a "George the Fifth" type 4—4—0, with loco boiler. I originally intended to have a "Claughton," but after conversations and correspondence with Mr. Greenly, it was turned down, principally owing to the difficulty of fitting a fire-box of sufficient depth. For the same reason a "Prince of Wales" was vetoed. The new engine is to have a feed-pump worked off the motion, injector, smoke-box superheater, and "all the latest improvements."

There is still endless work ahead in the construction of stations, signals, bridges, and other additions and improvements.

If there is anything you like about our little paper, or anything that you don't like, write to the Editor. He wants to hear both sides.

How does "grouping" affect your model railway? Have you brought it up to date?

Making Signals for "0" Gauge.

By "Father."

No decent model railway can be considered anything like complete unless it is properly fitted up with signals.

The models about to be described are not copies of those in use on any particular line of railway, but are such, that if made full size, would comply with official requirements, and the writer also ventures to think, that if properly made they will be of pleasing appearance to most model railway engineers, and do credit to their railways.

It has been said that it is a good thing to have the signals made to a rather larger scale than the other parts of the model, but there does not appear to be any reason to justify this.

One of the qualifications almost essential to the model railway engineer, is a keen eye to proportion, and to a certain extent, a sense of the artistic, so that if his signals and other things are not made the proper size he will not feel altogether satisfied with their appearance, which reason alone is a quite sufficient for keeping to scale in these little things as far as possible.

A plain signal is shown in Fig. 1. This is drawn to scale and is full size, the post being 20 feet high to the underside of the finial, $6\frac{1}{2}$ in. square at the top and 12 in. square at the ground line, these being the sizes generally in use in real practice.

The dimensions for the model are $5\frac{1}{2}$ in. high, $\frac{9}{64}$ in. square at the top, and a full $\frac{17}{64}$ in. square at the ground, sizes which are rather small for wooden posts; it is, therefore, better to make them from brass rod; the best size for this being $\frac{5}{16}$ in. square, which will be plenty large enough for the highest posts as well as bracket signals, and also the finials can be made from the same rod.

All posts are the same size at the top, irrespective of height, but are made larger at the ground line as the height is increased. The sizes for the models should be 8 in. to 10 in. high, $\frac{9}{32}$ in. square, and for anything higher than this and for bracket signals $\frac{5}{16}$ in. square.

The posts can be tapered by soldering about half a dozen of them on to a piece of flat stiff metal plate, keeping all the ends which are to be the tops in a line, see Fig. 2, and filing to the correct taper with a 14-in. second-cut file, and repeating the operation to taper the other side. The plate, of course, must be held in the vice or screwed to the bench while filing. It is obviously only necessary to file two sides of each post. Care should be taken to keep the filed sides nice and straight; any waviness will completely spoil the appearance of the finished signals.

Fig 2

The method of fixing the posts will depend on what the ground or foundation consists of. Alternative ways are shown in Figs. 3 and 4. If the base of the model is of wood covered with loose ballast, Fig. 3 is probably the best to adopt. The plate should be of brass about 1 in. square and $\frac{1}{16}$ in. thick. The post has a spigot passing through the plate and may be either riveted over or soldered. If the base or foundation is not less than say $\frac{3}{4}$ in. thick, a plain spigot as Fig. 4 may be used, simply fitting tight into a hole.

The finials may be made to suit individual taste, but the one shown in the drawing is a neat design, and is easily made by being turned from some of the $\frac{5}{16}$-in. square brass rod, held in the chuck. They are fixed to the top of the post by solder.

The various fittings are shown in

Figs. 5 to 14. Sheet brass a little more than $\frac{1}{64}$ in. thick will answer the purpose very well for all of them excepting 5, 10 and 14, and are so simple that description is not necessary.

The lamp, Fig. 14, is turned from a piece of rod, and a small piece of suitable shape soldered on each side to represent the front and back lenses. The rod-guides, Fig. 8, should have the holes slightly elongated to allow the rod to work freely.

The semaphore, or arm and spectacle, Fig. 5, is built up of four pieces. It is necessary for the arm itself, A, to be as light as possible. It should, therefore, be made of aluminium $\frac{1}{64}$ in. thick, the other three pieces, B, C, and D, are brass, B and D being $\frac{1}{32}$ in. thick and C same thickness as the arm A. The aperture for the glasses must be cut slightly larger in C and D than in B, in order to form a rebate or recess for the glasses. These three brass pieces are soldered together and form the complete spectacle. The arm A fits in between B and D, and is held in position by the spindle E and rivet F. When the arm is in the danger position, the pin K should be resting on the projection M on the lamp bracket, Fig. 13. The spindle E must be soldered in the spectacle. A hole must be drilled at H for the working rod.

Glass cannot be obtained thin enough in the correct shades of red and green for the spectacle, and celluloid is used instead. This can be purchased from firms whose advertisements appears in this paper.

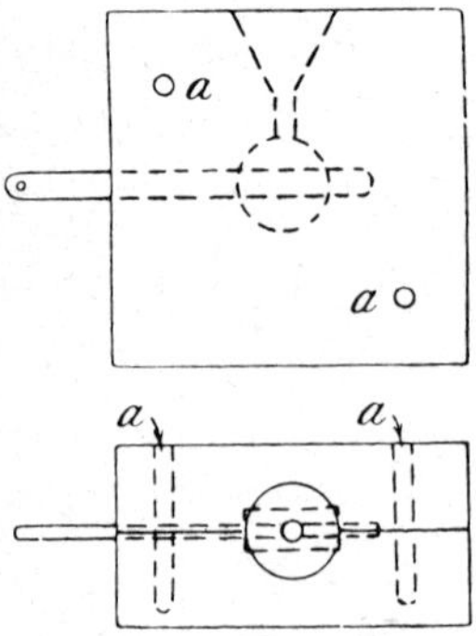

Fig. 15.

When the whole is fixed together it should be carefully filed up, especially round all the edges of the spectacle, in order to give it a nice neat finish before painting.

It is better to put the celluloid into the spectacles after painting, and it can be fixed with a very small quantity of rubber solution, as used for patching pneumatic tyres, etc.

The backshade, Fig. 6, is fixed on to the spindle by solder, but this must be the last job in assembling the signals.

All the fittings, excepting Figs. 10 and 11, are fixed to the post by solder. The balance lever and side cranks, Figs. 10 and 11, have to work on pins. These can be made in the following manner: drill holes about $\frac{3}{64}$ in. diameter nearly through the posts, plug them with soft wood, and use common pins of suitable thickness cut to correct length and filed to a point. These can easily be pushed into the soft wood and will hold tight, but can be taken out with a pair of pliers if required.

The rod connecting the arm to the balance lever, Fig. 10, is made of a thin piece of brass wire, having the ends bent at right angles so as to fit into and work freely in the holes in the arm and balance lever.

The balance weight is a lead casting made in a rough mould of hard wood (*see* Fig. 15).

When all the parts are made they can be soldered in their proper places on the posts, and the whole painted in correct colours before assembling the working parts.

It will be as well to get each signal working properly before soldering on the backshades, which will be the last job. These fittings, if made as described, will be suitable for any type of signal, such as bracket signals or a gantry with several arms.

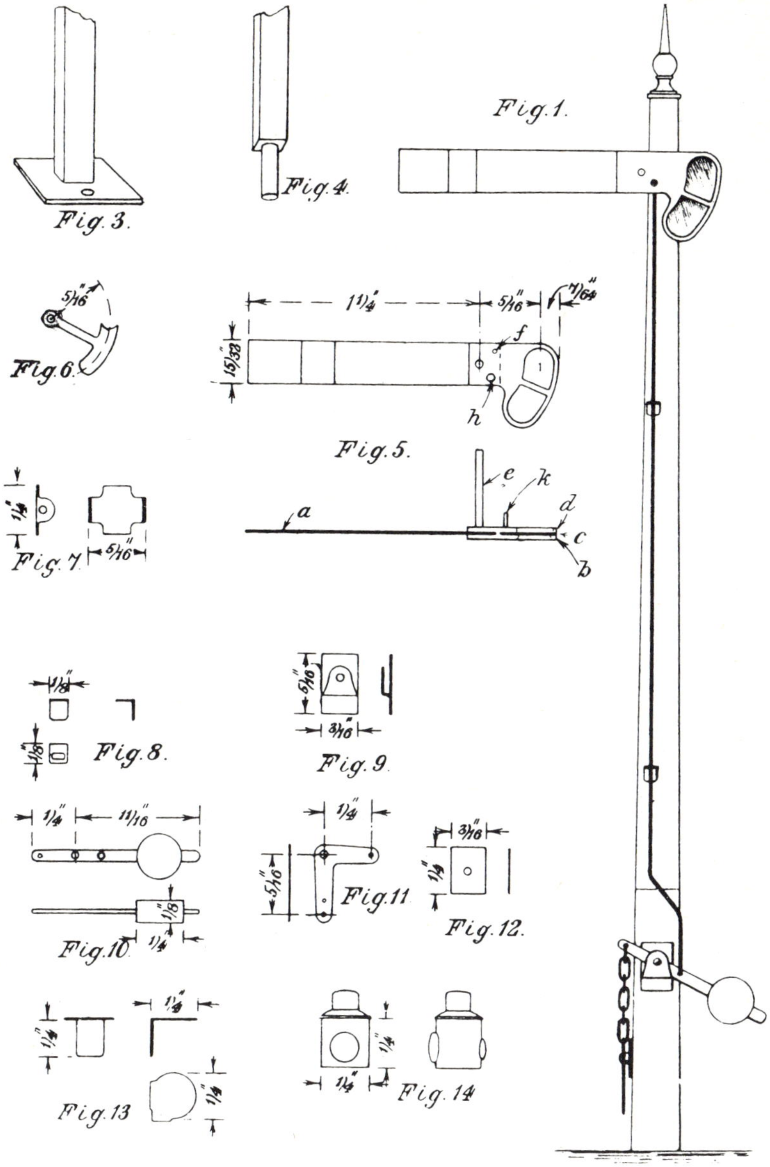

Components of a plain "0" Gauge Signal.

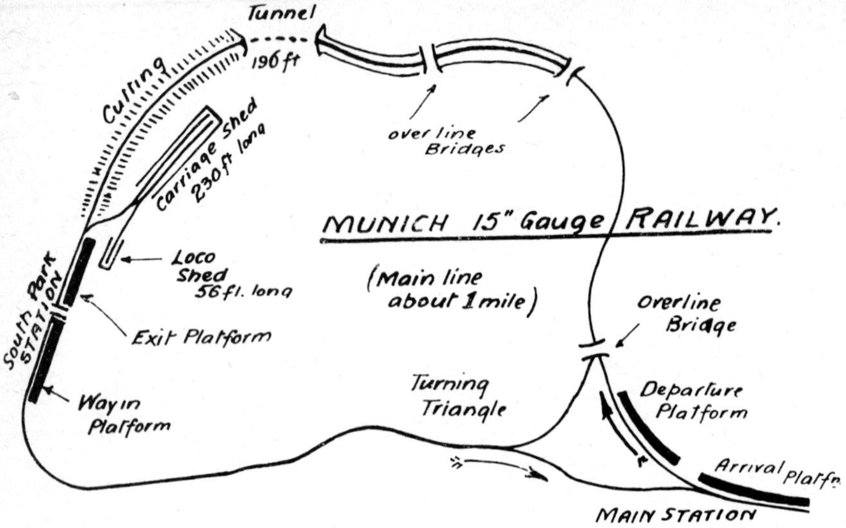

The Key-plan of the Line.

The Munich Miniature Railway.

The Munich Exhibition Transport Miniature Railway is progressing very well and we are now able to reproduce the key plan of the line. Engineer Dr. Flugel has made an excellent arrangement. There are plenty of overbridges over the line and a tunnel is introduced, which also helps to make the enclosed space more useful and getatable. The line is nearly a mile long. The terminus station is ingeniously planned on a triangle. At both this and the passing station at the South end of the park the platforms are arranged in sequence. This should obviate much of the trouble which has been experienced on other lines during "rush" hours.

Herr Roland Martens also reports that the locomotives are well under way and sends us an outline drawing of these interesting machines.

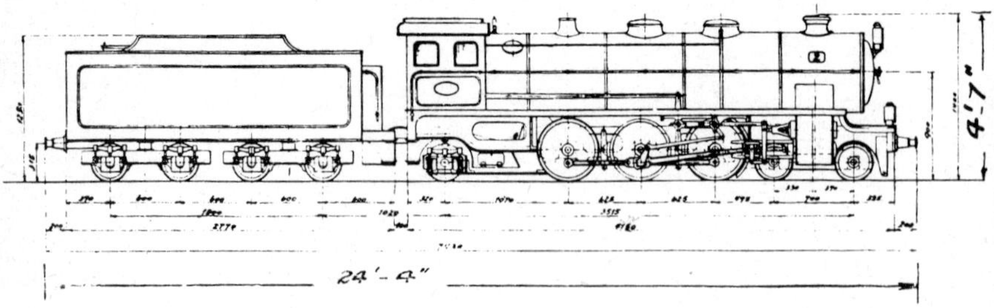

Herr Roland Martens' design for a Pacific 4-6-2 type (⅓rd scale) miniature locomotive, now being built at Krauss Loco. Co.'s Works, Munich, Bavaria.

A new Reversing Motor for Gauges 0 and 1 Electric Locos.

AN interesting motor for model electric locomotives has been put on the market. We are informed that it is now adopted as the standard for models emanating from the Continent in place of the permanent magnet-type motors previously used. This invention is the result of two years' experimenting. It has been brought to our notice by Messrs. Bassett-Lowke, Ltd., of Northampton, and they inform us that it is being made in three sizes, as follows :—

No. 1.—Small size, for 0 gauge locomotives of limited boiler capacity.

No. 2.—For large size 0 gauge locomotives or motor trains.

No. 3.—Suitable for gauges 1 and 2 locomotives.

All of these types will be stocked regularly by Messrs. Bassett-Lowke, Ltd., for those purchasers who may like to fit this new motor to special models which they may desire to construct. The motor can be worked by direct current at 4 to 6 volts, or alternating current at 10 to 12 volts.

The salient feature is that reversing from the track is effected by merely switching off the current and switching on again; reversing the polarity of the track is dispensed with. A lever is provided on the motor for hand operation. It enables hand reversal to be effected from the cab or the movement of the locomotive to be in one direction only.

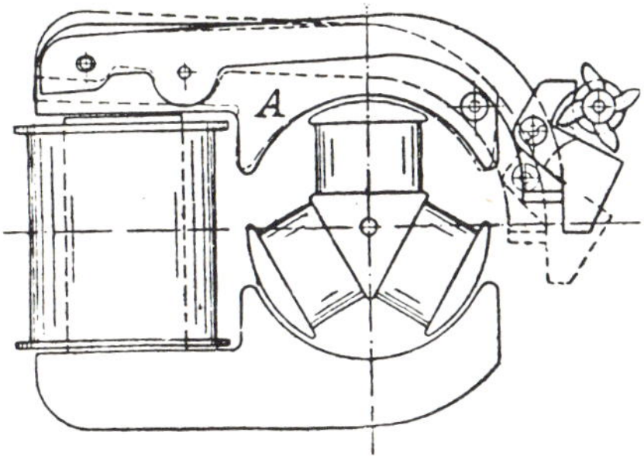

Fig. 1.—Motor, with movable pole-piece.

The motor is of usual form, having a series-wound laminated field-magnet and a tri-polar armature, as shewn in Fig. 1, but fitted with a movable pole-piece A, normally held

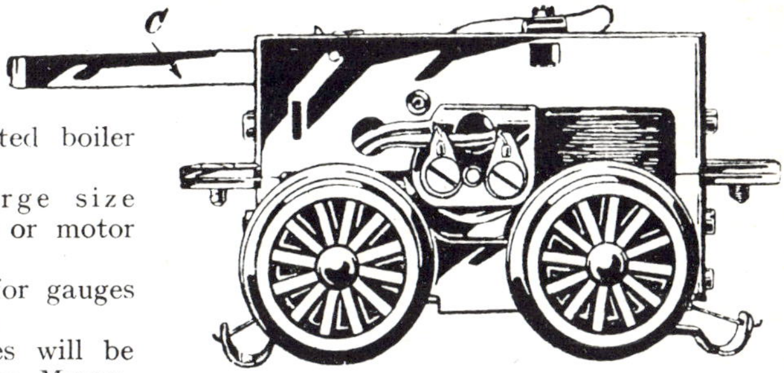

Fig. 2.—Elevation view of complete units.

so that its limb is a short distance away from the field-magnet core. Attached to the pole-piece is a system of lever-and-ratchet pawl. The latter engages with a star wheel fixed upon a shaft, which carries a commutator interposed in the armature circuit, and making contact with brushes. When current is switched on from the track, the limb of the pole-piece is pulled against the field-magnet core. Movement is thus imparted to the lever pawl and star wheel, the latter being rotated one quarter of a revolution.

If current is then switched off and then switched on again, the movement of the lever system repeats and the star wheel is rotated one quarter of a revolution again. Each movement of the star wheel rotates the commutator by this amount and changes the direction of current through the armature winding, thus effecting reversal of armature rotation.

Figs. 2 and 3 show respectively an elevation and a plan view of the complete motor unit. The motor commutator is of disc pattern and the brushes are carried in tubular holders with milled heads.

The reversing commutator and brushes are shown in Fig. 3 at B. The lever for hand reversal is shown at C, Figs. 2 and 3. When the motor unit is in position, this lever projects over the footplate inside the cab. If pushed in as far as it will go, the locomotive will run in one direction only, and does not reverse when current is switched off and switched on again. To reverse direction, current should be switched off, the lever pulled out to farthest extent and pushed in again. Current being then switched on, the locomotive will travel in the opposite direction. If the lever is pulled out and left in this position, reversal of direction is effected by switching off the current and switching on again. Movement of the lever out and in rotates the star wheel through one quarter of a revolution and thus substitutes hand operation for the automatic action to effect reversal. If the locomotive is standing with the reversing action in gear and is required to move on and not to reverse, current must be switched on, off, and on again quickly so as to effect reversal twice.

Messrs. Bassett-Lowke have sent, for our inspection, one of their L.N.E.R. No. 0 gauge locomotives, fitted with one of these motors. We have made some trials with it and found the working very satisfactory. Current was supplied from a battery of accumulators. With 6·4 volts the starting current was 2 amperes, running current 1·4 amperes. Trials were made also with loads of $1\frac{1}{2}$ lb. and 1 lb. in the tender. The amperes were practically as before, about 1·6 with the heavier load, and 1·5 with the 1-lb. load, starting current, 2 amperes. With 4 volts and no load, the speed was low, such as would be adequate for shunting purposes.

Manipulation of a locomotive fitted with one of these motors, affords interesting entertainment, and the whole unit is very nicely made and finished.

Messrs. Bassett-Lowke advise us that they are only fitting these motors to a few of their cheaper-type models. For their better-class scale models, they are now engaged in designing and constructing a special permanent magnet - type motor, which they hope will fulfil the requirements of advanced model railway enthusiasts. The new motor we have described is of Continental manufacture, but is guaranteed, provided the instructions sent with each are carried out. We understand that these motors will be fitted to practically all the Continental-made models sold by toyshops, in the future.

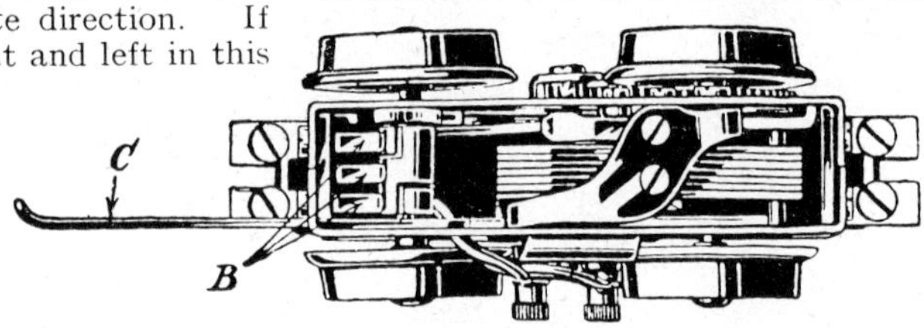

Fig. 3.—Plan showing Reversing Commutator.

The No. 0 size has a wheel base of 2 in., diameter of the wheels is $1\frac{1}{4}$ in.; the No. 1 size has a wheel base of 3 in., diameter of wheels $1\frac{3}{4}$ in. Inclusion of the reversing commutator and operating mechanism obviously causes the whole unit to be somewhat complicated by comparison with an ordinary motor. But it is arranged in two portions, held together by screws, removal of which enables the lower, that is the wheel part, to be detached so that the armature, gearing and reversing commutator are exposed and accessible. We have not had an opportunity of testing the sample with alternating current but hope to do so in due course.

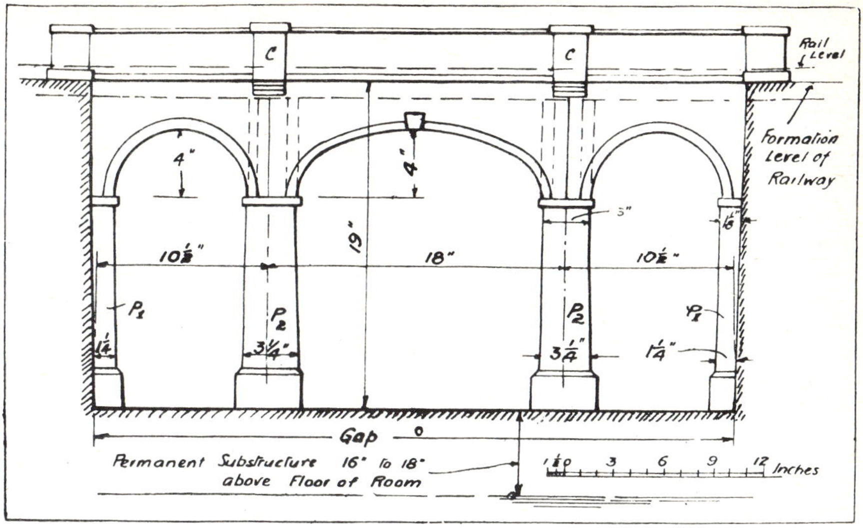

A Removable Model Railway Bridge.

A WEST country reader on his No. 1 gauge railway now under construction has a gap to bridge at the doorway of the room he uses, and while seeing the difficulties of employing a lifting bridge of the orthodox type, has suggested that a three-span brick or stone type of bridge, as illustrated in "Model Railways," Fig. 299, page 228, might be used.

In adopting his proposal, we suggest that the three spans of the bridge can be in one piece and rest on a permanent structure fixed to the floor. This stool would be not more than 18 in. high and would have to be stepped over when entering the centre operating space of the model railway. The line of this structure could be arranged to leave a space at A (Fig. 1) to act as a lobby inside the room. The individual arches may be of unequal span back and front, quite an unusual proceeding in so exaggerated a degree, but not an important matter in a model. The semi-circular side arches would, therefore, become ellipses at the back (the doorway side) and the centre arch would be flatter than shown in the drawing at the front. The abutments of the gap—mere cliffs on each side—could be made slightly taper to allow the removable bridge to wedge into position. Four plug-and-socket kind of bolts (good-fitting barrel bolts would do) could be fitted underneath the bridge to ensure the abutting ends of the rails properly registering with each other. Additional safeguards on the rails themselves may, of course, be arranged. The sides of the bridge would join at obtuse angles. This will not look out of place if masked by the corbelled-out piers (C) on the parapets. To lighten the bridge the piers P1 may be separated from the arched portion and fixed to the sides of the gap. Indeed the centre piers P2 may also be independent structures. The latter would, however, be quite loose, just resting on the step, with dowels or some other similar device to prevent their being displaced when the bridge is in position.

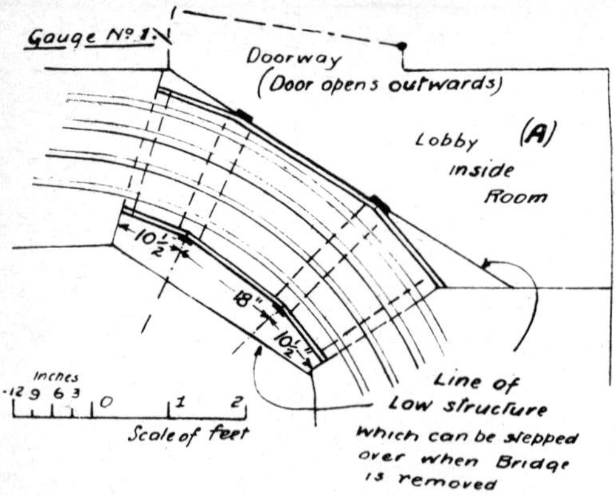

Fig. 1.—The corner of the room, and doorway.

imitation stone bridge chosen was considered the best. Personally, the writer thinks that it will "fill the bill" admirably. Of course, a single-span girder bridge could be used, but the line being on a curve, any such structure would have to be very wide and would encroach on the space marked A in Fig. 1. The smallest timbers should be used in the construction of the bridge chosen. Wide boards only shrink and twist. Smaller sections properly framed up will reduce warping and reduce the tendency for the bridge to fit badly after it has been in use some years. The piers need not be solid but box-like structures. Of course, the wood should be as dry as possible at the outset.

The under-sides of the arches can be made in sheet metal or cardboard as recommended in the book, "Model Railways." This construction will allow them to conform to the changing curvatures necessary at the back and the front of the bridges.

A bascule bridge for the prescribed position was thought out of place under the circumstances and the

The bridge may be distempered stone colour instead of being painted. Before doing this it should receive a coat of size, and when finished will be most realistic.

A G.N.R. Box Wagon.

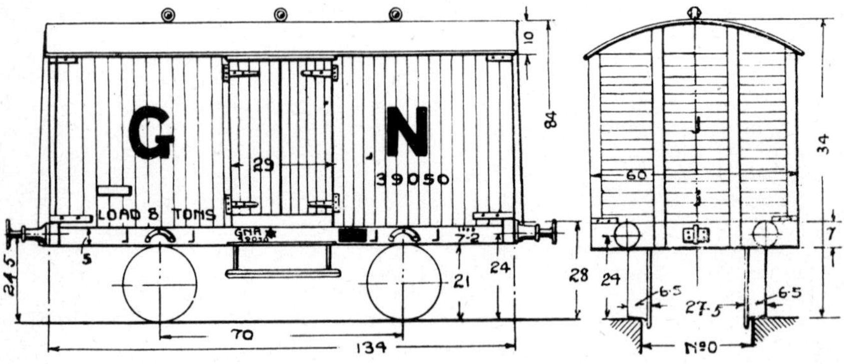

The above illustration shows the standard eight-ton box wagons used on the late G.N.R. These vehicles have flush sides and were painted a red-brown, with white letters. If made in wood, the boardings may be represented by scribed lines and have the strappings (L.M.Co.'s strips) glued on. The wagon requires standard axle-guards and wheels.

A Model Railway Weigh Table.

A CORRESPONDENT has asked us to publish the drawings of a weigh table for a model railway, and we presume that he includes the building which covers the machine, as well as the table itself. He has not indicated whether or no a working table is desired, but in the accompanying sketches we have shown a method whereby such a table may be made and which will weigh a four-wheeled truck with a degree of accuracy depending on how well the apparatus is constructed. Of course, the mechanism is much simplified in principle and is not a bit like a full-size machine in its details. Railway weigh houses are designed for two purposes. The tables used outside goods sheds for weighing the goods as received or delivered on carts or motors are set in the roadway, and in a model might be represented by a chequered plate let into the floor of the model. The other type of table is used for weighing railway vehicles when loaded with freight. Hence the tare weights of all goods trucks are painted in a conspicuous manner on the sides of the wagons, so that the tare can easily be deducted from the total weight to arrive at the " paying load " contained in the vehicle.

Concerning Dimensions.

In submitting the sketches herewith, the dimensions of vertical height will depend on the type and make of permanent way used. The depth of the frame, marked R in the drawing, must therefore be made to suit the rail, so that the surfaces in the finished model are flush throughout. This will also affect the building. This should fit over a floor which is level with the table. The base of the house outside may be, however, made the same as the general sleeper level.

The ends of the frame F will require to be grooved for the flanges and also have metal strips (P) at each end similar to those fitted on the table itself. As an alternative, the running rails on each side might be extended as far as the well in which the table fits. The table may be made of wood and fitted to a " steelyard " of metal. This is pivoted at V to the frame, the piece of rod which is drilled at the ends for the pivot centres being sufficiently long to give the table sufficient lateral stability. The table can be made shorter. As it is dimensioned it is long enough for a vehicle with a wheel-base of the scale equivalent of almost 14 feet. To counterbalance the table, the steelyard may be fitted with weights hung from a wire passing through the floor of the superstructure on which the railway is built. The magnitude of this weight can be found by experiment.

The Weighing Apparatus.

The rest of the weighing apparatus inside the cabin may be entirely made out of scrap or raw material. It is a spring-governed device actuated by a push rod (a stout needle with both ends pointed) from a cup fixed at the extreme end of the steelyard. This pressure is transmitted to the adjustable tension spring by a bell crank. The outer end of the spindle carries a light pointer moving over the surface of a vertical scale of quadrant form marked out in scale "tons," "cwts." and "quarters." For the rest, it may be made substantially as sketched.

While a stop has been shown at S, a strip of metal fixed to the surface of the frame to prevent the table rising above the rail level, no other attachment except the sort of " terminal screw " L fitted at the ends of the table has been suggested to put the table out of action and to relieve the weighing mechanism of the jar of a passing or entering vehicle. Instead of this device a lever or bolt might be fitted.

In addition, it would also be advisable to give the table a permanent

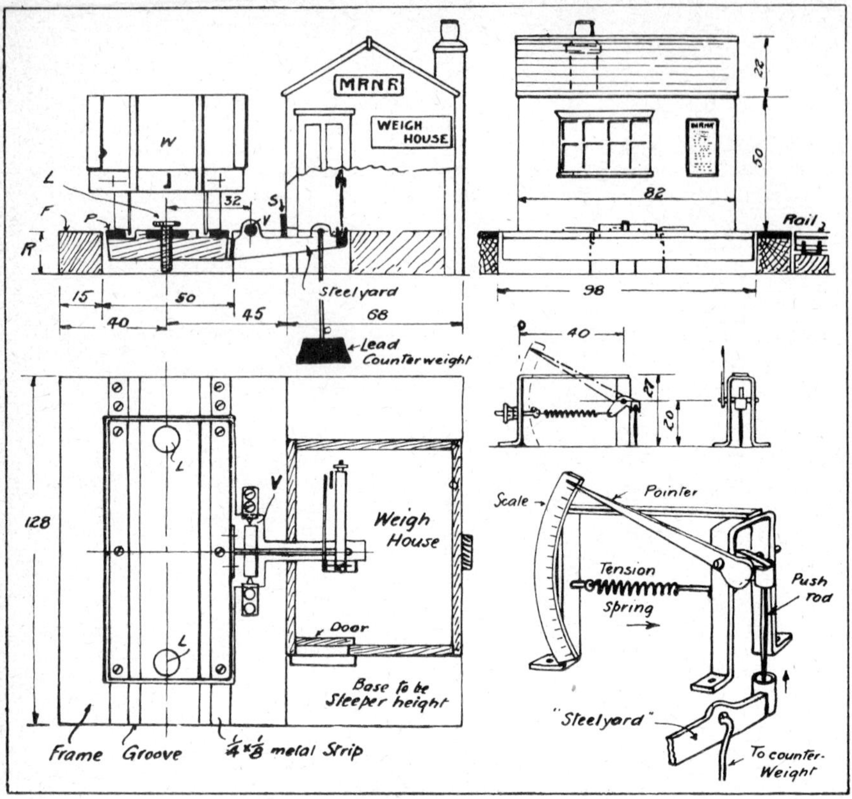

Design for a Model Railway Weigh Table.

counterbalance of, say, 5 scale tons, roughly an amount less than the tare weight of the lightest vehicle used. This would reduce the range of the spring and increase the sensitiveness of the apparatus. Further, it would lessen the jar occasioned when the trucks run on to the table. Of course, this weight would have to be added to the scale. The quadrant marking would, therefore, commence at five tons.

L.S.W.R. Locomotives.

The "Urie" 4—6—0 type express locomotive No. 742 with the new Maunsell (S.E.C.R.) type bell-topped chimney in place of the usual "stove pipe," was seen by us running on fast trains with the indicator house on the front of the smoke-box. We also travelled behind No. 334, a rebuild of the four-cylinder Drummond 6-ft. 4—6—0 of 1905. This engine was evidently just out of the shops. It has a very large boiler with a very short stove-pipe chimney of the "Urie" pattern, two cylinders and Walschaerts gear, and is an excellent prototype for a working model. Evidently the amalgamations are not yet lessening variety in locomotive practice.

No. 00 Gauge Electric Locomotive Motors.

By Henry Greenly.

THE introduction of the No. 00 (⅝-in.) gauge to the model world will certainly not react to the detriment of the ever-popular No. 0 gauge, but is simply a phase in the general tendency for reduction in the space occupied by a large lay-out. Twenty-five years ago clockwork locomotives were made in what was called the No. 4 gauge (2$\frac{13}{16}$ in.), and it was considered a rather risky experiment to attempt to make a 2-in. gauge model steam locomotive. Nowadays a 2½-in. gauge model locomotive is quite a large affair and in many cases takes the place of the 3½-in. gauge models which were considered small in those days. To some extent the increase in size of the modern locomotive has made it necessary to keep the gauge as small as possible. The latest "Pacific" type engine, or even a 4—6—0, requires a curve of nearly twice the radius commonly used for the small 4—4—0 and 4—2—2 type models of the pre-war decade. In any case to obtain "success" in a model 3½-in. or 4¾- in. gauge engine needs no great skill: almost anything made in a reasonably good manner and in the light of recent experience will "go." It is just a question of the relative efficiency of one model over another. The better made and better designed 3½-in. gauge engine will prove more efficient than the inferior one, and not a circumstance of success or failure.

What is exercising many model engineers who, for the most part, are interested in "railway operation" as a whole—a scheme in which the locomotive plays only its own part—is the problem of hauling a 300 to 400-ton train from point to point, accommodating such a passenger train at a platform, providing space for the marshalling of an 800-ton goods train, all within a room not exceeding 26 feet long, is exciting some interest. No. 0 gauge suffices where there is a space 20 or 25 feet long, but No. 1 gauge is out of the question. The writer remembers Mr. Stanley M. Hunter's No. 1 gauge Sydenham line. This was quite a

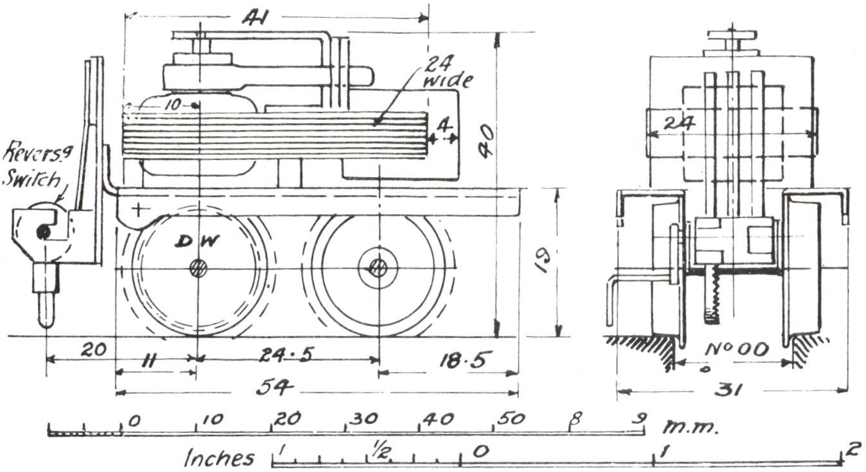

Fig. 1.—Motor with laminated fields, suitable for alternating current.

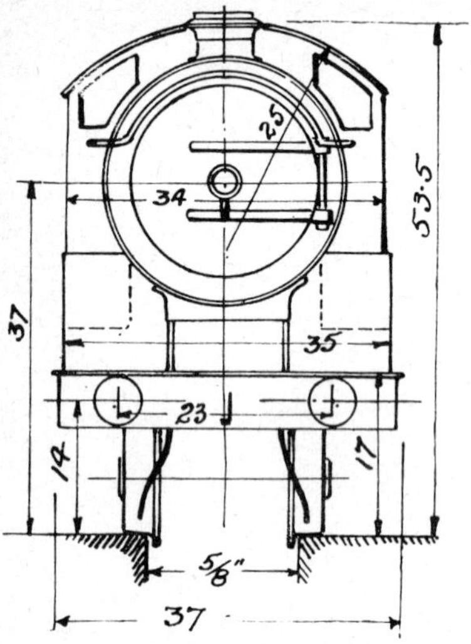

Fig. 3.—End view of 00 Gauge Electric Loco.

nice plan, but although a room 19 feet by 14 feet wide. was available there were evidences of congestion, and the size can be considered as an approximate minimum for a line in this gauge. Of course, by using nothing larger than six-wheeled tank engines and four-wheeled rolling-stock quite a considerable reduction in space and curve radius can be made. I well remember in 1900 seeing Mr. Fred Smithies famous 3¼-in. gauge steam locomotives careering round five-feet radius curves for hours at a stretch. But this " industrial " type of model railway, which sharp curves renders necessary, does not appeal to the average man. He must have model express locomotives—" Pacifics " for preference—long bogie carriages, " 70-foot diners " included, and trains of not less than six or eight coaches. This requires space, and ample space too.

As the models of No. 00 gauge railways on the market—marvellous value that they are—cannot satiate the above desires it is natural that the specially made model No. 00 gauge locomotive is receiving attention. For those who are not electrical experts the building up of locomotives around the electric mechanisms supplied by Messrs. Bassett-Lowke at about 5*s*. 6*d*. each is perhaps the best solution of the difficulty. Using my original standard scale of 4 mm.—I think it will be a mistake to alter this, as in the ever-present war of desires this scale will survive the same as the 7-mm. scale ultimately prevailed in the No. 0 gauge (1¼ in.)—it is just possible to get two of these motors into a 4—4—0 type express engine of the largest dimensions. Testing out the first No. 00 gauge electric train set—which by the way belongs to Mr. R. P. Mitchell—we found that by loading up the cheap four-wheeled coaches with halfpennies to a total of 300 tons it was possible to haul the train with the single driving-wheeled tank locomotive provided with the set. This was, of course, quite an unfair test. The wheels of these coaching vehicles are only of pressed tin, and the load represented 50 tons per axle. As many readers have no doubt already tried, fitting these coaches with turned wheels reduces the train resistance by at least half the normal amount. In this test the motor on six volts warmed up to danger point. Therefore, it was concluded that two motors, which would nearly halve the current consumption, the use of turned wheels and a reduction in the load per axle, both of which should again cut down the power required by a half or a third, there was no insuperable difficulty in building a locomotive with steam outlines capable of hauling a six or eight-coach train at scale speed over a lengthy run.

To this end some designs for motors—the parts of which could be more or less standardized—were prepared and the chosen arrangement, as applied to a 4—4—0 type N.E. railway locomotive of the No. 1238 class R1, is illustrated in Fig. 2. The motor is a duplex one, each armature driving one of the coupled axles. The motor is arranged to be housed in a boiler barrel of about 6 ft. 1½ in. diameter,

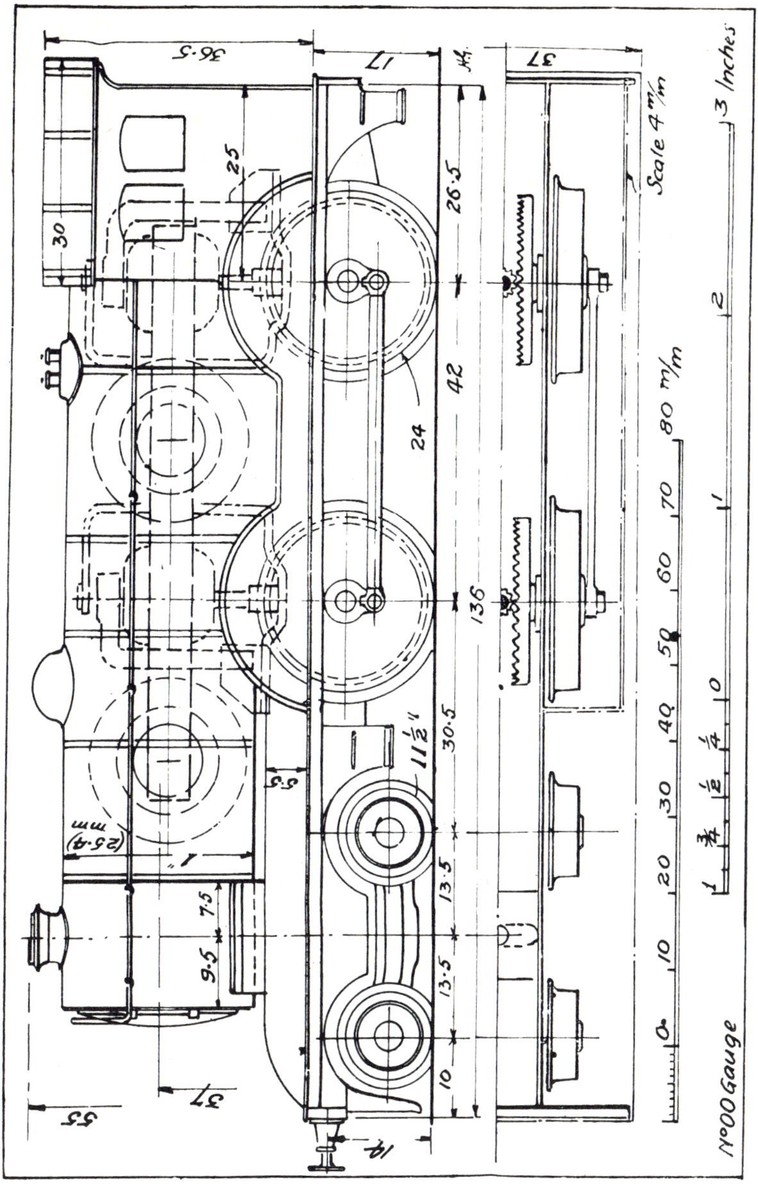

Fig. 4.—Elevation and part-plan of 00 Gauge Electric Locomotive, with double motor.

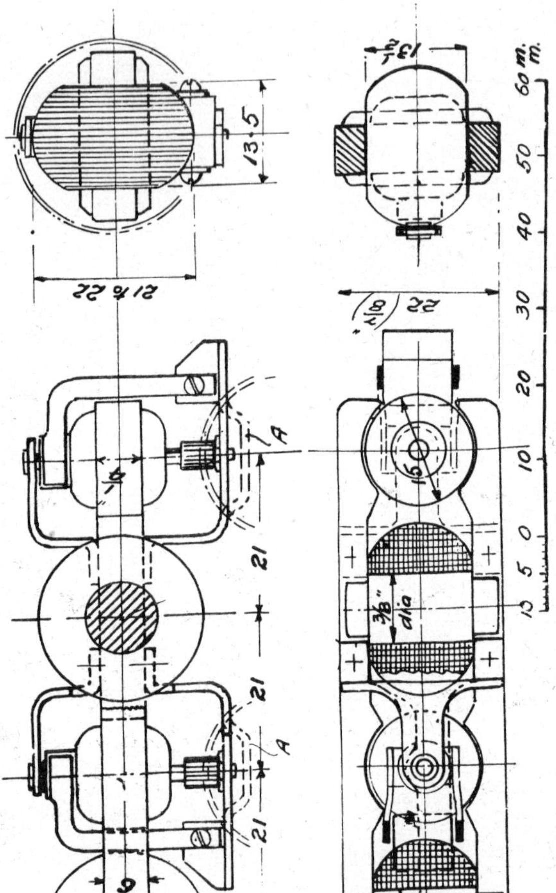

Fig. 2.—Design for Double Motors for 00 Gauge Electric Locomotive.

This arrangement halves the current-consumption per motor and reduces heating in windings.

i.e., a 1-in. tube. The field carcase can be made up completely and then be taken apart for the operation of winding the cores. The "commercial" motor shown in Fig. 1 has laminated fields because of its frequent use on alternating current. Where an automatic polarized reverser is to be fitted and the line current is a direct one of 4 to 8 volts, supplied from accumulator, there is no reason against using solid wrought-iron or a mild steel for the field-magnet yokes and cores. The same armatures as employed in the standard motors may be used, or ones alike both in size and construction. The tunnel gap should, however, be reduced to half a millimetre or less. This is entirely a matter of workmanship, and superior skill will be reflected by improved efficiency in working. For an express engine wheels of 24 mm. ($\frac{15}{16}$ in.) with 16 spokes are necessary, and it is up to some model-making firm to produce these. I have received a sample diecast wheel 20-mm. diameter from the Blenheim Company, Egham, Surrey. This is quite satisfactory for goods or mixed traffic engines, but something bigger is necessary for passenger locomotives. Another point to consider is gear transmission. The ratio of 1 to $4\frac{1}{2}$ is hardly low enough for real electrical efficiency. I would prefer 1 to 6, and the only way to accomplish this is to use a finer pinion. The crown wheel can be increased to $\frac{7}{8}$-in. diameter where a 24-mm. wheel is employed. With these proportions and a boiler pitched 37 mm. above rail level—as shown in Figs. 3 and 4—the bottom bearing bracket may require to be made as shown at A A in the sketch (Fig. 2).

I have tried modifications of the design in the G.N.R. "Pacific" engine and see no reason why it should not make an excellent basis for a standard type of No. 00 gauge motor. At any rate, I understand that an experimental motor is to be made up to demonstrate the possibilities of the scheme.

Model Making in Czecho-Slovakia.

Mr. May's Model 4-6-2 type tank engine chassis.

For some time past we have had communications with Mr. Alfred May, who resides in a small town in the Czecho Republic, on the subject of $3\frac{1}{2}$-in. gauge engines. The full-size drawing for the model London and South Western Railway, Walschaerts valve gear, was made at his request, and he has used this and other information in the making of the model 4—6—2 type tank engine, the chassis of which is now complete and is illustrated in the accompanying photograph.

This locomotive has two outside cylinders 28-mm. bore × 38-mm. stroke ($1\frac{3}{32}'' \times 1\frac{1}{2}''$), worked by correct type piston valves with inside admission. Mr. May is now considering the boiler design and discussing with the writer the arrangement of the superheater.

Laying "0" Gauge Track.

By Geo. Winteringham.

IT is assumed that the track will be nailed down to a wood foundation of some sort, and that the plans are prepared already for commencing work on a simple track, consisting of a single line of rails laid near the four walls of a room and having curves of about four feet radius at each of the four corners.

It will be best to put down the sleepers for the four curves first, and lay the straight parts in afterwards. To do this satisfactorily as well as expeditiously, it will be necessary to make a jig in the form of a radius-rod. (*See* Fig. 1.) This will also be used later on for laying the rails on curves. If the track is eventually to be made more elaborate by the addition of curves of various radii and points and crossings, etc., it will be worth while to make this radius-rod adjustable, and also to fit it with a pivot arrangement, as shown in Fig. 1. This avoids any slackness, which is a most important point while using it for laying down the rails. But if, on the other hand, it is only to be used once for the simple track with four curves, a plain lath with a bradawl put through it for a pivot will answer the purpose perfectly.

The adjustable rod consists of three pieces of lath about 1 in. wide by $\frac{1}{2}$ in. thick. Clean pieces of wood, free from knots, should be chosen. The middle portion F may be of any length to suit requirements, and can be adjusted to suit various radii by means of the screws H. The pivot is made of two pieces of metal plate about $\frac{1}{8}$ in. thick. The piece K is 5 in. by 1 in. and is screwed on to the under side of the rod. The plate L may be about 2 in. square and fixed to a piece of wood M about 3 in. to 4 in. square by a couple of screws. The screw N should be a nice fit in the plate K, so as to allow it to work round without slackness, and be screwed tightly into L, passing through the block M and ending in a point about $\frac{3}{16}$ in. long. In use, this point is placed on the centre from which the curve will be struck and the pivot fixed down by means of a couple of screws put through the holes P.

The recess A is for keeping the sleepers in correct position while being nailed down.

The gauge which is attached to the jig when being used for laying rails is

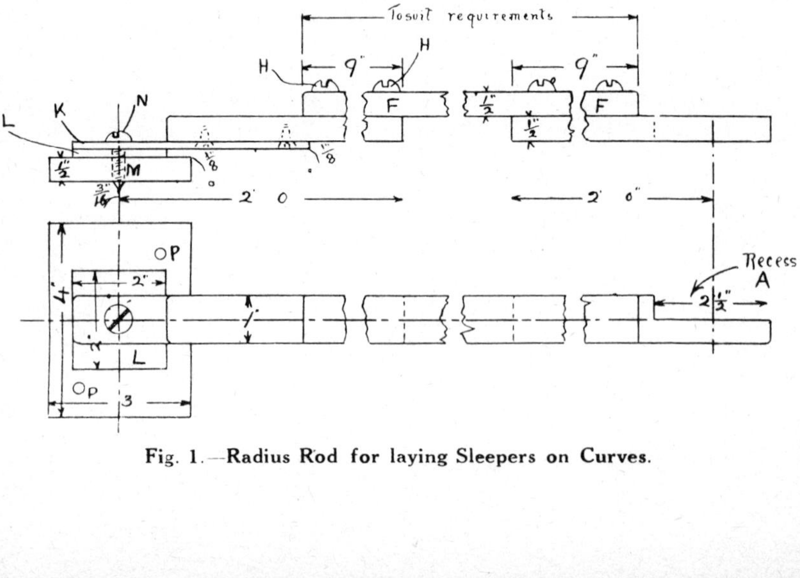

Fig. 1.—Radius Rod for laying Sleepers on Curves.

shown in Fig. 2. This is made from a piece of sheet metal about $\frac{1}{32}$ in. thick, and is fixed to the radius-rod in the recess A by means of three screws.

It is good practice to increase slightly the gauge of track on curves. Therefore this gauge (Fig. 2) is shown $1\frac{5}{16}$ in. between rails, an increase of $\frac{1}{64}$ in. on the scale gauge of $1\frac{19}{64}$ in.

Work may now commence by marking out the centre lines of the straight portions of the track, projecting the lines until they meet, as at A, Fig. 3. Mark off the two points B and C four feet from A. The points B and C are where the curves commence. The centre of the curve is D, exactly four feet from B and C. When using the radius-rod the centre of the pivot must be exactly on D.

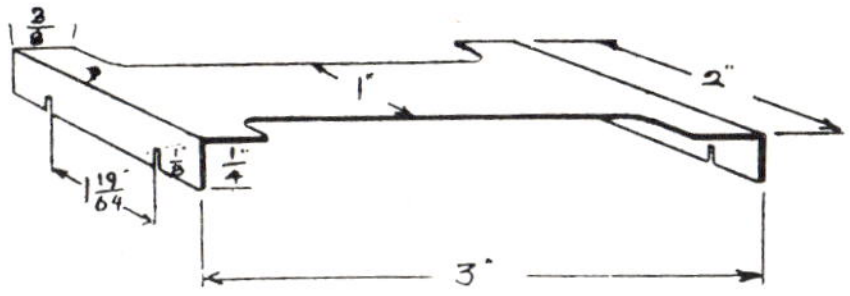

Fig. 5.—A useful Rail Gauge.

Anything in the shape of a box or table may be used as a support for the pivot, or a piece of wood about 4 ft. 6 in. long may be fixed by screws, or a clamp to the foundation boards of the track.

The above explanation of marking out is given with the hope that it will be of some assistance to those model railway engineers who have not had any previous experience and are about to lay out a track for the first time.

Having fixed up the radius-rod, the sleepers can now be nailed down, commencing either at B or C, and working round the curve. The best kind of nails to fix the sleepers will be $\frac{1}{2}$-in. panel-pins, two being used for each sleeper, and they must be spaced

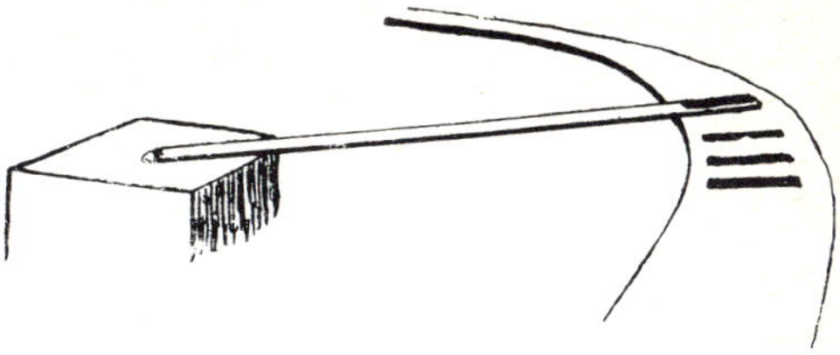

Method of using Radius-Rod.

$\frac{11}{16}$ in. each side of the centre line of track, so that they will come under the centre of the chairs and thus be out of the way of the two pins which will be used for fixing the chairs down. Take care to space the sleepers exactly the right distance apart in order that the chairs already soldered on to the outer rails will come on to their proper places on the sleepers. The exact spacing can be ascertained from a length of rail which already has the chairs fixed on, a piece of wood may then be cut the correct width and used as a gauge between the sleepers while laying them down. If preferred, a length of rail with the chairs fixed on can be used as a gauge.

When the sleepers are correctly nailed down on all four curves, those on the straight parts of the track may also be fixed in the same way, care being taken to get them in a straight line. A thin cord stretched along between two nails will help to ensure this.

Laying the rails is the next job, but before commencing, the rail-gauge must be screwed into position in the recess A of the radius-rod. (Fig. 1).

Do not commence with the ends of the rails exactly at the point where the

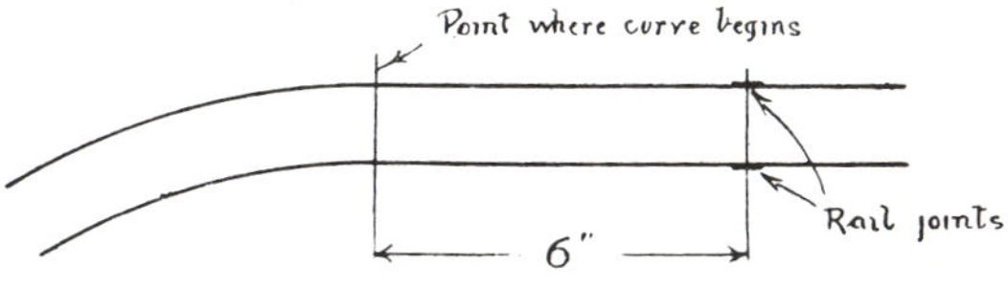

Fig. 4.—Showing starting point.

curve commences, but about five or six inches along the straight. (*See* Fig. 4.)

The radius-rod, with gauge fixed, can now be brought into use and the outer rails fixed down, soldering the

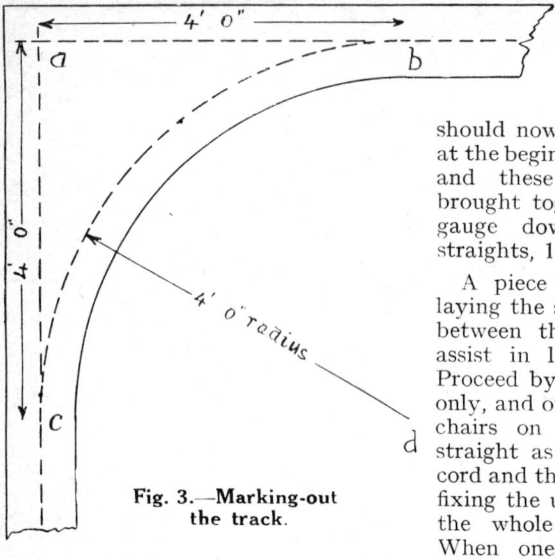

Fig. 3.—Marking-out the track.

joints together with fish-plates, or down on to chairs, as the laying proceeds, but do not fix down the five or six inches, referred to above, at the beginning of the curves.

It will now be quite easy to find the correct lengths for the inner rails of the curves, and also the spacing of the chairs on the rails, the latter being taken from the spacing of the sleepers.

To ensure getting the chairs in their right places on the rails, make a short jig (Fig. 4, Feb. issue), but having only three stops, two as B and one as C. Put three chairs and a rail in the jig, taking care that the end of the rail projects the correct distance beyond the first chair, now solder on the chairs, move the rail along the jig two spaces, solder on two more chairs, and so on until they are all fixed. The inner rails of the curves may now be spiked down.

Another rail-gauge is required for the straight track, and Fig. 5 shows a good type which will hold the rails in position while being spiked down.

This gauge can be made from thick tin or any other suitable metal plate. At the commencement of each curve 5 in. or 6 in. have been left unfixed. These ends should now be laid down. The gauge at the beginning of the curves is $1\frac{5}{16}$ in., and these ends must be gradually brought together so as to bring the gauge down to the standard for straights, $1\frac{19}{64}$ in.

A piece of fine cord—as used in laying the sleepers—may be stretched between the ends of the curves to assist in laying the track straight. Proceed by laying in one line of rails only, and only spike down a few of the chairs on each rail, keeping it as straight as possible by the stretched cord and the use of your eye, gradually fixing the unspiked chairs as you find the whole length coming straight. When one rail is got down quite straight, the other follows by using the gauge shown at Fig. 5.

Suitable pins for fixing down the chairs can be purchased from advertisers of model materials. They need not be more than $\frac{3}{8}$ in. long and should be a little less than $\frac{1}{32}$ in. diameter, and have rounded heads for the sake of appearance.

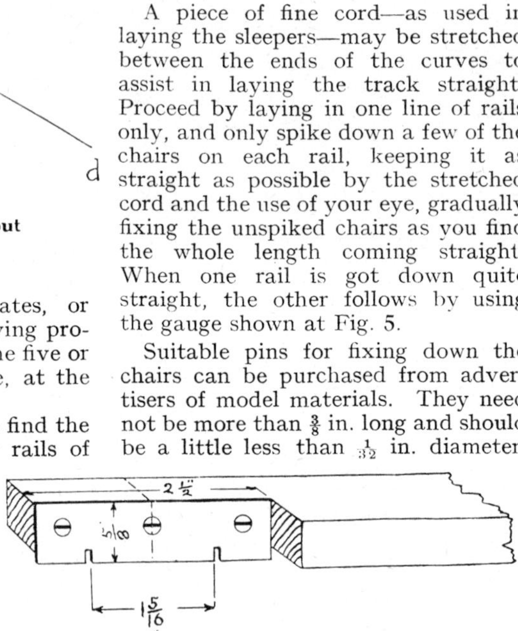

Fig. 2.—Gauge attached to the jig.

It will be recollected that the chairs were to be soldered to the rails with the burrs around the holes uppermost. The reason for this is two-fold. If they were on the underside, the chairs would not go down nice and flat on the sleepers, and secondly, when they are uppermost, the heads of the pins come down on the top of the burrs and cause them to close in round the pins, thus making them a tight fit.

Rail joints, of course, will have been soldered up during the process of laying.

Queries and Replies.

(11) Design for a No. 0 Gauge Steam Tank Locomotive.—A. W. (Essex) writes for particulars for making a model 4—4—0 type steam locomotive in No. 0 gauge.

This matter cannot be replied to fully within the space of a reply to query. There are more than the ordinary difficulties to be encountered in making a successful working model steam locomotive in gauge No. 0 ($1\frac{1}{4}$-in.). Unless you have had some experience, we therefore cannot recommend you to attempt so small a model. The scheme that admits of success with the least trouble is the geared tank-engine model. An outside-fired boiler is arranged within the side tanks. On the back of the boiler in the cab a reversing oscillating cylinder is fitted up to gear about three to one on to one of the driving axles. A member of the London Model Railway Club, Mr. Stanley M. Fish, has built several interesting and successful model locomotives on these lines. It is essential that the boiler should be made of the lightest tubing consistent with the strength required. We reproduce a drawing of one of the above-mentioned models. To get the boiler high enough up (the flame of the lamp cannot be reduced to scale), the vertical scale of the model is about 8 mm. to the foot.

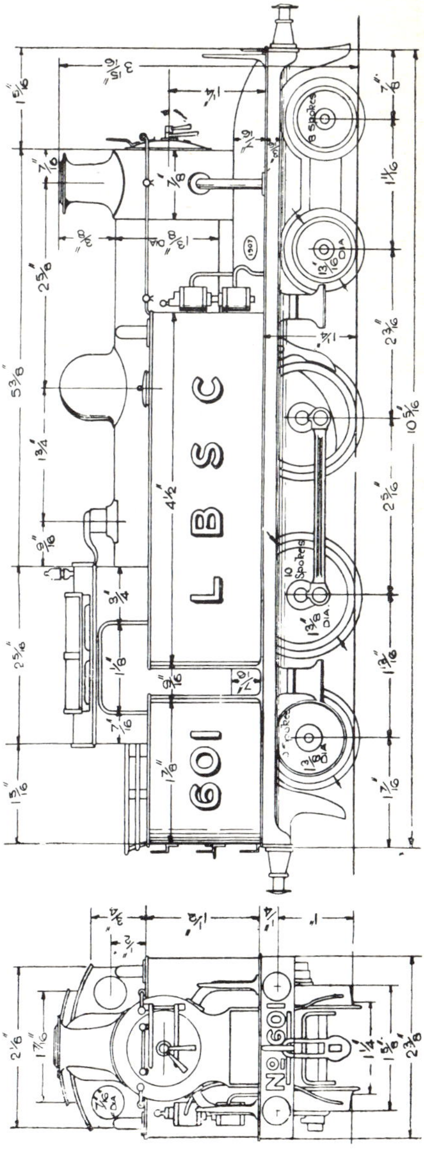

Mr. Stanley M. Fish's Model L.B.S.C.R. No. 0 Gauge Steam Tank Locomotive.

(12) Plan for "O" Gauge Railway.—F. M. (London, S.W.) has written for plans to suit a small room. We have suggested the orthodox point-to-point and continuous systems but lastly he states he now has a room 6 ft. × 10 ft. and sketches a sort of figure-eight plan.

Since sending you the post replies to your query we find that independently of the fact that there would be difficulty in operating the railway on a system laid out in the manner shown in your letter, your suggested line could not be got in the space unless you use curves less than 2 ft. radius. Therefore, you must do something else. We suggested various plans, but on further consideration submit the accompanying scheme.

The room is very small and we, therefore, have planned an oval main line with elliptical ends. At the end A a three-road station—a combined terminus and passing station—

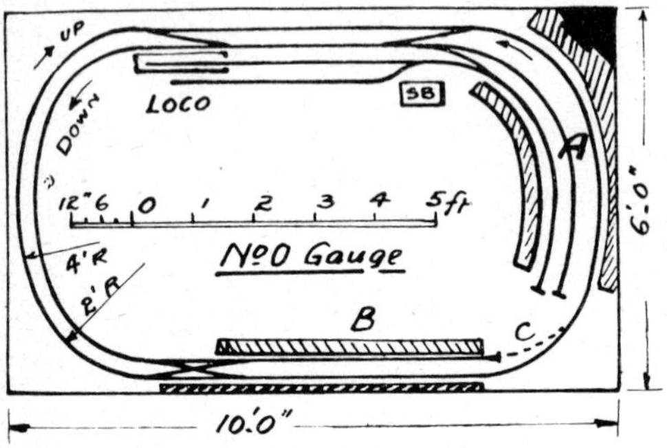

Suggested rail-plan to suit a small room, for "0" Gauge.

is fitted up with the large building in the corner of the room. The plan is peculiar, but allows its trains to run continuously or to work between the terminal roads of A and B, without having to back into the arrival station as would be necessary in your proposed plan. Possibly the connecting loop C would be an advantage, but everything depends on the particular system of working. Another modification would be to place the down platform at A between the two terminal roads. Other readers may be able to work on this plan and produce other variations. It is quite a usual difficulty, but we think the scheme has some merits where proper time-table working is desired. It is easy to make wonderfully complete plans, regardless of space limitations, but the trouble commences when a complete L.M.S.R. system is required in a space 10 to 12 ft. square.

(13) Alternating Current for Model Loco. Motors.—G. H. (London, N.W.) writes: (1) In what respect does a model motor which is designed to run on alternating current differ from one which will only run on direct current? I notice that some are advertised to work off both supplies. (2) Are these motors as powerful? (3) Can the locomotives fitted with these motors be reversed in the same way?

(1) There is no difference in the general scheme except that it is necessary to make the field and armature coils of laminated plates where the motor is to run on A.C. to prevent undue heating due to eddy currents. (2) On A.C. the motor will require a slightly higher voltage as the average impressed E.M.F. is lower than where the current is continuous. (3) No, only by a hand reverser, some scheme which depends on a "trip" on the side of the line or an impulse arrangement in which the stoppage and renewal of the current operates a separate device. Both of these latter devices are quite unsatisfactory from point of view of the amateur who requires a fully automatic system of control. We have no further data of the loco referred to in your letter, but we know that there are hazy ideas extant on this subject. In the ordinary way a series wound motor operating on alternating current cannot be reversed by commutating the line current. A polarized reverser depends on the direction of the current, and a current which is alternating in direction cannot be tied up to a polarized reverser.

(14) Coupling a Tender to the Engine.—L. H. P. (Horsham) sends a batch of questions relating to model locomotive construction, the gist of which can be gathered from the following replies.

You can obtain a coloured plate of a N.B.R. engine from the *Railway Magazine* office, Tothill Street, Westminster, S.W. 1. Before the amalgamation, this Company's engines were painted brown. It is always better to use sprung vehicles, and in No. 1 gauge no difficulties arise. Yes,

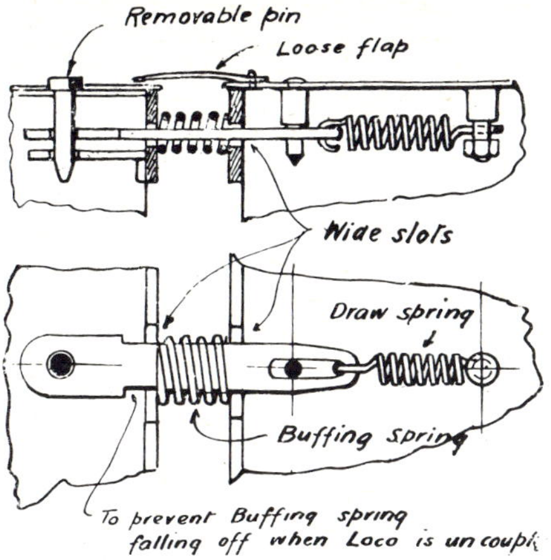

wheels can be coupled just the same as when springs are not used, but where three or more axles are coupled, the rods must be jointed or made in separate units. (*See* "Model Steam Locomotives," by Greenly.) Model loco wheels should be made a "force fit" on their axles. They are often further secured by recessed screwed nuts. The arrangement of transmission between electric motor and driving axles of the locomotive depends on the type of motor used and the disposition of the various wheels.

The enclosed sketch shows a good method of coupling a tender to the engine. Many of the schemes employed in commercially made models are poor in design. The arrangement provides for both buffing and drawbar springs.

(15) How to procure Motors.—C. H. (London, S.W.) writes:—" Kindly let me know the makers of motors. I wish a similar one to that published in February issue, pages 48 and 49.

The motor illustrated in this article is a specially made one, but if you purchase a complete armature and commutator you should have no difficulty in building it. You should be able to get an eight-pole drum armature from Bond's, Ltd., 254, Euston Road, London, N.W. 1, if not the complete motor. The windings will depend on the exact details of design and system of auto-reversing. (*See* the tables in "Model Electric Railways and Locomotives.") For a series-wound and shunt polarized reverser use No. 22 enamelled wire on the armature and No. 20 on the fields.

Answers to Correspondents.

J. E. D. (Oldbury).—It is difficult to diagnose the trouble with your electric loco seeing that you say that the magnetism in the permanent field magnets is good. Possibly the gearing is badly fitted and is absorbing too much power. You can send the locomotive to Mr. Henry Greenly, Ashley Road, Farnborough, Hants, with return carriage paid and 1*s*. fee, and he will test it and give you a report. Another source of trouble may lie in the cleanliness and adjustment of the brushes and commutator.

* * *

S. V. Somers (Shipley).—It is not difficult to convert a clockwork locomotive into an electric one, but you should find out the exact make of locomotive. Many of the electric mechanisms are arranged to fit the superstructures of clockwork locomotives with very little, if any, alteration. Send your locomotive to Messrs. Bond's Ltd., 254, Euston Road, London, N.W. 1, and ask if they can supply an electric mechanism to suit it. The other alternative is to sell the loco through our "Sales" columns, and put the value received towards a new electric engine.

* * *

R. R. S. (Devon).—Although not a strictly defensible process from a mathematical point of view, the scale speed of a No. 0 gauge train may be considered as being directly proportional to the linear scale, viz., 1-80th of the original. Therefore, three-quarters of a mile per hour equals a real train going 60 miles per hour.

00 Gauge.

To the Editor Model Railway News.

Sir,

In view of the interest that you anticipate will be taken in this new gauge, as expressed in your editorial of the current number, may I suggest that, if not too late, an effort be made by the manufacturers concerned, to arrive at some decision as to what scale is going to be adopted as the standard for this gauge.

It is a little discouraging, after reading Mr. Stewart-Reidpath's article in your first number, to find in the next issue that an authority of Mr. Henry Greenly's calibre is not entirely convinced that 3½ mm. to the foot should be the standard; and further, that one of your advertisers is marketing a 5-foot driving wheel, 20 mm. across, which is equal to a scale of 4 mm. to the foot, and I imagine that many who desire to make a start in this gauge will progress very "ca' cannily" until they know which scale will be generally adopted.

In such small models, the difference of half a millimetre is considerable, as a glance at the enclosed sketch will shew; and the beginner who lays out

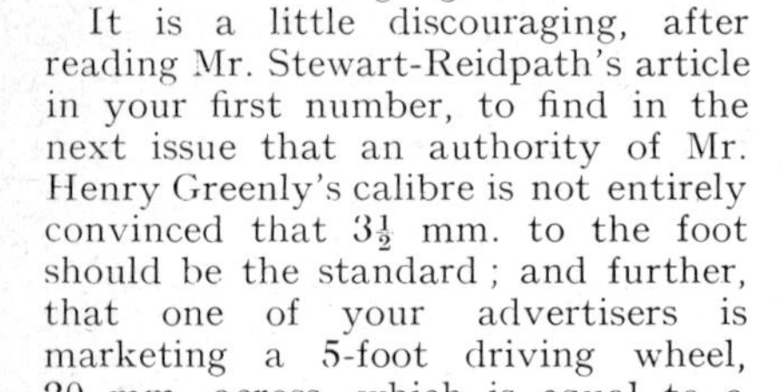

Comparative Diagram of 4 m/m and 3½ m/m scale Engines shewing difference between the two Scales——

his system to the smaller scale, and unwittingly buys a 4-mm. locomotive and rolling stock, is going to find himself pretty badly "stung."

It is, of course, possible that the two sizes will develop independently; the smaller being for strictly-to-scale models, and the larger for the tin-plate-toy variety, but seeing that this gauge is so eminently fitted for realism in lay-out, and that the easy curves and "flat" points and crossings will permit of the use of a wheel tyre somewhere nearer the scale mark than, say, the average 0-gauge atrocity, the need for the latter product, except perhaps for the crudest of toys, hardly arises.

However, if it is now too late to concentrate on one scale only, I submit that it would help to mend matters a little, if a distinctive name for each scale were adopted, as I feel sure you will agree that simply "00 gauge" for both sizes, is far too misleading a description in view of the big discrepancy in the respective dimensions.

Yours faithfully,

Blackheath. H. Chase.

Standard Gauges and Scales.

To the Editor Model Railway News.

Dear Sir,

I submit the following list for reference purposes:—

Gauge		Track		Scale to 1 ft.
No. 00	=	$\frac{5}{8}$ in.	=	3½ mm.
,, 0	=	1¼ in.	=	7 mm.
,, 1	=	1¾ in.	=	10 mm.
,, 2	=	2 in.	=	$\frac{7}{16}$ in.
,, 3	=	2½ in.	=	½ in.
		3¼ in.	=	$\frac{11}{16}$ in.
		3½ in.	=	¾ in.
		4¾ in.	=	1 in.
		7¼ in.	=	1½ in.
		9½ in.	=	2 in.
		15 in.	=	3 in.

Yours truly,

London. C. A. S.

Lever Control for Reversing Clock-work Locos.

To the Editor MODEL RAILWAY NEWS.

DEAR SIR,

A gadget for reversing the loco was described in the December 14th, 1922, *Model Engineer*, but lacked any means of operating it in an off position, It was always in action. This appliance was a piece of flat brass, bent to a right angle. In the corner a piece of brass tube was soldered and cut off so that it fitted between the rails. The horizontal end, being weighted, would drop and hold the short end up to catch the lever on the engine. The engine would travel past the catch before starting back and the brass would tip up on the return and not act but immediately the engine had passed would flop up again and reverse any train that might happen to come along.

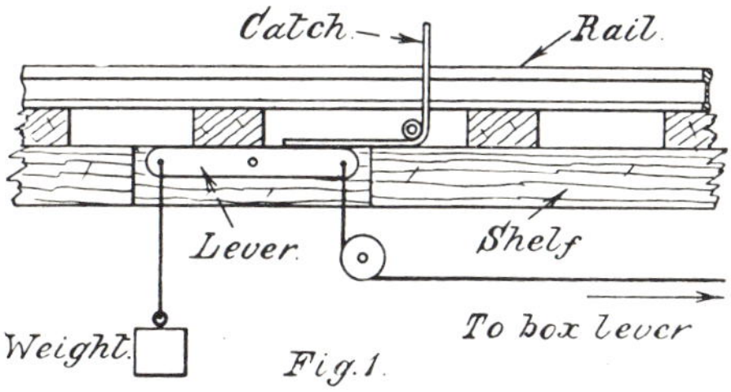

The box-lever pulled.

(I should say that a wire is threaded through the rails and brass tubes on which it swivels.) I have adopted this catch with an addition. Beneath the horizontal end I have cut a slot in my shelf on which the railway runs, and across this slot have fastened a piece of wire on which is pivoted a flat lever made of a piece of thin steel or brass $1\frac{3}{4}$ in. long $\times$ $\frac{1}{4}$ in. wide. This lever is weighted one end and the other is connected to the box-lever frame by a cord over pulleys, the one end resting lightly against the reversing catch underneath. When the box-lever is pulled the catch is as shown in Fig. 1, but when released, the weight pulls the lever down and

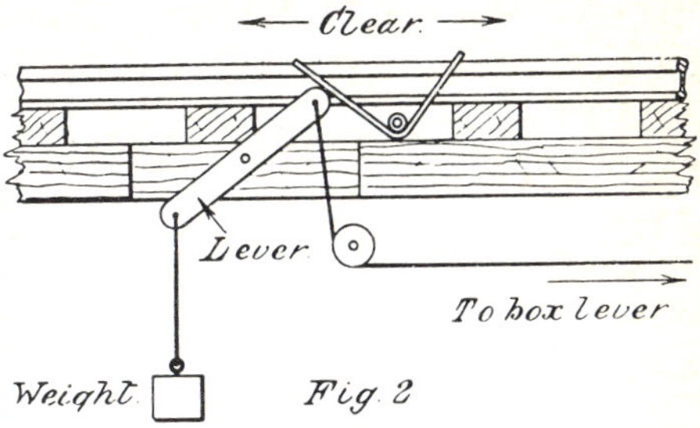

The lever released.

lifts up the catch to the off position and the line is clear. (Fig. 2.)

This catch only operates one way, of course.

A description of my railway will be sent along as soon as photos have been obtained. Wishing the MODEL RAILWAY NEWS every success.

I remain, Yours faithfully,

ARTHUR PETERS.

Finishing Models.

To the Editor MODEL RAILWAY NEWS.

DEAR SIR,

With reference to the query regarding the painting of rolling stock, which is raised on page 74 of this month's issue, perhaps the following notes may be of use.

GOODS STOCK.—To avoid the grain of the woodwork showing, use a fine-grained wood such as cedar, mahogany, or satin walnut, and sandpaper it thoroughly before the component parts of the wagons are cut out. Do not attempt to sandpaper the sides, ends, etc., of wagons after they have been cut, as the sharp edges will almost certainly be destroyed. Scribe board lines *after* cutting out. If these are scribed before, it may be found that they are very slightly out of parallel with the top and bottom edges of the wagon due to the thickness of the pencil lines marking them.

Use flat paint for all woodwork of goods stock. Stir it well and apply it thinly. Two or three thin coats are much better than one thick one. Do not use too small a brush, as this tends to produce a blotchy appearance.

A ½-in. or 1-in. flat brush is a good size for applying the ground colour. Keep all paint covered when not in use so as to exclude grit, which will, if present, leave a rough surface on the paint. Keep brushes scrupulously clean for the same reason, and when wagons are set aside to dry, put them in a box or cupboard as free from dust as possible.

For lettering, I use a small coach-

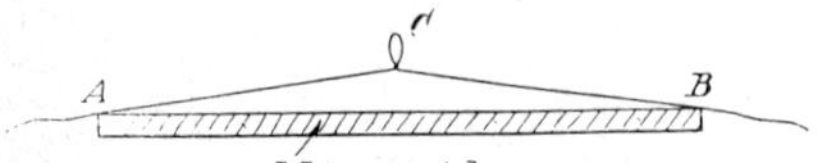

builder's lining brush. These can be purchased in various sizes for a few pence, and for the smaller gauges the two smallest sizes are most useful, the larger being used for the initial letters and the smaller being kept for detail work, such as the tare weight and number. With a little practice, I find no difficulty in reproducing letters 3-in. to 4-in. scale height in No. 1 gauge—*i.e.*, 2·5 to 3 mm., the main thing is to see that the paint is of the right thickness. If too thin it will run too freely and produce a broad blurred figure. If too thick it will hardly leave the brush. Flat paint being very quick-drying, it may be found that during the course of lettering the side of a wagon the paint in the tin into which the brush is dipped thickens on the surface. If this is so, the tin should be stirred again.

In lettering wagons, where there is no mark, such as a scribed board line, to regulate the size of the letters, it is well to make a chalk mark so as to keep the letters all the same size. On a flat-sided wagon, *i.e.*, one without raised timber framing, this can be done by means of a thread which has been well rubbed in chalk. A loop C should be tied in the centre, the thread adjusted over the spot where the chalk line is required, the two ends being held down firmly at A and B, and the thread pulled up by the loop, which is then let go suddenly, so that the thread will hit the wagon side for its whole length and deposit some of its chalk on the wagon. The sketch will make this clearer.

In the case of wagons with raised framing on the sides, it is best to draw as fine a line as possible with a sharpened piece of chalk. In spacing letters, do not chalk in the whole letter, for this tends to obscure the letter during painting. A small mark denoting the centre of each letter is quite sufficient.

Trusting the above rough notes will be of use.

Yours very truly,

E. A. O. HUTCHISON, *Lieut. R.A.*

Terminus Planning.

To the Editor MODEL RAILWAY NEWS.

DEAR SIR,

I should like to point out that I think Mr. H. D. Pinnington, in "Terminus Planning," page 61, has overlooked the fact that in my design, in the January issue, goods trains do not interfere with the working of passenger trains either " in " or " out " of No. 4 platform.

On my line a goods train averages 7 ft. long, *i.e.*, 1 ft. locomotive length and 12 wagons, approximately 6 in. each, occupy 6 ft. Assuming such a train in use is entering the goods line at G, then it would over-run any points near S.B., and arrive on platform 4 line, thus interfering with the working of passenger trains either " in " or " out."

No real ob ect is served by the points and slips (at G) *crossing* all sidings, as amoun of siding space is too short to hold many trucks, also no use for siding at S.B.

As a matter of interest I should like to state that I have two 4-coupled spring-motor locos, either of which will pull 18 wagons (4 wheel) and one bogie wagon (8 wheel). This is equal to 20 wagons of 4 wheel each.

I am, Yours truly,

J. A. DEAN.

Manchester.

Model Railway Club.

The meeting on February 12th was a Track Night, at which good progress was made in improving and preparing the Club's 0 gauge track in connection with the forthcoming exhibition. February 12th was a Lecture Night, "Ten-minute Talks on Model Railways." Messrs. Pitt and Kerr discoursed on Point and Switch Making, in an informative and illuminating manner; and, what was especially interesting, from two different points of view, the former treating of the subject from the standpoint of a 2½-in. gauge outdoor railway, while the latter dealt with the requirements of an indoor 0 gauge layout. Mr. Fish followed on a subject of which not much is heard—Substructures for Model Railways, giving many ingenious and money-saving hints. Mr. Pond next spoke on Sheet Metal Working for Model Locomotive Builders; but he did more than speak, for, in his hands, tinplate assumed various shapes in the most tractable manner, and that with the simplest of tools. A very valuable demonstration. Mr. Smart, senior, wound up an unusually instructive evening with a short reminiscence of models and model makers in his earlier days.

The Club's Exhibition is being held this year at the Kingsway Hall, Kingsway, W.C. 1, on Friday, April 17th, from 2 p.m. to 10 p.m., and Saturday, April 18th, from 10 a.m. to 10 p.m. There promises to be a good show of models, and a strong attendance is expected.

A programme of shed visits, etc., including some innovations, is being arranged for the Spring and Summer.

Fixtures for April:—Thursday, April 9th—Track Night. Thursday, April 23rd—Lecture, "Mechanical Drawing," by Mr. J. C. Cosgrave.

Particulars of the Club can be obtained from the Hon. Secretary, R. Henvey, White Cottage, Shirley, near Croydon.

R. H.

Wimbledon Model Railway Club.

On February 28th a large party of members of the Wimbledon and District Model Railway Club visited the Southern Railway School of Signalling at East Croydon. The Signalling instructor, Mr. W. C. Collins, welcomed the party on behalf of the Company, and then gave a short description of the School and the various courses conducted there. The School was started in 1913, and since that date over one thousand men have passed through. The classes are divided into grades, such as (1) Clerks, (2) Permanent-way men, goods porters and ticket collectors, (3) Higher grades, and (4) Technical lectures for signalmen.

Mr. Collins then explained the operations involved in despatching and receiving trains, including junction and siding work, illustrating each step by means of the model railway attached to the School. This line of 2½-in. gauge is laid with small-scale permanent way and is fully signalled. All points and signals are interlocked, working in connection with full-sized Tyers' "block" system and Sykes' "lock and block" instruments. The rolling-stock consists of a 4—4—2 tank loco and goods and passenger vehicles.

Single-line working on the staff system was then demonstrated by means of the model, after which much useful information about track-circuiting and the slotting and interlocking of signals and points was given. Members then had the opportunity of inspecting full-sized semaphore and disc signals at close range. This brought us to an explanation of the bell codes in use, in connection with which Mr. Collins mentioned an ingenious "word-system" he has devised to assist students in memorizing the many "calls." For example, "Cancel train" is seven beats—code word "washout" (seven letters), and so forth. We then passed on to a short description of the Westinghouse brake, and in this connection we learnt that the Southern Railway fit the vacuum brake on steam-hauled stock and Westinghouse brake on electric stock. As the steam-hauled stock go through the shops, the Westinghouse is also being fitted, as this is the system that will eventually be adopted. At the conclusion of this very interesting visit, a hearty vote of thanks to Mr. Collins was proposed and carried. Then (with permission, of course) several members tried their hands at working the levers and instruments, not with conspicuous success, one fears, the strict rotation in which the levers and plungers have to be moved being very complicated. Each signalman has to keep a train register book, in which are entered all train movements. But it was noticed the "temporary signalmen" were not prepared to go to that length.

This visit is one of a series that have been arranged in the Club's 1925 programme, the intention being to give members a real insight into the practical working of our home railways, which, with all due respect to everyone else, are the best in the world.

April Fixtures.—April 6th—Lecture on "Modern Boilers" by Mr. Robt. Clark. April 20th—Test Track Night and Demonstration on "Metal Cement" by Messrs. British Laboratories. April 25th — Visit to Messrs. Stuart Turner's Works, Henley-on-Thames. (Meet outside Works.) Meetings held at Red Cross Hall, Church Road. Hon. Secretary, R. Shephard, 27, Bernard Gardens, Wimbledon, will supply full particulars to those interested.

Mr. Wavell Dewis, 22, Sandfield Road, St. Albans, will be pleased to hear from any other reader in his neighbourhood with a view to forming a local Model Railway Club.

Construction and Repairs.

Readers in the West Country who desire any locomotives or model railway necessaries, building or repairing, may like to know that Mr. F. W. E. Stevens, of Sunnyside Cottage, North Street, Cheddar, is prepared to undertake such work. While inviting enquiries of any kind, he specializes in gauges 0 and 1.

Model Railway Drawings.

Messrs. Edwards Bros., 7, Fairoak Road, Roath Park, Cardiff, send us their list of full-size outline drawings of model railway rolling stock and locomotives which they are prepared to supply. This covers a very extensive range of engines and vehicles of all the principal railways, in gauges 0 and 1, and should be a very useful source of supply for many of our readers needing drawings to build from. Several drawings of new rolling stock recently put into service by the grouped Companies are included in the list, and Messrs. Edwards Bros. inform us that they are prepared to supply detailed drawings for both gauges of any new vehicle which may appear.

A Model "Caerphilly Castle."

A very neat little model of the "Caerphilly Castle" in the form of a paperweight has just been brought out by the Publicity Department of the Great Western Railway, for whom it is being manufactured by Messrs.

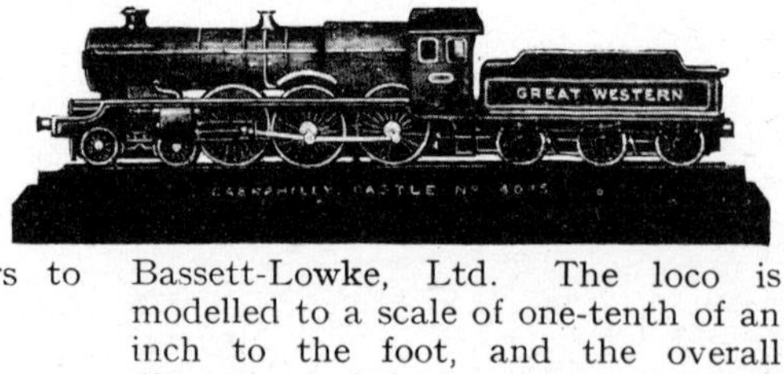

Bassett-Lowke, Ltd. The loco is modelled to a scale of one-tenth of an inch to the foot, and the overall dimensions of the base-plate on which it is mounted are 7 in. long by $1\frac{1}{8}$ in. wide. The model is nicely painted in the correct colours, and makes an exceedingly pretty little ornament which will please every model railway engineer. It may be obtained from Messrs. Bassett-Lowke's London branch, or from Northampton, price 5*s*.

The MODEL RAILWAY NEWS

Editorial and Publishing Offices :
66, FARRINGDON STREET, LONDON, E.C. 4.

Single Copies, post free, 7½d. Annual Subscription, 7s. 6d.

Vol. I. No. 5. MAY, 1925. Price, 6d.

Notes of the Month.

EVERYBODY who visited the Model Railway Club Exhibition is agreed about its success. It was a fine show, well-organized, and enthusiastically supported on all sides. It went just like the Cornish Riviera Express ; a big crowd awaiting the departure, a punctual start, and a splendid run to the other terminal. The doors were to open at 2 p.m., on the Friday ; at 1.59 the commissionaire took up his post, rather astonished to find a crowd of enthusiasts already demanding admittance, and on the stroke of the clock the show opened. It remained crowded all through the afternoon and evening, and the busy scenes were repeated throughout the Saturday. Unlike many other exhibitions, everything was ready in good time on the opening day. Careful organization by the executives and good team work on the part of the members ensured this, and it added considerably to the pleasure of the earlier visitors.

* * *

Running tracks were installed on each side of the hall. On one of these, Mr. Lawrence, well known as "L.B.S.C." was demonstrating the efficient working of Mr. Kirk's 4—6—2 Pacific, which has just come out of the shops after some slight repairs. Mr. James Crebbin's ever-popular *Cosmo Bonsor* was also doing duty under the charge of Mr. W. B. Hart. On the other side of the hall, the Club's co-operative 0-gauge track was in constant operation, and aroused much interest. But, whisper it gently, derailments at the crossings were of frequent occurrence. They naturally added much to the excitement of the day, but there is evidently scope for the Club's platelaying gang to get busy in the near future.

* * *

The success of the competitions was only partial. Some excellent work was shown, but for several of the events no entries at all were received. In one respect this is not to be regretted, because the multitude of non-competing exhibits made one realize that the members as a whole are happily more concerned with putting up a good all-round show for the credit of the Club than with the winning of individual prizes. Competitions, however, have their rightful place in such an exhibition, and it is good that meritorious work should receive suitable recognition. Those who have been familiar with the work of members of the Model Railway Club over a period of years, will agree with us in the opinion that the level of design and craftsmanship is distinctly rising. More attention is being paid to technical accuracy of detail, and some really excellent workmanship was to be seen on some of the exhibits. Some of the younger members show decided promise in this direction. There is a tendency in some quarters to miss a representative finish by the use of varnish instead of flat paint, while in other cases a certain slovenliness in finish mars an otherwise well-made model. We know how difficult the proper painting and lining-out processes are, but this very difficulty should call for greater patience and greater care than they sometimes receive.

* * *

We hope in our next issue to give a fuller account of this exhibition. There is no doubt it has given a distinct impetus to public interest in model railway engineering, and that the Club itself will receive new recruits for its membership goes without saying. We understand that during the past year it has grown by some 25 per cent., and hope this rate of increase will be well maintained. We congratulate the members of the Model Railway Club very cordially on the success which has attended their efforts on this occasion. There is no need to mention individual names; it was a co-operative effort in the best sense of the word, and everybody we met there was doing his best to make visitors welcome, and to give them an instructive and enjoyable time.

* * *

The Model Railway Club have two fixtures in May. On the 14th, there will be a track-night, and on the 28th, Col. Henvey, the Honorary Secretary, will give a lecture on "0-Gauge Methods."

* * *

The Manchester and District Model Railway Club report a well-attended meeting on April 14th, when Mr. Theo. Horn exhibited several 0-gauge models, and also an 00-gauge wagon. Mr. J. A. Dean, the Hon. Secretary, also showed an 0-gauge low-sided wagon, which has been in continuous use since 1919. The next meeting will be held on May 12th, at the Clarion Café, Market Street. The Club Room is on the third floor, and visitors will be cordially welcomed.

* * *

Those of our readers who are interested in the question of correct scale for 00-gauge models may like to exercise their ingenuity in inventing a trade name for models to the 3½-mm. scale. Messrs. Marshall, Stewart & Co. are offering a prize of 10*s*. for the most appropriate name submitted.

* * *

Mr. Tibor Singer (New York) writes :—" Allow me to be one of the first in the United States to congratulate you on the excellent appearance of the MODEL RAILWAY NEWS, the second issue of which I received yesterday. In connection with Mr. Greenly's article in the January number, it seems to me that as at present, clockwork locomotives once they are started, are uncontrolled as regards to speed, it would seem better to have a down grade from the terminus in order to give a good start to a heavy train, and an up grade into the terminus, in order to slow the train at its entry to the station limits where it has to cross many switches, and where the curves are generally sharper than on the main line. This arrangement would, of course, only apply where the plan is non-continuous, and where the line is somewhat shorter than the total length of run possible by the weakest locomotive. This is the scheme Mr. Wilson and myself have adopted on our railway, which was described in the July, 1923, number of *Everyday Science*. I wonder if it would be too much trouble for you to let me know whether there is a good model of a G.W. locomotive, 0 gauge electric, made, besides the 4—4—0 by Bassett-Lowke. The various manufacturers seem to have slighted the G.W.R. in choosing their prototypes. There are, of course, the standard tank engines supplied in G.W. colours as well as the others, but these can hardly be called models. I should like to get a G.W. engine, preferably a 4—4—2 or 4—6—2 tank engine."

NOTABLE MODEL RAILWAYS

Mr. N. Evans' "O" Gauge L. & N.W.R. Model Railway.

MY model railway is laid in a loft measuring 26 ft. × 11 ft. over a stable. As the roof and walls are not plastered, the place is somewhat damp, and therefore it was decided to have brass rail. The track is laid throughout in "Lowko" track—hollow brass rail and brass chairs spiked to tarred sleepers. The rails, being hollow, exert a slight outward spring, which, in my opinion, makes this track superior to the track with solid rails and slide-on chairs, as the chairs do not so easily tend to become loose. All the track and points are home-made, and the track is laid double on the main line, as will be seen from the diagram. Super-elevation is obtained on the curves by placing under the sleepers long strips of wood about $\frac{3}{16}$ in. × $\frac{1}{8}$ in., which came out of an old parasol. These can be bent to the curve quite easily, and they are tapered down gradually at the end where the transition curve begins, to provide gradual entrances to the curves. The curves on the main line are laid to a mimimum radius of 3 ft., but they are, of course, larger where possible. On the goods sidings, an absolute minimum of 2 ft. 6 in. is adopted, but this sharp radius only occurs in two places.

It will also be seen from the plan that a great part of the line is on an incline. This model railway plan is, no doubt, open to criticism on account of these inclines, but it seemed to be

A Goods entering Euston,.and a Passenger Train on its way from Crewe to Liverpool.

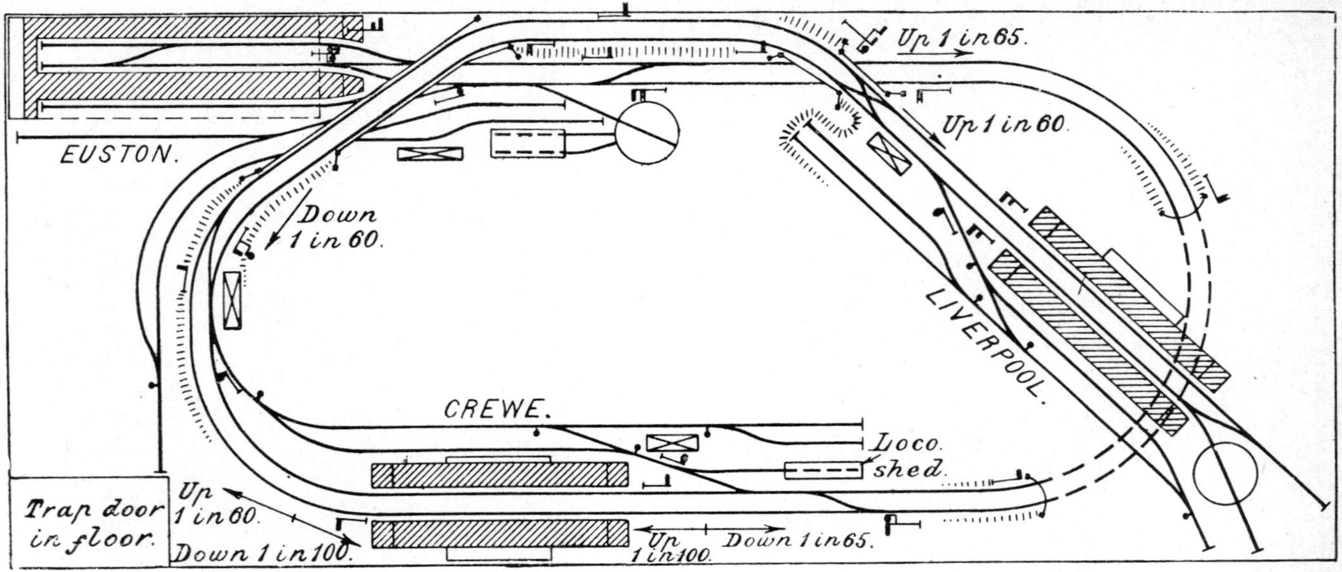

Lay-out of Mr. Evans' "O" Gauge Model Railway.

The gradients, which may at first sight seem rather frequent, were introduced as the only practical means of getting a long run between stations. Between the ends of the platforms of Euston and Crewe is 32 ft., between Crewe and Liverpool 18 ft., and the total length of continuous track from buffers to buffers of Euston and Liverpool measures about 75 feet.

General view of Euston Station. An Engine is taking water on the left-hand side of the picture.

the only way to get a good long run between each station, and to have all three stations of fairly reasonable size. Between the ends of the platforms of Euston and Crewe measures about 32 ft., and between the ends of the platforms of Crewe and Liverpool measures about 18 ft., whilst the total length of continuous track from buffers to buffers of Euston and Liverpool measures about 75 ft. As the steepest gradient is 1 in 60, the inclines do not trouble me very much, as my 4—4—0 George V loco starts easily from Crewe, when fully wound, and goes up the gradient of 1 in 60 immediately following, quite merrily with two eight-wheel coaches and a 12-wheeler dining car.

As the lower-level track passes under Liverpool station, it is to enter a tunnel about 3 ft. on each side of Liverpool and "hills" will be built to make more realistic this means of "getting rid" of a track whilst it passes under a station. As this part of the line is not yet completed, no photographs are, of course, available to show the tunnel, hills, etc., but as soon as it is finished, more photographs will be taken.

The embankment, seen in the photographs, at the back of Euston yard, was made of brown paper, carefully tacked to the wood. Hot carpenter's glue was then applied, and the small gravel sprinkled on, enough sticking to the paper to give a realistic effect. When dry, patches of grass were painted on in green paint, but these, of course, are hardly noticeable in the photographs. The glue, when dry, makes the paper quite stiff.

Of course, it is hardly correct for Euston to have a large box-girder bridge spanning its yard, but the effect of the two trains, seen in one of the photographs, is quite realistic. The abutments for this bridge were made of wood and coated with hot glue, and fine light grey chippings thickly sprinkled on. When dry, the loose were shaken off, and a stucco effect was the result. This stucco was also employed for Euston signal cabin. (The fine chippings are a kind of dust, obtainable from a dealer in concreting materials ; the dust is used sometimes instead of sand, for mixing with cement and rubble for making concrete.) These fine chips are also used for ballasting.

The points and signals at Euston are all worked from the one lever frame of 24 levers ; all the signals are home-made, being constructed on a sort of "mass-production" system, which can hardly be described in these short notes. The signals are connected to the lever frame by thread passing through guides, and a description of their construction may not be out of place here. Strips of boxwood, a full $\frac{1}{8}$ in. square, are cut from an old broken foot-rule, and cut off at lengths in proportion to the number of threads they are to carry. For example, for four threads they are about $\frac{3}{4}$ in. long. One is placed lengthways in the vice, flush with the top of the vice, to prevent splitting, and fine gimp pins, cut off to about $\frac{1}{4}$ in. long, are driven in as close to each other as possible, *i.e.*, with their heads touching ; about $\frac{1}{8}$ in. is left projecting. One more rail is put in than the number of cottons the post is to carry, so that each cotton is passed, so to speak, between two nails. The head is cut off one gimp pin, to make a double-ended nail, and this is driven into the bottom of the post, in the vice, to fix the post to the ground. They are now ready to be painted black. This must be done carefully and thinly, so as not to make the nails sticky, and, therefore inefficient. In the general view of Euston station a row of these can be seen at the bottom of the embankment, and even if they are not quite "real practice," *i.e.*, with pulleys, the result is quite effective, and I find that with these there is no need for any auxiliary weights for the signals, the balance weights returning them to danger quite satisfactorily.

From the plan of Euston, it will be seen that up trains can run either to the main arrival or local arrival platforms. After the "passengers" have alighted from the express trains, a small tank loco shunts on from the engine-shed road, and pulls the train out, either to shunt it on to the carriage siding, or to pull it over the crossover, and shunt it into the main

An Express leaving Euston.

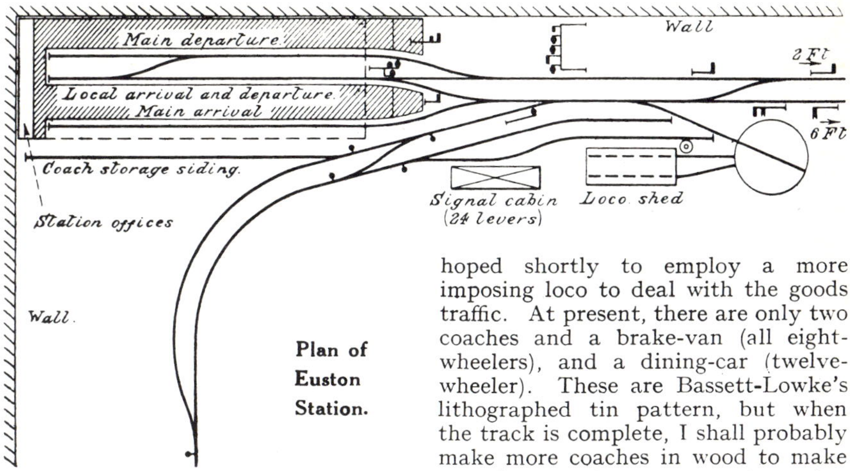

Plan of Euston Station.

departure platform. The express loco which has brought the train in can now shunt straight to shed for coaling and watering, and the tank loco also returns to shed. Then the loco which is to haul the down express can come out of shed on to the up line, go over the crossover, and back on to the train. Local trains worked by a tank loco can run straight to the local platform; the engine can uncouple, shunt to the buffer-stops, and pass up through the main departure road *via* the crossover in the station, and shunt straight to the front of the train. The manipulations of the loco in the station are done through an opening left in half the centre span of the roof, which is done in three V spans. The coaling of locos is done from coal wagons on the siding nearest the loco shed; two such wagons can be seen in the photographs. Goods trains can run into the goods department, best seen in the plan of Euston, and all shunting can progress without any interference with the passenger trains.

The only locomotives in use at present are those seen in the photos; a 4—4—0 George V clockwork loco and a pre-war 0—4—0 Peckett saddle-tank loco, both by Bassett-Lowke. But a 4—6—2 clockwork tank loco is in course of construction, and it is hoped shortly to employ a more imposing loco to deal with the goods traffic. At present, there are only two coaches and a brake-van (all eight-wheelers), and a dining-car (twelve-wheeler). These are Bassett-Lowke's lithographed tin pattern, but when the track is complete, I shall probably make more coaches in wood to make up a four-coach express train, and a three-coach local train.

Euston station may not be as convenient to operate as those stations with scissors crossings, etc., to enable trains to arrive at and depart from all platforms, but there are, I think, comparatively few of us who can afford, or who have time to make, such coaching stock that justifies laying down such an arrangement. All extra crossovers, etc., take up space, and in laying down this line, my chief object was to get as long a run between each station as possible, and to have, at the same time, three moderate-sized stations.

N. H. B. (Manchester).—We note with regret that you have asked three engine drivers the purpose of the snifting valve used on their engines, and "have drawn a blank," as you put it. The writer is afraid that the larger part of the younger generation of drivers are, compared to the days when engine men were also trained fitters, mere "regulator pushers." The snifting valve is used on piston-valve engines, to prevent a vacuum being formed in the steam chests when the engine is running with the steam off. Air is drawn in—sometimes a little steam—when the pistons are acting as vacuum pumps.

Semaphore Type Ground Signals.

THIS design, arranged for No. 1 gauge model railways, is based on the newer pattern of "Tommy Dod" in use on the Southern line (L.S.W.R. section) in the Woking district. The arm is arranged on a post the top of which carries the lamp, and a short semaphore painted vermillion with the usual white stripe faces the driver who is backing into the siding. On top of the semaphore a double spectacle plate is fixed. In the "on" position the left-hand plate is pierced with a small hole in the centre, thus showing a small white light. The adjacent spectacle has a green glass. In the prototype this is slightly oval to allow for errors in the movement of the wires and levers operating the signal. To ensure that false indications cannot be given the lamp case at the back of this light is in the "on" position extended, so that the glass is effectively blanked off. There is the usual back light, but from the examples examined this light in not obliterated on the movement of the signal, as in the case of main-line signals.

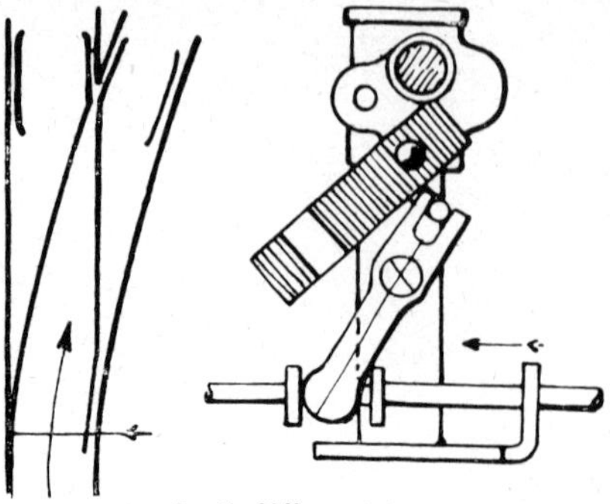

In "off" position.

The mechanism suggested for the model consists of a lever operated by washers soldered on to the point rod. The exact proportions of this lever will depend on the amount of movement provided by this rod. This lever is pivoted to a boss on the post, and a rounded lower end where it engages the washers and a forked upper arm. This fork fits in a piece of bent wire soldered on to the back of the semaphore The leverage as arranged allows the signal to be put on either side of the points. It should, of course, face the train that is backing into the points or over the crossover, as the case may be. The base of the post (a piece of sheet metal) is shown to be upturned at one corner as a guide for the point rod.

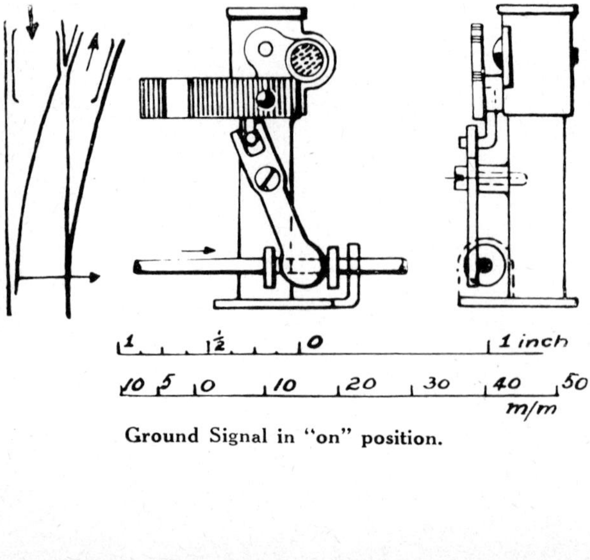

Ground Signal in "on" position.

For No. 0 gauge the signal can be made about three-quarters of the size shown in the drawings except perhaps in the matter of height. As the same permanent way is often used for both scales, the accessories which depend on height have to be modified to suit.

H. G.

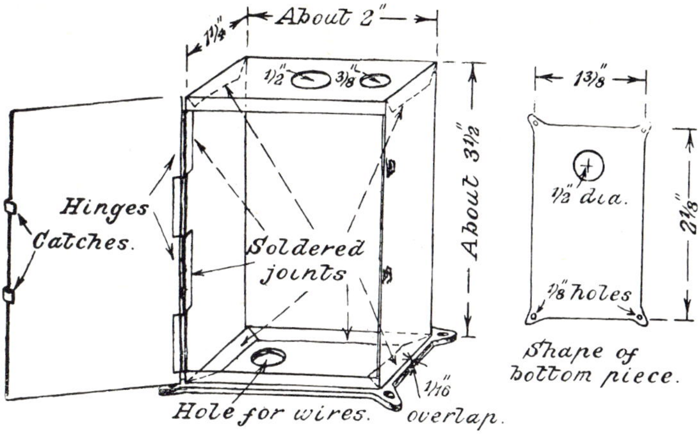

Fig. 1.—The box, or frame.

A Controller for Electric Model Railways.

By Brian. T. Cooke.

I HAVE usually observed, in model electric railway systems, that the locomotives, rolling stock, etc., are in perfect detail, but that the same cannot be said of the control apparatus. Why not make this part of the equipment as "true to life" as the remainder? In actual practice, in most instances, at any rate, the principal portion of the control gear is the "controller." Even although this is so, I do not recollect ever having seen a model of this interesting piece of apparatus in use on a model railway. It seems to me that such a model would greatly enhance the appearance and interest of any electric system, so, in view of this, and in the hope that I may interest some of our readers in this direction, I offer here a design for a model controller which can easily be made, with a little care, trouble and patience, by any enterprising "model railwayist."

Of course, it will be understood that this is only the "bare idea." Space does not permit of a very detailed description here, but the individual constructor will be able to enlarge on and adapt the idea to suit his own convenience. The controller described here is suitable for use with alternating or direct current, up to a pressure of about 16 volts, on any system using either auto-reversers, permanent magnet motors, or separately excited fields. The method of connecting and the connections performed by the controller are fully shown in the diagram of connections, Fig. 5.

The *box* or frame, with its hinged front, is illustrated in Fig. 1 and is of a fairly stout gauge of tinplate. The only important point in the construction of this is that the bottom is a separate piece, shaped as shown, cut from sheet-iron about $\frac{1}{16}$ in. thick, and soldered on.

The *main drum* is illustrated in detail and assembly in Fig. 2 and needs special care in its construction. The shaft, of $\frac{3}{16}$-in. square steel, turned down to $\frac{1}{8}$-in. diameter at the ends, is insulated on the square portion with Empire tape, shellac varnished. The clamps, which also serve to connect the segments together correctly, are cut from sheet copper, $\frac{1}{64}$ in. thick, to the shapes shown, bent to fit the square shaft accurately,

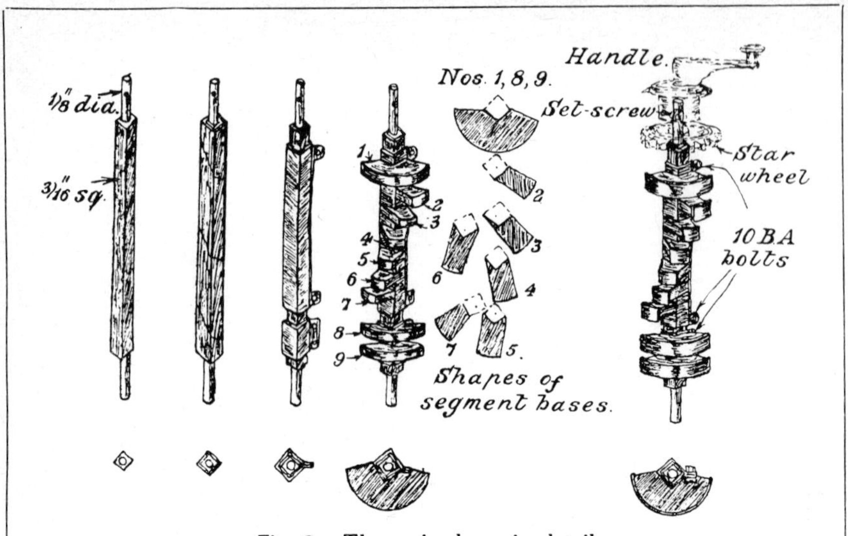

Fig. 2.—The main drum in detail.

and fitted with 10 B.A. bolts and nuts. To these clamps are soldered the segment bases, which must be cut accurately to the shapes shown from $\frac{1}{16}$-in. thick sheet brass. The final step is to solder the segments, of $\frac{1}{8}$-in. × $\frac{1}{64}$-in. thick sheet copper, to their respective bases, and when this is done the drum is complete, and should be painted black on all parts, except the segments and the ends of the shaft.

The *reverse drum* is the next part to consider, and is of hard wood, with $\frac{1}{8}$-in. diameter steel spindles forced into the two ends, so that it will run in the bearings, as shown in the assembly sketch, Fig. 3. The segments, as shown, are of $\frac{1}{64}$-in. thick copper sheet, and are fastened on with $\frac{1}{4}$-in. No. 2 wood screws, countersunk.

The *fingers*, of which there are two sets, one set for each drum, are illustrated in Fig. 4. They are screwed on to a "board" of hard wood by $\frac{1}{4}$-in. No. 2 round-headed wood screws, and the wires from outside are connected by soldering, as shown.

The minor parts, such as bearings, star-wheel, roller, handles, keys, etc., need no explanation, but can be easily constructed from the sketches herewith.

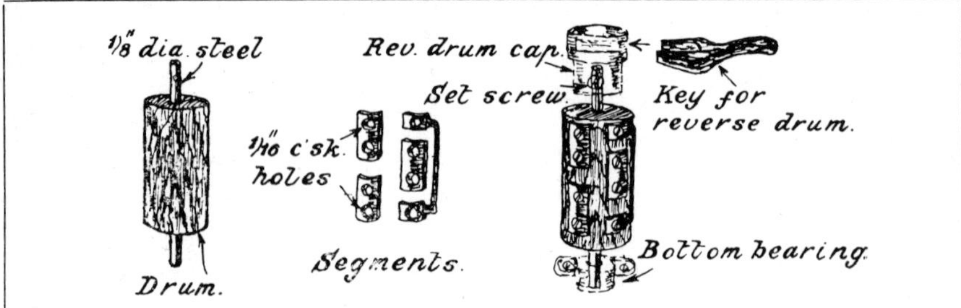

Fig. 3.—Assembly sketch of reverse drum.

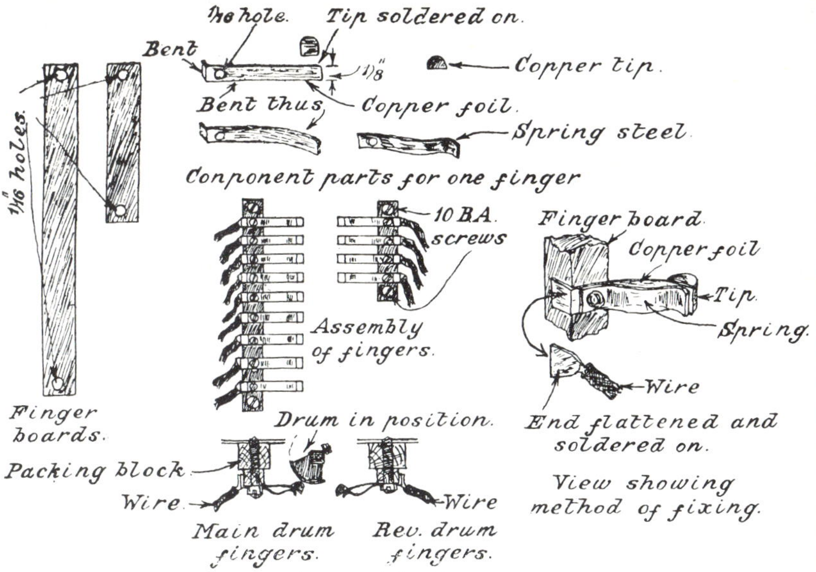

Fig. 4.—The Fingers.

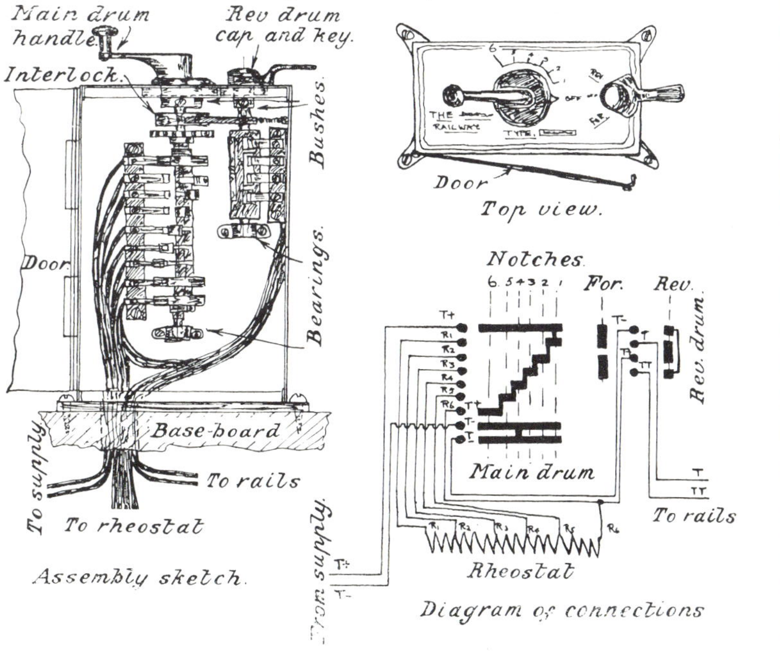

Fig. 5.—The method of connecting, and the connections made.

The model having been completed to the maker's satisfaction, it should be painted grey, with black handle and key, and the operating positions of the drums marked on the top with black.

If considered necessary, an interlock may be fitted between the drums, as is done in actual practice, to prevent the main drum being moved when the reverse drum is in the "off" position. However, space does not permit of it being described here, but perhaps space for a little more on this subject may be granted, by the courtesy of the Editor, at some future date. Meanwhile, if any model railwayman thinks of making one of these controllers (and I can assure you that any who do will find it well worth their while), and is "stuck" for want of sufficient information, I shall be very pleased to tell him all he wants to know, if he will write me, c/o the Editor.

Miniature Railways in Australia.

Mr. J. J. Mahony, of Melbourne, in communicating with the writer on his intentions for next season, says that his 7¼-in. gauge "Pacific" has been plugging away all the year with loads of upwards of 30 children. To make the carriages more stable when used by adult passengers, he has now arranged them to fit a 12-in. gauge line. This scheme has proved quite successful, and should he at any time be able to build another engine, he could make it to suit the larger gauge. These new rails are of 12 lb. per yard F.B. Section, and run parallel and outside the 7¼-in. gauge track, as shown in the accompanying picture.

Showing the 12 in. gauge line for carriages.

Mr. J. J. Mahony on his 7¼ in. gauge "Pacific."

A Working Model Water Crane for "O" Gauge.

By R.H.

THIS is a simple model to make, provided a lathe is available. It is made of scrap, except the counterweight, which is a $\frac{1}{2}$-in. phosphor bronze ball, as used for pump valves. The maker could, of course, turn a ball for himself. Dimensions need not be adhered to exactly, the various screwed parts being of a size to suit existing tackle.

The column is turned slightly taper, screwed at the bottom, and back-nutted to the square base-plate. A hole is bored a nice sliding fit for the hollow tee-piece. The top is filed as shown, so that the weight of the tee-piece tends to turn it away from the track. The copper pipe for the hose is tinned inside, filled with solder, and then bent. The tube must be well annealed first. The hose is made of fine cambric, and bound on to the end of the copper pipe, which has a small wire soldered round the mouth to

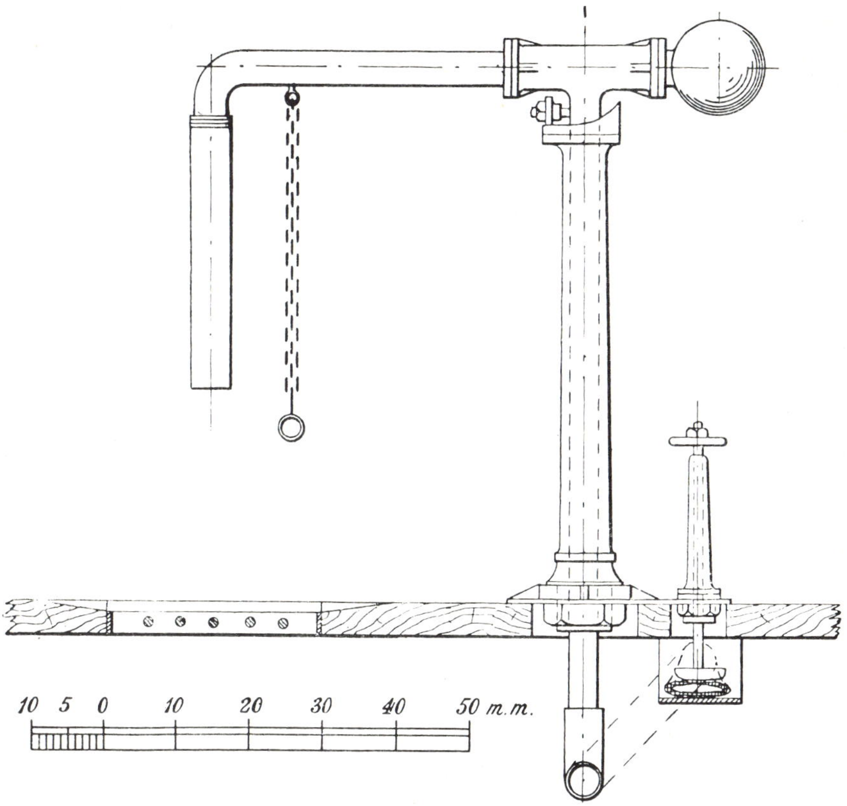

General Arrangement of Model Water Crane.

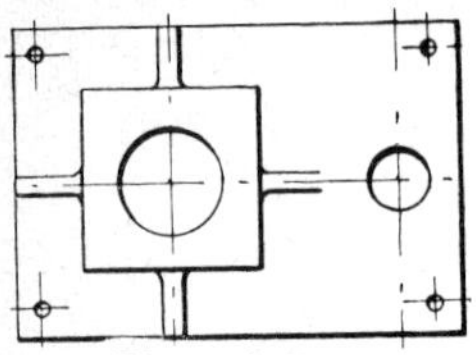
Plan of Base.

prevent the hose slipping off. A chain with ring is fitted to the copper pipe.

The tee-piece is turned out of brass, bored axially for the copper pipe, which, with a spigot fitting into the counterweight, is then soldered in. A hole is bored at right angles to take the long stem, which, in my case, was bored and turned from the solid, but which might be made of treblet or other tube. This joint is preferably hard-soldered. A small roller is fitted, as shown, to run round the top of the column.

The base-plate consists of two pieces of brass plate, shaped as in the plan, and sweated together. Holes are made for the main and valve columns. The base-plate is a casting in the real water crane, and the appearance of the model is much improved by adding small angle-pieces, as shown. This would be a fiddling job if each piece were separately shaped and sweated in position. It is, however, easily done as follows. Make four cuts with a hack-saw, and don't be afraid to cut well into the upper square of the base-plate. Insert four bits of brass of any reasonable size, just thick enough to fit the saw-cuts snugly. Sweat up the whole base-plate, and trim off with a fairly smooth file. The angle-pieces shown in the tee-piece (which in the original is also a casting) were made in a similar way.

The valve column is turned, drilled, tapped $\frac{1}{16}$ Whitworth at the bottom, and counter-drilled $\frac{1}{16}$ clearing size. It is externally screwed at the lower end, and back-nutted to the base-plate similarly to the main column. The valve-spindle is a $\frac{1}{16}$ wire, screwed for about half its length, and fitted at the top with a little German silver hand-wheel. At the other end, a small mushroom-head is screwed and sweated on. On screwing the spindle down, it pinches a rubber tube leading from the bottom end of the tee-piece through a stirrup made of brass plate screwed to the base board upon which the crane is fixed. This "valve" would naturally be hidden from sight.

A small grating is fitted in a square hole in the base-board to receive overflow and drips; and the base-board round the crane is painted and lined out to represent flag-stones.

Water cranes vary very much in size and design. This one is intended to stand at the end of a passenger platform, and the height will be found about correct.

The scale of the model is 7 mm. = 1 foot.

Why Do You?

Why do model railway builders and owners limit their interest almost entirely, so far as I have observed, to the usual form of steam or electric railway? It seems to me that there is a wider field, and that much pleasure could be derived with railways of other kinds. For example, the suspended overhead type, such as runs between Barmen and Elberfeld, in Germany, over the river Wupper. The trains run suspended from a rail carried upon inverted V arches. Illustrations and a description were published in the *Model Engineer* of October 13th, 1904. There is the cable-operated type. Many years ago there was a cable railway working from Fenchurch Street, in London, to Blackwall. A model railway of this type, with winding engines and gear for driving the cable, would surely be an interesting scheme. The Telepher type is another, the carriages and locomotives or motor-coaches running suspended from an overhead cable. There is also the mono-rail type, capable of various modifications. Motive power may be steam, electricity, or compressed air.

"O" Gauge Points and Crossings.

By George Wintringham.

POINTS and crossings can be constructed very easily with the type of rails described in the first three numbers of this paper, but before going into details it will be as well to say a few words regarding the radius

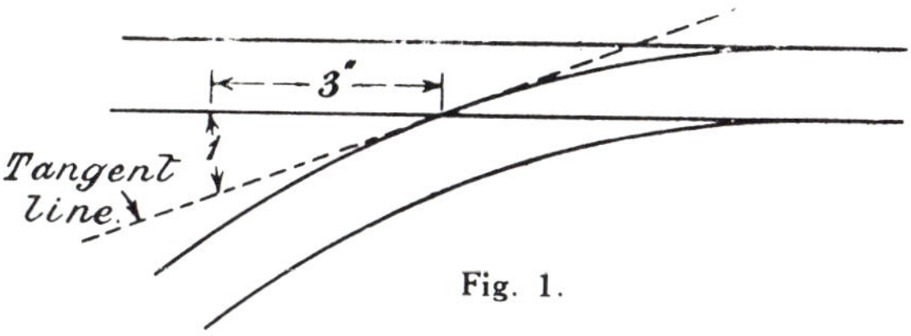

Fig. 1.

of curves, as they are a very important factor.

First of all, curves should always be of the largest radius that can be got in, because if they are too sharp your scale model rolling stock will not run round them, but will jump off, and give all sorts of other troubles, such as buffer-locking, and bogies swinging too far and fouling underframes, etc.

The radius of curves in connection with points and crossings is dependent upon the angle of the crossing—the angle usually being referred to as one in so-and-so, as 1 in 8 or 1 in 12, as the case may be. The method of measuring the angle is shown in Fig. 1, where the angle is 1 in 3.

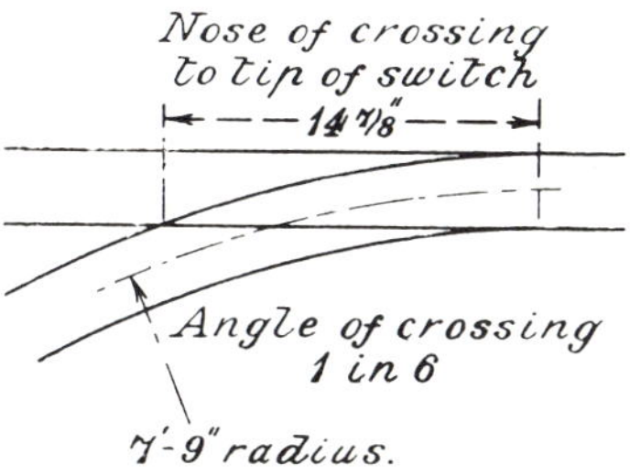

Fig. 2.

Perhaps the most usual angles to be found on real railways are 1 in 6 to 1 in 8, but they are more acute for main line junctions and other positions of importance. For models, however, 1 in 4½ and 1 in 6 will, in most cases, meet all requirements.

The radius of a curve on an 0-gauge crossing of 1 in 4½ is 4 ft. 4 in., and for a well laid-out model railway of 7 mm. scale, I recommend this as the sharpest curve allowable, whether it is in connection with points and crossings or otherwise.

Crossings of 1 in 6 are preferable, and should most certainly be installed wherever space admits.

Obviously, the more acute the angle of the crossing, the greater will be the radius of the curve, as well as

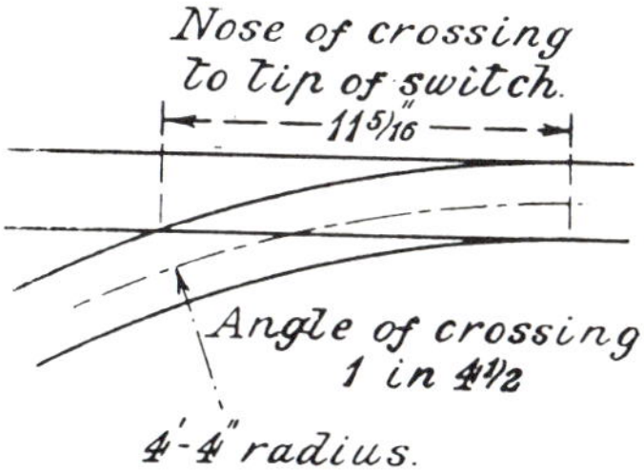

Fig. 3.

the overall length from the switches to the crossing.

The leading dimensions of 1 in 4½ and 1 in 6 points and crossings will be found in Figs. 2 and 3.

A complete set of switches and a 1 in 6 crossing are shown, half size, in Figs. 4 and 5, but the intermediate curved part has been left out owing to space limitations.

The sleepers for the points and crossings are graduated in length, beginning from the tip of the switches

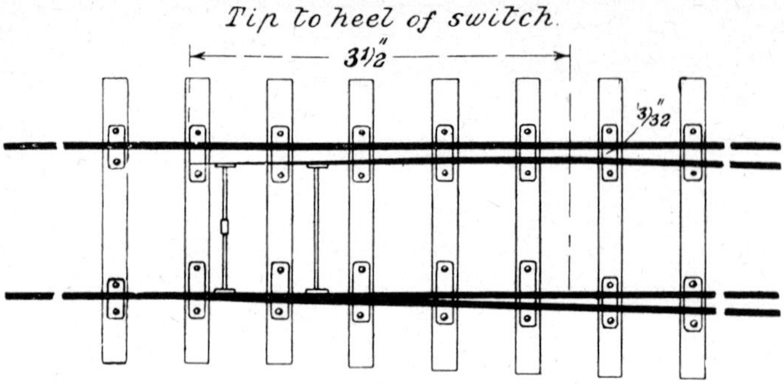

Fig. 4.

and gradually increasing until clear of the crossing, the longest one being $4\frac{1}{4}$ in. The width should be $\frac{1}{4}$ in. to $\frac{9}{32}$ in., in order to accommodate the larger chairs, some of which are placed diagonally.

The drawing shows the sleepers arranged so that the crossing can be used as either a right or left-hand one, but the actual arrangement of sleepers will, of necessity, vary and must be left to the judgment of the engineer in charge.

The chairs are made exactly in the same way as described for the plain tracks, the only difference being that they are larger and vary in size according to the position they occupy on the crossing.

It will be best, and save a lot of time and trouble when making points and crossings, to draw them out full size on a board or stiff piece of paper, as the rails can then be cut and bent to the correct shape without any difficulty.

Care must be taken in filing up the switches to make them a clean fit

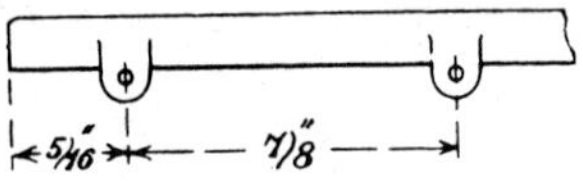

Fig. 6.

against the stock-rails.

In making the crossing, the splice rails must be nicely fitted together and soldered, and finished up with a smooth file.

Fig. 7.

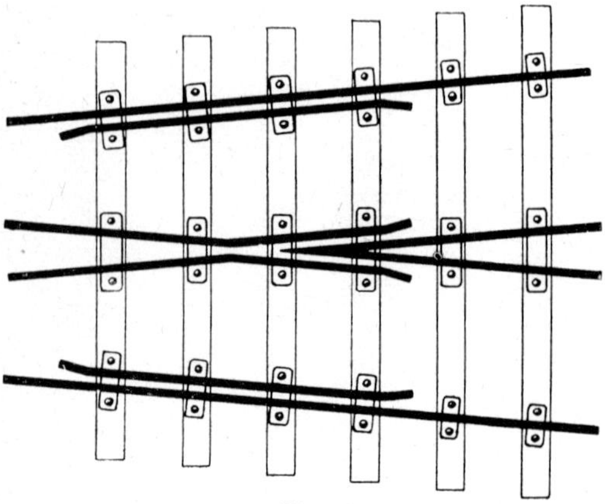

Fig. 5.

With this type of rail, the connecting rods between the switches cannot very well be fitted through holes in the rails in the orthodox way. The best way to do this is to solder—silver solder preferably, as it is stronger—two small lugs on to each switch, *see* Fig. 6. The connecting rods can be shouldered down a little at each end, put through the holes in the lugs, and then rivetted over, leaving just the smallest amount of slackness.

A lug, Fig. 7, must be fitted to the front connecting rod for attaching the working rod from the point lever. This lug may be made from a thin piece of metal bent round the rod and then soldered.

Having got all the parts finished, they may be soldered into the chairs and then the whole spiked down on to the sleepers.

If care has been taken with making and laying this type of track, and most particularly with the points and crossings, the whole will give the greatest possible satisfaction, and there will be no more derailments on account of the small wheel dimensions than there are on those models laid with out-of-scale rails and absurdly exaggerated wheel flanges and treads. Moreover, the whole running of the locomotives and rolling stock will be found incomparably better.

New L.M.S.R. Box Wagons, with Corrugated Ends.

SOME new box wagons are now running on the L.M.S.R., with ends made in pressed steel, in place of the usual timber-framed and sheeted construction. Railway companies, in the past, have experienced considerable trouble owing to the ends of wooden-covered wagons being damaged by the load. To mitigate this, Mr. R. W. Reid, the carriage and wagon engineer of the above line, has, in collaboration with the Leeds Forge Co., Ltd., designed and made a large number of pressed steel ends, which are being embodied into the latest wagons.

The drawing for the model No. 1 gauge wagon reproduced herewith gives a good idea of the arrangement. In a model, sheet-metal might be employed, as in the prototype. Aluminium is a very suitable material, as it is easily shaped. Otherwise, the corrugations can be imitated by gluing strips of wood on to wooden ends, finishing them off to a smooth and rounded form, with fine glass-paper. In the prototype, corrugations are pressed outward only—not alternatively inward and outward—from the surface of the ends.

The new wagons to which these ends are fitted, have disc centres to the wheels. These centres are pierced with three holes.

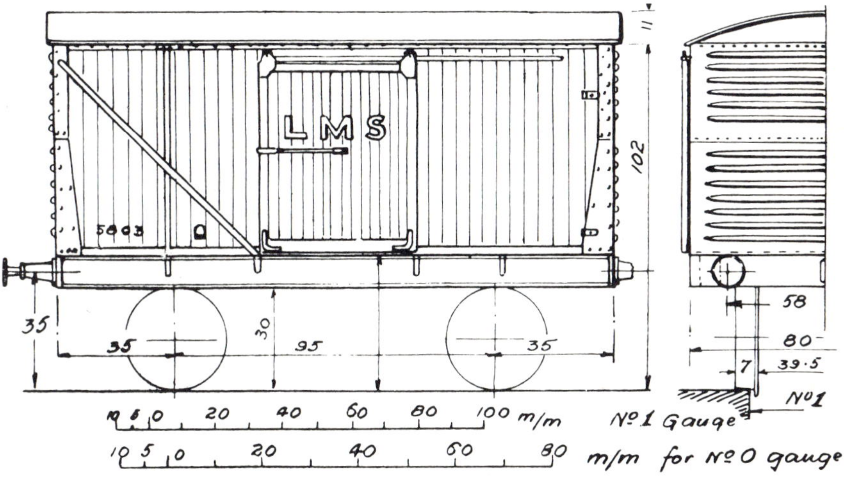

Notes on a No. 1 Gauge Model Railway

By

J. FRANCIS PARKER.

Express Train passing the country station.

I AM sending you a few notes, supplementary to my article in your previous model railway publications, on my line since it has been fixed in its new home.

My brother and I were fortunate in having the exclusive use of three small attics and a dark gable, and so the line has been put on trestles and shelving in a permanent manner.

Surveying the site proved quite an interesting task, as I was limited by difference in level, and slope of the floors, sloping roof, and many massive oak beams which had to be avoided. Altogether, so far, we have cut nine tunnels through the lath and plaster walls! and these had to be situated so as to avoid the oak beams. In one place there was just exactly enough room for a single line track between two beams.

The "Scherzer" type lifting bridge.

The line itself is a continuous track 100 feet round, with a loop and sidings. Eventually we hope to link up the goods siding with the inner siding on the opposite side of the room in order to form a second loop, thus providing double line for half the length of the main line.

Coming up to view the railway, one passes first under the lift bridge over the stairs (three-feet span), and sees the viaduct 12 feet long, opposite. In the second room on the left is the main station with sidings, etc., and on the right the country station with goods siding. In the third attic are engine sheds, and a Scherzer-type lift bridge (three-feet span). This bridge was made in order to keep a small tank room accessible, and is pivoted instead of rolling. It took us both about three weeks to make, from designing to fixing.

Up to the present very little scenery has been put up, but eventually we hope to have this very complete. The present job is signalling and locking gear for the bridges. We have very nearly had some serious accidents through the lifting bridges!

Lifting bridge and tunnel entrance.

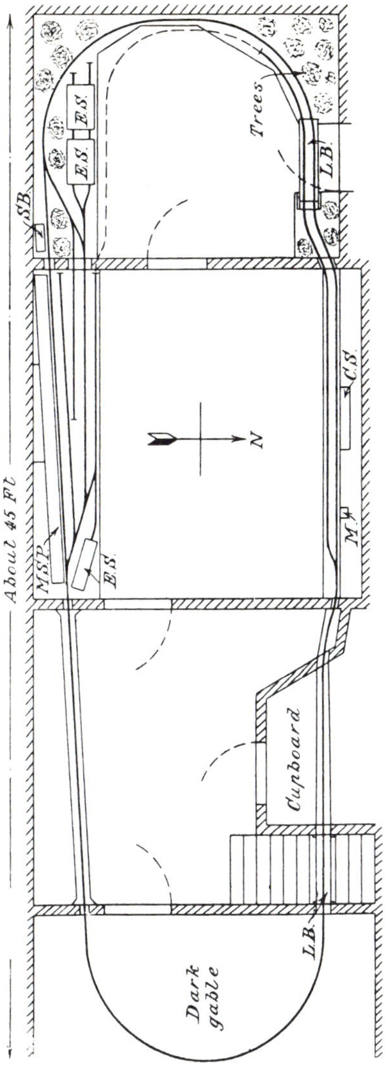

Lay-out of Mr. Parker's Model Railway.

Gradually the old track is being replaced by solid brass permanent way, and the resulting improvement in running is immense.

The latest additions to the rolling stock are three new bogie vestibuled coaches, and one rebuilt to match. These form a set, and with restaurant car and mail van make quite a smart-looking train. The coaches are fitted with electric light, controlled by one switch, and the cables between them are joined by means of necklace fasteners.

The "Claughton" makes no fuss about this load, so I hope to make some more carriages some time. I find it pays to make about three at once, because then the parts can be got out in lots, which saves time.

The three last took me about six months of spare time to make, including painting, and there are about 100 pieces of material in each. The tare weights are only slightly over scale.

I have only three professionally built coaches, mail van, restaurant car, and short bogie brake.

On a test recently we got the "Claughton" up to a scale speed of 116·75 m.p.h. on 5′ 6″ radius curves! She would have done more had the curves permitted.

We have not definitely decided upon future extensions of the line, but space will only allow of these in a vertical direction. For some time yet we shall have as much to do as we can manage.

What has become of M. Emile Bachelet and his Levitated Electric Railway? In 1914, M. Bachelet had, in London, a very interesting model railway, working upon an extraordinary system. The car did not run upon rails, but floated in air above the track, being levitated by the electrical repulsion effect of alternating-current electro-magnets upon the metal floor of the car. This provided support. Propulsion was obtained by means of solenoids, coils of wire carrying an electric current, placed at intervals along the track, and through which the car was sucked. The model caused a considerable amount of interest. Then came the war. M. Bachelet and his model seem to have disappeared.

A Fine Model Terminus Station.

JUST prior to the outbreak of war, two gentlemen, well-known in model circles, were busy equipping a $1\frac{3}{4}$-in. gauge line with the best of everything that could at that time be obtained. Among other very interesting features, such as a 12-ft. model Forth Bridge the terminal station illustrated in the photographs on the opposite page is worthy of special mention.

The roof truss was arranged on the "St. Pancras" principle, and covered four roads and three platforms. In Fig. 1 a corridor train, headed by a model French "Nord" 4—6—0 type locomotive, is shown just running into the arrival side. The porters and taxi-cabs are grouped in a most realistic fashion. The second picture shows the construction of the roof girders in detail. These were built up of segmental aluminium castings and glazed outside.

We have to thank Mr. Fred Hart, the late Hon. Secretary of the Reading Society of Model Engineers, for these fine photographs. As the line is now disbanded, it is important that this excellent workmanship model should be recorded, and we hope to be able to illustrate other features of the railway in future issues.

A Model Locomotive for India.

Messrs. Bassett-Lowke, Ltd., have just sent us a photograph of a locomotive completed last week for one of their customers in India.

This model, which is based on the N.B.R. outline, but with the addition of an extra coupled wheel in place of the trailing wheel under the cab, is built to a scale of $\frac{3}{4}$ in. to the foot, on $3\frac{1}{4}$-in. gauge. The model is 4 ft. long over engine and tender and is fitted with a dual system of firing, viz.:—two Primus burners with pressure tank in tender and methylated spirit with spirit container at back of tender. The two cylinders are B.L. standard No. 6 short-stroke cylinders, $1\frac{1}{2}$-in. stroke, 1-in. bore and the motion is inside single-link motion reversing from cab. The coupled wheels are 5-in. diameter, and the tender and bogie wheels $2\frac{5}{8}$ in. The whole of the axles, both engine and tender, are mounted on springs and the axle boxes are of gunmetal.

A special arrangement will be noticed on the side of the cab for stopping the locomotive by means of a ramp fixed alongside the rail.

The boiler is filled by a duplex hand-pump or a mechanical pump driven from the main driving axle. A large head light is fitted, and also two tail lights at the rear of the tender, supplied with electric light from a small accumulator carried in the back compartment of the tender.

The model is finished in the old C.R. colours and, as will be seen from the photograph, is quite a handsome production. The model gave excellent results under tests.

A view showing in detail the construction of roof girders.
(*for description see opposite page*).

A French "Nord" 4-6-0 Locomotive running into the Arrival Platform.
(*for description see opposite page*).

Queries and Replies.

C. S. (Margate) sends a plan of his line now in course of construction. The main idea of the railway is serving a market town ("Oakvale") and a mining district at "Ashley." The triangle at the junction is designed to save a turn-table at "Oakvale."

It is difficult to criticize your plan in a constructive fashion. The destructive method would be quite easy. The whole trouble is that you have not drawn the plan to scale. If the junction at Taunley is anything to go by, and if laid with the smallest curves practical in No. 0 gauge, the whole lay-out (we only reproduce a small part) would occupy a room 55 ft. × 42 ft. Plans sent in should be laid out to scale and also all fixed obstacles—physical difficulties we might call them—should be noted.

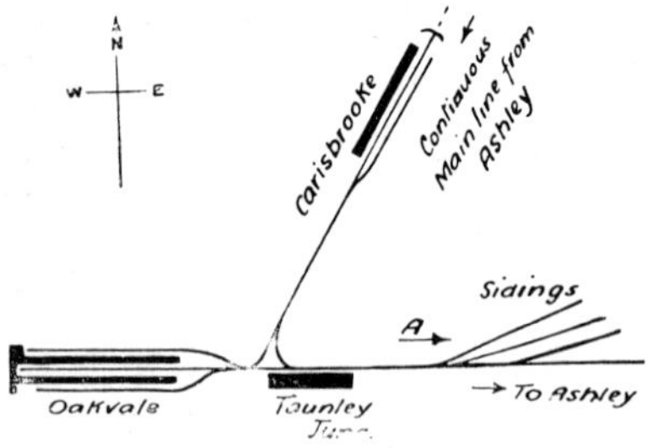

Fig. 1.—Portion of original lay-out.

If this is done, readers will discover many of the faults for themselves, and will not need to bother us with impossible schemes. One or two points of the plan can, however, be dealt with. The type of terminal station should be avoided as wasting space. Only one island platform is necessary. The two other roads may be laid together. The "Taunley" junction station is rather too near to the terminal station, and, further, a train approaching the sidings from "Carisbrooke" (as at A) would have difficulty in dropping and shunting in

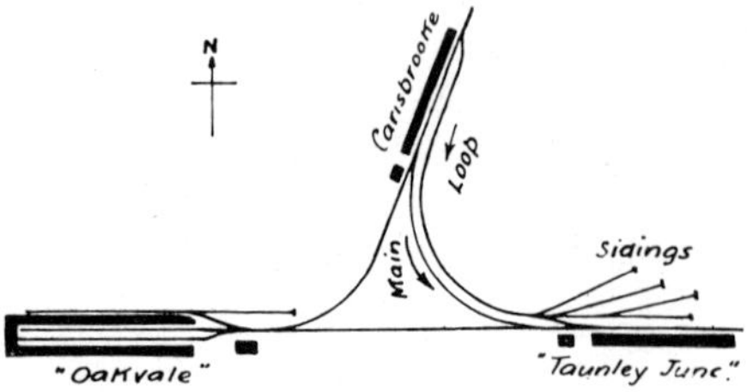

Fig. 2.—Suggested improved lay-out.

trucks off its train, without the help of another engine. It would be better to double the line from "Carisbrooke." The junction station could then be placed nearer the sidings and the control of the triangle junction could be divided between the signal boxes at the three stations. The doubled line would allow the loco with a train travelling in an easterly direction to run round it here and push wagons into the sidings. Other trains could be marshalled from this reception loop clear of main-line trains. The entry and exit to a reception loop controlled by two separate stations or boxes is not an impossible scheme in real practice, and actual examples may exist.

F. A. W. C. (Wandsworth) writes, sending a plan of his room, for an idea for a suitable lay-out in No. 0 gauge.

The room you have at your disposal is really only suitable for No. 00 gauge, if you require a very elaborate plan. However, for a simple plan, such as we reproduce herewith, the space will suffice. The curves cannot be of much larger radius than 2 ft. 6 in. but you can, as far as possible, make them with transitional entrances. On the eastern side there is no need to introduce any absolutely straight track at all. The main station on the north side can have a platform 5 ft. 6 in. long and a slightly shorter

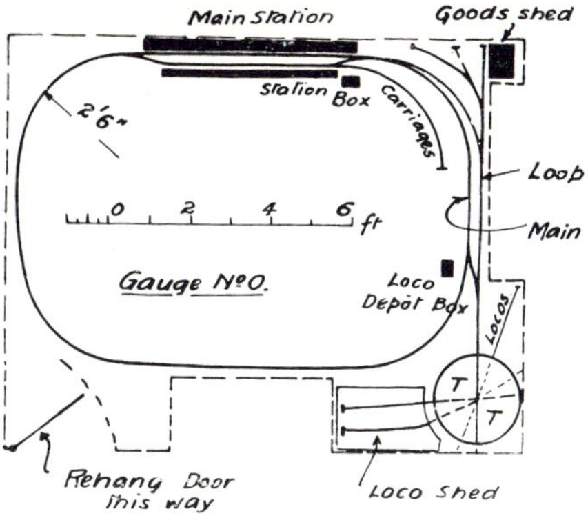

A lay-out for "O" Gauge.

loop-r platform. A carriage siding is provided and a rather small goods yard. Curves in the latter may be 2-ft. radius. Entrance to this yard and the locomotive depot is obtained from a loop-road from the main line between the station and the loco yard. The engine shed must be of the radial type, served by the turn-table. This saves much space and provides room for storing up to three engines easily.

L. E. P. (London, S.E.) requires a plan for a No. 0 gauge railway in a $16\frac{1}{2} \times 11$ ft. room, of the shape illustrated and proposes 2-ft. curves.

The space available is not at all difficult to fill satisfactorily. It allows for a combined continuous and point-to-point plan. In any case, however, we would advise you to use 3-ft. not 2-ft. radius curves on the main line, as we presume you will not employ tinplate track. For a permanent line, solid steel rails such as supplied by Mills Bros., Sheffield, or Bond's, Euston Road, are much to be preferred, and are a cheaper proposition in the long run.

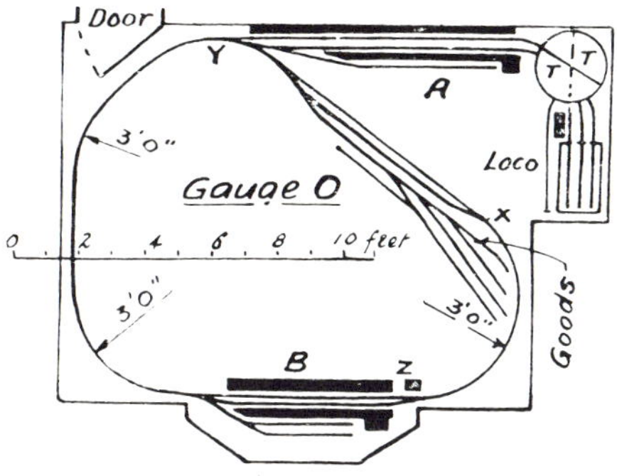

Plan for a $16\frac{1}{2} \times 11$ ft. room.

The main terminus is at A, but the junction-box controlling it may be placed in the main operating space at Y. Another box is required at the south-east end of the goods reception loop siding, but this could be worked by the man in charge of the low depot operating space. If it is essential that only one operator be provided for, the line could be doubled from X to Z. The station box at B would then control the points at this end of the loop siding. Only one goods depot is advisable. Goods trains leaving the yard would work round to it again, and would then be considered as arrival goods. The lay of the loco department at A is obvious from the sketch. It makes use of the alcove at this point. The station at B is a a combined terminal and posting station.

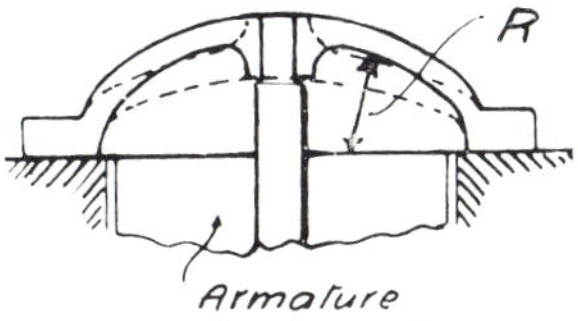

Fig. 1.–Showing alteration of bearing caps.

G. W. R. (Durham County) sends his design for an electric traction-motor for criticism.

We appreciate your sending the design along for criticism and also congratulate you on it. To obtain the most room for the end-windings of the armature and to allow you to use an eight-pole drum armature, we suggest that you alter the outline of the brass bearing caps from that shown in dotted lines in Fig. 1 to the full lines on the drawing. The bearing boss is then inside and greater space is obtained at R. Should you still find that clearances are insufficient, you can reduce the length of the armature $\frac{1}{8}$ in. ($\frac{1}{16}$ in. each side). The windings do not turn immediately and there will, therefore, be no loss in efficiency that could be measured.

The projection of the pole-pieces beyond the yokes (P, Fig. 2) is not good. It tends to increase outside magnetic leakage (A). You are using wrought iron and, therefore, you can

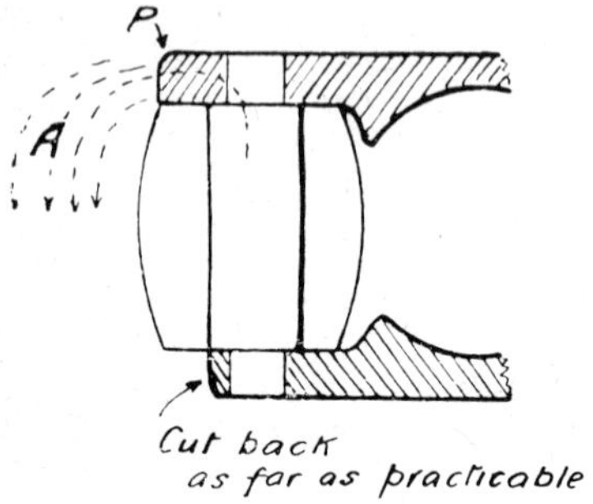

Fig. 2.—Suggested improvements at pole-pieces.

easily cut the pole pieces back to the level of the yokes. Also round off the ends in all directions. A stream-line flow for magnetic lines of force is just as important as in a fluid transmission device, aeroplane or ship.

R. V. H. (**Worcester**) asks for a sketch of a steam regulator for a No. 0 gauge locomotive.

The accompanying sketch illustrates an idea which is as good as any for a No. 0 gauge model steam locomotive. An angle union cock (ordinary plug-cock) can be fitted on the back of the

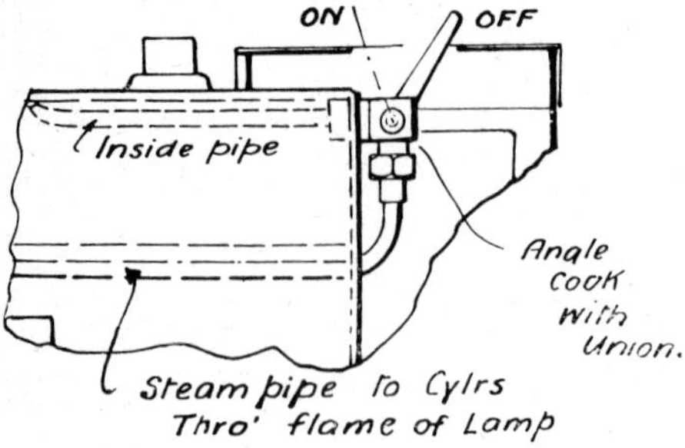

boiler in the cab. It may have an internal pipe leading to the top of the boiler near to the middle. A handle is then arranged to pass through the roof of the cab, as shown, and the steam pipe is led forward to the cylinders through the flame of the lamp. The union nipple will require silver-soldering to the steam pipe: soft solder is admissible.

C. F. P. (**Yorkshire**) writes:—

"Would a small inexpensive dynamo run an electric railway, and how would it be worked? I am told by one firm that steel rails are less satisfactory than brass for carrying the current."

It is hardly any use putting a dynamo in of lesser size than used on motor cycles or small cars. Model dynamos under 10 watts are not sufficiently robust for constant duty. The dynamo should be of the shunt-wound type and be fitted with an automatic cut-out. It should also be used, if a source of power is not available continuously, by charging accumulators which, in turn, will supply the railway. Of course, there is no objection to using a small low-voltage dynamo direct. If you have no power then you must rely on accumulators. Now that wireless is universally used, it is not so difficult to get the cells periodically charged in country districts.

If you use the solid steel rail as supplied by Bond's, Ltd., 254, Euston Road, N.W. 1, or by Mills Bros., 89, Ellesmere Road, Pitsmoor, Sheffield, no difficulty will arise due to the lower conductivity of steel. The sectional rail of metal is so large. (*See* "Model Electric Locomotives and Railways" for fuller details.) Steel rails are used in real practice, where the amperage carried is proportionately large. Several No. 0 gauge electric railway enthusiasts insist on specifying steel rails, and say that they are less troublesome in picking up dirt. This, however, is a debatable point. You would need a small engine to drive the dynamo; a gas engine running off the house supply could be installed.

OUR MAIL BAG

The "Boiler War."

To the Editor, MODEL RAILWAY NEWS.

DEAR SIR,

By the time you receive this Mr. F. A. Evans will have given his demonstration to the Wimbledon M.R.C. on "Torrid Oil Burners," and doubtless proved his claims for them.

During the late "boiler war" in the *Model Engineer*, it became a straight tussle between coal and methylated-spirit firing, and little or nothing was said about oil fuel.

The only argument that I have seen put up against paraffin burners is their so-called unreliability and constant need of attention. Regarding the first, the burners on the market now are so improved that with a little common sense in the using of them, they are just as reliable as any other method of firing. Is it not a fact that even coal and "meth." require a lot of attention, and isn't this true of our big locomotives ? If anyone disbelieves this, let him try for a chance to fire one for an hour.

If any of our modellists want a loco that requires no attention to the fire-box, by all means run some of L.B.S.C.'s "electric abortions," or those that want a key to wind them, but leave steam alone.

I have never owned a coal-fired loco and, although I am a very great admirer of L.B.S.C.'s creations, I have no great desire to do so. I am satisfied with oil every time. No smell, and a "meth." burner indoors can make some, and no dust. I have had steam locos of all gauges, and internally and externally fired, and as regards the "spirit" firing, it is a wash-out. The so-called vapour burners go out in the least draught, and the wicks on the other sort burn out or overflow. There have been some nasty flare-ups on my line at times.

I am only one of hundreds who had this trouble, but in my case, I could not go to the expense of having a coal-fired boiler fitted. So I struck the happy medium and went in for oil.

I venture to say that, providing your cylinders are *cylinders* and your boiler a good steamer, that no matter if internally or externally fired, you will get far better results from one oil burner than half-a-dozen wicks will give you. And this at about one-tenth of the cost.

Mr. L. G. Day's Oil-Fired $\frac{1}{2}$-inch Scale Locomotive.

I have found from experience of externally fired locos, that two of the smallest burners placed tandem fashion give the best results and spread the flame under the boiler, for, as we know, the brass boilers are not of the strongest.

I enclose photos of my present engine, which is ½-in. scale, and oil-fired. She will haul nine stone easily on a rusty track when required for showing off. For ordinary purposes a live five-stone driver is usually up. As these two weights represent respectively 630 and 350 scale tons, it is enough for me, and, I think, proves that oil has some "pep" in it.

The Two Oil-Burners.

As the photo shews, there are two burners, slightly staggered, and they are attached to the tender with the usual coil in the pipe, *and not to the back beam of engine.* Should the burner require special attention, it is only necessary to undo a union in the water pipe and lift the engine off the burners.

There is no laying the engine on its side, which is a rotten process at any time, and if in steam a tricky job.

I find that my loco with only one burner will keep a head of steam at 45 lb., and with the two from 75 to 90 lb., and weather will not affect it.

I have run locos outdoors with the flames from the "meth." burners playing out under the firebox at every little gust of wind and living in hopes of a flare-up every minute.

I have, in six months, only had one burner fail me, but I always clean them after *every* run. The method of fixing makes it no trouble, they are easy to get at. Perhaps I should mention there is no axle across the firebox for the trailing wheels, each one is contained in its own bearings.

In conclusion, I would advise all who are fed up with "meth.," before they go to the expense of a coal-fired boiler, to give oil a chance.

Like me, they will not regret it, and where running expenses must be low, will find it a saving to their pocket.

I am not going to say they will equal coal results, as per L.B.S.C. standard, but they will get satisfaction in more ways than one.

Wishing your splendid magazine every success.

Yours faithfully,

L. G. DAY.

Margate.

A Beginner's Model Railway.

To the Editor, MODEL RAILWAY NEWS.

DEAR SIR,

I am writing to say I am very pleased with the MODEL RAILWAY NEWS. I have an 0 gauge line at present in an incomplete state, as to make haste slowly has been my plan, and cost had to be taken into consideration. A description of the line, I hope, will be of interest. The line starts in a bedroom on ground floor and runs out up a short garden. The indoor part comprises a small dead-end station of three passenger roads and one goods siding. It runs half-way up the yard at the time of this letter but will later be extended into a wood shed at the other end.

The station is in two sections and is raised on boxes or anything handy, and is, I am sorry to say, laid in tinplate track, which I used on account of keeping the expense down. I shall relay this track as soon as means allow. The outdoor part is laid in rustless rail which, nevertheless, has rusted a deep red rust. I have about 10 ft. of this track laid at the present so you will see I have only a short run so far, with about 8 ft. tinplate indoors.

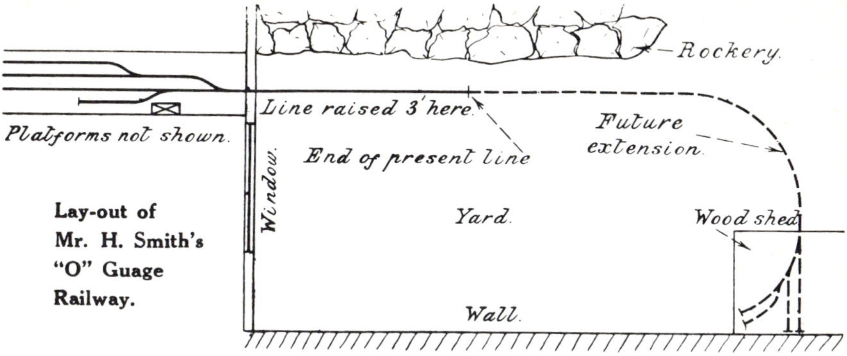

Lay-out of Mr. H. Smith's "O" Guage Railway.

One objection to having a portable line is you cannot get good scenic effects. I put this line down last October, and have had it running on Sundays ever since. I have run a train service on the outdoor part all through the winter, sometimes on quite wild blustering nights, and have not had the Owencarry disaster repeated on my line so far. High walls protect the line from too much wind.

I enclose a plan of the line, and as soon as I can I will send some snapshots. I have found a great deal of interest in this railway, although I am only a novice. I have very few tools and have done all the work with only an old pair of scissors, a screw driver, a hammer, a pair of pliers, pocket knife, etc., and a few odds and ends. I have had no plane. The station building and signal box are made of strong card braced with blind laths, and mica for windows. I have one signal put up, which is an advanced starter, and is lit by a pocket lamp placed on a footbridge, the signal being placed just in front. The station wall, etc., are covered with miniature adverts and posters. I have kept to scale as much as I could, and have managed to get quite a realistic station. If any reader could suggest any improvements to make my line more interesting I should be glad to hear from him, as I have been ploughing a lonely furrow with my line up to now. My rolling stock is small: I have three-passenger coaches and two locos, both clockwork, but I have no goods stock yet. The first loco is a 0—4—0 Hornby tank, a realistic little engine, but not very powerful. It will just manage three coaches. The other is a G.N.R. No. 440/294 of German make, and is a powerful engine having small driving wheels $1\frac{1}{4}$ in. I should say she will pull four heavy coaches. I intend to have the L.M.S. coaches in future, as those I have are very short bogie-coaches with tinplate wheels, which leave much to be desired. I have not had any trouble with these engines and they run quite well on the track coated with rust and pull their loads, even the less powerful Hornby tank. I shall try steam in future.

Yours faithfully,
H. SMITH.

West Jesmond.

Making Lead Wheels without Moulds

To the Editor MODEL RAILWAY NEWS.

DEAR SIR,

The writer, possessing a small G.O. indoor railway, and requiring some rolling stock, found it was financially out of the question to procure them commercially, so some method had to be discovered to enable me to make them myself, and that economically.

I set about making the bodies of the stock in the usual fashion, but now the metal parts required some thinking. Casting axle-guards in lead was not successful, so they had to be

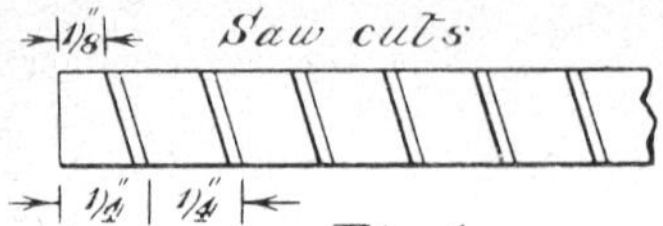

Fig. 1.

bought commercially. The buffers were turned from brass rod, which proved a laborious job when making about four dozen. Two or three shaped tools on a lathe with a large tool-rest would make the production of 48 a matter of minutes.

The wheels were now taken under consideration. Many experiments were tried before the following idea was thought of. A few pieces of $\frac{1}{4}$-in. square brass rod were obtained from a wireless store at a penny per length, four bits of brass tube about 2 in. long by $1\frac{1}{4}$ in. inside diameter, and some old lead pipes. The brass rods were now centred and saw-cuts made on each face at a slight angle, about $\frac{1}{4}$ in. apart (Fig. 1). The brass tubes are now made smooth inside, with fine emery, taking care there are no

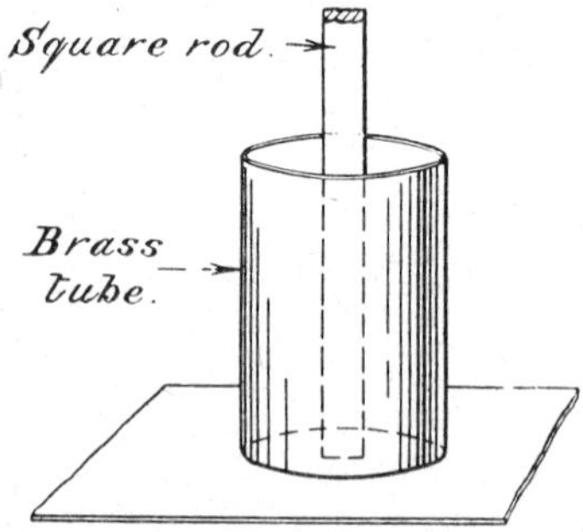

Fig. 2.

dents or marks inside the tubes. A piece of sheet steel was placed on the bench with the four tubes on it; the rods are placed inside the tubes and in the exact centre (Fig. 2). The lead pipes are now melted over the fire, in an old iron ladle, and poured into the tubes. The finger should be placed on the end of the rods, to keep them in position while the lead is poured in. After the metal has set, t is immersed in water, when the rod with the lead casting will easily lift out. It is then placed in the lathe and turned with a tool made from $\frac{3}{16}$-in. $\times$ $\frac{3}{8}$-in. strip steel, filed to the required wheel section (Fig. 3). The rod is now taken off the lathe and the wheels sawn off. They can now

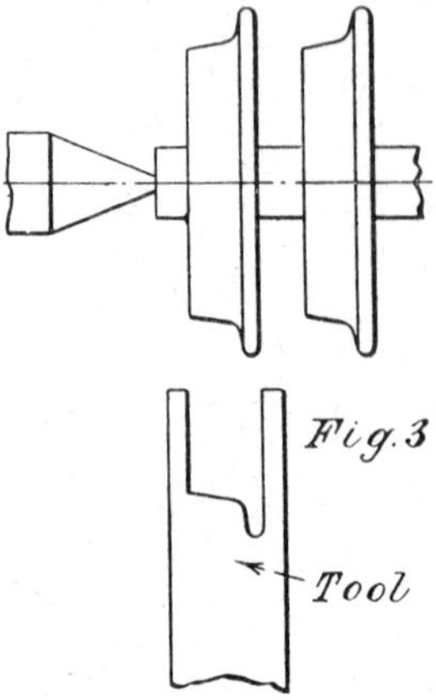

Fig. 3

be bored and screwed for axles. Before mounting on the axles, a piece of rod is chucked and screwed same size. The wheels can be again mounted on this rod, and the wheel face grooved to represent the pressed-steel pattern wheel. The features of this method are, cheapness and true-running, and it allows the axles to be screwed on, which is almost impracticable with ordinary lead wheels.

Yours truly,

Aberdeen. W. RONALD.

Springing O Gauge Bogies.

To the Editor MODEL RAILWAY NEWS.

SIR,

There is one point in the running of 0 gauge model locomotives that I should like to see treated fully in your columns.

In most of the model express engines of this gauge that I have seen the bogie is simply hung on a loose bolt with nut and lock nut, and follows the track—or is supposed to. But I have been trying to make wheels with reasonably small treads and flanges, and with this loose type of bogie it is next to impossible to make the wheels keep the track when crossing points or crossovers, no matter how well laid the line is.

Can you persuade someone to give us a practical article on the springing of 0 gauge bogies? I think the subject was touched on lately in the *Model Engineer*, but this seems such an important question that it should be fully discussed and improvements worked out in your new paper. When my engine left the rails it was always due to the jumping of the bogie wheels.

Also could an article be written on how to make simple die castings or stampings in white metal suitable for axle-guards and W-frames and chairs?

Yours faithfully,
H. A. Cox.

Cranwell.

[We shall be glad if readers will contribute their experiences on these points.—Ed., M.R.N.]

Cradle for Locomotives.

To the Editor Model Railway News.

Dear Sir,

It is frequently a great convenience to be able to place a model loco upside down to clean or adjust the works, and I always have one standing on the work bench. Obtain a piece of deal, 15 in. × 5 in. × ½ in., cut a V-shaped piece out at each end, saw across at AA, nail or screw the two V-pieces to the ends of the long piece as per sketch. Struts at BB are an advantage. The V's should be padded with felt or other soft material. To use, turn the loco upside down and place the boiler in the V's. The dimensions are suitable for ½-in. scale and would need altering for larger or smaller models.

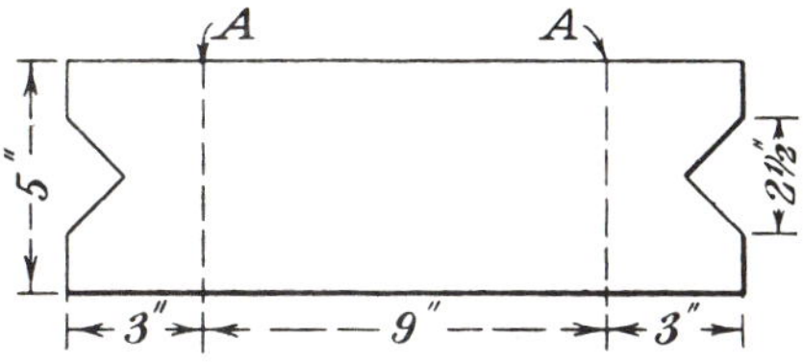

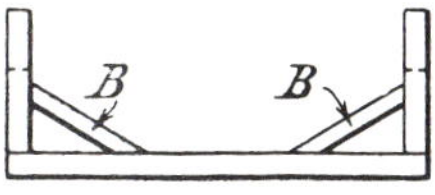

Yours truly,

Ingatestone. Hugh Conybeare.

The Effect of Grouping.

To the Editor Model Railway News.

Dear Sir,

You ask in the current issue of the M.R.N., "How does grouping affect your model railway?" In answer I may say that grouping does not affect my model railway at all, and I shall take the greatest care that it shall not. I have no use for grouping, which has ruined my interest in full-size railways. I have now only my London and North-Western Railway Junior.

I am sorry that you have not given my line its correct title at the head of my article which you publish this month.

My reference to the title in the course of the article is, therefore, without meaning.

I consider it a tragedy that England's premier railway is becoming thoroughy "Midlandized," and the rapid disappearance of the old chocolate and white stock at Carlisle station gives me nothing but pain. A red train looks all right on the Midland line, but quite out of place on the L.N.W.R. I do not see that the L.N.W. has been in *any* way improved by being taken over by the Midland. Perhaps other railway enthusiasts feel the same way as I do about it, or am I the only thoroughly crusted old Tory in this respect? I can only say that I can find no good word to say for grouping.

Yours faithfully,
Hugh Simpson,
Major, late R.A.

Carlisle.

The Exchange of Locomotives between the G.W. and L. & N.E. Railways.

To the Editor, MODEL RAILWAY NEWS.

DEAR SIR,

A Great Western locomotive of the Castle Class will take the 10 a.m. Scotch Express from King's Cross from 20th April until the 2nd May, and a L. & N.E. Pacific Class engine will haul the 10.30 a.m. Riviera Limited Express from Paddington during the same period.

The actual trials will be between the 27th April and the 2nd May.

Each engine will be manned by the engine driver and fireman of its own company. These men started at the beginning of April to travel over the respective routes in order to learn the nature of the line over which the trials will be made.

Much interest is being taken at home and abroad in these trials.

The particular feature of interest being the type and sizes of piston valves employed in relation to the diameter of cylinder.

The usual continental practice is to design the piston valve as half the diameter of the cylinder.

The G.W. engine has very large piston valves, using a long stroke and large exhaust passages.

This enables the steam to be used expansively, 17 per cent. cut off being the usual : that is to say, that steam is admitted to the cylinders for $\frac{17}{100}$ part of the piston travel and the other $\frac{78}{100}$ is used for the expansion of the steam.

Mr. Churchward maintained that when steam had finished its work, it should be got rid of as quickly as possible. Hence the use of large piston valves.

He also adopted what is termed the jumper exhaust nozzle."

When the pressure of steam in the exhaust pipe is excessive, the whole of the nozzle lifts and thus gets rid of the exhaust steam.

Any reader who witnessed a G.W. express engine starting will notice the hammer blow sound of the exhaust.

This denotes the lack of back pressure on the pistons.

The Pacific engines of the L. & N.E. Railway are fitted with small piston valves in comparison to the size of the cylinders, namely 8-in. piston valve to supply the 20-in. diameter cylinder, whereas the Great Western use a 9-in. piston valve for the 16-in. cylinder.

The piston valve stroke is also shorter : the result is that the valves cannot with advantage be linked up more than between 35 and 40 per cent. of the stroke. It is for this reason that the drivers work the engines more by means of the regulator.

Whether the using of the steam expansively will compensate the Castle engine for the huge boiler used by the L. & N.E. locomotive remains to be seen.

Yours truly,

J. C. CREBBIN.

King Edward VII Sanatorium,
Midhurst.

Points from Letters.

H. S. (Carlisle) writes :—" A passenger on a railway journey was obliged to change at a junction, and, as the particular connection was not good, had some time to wait for his train. Walking about the platform he noticed a cat without a tail. He was a man of few words, but feelng bored, and obliged to speak to some-one, addressed a porter, pointing to the cat : 'Manx'? The porter, likewise a man of few words, replied, 'No, 2.15.'"

Mr. D. ENGLAND (Sutton) writes :—" It may interest those readers who have model L.B.S.C. railways to know that No. 430, the only re-maining 'Jumbo' C1 goods loco, has been scrapped. Alas! Also that 424, a superheated Atlantic, has 'Pop' valves. D1, No. 244 has come out of the shops with rivets on the smoke box à la S.E.C.R. I hear that this is to be standard on the S.R."

The Wimbledon and District Model Railway Club.

ON March, 28th an interesting visit to Battersea Loco Depot, S.R., took place. The round-houses and yard were thoroughly inspected a Stroudley 0—4—2 tank, minus wheels, and a "Mogul" goods loco, with sand-dome on boiler, being noted. Some amusement was excited when Mr. Stoakly produced a photo taken on his model 0-gauge line, and a fireman immediately recognized it as being taken near Purley. He borrowed the print to "take in" his mate!

Events for the month:—May 4th—Lecture by Mr. H. H. Hudson, on "Cardboard and Model Railways." May 18th—Test Track Night. Both held at Red-Cross Hall, Church Road, 7.30 p.m. May 23rd—A visit to Old Oak Common Loco Depot, G.W.R.; meet Willesden Station, L.M.S., at 2.45 p.m. Hon. Secretary, R. Shephard, 27, Bernard Gardens, Wimbledon.

The Manchester and District Model Railway Club.

AT the first meeting, on March 24th, some very fine specimens of models were shewn, Mr. R. E. Priestley exhibiting the following gauge 0 models:—L. & N. W. R. 10-ton open wagon; Colman's mustard van; M.R. cattle wagon; L. & N.W. timber bolsters (one pair); L.&.N.W. 10-ton goods brake van; L. & Y. flat wagon—above wagons made of wood and L.M.S. fittings—L.M.S. 57-ft. bogie corridor coach, in course of construction, bogies by L.M. Co.; L.M.S. bogie parcel van, sides in course of construction; one side of frame of an L.M.S. (L. & Y section) Baltic 4—6—4 tank locomotive; firebox and cab of an L.M.S. (L. & Y. section) 4—6—0 class 8 locomotive; also straights, curves and points in steel tracks.

Mr. R. A. Mills showed the following 0-gauge models:—Private-owner flat wagon; private-owner covered van; and brass fan-shaped points in course of construction.

Mr. T. R. Ansley showed a L. & N. W.R. motor coach, gauge 1, and almost "ready for the road." The only difference from the original is that the motor is electric instead of steam driven.

In all cases the models were made by their owners and may be described as super-detail models.

Later meetings were held on April 14th and 28th at the Clarion Café, Market Street, Manchester.

* * *

An interesting ceremony takes place once every week, at King's Cross terminal station, London. It is the trial of the hydraulic buffer stops. A locomotive slowly pushes in the stops and is then pushed back again. It is a sight quite worth seeing, especially if the locomotive is one of the big Pacifics, or other big engine.

A number of specially constructed refrigerator vans, for carrying cheese and perishable goods between Italy and London, *via* the Zeebrugge-Harwich Train Ferries, have been built by an Italian firm. The tare weight is 15 tons, and the carrying capacity is 14 tons. They are fitted with the Westinghouse Air Brake and the Hardy Vacuum Brake. These cars will deliver goods direct from Italy to Bishopsgate Goods Station, (L.N.E.R.).

In a paper on "The Prevention of Railway Accidents," read before the G.W.R. (London) Lecture and Debating Society, Major H. A. Watson stated that the 10-mile installation of Automatic Signalling between Alne and Thirsk, on the North-Eastern Railway, had carried a heavy traffic for twenty years without a single case of one train overtaking another.

Superelevation on Curves.

A CORRESPONDENT recently queried the practice of starting the superelevation on the straight track preceding a curve of given radius. We pointed out that this is necessary where a curve of fixed radius is placed tangential to a straight section. The superelevation is necessary on the curve and obviously cannot attain its full value immediately. Therefore it must be started on before the curvature. But all tangential curves are bad in principle. To provide elliptical entrances to curves is the only sound practice. As the curves then commence with an infinitely large radius and finish with the minimum, inversely the superelevation can start just in front of the curve and attain its maximum at the minimum radius. Further, in settling on the amount of the superelevation, the *average* top speed must be considered. A given superelevation suits only a certain speed and varies as the square of the speed. If the average speed is not taken, it would be excessive for a train which happens to be going slowly over the curve. If the absolute maximum speed is four miles an hour (value $4^2 = 16$), the possible slowest speed—disregarding stopping on the curve—may be $1\frac{1}{2}$ m.p.h. (value $1\frac{1}{2}^2$ = about 2). This represents a possible difference of one in eight in the amount of the superelevation. The writer would therefore recommend a value of about nine, and as the square root of nine is three, would work out the superelevation on a speed of three miles per hour. The formula used by the correspondent was that given in the new book, "Model Railways."

H. G.

Marking Model Railway Plans.

It is proposed to mark all plans with the compass line, so that reference to directions can be more easily made. Even if not marked, it will be taken that the top of the plan is the North.

A Rail for Outdoor Tracks.

THE accompanying sketch illustrates in section a steel rail which is suitable for outdoor model railway systems of from 6 to $7\frac{1}{4}$ in. gauge. It will be noted that the section is of a more suitable shape than that known as "double-bulb," as the edges are only slightly rounded instead of being almost circular. The weight is approximately 1 lb. per foot run. It can be obtained through Messrs. Mills Bros., 69, Ellesmere Road, Sheffield.

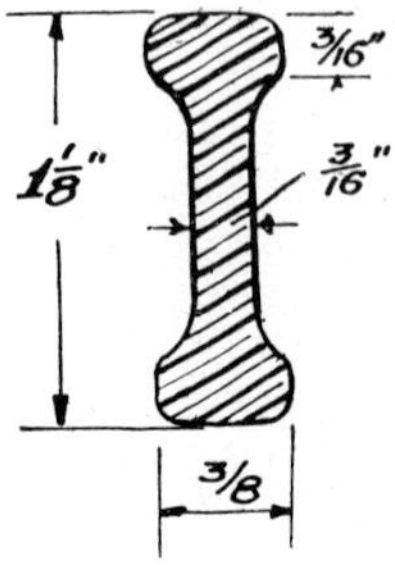

A Miniature Railway for Wembley.

IN connection with the Exhibition at Wembley this year, the Eastern grand bandstand, which has a diameter of about 250 feet, is going to be converted into a children's paradise, to be known as Treasure Island.

The bandstand will be converted into caves and the upper part into a dovecot, and immediately round this, will be a circular lake and sandy foreshore. Round the breakwater will be anchored small model boats, and at the end of the breakwater, a small lighthouse, with revolving light.

On the outside of the beach will be a $9\frac{1}{2}$-in. gauge, 2-in. scale, miniature railway, with an "Atlantic" type and a tank locomotive, each carrying a train of about 20 children. The scenery *en route* will represent a portion of the Rocky mountains, and the main station will be a model of Banff station on the Canadian Pacific Railway.

Messrs. Bassett-Lowke, Ltd., have secured the contract for the engine and cars, and they are being constructed at their works at Northampton.

The MODEL RAILWAY NEWS

Editorial and Publishing Offices:

66, FARRINGDON STREET, LONDON, E.C. 4.

Single Copies, post free, 7½d. Annual Subscription, 7s. 6d.

Vol. I. No. 6. JUNE, 1925. Price, 6d.

Notes of the Month.

ONE of our readers takes us to task for giving what he describes as "just a wee bit too much" space to electric locomotives. Is that the general opinion, or only just an isolated complaint? We admit that our correspondent puts his grumble in a very friendly way, and goes on to add that the M.R. NEWS is "simply splendid." We want, however, to give the majority of our readers the right kind of matter, and we do not wish to overdo any one section. We endeavour to vary our contents so that all our readers will find something in each issue to interest and help them, but it is almost impossible to obtain a perfect balance. This is our sixth monthly issue, and it is perhaps an appropriate time to take stock of what we have published during this period. Will our readers kindly write and tell us if the M.R. NEWS is giving them what they want? We are not asking for testimonials, but for a frank expression of opinion, and perhaps suggestions for improvement. Is there is anything we can do to make the journal more interesting or more helpful? Do our readers want more illustrated descriptions of model railways, or do they want more working drawings of locomotives or rolling stock? Do they want more steam matter, or more clockwork or electric matter? We cannot promise to carry out all the suggestions we receive, but letters of constructive criticism will be helpful and will be carefully considered.

* * *

So far as the design and construction of steam locomotives is concerned we may point out that this department of model railway engineering is, and has been for many years, the special province of the *Model Engineer*. Every week in that journal "L.B.S.C." contributes from two to three pages of most excellent notes on the practical side of steam model loco building, while Mr. Greenly frequently supplies designs and articles on the same subject, and Mr. Chas. S. Lake keeps the readers regularly posted with photographs, drawings and notes on the happenings in the real locomotive world. In addition to these regular features, articles on first-class model locomotives built by the readers of the *Model Engineer* frequently appear. The steam man is so well supplied with helpful matter therein that there is no need to cover the same ground in the M.R. NEWS.

We suppose there will always be a divergence of opinion as to the advantages of steam, clockwork or electrical propulsion; even if opinions agree there will be a divergence of interest, because some of our readers use one kind of power and some another. Similarly there will always be a difference of interest in the various gauges, because some have adopted one gauge for their system, and others have adopted something larger or smaller. But even so, there is the possibility of a reader changing his system over from one type of power, or from one gauge, to another, and, therefore, we think we may fairly assume that all the matter we publish has some degree of general interest. Where there is a real common ground is in track-planning, and the hundred and one designs for locomotives, rolling stock, buildings and accessories, which in external appearance at any rate, are the same for all kinds of power, and for all gauges. So that while one reader may be a specialist in steam, clockwork or electric power, he has a real interest in the doings of his fellow-readers in the lay-out and equipment of their model railways, even if other power be used.

* * *

Now, having asked how we can help our readers, we want to say a word about how our readers can help us. We want more of our readers writing in to give practical working hints to others. Everybody finds out a neat or simple way of doing some little job, or of getting over a difficulty, which some other reader would like to know about. Send us a few lines and a sketch or a photograph. We have had some excellent articles on complete model railways, and have more of these to follow. We join with our readers at large in expressing appreciation of these interesting contributions; but even those who have not a fine model railway to describe can send us some small item of practical interest, or a letter discussing the design or contribution of another reader, and it is in this community of interest and of sharing in the contents of our journal that its future largely lies.

(Left) Mr. H. G. Kerr holding his clockwork loco. (approx 2 in. long) and Mr. L. Lawrence with his "Vindictive," a Southern Railway pattern loco., at the Model Railway Club Exhibition.

* * *

H. P. L. C. (Rottingdean) writes:—"Old window blinds make splendid material for model railway sacks, and look very neat in the original colour or painted."

NOTABLE MODEL RAILWAYS

Rev. H. A. Turner's "OO" Gauge Railway.

SOME 12 or 13 years ago I built a model railway 0 gauge to the scale of $\frac{1}{4}$ in. to the foot, but, on removal to the South, it was necessary to part with it. I have often wished to build a line on a much smaller scale, and when the miniature table railway sets appeared on the market I saw the opportunity had come. As I needed clockwork mechanism and wheels, I began by buying one or two of the small locomotives, the driving wheels of which I coupled, after infinite labour, with very tiny jeweller's drills and screws.

My rails I made from 13-gauge tinned steel wire, which works up very well into points, etc. I procured 3-in. wide battens, and at intervals of four or five inches pinned tin sleepers. To these I soldered the wire, and then added, at the correct distance, cardboard sleepers, painted black and glued to the batten. I then painted the battens with glue between sleepers and the correct distance at each side, and spread on silver sand for ballast.

The idea was to make a model system, complete in every detail, as a side-show for my annual sale of work. This was done. The line had five stations, two of them termini, each with goods yard and four sidings, and shunting neck, a goods shed, cattle dock, station buildings, etc., and a signal box with tiny levers, made from the same wire as the rails, which worked the signals. The line was single and was 63 feet run from end to end, in the form of a flat U, and was signalled strictly in accordance with Ministry of Transport regulations. About midway was the principal station, with passing loop and two platforms, and a large goods yard behind, and long shunting neck. There was also a bay platform, which served the branch. I made this take the form of a " fly-under junction." Immediately at end of the passing

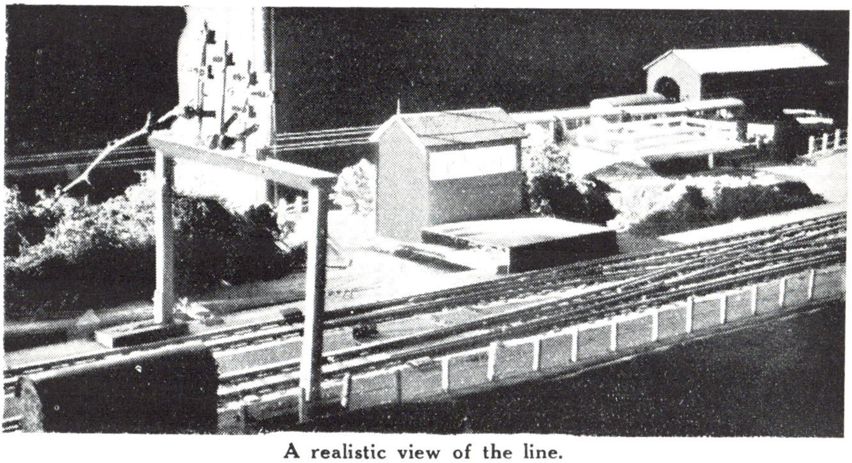

A realistic view of the line.

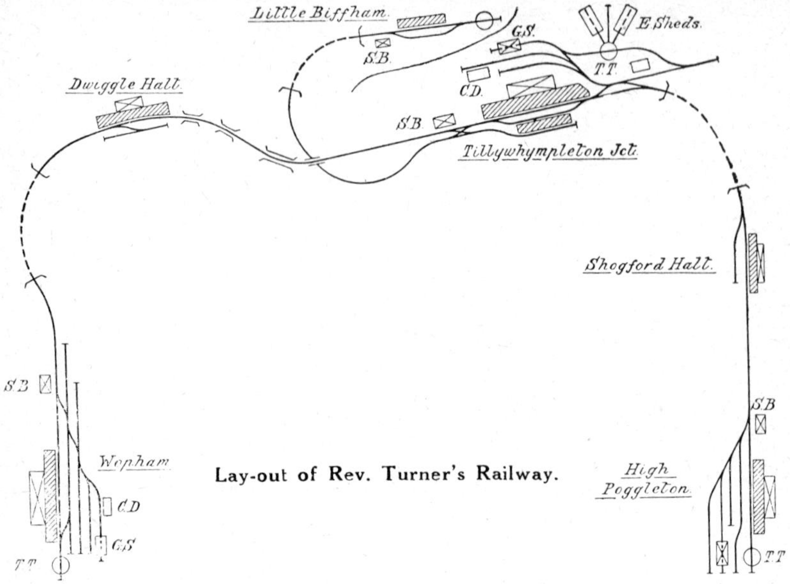

Lay-out of Rev. Turner's Railway.

loop, which, by the way, had catch-points interlocked with the starting signals, was a "scissors" crossing, protected by eight signals, on two gantries to connect main line with branch and bay platform with main, and *vice versa*. The branch then curved away downa 1 in 30 incline, passed under the main, by a skew bridge, and soon entered a tunnel, some distance beyond which was the branch terminus. At the main station were two engine sheds, with coal siding and engine-coaling crane and turn-table. The main station had two signal boxes, one with 10 levers working all signals at the scissors crossing end, and another with six levers working signals at the other end of the station. Imitation "controlled" distants were provided on the home signal posts respectively, as this was a very short section. All distants were "fixed."

Scenery was crumpled and stained "*Daily Mail*," and I know of nothing more realistic in an inexpensive way.

There was a large-span bridge, and two other skew bridges, all finished to represent ferro-concrete, likewise all tunnel mouths and retaining walls. Necessary greenery was provided by moss, and sawdust, dyed green. There were two telegraph wires throughout, and four from the main station to the skew bridge carrying main over branch, where two wires went off down the branch.

Telegraph poles made from the thin topends of basket withies, cross-bars of thin galvanized wire, and the insulators the smallest brass beads I could get, painted white. Each insulator had to be fixed with a dab of glue and tied on with cotton, a tiresome job! Wires, gray cotton, passed through the beads. All signal posts made from Bryant & May's "take me" matches bored for No. 0 brass screws for the board and spectacle plate, of zinc, and the counter-balance weights were small discs of lead punched from the sheet and rivetted to the counter-balance lever. Signal wires black silk.

The line was fenced throughout with over 1,300 small match ends, and two lines of grey thread for wires, another tiresome job! There were two tunnels on main line and one on the branch.

As these small locomotives have no reverses, unfortunately, I had to provide a turn-table at each terminus (the pit boarded-in pattern), and of course at the branch end, as well as at the engine sheds. Each goods yard had its crane, a workable one.

The station buildings were made from the cardboard from old boot boxes, windows painted black, and the rest painted with glue, sanded, and, when dry, painted cream to represent roughcast.

Every item was to the scale of $\frac{1}{8}$-in. to the foot.

Luggage barrows for platforms, with tiny wheels (the circular bosses of clock-hands with the hand cut off), $\frac{1}{8}$-in. diameter. Small station seats and station lamps of bent wire, and a large bead with black shade (a disc of paper) to represent electric light standards.

Between the two termini and the main central station were two small halts, each with a siding, but no passing loop and, therefore, not signalled.

There were 39 signals altogether, and 41 points. All the points at the main station, including the scissors crossing, were of the correct type, with "frog," etc., but elsewhere of the "continuous-rail" type. Ground discs, G.W.R. pattern, were provided for all sidings leading off main line, and catch-points also.

For the stock I bought many dozens of the commercial four-wheel coaches, which I stripped. I made four bogie coaches by soldering the bodies of two four-wheelers together and making bogie trucks, which I fitted with small brass wheels turned from the solid, journal to journal. Others I cut down to open wagons of varying height of sides and re-assembled. Two I cut to make goods brakes, one single-ended, the other double-ended. Fourteen I cut to represent cattle wagons, and painted accordingly. Six were left as bought and simply re-painted to represent box wagons.

I made a close-coupled train of three four-wheel coaches, with no buffers between coaches; a mail van with net opening and worked by the usual plunger and roller from ramp, but I was obliged to weight the vehicle down very heavily, as the action of the ramp tended to lever the vehicle off the track. One bogie coach was fitted to act as a slip-coach, the hook being hinged, actuated by a trigger.

I also made two six-coupled goods

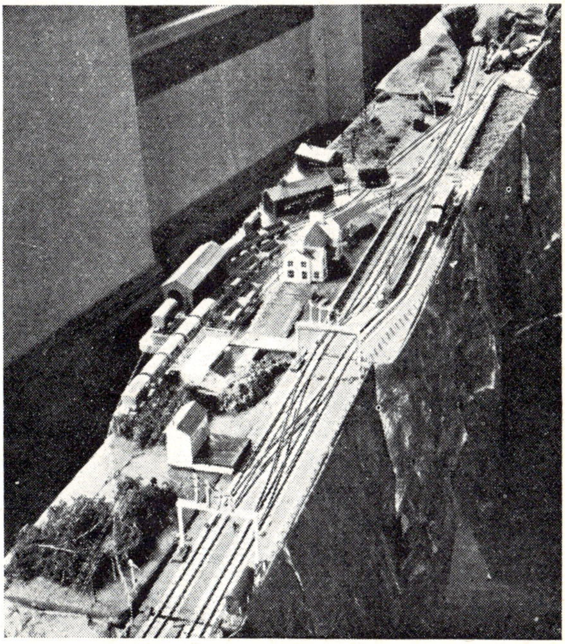

A section of the track, showing goods yard and siding on the left.

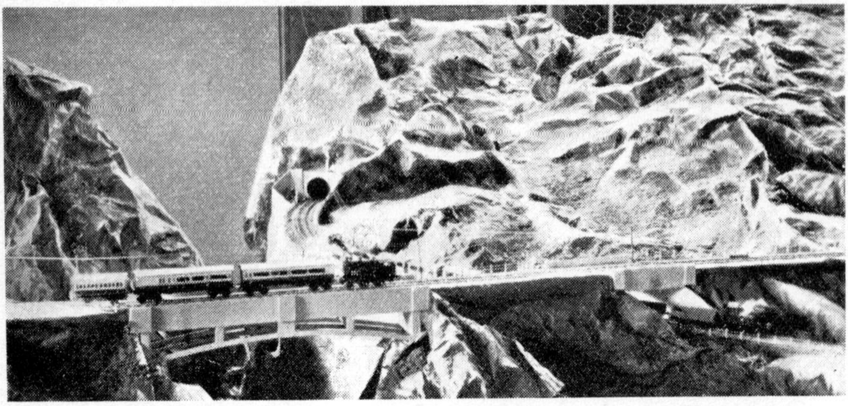

A train crossing the large-span bridge. A tunnel can be seen in the background, and a skew-bridge on the right of the picture.

tank locos for playing with (no mechanism); boilers (bits of brass tube), boiler ends (a threepenny piece—just the right diameter) and chimneys (·22 cartridge case upside down), the whole soldered together. The show was most successful, everything working perfectly. Every train was correctly signalled, my little girl of 12 working the signal boxes most efficiently. The biggest load run was a train of two four-wheel bogie coaches, the close-coupled train of three four-wheel coaches, and one extra four-wheel coach—all on brass-turned wheels—a train of 16 axles, which the best of my four-coupled locos pulled on a line not by any means level and abounding in curves, though I purposely made all my curves of a fairly generous radius.

The complete stock was:—

Three four-coupled clockwork locos; two six-coupled push locos; four four-wheel bogie coaches; one close-coupled train of three four-wheel coaches; three four-wheel coaches (as extras); one four-wheel mail van; two goods brakes; 14 cattle wagons; six box-wagons; and 27 open wagons with sides of varying height.

Engines, painted dark blue—passenger with fine yellow lining, goods plain blue; coaches, dark blue lower panels, white upper, with very fine blue lining; all van-ends, vermilion. Every vehicle had a small white panel on ends, on which was painted a tail-lamp when necessary. Goods stock, grey, with black lining to represent iron work.

The line is now dismantled. I am shortly moving to a country vicarage, when I hope to re-erect it in a different lay-out, in a disused attic, with possible improvements and additions.

The fact that everything is so tiny adds very greatly to its prettiness, and I would not go back to the larger size on any account.

The first of the one-third full-size Pacific locomotives being built at Colchester for Capt. J. E. P. Howey and the late Count Zborowski, has had its preliminary steam test. It developed 34 I.H.P. at 280 revolutions per minute.

A. Jobson (Tredegar).—You will find various designs of slip eccentric valve gear in "Model Steam Locomotives," by H. Greenly. Price 6s. nett. We cannot supply further details without a dimensioned drawing of the existing model.

Fig. 1.—Perspective drawing of finished stage.

Model G.W.R. Type Loco. Coaling Stage.

By Edward Beal.

THE booklets recently written by Mr. W. G. Chapman and issued by the Great Western Railway Publicity Department will not have escaped the notice of ardent model railway enthusiasts, and those who have had the privilege of reading "The 10.30 Limited" and "Caerphilly Castle" for themselves will doubtless have found many profitable suggestions as to model railway procedure. Two of the most interesting chapters of the latter work are entitled "Fuel and Water" and "The Engine Shed" respectively, and give some details of the standard type of locomotive coaling stage employed on this great system. Some years ago, the manufacturers of model railways put on the market an accurate scale replica of the Great Western water tank, but for some reason unknown—possibly that of the expensive price at which such a model would need to be sold—no firm nas yet attempted a coaling stage model. In the light of Mr. Chapman's two sections already mentioned it ought to be easy for any amateur to proceed, especially in view of the perspective sketch and photos which Mr. Chapman gives.

"A coal stage," we are told, "consists of an elevated platform about 13 feet above the rail level of a road running alongside. On the other side of the stage is an elevated road rising from rail level to within one foot of the platform level and laid more or less parallel with the stage road. Beyond the stage this elevated road rises on a gradient of 1 in 80, so that wagons shunted to the top can be lowered by gravity to the stage as required. Coal from wagons is shovelled into trollies, each of which holds five to ten cwt.; from these it can easily be tipped from the side of the platform on to the tenders of engines standing on the coal stage road below. Special balanced tip-platforms are employed, which normally assume a vertical position. When a trolley is pushed against one of these platforms it tilts outwards over the road until the weight of the trolley forces it to the horizontal position. The trollies are run between the guide rails secured to these platforms, the ends of the rails being turned up so as to form semi-circular buffers. On the top of the coal stage building is situated a tank (or tanks) of considerable capacity, which form the reservoir for the water supplied to the engine shed."

Description of Stage.

In the case of a model, of course, as applies also in the cases of different railway companies, considerable margin is allowed in designing these appliances, as required by local conditions, the exigencies of the track layout, and so forth. The writer has recently practically completed such a model for his own 00 gauge system, photographs of which he hopes to forward later. Some general idea, however, may be gathered from an examination of the rough perspective drawing shown in Fig. 1. The loaded wagon track may be led to the stage building on either an up or a down gradient, which should in either case not exceed 1 in 40. It ought not to be difficult for any standard clockwork or electric locomotive to negotiate this incline with half-a-dozen coal wagons, particularly if these are run down to the stage by gravity when loaded and taken away when empty on the up-grade. The wagon track passes through the stage and terminates on the opposite end outside in buffer-stops. The locomotive coaling track passes alongside the stage at the lower level and is served by two tipping platforms, which in the case of the writer's model are of the dummy type only. A large water tank is situated on the buffer-stop end of the roof of the building and occupies the entire width and about a third of the length thereof. A locomotive standpipe is located just beneath the tank in such a position as to serve the locomotive track near by. This standpipe is complete with dummy draining-well and lever control. A dwarf wall retains the sides of the embankment under the wagon track on the outer end of the stage, while at the inner end a portion of the embankment is removed and so buttressed as to provide a suitable recess for a workmen's lavatory building. Other details include scale gas lamps and a ladder and gallery for access to the top of the tank.

The whole scheme is given in the working drawings, of which Fig. 2 shows the entire side elevation of the stage. For gauges 00 and 0 the building may be constructed of stout cardboard, if for indoor use. For the larger scales and for outdoor systems thin wood, as sold by the model manufacturers, may be employed. For the pilasters and plinth and facia strips, the writer used the stout cardboard picture-framing strips, as sold by the manufacturers of *passe partout* binding tape. These can be secured in various widths ready cut to size, from $\frac{1}{4}$ in. to $\frac{1}{2}$ in., $\frac{3}{4}$ in. and 1 in., and for model railway buildings nothing more useful and cheap can be imagined. On the side opposite to that illustrated there are eight windows, three at the top and five at the base. The water tank may be built up of the same material, though should a suitably sized tin be at hand this might more realistically be used, particularly if it is provided with rounded corners like sardine or fancy biscuit tins. The best adhesive to use on such work as this is Seccotine, though Necol is also very good if in proper condition and not too stiff.

The building is erected upon a flat oblong piece of pasteboard or cardboard $19\frac{1}{4}$ in. by $8\frac{3}{4}$ in. (for 0 gauge) and the track is fitted down to this base without the intervention of sleepers. The base itself should be as thick as the standard railway sleeper for all gauges except No. 00. In this case it may consist of cardboard to a

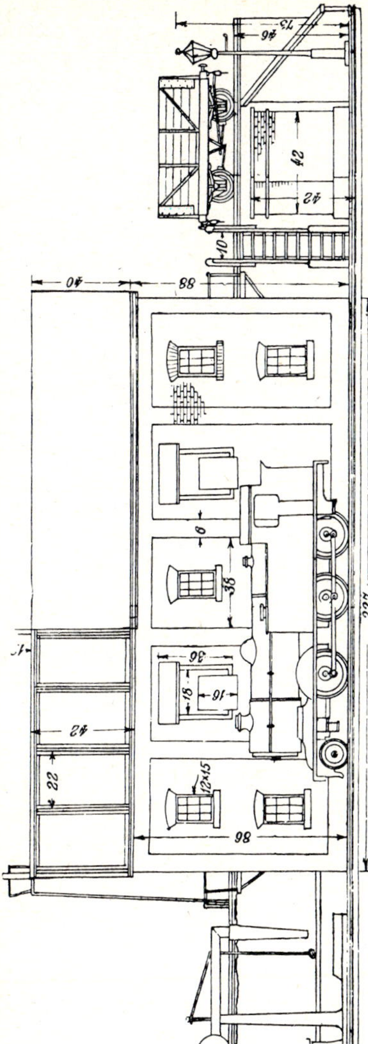

Fig. 2.—Side Elevation.

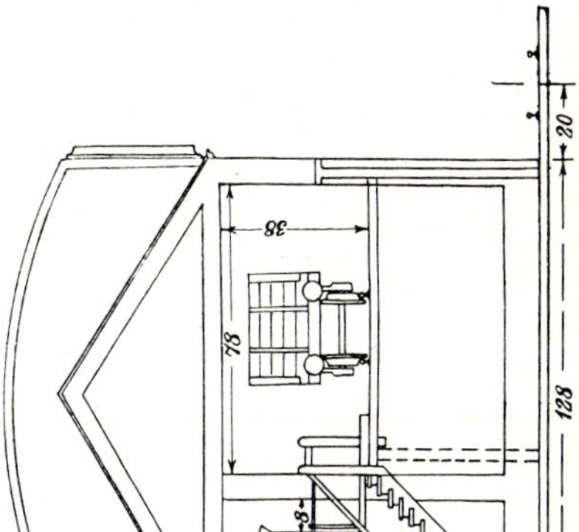

Fig. 3.—Elevation from Staircase end.

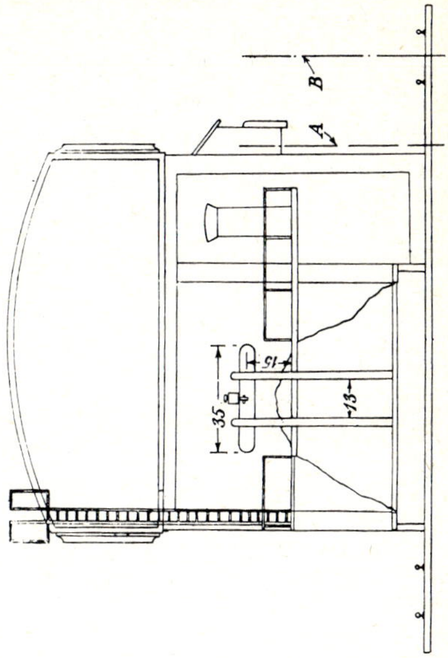

Fig. 4.—Elevation from Buffer end.

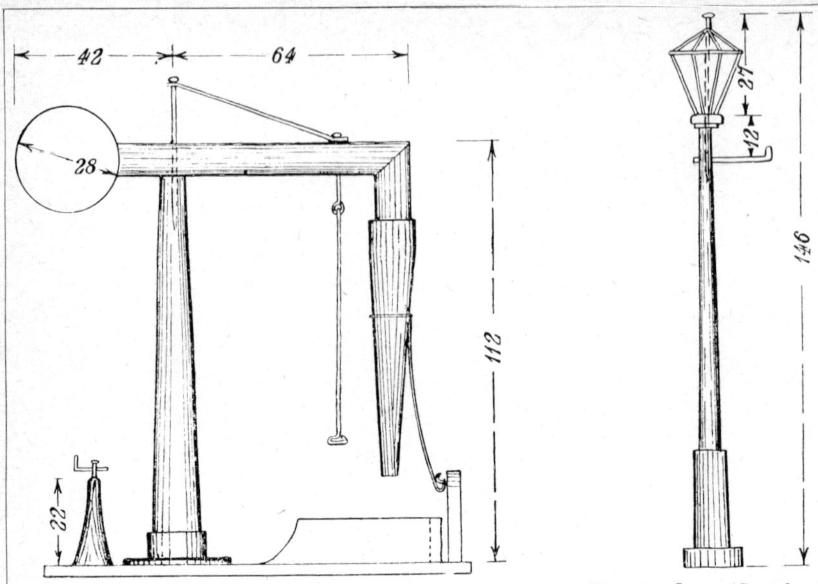

Fig. 5.—Standpipe. Fig. 6.—Lamp Standard.

(These drawings dimensioned for "O" gauge.)

thickness identical with that of the height of the tinplate sleepers from the ground-level, and the standard pressed tinplate track as sold is treated in an especial manner. The method is made clear in Fig. 8. The track is trimmed off with shears flush with the ends of the sleepers so-called and the raw edges are filed even and flattened out with pliers. This track can then be glued straight down to the base, the advantage being that the entire model can be easily installed in place on the railway, the ordinary standard track being joined up and the level of the rail-top being identical in each case. In any case, the dummy "embankment" is a great impediment in the way of using this type of track for model buildings. If the standard 00 gauge brass rail is employed, of course, the method of procedure with the base will be the same as in the case of 0 gauge permanent way.

Figs. 3 and 4 are more or less self-explanatory and show the two ends of the stage building. These drawings, like that of the side elevation, are dimensioned for 00 gauge, and while Fig. 3 gives the approach and elevation at a point just beyond the ladder, Fig. 4 shows the buffer-stop end. It should be noted that the locomotive coaling track has its centre at a greater distance from the building than that of a possible passing track on the off-side of the stage. In Fig. 4 the ladder and tank-gallery are shown, as well as the rear battens off the buffer-stops, which come down in line with the embankment surface as far as the top of the dwarf wall. A and B are the centre lines of the standpipe and delivery tube respectively. In Figs. 5 and 6 an attempt has been made to give larger sketches of the latter fitment and the lamp-standards. The standpipe may, of course, be properly made from brass rod and tubing if so desired, the delivery pipe being in this case of rubber tubing. For a dummy model a couple of penholders are all that will be required. In the 00 gauge, use the thinner ends of these and for 0 gauge the other ends. The dummy counterweights are simply round discs of cardboard glued in place one above the other till a suitable thickness is obtained. A heavy household pin acts as the pivot on which the pipe turns and is a tight fitting into the upright post. A second pin is bent into a loop underneath after having been passed through the horizontal pipe near the end. In place of a chain a straight length of thick wire may be substituted, having the lower end shaped to form a handle. The flexible delivery pipe is a piece of black paper rolled into a tapered shape and fixed on the nose of the standpipe. The draining-box beneath consists of three pieces of cardboard strip glued upright on their edges.

In the case of the lamp standard (Fig. 6), a solid block of cardboard is made by gluing together about six thicknesses of strip. This is then trimmed to the shape shown in Fig. 9, with the aid of a safety-razor blade. The upper (unshaded) portion is painted dead white and the lower part black. The frame-lines are then drawn in with a pen, being black on the upper surface and white on the black surface below. A pin is passed right through the block from top to bottom, and the head of the pin acts as a finial. A roll of paper is fixed at the base of the post and another pin is halved and bent to shape to serve as the ladder-rest. A dozen of these standards can be made in an hour, and if painted dead white with black on the lower portion of the post they are most realistic.

Fig. 7 gives a rough sketch of a section of the staircase. This method the writer has found by far the simplest for all kinds of model railway ladders. Two thick strips are pinned down to a board flat, one above the other, to serve as step-rests, and are cut out to receive the treads as shown (B). The treads are then cut and in order that they shall all be alike in length (the width not being so important) they are all cut from one piece, say, four inches long by one inch broad, the one inch to be the length of the steps. The step-rests are then placed on their lower edges flat and the top and bottom treads glued in, the other treads being added later.

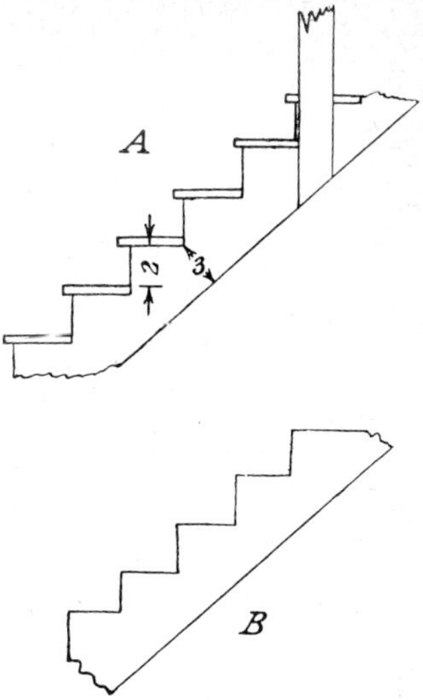

Fig. 7.—Simple method of making model staircase.

The most important work of all is the finishing off of the model. The best thing for the writer to do is to describe the method he himself followed. The tank outside and inside was given one coat of quick-drying black enamel. For the other work three tins of oil flatting were bought: one black, one white and one brick red. A portion of the black and white was mixed to form the slate-gray for the roof. The various fittings were all made loose so that the walls were left clear for painting. The walls were then given one coat of brick red, the guttering one coat of black, and the roof a coat of slate-colour. This was allowed to dry and the brick lines were afterwards drawn in with the utmost care and precision with a pen and ruler. This proved to be a very much less tedious job than was anticipated, the whole being completed one Monday morning. The horizontal lines were done with a straight-edge and the vertical lines by free-hand. The courses were spaced at one-sixteenth of an inch and the " bricks " were drawn about one-sixth

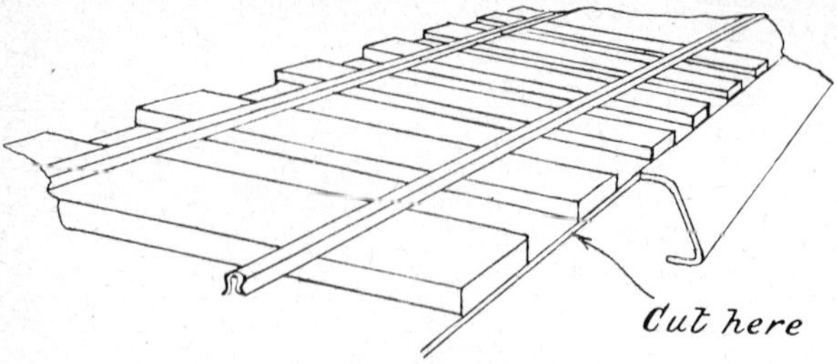

Fig. 8.—Cutting tinplate track ("00" gauge).

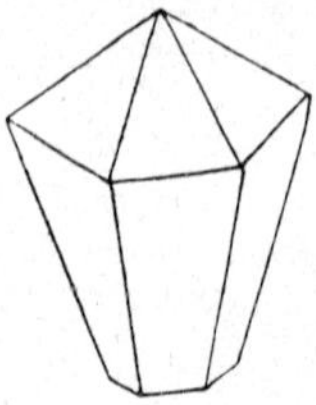

Fig. 9.—Cutting blocks for lamp standards.

of an inch long. For the rough "earth" portion of the embankment, a cardboard form was first made to the correct shape and then glued into position. The whole of the "rough" surface was then given a thin covering of "glitter-wax," which sets quite hard and takes a flat black paint nicely. The tank-ladder and handrails are another matter, especially for 00 gauge. For a larger scale the ordinary signal ladders and gallery can be used. The writer's method was to cut two very narrow strips of thin cardboard, about 1-16th in. wide and about 4 in. long. These were pinned on the top of a blotting pad and given a coat of seccotine, which was worked in with the finger. The "spells" were then stuck on, all being cut exactly the same length in the manner already described, and the ladder left to dry. Before finally leaving it, a penknife was passed underneath the strips to separate them from the blotting pad. When thoroughly dry a perfectly strong ladder was the result. The window panes are of thin strips of white paper—stamp-edging being very suitable. The insides of the tip-platform housings are painted dead black, as also is the outside. The Bavarian-made tinplate pressed track, which the writer uses, after having being cut as described, was given a coating of dead black paint all over, excepting the rails. These were finally rubbed over with a dry cloth to remove any spots of paint, and a most realistic and cheap type of track was thus easily made. The lower tracks should be electrified, if electric traction is the order of the day; but the wagon track need only have two rails inside the building, as locomotives are not allowed inside the coal-stage itself, unless under exceptional circumstances. The standpipe may be painted red with black mountings.

Drawings are dimensioned for 00 gauge unless otherwise stated. For 0 gauge multiply by two, and for 1 gauge by three.

London without Steam!

Mr. C. S. Harkness, the great American railway director, has recently arrived in London with some interesting ideas. He thinks that we shall have to follow New York's lead, and abolish steam locomotives from London altogether, in order to keep as much dirt and smoke as possible away from the city. His scheme is that the steam locomotive should be replaced by an electric one, forty miles from London, and the run completed by electricity, which is actually done in New York. He is certain that electricity will be exclusively used, in the future, all over the country, and he mentioned an American railway system where electricity had effected a saving of a million-and-a-half dollars a year. Although he thought we would have to follow America in so many things, he admitted that the English sleeping car is so superior to the American, that they intend copying our carriages.

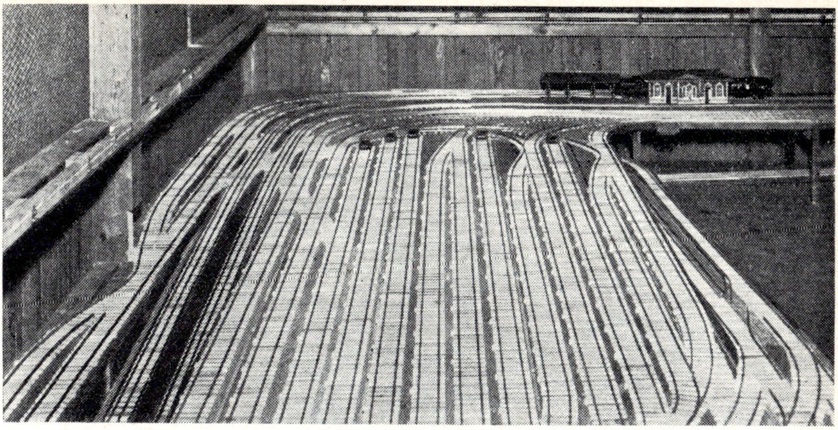

North half of main station, showing approach tracks and coach yard. There are nineteen parallel tracks.

A Large 2 in. Gauge Model Railway.

By Arthur W. Line.

THE subject of this article is without doubt one of the most comprehensive amateur-built model railway systems ever constructed. It was built about four years ago by C. Stuart Abbott, of Jamestown, N.Y., at his summer home on Lake Chautauqua.

Practically all the station and yard trackage was laid out in a large pavilion on the grounds, long runs being obtained by continuations of the trackage, double and single, through and around other adjoining buildings and shops.

The lower portions of the pavilion walls were solid. The upper portions of the sides were open (except for wire netting) during the summer months. Large shade trees, shrubs and flowers with the lake a few feet distant made an ideal setting. No plans were available, but the illustrations will give some idea of the great amount of trackage, the enormous amount of detail work and the high quality of workmanship.

Most of the tracks were laid upon platforms and shelves of suitable widths and at a height of about two feet above the floor. At certain places trestles were built in order to bring the tracks down to floor level at the doorways in one corner of the pavilion. The track gauge was two inches and too wide in proportion to the width of the rolling stock used, which consisted mainly of commercially made toys of Lionel and Ives makes, some of which were modified and improved by Mr. Abbott. The rails were of tinplate, spiked to untreated ties and were laid very neatly, as can be seen in the several views shown.

Shortly before the writer first saw the railway, almost all the tinplate rails had been torn up to make way for solid brass rails and $1\frac{3}{4}$-in. gauge and a greatly simplified track layout.

The power used was electricity at four volts and was derived from the local electricity supply at 110 volts, 25 cycles, by means of small transformers. The motive power consisted of four steam outline 4—4—0 locomotives and four 0—4—4—0 electric locomotives. In addition to these, several passenger cars were equipped with motors. About 50 cars were in operation, consisting of day-coach, baggage and observation types of passenger equipment, also several types of freight cars.

Entrance to tunnel through stage.

Trackage on north side of pavilion, and long trestle leading to subway under main station.

Central portion of main station. Note overhead rolling work-platform and method of working on tracks.

Design for a $2\frac{1}{2}$ in. Gauge Baltic Tank Locomotive.

By Henry Greenly.

THE advantage of employing standard parts is made more evident when designs for both free-lance and prototype models have to be prepared—more particularly perhaps in the case of the former. A large amount of drawing work is eliminated, as reference can be made to the separate details for all the component parts. True, like a model railway, the standardization will never be complete, as locomotive design is always progressing, and further, Walschaert's gear has created many difficulties. No one arrangement will suit all types. The lengths of the main links or rods must be altered to suit individual designs, and the accommodation of the reversing arm may require special attention. All these points are common to real practice as well as models.

The accompanying design for a Baltic tank has been prepared in response to a special request, and embodies a feature which is not present in any prototype design of which I know, viz., the wide firebox. Before the war, in 1913, I introduced this into one of the three engines built for Mr. Roland Martens, and I endeavour as far as possible, to apply it in every case possible. The large firebox capacity obtained is so very valuable, as well as the increase in grate area which accompanies it. The present design is based on the new "J.R." $2\frac{1}{2}$-in. gauge parts and cylinders. For the first time this design of cylinder is available in a finished form—in cast iron as well as gunmetal and with accurately made piston rings.

Fig. 3.—Photograph of "J R." Piston-valve type cylinders for Walschaert's models.

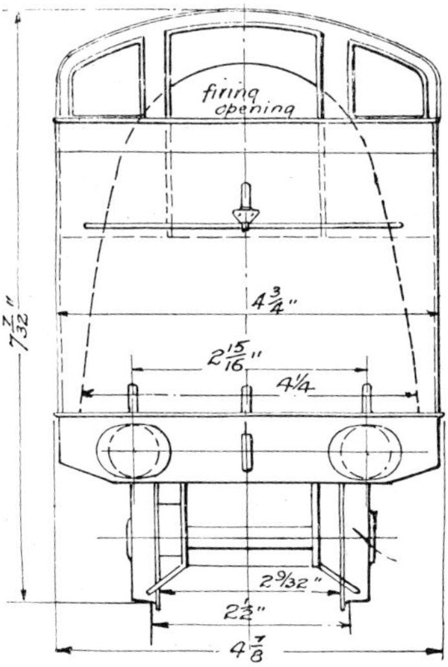

Fig. 2.—Trailing end view.

The main details are the same as the "Junior Mechanics," "Atlantic" and "Pacific" tender locomotives. The driving wheels are smaller, but there is, of course, no objection, except that the total length of the model will be increased, to employing the standard 6-ft. to 8-ft. express driving wheels (3-19-32nds in. diameter).

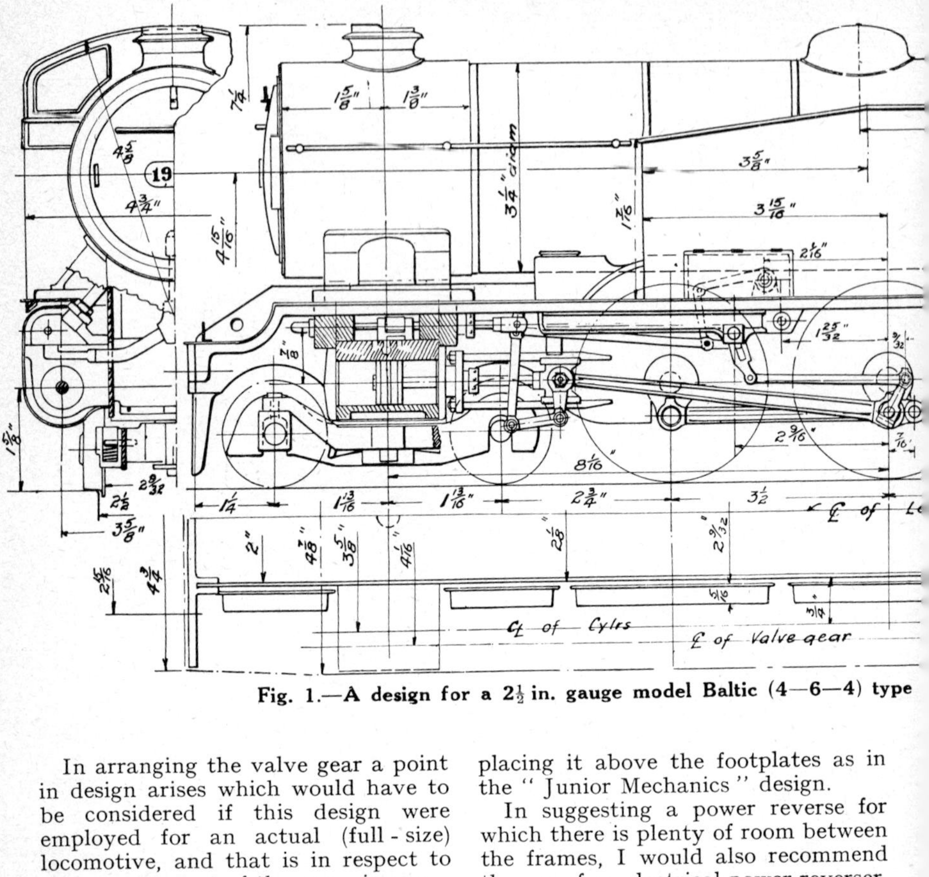

Fig. 1.—A design for a 2½ in. gauge model Baltic (4—6—4) type

In arranging the valve gear a point in design arises which would have to be considered if this design were employed for an actual (full-size) locomotive, and that is in respect to the arrangement of the reversing arm. It would be necessary to throw the weight of water carried well forward to prevent the trailing bogie being over-loaded, and while the forward part of the side tanks would have to be cut away to accommodate the lifting links, the ordinary method of connecting the gear to the cab would have to go. A power reverse would be necessary unless, of course, the G.N.R. Pacific type of gear is used. Even this gear, although it eliminates the lifting link, would introduce mechanical difficulties—a working model. In the one-third size working models for the late Count Zborowski, I thought it was advisable to alter the reversing arm by lengthening it and placing it above the footplates as in the " Junior Mechanics " design.

In suggesting a power reverse for which there is plenty of room between the frames, I would also recommend the use of an electrical power reverser. This would allow the speed of the locomotive to be controlled from the track. This scheme I would like to elaborate, should it be of any interest to " steam " men.

Where the side tanks are not actually carrying water it would, of course, be quite easy to fit up the same gear as on the standard Pacific as the reversing rod can easily pass behind the tank plates.

Firing a tank engine does not offer any insuperable difficulty so long as there is a large opening in the back weather-board of the cab, and the cab and the tank in the rear bunker has a sloping top as shown at C in the general arrangement drawing. Owing to the

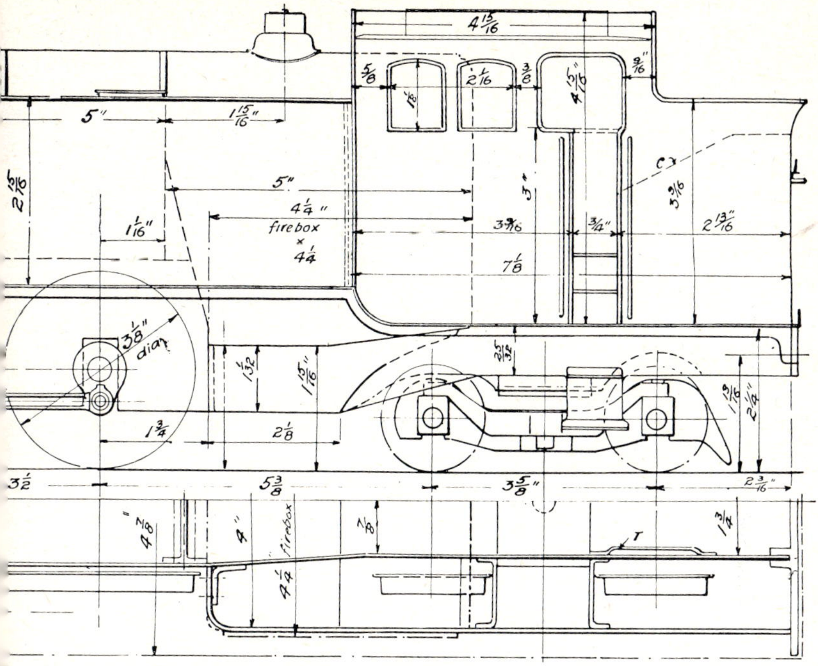

ne with Wootton fire box and Walschaert's valve gear.

use of $3\frac{1}{8}$-in. driving wheels, it is not necessary to crank the weigh-shaft to clear the underside of the boiler barrel as shown in the standard Walschaerts gear drawing, No. J.R. 303, I have lately issued. The saddle-side casting will also have to be mounted on a rectangular casing, 3-16ths in. deep, unless, of course, the footplate is raised to $3\frac{1}{8}$ in. locally at the cylinders.

The main frames at the trailing end also require special attention. There is no objection in placing the firebars on top of the inside frames transversely. This would save all further fixing. In that case the inside frames could be made to follow the line of the foundation ring. They will require to be set in to $1\frac{3}{4}$ in. to suit " narrow " standard buffer plank. At the trailing bogie wheels the frames can be cut away to allow for a further lateral movement of this wheel and the cut-away portion reinforced by a dished plate, as shown at T in the plan. The bogie-pin stretcher casting at the trailing bogie will have to be modified in the machining by slotting as shown in the sketch, Fig. 4, the flange fitting over the outside of the narrowed-in main frames, instead of inside as in the normal case.

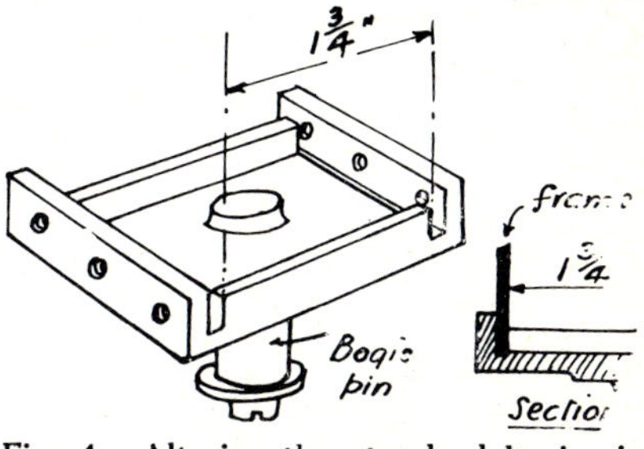

Fig. 4.—Altering the standard bogie-pin stretcher to suit "narrowed in" frames at trailing end.

The New L.M.C. Catalogue.

WE have received the Leeds Model Company's catalogue of model railways, fittings and accessories. This is a most interesting production, and anyone who is contemplating additions to his railway system should certainly procure a copy. The Company divide their scale model locomotives into four classes (*a*) free-lance design, (*b*) scale models of actual types, (*c*) super-detail exact-scale models, (*d*) exhibition or "glass-case" models. The first class are particularly suited to the private owner, who has definite conditions to which he must conform, and who is bound to consider cost. The scale models illustrated in the catalogue range from a standard 0—4—0 saddle-tank locomotive, which is priced at £2 5*s*., to a super-detail L. & N.E.R. 0 guage Pacific, for which £45 is quoted as a basis, and extra details are added as required at so much per unit, thus giving the customer unlimited range. The workmanship seems thorough throughout, and most of the locomotives listed are built in both 0 gauge and 1 gauges.

There is also illustrated some excellent rolling-stock, in three series, scale model with lithographed sides, hand-made, and super-detail exact-scale models. We have had forwarded for review one of the most interesting items, a three-coach articulated set train, copied from those in use on the G. N. section of the L. & N.E.R. Of this otherwise entirely satisfactory model, we have no criticism to make, save that the windows seem a little too white to be truly realistic. This is a small point, and it is, of course, extremely difficult to render glass by lithography, but the result would be more satisfactory if the unnatural pallor were somewhat dimmed. In addition to passenger coaches, every kind of goods rolling stock is included. Great attention has been paid to the exact reproduction of signalling to ensure realism, with very commendable results, and track problems have also been carefully studied. Sets of parts, separate fittings, clockwork and electric mechanisms, scale model stations, bridges, signal cabins and engine sheds, raw materials and sundries of all kinds are fully dealt with, and there is a list of transfers and complete locomotive and rolling-stock outline drawings. Altogether, this catalogue of 116 pages should prove extremely interesting to the model railway engineer. The price is one shilling, post free, from the Leeds Model Company, Ltd., Hunslet, Leeds.

The Earl Model Co.

A neat little illustrated catalogue, recently issued by the Earl Model Co., Bayley Lane, Coventry, contains an interesting range of scale-model rolling stock in gauges 00, 0. and 1, permanent way in 00 gauge, model railway buildings, model bricks, sundry fittings and materials, and full-size blue-prints for wagons and brake-vans in various gauges. The price of the list is 4*d*., post free.

L. R. (Nutfield).—We beg to recommend you to write to Messrs. Bonds, Ltd., 254, Euston Road, London, N.W. 1. They have a very good selection of electric loco mechanisms.

N. E. (Ross).—We have returned your signal plan with the note that advance starting signals should be placed a train's length in front of the starter or any points or crossovers near the starter. While it is not usual in full-size railway practice to make one distant serve for two home signals, you may do so in model practice. The distant should only be capable of being pulled "off" if the main line signal is "line clear." It should be locked in all other combinations. The driver will, therefore, be slowed up if he is to pass into the facing siding or branch line.

Queries and Replies.

MODEL RAILWAY PLAN.

H. J. (London, S.W.) requires a plan for a room of the shape illustrated, something on the lines of the Mill Hill scheme·

You do not state the gauge of your proposed railway for the room 20 ft. 6 in. long × 11 ft. 8 in. wide, but we presume it is to be a No. 0 gauge line, seeing that you require a plan as comprehensive as that made by the Mill Hill School Society. This plan cannot be got into the available space without introducing sharp curves, but we have shown a formation in the accompanying sketch, which introduces both point-to-point and continuous working, with one terminal station at A, in the centre of the Eastern end of the room. Behind this terminus the main line can be hidden by a tunneled section on a large-radius curve. Both ends of the plan are elliptical, the maximum radius being about 7 ft. and the minimum 3 ft. 3 in. or 3 ft. 6 in. Two smaller stations, B and C, are shown, the latter being the larger of the two, and being the site of the goods depot. Here the road is doubled to provide a run-round loop. A locomotive turntable is arranged for, but this is not an absloute necessity, as engines can be turned by sending them round the main line through stations B and C. The base of the railway should be at least 3 ft. 6 in. above ground level, as there are operating spaces. If the trestles on which the line is laid are too low, getting from one space to another is a more awkward proceeding. Lifting bridges could be made to allow easy access to the spaces on the North and South sides of the terminus A, but if such can be avoided, difficulties in making and maintaining the track will be lessened. Of course, fixed bridges of the single-span girder type may be used at G and H to span gaps in the substructure of the model railway. These will form the least obstruction to a passage from one space to the other.

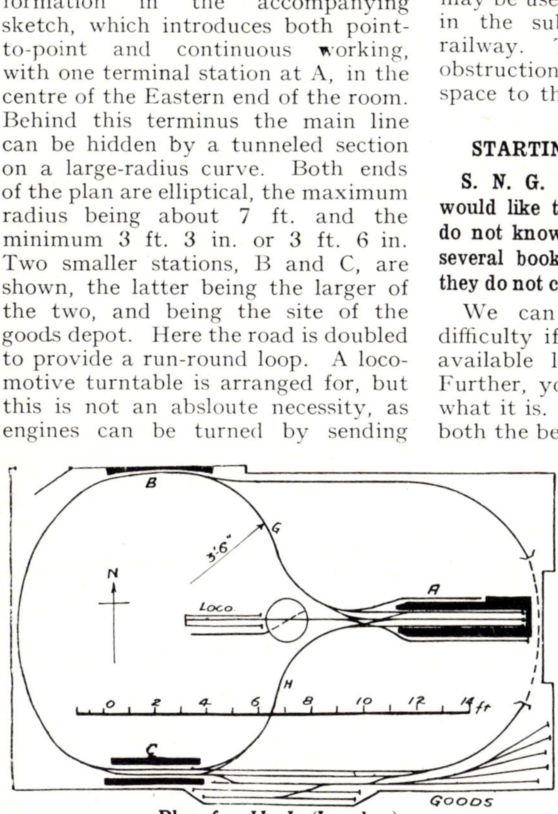

Plan for H. J. (London).

STARTING A MODEL RAILWAY.

S. N. G. (London, N.W.) writes:—"I would like to start a model railway, but do not know how to begin. I have read several books on model engineering, but they do not contain practical information."

We can hardly appreciate your difficulty if you have perused all the available literature on the subject. Further, you do not indicate exactly what it is. We are doing our best for both the beginner and the experienced model railway man, but the hobby has so many phases of interest, that we cannot hope to cover them all in even a year's issue of our journal. In addition, we may mention that, living in London, you can join one of the model engineering or railway clubs, the meetings of any of which you can first attend as a visitor.

In commencing a railway, you must first

settle what type of line would suit you best. The indoor line is, to a great extent, bounded both in character and size by the space available. If a comprehensive system is desired, then you will be limited to clockwork or electricity as a motive power. Steam engines are possible in No. 0 gauge, but No. 1 gauge is to be preferred. The latter size requires a room at least 20 feet long. The $2\frac{1}{2}$-in. gauge steam locomotive is an outdoor model. It is not really suitable for passenger hauling, and the paramount interest is usually centred in the locomotive itself where this gauge is used, the railway being more or less of a testing track. For riding behind, the 1-in. scale locomotive is the smallest size to be recommended.

E. A. S. (Manchester) suggests using a small, single-cylinder, vertical engine, direct-coupled, for driving a dynamo to supply his electric railway with current.

It is quite possible to run a model electric railway from a steam-power plant, but the engine in question would not do so continuously or satisfactorily unless it is belt-driven. Further, an auto cut-out switch is necessary on the switch-board to prevent the accumulators running the dynamo, should the voltage of the latter fall below that of the accumulator. It would be possible to run the railway direct, without the intervention of accumulators, so long as the engine is properly governed and is supplied with a steady head of steam. Probably this is the most satisfactory method. A small single - cylinder slide-valve engine should be belt-driven. Balancing difficulties arise in direct - driving model dynamos. The average limit of engine-speed is about 1,500 revolutions, and the average dynamo requires 2,500 revolutions per minute, at least.

G. M. B. (London).—*Q.* **I want a book that deals fully with the modern steam locomotive. I have bought such books as "The Locomotive Simply Explained" "Caerphilly Castle" and "10.30 Limited," but they do not seem to explain things enough. Being of a rather non-mechanical turn of mind, perhaps I am slow at grasping the whys and wherefores that appear quite simple to other fellows.**

A book that fully and comprehensively explains the locomotive (not one in which this appears : "Owing to lack of space we cannot go into the details of ") is what I am after. Something that starts as simple as A B C, and leads you on until, towards the end, you are quite conversant and familiar with technical terms, etc.

I shall be glad if you will inform me whether there is such a book. Perhaps other readers of the "Model Railway News" can put me wise ?

A. You will find exactly what you require in "The Locomotive of To-day," post free 3*s.* 9*d.*, from our publishing department.

The Wimbledon and District Model Railway Club.

The visit to Messrs. Stuart-Turner's works on April 25th, proved of exceptional interest. A 0—6—0 outside-cylinder coal-fired loco in for repair was well examined, and a detailed inspection of the machine-shops, foundry, testing and erecting shops was thoroughly appreciated. An $\frac{1}{8}$-h.p. gas engine and dynamo plant, and model boats in a testing tank were set working for our special benefit—also a demonstration of brazing. In the test shop, 143 electric lighting sets for the P.O. were noticed—a set on a 40 % overload test was explained.

Fixtures. — June 8th. — Lecture — "French Railways," by Mr. J. Cook. June 15th.—Test Track Night. June 27th.—Visit to Domestic Sanitary Laundry, Ltd., Kingston. Meet Kingston Station (S.R.), 2.45 p.m. Meetings held at Red Cross Hall, Church Road, Wimbledon, 7.30 p.m.

The Secretary will be pleased to receive suggestions for the proposed shunting track. Members are reminded that "subs" are due within two months of joining. Seniors, 10*s.* Juniors, 5*s.*

Hon. Secretary, R. Shephard, 27, Bernard Gardens, Wimbledon.

OUR MAIL BAG

Realism in Model Railways.

To the Editor, MODEL RAILWAY NEWS.

DEAR SIR,

After reading the contribution by "The Looker-on," in the February issue, on "Realism in Model Railways," I have thought I would just like to send you a few photos of parts of my 2-in. gauge model railway, showing the amount of realism and detail I

North end of Station.

have put in up to a limit, without overcrowding, but I must urgently remind model railway enthusiasts that a large degree of patience and knowledge is required to ensure that realism. Although I have never worked on the railway, I have quietly studied realism in my working up of this model railway after being an enthusiastic admirer of railways all my life.

Tunnel face and part of platforms with some equipment.

A few home-built trucks, and goods depôt.

I may mention before closing that I have had several real railwaymen pay me a visit, and they all quite admire the realism I have put in, coupled with the smallest detail practicable, and if any model railway enthusiasts living in or near Birmingham, I shall only be too pleased to shew them my work. I am working at home at the address given if you care to publish it, and any time

Station from the South End.

suitable to them, I shall be at liberty to shew them.

I remain,
Yours truly,
W. PRETTY.

246, Wellington Road,
Perry Barr,
Birmingham.

Scale for "OO" Gauge.

To the Editor MODEL RAILWAY NEWS.

DEAR SIR,

I regret that I have been busy with model locomotives of an entirely different character to those used in the above gauge and not replied to Mr. Stewart-Reidpath's letter published in the March issue. I note that he has exactly halved the 7-mm. scale as fixed by me some 18 years ago, but I would point out that as I have to work for the average model maker of average skill it has been my practice to coarsen detail as the scale gets smaller. We must realize that tracks (even the Southern) are not perfect and, further, that the proportionate degree of error grows as the scale is made smaller. In fixing a scale it is important to get sufficient space between the outside of the tyre and

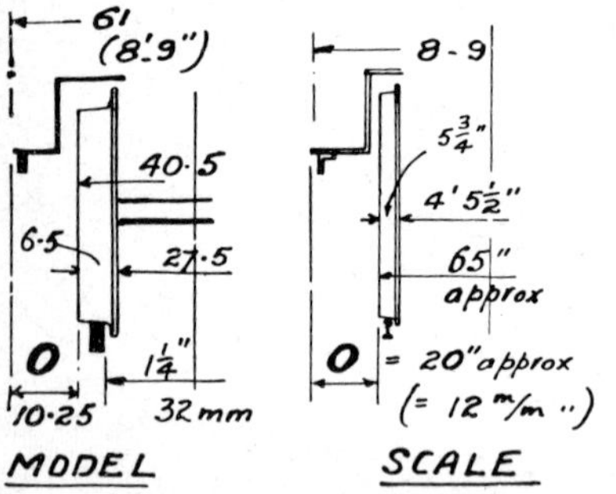

Fig. 1.

the outside of the vehicle. Don't worry about the exact scale equivalent of the gauge. Such an equivalent can produce the most atrociously out-of-scale working models. The width over the outside of the tyres should be correct.

Of course, in No. 00 gauge, everything depends on the minimum tyre width that the amateur can provide a workable track for. As far as I am concerned this has not yet been settled, except for the cheap "Everyman's" track such as is now on the market. The use of electric traction must be considered.

It would be quite easy to "make everything exactly to scale," but this is admittedly not possible. With the 3½-mm. scale, the tyre is nearly a foot wide. It would be just as simple for some one to ask me to make a watch. The "ticker" would be as unsatisfactory as the average novice's attempt to produce a perfect-scale track in No. 00 gauge. There must be a coarsening of detail to make the working model possible to the man in the street. I cannot, of course, fall out with Mr. Stewart-Reidpath's settling to use half my own 7-mm. scale for a railway which is half the gauge. The 7-mm. scale is based on width over outside the tyres, *not on the gauge of the railway*. In settling on 19 mm. over the outside of the tyres instead of half of 40·5 he had reduced the tyre width slightly. It is essential that the overhang of a loco-wagon coach, as shown at 0, Fig. 1, should not be less than scale. Otherwise there will be endless difficulties as the work of providing for models of all types are concerned.

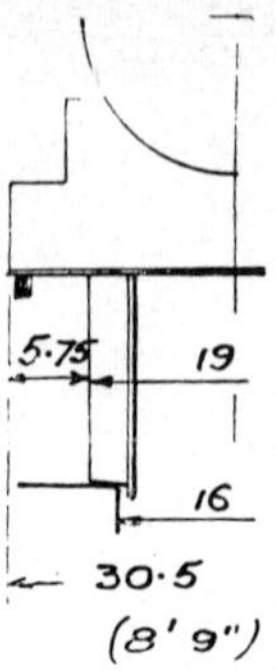

Fig. 2.—The 3½ m/m scale.

The difficulties are not immediate in their incidence. Great latitude is possible with the ordinary simple inside-cylinder engine of English design, but when it is necessary for an unskilled model maker to tackle a Walschaerts gear engine in No. 00 gauge and finds that he has a space only of 5·75 mm. or less than a quarter of an inch in width, in

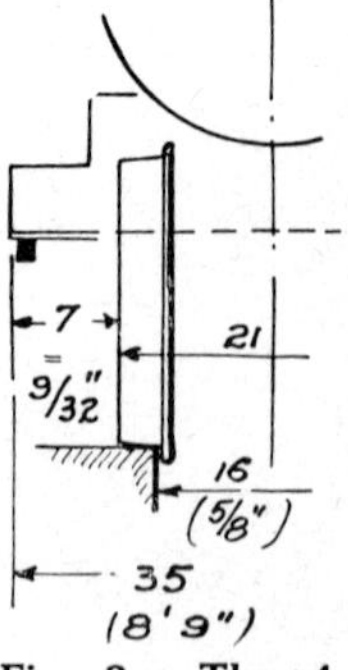

Fig. 3.—The 4 m/m scale showing increased tyre width and increased space available for outside motions.

which to fit coupling and connecting rods and all the rest of the links required, that he will be tempted to widen the footplates of the engine. By using the 4-mm. scale $3\frac{1}{2}$-mm. tyres are possible and the space for outside work is increased to 7 mm. (9-32nd in.). The appearance of an outside geared locomotive will be enhanced by the increase of scale.

As soon as I can find time I would like to be able to refer to the subject again. In settling on 7 mm. as the scale for No. 0 gauge, in the desire to use a round figure I did not apply the principle of scale overhang completely. To be right the scale should have been $7\frac{1}{8}$ mm. to the foot, when using 6·5 mm. tyres.

Yours faithfully,

HENRY GREENLY.

Farnborough, Hants.

Simple "OO" Gauge Track.

To the Editor MODEL RAILWAY NEWS.

DEAR SIR,

I feel I need scarcely attempt to congratulate you on the M.R.N., because, after reading it, I think ordinary praise and sweet words are not sufficient. I consider it a model railwayman's paradise.

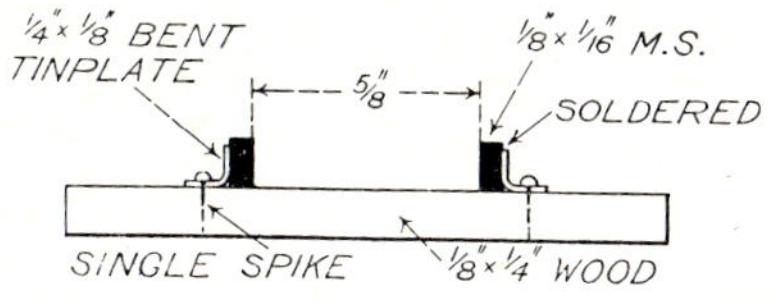

My real object in writing is to tell you of the sort of track I use on my 00 railway. The drawing will explain. The rails are $\frac{1}{16}$-in. × $\frac{1}{8}$-in. mild steel, supplied by Mr. J. Heath, an advertiser in the M.E. The chairs are "cocoa-tin." I trust this will be of some use to you.

Yours truly,

G. A. MCCULLAGH.

Belfast.

On Several Matters.

To the Editor, MODEL RAILWAY NEWS.

DEAR SIR,

I am back in my old home for a couple of months and unearthed two locos of a 1 gauge railway I had in 1910.

I attended the Model Railway Club exhibition on the invitation of Mr. Goodlet, of "Kay Models," who have some work in hand for me.

I was very much struck with the high standard of exhibits and was also very pleased to see a number of G.W.R. models in many gauges, by both amateurs and the trade—excellent, better and better.

At present my 0 gauge G.W.R. has only progressed as far as two locos, a Castle express and a Pannier tank shunter, G.W.R., and a train of six corridor coaches by Bassett-Lowke. "Kay Models" have all in hand; the latter are being re-painted by them.

I have made two resolutions with my railway to be :—

1. No curve under six feet radius and reverse curves 7/9 radius.
2. All buffers to be permanently touching on the straight when coupled up. This for passenger stock only.

In looking over photos of various model trains, I have always been struck with the distance between the coaches. This, to my mind, *entirely spoils* the whole effect.

I am hoping to overcome this by having spring draw-hooks instead of spring buffers, so made that the buffers just touch when coupled up, inside buffers will touch on a curve—couplings extended, of course—and outside buffers gaping. Future coaches I hope to have fitted with oval spring buffers by the Sheffield firm of Milbro, as well as ample spring couplings.

I saw the L.N.E.R. "Pacific" hauling the "Cornish Riviera" express passing my house the other day. I was very much struck with the noise she made, more of it, and entirely differing from the beat of the G.W.R. two and four cylinder classes.

This, of course, owing to her three cylinders.

There are two other points which add interest to Mr. Crebbin's letter in your last issue :—

1. The two engines are driven differently. The G.W.R. drive with regulator wide open and "work on the cut-off," keeping that as early as possible, thereby gaining economy. The L.N.E.R. (G.N.) drive with a late cut-off and "drive with the regulator."
2. G.W. use Welsh steam coal, L.N.E. any coal, *i.e.*, not special coal.

I suppose we shall never know the real result of this most interesting interchange.

With regard to grouping and models, I entirely sympathize with Major Simpson. I agree that it must be galling to see the smart livery of the old L.N.W.R. changing to the Midland red.

But for the trade, I suppose it vastly simplifies their problem, by reducing the enormous range of models in stock demanded by numerous folk like me.

In the near future there will only be two (or three) models demanded of each of the four groups.

Wishing your paper the best of luck,

Yours sincerely,

"Sparks."

South Devon.

2½ in. Gauge Signal Post Finials.

To the Editor, Model Railway News.

Dear Sir,

The following is a description of a quick and easy method for making finials which mean so much to the realism of a scale model signal, especially if they are on a level with the enthusiastic operator's eyes!

Take a boot button, and grip it in the vice by the loop. Drill a hole in the top to take a loud-tone gramophone needle, point upwards.

Take a piece of tubing about ½ in. long, and solder to a square of thin

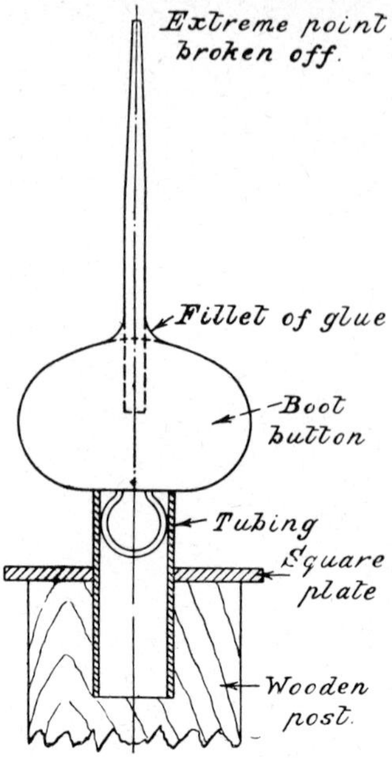

Enlarged Sketch of Finial.

brass about 1-16th in. larger than top of post. Glue loop of button into one end of tube, and drive other end into top of post (*see* sketch).

The only fault about the M.R.N. is that it is not published often enough.

Yours truly,

"Lord of the Isles."

Constructional Articles.

To the Editor, Model Railway News.

Sir,

After congratulating you on the first three numbers of your journal, and trusting that it may be a financial success, may I venture to offer a few suggestions?

I believe that your paper appeals principally to the man who makes things as opposed to the one who buys things ready made. Most of the model firms sell more complete articles at Christmas than at any other time. The rest of the year, their sales are to enthusiasts and firms requiring models; at least, so I am told.

According to this theory, articles describing railway systems made of complete parts, are of little interest; an example is the first one in the March number.

Cannot you give more articles of the type of Mr. Spade's, on body building? Personally, I think that the best article ever written, was that published in the *M.E.* by Mr. Stevens, on the making of his track. It was full of hints which were worth pounds.

Some subjects worth consideration are :—

(1) Point operation, including levers.
(2) Hints on making Greenly's All Level Points.
(3) Details of winding and where to get material for small electric motors of various types.
(4) Settle the question of whether 3·5 or 4 mm. is to be standard for 00 gauge.

These sort of articles would certainly appeal to the Colonial reader who has to write to England for most of his material, and to whom it is very vexatious to experiment and then find that he has omitted to get some essential part.

I shall have to send you an article describing his troubles one day.

Yours faithfully,
W. B. Cushion,
Squadron Leader, R.A.F.
Simla, India.

Points from France.

To the Editor, Model Railway News.
Dear Sir,

During a recent visit to Calais for the purpose of taking railway photographs, I noticed an arrangement over the right-hand buffer of the locomotives on the expresses which I had not seen previously, and on making enquiries I found it was a post-war method of indicating the train numbers by means of a box placed over the buffer, which can be read easily by day and also by night by the signalmen or stationmasters as the train approaches.

I am enclosing a photograph showing this attachment, and the train number, in this case is 2250, which leaves Calais at 15.00 o'clock and runs to Brussels and is composed of first and second - class corridor coaches and restaurant car. The number box is electrically illuminated and the spaces containing the figures are just plain white lights. I am also enclosing

Method of indicating Train Numbers.

a snapshot taken the other day at Calais, of one of the P.L.M. coaches on the ordinary Riviera Rapide, where I noticed that, in addition to the ordinary number of the coach and the destination plate, there was a series of letters and figures painted on the panel, which my friend, Mr. G. P. Keen, who, as readers of the Model Railway News know, is a specialist in the knowledge of rolling stock, has deciphered for me.

The interpretation is as follows :—

P.L.M., of course, means Paris-Lyons Mediterranean Railway.

A. means first-class compartment, and the 2 above it means there are

Lettering on the Riviera Rapide.

two first compartments in the coach.

C. means third-class, and the 2 above this means there are two third-class compartments in the coach.

L. means Lits Salon, and the 3 above it means there are three on the coach.

F. means brake wheel.

Y. means that it is fitted with electric light.

I. means a vestibule connection.

187 is the number of the coach.

43T. is the weight, 43 tons.

It may interest readers the next time they go on the Continent to look out for these marks on the coaches and try and decipher them.

Yours faithfully,
W. J. BASSETT-LOWKE.

A Suggestion.

To the Editor, MODEL RAILWAY NEWS.
DEAR SIR,

I was very interested in Mr. F. Spade's article on coach building in the March issue of your paper. I would like to suggest that a series of similar articles dealing with methods, both simple and elaborate, of constructing and finishing coaches is greatly needed, and would be greatly appreciated, by model railway engineers, especially to those interested in the 7-mm. scale.

May I take this belated opportunity of congratulating you on your excellent and long-wanted enterprise, and of wishing it every success.

Yours truly,
T. W. H. ADAMS.

Harlesden.

L.N.E.R Signals and L.M.S.R. Locos.

To the Editor, MODEL RAILWAY NEWS.
DEAR SIR,

On the Great Central section of the L.N.E.R. in the vicinity of Manchester, the distant signals have been fitted with orange, instead of red, "spectacles" to distinguish them from the home signals at night. Where this has been done the arms have been painted yellow with a black band. If this could be done on one's model railway it would certainly help to bring the system up to date. On the L.M.S.R. (L.N.W. section) many of the "Prince of Wales" 4—6—0 two-cylinder locomotives have recently been fitted with Belpaire firebox and Ross "Pop" valves. This would help to modernize a model North-Western system if it could be reproduced in miniature on the "Princes," but this is, of course, a very much bigger job than the first-mentioned idea for bringing things up to date.

Wishing the MODEL RAILWAY NEWS all the success it deserves.

I am, yours truly,
RONALD H. WILD.

Plan for a Small Room.

To the Editor, MODEL RAILWAY NEWS.
DEAR SIR,

I noticed in the first issue of your magazine, "Some Beginners' Questions," among which was: What space is necessary for a reasonably good system ?

Now, in designing a model railway, the first things to keep in view are: Firstly, to have as large curves as possible. Other considerations are: arranging goods sidings and platforms of suitable length (which should not be less than four feet), etc.

My room is 12 ft. × 11 ft. 6 in., and for it I have designed a very

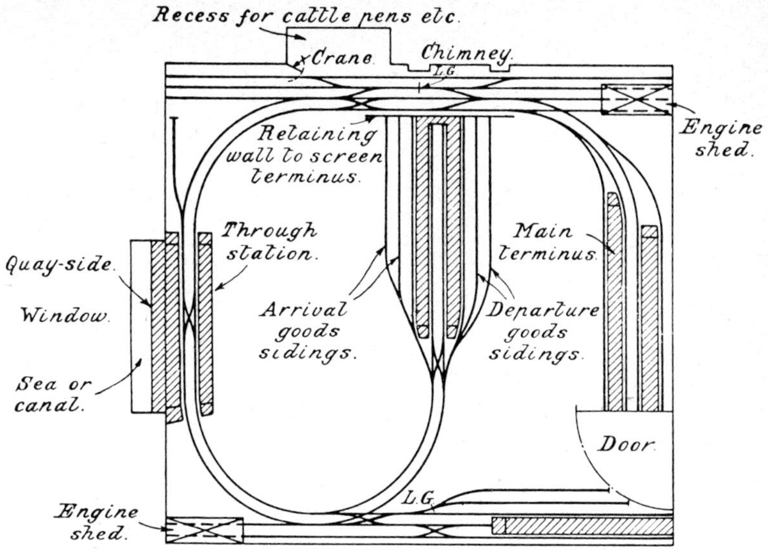

Mr. Doherty's plan for a room 12 ft. × 11 ft. 6 in.

complete gauge "0" system, which I show herewith. The minimum curve is three-feet rad us, and each terminus has its own goods yard.

Perhaps the plan is a little bit complicated, but I am sure a very good system can be obtained in a room which is 12 feet square.

Best wishes for the success of your paper.

Yours sincerely,

P. T. Doherty.

Streatham Hill, S.W. 2.

Reminiscences.

To the Editor, Model Railway News.

Dear Sir,

I have seen letters by Colonel Hamilton and one or two others, stating they wished more steam could be used, and some letters not liking clockwork.

When I first started, I had dreams of seeing various types of locos running about, without considering how I was to control them.

Then, when I started my ½-inch line, I was determined to have a really scale steam loco, and thought the whole railway, to look real, must be outside, on embankments. I had not gone far, however, before I came to the conclusion that, at any rate, one station would be better in a shed and run out through a tunnel.

After running the line, I found it impossible to run and look after, with two operators, more than two locos.

My idea was to have a model of a steam railway, but if one wants to have a system, steam locos cannot be left in stations, in steam, unattended ; so the only thing I think to do is, on this sort of railway, perhaps, have a coal-fired or other fired loco boiler, also some externally fired ; have other locos with steam outlines in clockwork and electric. Certainly have an electric one for shunting at the principal station, as it is difficult to do it without assistance in any other way. Clockworks can work between stations if one does not wish to electrify the whole line. In any case, they might be useful, should the electric not always work.

If electric is too expensive or complicated, then I have found one can shunt with clockwork locos, without leaving the signal box.

Another point that I think should be altered, if possible, is all steam locos, lamps, and clockwork locos, catches for stopping and reversing, should be arranged to clear a third rail of 1/8 or 5-32nds above running rails, so these locos do not foul the third rail.

Of course, if the all-level system is adopted, it does not matter if one makes the points insulated. With the raised, the line can be electrified at some future date and not allowed for, except in insulating the up and down roads.

Yours sincerely,
Wakefield. C. GEORGE HARRISON.

A Correction.

To the Editor, MODEL RAILWAY NEWS.
DEAR SIR,

I would like to point out that, in the plan of Mr. W. A. Gosheron's railway, given on page 68 in the March issue of the MODEL RAILWAY NEWS, there is no connection between the inner and the outer circles, whereas, in the foreground of the photograph shown on the previous page, there is a cross-over shown. Also, I would like to venture to suggest that the aforementioned crossover be moved to the position A, shown on the plan enclosed.

Yours sincerely,
D. A. P. WEST.

Beckenham.

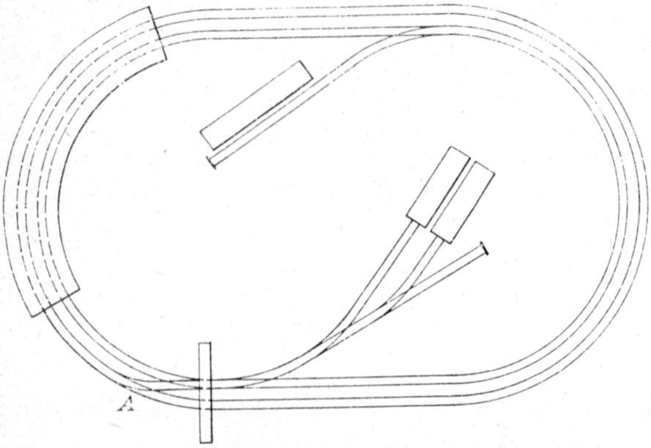

The corrected lay-out of Mr. Gosheron's Railway, with a new suggestion.

Simple Turntable for "O" Gauge Electric Railway.

To the Editor, MODEL RAILWAY NEWS.
DEAR SIR,

I wish to say how pleased I am with the MODEL RAILWAY NEWS, and to congratulate you on getting up such a necessary magazine.

My father, a doctor, started me off on railways (in model form) at four years of age, by building an 0 gauge line. I am now 15½ and own an 0 gauge electric railway and a 2½-in. gauge.

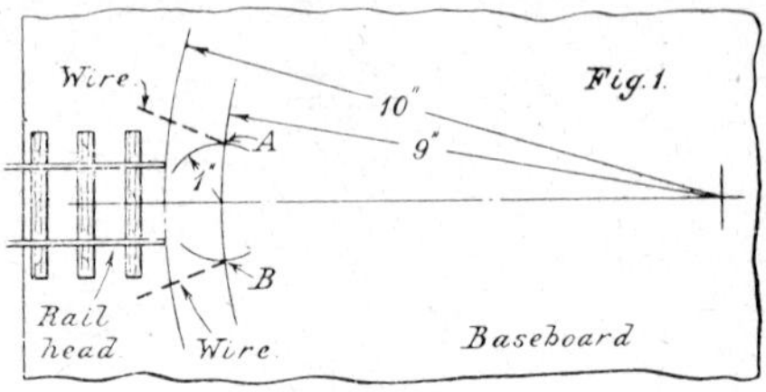

Fig. 1.

Recently, I completed a simple electric turntable for my 0 gauge, which I venture to describe, trusting that it may be of use to some reader.

Make a smooth-surface baseboard—an old drawing-board or pastry-board does very well. It should be at least 25 in. long and over 12 in. wide. Mark out a circle or two arcs, 10 in. radius, and inside another of 9 in. radius, and mark the centre of each rail-head on the inside circle. Having obtained the positions of the rail-heads on the baseboard from each mark, draw an arc cutting the 9-in. radius 1 in. on either side. (See Fig. 1.)

Channel out a groove from each of these points (A and B) to clear the 10-in. radius. These channels are to take the wires. A large-headed brass screw should be put at A and B and the wires from the screws laid in the channels and connected to the running rails in the one case, and the electric rail in the other case.

The turntable is made of a piece of board 20 in. × 4 in. × ½ in., suitably curved at the ends. At both ends, 1 in. from the extreme end, mark two points on the underside, 1 in. on either side of the centre line (Fig. 2). At each of the four points, screw in brass screws similar to those used on

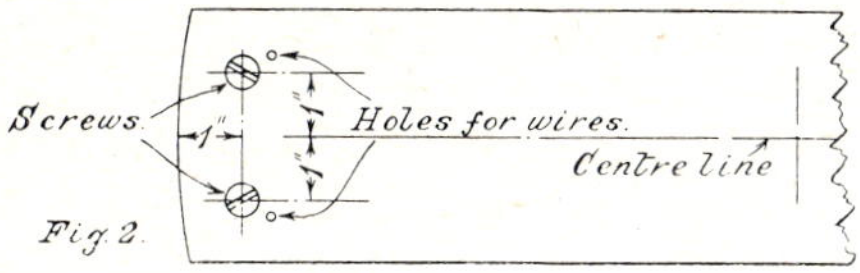

Fig. 2.

the base, and pass the wires up through holes to the upper surface.

Now lay down the track and pivot the turntable with an ordinary screw, taking care also that the screw surfaces are level with the wood and slide nicely over each other. Some kind of railing and buffer-stops at the blind end can be fitted. Then lay down the centre line; screw down the rail-head or heads to their respective

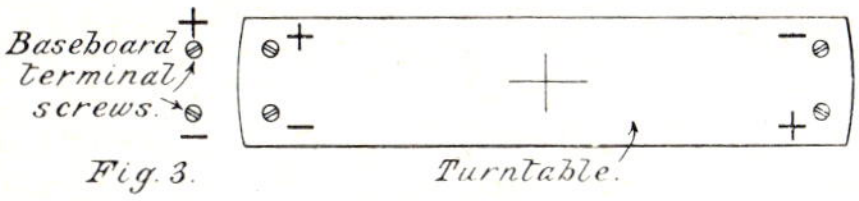

Fig. 3.

positions on the baseboard, and connect up the terminal screws as shown in diagram (Fig. 3).

The whole should be painted red oxide or grey. If 20 in. is too long for the purpose, it can be shortened to 18 in. or 16 in., etc., as required..

I have also just done a plan for an electric-type 0 gauge 4—6—4 electrically driven loco, which can be built up with an ordinary mechanism. If you think it will be any use, I will send it up.

Yours truly,

S. C. Suggit.

Baldock.

The Possibilities of Gauge "OO."

To the Editor, Model Railway News.

Dear Sir,

After reading Mr. Reidpath's article on gauge 00 tactics, it occurred to me, that of all the many gauges used in model railway practice to-day, in none of them, not even in the passenger-carrying gauges, have we anything so realistic.

I give herewith a sketch of my own "lay-out." "A" is the main line; "B" is the suburban, with a branch line "C." The line runs from "Huntingdon Terminus" (H. T.) through "Mannington Halt" (M. H.) to "Abbeville Junction" (A. J.), whence one line goes on to "Desborough Station" (D. S.) and the other to "Wick" (W. S.).

"T" is a short line connecting the main and goods to a turntable in preparation for the next train out. I found it necessary to couple the two centre coaches of each train by their loop ends, to permit the coupling of engines at either end. The turntable I made by fitting a "straight" on a pivot in a bowl-shaped block of wood. This "straight" should be a "brake" rail.

I do not pretend that this system is anything like the last word in arrangement, but it shows what can be done with a little thinking, a little outlay, and a lot of care.

A. Dobson.

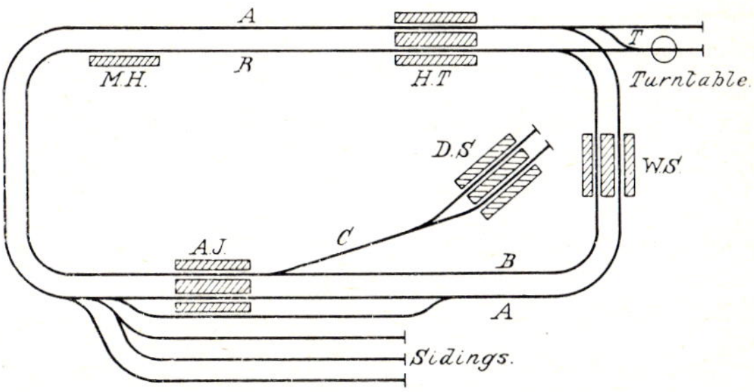

Mr. Dobson's Lay-out.

A Lay-out Competition.

WE have been considering various schemes for practical model railway competitions among our readers, and, although we hope to announce others in the near future we think that, at the outset, a railway-planning contest will prove most interesting and useful to our ever-growing circle of supporters.

In submitting the details of Railway Plan Competition No. 1, we are not stipulating that the plan shall be modelled on any full-size system. This may come later. Our sketch shows an attic-room of average dimensions suitable for quite a good No. 0 gauge formation.

The main conditions to be observed are as follows :—

(1) The plan is to show a suitable No. 0 gauge railway system of a practical character.

(2) There should be at least one passenger station and one goods yard and, in addition, a country station is desirable.

(3) It should be possible to work local and fast passenger trains in and out of the station in a railway-like manner.

(4) Goods working—both through and pick-up—is also to be capable of accomplishment, with some pretence to realism.

(5) One example of time-table working may be described with advantage, but in doing this, it must not be assumed that engine power and rolling stock is unlimited in amount.

(6) Main-line points and curves should be at least 3 ft. radius. In goods yards the minimum radius may be 2 ft., although 2 ft. 6 in. radius points are desirable where they are traversed by locomotives. Six-foot ways to be the standard 7-mm. scale dimensions.

(7) Double-line working is not essential.

(8) Signalling, if shown, should be

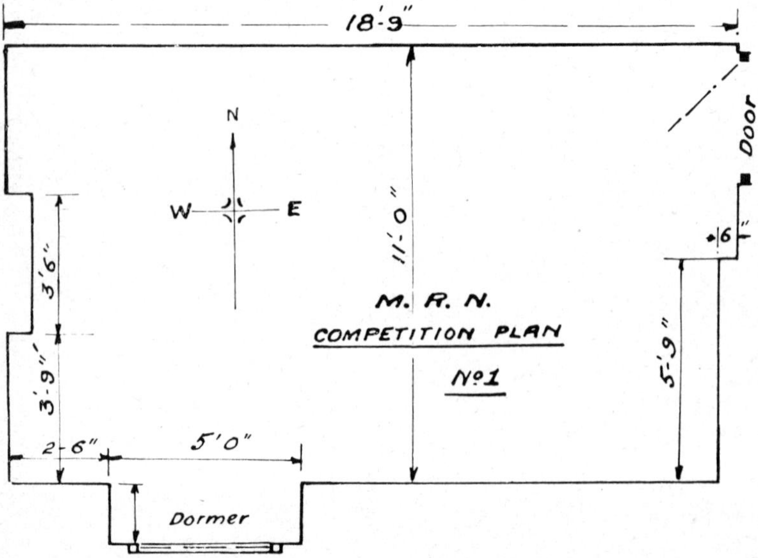

The attic in which the railway is to be laid.

of practical form. Distant signals may be eliminated on short sections.

(9) If the line is to be electrically operated, the sections should be indicated.

(10) Plans must be drawn to scale, and the description should be as concise as possible.

Conditions and Prize.

This competition is arranged more to interest our readers than as a contest for prizes. However, to add a spice of excitement to the result, we propose to award, to the best plan submitted, any goods to the value of ten shillings and sixpence, chosen from the catalogues of any one of our advertisers. All entries must reach this office by Friday, June 12th.

The Model Railway Club.

In our last issue we gave a general account of the Club's very successful Annual Exhibition. We now give some further details, which testify to the excellent quality and variety of work on view.

Among the principal steam exhibits were :—Mr. Pitt's ½-in. 4—4—2 tank ; Mr. Attenborough's ½-in. L. & N.E.R. " Pacific " and two coaches ; Mr. Straker's " Pacific," and Mr. Kerr's tank (both 0 gauge).

The 1 gauge clockwork models included Mr. Norman's three N.L.R. locomotives and surburban block-train—a nice piece of work ; Mr. Templer's G.N.R. " Pacific," a model shewing exceptionally full detail ; and Mr. Mackinnon's wagons. In 0 gauge, Mr. Kelly's North Eastern " Pacific " and a locomotive of the same type of the C. de f. du Nord. Mr. Muntz's G.W. railway coaches, one of which is an efficient slip-coach ; Captain Layland-Barratt's G.W. locomotives and coaches—a good and well-arranged display ; Mr. Bindon-Blood's two G.W.R. locomotives, and a track exhibit comprising slips and scissor crossovers ; Mr. MacLeod's range of Caledonian and L. & N.W.R. locomotives. Other notable exhibits were Mr. Keen's comprehensive display of locomotives, wagons and coaches, including a nearly finished observation coach, which must surely be a record for completeness of internal and external detail ; Mr. W. R. S. Smart's Southern Railway locomotives and wagons, and a new departure in model work, a " Garratt " 2—4—2+2—4—2 locomotive and a 4—2—2 American locomotive of the Lehigh Valley RR. Mr. Fish exhibited a group of Southern Railway (L.B. & S.C. Section) locomotives ; Mr. Forrest, coaches ; Mr. Lance, coaches ; and Mr. Thompson, wagons and brake-vans.

Mr. Kerr also exhibited Caledonian locomotives and rolling stock in 0 gauge, while in 00 gauge he showed several very neat engines, fitted with home-made reversing mechanisms. Other 00 gauge exhibits were Mr. Brewer's old-time locomotives, including the " Cornwall," while Mr. Chase showed some beautiful cardboard models in both 00 and 0 gauges. Colonel Henvey exhibited an 0 gauge 0—6—4 tank and a water crane, and an unfinished narrow-gauge locomotive (½-in. scale, 0 gauge) with a novel system of controls.

Among the electrical exhibits were Mr. Pond's 0 gauge electric locomotives and tube train, and Mr. Lee's ½-in. 4—4—2 tank.

The prizes were awarded as follows : Six-coupled hauling competition, Mr. MacLeod (12 lb.) ; 0 gauge coaching stock, Mr. Lance ; 0 gauge wagon, Mr. Kerr and Colonel Henvey tied ; best 1 gauge exhibit, Mr. Norman ; 1 gauge wagon, Mr. Mackinnon ; drawing competition, Mr. Harrison.

Certificates were also awarded to Captain Layland-Barratt for the best general exhibit ; Mr. Keen for general excellence ; Mr. Smart for originality, and Mr. Kelly for his " Nord " Pacific.

The prizes were presented by Mrs. Percy Keen, to whom a vote of thanks was passed with acclamation.

The trade was represented by Messrs. Bond, Ltd., Bassett-Lowke, Ltd., the Leeds Model Co., and Kay Models; while Messrs. Percival Marshall had a stand for model engineering literature. A feature of the trade exhibits was an advanced specimen of an English-made steam locomotive for 0 gauge, by Bassett-Lowke, Ltd., which put up a good performance on the track. This will be illustrated in a later issue.

Fixtures for June:—June 6th, Visit to Nine Elms; June 11th, Track Night; June 25th, Lecture by Mr. S. H. M. Fish—"Models of long ago."

Particulars of the Club may be obtained from the Hon. Secretary, R. Henvey, White Cottage, Shirley near Croydon.

The Manchester & District Model Railway Club.

The fifth meeting of the above club was held at the Clarion Café, Market Street, Manchester, on the 12th May.

The meeting was well attended and two new members were enrolled.

An 0 gauge G.N. 0—4—0 tank loco body, made entirely of wood, was shewn by Mr. Hines, who also showed a number of signals and a loading gauge.

A short paper, "Model Railways in Summertime," was given by the Hon. Secretary.

The next meeting takes place on Tuesday, the 9th June.

A visit to the L.M. & S. Co.'s central room at Victoria Station, Manchester, has been arranged for Saturday, the 16th inst.

A visit to the Manchester Ship Canal Co.'s locomotive sheds at Mode Wheel, has been arranged for Saturday, the 23rd inst.

Arrangements are being made for visits to Trafford Park and Gorton locomotive sheds (L. & N.E.R.) and Newton Heath loco sheds (L.M.S.).

Any further information may be had from the Hon. Secretary, J. A. Dean, 29, Gorse Lane, Gorse Hill, Stretford, Manchester.

Special Model Work.

Mr. George Winteringham, whose work is well known in the model railway world, asks us to state that he is prepared to undertake any special model-making orders, either of a railway character, or otherwise. He would be particularly interested in building to 7-mm. scale. Enquiries addressed to him at "Compages," Taunton Road, Lee Green, London, S.E. 12, enclosing a stamped addressed envelope, will receive prompt attention.

Model Building Materials.

We have received a sample packet of model building materials from the Multum-in-Parvo Co., Ltd., 144, Falkland Road, Hornsey, London, N. 8. The packet contains sheets of printed papers representing realistic brick and stone walls and roof tiles, and also silver paper for window glazing. Although sold as "Doll's House Paper," this material will be found very useful for model railway buildings, such as stations, signal boxes, embankments, and tunnel facings. The price is only 6*d.* per packet, plus postage.

A Royal Model Railway Ride.

When His Majesty King George visited Wembley, he delighted the children by joining them in a trip on the miniature railway which encircles Treasure Island. We believe this is the first occasion on which model railways have been patronized by the Royal family, and this recognition of their fascination should do much to stimulate public interest in the joys of the miniature railway.

The MODEL RAILWAY NEWS

Editorial and Publishing Offices:
66, FARRINGDON STREET, LONDON, E.C. 4.
Single Copies, post free, 7½d. Annual Subscription, 7s. 6d.

Vol. I. No. 7. JULY, 1925. Price, 6d.

Notes of the Month.

OUR rail-planning competition has proved eminently successful — so well entered for that our chief difficulty has been to say which is the best plan among the many entries received. As the main object of the competition is not the prize but the stimulation of ideas on this absorbing part of the model railway hobby, we hope to be able in a future issue to publish plans other than the one we have picked out as the best. Many of the lay-outs entered for the competition have included suggestions which are quite useful. In some cases the main scheme has been really good but the winning plan has scored because it has been more completely and most carefully worked out.

We have pleasure therefore, in awarding the prize to

Mr. NORMAN AXFORD,
30, Stanley Road,
Edmonton, London, N. 9;

and in reproducing his plan on page 223. His arrangement displays great ingenuity, and although it is open to criticism—all model plans which are laid in an extremely small space have some disability or other—more particularly in that goods-train accommodation and operation has been made subservient to the demands of passenger traffic, it is possible to obtain quite a representative service. In spite of the introduction of the reversing loop line, Mr. Axford has reduced his operating spaces to two.

We have to commend specially the efforts of the following competitors.

Mr. H. M. PEARSON (Golders Green, London, N.W.), for a two terminal station plan with a continuous main line.

Mr. H. D. PINNINGTON (Liverpool), for a two terminal point to point (non-continuous) plan.

Mr. L. E. BREWER (Eltham Park, London, S.E.), for a single terminus plan with a continuous main line with two other stations having terminal roads.

Mr. N. F. STEVENS (Birmingham), for a non-continuous (terminal to terminal) plan with one passing station. The main line is in the form of a volute and should be quite a good scheme for a clockwork railway. A time table is included.

Mr. E. N. HORTON (Nottingham), for a non-continuous plan with two terminals and two passing stations. The reversal loops cut up the operating spaces into three separate compartments, which characteristic some users might object to.

Other useful plans were sent in by G. Clark (Stroud Green, London); F. W. H. Adams (Harlesden, London); J. N. Edwards (Clifton College); Alan J. Thorn (Highgate, London); H. L. Warren (Mill Hill School); H. F. Inskip (Plymouth); B. J. Holden (Steyning).

Some of the other plans received show great ingenuity and knowledge of railway matters, but fail from a competition point of view, by showing rail formations which could not be got into the space. Among other faults that we may mention are the placing of stations in positions in which it would be impossible to get at the trucks or coaches to uncouple them. However, on the whole, we are highly delighted with the response to our competition and can congratulate the younger entrants on their efforts.

An Interesting Catalogue.

We have received from Messrs. Jackson Rigby Engineering Co., Ltd., Station Road, Shalford, near Guildford, Surrey, a copy of their catalogue of model steam engines, fittings, J. R. lathes and accessories and a temporary list of parts and castings for model locomotives.

A very interesting item amongst their various specialities is the model high-speed stationary steam engines working on the "uniflow" principle. These are made in several designs and sizes, the 1-in. bore by 1-in. stroke single acting, the twin-cylinder model having cylinders 9-16th in. bore × $\frac{3}{4}$-in. stroke for boats up to 4 ft. length, and $\frac{3}{4}$-in. bore × 1-in. stroke for boats of greater length than 4 ft., and the small model having a cylinder 7-16th in. bore × $\frac{1}{2}$-in. stroke. Any of these are supplied as castings, fully machined parts or finished engines. The J. R. 3-in. centre screw-cutting lathe is a good and inexpensive tool, very suitable for home use. It is supplied either as a bench lathe to be worked by a separate foot motor or as a pedestal lathe with treadle complete or arranged for power or electric drive. The standard parts and castings for model locomotives are to suit $2\frac{1}{2}$-in. gauge, half-inch nominal scale models. They are supplied as castings, machined only or completely finished. Amongst these are, main axle-boxes, buffer planks, parts for bogies, wheels, axles, pony trucks and boilers, also drawings for Atlantic or Pacific classes and detailed arrangements of Walschaerts' valve gear. A speciality is cylinders of outside piston-valve type. The firm have an excellent reputation for the design and quality of their products. The price of the complete list is 6*d*.

The Railway Year Book.

Since the "Railway Year Book" was first published, 28 years ago, many revisions and additions have been necessary. This time, attention has been given to the further development in grouping associated with the Irish section, dealing particularly with the Great Southern Railways Company, with which practically all railways in the Irish Free State, except the Great Northern, are in the course of amalgamation. Information regarding the various British railways has been thoroughly brought up to date and amplified, and a comprehensive index to the whole work has been included for the first time. In view of the great mass of material covered, and the necessary complications involved in railway information, this addition greatly increases the value of the Annual as a reference book. The general arrangement of the contents is excellent and comprehensive, and any student of real railway practice will find it invaluable. It is published by the Railway Publishing Co., Ltd., 33, Tothill Street, London, S.W. 1. Price 5/–, by post 5/6.

Mr. R. Hughes, of 36, Rendlesham Road, Clapton, E.5, is building a portable model railway, and would like to hear from any other reader who is similarly engaged.

NOTABLE MODEL RAILWAYS

Mr. C. E. Howie's Gauge 1 Railway.

THE lay-out of this railway, which is probably the longest and most complete in Germany, is a double-track gauge 1 " Lowko " track, with the largest obtainable curve radius (11 ft.) all over. The total length of the lines all round measures 140 ft. or 42 metres per line, both lines measured inside wall circumference of our house, passing through six rooms and one corridor. This does not include numerous tracks in Station Room No. VI (*see* Fig. 2), but only means the length of one through line of the double track. The system of points and switches incorporates all possibilities; therefore, trains can be directed any way without running into a dead position. Whatever way they go, besides the main line, they will always come back to their home rail without any complication at all.

The water basin is about 10 ft. long and gives the appearance of a sea harbour with docks, landing stages, cranes, etc. It is about 2 ft. wide and 1 ft. deep, so that steamers are fully free to move.

The station is situated and modelled on the lines of " Harwich " (Parkeston Quay), after which it is called.

Rolling stock, five steam engines, by several makers (Bassett-Lowke, F. Smithies, etc.), of Sir Gilbert Claughton class are doing the hard work. They are equipped with all possible modern

A Corner of the track.

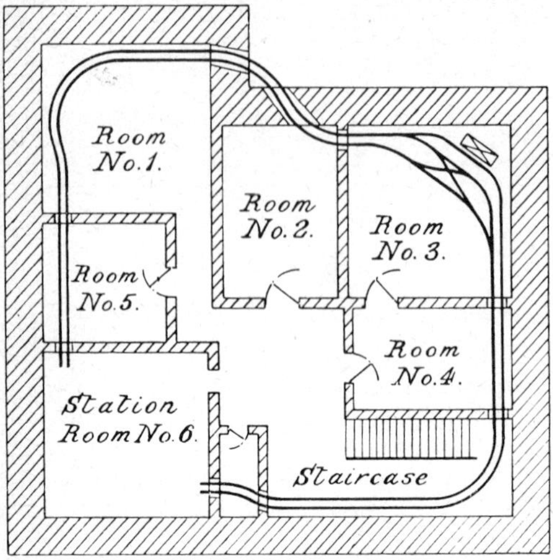

Fig. 1.—General lay-out.

fittings. Of course, the proper type of lamp is not yet found. Petrol and methylated-spirit lamps are neither really satisfactory.

Six large clockwork engines, latest models of the L.N.W., G.E.R., M.R., L.M.S.R. types are always ready to start and will just complete one all-round journey, with four to five corridor coaches. Besides one complete good-looking goods train, we are able to make up :—

Three L. N. W. express Corridor trains with six coaches each.

One L.M.S. express corridor train with five coaches.

One M.R. express corridor train with four coaches.

One G.N. express corridor train with three coaches.

Of course, it is very difficult to give a real picture of the lay-out by writing —it must be inspected in order to get the right idea. Fig. 1 shows the general lay-out of the line running through the six rooms and the corridor, the Station Room No. 6 being shown in detail in Fig. 2.

I have numerous visitors from all parts of the country, who are interested to see the railway and happened to hear about it by chance. Any readers of the M.R. NEWS who happen to be on a trip through Germany are always welcome, and I will show them my

Harwich Station—showing a ship at the Quay.

Rolling Stock in a siding.

lay-out with the greatest pleasure. They are requested to announce their visit by a post-card addressed to C. E. Howie, 7, Thomaestrasse, Wiesbaden, and I shall be pleased to receive them personally.

I may as well state that every article used in the construction of this railway, as well, of course, as all rolling-stock and fittings of every kind, is of British manufacture.

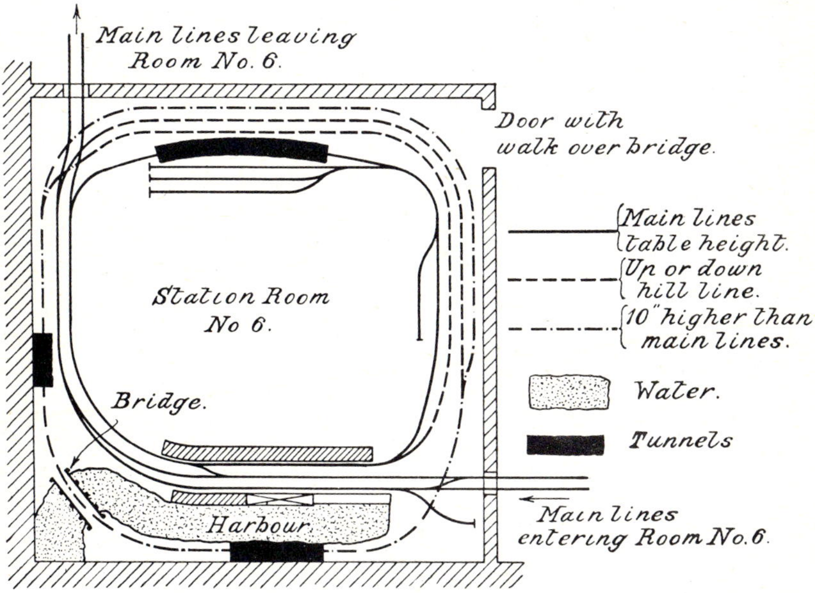

Fig. 2.—Room No. 6 in detail.

WITH THE CLUBS

The Model Railway Club.

The Shed Visit season is now in full swing, and visits have already been paid to King's Cross, Old Oak Common, and Nine Elms. Last month's lecture was by the Hon. Secretary on "0 Gauge Methods," and was well attended.

Fixtures for July:—Thursday, July 9th, Track Night. July 23rd, Lecture by Mr. S. H. M. Fish, "Models of Long Ago." Saturday, July 4th, Shed Visit to Neasden. July 25th, Shed Visit to Bricklayers' Arms.

The Club has organized a small stand at the Locomotive Centenary Exhibition, which is being held at the Faverdale works of the L. & N. E. R. at Darlington for a fortnight from July 2nd. This promises to be exceptionally interesting as a large and unique collection of railway relics, models, prints, etc., will be on view.

Particulars of the Club may be obtained from the Hon. Secretary, R. Henvey, White Cottage, Shirley, near Croydon.

Wimbledon Model Railway Club.

This month's "time-sheet":—7.30 p.m., July 6th — Lecture: "Feltham Marshalling Yard," by Mr. R. Shephard. 7.30 p.m., July 20th—Test runs on the Club Track. Both at the Red Cross Hall, Church Road. 2.45 p.m., July 25th—Visit to L.N.E.R. Loco Depot, King's Cross; meet No. 1 platform, King's Cross Station.

On Saturday, May 23, an instructive visit took place to the G.W.R. Loco Depot at Old Oak Common, the running sheds and other points of interest being thoroughly inspected including the footplates of various locomotives.

The Hon. Secretary, R. Shephard, 27, Bernard Gardens, Wimbledon, is always pleased to supply full particulars to prospective members.

The Manchester and District Model Railway Club.

The sixth meeting was held at the Clarion Café, Market Street, Manchester, on the 9th of June. The attendance of members was the largest of any meeting held so far, five new members being enrolled.

Club Photographic Album.—As a record of Club visits and railway matters of general interest, a photographic album has been instituted. The Secretary will be pleased to receive photographs from members for insertion in the album. It is requested that the photographs be printed on gaslight paper and a pencil number on the back, particulars of the photo being given on a separate sheet enclosed with the photographs.

Diary for July, 1925.

4th.—Club visit to Chester (G.W.R.) Locomotive Sheds. 1.35 p.m. train from Exchange Station, Manchester. Members going meet on platform at 1.20 p.m. 14th.—Club meeting at Headquarters, the Clarion Café, 7.30 p.m. It is hoped that the discussion on the "Club Track" will be settled at this meeting. Will members, who have not done so, please let the Secretary have the June quarter subscription. 18th.—Visit to Crewe Loco Sheds. Train, 2.15 p.m., from London Road Station, Manchester. Members meet on platform at 2 p.m. Joint visits with the Stephenson Locomotive Society can be arranged for the following locomotive sheds:—4th.—Darlington. 11th.—Wolverhampton. 25th.—Barrow.

Members desirous of going are requested to let the Secretary know early.

Special Note *re* the 14th inst.—Members are requested to bring a model along with them to the meeting, as it is desired to obtain a Club photograph.

Mr. Walkley's Model Two-road Level Crossing.

Getting Down to "OO" Gauge.

By A. R. Walkley.

As mentioned in an article in the *Model Engineer* last year, the writer has been greatly struck with the possibilities of a really ambitious lay-out in the 3·5-mm. scale, popularly known as "double-0" gauge. With the assistance of the writer's brother, a considerable amount of experimental work has been carried out during the last two years, before definitely deciding to adopt this small scale. However, the conclusion has now been reached that "making a few feet look a mile" is quite a practical proposition and an absorbingly interesting one at that. As Mr. Percival Marshall recently remarked, the building of a model railway affords scope for every kind of craftmanship and individual taste—and the construction of a model line through an actual section of "country" is rendered possible by the area advantage of 00 gauge.

In the railway to be constructed, the following points are considered essential and will be strictly adhered to :—(1) electrically driven locos with remote control (including reversing); (2) all signals and points connected to a central control point, with the rods and wires going first through dummy signal-boxes where possible; (3) auto-couplings fitted to all vehicles or, in the case of "set" trains, at each end; and (4) any other working components, such as level-crossing gates, cranes and so forth, to be controlled from the same central control board. It is realized this will entail quite a considerable amount of extra work, but it is felt that the general effect of a small-scale railway is completely spoilt if such an out-of-scale object as the human hand has to be spread o'er the landscape at frequent intervals. Experience with an 0 gauge railway on the remote-control system (*see* the *Model Engineer*, July 10th, 1919), has been a factor in deciding to develop remote control still further.

Methods of making rolling-stock, signals and auto-couplings have been more or less decided upon as the result of much experiment, but as regards

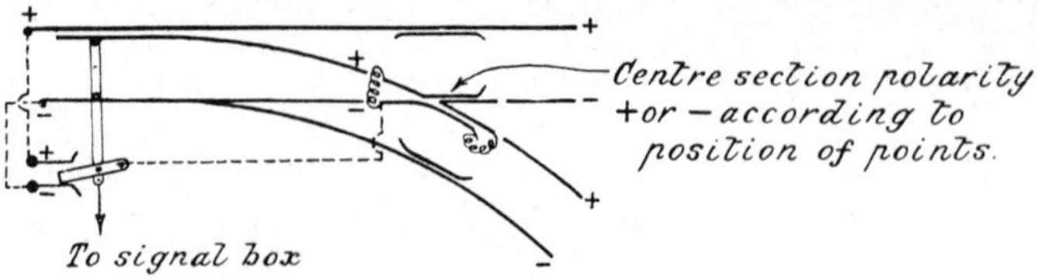

Fig. 1.—Insulated Rail System Point Wiring.

track the question, at the moment of writing, is still an open one. There are two types in view—the orthodox third-rail system and the "insulated rails and wheels" idea. Some time back, in answer to a letter of Mr. G. R. Stevenson's in the *M.E.*, the writer suggested that the extra detail work required in insulating the wheels seemed hardly worth while, but he has recently reconsidered this view, especially as a simple way of insulating at points (probably not original!) has been devised, the same remarks applying to wheels. From Fig. 1, it will be seen there are no dead sections other than the small insulating gaps, and the switch arm (which can be very small indeed) alters the polarity of the "centre section" as required. (*Note.*—Rails broken as shown and operating rod insulated.) If the supply current be reversed the switch follows suit. Any reader who can spare time from "cross-word" activities might care to plan the switching for a double-scissors crossover on this system.

An experimental single turn-out has been built up in this way, and no difficulties in construction were encountered. The rails and sleepers are brass strip and laid to gauge by soldering in the accepted manner, the sleepers then being slit up on the centre line by a fairly coarse metal fret-saw or fine hack-saw—a much quicker job than it sounds, by the way.

The separate parts, either points or rails, are then pinned or screwed down to gauge, in this case to battens. Plastic wood or similar filling is then inserted in the sleeper "cracks," sleepers painted dead black and who is the wiser? Insulation tests with H.R. phones and battery (it is quite all right, we are not switching on to another subject), show that this method will be satisfactory for low-tension supply at any rate. As regards wheels, ebonite "Mansell" pattern for coaches and wagons are suggested, with proper spoked wheels in metal with insulating bushes for the locos. With the Editor's permission

"OO" Rolling Stock.

these particular features might perhaps be described later on, as they are really only at the paper stage at present. However, the extra work required would be well repaid by the clean appearance of the track with the third rail eliminated. (Thanks for the suggestion, Mr. Stevenson.)

A short description of the photographs may be of interest. Ransomes and Rapier Wharf Crane :—3·5 mm. scale. All brass construction, jib fretted from sheet brass, corrugated cab formed on "home-made" press, which consists of cast-iron plates cut and filed to shape and operated by bench vice. Built-up H section bed-plate. All controls taken down a central column (carefully covered by the front girder in photograph !), and will be connected to the aforesaid central control board via Bowden cable. Three movements—turning, luffing and hoisting—with positive stops on each. Sliding cab door—note the regulation daubs of whitewash. Rolling stock, etc. :—The two goods vehicles are a brake van and coal wagon built from 1-mm. three-ply with battens, etc., of spruce veneer strips. Handrails, glass windows, "Marshall-Stewart" die-cast axle boxes on brake van. Auto-couplings are fitted but will not be described now, as they have not yet been "passed for service." The loco speaks for itself, and will not have a permanent position on the line. The coal-office is built up from thin wood, bricks and slates imprinted in the usual way—quite a business in this size. All 3·5 mm. to one foot, except loco, of course.

Two-road level crossing lay-out, 3·5-mm. scale. This makes an effective model and gives some idea of the detail work possible in double-0.

Gates are fretted from sheet brass, posts have proper hinges and operation is by rods and cranks below. The signals have scale fittings, including ladders, spectacle-glasses and back-plates. The moveable stop-gear in the roadway will be noticed. Telegraph poles are square brass rods with cross-battens of thin steel wire. Insulators

A model Wharf Crane, 3·5 m/m scale

(or "blobs" would better describe them—improvement is desired here) are a mixture of white paint and glue and the "blobbing" process is much simplified by holding the posts upside down during the operation.

The lone poplar tree represents a terrific effort by the natural history department, which, as yet, has not really got into its stride. There appears to be some mystery attached to model tree culture !

This model was mounted on the temporary stand for exhibition purposes and gained a prize at the Wimbledon and District Model Railway Club's competition last year. The writer wishes to thank Mr. W. P. Ashdown, a fellow-member of the club, who is also a keen 00 enthusiast, for his kind assistance in taking the photographs illustrating this article. In passing, it may be mentioned that Mr. Ashdown is experimenting with a type of track with wooden sleepers which will probably prove more suitable for an "insulated-rail"

Another realistic aspect of the model level crossing.

system than that described earlier in these notes.

In conclusion, as one of the first to experiment in double-0 gauge, the writer hopes to see a great development in the near future and looks forward with interest to seeing the results of other readers' experiences described in these pages. It seems unfortunate that there are no locos or mechanisms (clockwork and permanent-magnet motors) comparable in price and finish with the typical 0 gauge productions now to be obtained. Despite expert opinion the writer ventures to suggest that, in view of the advances made recently in the manufacture of special magnet steels, it should be possible to produce a permanent-magnet motor of sufficient power—in any case, units of this character would do much in obtaining converts to "the smallest gauge."

"The Mechanical Age."

The July issue of the *Mechanical Age,* a threepenny monthly magazine of popular engineering, is a special railway centenary number, and should be of particular interest to readers of the MODEL RAILWAY NEWS. In addition to an unusually fascinating account of the early history of the railway, there is a description of a model 00 gauge clockwork loco by Mr. Edward Beal, who described the coaling stage in our last issue. There are also general articles dealing with an exceptionally wide range of subjects, including electricity, ships and wireless, as well as an exciting serial and prize competitions. Altogether, the *Mechanical Age,* which is published to-day, is well worth the threepence which will procure it from any newsagent, or fourpence, post free, from this office.

R. B. (Apsley).—You will be advised to employ six volts, as the average voltage required is four volts. This extra two volts will allow for the voltage drop in the transmission of the current to the rails. For an indoor railway, ordinary rail and chairs may be used for the conductor rail. The wooden substructure will sufficiently insulate the conductor. See "Model Electric Railways and Locomotives," price 6s. 6d. post free, for descriptions of the various systems that are applicable to indoor electric lines and for the many different methods of control. Messrs. Bond's steel rail will suit your purpose excellently.

Building a 1 in. Scale "Pacific" under Difficulties.

By W. H. CROTHALL.

IN response to a request from our Editor, I will endeavour to describe the building of a 1-in. scale "Pacific" type locomotive. Before proceeding I would like to mention that the model is being built from scrap, the only exceptions being the steel for engine frames and the wheels. Hand tools only are being used, and a kitchen table is performing the duty of a bench.

Having purchased two blue-print drawings and the mild steel sheet for the engine frames, a start was made. The outline of the frames was marked out on the metal, two pieces rivetted together, and the most accessible parts cut out with hack saw and chisel, the remainder being drilled out in accordance with instructions contained in Greenly's "Model Steam Locomotives." The frames were now completed by the generous use of the file. The buffer beams were next proceeded with. These are made from a piece of steel plate from the scrap box. They are fitted in position by pieces of ½-in. angle iron obtained from an Army General Service Wagon which had been condemned.

I now had to find something with which to make the buffers. In the garden I discovered two wheels belonging to a child's perambulator. The hubs were removed, and, after measuring up, I found I could make four buffer stocks from them by cutting each in half (*see* Fig. 1). Buffer heads and shanks are made in one. These were once bolts holding two beams belonging to an Army hut. The round heads were filed flat, and the bolt reduced at one end to allow spring to fit (*see* Fig. 2). A piece of steel plate found on the road side was converted into two draw hooks, one for the engine and one for tender.

Wheel castings having been ordered but not delivered, I set to work on the foot plating. This is made from galvanized iron sheet, and was once part of a water tank. Angle iron, taken from the aforesaid wagon, was used to attach plating to the frames. The edging under foot plating is of strip brass, ⅜ in. wide and 3-32 in. thick. This material is extensively used by house furnishers for hanging curtains which run along a rail, the fittings of the device employed comprising the strip brass in question, and some small wheels.

The engine bogie next called for attention. A search in the scrap

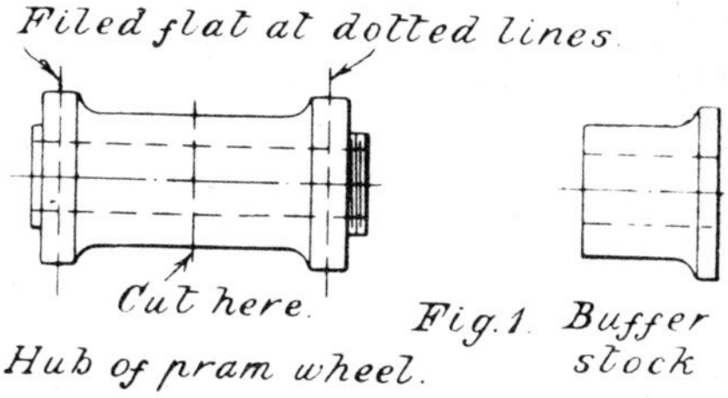

Fig. 1.—Making Buffer Stocks.

box produced some steel plate of required dimensions. Greenly's most useful book was again consulted, a design for the equalizers being desired. Having found the most suitable pattern, and also a piece of steel, which proved to be very hard, the equalizers were eventually made as per Fig. 3, reproduced here half size. The springs were taken from two broken cycle bells.

The wheel castings having by this time arrived, were put in hand. They proved to be exceptionally good castings, and when cleaned up by the file and some emery paper, were handed over to a friend to be bored, as my small hand-drill could not manage the job.

Failing to acquire anything suitable for axle boxes, I had to purchase

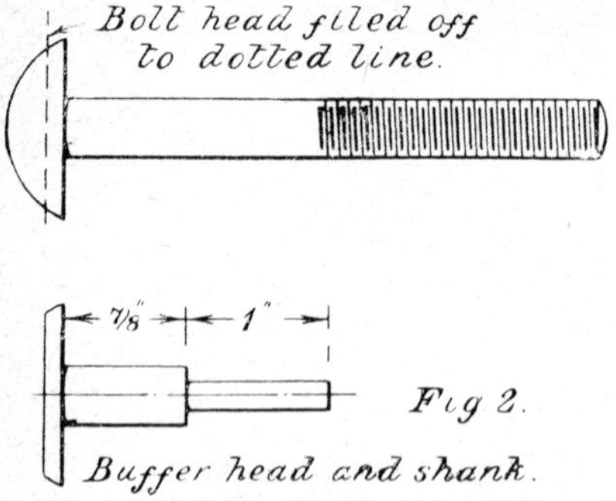

Fig. 2.—Buffer Heads from Bolts.

them. Having trued them up, I again had to call upon my friend, who very kindly bored them for me. I was more successful regarding the axles. These were found after a diligent search among the scrap heap in a motor works. Having fitted them, I next turned my attention to the tender.

The method adopted for making the under frames and bogies was the same as for the loco. I would like to mention, before proceeding further, that the tender is of my own design, and follows no particular railway company's pattern. It is carried on two four-wheeled bogies. The base, end and sides are made from oven plates taken from a large kitchen range. These plates proved to be very good steel, and worked up well. The outline was marked out and the hammer and chisel brought into play. Having been finished off with the file, the plates were now ready for assembling, They were held in position by $\frac{1}{2}$-in. angle iron, the source of supply again being the Army wagon. The tank is made from an Army biscuit tin, and, being of very simple design, calls for no comment. Buffer beams, buffers and draw hook having been fitted, the tender now awaited its wheels and axle boxes to complete it.

Having got thus far, I again turned my attention to the engine, and commenced to build the cab. The thin sheet-iron used for this once did duty in an ordinary gas oven. I made a slight deviation from the blue print, and adopted the design used on the L. & N.E.R. "Pacific" locos (G.N.R. section). Some $\frac{1}{2}$-in. angle brass, which I had the good fortune to acquire cheaply, is used to hold the cab together. The windows will eventually be glazed. I propose using mica or thin glass for these.

Horn stays were now made, steel plate from the scrap box being used. These are riveted to the frames. I will conclude by giving a few principal dimensions :—

Engine—			
Length of frames	...	...	41 in.
Thickness ,,	...	...	3-16 in.
Distance between	...	...	$3\frac{3}{8}$ in.
Width, over buffer beams		...	$9\frac{1}{2}$ in.
Tender—			
Length of frames	...	...	$23\frac{1}{2}$ in.
,, of body	...	...	22 in.
Height ,,	...	...	$6\frac{1}{2}$ in.
Width (inside)	...	...	9 in.
Wheels—			
Coupled, diameter	...	...	6 in.
Bogie and tender	...	...	$3\frac{1}{4}$ in.

The loco will be driven by means of an electric motor placed in the boiler barrel. I hope to give some further particulars of this model in a later issue.

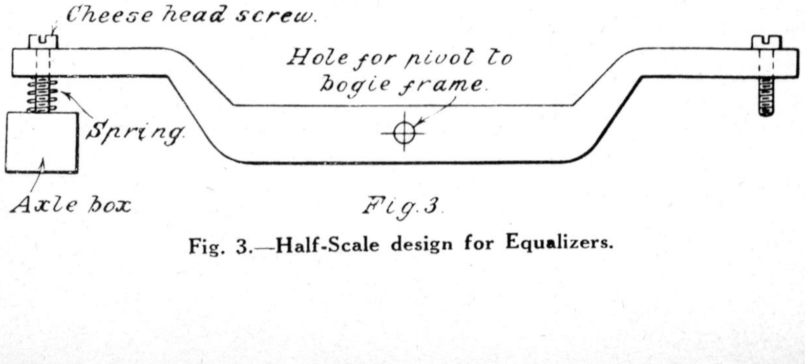

Fig. 3.—Half-Scale design for Equalizers.

A $1\frac{3}{4}$ in. Gauge Electric Locomotive.

By A. W. Line.

THERE is here presented a brief description of the writer's $1\frac{3}{4}$-in. gauge electric locomotive, which has been on exhibit, together with a 10-car freight train, in the New York Central Railroad's Transportation Exhibit, at the Grand Central Terminal, New York, for over a year.

The locomotive was first built 12 years ago but has been rebuilt and overhauled, also painted and lettered several times. Space will not permit an account of the various changes in design and the improvements which have been made. Of the original form only the axles, main axle boxes and frames, the motor and some of the gear wheels remain. The cab, roof, equalizing gear and pony trucks have been entirely rebuilt, the gear ratio changed and all wheels renewed. The locomotive was originally built to carefully designed drawings, but all changes were made to detail drawings and no drawings have been made as it exists to-day.

The model is built to $1\frac{3}{4}$-in. gauge, $\frac{3}{8}$-in. scale North American clearance limits and is of free-lance design though moulded somewhat on the lines of the Boston and Maine Railroad "5000" class electric locomotives operating through the Hoosac Tunnel. The truck frames and crossties are cut from hard sheet brass and the main axle boxes are white-metal castings. The driving wheels are turned from hard close-grained cast iron and the pony wheels are turned from mild steel bar. The pony truck frames are of hard sheet brass, the axle boxes are brass castings and the wood bumper beam is attached directly to the pony truck frame instead of to the main truck frames on account of the sharp curvature. The pony truck also carries the couplers and safety chains, the footboards and flag sockets. All flanges are of scale width and slightly over scale depth. The helical springs shown on main trucks are too stiff to function and are considered as dummies, but perfect flexibility is provided by equalizers, which are pivoted under concealed knife edges at their centres. The pony trucks have no springs on axle boxes nor any guiding springs, but a portion of the weight of the cab and main frames is transmitted to them through centrally located leaf springs, thus giving great flexibility. The locomotive has excellent riding qualities, and although the flanges are very small for this gauge track, derailments were very infrequent even over rough track on curves and at high speed.

The cab is made of heavy tinned sheet iron applied to a bar brass frame. However, hard sheet brass is a better material for metal cabs.

The driving wheels are 1 5-16th in. and the pony wheels are $\frac{7}{8}$ in. diameter. The wheel bases are: pony to front driver, 2 in.; between drivers, $2\frac{1}{4}$ in.; pony to second driver, $4\frac{1}{4}$ in.; total wheel base, 11 in.

Power is derived from a single Westinghouse 8-in. fan motor wound to run on 50-cycle current, but it also operates on 25 and 60 cycles and on direct current. On 60-cycle current the power is slightly less, but on 25 cycles the power is considerably more, while on direct current a great increase of power is obtained.

The motor is mounted above the frame of one truck and occupies one end of the cab, the remainder of the cab containing three-speed rheostat, reverser and wiring for the motor, headlights, cab-light and four corner lights used as classification or tail lights as required. The motor shaft is at right angles to the axles and drives a countershaft through four-to-one ratio, 32-pitch bronze bevel gears. This shaft, in turn, is connected to the second driving axle through a two-to-one ratio ladder-chain reduction gearing, the countershaft carrying a 10-tooth sprocket and the driving axle having a 20-tooth sprocket. Each driving axle carries a 32-pitch, 36-tooth bronze spur gear and the two axles are connected through a similar gear on an intermediate jack-shaft between the wheels and inside the truck frames. The gear ratio of motor shaft to driving axle is eight to one. The other truck, while provided with current collectors, is at present only a carrying truck, but later on will be geared to the motor in order to give more adhesion.

The current collectors, four in number, are of the third-rail over-running type. In the centre of each side frame is mounted a metal-faced fibre insulating block. The collector gear is attached to these blocks, the brackets being milled and filed from solid steel. The holes for the attaching screws are slotted to allow for vertical adjustment of the shoes to exact level

Mr. Line's $1\frac{3}{4}$ in. gauge Electric Locomotive.

of the third rail. A coiled spring on the hinge pin presses the shoes down on the conductor rail. When not in use and folded back the shoes are kept up by a catch made of watch spring. The shoes are of steel to resist shock and wear, and the whole collector gear is modelled after those in general use.

A pantagraph collector will be added later on.

The motor develops ample power for the $1\frac{3}{4}$-in. gauge, and the locomotive really requires more drivers and more weight to utilize it fully. Enough cars to load to full capacity were never available, but 12 eight-wheel cars loaded to represent 20 cars is a fair load with the present four drivers. With eight wheels geared to the motor and using direct current, the estimated load is about 40 cars.

Lack of space prevents mention of further details, but interested readers are referred to American Modelmakers' News-letter No. 20, appearing in *Everyday Science and Models* of October, 1922, where views of the top of the locomotive and the trucks are shown, and results of electrical and hauling tests are given. Also a full-page illustration of the locomotive is given in the July, 1922, issue of *Everyday Science*.

Model Connel-Type Cantilever Bridge.

By. H. Greenly.

AMONG the many girder - type railway bridges that are really imposing, as well as novel in their construction, the Connel Bridge, near Oban, on the Caledonian section of the West Coast group of lines, is a noteworthy example. This structure has long been a favourite of mine and, while I am surprised that it has not been modelled more frequently, I have to plead guilty to never having made a drawing of a cantilever bridge of this kind.

The Connel bridge is claimed to be the second longest single-span railway bridge in Europe, the clear length being 600 ft. As most readers know, the cantilever principle is used to reduce the length of the centre portion of a girder bridge. The overhanging cantilevers virtually throw out the abutments and, to fill the gap in between, a relatively short centre girder is then required.

As it is impracticable on the average model railway to build a model of so large a bridge exactly to scale—a structure such as the Connel Ferry bridge would be over 18 ft. in No. 0 gauge, without counting the stone arches leading to it—in preparing the accompanying sketches I have had to reduce very much the bridge in all dimensions except perhaps width, and have much simplified the construction. The details have been coarsened to make the job a less difficult one to the amateur model maker and to allow strip wood to be used throughout.

The side girders may be made in one piece, and I suggest the gig method described in my book "Model Railways." This part of the structure would be made on the flat, omitting the four main posts and the diagonal strut to the "stone" abutments. The lower horizontal member at the floor level would be a single member instead of a double one and the structure would then be completed when the girder is fastened to the $\frac{3}{8}$ in. × 3 11-16th floor board on which the track is laid. In laying the pieces in the gig the inside would be uppermost to allow for this system of construction. The main posts are inclined forward at the top and outward at the base, and to make a satisfactory top joint at the

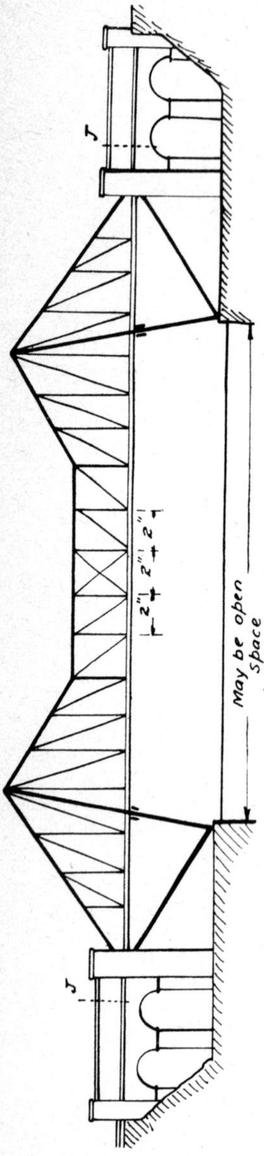

Fig. 1.—Diagram of the complete model Cantilever Bridge.

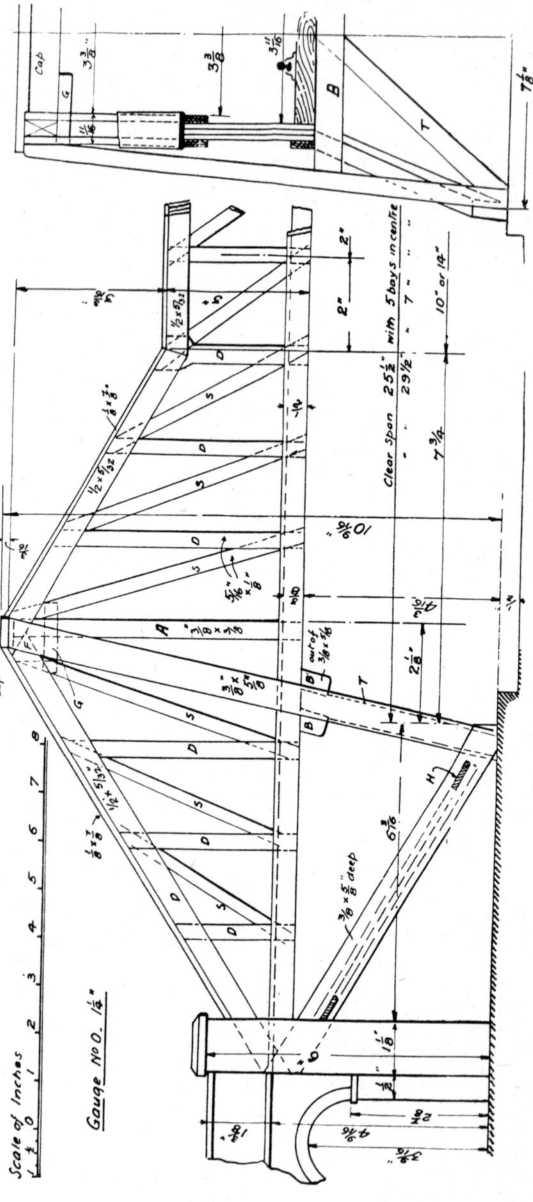

Fig. 2.—General constructional details.

top of the cantilever the side members are first tacked to the $\frac{3}{8}$ in. × $\frac{3}{8}$ in. post (A) which has a filling up or packing block about $\frac{1}{2}$ in. wide fixed to it. A block (G) out of 5-16-in. wood, is fitted inside each girder. This is shown with a plain face but actually it will have to be notched to suit the various members against which it abuts. The two-piece cross cap is then used to joint the two side girders and the pieces G together. The main post is fixed on outside and, by using long fine screws right through into G and the cap, a firm connection should be established. There are, of course, many other methods of connecting the two cantilever girders at the top, and a metal connection, including some long stay bolts made of $\frac{1}{8}$-in. wire, would make a good tie. The introduction of such fittings into the construction will depend on the completeness of the maker's metal-working tools.

The main posts are tied to the underside of the floor by the beams B B, between which are fitted the struts T, which run from the base of the posts to the centre of the floor, as shown in the end view. The main diagonal member may be cross braced more or less for a matter of appearance and fidelity to the original, by strips in the form of an X, which are let into diagonals at H.

With reference to the centre span, this may be made with five or seven bays. An odd number is necessary, as the bracing in the centre bay should be in the form of a cross.

Making the abutment arches is a simple matter, and methods are fully described in the aforementioned book. The floor boards should be extended to carry this part of the bridge, but if the structure is to be made in such a way as it can be lifted out of its setting, the jointing up with the permanent part of the line may be made just above the second arch, the side walls of the abutment arches (*see* J, Fig. 1) being fixed to the substructure of the railway. The Connel bridge has three arches at each end, but I have only suggested the use of two.

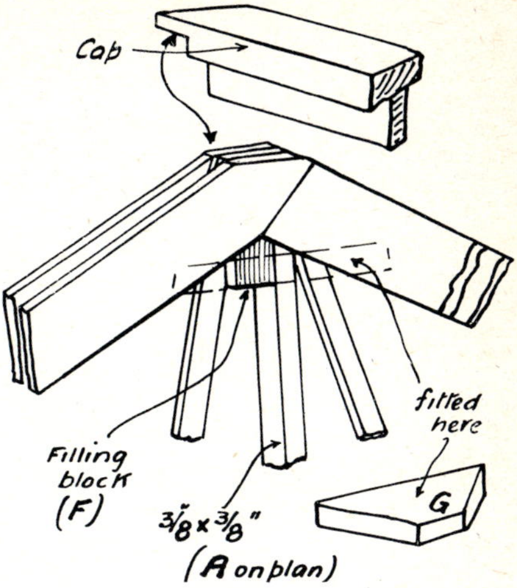

Fig. 3.

Construction of cross-cap joint.

The bracing members marked S and D in Fig. 2 are respectively single and double strips of 5-16th in. × $\frac{1}{8}$ in. wood.

Point Levers

We have received a sample of a point lever for 0 gauge systems from the Miniature Reproductions Co., 21, Industry Road, Darnall, Sheffield. It is of neat design, effectively painted in vermillion and black, and works well. It is of the weighted-arm type, the throwing over of the arm operating a bell-crank plate pivoted in the base. It locks positively in both directions. The price is 1*s*. 9*d*. each, plus postage.

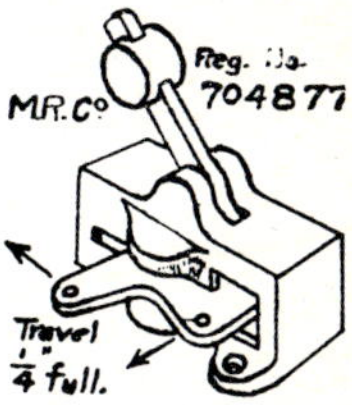

Kenneth Manhive, of 7, Lorrimore Road, Walworth, S.E.17, wishes to form a Model Railway Club for juniors. He would like to hear from other readers who are interested.

Queries and Replies.

F. J. A. (Cardiff) wishes us to criticise a draft model railway plan he sends, and to suggest which gauge, No. 0 or 1, he should adopt.

As a general idea for a *system* in a space of the shape shown in your sketch, your scheme is excellent. There are possibilities in it. From the main terminal stations, A and B, point-to-point working could be arranged. The station, J, could be an important junction, with a branch line to R, from which place direct trains or connections could be made to either A or B. The station, W, may be a minor wayside station with a junction signal box. A goods depot and loco shed might be arranged at B, as we have added to your plan. However, the size of the available space (6 ft. × 10 ft. 6 in.) will preclude anything larger than a No. 00 gauge line. There would not be room enough for a sufficient length of platform in No. 0 gauge, while the No. 1 gauge plan is almost impossible, even if desirable station dimensions were disregarded altogether. For instance, the branch line from J to R would have to be all platform to accommodate an engine and one coach. A three-coach train would be in both J and R at the same time.

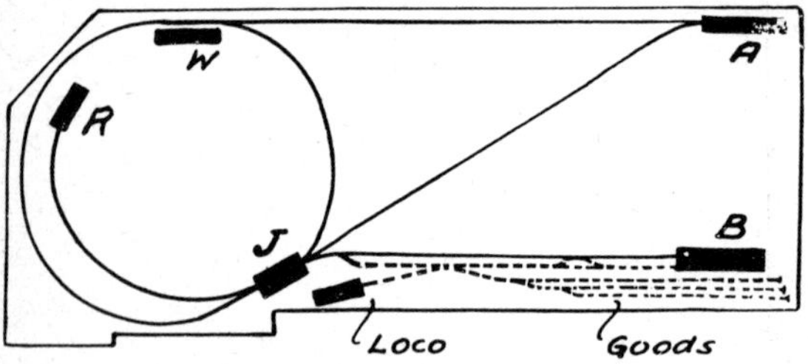

F. J. A's. Model Railway Plan.

We do not know of the existence of a model railway club or society in Cardiff, but at one time, within recent years, there was some activity in the hobby among members of the local Y.M.C.A.

L. S. (Nottingham) writes :—" I have a model clockwork locomotive which slips badly, even when running down hill. I have tried powdered resin on the rails, but this is only a temporary cure.

The model locomotive evidently has a motor which is geared for an express engine with a large diameter of driving wheel, and is provided with a small diameter wheel. This would increase the tractive effort for a given weight on the driving wheels. Also, the superstructure being too light for the tractive effort, the present arrangement of the spring and wheels provide, if you wish to use that effort—with 1 in 40 grades it is advisable—you can weight the superstructure until slipping is overcome. However, as you give us not the slightest information as to its type and its construction (not even the gauge) we cannot advise in definite terms. We presume it has at least four coupled wheels. If it is one of the cheaper models obtainable in which the wheels are not coupled, and at least half the weight is on the idle wheels, the slipping trouble with a powerful motor is more or less inevitable.

G. E. F. (Gillingham) writes :—" I am constructing a four-coach train and intend to illuminate it by small bulbs from pocket lamps, carrying the batteries in clips in place of the usual gas cylinders."

Yes, it is possible to light successfully a coach with the separate cells of pocket torch batteries. The full candle power of a 4·5 lamp is not necessary in a small coach and, as you suggest, you could take a pocket battery to pieces and clip the cells to the underside of the wooden underframe of the model carriage. Connecting the two cells in series you would obtain a voltage of only two-thirds that of the complete battery. The power of the light will be lessened, if the standard 4·5 volt bulb is employed, in a rather greater proportion but the illumination should be ample. The clips can be arranged to provide for almost instantaneous renewal. With reference to the lamps, of course only one bulb can be used, unless, of course, several lower voltage and lower candle-power lamps are employed, connected in series. However, it is worth while experimenting with the reflecting-lamp scheme. In this one light only is used, and by a system of mirrors the effect of several lights is produced. Such an arrangement of mirrors could be concealed in a double roof.

T. B. R. (Charterhouse) writes, enclosing a station plan for criticism and a suggestion for avoiding the double (scissors) crossover. He also asks what is the best conductor rail scheme for a short length of outdoor track.

Generally the plan is good as long as you can find room for the engine shed standing at right angles to the main line. In some sites it might be better to arrange the shed in a parallel position, as shewn by the separate sketch, Fig. 2. With regard to the double crossover, this is a most useful arrangement, and we hardly see how you can leave it out without lessening the efficiency of the plan.

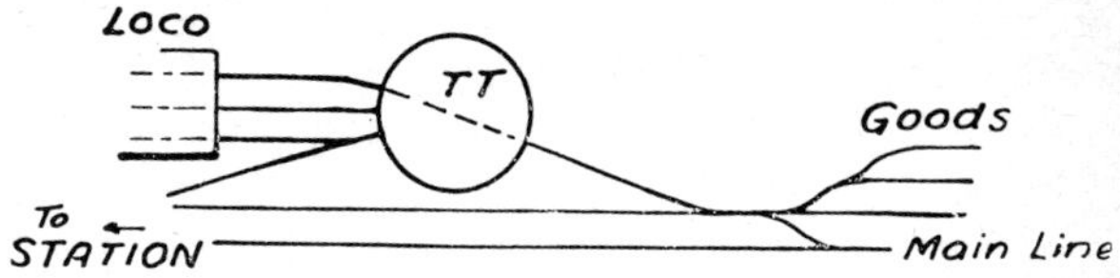

Fig. 2.—Alternative arrangement of engine-shed roads.

The carriage-siding points could be made as a slip point from a crossover, running across the reception road, as shown in Fig. 3.

For outdoor electric lines, there is no manufactured accessory which would provide a first-class means of insulating the third rail. Using brass rail and making special ebonite blocks (chairs) is the most satisfactory solution, but it involves a considerable amount of labour. These chairs could be placed at intervals of 6 in., say, at every fourth sleeper. You can, of course, use strip screwed down to

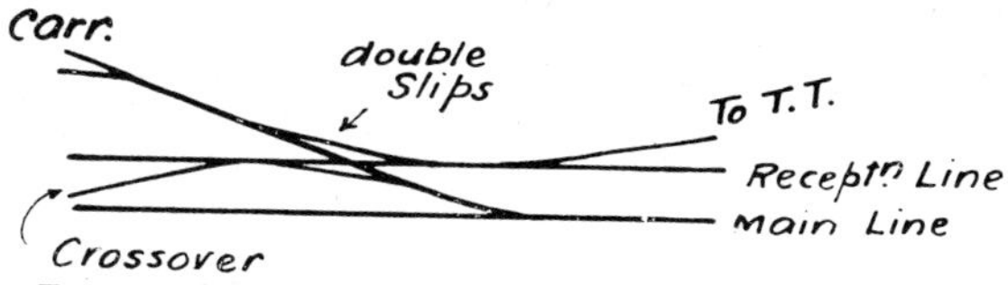

Fig 3.—Using a double slip point and crossover instead of scissors crossover.

ebonite or wood blocks. This is the next best scheme for outdoor work. Possibly some of our readers have ideas on the subject which they have tried out and in that case it would be very interesting to hear from them, and to pool the various experiences.

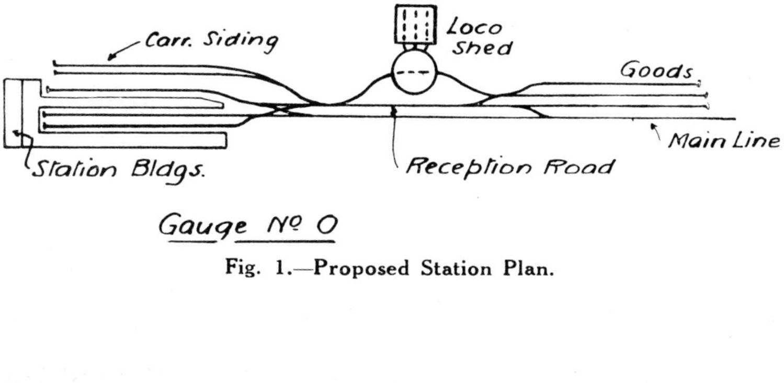

Fig. 1.—Proposed Station Plan.

OUR MAIL BAG

Grouping.

To the Editor, MODEL RAILWAY NEWS.

SIR,

For over five years I have waited for the MODEL RAILWAY NEWS, ever since the *Models, Railways and Locos* faded into another paper. I think the need for it really exists, and much entertainment can be derived from a model railway, it being a continuous hobby, in that however complete the model may be, something else can be added, and doing it forms an interesting pastime. Model railways are all the time as one complete whole, where the beginner, relatively speaking, is soon on a level with older modellists. Thus any part of the subject can be dealt with to the interest of all, as no elementary section is needed to divide one person from another.

I am very pleased to note a page (158) devoted to the group railways and locos. Perhaps this page can be continued, as descriptions or views of various locos, bridges, railway junctions, etc., might assist some model builders. Possibly, readers could help by taking photos of railway scenes worth sending in.

The MODEL RAILWAY NEWS offers a varied and interesting menu to all, thus giving the feeling that it represents readers' points of view, and not just written by any one party to air his own views only.

Should the grouping affect models at all? Some may still desire to retain one of the out-of-date companies, whilst others will preserve their own private colourings and titles. But modern progress still goes forward on the railways, and a "grouped" model to remain up to date, will eventually add "group" stock.

I remain,

Yours faithfully,

A. PEACOCK.

Birmingham.

A Timber Bridge.

To the Editor, MODEL RAILWAY NEWS.

DEAR SIR,

Allow me to congratulate you on the publication of our paper, and I hope it will be the great success you hope. I noted in the March number an article on model station overbridges and as there is at Newton Heath (formerly L. & Y. Ry.) station, a bridge entirely built of timber, I took the trouble to go and get a photograph which I trust will be of use to some model engineers.

Wishing you all the success possible.

Yours faithfully,

Manchester. GEO. W. SMITH.

Timber Bridge at Newton Heath.

The Selborne Model Railway.

To the Editor, Model Railway News.

Dear Sir,

Many old readers of *Models, Railways and Locomotives* will remember my notes and photographs describing the above model railway when situated at Keighley (Yorks).

This railway was packed away for removal in 1918 and is now just being unpacked and re-erected.

Unfortunately, the space now available is much more limited than on the former site and, in addition, the writer has much less leisure than formerly. Progress will, therefore, be very slow, but reports and photographs will be sent in from time to time as the new line takes shape.

My new address is "Kynance," Rhuddlan Road, Rhyl, North Wales, where "model railwayites" are welcome to call, but it will be some time yet before anything of interest will be on view.

If Mr. W. R. S. Smart, whom I have had the pleasure of visiting in London on three or four occasions, cares to write to me, I should be delighted to hear from him.

Yours truly,

J. C. Robinson.

"The Other Fellow."

To the Editor Model Railway News.

Dear Sir,

A reader of your excellent journal, also of the M.E. since its commencement, I note you ask for readers' views as to what subject is of most interest. Personally, I like to read about "the other fellow's" equipment and see views of what is being done by those who are going in for track work with correct signalling and points, etc.

I should like to mention the very kind assistance I have received from Mr. Crebbin, Mr. Greenly, "L. B. S. C.," and others, who have written letters from time to time on injectors, valve setting and other details connected with operating ½-in. scale spirit and coal-fired locomotives.

I am, Yours faithfully,

Louth. Samuel H. Boswell.

"00" Gauge.

To the Editor, Model Railway News.

Dear Sir,

After reading all the articles appearing in your columns about 00 gauge, I take the liberty to give you my idea about it.

The 00 gauge, equal to 16·5 mm. at the rate of 3·5 mm. per foot, makes 16·5 divided by 3·5 = 4·6 ft. or 4 ft. 8 in. If then the gauge of rail is reduced at the rate of 3·5 mm. to the foot, I find it absurd to make the rest to 4-mm. scale. It becomes then just like the Ravenglass and Eskdale Railway engine, River Esk, 2—8—2 type, which is 4 in. to the foot model upon 3 in. to the foot gauge. This is no more scale model of British engines; it becomes American loading gauge with British practice.

Mr. H. Greenly, whom I only know through the articles from him appearing in the *Model Engineer* and Model Railway News, is absolutely mistaken about the diameter of driving wheels. In his 4—4—0 model 4 mm. to the foot, described in April's issue, driving wheels are 24 mm. diameter. This is the size of a 6 ft. 8 in. express engine, reduced to a scale of 3½ mm. to the foot, and only a 6-ft. driving wheel, reduced at a scale of 4 mm. to the foot. A 6-ft. wheel is rather a wheel for a mixed-traffiic engine, since it is nearer 5 ft. 8 in. than 6 ft. 8 in. Thus this should be my idea about driving wheels for 3½-m/m. model:—

6 ft. 8 in. = 24 mm.; 5 ft. 8 in. = 20 mm.; 4 ft. 8 in. = 17 mm.

If I give you my idea about 3½-m/m scale it is on account of the interest in this scale, and also in the hope it should help to bring all those interested in this scale to adopt the 3½ mm., which is the only pure scale.

With many congratulations for the Model Railway News, which is come to fulfil a hole for model railwayists.

Believe me, dear Sir,

Faithfully yours,

Joseph de Volder.

Morhée, Orne, France.

Chester Station, on Mr. F. W. Shaw's line.

Mr. Shaw's "0" Gauge Railway.

To the Editor, MODEL RAILWAY NEWS.

DEAR SIR,

I have pleasure in enclosing some photos of my line, which give a much better idea of the railway as it now is than those which you published in the March issue of MODEL RAILWAY NEWS.

So far, no reference has been made in the magazine to the lines of Messrs. Robinson, W. R. S. Smart, the King Brothers, of "Muddle Puddle" fame, Jubb, or any others of the star turns of the late *Models, Railways, and Locomotives*.

I hope you have some news of these very interesting model railways to tell us sooner or later.

Crewe, from the South.

Crewe, from the North.

With best wishes for continued success of MODEL RAILWAY NEWS.

Yours faithfully,

F. W. S. SHAW.

Birkenhead.

Rails for Electrical Control.

To the Editor, MODEL RAILWAY NEWS.

DEAR SIR,

I note that in your May issue, page 152, in replying to C. F. P., Yorkshire, you say that no difficulty will arise due to the lower conductivity of steel if steel rails are used instead of brass rails for a model electric railway.

From practical experience, I find that in the actual performance of model electric locomotives, using low voltage current, there is a marked difference in running on brass and steel track.

A case which I have in mind was in connection with an oval track of 63 feet total length, of which the outer lengths were laid with mild steel, tin-coated rails, supplied by the L.M.C. which, as your readers know, are of ample section, the centre rail being of brass. It was found on this track that electric locomotives slowed down very considerably at points far from the main supply. This trouble was, however, cured by running copper cable track feeders to various points.

Subsequently the track was relaid with all brass rails and with no auxiliary feeders, when it was found that the locos ran perfectly round the whole oval, there being no drop of speed or power noticeable at points far from the switch.

I do not maintain that the area of the steel rails was not equal, theoretically, to carrying low voltage currents over a considerable distance without any drop of voltage, but I do say that in practice a difference is noticeable, and I suggest that this may be largely due to the comparative difficulty of making the steel joints perfect from an electrical point of view, without the trouble of bonding.

In reference to dirt on the rails, to which you also refer, it is, of course, obvious that a certain amount always collects on either steel or brass rails. A good method of removing this is by rubbing with a rag, with metal polish. The use of sand paper or emery cloth should not be encouraged, as unless these are very fine, they scratch the rail surface, and in the case of tin-coated steel rails, the coating will in time be removed.

Yours faithfully,

Leeds. REX F. STEDMAN.

"0" Gauge Track.

To the Editor, MODEL RAILWAY NEWS.

DEAR SIR,

After reading Mr. Winteringham's articles on 0 gauge track, I have been wondering how a small type of H section drawn brass would do for track, instead of $\frac{1}{8}$ in. × 1-16th in. which he suggests. The "L.M.C." supply T section, $\frac{1}{8}$ in. × $\frac{1}{8}$ in. outside of 20 S.W.G., but I have not come across any H section so small. For this type of track, it might be possible, even, to cast slide-on chairs. My suggestion for the rail would be as in the diagram :—

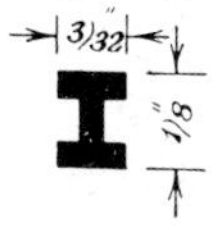

This would be in 20 S.W.G., making the centre portion of the H 3-56th × 1-28th in. approximately. I think this would be an improvement, and a firm making this would probably have some demand for it for bridge-building purposes, as well.

Yours,

Streatham. H. L. P.

A South African Model Railway.

To the Editor, MODEL RAILWAY NEWS.

DEAR SIR,

The M. R. NEWS has come as a very useful friend to us isolated model railway enthusiasts. I only hope it gets the full support it deserves.

About 21 months ago I started on a No. 1 gauge line. A friend suggested making the rails locally. To this end we finally decided on the type illustrated in Fig. 1. These are made from 2 ft. 6 in. by 1 in. strips of 22 s.w. gauge plate, bent in a machine in the Carbide Works drum shop. There are five sleepers per length, and when fixed are very firm. The fishplate is a piece of similar material pushed in the grooves and squeezed tight with pliers. It rests on a sleeper in each section of rail.

After experiments with a Bassett-Lowke 0—4—0 steam-tank loco and then a clockwork one of the same type, both for 1 gauge, I decided to try the 0 gauge, and relaid all my line. I

Goods Train crossing a bridge on Mr. Roberts' Railway.

find this quite satisfactory out of doors.

The present layout is about 100 feet long and has two intermediate stations. The terminal stations have not yet been put down. An additional 50 ft. of track will be laid to connect them. The present layout is something like Fig. 2.

Following the South African practice, my line is single-line tablet working. The weather out here is not bad for very many days at a stretch and I find the out-of-doors line much more realistic. Dust is the only drawback, and it can be cleaned from locos without much effort. A loco does not look so spick and span returning to its depot as when it left, which in this country, with dust-storms, etc., is more like the real thing. The yard has a gentle slope, hence all the bridges over drains to lead off storm water into a neighbouring field. Through lack of these bridges and drains I had several wash-aways in the early days.

The points used are tinplate, and for out-of-door lines do not work satisfactorily. (I shall get the scale model type in future.) They are laid in cement and painted with bitumen solution before being put in. The rails themselves are firmly laid in the earthworks. I laid a test section with

Fig. 1.—Rails.

ballast, but a heavy rain scatters it all over the place. I am thinking of mixing small broken stone with cement and making the ballast permanent.

Through the medium of the M.R. NEWS, I have discovered other model firms and have written them. Upon receipt of their lists I hope to be able to make a wider selection than hitherto and increase my locos and rolling stock as time goes on.

Yours faithfully,

NORMAN H. ROBERTS.

Natal, S. Africa.

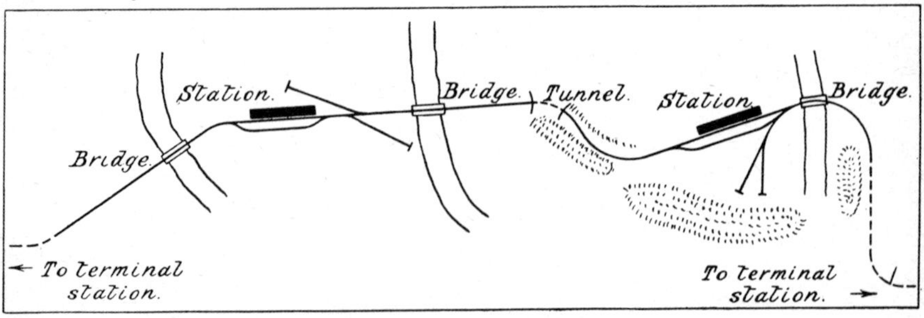

Fig. 2.—Lay-out of Mr. Roberts' line.

The want of Competition.

To the Editor, MODEL RAILWAY NEWS.

DEAR SIR,

Some time ago, in a letter to Mr. Greenly, I expressed the opinion that a periodical like *Models, Railways and Locomotives* was badly needed by the model railway world. I was delighted when I heard the news that the MODEL RAILWAY NEWS was to appear, and now having had six issues, permit me to say that it is filling the want nobly and adequately.

I should like to take this opportunity of thanking "Sparks" for his kind sympathy, which is deeply appreciated. I would like to congratulate "Sparks," as the G.W.R. is evidently "his" line, on the fact that that line, which I have always admired immensely, is less spoiled by grouping than any other; in fact, one may say it is the only one of our great companies which has been allowed to preserve its identity. So good luck to the G.W.R.! I may add that it is not only for sentimental reasons that I am against grouping. I cannot see, and have not yet found anyone to prove, that it has done any good at all to the public, companies, officials, or servants. Railwaymen are reticent about it, but one can sometimes worm out a candid opinion on this subject, and all that I have met preferred the old order. Taking the Stock Exchange quotations, the G.W.R. seems the most prosperous of all, so where is the much talked-of economy?

I have had several instances occurring to me personally lately, in connection with the carriage of parcels and goods, which point strongly to the conclusion that our railways are very far from being improved by this scheme, which appears to have been the fancy of some politician or politicians who wanted a new toy to play with. The abolition of competition has meant the abolition of the need or desire to give the public good service.

Yours faithfully,

HUGH SIMPSON.

Carlisle.

A Beginner's Lay-out.

To the Editor, MODEL RAILWAY NEWS.

DEAR SIR,

We are sending you a plan of our lay-out for our model railway, which we purpose to put further extensions to.

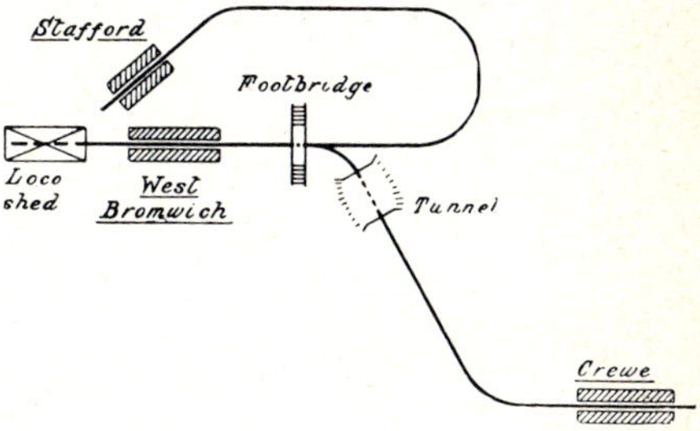

Messrs. Williamson's Layout.

Our room is $14\frac{1}{2} \times 13$ feet and, as you will see by diagram, we have three termini. We have, so far, one loco shed, three stations, which are Stafford, West Bromwich, and Crewe, one foot-bridge, which has signals attached to it, one tunnel, and trees. Each station is fitted with accessories, such as porters, chocolate and weighing machines, fire alarms and booking offices. We have also sacks and barrels for the goods trains, and gradient posts.

Our rolling stock numbers five, and we have one engine, but we intend to obtain another engine as soon as possible from the Clyde Model Dockyard, Argyll Arcade, Glasgow.

When further extensions are made we propose to make a junction at Crewe.

Yours truly,

SAM WILLIAMSON,

ALEX. WILLIAMSON.

Coatbridge.

Suggestions for Mr. Smith.

To the Editor, MODEL RAILWAY NEWS.

DEAR SIR,

I read with great interest the letter by Mr. H. Smith in the May issue of the M.R. NEWS. As one who also has "ploughed his lonely furrow," I shall be delighted to place my limited

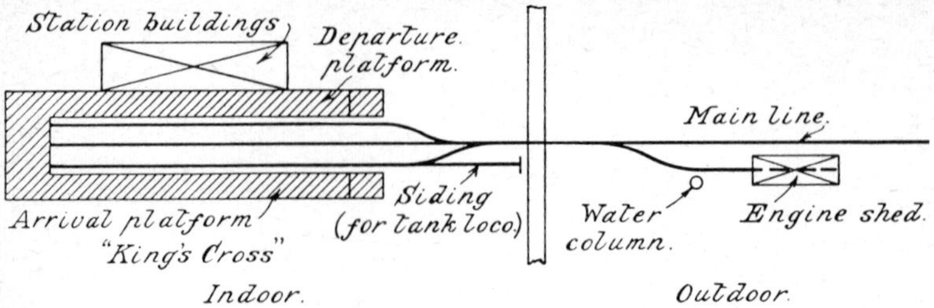

A suggested emendation for Mr. H. Smith's terminus.

experience at the disposal of your correspondent.

Taking into consideration the restricted track available at present, and having acquired some passenger rolling-stock, I would suggest that Mr. Smith gives up the idea of goods traffic meantime, and works out a fairly complete passenger-carrying system. I made the mistake of trying to run passenger and goods trains on a small line with separate sidings and stations; and the result was far from satisfactory. I submit a sketch for the terminal station which Mr. Smith may find more suitable than in its present form.

This plan provides for "arrival" and "departure" platforms, with centre siding for spare carriages. On the arrival of a train, the tank loco leaves its siding and, after the "passengers" have alighted, shunts the train on to the "departure" line—the loco returning to its siding. The G.N.R. engine now proceeds to the shed to take in water, and is ready to take the train out again. This, I believe, is in accordance with actual railway practice.

At the other end of the line I should suggest making a small country station and loop line. The same engine would then work the main-line trains between the two points—changing direction by means of the loop at "West Jesmond," and reversing at "King's Cross" with the assistance of the tank loco, as indicated.

A point frequently overlooked in the selection of rolling-stock is to have the carriages as nearly as possible of the same group or company as the locomotive. In this connection, Mr. Smith would possibly find the L.N.E.R. two or three-coach articulated set recently produced by the Leeds Model Co., Ltd., very serviceable. These would be in keeping with the G.N.R. loco, and possess the added merit of saving space.

I shall be interested to know how the railway progresses.

Yours faithfully,

T. A. FORSYTH.

Glasgow.

A Model Tank Loco.

To the Editor, MODEL RAILWAY NEWS,

DEAR SIR,

I have to congratulate MODEL RAILWAY NEWS on its successful start in life. I am enclosing herewith photograph of a 4—6—4 tank locomotive, half-inch scale, which may be of interest to your readers in view of the drawing of a 4—6—4 tank locomotive appearing in the June issue. There are no striking features of novelty about the locomotive shown in the photograph. It is a rebuilt Sir Sam Fay, adorned with some of Messrs. Bond's fittings. The conversion was made owing to the difficulty of maintaining a satisfactory joint in the flexible connections between the tender and the locomotive. This difficulty is now overcome in an obvious manner. The numeral on the side sheet of the tank is one of the brass numerals which adorned many of us during the war. These numerals are $\frac{3}{4}$ in. in height, and are very suitable for the purpose indicated, besides being cheap to purchase and usually of good finish. The boiler is of the water-tube type and is fired by a tandem torrid burner. I have been successful on short runs in getting the locomotive to haul on a ball-bearing driving wagon a load of 13½ stones. The valve gear is the standard Greenly motion; and what is perhaps peculiar is that the reversing lever may be "notched up" during the running, and the locomotive will proceed on its way in a satisfactory manner. I believe this is somewhat unique with regard to models.

The rebuilt Sir Sam Fay.

The model has now been disposed of to make way for a one-inch scale 0—4—0 locomotive of the type shown in the issue of the *Model Engineer* for December 22nd, 1910.

The auxiliary blower used for steam raising comprises a bent piece of copper tubing, one end of which is clamped to the blast pipe, and the other end of which terminates in the nozzle of a bicycle valve supported by the front buffer beam. The cap for the valve can be seen to the left-hand side of the front draw hook.

With every good wish for the continued success of M.R.N.

I am,
Yours faithfully,
J. H. H.

Winchmore Hill.

Cardboard and Model Railways.

To the Editor, MODEL RAILWAY NEWS.

DEAR SIR,

I note, on page 159 of the May issue, Mr. H. H. Hudson was down to lecture on the above subject, and I hope you will give us a good *resumé* of his lecture in "Ours."

I am reminded by the title that I would like to give a hint to some of my brother "Railwayacs," who may possibly never have thought of it, and that is, that very realistic models can be made, in cardboard, of locomotives, and, if carefully made to scale, can be placed around about the loco. shed, water column, coaling stage, etc., and give the appearance of a wealthy "Company." The only drawback is that the setting-out and drawing of the various parts take up some considerable time and patience: properly shaping chimney and dome being rather a tricky job. In pre-war days, I made up a G.N.R. Atlantic, an L.N.W. Precursor and a Precursor tank in gauge 1, and they were frequently taken, at a glance, for scale models in metal.

I seem to remember that some time ago a box was put up, at the price of 1*s*., a set of coloured designs in card of Johnson's Midland Single 4—2—2, with chimney, dome and safety-valve casing already made up in compo. and a length of bright steel wire for handrail, and when built up and varnished it looked all that could be desired. Unfortunately, however, it was not up to any model railway gauge. If some firm would take the matter up and produce some good coloured designs of some of the locos on our principal railways, with ready moulded dome, chimney and safety-valve in, say, 00, 0, and 1 gauges, they should take well with our fraternity. I have recently heard that a firm is about to exploit card-board designs for railway buildings and rolling stock, but whether they include locos, I am unable to say.

May I add, to this already rather long letter, a few words of protest against the designation of our younger generation of drivers as "mere regulator pushers" (page 135, *May* issue). I consider it a gross libel on a fine and intelligent body of men. I have travelled much, and I am positive that I am not exaggerating, when I say that the number of drivers on railways in England, Scotland, Ireland and South Africa, whom I have held in conversation, runs well into the thousands, and, with very few exceptions, I have found them to be highly intelligent men, well grounded in their craft, in very many cases well up in the properties and best uses of various metals—the advantages of super-heated steam—the relations between sizes of piston, stroke and wheels and their effects on draw-bar pull—simple *v.* compound—the merits and demerits of different valve-gears and a thousand and one other subjects; revealing the intelligent love of the man for his steed. There are, however, right and wrong ways of approaching a driver. Let me illustrate:—

A man standing on the departure platform in Glasgow Central station when one of McIntosh's splendid gee-gees backed on to a W.C.J.S. train watched the fireman coupling up three pipes and asked the driver what all those pipes were for. "Oh," said our friend the driver, "don't you know? Well, you see, having plenty of hot water at hand and nothing much to do on the road, we make tea, coffee and cocoa on the engine and pump it with this (pointing to the Westinghouse donkey) through those pipes to the restaurant car." The man walked slowly down the platform pondering on the wonders of modern inventions, whilst the driver mounted to the foot plate with his tongue in his cheek.

With all due respect for N. H. B. (Manchester), it is just possible that he asked for what he got.

With many thanks for your splendid successor to our old friend *Models, Railways and Locomotives.*

Yours truly,
E. J. L. B.

Coventry.

"Experientia Docet."

To the Editor, MODEL RAILWAY NEWS.

DEAR SIR,

We are venturing to send you a description of our railway, hoping it will be a help to beginners who have only limited space and means (as is the case with us) for their systems.

The plan is designed to facilitate long-distance runs in a small space. There is a double-line service between two termini, Robcombe (A) and Ralton (B), while large ovals enable long through runs. A local line runs from Robcombe up an incline to Mickdon (C), which is meant to represent a local terminus. (*See* plan.) Branching off from the top of the incline in Tunnelhill High Level station (D), is another line, passing the main line by a lift bridge (L.B.) (constructed from Meccano) and joining it near Squarelands station (E). A goods loop (L) is situated between the termini, with sidings (S). Carriage and engine sidings (C.S.) and (E S) are at Robcombe. This briefly is the plan of the lay-out.

The track is unfortunately laid on the floor, which makes "train-running" slightly inconvenient, but we have with moderate success run to a time-table. The track is unhappily laid in tinplate, as the cost of permanent way is prohibitive for the limited means of two schoolboys.

The locos are of a varied nature, representing the collection of several years. They are:—

One 4—4—0 (George V) L.N.W.R. loco for heavy expresses.

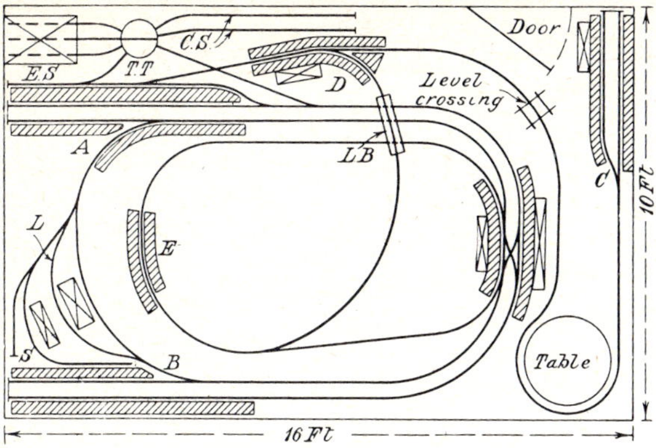

Plan for a limited space.

One 4—4—0 M.R. loco for lighter fast expresses.

Two 0—4—0 G.W.R. locos for "mixed traffic."

Two 0—4—0 shunting tank locos (used for local services).

One 0—4—0 shunting tank L.N.E.R. (used for pilot on incline).

The passenger coaches consist of a four-coach set of large four-wheeled bogie Midland coaches and guard's van; three smaller G.W. bogie coaches, and a home-made G.W. restaurant car, painted in the new colours three local G.W. coaches and guard's van.

There is a plentiful supply of goods rolling stock, including a M.R. high-capacity (home-made) truck on four-wheel bogies, and two brake vans. The signalling is not yet complete, but we hope to finish it shortly if funds will permit.

Yours truly,
R. R. Skelton.
R. M. C. Howard.
Paignton.

A Nigerian Story.

To the Editor, Model Railway News,

Dear Sir

Here is a photo of an excellent little model loco which may interest you.

It is a good many years ago since they were supplied, but none the less interesting.

They are a representative model of a type of mixed-traffic locomotive that we found most serviceable in Northern Nigeria, especially on the Baro-Kano section.

To propitiate one of the native chiefs, an Emir, it was decided to present a model of the engine, that would travel through his territory, together with a suitable circular track of rails where the engine could run in steam for his delight.

The presentation ceremony was a great palaver at which the Emir, with his head men, attended in state with their umbrellas. They sat in a circle round the track, and after the little models had completed a few circuits and they had appreciated the novelty, they danced around about in high glee.

Yours sincerely,
London. C. E. Williams.

This Model was presented to the Emir of Katsena.

The Winning Gauge '0' Lay-out Design.

By N. AXFORD.

THE principal feature of this design is that the main terminus is raised above an outer continuous main line and an inner loop.

It will be seen that trains can leave any platform of the terminus, descend the grade by the down track, to platform "C" of the passing station. Thence they proceed on to the outer of the three tracks on the left of the design, which, it will be seen, is a continuous track, level, and with a minimum radius of 3 ft. 6 in. Thus, high speeds may be obtained with as many times round as desired, each time passing through platform "D." The train is then diverted on to the middle track of the three on the left of the design, when it will traverse the loop, returning by the inner of the above three tracks, and can then either run through platform "B" and up the embankment to the terminus; or it can run into platform "A." In the latter case, when the train is due to return to the terminus, it leaves platform "A," traverses the loop in the opposite direction, and reaches the terminus through platform "B."

It should be noted that if only one operator is available, the cross-over at the left-hand end of platform "C" can be left set so that any train despatched from the terminus will then pass through platform "C" on to the continuous main line, through platform "D," on to the loop, and through platform "B" back to the terminus, a total run of 164 ft. (approximately).

Terminus.

Locos from the loco department can reach any road of the terminus and *vice versa*.

Goods trains are received and despatched from platform 1.

A run-round loop clear of the main lines is provided, so that trains can be marshalled, the loco run round, and the train backed into platform 1 ready for despatch.

The space "O" is provided so that easy access can be obtained to the window.

Passing Station.

This is intended to have the offices arranged on an overbridge, with stairs down to the platforms.

Goods trains shunt back on to road "E" and can then be marshalled clear of the main lines.

The provision of a cross-over as shown dotted at "S" would allow of the despatch of a train from the terminus direct round the loop and back, whilst another was circling the continuous track.

General.

The line is intended to be used with electrical control and, as trains proceed in one direction only on the outer continuous track, this is shown as fitted with automatic track-circuit signalling, which can be arranged to make the section ahead dead when the signal is on.

Signalling is fairly complete, but no distants have been shown.

No main-line curves are less than 3 ft. radius, and no sidings less than 2 ft. 6 in. radius.

The grade from the terminus commences at the signal gantry at the right-hand end of the station, and finishes at the left-hand end of platforms "B" and "C" giving a fall of 1 in 36. If this is thought too much, it could be halved by grading the continuous track and loop, instead of having them level.

Platforms may be thought too long, but I think you want room for at least four coaches and a loco for realism.

The controls would consist of an up and a down controller for the terminus, and three for the passing station; (*a*) continuous track and down main, (*b*) loop, (*c*) up main. Small sections normally dead, controlled by push buttons would be provided in the stations where necessary.

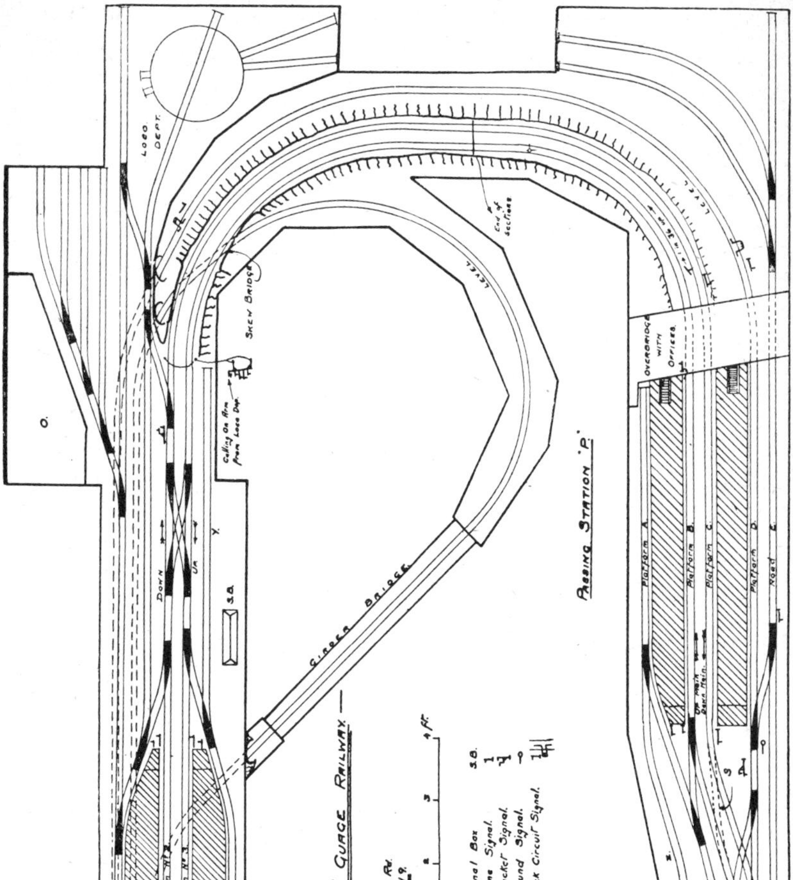

Mr. N. Axford's winning design in our Gauge "O" Track-Laying Competition.

(A sample time-table for use with this lay-out will be found on the next page.)

SAMPLE TIME TABLE FOR USE WITH DESIGN FOR GAUGE O RAILWAY

By N. Axford.

Station T.													
Platform 1	dep.	—	9.00	—	—	—	—	9.17	—	—	—	—	—
,, 2	,,	—	—	—	—	9.09	—	—	—	—	9.22	—	—
,, 3	,,	—	—	—	—	—	—	—	—	—	—	—	9.31
,, 4	,,	—	—	9.04	—	—	9.12	—	—	9.20	—	—	—
Station P.													
Platform C	,,	—	pass	pass	—	pass	9.13	pass	—	9.21	pass	—	pass
,, D	arr.	—	9.03	9.05	—	—	—	9.19	—	—	—	—	—
	dep.	—	shunt to	9.08	—	pass	9.14	shunt to	—	9.22	pass	—	pass
,, E	arr.	—	9.04	—	—	—	—	9.20	—	—	—	—	—
	dep.	—	stop	—	9.07	—	—	stop	—	—	—	9.30	—
,, A	arr.	—	—	9.09	—	—	—	—	—	9.23	—	—	—
	dep.	9.01	—	stop	—	—	—	—	9.18	stop	—	—	—
,, B	arr.	9.02	—	—	pass	pass	—	—	pass	—	9.24	pass	pass
	dep.	9.04	—	—	—	—	9.15	—	—	—	9.25	—	—
Station T.													
Platform 1	arr.	—	—	—	9.08	—	—	—	—	—	—	9.32	9.33
,, 2	,,	—	—	—	—	—	—	—	9.19	—	—	—	—
,, 3	,,	—	—	—	—	9.11	—	—	—	—	—	—	—
,, 4	,,	9.05	—	—	—	—	9.16	—	—	—	9.26	—	—
Train description		Local	Goods	Fast	Goods	Exp.	Local	Goods	Fast	Local	Fast	Goods	Exp.

Position at start. Local in platform A (motor train, no loco). Loco on siding Z. Goods in platform 1 with loco. Express in platform 2 without loco. Express loco on turntable. Fast in platform 4 with loco.

RUNNING ARRANGEMENTS FOR USE WITH TIME TABLE.

Terminus "T."

9.00 Despatch goods from No. 1.
9.01 Loco from turntable to No. 2.
9.04 Despatch fast from No. 4.
9.05 Receive local in No. 4.
9.08 Receive goods in No. 1.
9.09 Despatch express from No. 2.
9.11 Receive express in No. 3.
9.12 Despatch local from No. 4.
9.13–9.15 Goods shunting.
9.16 Receive local in No. 4.
9.17 Despatch goods from No. 1.
9.18 Loco from No. 3 to turntable.
9.19 Receive fast in No. 2.
9.20 Despatch local from No. 4.
9.21 Loco from turntable to No. 2.
9.22 Despatch fast from No. 2.
9.23 Loco from No. 2 to turntable and back to No. 3.
9.25 Receive fast in No. 4.
9.31 Despatch express from No. 3.
9.32 Receive goods in No. 1.
9.33 Receive express in No. 2.

Follow with necessary shunting to attain first starting positions of trains.

Passing Station "P."

9.00 Pass goods through C.
9.01 Despatch local from A round loop.
9.02 Local from loop in B.
9.03 Receive goods in D, shunt back to E.
9.04 Despatch local from B to terminus.
9.05 Fast through C round main to D.
9.07 Goods from E, round loop through B to terminus.
9.08 Fast from D round loop to A.
9.09 Express C to main, through D to loop, through B to terminus.
9.11 Loco from Z to A.
9.13 Receive local in C and despatch round main.
9.14 Local in D and despatch round loop
9.15 Local in B and despatch to terminus.
9.18 Despatch fast from A round loop through B to terminus.
9.19 Goods through C round main to D.
9.20 Shunt goods back to E, and loco from A to Z.
9.21 Local in C, despatch round main.
9.22 Local in D, despatch round loop.
9.23 Local in B, despatch to terminus.
9.24 Fast through C, D and to B.
9.25 Fast from B to terminus.
9 25–9.29 Goods shunts.
9.30 Despatch goods from E, round loop through B to terminus.
9.32 Express through C, D and B to terminus.

The MODEL RAILWAY NEWS

Editorial and Publishing Offices :

66, FARRINGDON STREET, LONDON, E.C. 4.

Single Copies, post free, 7½d. Annual Subscription, 7s. 6d.

Vol. I. No. 8. AUGUST, 1925. Price, 6d.

Notes of the Month.

THE appearance of Capt. J. E. P. Howey's "Green Goddess" 15-in. gauge L.N.E.R. type "Pacific" locomotive at Eskdale created quite a stir last month. By the kind permission of Sir Aubrey Brocklebank, Bt. who controls the R. & E. Railway, the owner of the new engine was allowed to use the line after the last 6.30 p.m. train, and the light nights of the North allowed running until midnight during the 14 days this engine was at Eskdale.

Both owner and designer must congratulate the builders, Messrs. Davey, Paxman, Ltd., of Colchester, on the excellence of the job as a whole. The engine ran perfectly, starting work the same day as it was unloaded from the trucks. Although not "all out," a speed of 35 miles an hour was obtained with an ordinary train. On test loads, 33 empty coaches were hauled without the least difficulty, and a 34-ton stone train was negotiated with only one stop. The Eskdale railway is an exceptionally difficult line, for a strange driver more particularly, but Capt. Howey handled the engine with exceptional skill and judgment.

As the technical details of this engine worthy of note are so numerous, it is proposed to deal with the various novelties and improvements involved in the design in the *Model Engineer* in due course. The second engine is nearing completion at Colchester, where any reader interested may see both of them by arrangement with Mr. Greenly and Messrs. Davey, Paxman, Ltd. The satisfactory results obtained with piston valves with a long stroke and Walschaerts valve gear will undoubtedly make this combination of mechanisms standard for new 15-in. gauge engines. The only thing yet to be discussed is the rival merits of Mr. H. Greenly's simple vacuum brake and the straight-line Westinghouse brake.

* * *

We have received the first number of the Wimbledon Model Railway Club's new official journal "Railway Pie," obtainable from the Secretary at 4½*d.*, post free. It is a most enterprising production, and, though it modestly aims only at interesting the members of its own club, actually it succeeds in providing interesting reading for any model railway enthusiast. Among other items, we liked particularly the very sensible (and badly needed) warnings in "Don't," and the interesting notes on cardboard modelling. Altogether, the Club are to be congratulated on their journal—good luck to it !

Capt. J. E. P. Howey's 15 in. Gauge Pacific "Green Goddess" on Trials at Eskdale.

Cardiff Model Railway Club.

Mr. H. R. Evans writes:—

"I would be infinitely obliged if you could find space for this letter in your splendid successor to our old friend 'Models, Railways and Locomotives.'

Sir Berkeley Sheffield taking a curve.

My object in seeking your assistance is to form a Model Railway Club for Cardiff; something which I feel certain is needed here.

If there are any of your readers who are interested will they please write to me at my address: Cold Maur, Lake Road East, Cardiff?

In my humble opinion there are not enough of these clubs, and it would be a good thing for us enthusiasts if there were more.

Thanking you for your patience, and with all the best wishes for the success of our new friend — The Model Railway News."

(Cardiff readers, please note and respond. Ed.)

NOTABLE MODEL RAILWAYS

The Normanby Park Railway.

JUST outside the delightful park at Normanby, the residence of Sir Berkeley Sheffield, Bart., is the nucleus of a 1 in. to the foot scale model railway, photographs of which we are able to reproduce herewith.

The hub of the system is a picturesque red-roofed building which serves as loco and carriage sheds, fuel stores, etc., and for convenience the line within is raised about one foot above the ground level. Leading out of this building a single line runs very shortly to a turntable, the diameter of which—about six feet—is capable of accommodating any of the present " stud " of locos. The turntable connects to the main line by way of a pair of points.

Full use of nature's water supply has been made by erecting adjacent to one side of the engine house a water tower. This fills automatically from the roof of the house, the rain-water being led down underground and up again into the tower. Along the length of the " sheds " the main line is raised above the ground level on trestle supports, this being a more comfortable height for filling up the tender, preliminary coaling up and generally looking round the engine. Two benches form a platform from which the driver can mount the tender and the passengers mount the vehicles. The main line is 420 ft. long and has its terminus near a by-road on the estate in a cutting about three feet

Full speed along the embankment. Miss D. Sheffield driving.

Leaving the shed, the G.N.R. in steam, and the G.W.R. "Great Bear" steam raising.

deep. In one direction the line runs over grass land for some little distance and finishes on a bank about five feet high. From here it is intended to make extensions in the near future, and plans are now being considered.

There are three locomotives in use, 1 in. scale, supplied by Messrs. Bassett-Lowke, Ltd.

No. 1 is a model of the old L.N.W.R. "Precursor" 4 ft. 8 in. over-all with two cylinders and Joy's valve gear; all the usual fittings, including one injector and one mechanical pump worked from the axle.

No. 2 is a nondescript type, 4—6—2, but has the general G.N.R. character and detail. The length is 4 ft. 9 in. over-all, the driving wheels are $6\frac{1}{2}$ in. diameter and it is fitted with four high-pressure cylinders, $2\frac{1}{8}$ in. × $1\frac{1}{8}$ in.; the usual cab fittings with one injector.

No. 3 is the finest of all the models, and is a scale model of the G.W.R. "Great Bear" 5 ft. 11 in. over-all. It has four high-pressure cylinders, $2\frac{1}{4}$ in. × $1\frac{1}{4}$ in., the driving wheels are $6\frac{1}{2}$ in. diameter; the usual cab fittings, including one injector and one mechanical pump worked from the axle.

The rolling stock at present comprises three high-sided bogie wagons and four flat-topped wagons for passenger carrying, also some covered and open box wagons.

Sir Berkeley Sheffield and his family are all enthusiastic drivers and some excellent runs are made. The track is made of brass vignol section attached to sleepers by means of brass chairs. All the earth work was done by the Estate Department and the track laid under the supervision of Messrs. Braunston and Walter, of Messrs. Bassett-Lowke, Ltd.

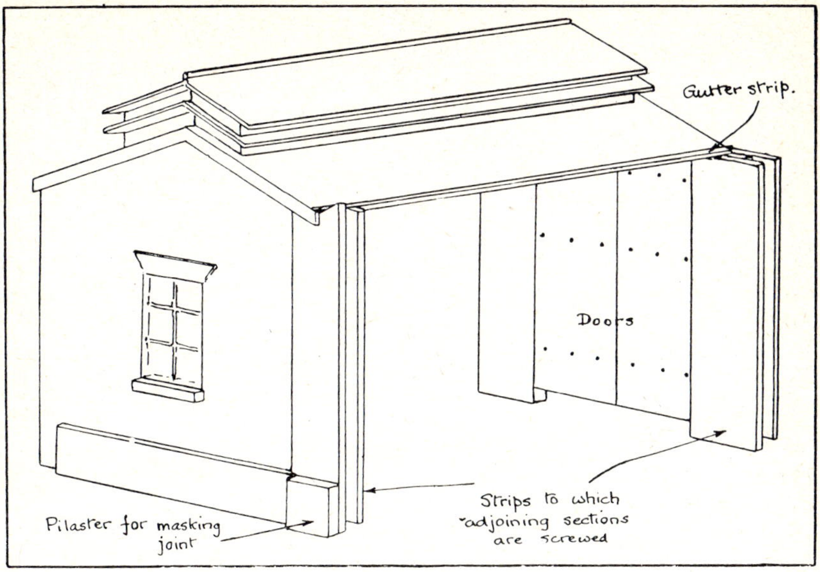

Fig. 1.—Perspective view of a centre section.

An Easily Enlarged Running Shed.

By Lieut. E. A. O. Hutchison, R.A.

THE question of locomotive accommodation is one which becomes very troublesome as a model railway is extended and more engines are acquired, and the following notes and sketches show a type of running shed which can readily be extended from a two-road structure to one of any size.

Briefly, the idea is that the shed is made in two halves, longitudinally, so arranged that they may be taken apart without any difficulty, and extra sections added between them, as occasion demands. Each additional section is composed of two ends and a single-span roof, a floor being added if thought desirable, though one is not recommended. Assuming that ordinary care is taken in making the building, there should be no difficulty in masking the joints between the sections and, at the same time, making them readily detachable.

Referring to the sketches, Fig 1 shows a rough perspective view of a centre section. It will be noticed that the farther vertical edges of the ends are plain, the nearer edges having the joint-strips fixed to them. Fig. 2 shows a general end-view of two centre and one side section. the

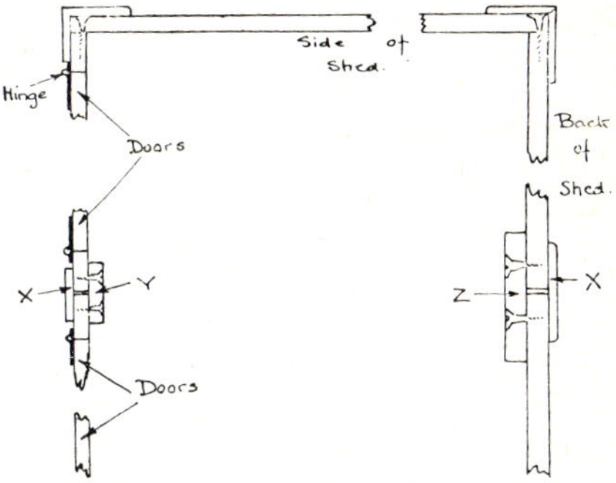

Fig. 3.—Sectional Plan of Joints.

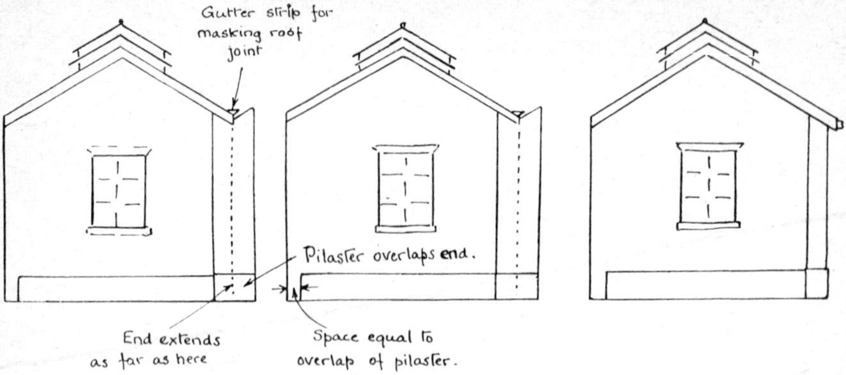

Fig. 2.—General end view of two centre and one side section.

sections being taken apart to show the arrangement at the joints. The small triangular strips, intended to

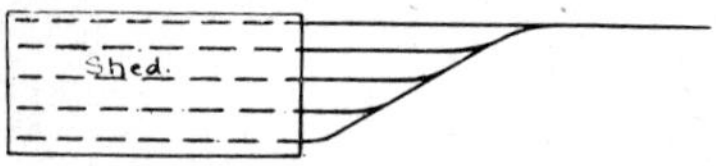

Fig. 4.—Roads converging.

represent the guttering between the roof spans, which are used to mask the roof-joints, should be noted. Fig. 3 shows a sectional plan of the joints. It will be seen that the sections are screwed to the strips Y and Z from the inside. This presupposes that the building is not floored, and is located on the baseboard of the railway by blocks or other means, so that it can be lifted clear. If a floor is required, the design will have to be modified, either by removing the pilasters XX when it is required to enlarge the shed, screwing the sections from the outside, and then re-fitting the pilasters, or else by making the roof separately and fitting it after the ends are in position. There does not seem to be any object in providing a floor in the case of a permanent or semi-permanent railway.

If it is anticipated that extensive enlargements will be made, care must be taken to leave enough space in front of the building, particularly if the roads converge as shown in Fig. 4. A glance at Fig 5 will show that if the shed is enlarged as shown by the dotted lines, points at A will be too close to the shed to allow of the new roads being laid, and will require to be moved back to B. The extra road space in the lay-out involved

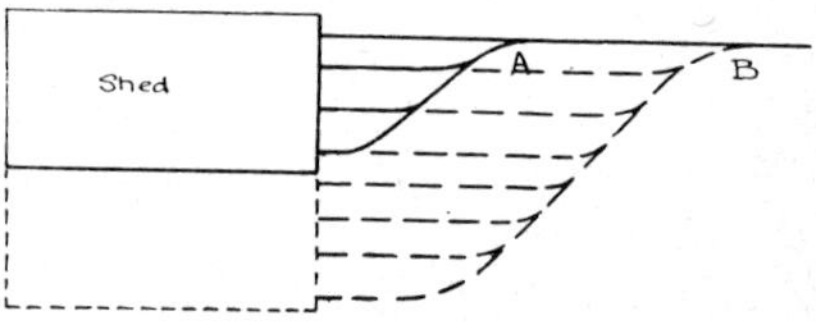

Fig. 5.—An improvement.

thereby is not wasted, however, as it can be utilized as sidings for engines which are waiting for their trains.

P. McC. (Sheffield).—A space only 6 ft. 10 in. × 4 ft. 8 in. wide is unsuitable for anything other than No. 00 gauge. The cheaper gauge No. 00 models are supplied by Messrs. Bassett-Lowke, Bonds, Ltd., and other advertisers. You can obtain rails both for clockwork and electric models, either in straight or curved sections. Please consult our advertisers' catalogues. The plan will have to be dictated by the limits of the sections obtainable.

The old L.B.S.C. model, since improved upon.

An "0" Gauge Railway in a small space.

By F. N. Lance.

Upon reference to the log-book of my model railway, I find that it is only 4½ years since the day when, with unbounded enthusiasm but little practical experience, I laid down the scheme for my proposed line.

The records for the first year seem like echoes of the dark ages. Model railway accessories were expensive and difficult to obtain. The Southern Railway had not come to inspire the humorists of the newspaper world and the Model Railway News was not at hand to guide the neophyte in the right direction. So, after about a year's activity, I had made so many errors and gained so much rather bitter experience that I desired to scrap the whole business and to begin again. The only relic of the old L.B.S C. line is a photograph (enclosed) in which can clearly be seen the faultiness of cardboard buildings and non-scale permanent way.

When I set out to re-design the track layout of the new railway I took advantage of the experience I had gained from the first attempt and paid special attention to large radii curves, long platforms, ample accommodation for stock, and the avoidance of cramping too much detail in a confined space. The plan produced in Fig. 1 contains about as complete a railway as is possible in a room measuring only 8 ft. × 12 ft. with a single-line extension down a passage.

The main features of the layout are a principal station, "Kirkdale," with four roads, the two inner ones forming part of a double-track continuous loop. No. 3 road is a relief line for the outer circular track in one direction and in the other direction is an approach road to the "fly-over" reversing-loop. No. 4 road is a shunting spur which

Kirkdale Station from the tunnel-head.

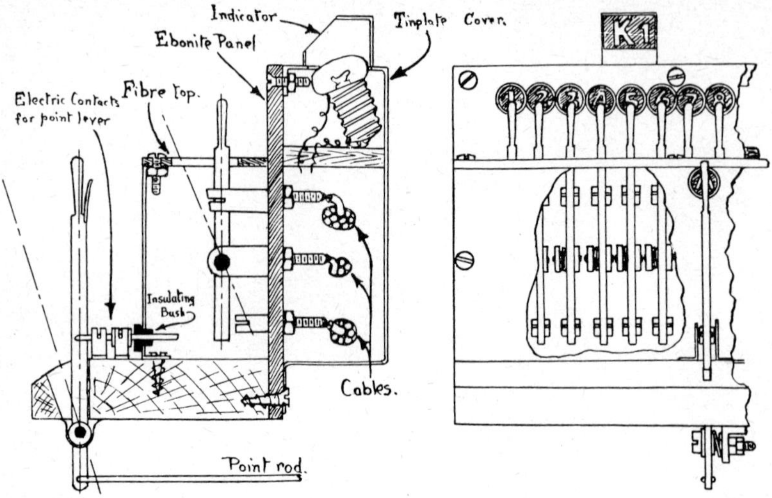

Fig. 2.—Showing the working of signal levers.

allows for shunting operations from the two carriage sidings, the goods shed and the two engine lines to be carried out without fouling the through road.

All the platform lines are capable of dealing with terminal trains. The "fly-over" loop with the two platform lines (2 and 3) used in connection with it and a single-line branch to an "underground" station, "Deepdene," is equipped with electrified centre and side rails so that it can be used to run a two-car electric-train of District Railway design.

The photograph of Kirkdale Station is taken from the tunnel-head and shows the engine-roads to the right with a loco. and some rolling stock.

At the other end of Kirkdale Station is a small goods-yard and a car-shed which is intended to protect from dust any newly painted rolling-stock.

Points of interest in the permanent way are a double slip in the sidings and a single-slip on the main line (for run-round purposes). These were made quite easily by soldering the

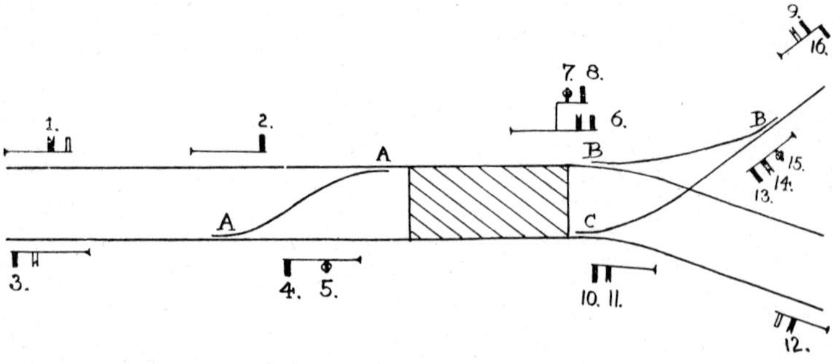

Fig. 3.

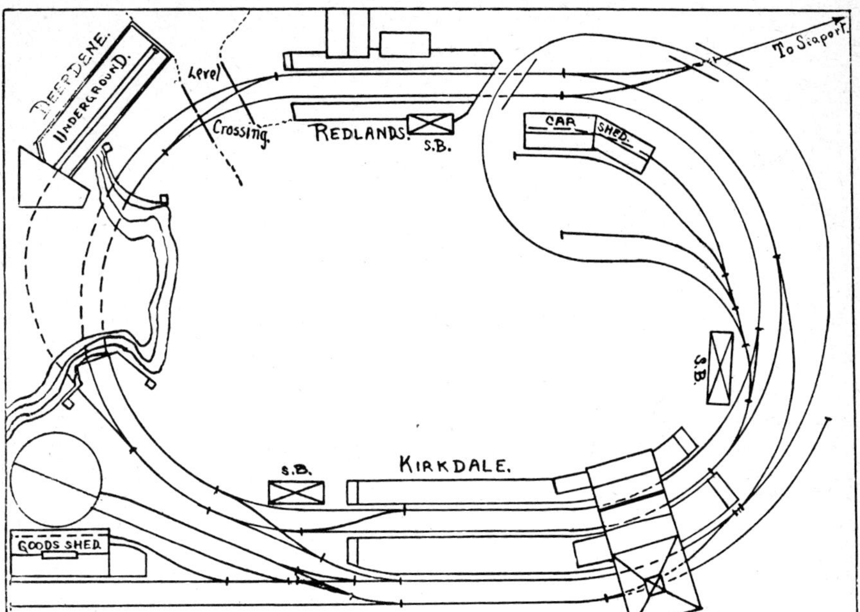

Fig. 1.—Plan of the line.

rails at the frogs to pieces of stout tinplate beneath, which makes it impossible for any part to shift its position. Sleepers are laid at intervals of one inch, but for economy chairs are only fixed to alternate sleepers.

Readers may be interested in the signal-cabin at Redlands Station. It is equipped with 19 levers, controlling 16 electrically operated signals and three mechanically operated points, all of which are interlocked to prevent conflicting movements.

Each signal-lever in the box is in effect a knife-switch that engages with one connection in the " off " position and with another in the " on " position (*see* Fig. 2). In the wiring-diagram (Fig. 4) the top row of contacts represents the connections closed in the normal position and the bottom row those made when the lever is pulled. The middle row represents the levers themselves.

In order to understand the wiring diagram it is necessary to know that from each signal (shown by a number within a circle) there is a return lead, not drawn in the diagram, to the — ve terminal of the battery.

Distant signals mounted upon the same post as a " home " signal are controlled by that signal by means of the usual mechanical arrangement on the post itself.

It can be seen that by

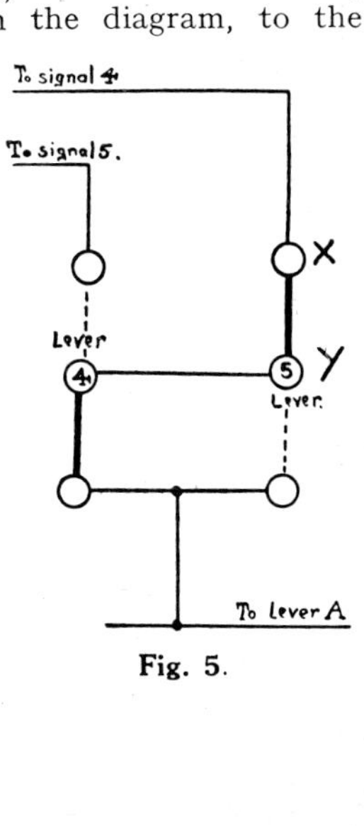

Fig. 5.

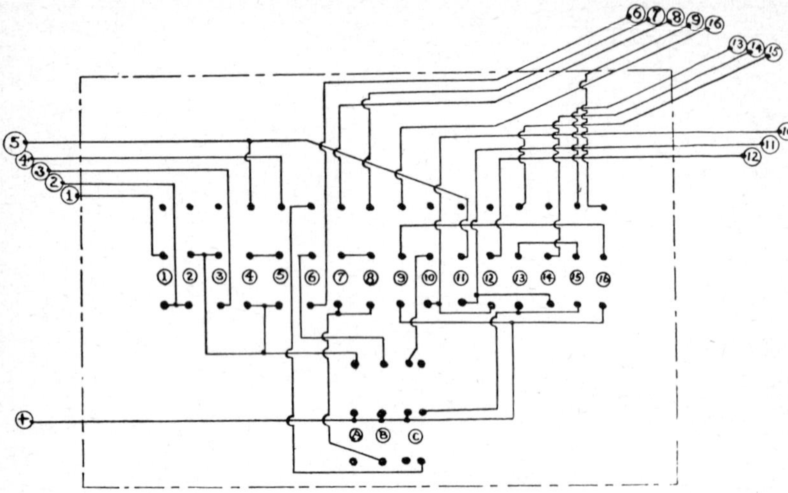

Fig. 4.—Wiring Diagram.

electrical means the interlocking can be carried out more simply and in a smaller space than with a mechanical frame.

INTERLOCKING OF REDLANDS BOX.

Signal	*Point A*	*Point B*	*Point C*	*Remarks*
1	—	—	—	Pulled after 2
2	Normal	—	—	—
3	Normal	—	—	—
4	Normal	—	—	Locked against 5
5	Normal	—	—	Locked against 4
6	—	Normal	—	Locked against 13, 15
7	—	Pulled	—	Locked against 8
8	—	Pulled	—	Locked against 7
9	—	—	—	Locked against 16
10	—	—	Normal	—
11	—	—	—	Pulled after 4
12	—	—	—	Pulled after 10
13	—	Normal	Pulled	Locked against 6, 15
14	—	—	—	After 4
15	—	Normal	Pulled	Locked against 6, 13
16	—	—	—	Locked against 9

To explain the idea to those who may be thinking of fitting up a box on similar lines let me take an example—that of signals 4, 5. From the table, it is found that both 4 and 5 can only be lowered when point A is normal and that only one of these two signals may be worked at one time. Accordingly, if we follow the current round from the + ve of the battery we arrive at the centre contact of lever A. The circuit, as is required, is only completed when A is in its normal position, when the current passes on from the top-contact of A to a lead joining the lower contacts of 4 and 5 levers. To avoid confusion the part of the diagram in question is reproduced alone in Fig. 5. Notice that, as the levers 4, 5 are connected electrically and the top contacts are joined to the respective signal solenoids, the circuit is only completed when one lever is pulled and the other is not pulled. In the position shown signal 4 would be lowered. If now an attempt be made to lower signal 5 the circuit between the points XY will be broken and signal 4 will return to danger.

If the wiring diagram is studied carefully in conjunction with the table other methods of overcoming difficulties will be discovered. For example, an extension of the scheme outlined above to permit the pulling of one only of three signals can be observed in respect of levers 6, 13, 15.

The only other feature of Redlands Box is that the three points are moved mechanically, the electrical contacts only being used for interlocking purposes. In the case of lever C it is necessary to have two sets of contacts insulated from one another to enable the interlocking to be complete. The extra complication of locking-bars to facing-points has been purposely avoided for the present.

The locomotive stock at the moment consists of a home-made 4—4—2 tank Southern B17 and a commercial L.N.W.R. George V, with a steam Brighton " Terrier " and an electric loco of the type used on the electrified lines to Sutton and Coulsdon North under construction.

Model Locomotive Sheds.

By H. G.

THE type of locomotive shed with a roof arranged longitudinally—called the gable-ended shed—is perhaps a better construction than the building with a saw-toothed roof where only one or two roads have to be accommodated. Of course, two or more separate longitudinal roofs could be arranged for a shed with four or six sets of rails if desired, but the saw-tooth roof would be a simple construction in the end. The accompanying illustration shows a shed made from one of my drawings by Messrs. Mills Bros., Sheffield, for one No. 0 gauge express engine. In designing a shed the chief characteristics should be a roof with louvre and chimney ventilators, and also to relieve the monotony of the long wall with few windows in it, the sides should be panelled out by adding a fairly deep raised plinth and vertical strips of wood to form pilasters.

A Gable-ended Model Locomotive Shed.

An L.M. & S. Railway Model at Wembley.

This "O" Gauge Model—which is electrically operated—was made by Mr. A. W. G. Kerswell, a dentist, and is now being exhibited in the Palace of Engineering at Wembley. It is grouped within a space of 10 feet by 6 feet, and has 100 feet of track. There is a snow plough, there are break-down vans, and 8 L.M.S. Locomotives of various types. "Croid" glue was used for the scenery, which, though rather cramped, represents a very ambitious effort at realism.

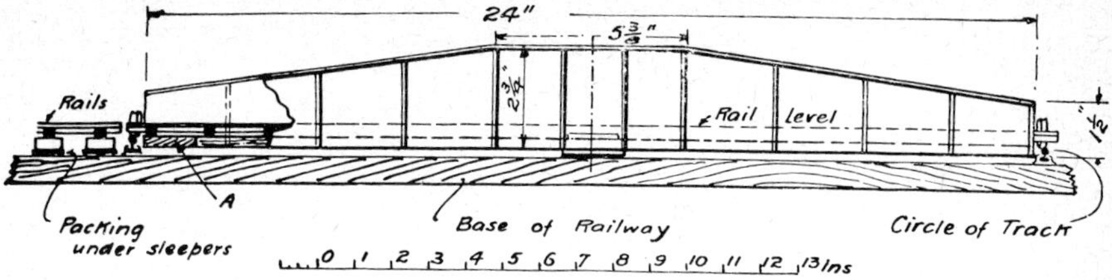

Fig. 2.—Model "O" Gauge 24 in. side girder Turntable.

Model Railway Turntables.

By Henry Greenly.

FROM the point of view of picturesqueness the type of turntable which is sunk in a circular well is, perhaps, the best, but as a rule the construction of a turntable is an after thought. The base of the railway is already laid and difficult to alter and, therefore, the G.W.R. "all-level" arrangement is the only possible scheme. The pit is necessary in the under-girder type to obtain depth sufficient for a girder frame of adequate strength. Usually the girder is designed to carry the complete locomotive without reference to the supports of the end wheels. When correctly set, the locomotive should almost balance on the centre pivot, the wheels on the circle of rails taking very little load. Two men can then easily turn the heaviest engine.

As in the side-girder type of turntable a certain amount of depth is required for the floor of the structure, either, as in the full-size example, the site is slightly saucer shaped or where an existing and exactly level base has to be contended with, the writer usually arranges a slight rise in the level of the tracks leading to the table. This can be accomplished by using thicker sleepers or packing up standard ones. Difficulties in this respect are reduced where ready-laid permanent way on battens is purchased. Ordinarily, with a 5-16th in. thick turntable floor, an $\frac{1}{8}$-in. to $\frac{1}{4}$-in. rise is usually enough. As shown in the sectional view of the No. 0 gauge turntable (*see* Fig. 4), the total height from the base-board to the under side of the chairs is 7-16th in. With $\frac{1}{4}$-in. sleepers, 3-16th-in. rise is necessary to the turntable. At the ends the table rails project over the surface of the circular-track rail. The four wheels supporting the outer end may be plain rollers fitted to metal brackets having their spindles placed truly radial to the centre of the table. For pivoting a thick metal plate countersunk for an upturned pin fixed to the base is fixed to the top of the floor, a plate being screwed on under the floor with a hole in it drilled an easy fit for the pin.

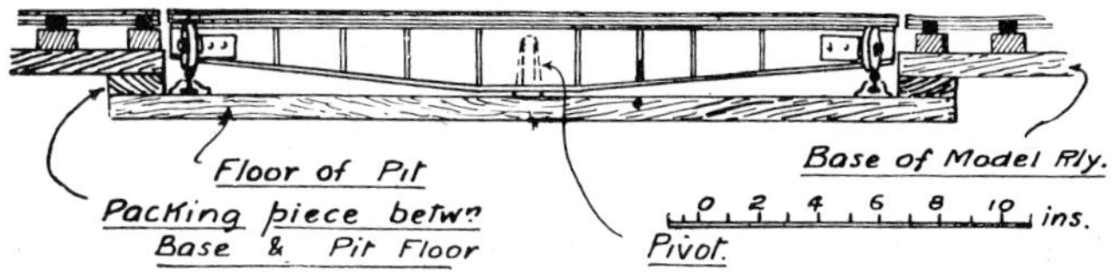

Fig. 1.—Sketch for an "O" gauge pit turntable.

In full-size practice it is always better to provide a turntable rather longer than actually required, not only with an eye to future developments, but to make it easier for the driver and fireman to turn the engine.

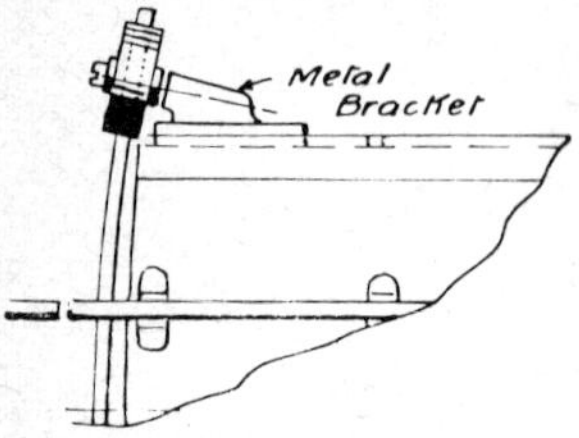

Fig. 3.—Plan of corner, showing end roller wheels.

The model maker has only to consider the first-named contingency. This will be the more difficult of the two, as providing space for a turntable at all is usually the trouble on the average indoor system.

Model turntables are easily made out of wood to represent plate girders by glueing strips on to the surface of the wood. The track can then be laid directly on to the girders or wooden

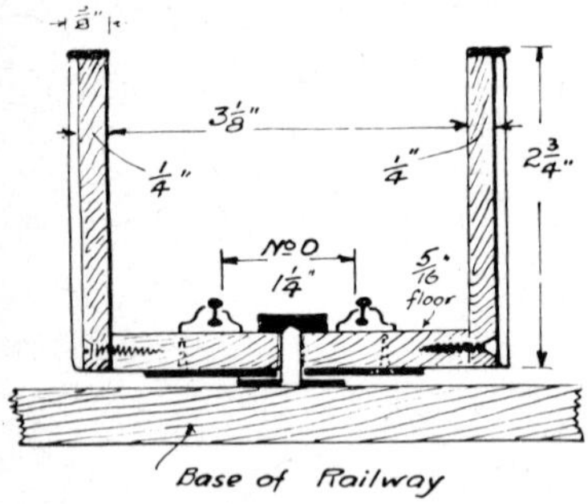

Fig. 4.—Section through centre of turntable.

floor without the intervention of sleepers. In the pit type of table, this is, of course, not so important, as sleepers placed close together may be made to form the floor. A three-piece floor is desirable in the turntable shown in Figs. 2 to 4. The centre "plank" may extend nearly to the ends of the girders and have its grain running the same way as the rails. At the ends, pieces about $1\frac{1}{2}$ in. wide may be fitted with the grain running across the table, as at A, Fig. 2. This will tend to prevent the floor from warping and causing the side girders to move from their normal vertical position. If a central hole of a diameter slightly larger than the width of the table can possibly be cut in the base-board of the railway it will

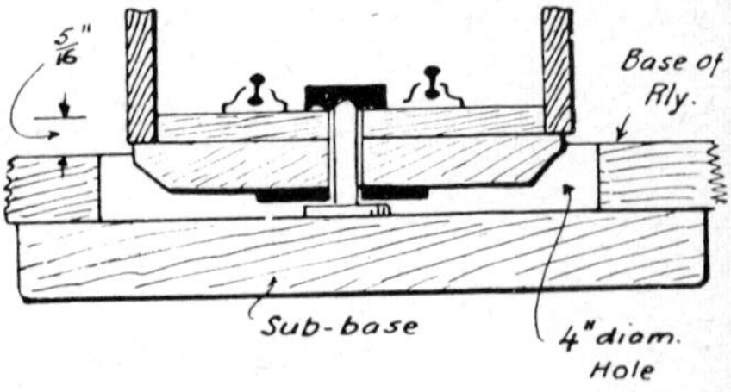

Fig. 5.—Arrangement of pivot with small circular pit to clear a strong central cross-beam.

pay to fit a stout cross member at least 2 in. wide under the floor as sketched in Fig. 5 herewith. A thinner floor (say $\frac{1}{4}$ in.) can then be used.

J. Francis Parker (Worcs) writes: "I am very glad to hear that the G.W. loco, 'Pendennis Castle,' has done very much better than her rival, the 'Flying Fox,' in the recent loco trials. A friend of mine, at Hitchin, has quoted the following remarks made to him by the district loco superintendent and a driver, respectively:—'Since the amalgamations we have tried G.E. 460's, G.C. 460's, N.E. 460's, 442's and 462's., but "Pendennis" isn't in the same street, she beats the lot!' and the driver, 'Some of our men laughed when they saw the little 460, but we soon found that she was a rattling good engine. I would never have believed she could do such good work.' My friend also states that 'Pendennis' was maintaining a steady 50 m.p.h., with 16 coaches on the 1 in 200 up through Hitchin, with no sign of smoke, and apparently in something far from full gear. Mr. Collett is surely to be congratulated upon his marvellous production, and Mr. Churchward also."

Springing "O" Gauge Bogies.

By Ovidian

When thinking of the above, two main considerations should be taken into account.

(1) If the track is scale, perfectly laid, and the driving wheels are sprung.

(2) If the track is — *comme les autres*—slightly uneven, and the driving wheels are unsprung.

In No. 1, a single light spring round the centre pin, with appropriate washers, answers quite well ; or, better still, any of the designs by Mr. Greenly of small spring piggots with roller ends, work very well when reduced to No. 0 gauge. But the track should be of scale "section," as well as being perfectly laid, for these to answer well with scale wheel flanges.

But in No. 2 " the case is altered " somewhat. The writer's experience is that it is very difficult to lay model permanent way absolutely flat without the aid of an expert carpenter to fix the shelving. One finds that the joint, say, of the bridge across the door with its buttress is slightly peaked, and when this is reduced it crops up mysteriously further on.

If a super-elevated curve starts from the same place the trouble is increased. Under these circumstances the writer has given up trying to spring bogies from the bearing plate above them, because the rising of the front drivers up the approach to the peak lifts the bearing plate of the bogies about twice as high, plus the amount of the fall-away of the rails from the peak on the farther side as the bogies descend.

This causes an up-and-down motion like one feels when one goes on the ocean (*vide* Gilbert and Sullivan), which is too great to be overcome by small spiral springs, or the most reliable of the remedies for mal-de-mer.

If a small bracket (A) is made of 1-32nd inch material with two slots on the vertical face, it can be bolted to the front of the clockwork mechanism with allowance for adjustment vertically. This leaves a horizontal face projecting from the front of the mechanism. On this face a piece of light clock spring (B) is riveted (or bolted until satisfactorily tested) and allowed to cantilever on to the bogie stretcher behind the centre pin.

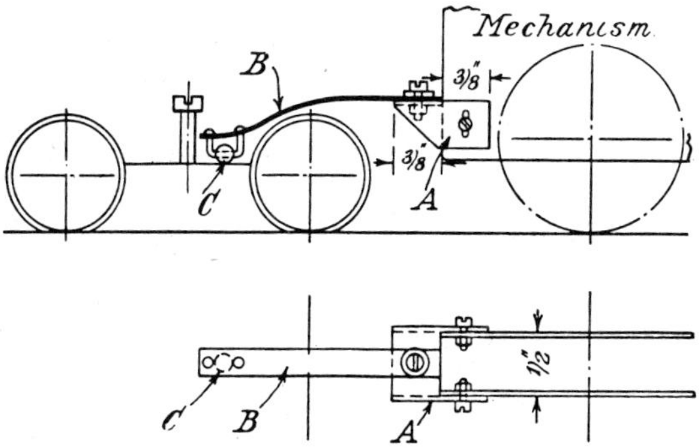

Two views showing the springing arrangement.

A drilled ball-bearing (C) can be attached by a U piece of 1-16th in. wire, shouldered off at the top ends of the U, and riveted on the underside of the spring end where it bears on the stretcher.

Failing the ball-bearing, a *round* glass bead with a hole in its *centre* can sometimes be purloined from one's sister's workbox.

Patience will be needed for trial and error in the strength of spring required. Only anneal the ends of the spring very slightly for drilling ; an evanescent blue floating across the metal is enough, and the drill should go through with a perceptible shearing sound. It is the easiest to have rather a weak pliable spring, ($\frac{1}{4}$ in. suggested but trial is essential), and, if it is not strong enough, extra leaves are easily bolted on top of it from the bracket end, of course, to make it ideal for holding down the bogies without tending to lift the "chassis."

An extra bearing plate may have to be put in, and parts of the "chassis" filed away, but this depends so much on the type of loco concerned that it will be left to the discretion of the works manager who is undertaking the job. Drill the holes in the front of the mechanism first, then make the small bracket with the slots in convenient position, so that the bracket fits snugly and avoids the various outcroppings usually encountered on a clockwork mechanism.

The writer had in mind an electric loco when penning the above, but sees no reason why a clockwork loco should not be fitted as suggested. The spring would not be so long when fixed to the front of a clockwork mechanism as from a cross-plate nearer the front driving axle of an electric loco, but if of lighter material should be quite satisfactory.

Design for an Automatic Reverser.

By E. W. Bentley.

THE permanent magnet is made by bending a bar of red-hot cast steel round an iron tube of the correct diameter—1 in. The poles must be $\frac{1}{4}$ in. apart. The pendulum consists of a piece of soft iron, $1\frac{1}{8}$ in. $\times$ $\frac{1}{2}$ in. $\times \frac{1}{8}$ in. thick, and two copper strips S each $\frac{1}{8}$ in. wide, twisted to shape and fixed as shown.

These copper strips have to carry the current and they must, therefore, be insulated from the iron core by means of a strip of cardboard C. The whole is held together with seccotine, and after being bound with insulating tape, is wound with enough No. 36 S.W.G. to take the required voltage.

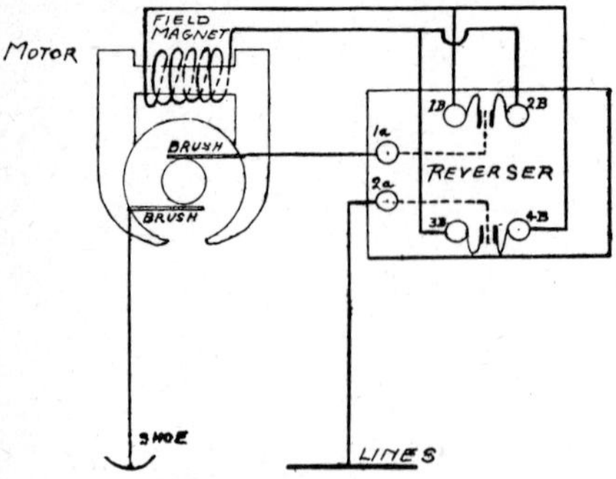

Wiring Diagram.

Two brass strips B hold the permanent magnet in position. They also carry current and must not touch each other. A few layers of insulating material are placed between them and the surface of the magnet.

The pivots P, which are made from thick copper wire, are soldered to the brass strips just mentioned. The four contacts E are made out of contact studs and copper foil. A piece 1 in. long and 3-16th in. wide of the copper foil is soldered to the stud and doubled back in the form of a V. A small piece of thicker copper is soldered to the part of the foil which makes contact with the pendulum.

One end of the coil of wire on the pendulum is connected to the shoe of the locomotive and the other end to the (wheels) frame. Refer to the lettering on the drawing (plan) and on the wiring diagram for other connections.

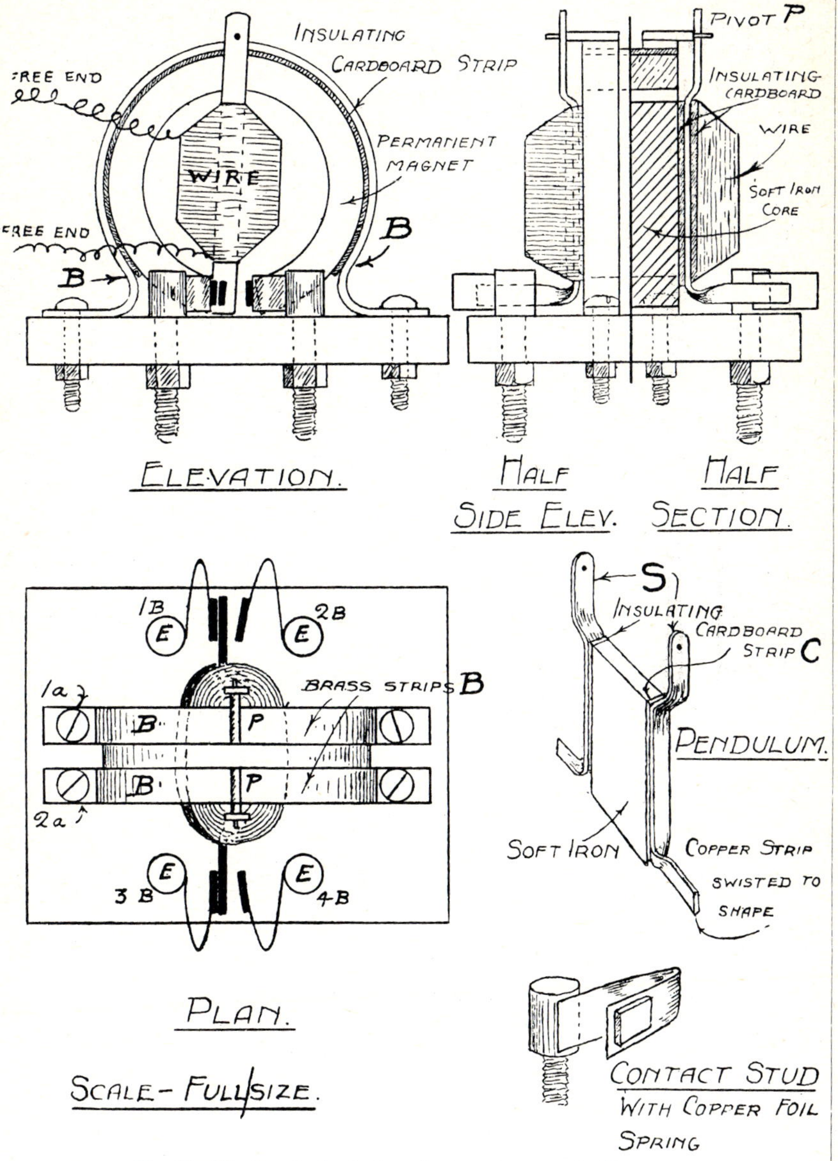

Mr. E. W. Bentley's design for an Automatic Reverser.

An "Electric" Explosion.

By Disgruntled.

It would appear that the time has come for voicing a plea for the popularity of the model electric locomotive proper, and it is with a view to appealing to any who entertain similar views that this is written.

To begin with I suggest that steam power in the usual form dished out to the public by the model vendors—certainly in gauge 0 and more or less in gauge 1—is not satisfactory out of doors, or without troubles indoors either, for that matter.

It is not that steam cannot be made to work outside by those who have the requisite skill to build their own models; but on the whole, let us say, the making of such models requires skill above the average, especially in experiment and design, and even then suffers from certain inherent drawbacks. Now it is here the so-called "purist" comes in, for by being practically debarred from being able to even partially scale the real motive power, he is driven (against his will) as the direct result to camouflage what is really an electric train with steam engine trappings, or perhaps the motive power has to be clockwork.

All the foregoing remarks are doubtless well-worn platitudes, but it is sincerely to be hoped that the souls of certain followers of these practices may be stirred by two straight questions:—

1. Why not model your locomotives on real electric prototypes and be done with make believe?
2. Are there not some exceedingly interesting electric locomotives well worthy of copying?

Now electric locomotives proper offer an enormous field for the model maker, especially the beginner in offering at least five great advantages, viz.:—

1. The external appearances are easy to make and the internal mechanism simpler than steam.
2. The difficulties of track circuits vanish with an overhead conductor.
3. In its proper form it can be made far more powerful than disguised as a steam engine.
4. Wheel arrangement and better weight distribution make it more stable and easier to run and handle.
5. Size of gauge and outdoor running do not need considering.

All the above are the result of experimenting with a model electric locomotive (gauge 0) based on Swiss design, and it was only after it had exhibited its powers that the advantages of this type of tractor were realized; and from the experience gained it would appear to be easy to have made this model twice as powerful and if anything, a little smaller.

The pantograph form of collector was found to give no trouble after a little experimenting, and the track remained out all winter, its insulation and earth-return circuits remaining intact (70 odd feet long). It is just as well to mention here and now that such circuits are no use for the disguised electric locomotive masquerading as a steam engine, as this article is intended for those who have the courage to install an overhead circuit and use either the bow or preferably the pantograph type of collector; and one is perfectly certain once it has been tried by anybody they will never revert to the camouflaged type with its persistent defective insulation and derailment short circuits.

[The above article represents the views of an "all-electric" enthusiast. What do our other readers think about it?—Ed. M.R. News.]

A Ninety-two Year Old Model.

By J. H. Alexander.

A FEW years ago my attention was drawn to an old working model locomotive which was constructed by a coal master, when he was a lad. I am sorry I have no photo of the model and am unable to give dimensions, but I enclose two freehand drawings which will show what the locomotive was like.

This model might be about 10 inches long and, perhaps, $3\frac{1}{2}$ inches from rail level to centre line of boiler. Fig. 1 is an elevation, and Fig. 2 is a longitudinal section, but the drawings are not to scale. The boiler was made of strong sheet brass soldered together, with the flanges of the end-plates overlapping the barrel. Just as in some early locomotives, there was inside the boiler not two, but one large flue terminating in front in a chimney; this passed up through the barrel. There was no smoke box. A weighted lever safety-valve and a dome with a screw cap were fitted on the boiler. The frames, like those in early locomotives, were made of wood and rested on four wheels, which were not coupled together.

One cylinder, with the slide-valve on the top, and the bore of which might be about $\frac{3}{4}$ inch, was fixed in front of the trailing axle, below its centre line, under the boiler in the horizontal middle line. A bent steam pipe was led from the dome to the cylinder, but there was no cock or regulator to shut off steam. The connecting rod was attached at the big end to a crank-pin on a dummy axle, which by spur gearing drove the front wheels; both spur wheels were of the same size. Spur gearing would increase the power somewhat. By means of a vibrating link, the slide valve was driven from an eccentric on the driving axle. There was no reversing gear on the model.

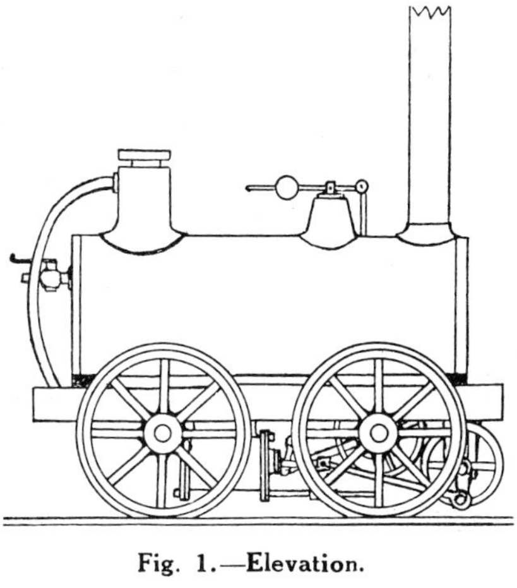

Fig. 1.—Elevation.

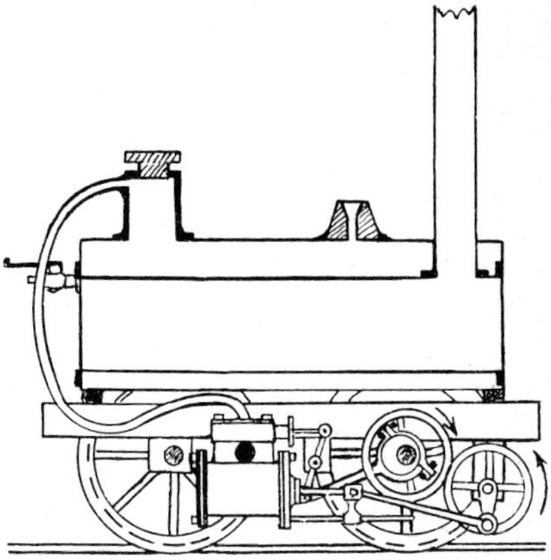

Fig. 2.—Longitudinal Section.

Action.—The boiler was filled with water through the plug-hole on the dome to about the level of the try-cock (which was set rather high). A round bar of iron, shorter than the flue, having previously been heated to a bright red heat, was pushed into the flue at the foot-plate end. When steam was up, the locomotive would run along rails or on a smooth floor. A plate fixed on the locomotive showed that it had been made as far back as 1833.

On Choosing Locomotive Types.

By G. B. Denty.

WHEN intending to build a new loco for a model railway, one of the first questions that has to be answered is, ' What is the most suitable type ? " With regard to this, the following considerations have to be taken into account :—(1) The track, (2) the traffic, (3) in the case of models, which only concern the M.R.N., the individual taste of the owner.

Model railway tracks usually have gradients of ridiculous steepness, and hopelessly inadequate curves. Engines with single driving wheels, apart from being obsolete, are useless for the former, and those with eight or more driving wheels are useless for the latter. Traffic can be divided into passenger, mixed and goods. Mixed traffic engines are useful, as passenger or goods trains can be hauled equally correctly with them.

In clockwork and electric locos, tenders are unnecessary; tank locomotives make just as good models, and provide better concealment for the mechanism. There are plenty of fine prototypes for tank engines, both for long and short-distance work. In the writer's opinion, tank locomotives should always be double-ended, especially in the case of models where it is advantageous for the overhang to be more or less equal each end.

0—4—0 T. Usually a small locomotive, largely used for contractor's work, although is equally well suited for shunting or motor-train working. Almost any curve can be negotiated by them.

2—4—0. A tender loco, much in favour at the close of the last century, when quite a large amount of express working was done by them. They are only used for short-distance passenger-train working nowadays, or for light goods traffic.

2—4—2 T. A good type of mixed traffic loco, with a flexible wheelbase.

4—4—0 and 4—4—2. These are essentially passenger locos, of which nothing further need be said.

4—4—4 T. Should make a good express passenger loco for a model, although not in extensive use in actual practice. The N.E.R. locos of this type should make good prototypes.

0—6—0. In common use for any kind of goods traffic.

0—6—0 T. Perhaps the most general service loco in existence. Its uses are legion, passenger, mixed traffic, goods and shunting work being equally well suited for it.

2—6—0. A mixed traffic loco that has become more or less common during recent years.

2—6—2 T. A mixed traffic loco that has gradually ousted the 2—4—2T.

4—6—0 and 4—6—2. Suitable for passenger locos where curves will allow.

4—6—4 T. An express tank engine, of which there are now several examples in the country.

F. E. D. (Birmingham).—On No. 1 gauge curves of 3 ft. 2¼ in. radius, slight super-elevation is necessary, more especially if locomotives, other than those propelled by clockwork, are used. The formula in Greenly's book, "Model Railways," may be used, but in all cases the "maximum speed," taken for purposes of calculation, should not be the highest speed it is possible to attain, but the average top speed. In No. 1 gauge, this is about two miles per hour, and the super-elevation would be about 1/16th in. As the super-elevation required varies as the square of the speed, putting the latter at three miles per hour would more than double the super-elevation. The length of the vehicle has little to do with the question, although a long vehicle should be sprung, to allow for sharp curves and super-elevation.

Queries and Replies.

THE ETERNAL GAUGE QUESTION.

V. C. D. (Sheffield) writes that he has a room with an adjacent loft not yet joined up to it, and requires our advice on the question of the most suitable gauge. No. 1 is being considered, but possibly No. 0 will give a more representative system in the space now available.

Unless you intend to make a large proportion of your locomotive and coaching stock, and are likely to attempt building a steam locomotive, we strongly recommend No. 0 gauge. You can do almost anything in No. 0 gauge where electricity is the motive power. As you are placed, with at present only one room, 16 ft. × 11 ft. available, No. 0 gauge will give you a fairly good system, and it would be possible to pierce the wall for a tunnel and run a line in and out of the loft which cannot yet be connected by a door to the adjacent room containing the railway.

No. 00 GAUGE ELECTRIC POINTS.

C. L. B. (Wimbledon). "My No. 00 gauge system is now part electric and clockwork, and I wish to add to it. Please advise.

We are not in possession of the details of the method whereby electric locomotives will collect the current in the track mentioned, and, therefore, if you require to purchase electric track for a No. 00 gauge without further experiment, you had better stick to the tinplate points now on the market and obtainable anywhere. In choosing these, see that the moving rails at the frogs fit decently. We have noticed some difference in finish in this respect. This precaution is more necessary where flanges of vehicles are reduced in depth. In any No. 00 gauge track which is made of strip brass soldered down to strip metal sleepers, some modification of the standard 1¼-in. gauge system of current collection at the frogs is necessary. The matter is now being experimented with by more than one amateur, but if you do not wish to spend either money or time in solving this particular difficulty, you had better stick to the present No. 00 gauge points. From an electrical point of view they are good and, considering the price at which they are sold, the mechanical construction is also reasonably good.

"Resistance" (Bradford) writes that he has a No. 0 gauge line worked off the A.C. mains through lamp resistances. He asks us to publish articles on improved lay-outs, electric signals, etc.

You cannot do much with a railway that is run direct from the A.C. mains, through lamp resistances, and you should consider some other scheme if you intend to improve it in the way suggested in your letter. You also appear not to know of the many schemes of control which have been used in the past, and would advise you to get all the literature on the subject and catalogues of trade firms that are available. We would strongly advise you to discontinue the use of the A.C. mains, except for charging the accumulators. Alternating current limits the character of the control over the trains and introduces many other difficulties.

T. G. N. (Marlborough), who sends a design for a fire-tube boiler without a fire-box, asks for an opinion of the same.

The defect of the scheme is the absence of a furnace (*i.e.*, fire-box). In addition to providing additional heating surface, the fire-box also gives space for the complete combustion of the fuel. This is very important in a small-scale model locomotive, as the vertical dimensions are so very much restricted. By arranging the tubes in the manner you suggest the height above the top of the oil burner is reduced. We strongly recommend you to adopt accepted practice—more or less—at the outset. When you have obtained sufficient experience you can proceed with experiments of a nature involving risk of non-success.

C. F. P. (Yorkshire) writes :—"I send you a sketch of the two attics I have available for a No. 0 gauge line. It will be electrically controlled."

The extra room is too narrow to allow of a terminal station at the apex of a triangle junction, and too short for a double-ended passing and terminal station, such as Rugby (L.N.W.R.). We have, therefore, devised a double-line continuous plan, with two stations, one in each room. The small room contains the goods and loco depots. Stations A and B could, of course, be transposed, but placing the larger one in the small room has really more justification, as it is adjacent to the main goods yard and locomotive shed. The terminal platforms of A and B are arranged so that short-distance trains may be worked from one to the other. Three control boxes are required at a, b and c, and these respectively govern sections A, B and C. We recommend 3 ft. 6 in. radius curves as the minimum on all main lines, and 3 ft. radius points on the locomotive and goods yards. The shorter sidings in the latter could have 2 ft. radius points, but no engine should be allowed to traverse these.

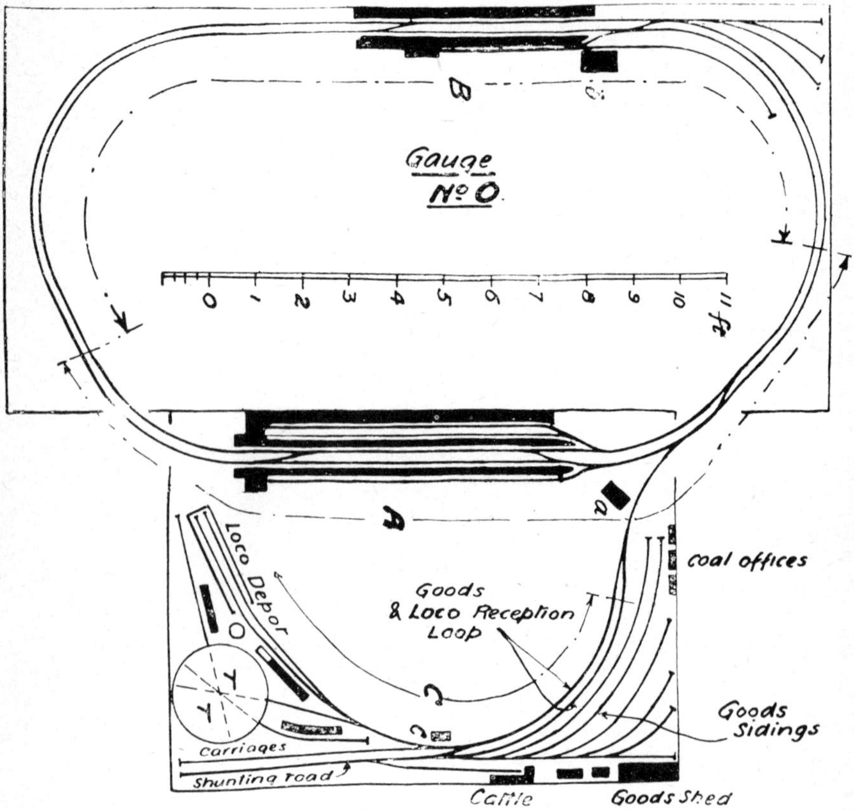

A double-line continuous plan for C. F. P.

OUR MAIL BAG

Mr. J. R. Smyth's "O" Gauge Railway.

To the Editor, MODEL RAILWAY NEWS.

DEAR SIR,

I herewith enclose some photos of my No. 0 gauge line, which I hope will be of some interest to readers.

Fig. 1.—York Station.

In the early numbers of *Model Railways and Locomotives*, and again in *Everyday Science* and the *Model Engineer*, photos of my humble efforts have appeared.

Many changes have taken place since then.

Fig. 1 is of York Station (ocal platforms). Part of the station buildings can be seen on the left, with the clock towe in the background.

Fig. 2 is part of the main line, south of York (some distance). There is a double set of rails behind the hurdle fence and behind that a field and sand dunes, etc. In the foreground one of the local lines can be seen. The loco is a G.W.R clockwork 0—6—0 T and immensely powerful. She walks away with 20 goods waggons or eight to ten bogie coaches with ease and despatch. She also takes the "mountain" portion of the line in a very gratifying manner.

I have constructed cranes and transit sheds, etc., with wool bales, barrels of port and other sundries scattered about. The model lights up at night (including searchlights), and looks very effective.

The docks are not yet completed.

The mountain section (with Carlisle Station), grade 1 in 36. Speed when descending terrific. The banking on the somewhat severe curves has to be

Fig. 2.—Part of the main line.

very heavy. This sometimes has disastrous results when ascending slowly, as there are no guard rails. At Thirsk Station, there are tunnel mouths and village on top of the mountain.

I am still slowly converting from tinplate to steel. There is only a little of the old tracks left now.

I am delighted that we have again a model railway magazine.

I am also pleased to see that Mr. F. W. Shaw has contributed. I had the honour of his company last year and a very "railwayfied" evening we had.

Wishing MODEL RAILWAY NEWS every success.

I remain,

Yours faithfully,

JOHN R. SMYTH.

Beckenham.

Lettering on French Rolling Stock.

To the Editor, MODEL RAILWAY NEWS.

DEAR SIR,

I saw, some days ago, your very interesting magazine for the first time. I had a great pleasure in discovering it, as I am deeply interested in model railways and railways in general.

In the June number I read the letter from Mr. Bassett-Lowke on French railways, and, as his remarks about rolling stock lettering are not quite exact, I think it will be of some help to your readers to correct them, knowing this question well, my indications being of official sources.

The lettering of rolling stock, which was different on all the French lines, has now been standardized, since two years, and is as follows :—

A*n* = First, *n* meaning number of compartments.
B*n* = Second.
C*n* = Third.
D = Brake van, with guard's look-out.
E = Brake compartment (without look-out).
d = Brake compartment, which may be closed for Customs.
L = Sleeping - Saloon. (On the P.L.M. the sleeping saloons with complete beds are lettered Lg, from the word *garni*).
c = Sleeping berths.
f = Hand-brake.
w = Air-brake (not usually indicated on passenger stock).
i = Vestibule gangways.
p = Open gangways.
t = Corridor and lavatory for coaches without intercirculation.
y = Bogie.

The coach seen by Mr. Bassett-Lowke would be read :—

$A^3c_2L^3g_2yfi$ = Three first class, of which two with sleeping berths, three sleeping saloons, of which two with complete beds, bogie, hand-brake, intercirculation.

I hope my explanations will be clear enough.

In the case some reader may travel on other lines than the P.L.M. I must indicate, before closing, that a lot of carriages are still running with the ancient lettering of their lines.

On the Etat :—

AA—BB—CC = Corridor coaches.
p = Intercirculation.

On the P.O. :—

T = Bogie (from the old word "truck" which was used for "bogie" at first).
S = Corridor, without intercirculation.
Y = Central look-out for brake van, viz., DY.

On the Nord :—

D = Composite carriages (1st, 2nd).
E = Brake vans.

Examples : — On the Etat, Bogie carriages = AAfpy, BBfpy, ABABfpy, etc. On the P.O., Bogie carriages = AT^8, B^9T, $C^{10}T$, $A^{3\frac{1}{2}}B^5T$., etc. Four-wheel corridor carriages = A^6S, B^7S, C^8S. On the Nord, First, Second, bogie brake = DEy.

In the ancient lettering the only two letters which had the same meaning on all the lines were :—

y = Bogie.
f = Hand brake.

I hope this letter will be of some use to your magazine, and shall be very pleased to give any information you may desire on French and Continental lines.

Yours sincerely,
EMILE ANDRÉ SCHEFER.

Sèvres, France.

P.S.—On coaches for international services, there is a special mark on the frame thus :—

R. I. C.	
All.	Schw.

meaning *Reglement International de Circulation*, and below the countries in which the car may pass: "All." = Germany, "Schw." (Schweiz) = Switzerland).

To the Editor, MODEL RAILWAY NEWS.

AR SIR,

I I may, I should like to make a few observations on Mr. Bassett-Lowke's very interesting letter and photographs in the June number, on Continental rolling stock and usages.

The "A^2," as he states, denotes that there are two first-class compartments on the coach, but the "c^2" does not mean that there are two third-class compartments. The general practice on the Continent is to build composite coaches having only first and second-class compartments, and this would specially be in the case of coaches run over other Companies' lines, as would be the case of the P.L.M. coach illustrated. There is such a vast difference in the quality of the comfort provided in the first and second classes and the third class. The "c^2" denotes, therefore, that both first-class compartments are "couchettes," as can be clearly seen under the figure "1" on the right of the photograph; third-class would be denoted by a capital "C."

The "L^3" denotes three lits-salons, and the "g`," of which no mention is made in his letter, means, if I am not mistaken, that two of these compartments are large (*grand*), holding usually three sleepers, whilst the third would, therefore, be a smaller compartment; the large ones might even hold four. The difference between the couchettes and the sleeping saloons is that in the former no bedding is provided.

I have just returned from England, and, during the course of my journey, travelled over six railway systems, namely :—Southern Railway of England, London to Dover; Nord, France, Boulogne to Laon; Est, France, Laon to Mulhouse; Alsace-Lorraine, France, Mulhouse to Bâle; Chemin de Fer Federal, Switzerland, Bâle to Chiasso; Ferrovie dello Stato, Italy, Chiasso to Milan.

It was very interesting to note the different customs and, especially, variations in signalling, etc. On the Alsace-Lorraine system we travelled on the right-hand track.

With best wishes,
Yours very truly,
D. H. P. MADGE.

Milan.

Locomotive Hand-rail Knobs.

To the Editor, MODEL RAILWAY NEWS.

DEAR SIR,

I have found this method of making hand-rail knobs for 0 gauge locomotives a successful and speedy one.

A length of one-sixteenth inch half-round brass wire was obtained, and a small piece cut off. This was bent

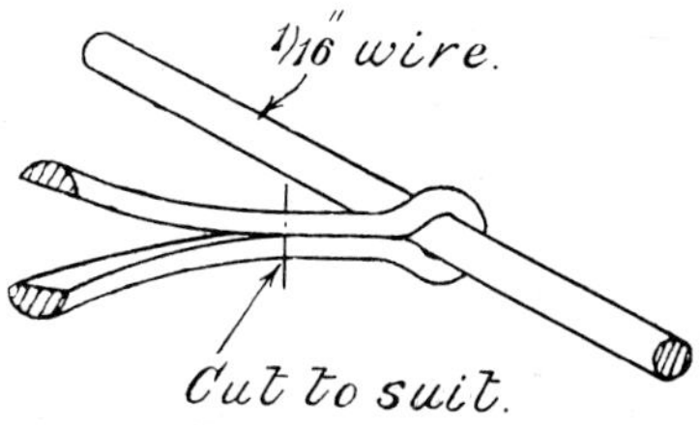

round the wire for the hand-rail till the ends met, and was then squeezed tightly over it with a pair of pliers. The ends were cut at a suitable length of about one quarter of an inch long (*see* enlarged sketch herewith), so that they could be sweated into a sixteenth hole in the boiler-barrel. After making a number of these, the hand-rail was then fixed in position.

Yours sincerely,

J. RINTOUL.

Glasgow.

An "O" Gauge Line.

To the Editor, MODEL RAILWAY NEWS.

DEAR SIR,

I am constructing a model 0 gauge railway, and enclose a photograph of the line in its present early stage of construction. In the foreground is the site of the main terminus.

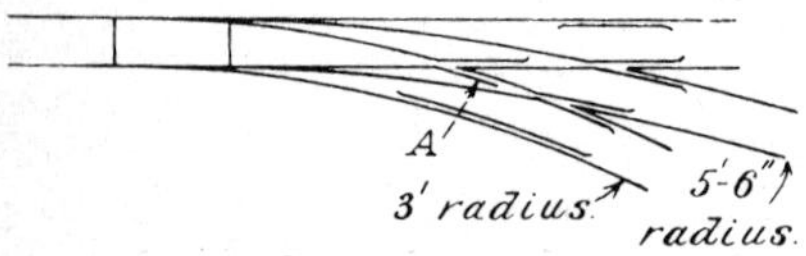

Just beyond the left of the photograph the layout necessitated a three-throw point. I enclose a diagram of the method I adopted to avoid this. I have never met the arrangement before in model systems. It will be noticed that the heel of the point blade marked A ends somewhat abruptly. This was inevitable owing to the comparatively sharp curves.

I hope to send you further particular as the work proceeds.

Yours faithfully,

T. GREGORY SMITH.

Watford.

"Railway Pie."

To the Editor, MODEL RAILWAY NEWS.

DEAR SIR,

I have read with great interest "E. J. L. B.'s" letter in the July number of the MODEL RAILWAY NEWS, on the lecture of "Cardboard and Model Railways" delivered by Mr. H. H. Hudson some time ago to the members and friends of the Wimbledon Model Railway Club. I should like to point out that this very interesting and unusual lecture is briefly reported in the Club's magazine *Railway Pie*. The first number is nearly out of print, but a few copies may still be had, price 4*d*. (postage ½*d*.).

It is not the intention of the promoters to run a rival to "Ours," as *Railway Pie* is only being published quarterly and can only be had from members. Next year it is hoped to issue a free copy to every member of the Club.

Trusting I have not taken up too much of your valuable space and wishing MODEL RAILWAY NEWS the success it has had since the day when you as its Editor and Driver opened the regulator for a non-stop run.

Yours faithfully,

R. SHEPHARD.

Hon. Sec. W.M.R.C.

Springing O-Gauge Bogies.

To the Editor, MODEL RAILWAY NEWS.

DEAR SIR,

In my opinion the main feature is that all four wheels should be sprung

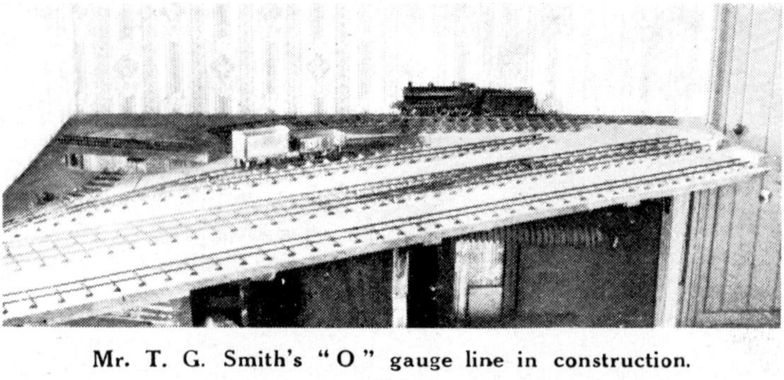

Mr. T. G. Smith's "O" gauge line in construction.

independently of each other. Of course, the bogie must be completely dismantled. A slot should be cut at each bearing and must be filed up to a uniform width. A small quantity of square brass rod should be procured about $\frac{1}{8}$ in. wider than the slots. Now cut the rod into four lengths and file two grooves so that they will slide comfortably in the slots.

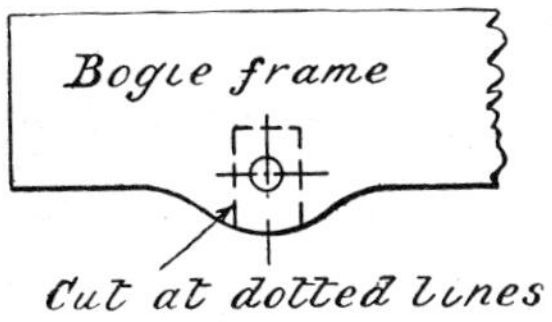

The slots should be made wider at the top and bottom than in the middle to allow for one side moving and not the other. Some watch spring should be bent to shape shown and softened and punched in the middle to allow it

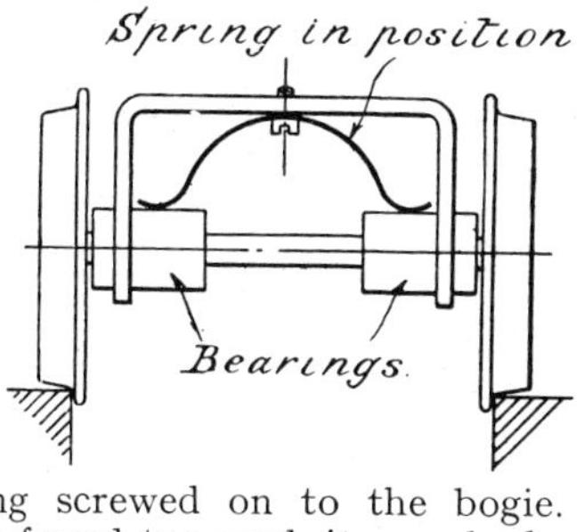

being screwed on to the bogie. If it is found too weak it may be loaded by another spring on top. Some stiff brass wire should be soldered across the bottom of the slots to prevent the wheels falling off when the engine is lifted up.

J. A. K.

Brackley.

Starting a Model Railway.

To the Editor, MODEL RAILWAY NEWS.

DEAR MR. EDITOR.

I note "S. N. G." finds a difficulty in starting a model railway. As I have a great sympathy with all beginners I will be pleased to give him a few practical tips if he will communicate with me.

But to enable me to do so it is necessary for him to let me know what he really wants. So I ask the following questions :—(1) Outdoor or indoor system ; (2) scale and guage ; (3) steam or clockwork (I don't deal in electric or freak systems) ; (4) what sized room has he ? And lastly has he a large supply of patience and dogged determination. If he will supply me with a stamped envelope and this information, I will be pleased to give him all the information in my power.

Faithfully yours,

WILLIAM HAMILTON (Col.).

Henley as a Prototype.

To the Editor, MODEL RAILWAY NEWS.

DEAR SIR,

Recently, when at Henley-on-Thames, I was struck by the suitability of the G.W.R. terminus there, for the prototype of a model railway terminus.

Owing to the brevity of my stay I was unable to procure any photographs or notes other than a few mental ones.

The station would be very suitable for the main terminus of a model railway although at the end of a single line, I think.

As far as I remember there are three running lines and a carriage line serving one island and one single-faced platform.

There is a span roof of the "peaked" pattern about 100 ft. long, and awnings of the "umbrella" type.

The station was flanked on one side by loco sidings with shed, turntable, and tank, and on the other by a goods yard of several tracks, with shed and milk dock.

The passenger platforms, of course, had the usual offices.

Perhaps an enthusiast in the Henley district will send photographs and plan of track lay-out to the "M.R.N." if any readers are interested.

Yours truly,

"LORD OF THE ISLES."

N.L.R. Model Clockwork Loco.

To the Editor, MODEL RAILWAY NEWS.

DEAR SIR,

The photo below is one of my North London Railway locos. These were constructed for me by Mr. Exley, of Bradford, to a scale of 10 mm. to the foot, and are operated by clockwork. An interesting feature is the covered keyhole, generally an eyesore on clockwork locos; a small lever in the cab operates a shutter inside the side tank which covers the keyhole. I am at present engaged in the construction of a gauge 1 N.L.R. line, and will send further details as the line progresses.

Yours truly,
H. R. NORMAN.

Brighton.

Lettering and Lining Models.

To the Editor, MODEL RAILWAY NEWS.

DEAR SIR,

In response to your invitation in the current issue of MODEL RAILWAY NEWS to send in helpful suggestions, I have the greatest pleasure in submitting, for publication, a hint *re* lettering and lining of models.

A medium-sized pen nib (of common or garden variety) is far more useful than a series of small pencil brushes, as it is possible to make letters of lines of any desired size or thickness, giving a more perfectly defined outline than can be obtained by a brush in the hands of an amateur.

The only point to be carefully noted is the correct consistency of the paint used, which must be determined by the nature of the surface to be operated on.

Trusting this will be of interest and help to many of your numerous readers.

Yours faithfully,
C. BENTLEY.

Leeds.

No. "00" Gauge Dimensions and Scale.

To the Editor, MODEL RAILWAY NEWS.

DEAR SIR,

I am very interested in your French correspondent's letter in the July issue. The criticism was expected, and I think the argument he puts forward will not bear the light of a thorough investigation. Any model loco engineer who starts with the idea of perfect scale reduction of any particular dimension is bound to come to grief.

It is fatal to some designs of English locos to work from the tread of the wheel. Take, for example, the design of N.E.R. No. 1230 class R1 loco referred to. If I had made the wheel 24 mm. diameter there would have been considerable difficulty in

A Realistic Gauge 1 N.L.R. Model Clockwork Loco.

preserving the scale outline of the body of the locomotive. This is the thing that strikes the eye first and the necessary compromises that must be made to preserve the true *tout ensemble* of the model include such items as wheel diameters. There must be more than scale clearance between wheel-flange and splashers, and material thicker than the scale equivalent is equally necessary. Therefore, if the correct height and radius of the wheel splashers are to be nearly preserved, the driving wheels must be proportioned to something less than the scale equivalent of the wheel of the prototype *over the flanges*.

A 6 ft. 8 in. wheel would be about 6 ft. $10\frac{1}{4}$ in. diameter over the flanges, say, 6·8 ft. Now, with $1\frac{1}{4}$-mm. flanges a 24-mm. wheel measures $26\frac{1}{2}$ mm. over the flanges. Four times 6·8 is 27·2 mm., and I am sure that we cannot quibble about half a millimetre or so, especially when clearances cannot be to scale.

Yours, etc.,

HENRY GREENLY.

At R.E. Railway, Ravenglass.

An "0" Gauge Scenic Truck.

To the Editor, MODEL RAILWAY NEWS.

DEAR SIR,

In the January MODEL RAILWAY NEWS there appeared a drawing and account giving the necessary instructions for making a model 50-ft. bogie scenic truck by Mr. Greenly.

I have since made this truck and find it a great success.

The articles used for building same are given with their cost price. They were all bought from the Leeds Model Company.

		s.	*d.*
1.	One pair of bogies (coach, tinplate)	4	6
2.	One set of four-coach buffers		8
3.	One pair of three-link couplings		8
4.	Two feet of $2\frac{1}{2}$ in. × $\frac{1}{8}$ in. wood		5

The over-all length of the finished truck is 328 mm., a scale length of 46·57 ft. which is not very far off the length of the prototype.

The width over all is 62 mm.

The height from rail to top of truck is 47 mm.

The height of the side rails is 15 mm.

The rails were cut out of one piece of wood with a fret-saw and then made smooth with a sharp knife.

I found trouble in fixing the rails to the body, but eventually fixed them with thin wire nails also bought from the Leeds Model Company.

The vehicle is painted L.N.W.R. chocolate with "L.N.W.R. 11431" painted in white on each side.

Yours sincerely,

St. Albans. B. J. ASHWELL.

Canadian Import Duties.

To the Editor, MODEL RAILWAY NEWS.

DEAR SIR,

An Englishman and an American were discussing the size of their countries.

"Why," said the American, "I could board a train in Kentucky at seven o'clock in the evening and at seven in the morning I would still be in Kentucky."

"Ah!" said the Englishman, "We have trains like that here too, but we don't brag of them."

By the way, could you tell me what the duty would be on model railway goods imported into this country from England?

Yours sincerely,

Canada. T. KAY.

[We are informed by the Department of Overseas Trade that a duty of 18 % would be charged on the cost of model railway goods, as well as a sales tax of 5 %, making a total duty of 23 %.—ED. M. R. NEWS.]

We much regret that pressure on our space prevents us printing in this issue letters from the following readers: G. H. McCullagh. O. H. Jacobsen, F. G. Hagborg, T. J. Henry, "A. P.," K. R. M. Biggs, "Great Western," W. O. Brown, F. Farrance and G. E. Tenton. We hope to find room for these in the September issue, and in the meantime thank our correspondents for their interest.

WITH THE CLUBS

The Manchester & District Model Railway Club.

The seventh meeting of the above Club was held on July 14th, 1925, at the Clarion Cafe, Market Street, Manchester. There was a good attendance and two new members were enrolled.

The following Locomotive Shed visits have been enjoyed by Club members :—

On Saturday afternoon, June 20th, 1925, several members visited the L.M.S. Loco Sheds at Newton Heath, Manchester.

On July 4th, members paid a visit to the G.W.R. Loco Sheds at Chester.

The subscription is 6*s.* per annum, but for juniors under 18 years of age it is 3*s.* per annum. If desired, a member may pay quarterly subscriptions of 1*s.* 6*d.* The entrance fee, either senior or junior, is one shilling.

The Secretary has been able to secure concessions in the way of discounts from certain well-known model railway firms, and the advantage of this has already been very much appreciated, and is better when the collective total amount of the members' orders are large. As an example, I quote the following :—

	s.	*d.*
A member has an order for 20/– worth of goods ...	20	0
He encloses 1/– for carriage...	1	0
His postal order costs ...		2
Post on sending his order and money		1½
Total	21	3½

Now, if the firm give the Club a discount of 10 %, the member gives his written order to the Secretary and receives a discount of 5 %, thus bringing his amount down to 19/– net. The order is then sent through by the Secretary together with any other members' orders and goods can then be obtained, carriage paid by the firm. It will be seen, by this example, that a saving of 2/3½ is effected for the benefit of the member.

Any further information may be had from the Hon. Secretary, J. A. Dean, 29, Gorse Lane, Gorse Hill, Stretford, Manchester.

The Wimbledon & District Model Railway Club.

The Club's latest venture, *Railway Pie,* our new official journal, has been very well received. Copies can be obtained from the Hon. Secretary, post free, 4½*d.* per copy.

Fixtures :—August 17th, 7.30 p.m. Red Cross Hall, Church Road—Test Track night. 3¼-in. gauge locos can now be accommodated. August 22nd. Visit to Acton works, Underground Railway—Meet 9.45 a.m., Acton station.

Members joining after July 1st obtain the benefit of half-yearly subscriptions, viz. : — Entrance fee, 2*s.* 6*d.*, and Seniors, 5*s.* 6*d.*, Juniors, 3*s.* Further particulars from the Hon. Secretary.

Members requiring photographs of their models should get into touch with Mr. W. P. Ashdown, the Club's official photographer.

The new passenger-carrying track has been successfully installed. Our thanks are due to Messrs. Lamb and Temple for this work, and also to Messrs. Ashdown, Ashford, Miller, Moore and Plummer for their assistance with the storage-chest for this track.

During Mr. R. Shephard's absence on vacation in August, Mr. C. G. T. Plume, 7, Kingsley Road, Wimbledon, will be acting Hon. Secretary.

A New Model L.M.S, 2—6—0 Loco.

A new range of steam gauge No. 0 model locomotives have been produced in Northampton. Hearing that the L.M.S. railway were about to introduce a new type of 2—6—0 mixed traffic locomotive this year, Messrs. Bassett-Lowke, Ltd., were able to obtain from the Company, through the courtesy of the chief mechanical engineer, Mr. Geo. Hughes, an advance drawing of this engine. In a consultation with Mr. Henry Greenly, the firm decided to adopt this as a standard, and also to introduce the model in the G.W.R. and L.N.E.R. type. This could be done with the least trouble by making the two latter engines modelled on the G.W.R. 4300 class and the L.N.E.R. latest editions of the No. 1000 (G.N.) class respectively.

The producing of a model of this description involves an enormous amount of preliminary preparation in the way of drawings, samples for trying out the relative capacities of boiler and lamp, and experiments in tool-making. This has all been gone through very successfully. The models are now in the course of construction at Messrs. Bassett-Lowke, Ltd.'s works at Northampton and will be on the market during September well in time for the coming model engineering season. In addition to the arrangement in three companies' types and colours, the models are to be made with three different motive powers.

First.—Clockwork. This will be a standard six-coupled movement of the new design with specially wide pinions and having a maximum length of run.

Second.—Steam. The same model, with modified Walschaerts valve gear. This is a very attractive engine indeed, and the sample has already received favourable comment by most critical model railway owners.

Third.—Electric. The models will be fitted with an entirely new permanent magnet motor mechanism which has been so designed as to be standard for this and other models, either four- or six-coupled.

These will be fully described in a later issue.

The first of the models to be ready was the No. 0 gauge L.M.S.R. (L.Y.) 2—6—0 type engine, as shown in the accompanying photograph.

This locomotive was shown for the first time at the recent Model Railway Club Exhibition.

The engine is built throughout of steel plate with brass boilers, solid drawn copper piping, and fitted with piston-valve cylinders. The cylinders are of special hard brass, with brass pistons and piston rods, and fitted with stainless steel piston valves in order to guard against rust or seizure in use.

The lubrication is of a special character and consists of a very large

The New Model L.M.S. 2—6—0 Mixed Traffic Steam Loco.

lubricator fitted in the smoke box, and with no cocks or other adjustments to mishandle. It is made specially accessible through the ingenious way in which the smoke box is fitted. This, instead of having a small door to open, has the door embossed on the front in dummy, and to get at the lubricator the whole smoke box slides bodily off the end of the boiler, this making the filling as simple as possible.

The valve gear is made throughout of brass, nickel plated to guard against rust, and the reversing is by special reversing block with a rotary valve so arranged that it can be used to regulate the speed of the locomotive in either direction as well as for reversing.

The wheels are of hard cast iron well nickelled. The lamp is of vaporizing methylated-spirit type, with an exceptionally large reservoir which will give a long run. In actual practice the locomotive takes four minutes to get up steam, and will then steam for 21 minutes without re-filling either the boiler or the lamp, that is, using cold water. If boiling hot water is used for filling the boiler, steam is raised in a little over one minute, and the locomotive will steam continuously for 25 minutes. The tender is of the six-wheel variety and is complete with dummy axle guards and proper coal plates.

This is propably the first occasion on which a model has been ready before its prototype—the real L.M.S. engine is expected to be on the road in October.

Answers to Correspondents.

H. B. W. (Aldershot).—It would appear that No. 00 gauge (⅝-in.) would be the best for one who is continually moving about the Empire. However, everything depends on your point of view, whether the *railway* or the *locomotive* has the greater interest for you. If you like the manipulation of the loco better than railway operation, then go in for 2½-in. gauge and only bother with a plain track, minus all buildings and structural accessories.

J. W. (London, S.W.) :—We do not think that even with two levels you would get a sufficiently good No. 0 gauge line into a room only 5 ft. 6 in. wide by 8 ft. long, and your second idea to fit up a portable or semi-portable track outside the room much to be preferred. You could design a non-continuous system having two very complete terminal stations inside the room which is to be devoted permanently to the railway.

R. M. H. (Guildford) :— Messrs. Twining, Ltd., Northampton, should be able to supply the drawings you require.

L. H. P. (Christ's Hospital) :—You should consult the history of the L.B.S.C.R. locomotives, published by the *Locomotive Magazine*, 2, Amen Corner, Paternoster Row, London, E.C. 4. Of course, if you require a drawing for a model, Mr. H. Greenly's list contains several full-size diagrams of various types of L.B.S.C.R. tank engines.

E. M. (London) :— We will get the information if it is at all possible, but cannot promise that we shall be able to definitely publish drawings in any particular issue of our journal.

J. C. W. (London, W.) :—You do not state the purpose or main idea underlying your proposed scheme Do you wish to leave the train to work by itself entirely? If so, it would be very difficult to arrange the clockwork to at all times synchronize with the progress of the electric locomotive over the separate sections. If you require to operate the line in a proper railway fashion, the scheme is not worth bothering about. After having used it a few times it would get exceedingly tame and uninteresting to watch it at work. Use one of the many systems outlined in Greenly's book, "Model Electric Locomotives and Railways," price 6/6 net, post free.

The MODEL RAILWAY NEWS

Editorial and Publishing Offices:

66, FARRINGDON STREET, LONDON, E.C.4.

Single Copies, post free, 7½d. Annual Subscription, 7s. 6d.

Vol. I. No. 9. SEPTEMBER, 1925. Price, 6d.

Notes of the Month.

THE net result of our answering queries on questions of rail-planning and suggesting formations to suit given spaces has been a large influx of letters asking for plans. Nearly all of the examples are plain, rectangular rooms, with perhaps a few obstructions in the way of chimney breasts, stairs and doorways. While we have every desire to help, there are only two or three of us on the staff here who are conversant with all that has been done in the past in the matter of rail planning, and repetitions are bound to occur sooner or later. Obviously, there is a limit to the types of rail formations that can be devised to suit the ordinary square room, and some day or other we shall have published examples of all of them. Therefore, before sitting down and taking the easier course of "consulting the Editor," readers who cannot at the moment fix on a suitable plan, should look through all our back issues, and other books on the subject. It will give the reader much greater satisfaction in the end to have designed a lay-out himself, and further, he is conversant with every condition, which a letter cannot convey. More than half the queries we get do not fully state either the exact nature of the difficulty, the number of locomotives available, the main scheme of the line, or the motive power to be adopted. Therefore, our efforts to satisfy are often in vain, and correspondence has to be entered into to get a real idea of the reader's requirements.

The recent competition should prove of great help in this ever-interesting problem of rail-planning, and we are from time to time publishing designs which have certain merits, although they may not be the winning entries. This month we are reproducing Mr. H. M. Pearson's plan on page 286.

Of course, there will always be difficulties on which it may be worth while to invoke our aid, but readers should make some attempt to design their railway and not simply send us a drawing of the available space and baldly ask us to fill it. We would prefer to criticize their attempts at planning. Once they have laid pencil to paper in this way and explained in a covering letter what their ideas are, we are better able to judge as to the type of line that will suit their particular case. Correcting mistakes and suggesting alterations which will be conducive to better working is fully within our province. In all cases a query coupon and stamped addressed envelope should be included, and every drawing and document sent with the query should be signed as a ready means of identification. A request for a postal reply, of course, needs the usual 1*s*. fee.

Those of our readers who have visited Wembley this year have, no doubt, observed how much the model railways there contribute to the public interest. The excellent working model railway installed by the Leeds Model Co. in the Palace of Housing and Transport is a never-failing source of attraction. It is surrounded by giants of the locomotive world, the famous "Pendennis Castle" of the G.W. Rly. being a next-door neighbour But in spite of the imposing appearance of the "big fellows," the little Leeds trains always draw the crowd directly they are set in motion. The movement of a model railway counts for so much. When at rest, the perfection of detail can be quietly admired, but it is the sight of a miniature train in motion which thrills the spectators, young and old alike. Directly a signal drops and a train begins to move, eyes open wide and there is a buzz of excitement. "Look, it is working!" "See that signal move," "There she goes," "Here she comes"—these are the involuntary expressions which testify to the emotions aroused by something that really works. The people come rushing round from the neighbouring stands at the sound of the moving train, and they, too, are thrilled in turn. There is no doubt that the Leeds exhibit is making many new converts to the fascination of the working model railway.

* * *

At Treasure Island, too, the miniature passenger-carrying railway is the most popular feature. Here, Mr. Terence Holder, the chief engineer of the line, is the busiest "pirate" on the beach. He tells us that since the opening, they have carried well over 100,000 passengers, and the locomotives between them have covered over 1,300 miles. There are three locomotives sharing the duty between them—a G.N.R. Atlantic named "Peter Pan," a S.E.C.R. tank, named "Alice," and Mr. Holder's own N.E.R. loco "Wendy," which only recently arrived on the scene, but is doing yeomen service. The track is about 240 yards, circular in form, with a siding and engine shed. The rolling stock consists of 10 ordinary passenger coaches, and six extra coaches borrowed from Mr. Holder's railway at Broome. We had a run behind "Wendy" with Mr. Terence Holder in charge, and he really let her go all out. It was a great run. Curiously enough, there are quite as many adult passengers as "kiddies." They enjoy it just as much, and it shows how a model railway, in whatever form we use it, tends to keep us young. The Treasure Island miniature railway is probably the hardest-worked line in existence. It is on the go all day long, and the sand from the neighbouring "sea-shore" is not the least of the many trials the busy little locos have to contend with. The running staff of this line deserve the greatest possible credit for keeping the wheels going round in such splendid style

* * *

Mr. Tibor Singer and Mr. J. Logier, both of New York, have been amongst this season's visitors from over the water. Mr. Singer is very interested in the development of a supply service to enable American model railway enthusiasts to procure British goods, and has been making a number of calls with this end in view. Mr. Logier is having a locomotive built by "L.B.S.C.," and hopes to take this back with him when he returns. He is putting down a model railway in his flat in New York, and has promised us a description when the installation is complete.

E. C. B. (Aylesbury). — We are always pleased to hear from old friends. Your request will be borne in mind, as the particular design is needed by others.

T. J. C. (Derby).—Consult the latest issue of the "Railway Year Book" for this information.

Mr. F. Malham, of 30, Marquis Road, Stroud Green Road, N.4, would like to get in touch with a Model Railway enthusiast in that district.

NOTABLE MODEL RAILWAYS

Mr. W. R. S. Smart's Southern Line.

SINCE the last description of the line, which appeared in *M.R. and L.* in March, 1917, improvements in the line have been carried out rather slowly; and we may perhaps divide this article under the headings of lay-out, rolling stock and general remarks.

Lay-out.

The general design of the lay-out has been preserved, with the addition of the lengthening of the line to Portsmouth. The whole line has been laid in steel rail, and the points built up from parts purchased in sets. The two crossovers were bought. In Victoria Station an additional road has been laid in on the arrival side, and the goods and local departure roads have been lengthened by about three feet each. Unfortunately it has been found impossible to do away with the bottle-neck outside Victoria without the use of another crossover, and the writer is of opinion that there are quite enough points at this particular spot for the trains to negotiate.

Clapham Junction has also had an additional road laid in. The new road is called the up slow, and leaves the up main at East Croydon North, and at the North end of Clapham Junction converges into two roads, one going to the main, the other to the loco yard. This road has been found to be of great value in holding a train when the terminus is congested.

East Croydon has also had a goods road installed on the up side. This road is fairly long and will hold nine wagons and a locomotive. The train of private coal-owners' wagons are usually stored here.

Victoria Station, with Havant on the upper line.

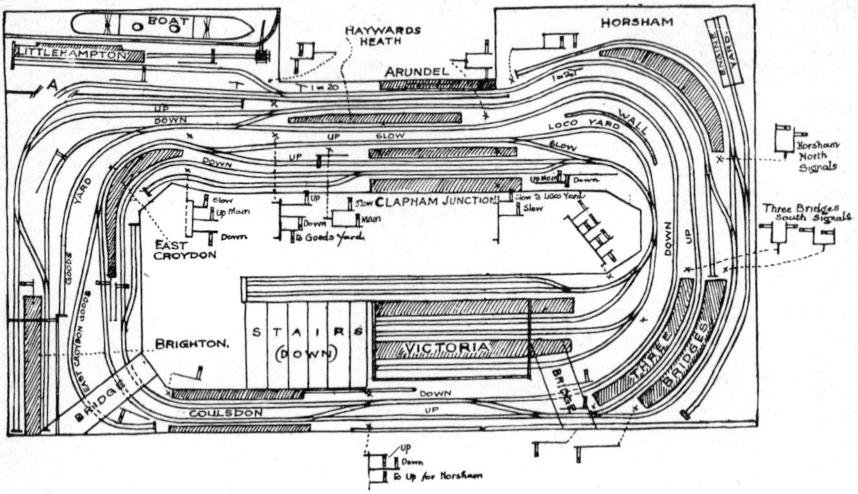

Lay-out of the line on the low level.

On the Southern Railway in the working of the Horsham via Three Bridges traffic, it is the practice, if the train is running on the main, to cross it to the slow at Three Bridges North. On this model line the down train crosses from the down main to up main at the north end of Three Bridges, thus appearing somewhat to follow the same practice. This is rendered necessary by the fact that there is not enough room for two lines from Three Bridges to Portsmouth and the traffic is, therefore, conducted upon a single road. Three Bridges Station has been enlarged. It now possesses a goods and loco road ending in an engine shed behind Horsham Station. The break-

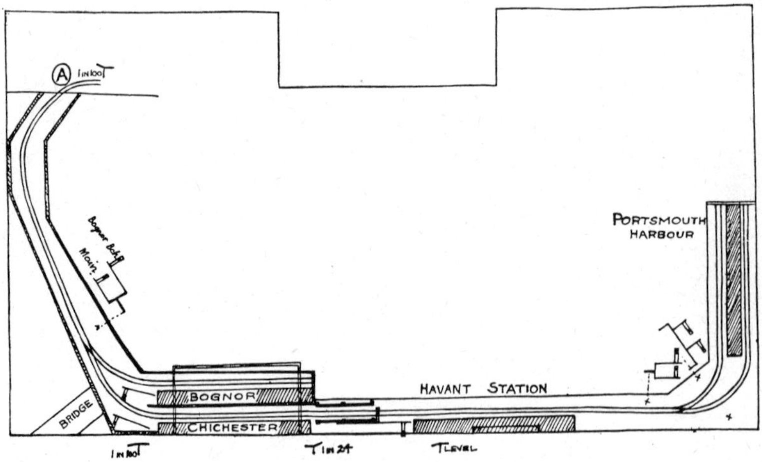

Continuation of line on high level.

down train is also kept here on a siding just long enough to accommodate it.

From Three Bridges to Brighton, the lay-out has not been altered, it being quite satisfactory. Returning to Horsham Station, a bay road, capable of holding four coaches and an engine, has been added. The line from Horsham platform to Arundel has been made straighter, resulting in a great improvement in the hauling of the trains up the bank of about 7 feet of 1 in 20. The old station of Portsmouth has been raised another 4 in. and renamed Littlehampton, and is situated on a short branch line. The main line at this point begins to cross the Brighton Yard on a viaduct.

In constructing the viaduct, by a stroke of luck there was sufficient room at the desired spots to erect piers for the viaduct without disturbing the position of any roads. Any alterations necessary on that score would have resulted in some difficult problems in planning to have produced any satisfactory result.

Clapham Junction.

Up Southern Belle approaching Clapham Junction.

Half-way across the viaduct a junction has been laid in. This has enabled two stations to be installed over Coulsdon Station. These stations are named Chichester and Bognor, the latter being on the branch; and both stations are covered by one roof.

After leaving Chichester the line climbs up the last bank and reaches Havant. This last climb was rendered desirable in order to give more room, in case of any derailment on the main line underneath. The total rise from Horsham being one foot. When Havant is passed, the line converges into two, and after negotiating the corner of the room, Portsmouth Harbour is reached.

It was at first thought that difficulty in working Brighton Yard would be experienced, due to the position of the viaduct. However, after a little practice, it has been found to be satisfactory.

Rolling Stock.

Locomotives.

Several new ones have been built, and the locomotives running are as follows :—

L.B. & S.C. Section (*B*).

A class, No. 651, 0—6—0 T	...	1
B 1 class, No. 177, 0—4—2	...	1
B 2X class, No. 210, 4—4—0	...	1
B 4 class, No. 61, 4—4—0	...	1
B 4X class, No. 52, 4—4—0	...	1
C 2X class, No. 441, 0—6—0	...	1
D 1 class, Nos. 216 and 361, 0—4—2 T		2
D 3 class, No. 369, 0—4—4 T	...	1
E 4 class, No. 495, 0—6—2 T	...	1
E 6 class, No. 413, 0—6—2 T	...	1

F class, No. 334, 2—2—2 ...	1
(Not now used)	
H 1 class, No. 41, 4—4—2 ...	1
H 2 class, No. 424, 4—4—2 ...	1
I 2 class, No. 11, 4—4—2 ...	1
T	
(Made by Bassett-Lowke)	
I 3 class, Nos. 21 and 90, 4—4—2	2
T	
K class, No. 339, 2—6—0 ...	1
L class, No. 333, 4—6—4 ...	1
S.E. & C. Section (A).	
No. 765, 4—4—0	1
S.W. Section (E).	
No. 464, 4—4—0	1
Free lance (with leaning toward S.W. practice).	
No. 36, 4—6—0	1
No. 420, 4—6—2	1
T	
Garrett Type.	
No. 251, 2—4—2—242	1
Gt. Western design	2
L. & N.W. design (purchased) ...	2
L.B. & S.C., 0—4—0 (Leeds) ...	1
T	
Total	29

NOTE.—These numbers do not include three locos belonging to my son.

Also a breakdown crane, No. 17.

Drawings have also been prepared for L. & S.W. Rly, "King Arthur" class; S.E. & C. Rly, rebuilt 4—4—0 class; S.E. & C. Rly, 2—6—0 goods.

These have been designed owing to the fact that the Southern Railway have lately moved engines from one section to another.

The A class terrier locomotive has been fastened to a coach and is run as a motor service between Littlehampton and Horsham; Horsham and Bognor; Bognor and Arundel.

Passenger services are run between Victoria and Brighton; Victoria and Horsham; Victoria and Littlehampton; Victoria and Bognor; Victoria and Portsmouth; Victoria and Coulsdon (local).

Coaches.

The majority of the coaches have been built from Leeds coach parts. A few coaches are of the tinplate variety, and four tinplate Pullmans have recently been acquired. The old three wooden Pullmans sustained a severe derailment, resulting in a crash upon the floor. They are to be rebuilt, but were originally made by my sons. One train may also be fitted experimentally as a triple set.

Wagons.

These have been built from Leeds parts and cigar boxes, and represent all classes of goods wagons. One or two varieties open and covered, including a couple of train ferry wagons.

The whole of the Brighton Section stock, with one or two exceptions, have been repainted in the colours of the Southern Railway.

The signals are still constructed with $\frac{3}{8}$-in. square posts. This is above the 7-mm. scale, but from actual experience, it has been found that 0 gauge scale signal posts require very great care to avoid breaking, and the slightly larger post is not very noticeable.

General Remarks.

The line is usually run to a time table, but it is not always that three operators are to hand. A very good selection of trains can be run by one or two operators without any arranging beforehand.

It is found that the four-coupled mechanisms are the best for climbing the Arundel bank, this one being somewhat severe, and several of the locomotives demand a pilot at Horsham.

In general, the four-coupled gives the best results. Passenger trains are usually limited to three coaches. On special occasions four or five coaches are used. It may also be considered that seven wooden wagons and a brake-van constitute a good load for a clockwork goods engine. Outside cylindered engines are found to haul less than an engine modelled after

Portsmouth Harbour Station, with Three Bridges Station and yard on lower line.

inside-cylinder practice. The amount of friction caused by the piston and connecting rods may be almost nil, but the effect can be seen in the hauling of a load. The same remarks may also be applied to six-coupled mechanisms, the crux of the matter being that the same size spring is fitted in both four and six-coupled mechanisms, due to the fact that a wider spring could not be fitted in the six-coupled one.

The scenery around the line is painted in flatted oil, cut out and fastened to a background made of plain blue wall paper. This gives quite a good effect.

It may be interesting to note that the writer's interest in model railway work is still going strong, notwithstanding the fact that he has now been actively engaged in it for about 30 years, and attributes a good deal of the "feeling-young spirit" to this splendid hobby.

H. H. Devonport.—Generally your plan is excellent, and we can see no important objections to any part of it. Write to Messrs. Mills Bros., 89, Ellesmere Road, Pitsmoor, Sheffield, and also to the Leeds Model Co., Ltd., Hunslet, Leeds, for samples of their No. 0 gauge track materials, sending the cost of postage.

An Interesting System.

WHAT will probably be one of the most interesting railways yet built is now in the course of construction at Edinburgh. The railway is being built to the order of Mr. W. Strang Watson and is situated in a large top room about 28 ft. × 18 ft. and is laid in "Lowko" steel rail.

A portion of Mr. Watson's track.

The gauge is $1\frac{3}{4}$ in. and the whole of the layout is to Mr. Watson's idea, whose chief interest in model railways is the signalling and interlocking.

The photograph shows a portion of the railway, which is built by Messrs. Bassett-Lowke, Ltd., under the supervision of Mr. A. Walker, and we hope later on to be able to give readers full particulars, plans and photos.

An "O" Gauge Goods Yard Crane.

By "SHUNTER."

THE photograph shows a model five-ton crane of 7-mm. scale, which was more or less made from scrap some years ago. When I say made from scrap, I refer chiefly to the wheels, as they came out of an American-type clock, which was picked up on the sea-shore down Portsmouth way.

The rest of the material consists of a little sheet brass or mild steel, some wire and a little piece of wood for the jib.

There should not be much difficulty in getting hold of the necessary wheels the same size as those shown on the drawing, but it will be best to get them before proceeding to mark out the frames, as any slight difference in the diameters can then be allowed for in marking the positions for the spindles.

The diameters of the wheels shown in Fig. 1 are the same as those taken from the clock, but the model would be more correct if the pinions were a little smaller and the spur wheels a little larger and all having smaller cogs. This remark applies to those on the slewing gear also.

The two side frames, Fig. 2, should be made from sheet metal about 1-16th in. thick. These are fixed together by the two parts, Figs. 3 and 4, Fig. 3 being the top one, The end spigots on these are to be made a nice fit in the holes in the frames and soldered in, and filed off flush on the outside; they may be slightly rivetted also, if preferred.

The pivot upon which the crane revolves is clearly shown in Fig. 5, and requires very little description. The big end of the taper spigot should be a nice fit in the wheel and the two washers and base, and soldered in, three or four holes must be drilled near the edge of the base plate for screws to fix it down. The frame should be a nice fit on the pivot, and revolve freely without any shake.

The slewing gear, Fig. 6, comes next. The bevel wheels are shown about the same size, but it would be better to have the one on the handle shaft smaller and the other as large as possible. Those on the original, shown in the photograph, I filed out of brass by hand, and the cogs are much too large and, as may be imagined, of rather irregular shape, so that the crane revolves in a somewhat jerky manner. However, a pair of wheels suitable for this can now be obtained from some of the model shops.

When this gear is completed it may be soldered into position between the frames, as shown in Fig. 1, taking care to get the pinion to gear properly with the spur wheel on the base of the pivot. The frame and slewing gear is now complete.

The chain drum, Fig. 7, requires a

The completed crane lifting a model gun barrel.

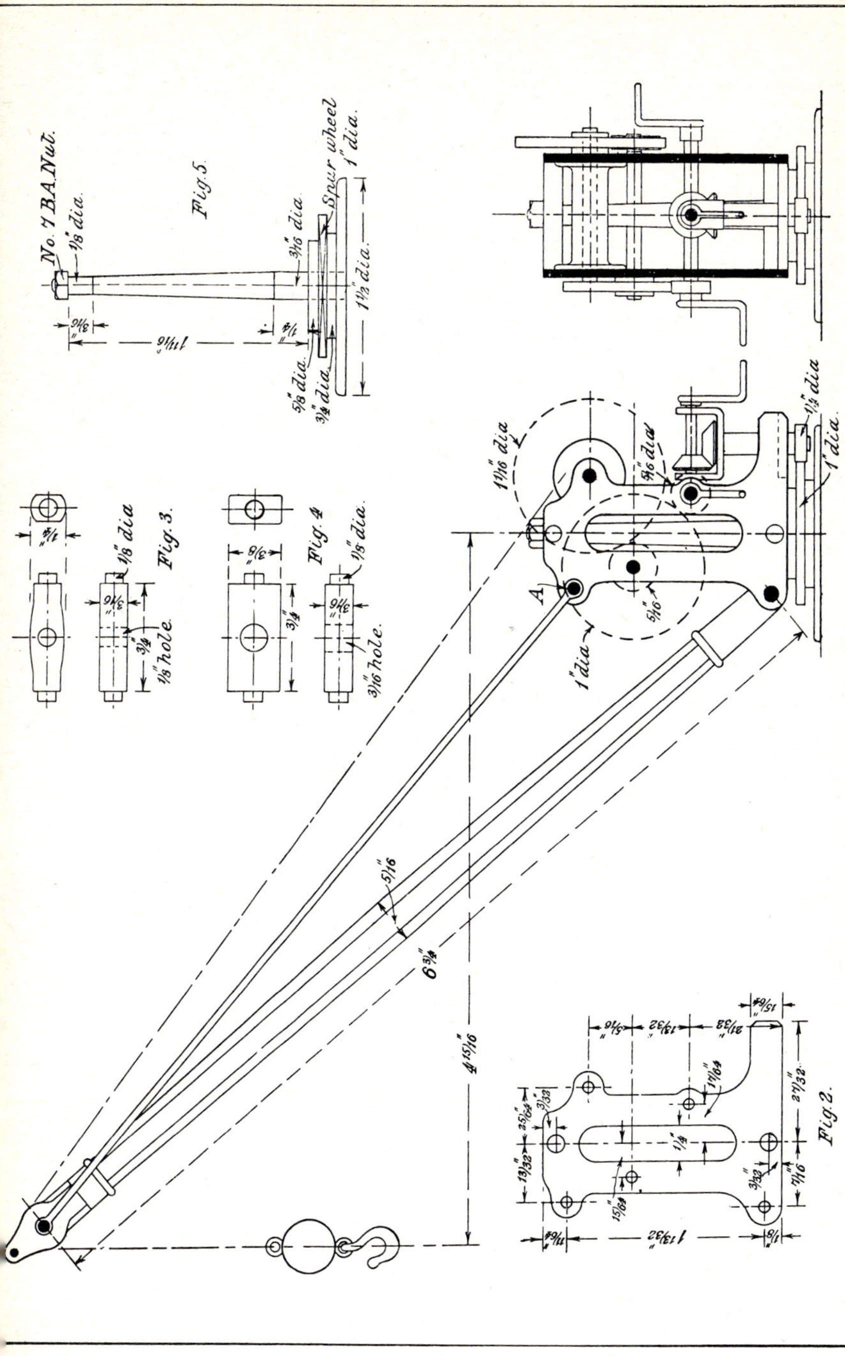

Fig. 1.—Showing side and end elevations of crane, and various constructional details.

small hole drilled through the side flange as near the barrel as possible for fixing the chain or cord. If cord is used, this hole must be countersunk on the outside to accommodate a knot to prevent the cord running out, but if chain is employed a small ring must be soldered into the hole, and the end of the chain fixed to it. Very small chain, oxydized, can be purchase from some model firms, and would give the model a much better appearance than the cord.

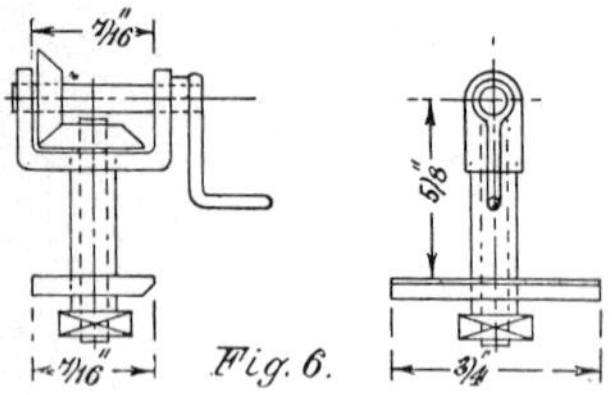
Fig. 6.

A small set screw must be provided in the centre of the barrel to fix it to the spindle. This, and all other spindles in the model, are mild steel about 5-64th in. diameter, or say 14 s.w.g. In the original all spindles are soldered into the wheels, but they should be made very slightly taper at the ends and driven into the wheels just a nice tight fit.

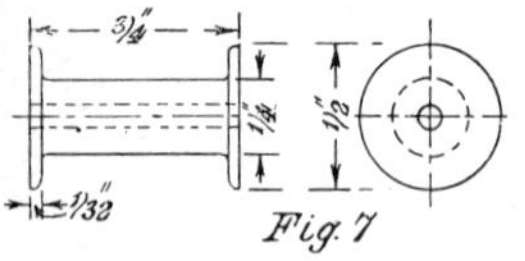
Fig. 7

The winch handles are made of wire about 21 s.w.g., bent to shape and soldered on to little pieces of round brass with holes in them to fit the ends of the spindles and soldered on.

The jib, shown in Fig. 1, is made of mahogany, or any other suitable wood. It should be carefully planed up octagonal in section and a slightly curving taper towards the ends. The ends must be rounded and made a tight fit on the top and bottom fittings. These are shown in Figs. 8 and 9. Care must be taken to make the pulley in the head, Fig. 8, a nice easy fit, but leaving no gaps at the sides for the cord to get jammed in. Fig. 10 is a stay between the frames (*see* A, Fig. 1), and the ends of the jib tie-rods are fixed to this.

The tie-rods are made of the same size wire as the winch handles. The eyes at the ends should be neatly formed and hammered or filed a little flat. They may be soldered into position on the ends of the pins upon which they fit or the pins may be slightly riveted over.

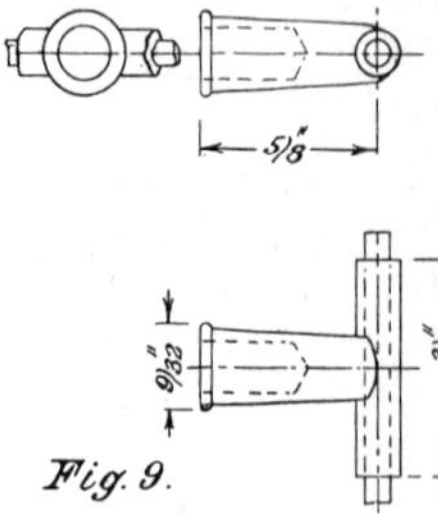
Fig. 9.

The hook can be made from a piece of 1-16th in. wire, bent to shape as near as possible, hammered flat in the widest part and then carefully filed up. Hooks of all descriptions are rather difficult to make, and small-scale ones require some patience.

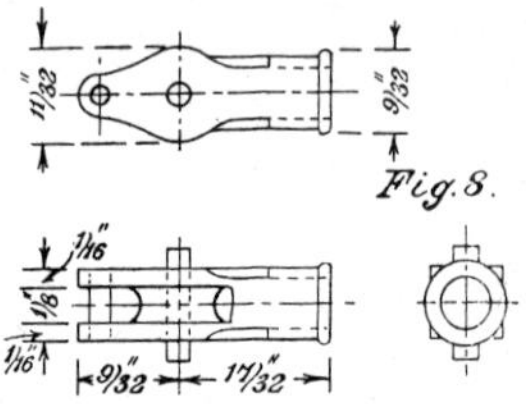
Fig. 8.

The ball is ⅜-in. diameter and turned from a piece of brass rod.

The finished model looks well if painted chocolate colour all over, excepting the wood part of the jib, which should be stone colour.

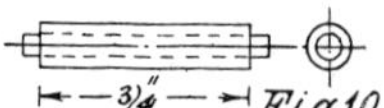
Fig. 10.

The ball, hook, and winch handles may be black.

G. R. G. (Victoria, B.C.).—We have just replied to a query giving a plan which is almost identical in requirements to your own. Please look through our columns. Foreign and colonial readers can remit for post replies by means of the international postal coupons. There is then no need to bother about obtaining English stamps.

Indoor Railway Scenic Effects.

A PERFECTLY flat model railway never looks entirely real. Although the line itself can be entirely level, the model earth should be made to undulate in a truly natural manner. Of course, there can be stretches of level country to provide a variation in effects. To obtain the best results it is just as necessary to carefully pre-determine the substructure of the system as it is to plan out the lines of railway. We are hoping to be able to illustrate a super-model model railway in the very near future. Our readers already have done some excellent things—in the way of beautifying their models, but we have yet to record a perfect example.

Blank spaces at the back or wall-side of the line—spaces which are not covered with tracks—may be in places inclined upwards to the painted scenery—the background, while the foregrounds may be dropped to a lower level, as shown in the section, Fig. 1. This scheme is usually possible at a corner of a room. The main substructure can be of the usual form—two sets of boards intersecting at right angles—and the hill at the back and the falling ground at the front may be made with a false work of odd pieces of wood and papier maché and made as indicated in the plan sketch, Fig. 2.

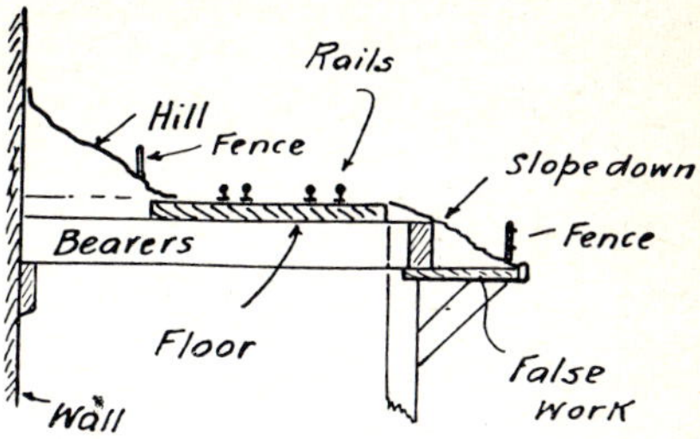

Fig. 1.

In building up rockery out of wet brown paper coated with thin glue to preserve the stiffness, don't make the boulders and projecting crags too coarse. Take note of the scale of things. A model rock 6 in. wide would represent one nearly of 30 ft. in the real article. Model trees, shrubs and plants, should all be slightly on the small size rather than of too large a scale dimension, more particularly those in the far background. Ornamental buildings in similar positions may be reduced in scale according to their distance from the line. This will help the perspective.

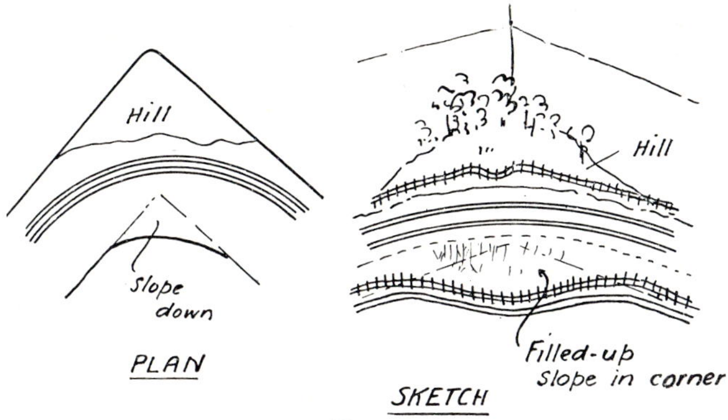

Fig. 2.

Economic Model Railway Materials.

By F. W. Shaw.

IN offering this article to your readers, I feel that many of them will think my time might have been better employed expounding my theories to my grandmother. However, everyone must make a start sometime, and it is more particularly for the beginner that these lines are written.

Painting Hints.

A red brick wall should really be red, and if it looks too gaudy, a few of Messrs. Bassett-Lowke's very excellent miniature posters will soon tone it down. Never be afraid to use plenty of paint or enamel. Messrs. Woolworth's supply sixpenny tins of assorted colours, which are just the thing for green fields, drab goods yards, grey overbridges in steel, and similar work. For such fine work as signal posts, etc., paint of a much better quality should be used, but for large surfaces, such as baseboards, judiciously used, Woolworth's paint, at small expense, gives an excellent *tout ensemble*. I don't suggest paint alone for scenic purposes. Naturally trees, fences, embankments, etc., should not be neglected, the paint merely hiding the bare patches and knitting the whole together.

Bricks and Buildings.

There are on the market several varieties of brick paper, most of which are, unfortunately, much overscale for small gauges, but Messrs. Hobbies supply one variety in particular which is made up of quite good-sized bricks in sheets 3 ft. and 2 ft., at the reasonable price of threepence per sheet. This firm also markets a tile paper in grey, which makes good platforms or cattle docks. Used for the purpose for which it was designed, these tiles are much too big and a more satisfactory method of making roofs is to paint the work a light grey, and rule slates on in indian ink after. Some model makers go to the trouble of glueing strips of card together, overlapping at each edge when making a roof and, if time is no object, the result comes out very well indeed.

An unusual method to use when making buildings in "pebble dash" or roughcast, is to glue coarse sand paper over the surface of the model and wash over with thin paint after, the colouring being left to the choice of the maker. One or two buildings made in this way give an air of realism to a model railway. which no commercial brick paper can ever attain. Apart from its excellence for signal posts, Hobbies stripwood makes very good door and window frames, and this wood has the advantages of being easily obtained, cheapness, and being easily "worked." It is rather putting the cart before the horse by describing the "trimmings" before the building materials, but, as a general rule, station buildings and similar erections, for indoor use only, can be best made of stiff cardboard, such as any stationer supplies. Old razor blades, Clemaks for preference, as these blades have a thick top to catch hold of, give a good, clean cut when making doors, windows and so on. The windows themselves can be made of old negatives in glass or celluloid.

Cigar-Box Uses.

It is a useful plan to keep friendly with the local tobacconist, and about once a fortnight, for the modest sum of twopence, he will be able to let you have an old cigar-box. If this is left in the bath overnight, the next morning it will emerge cleansed of its labels and, after having been dried, under pressure, to prevent warping, the wood is just the material for all sorts of odd jobs on a model railway.

Mr. Martens' Miniature Railway advertising train.

The Munich Miniature Railway.

THE miniature railway at Munich has been opened, and the "Pacific" locomotives are quite a success, pulling ten bogie coaches with ease. Mr. Roland Martens, who has had charge of the construction of the locomotives, writes :—

"The engines are running exceptionally smooth and steady, and take curves of 25 metres radius with ease. The boilers are steaming perfectly and the motion is excellent. It is a pity we have no long non-stop on which we could let the engines go at high speed. I wish I could see them on your R.E. (Eskdale) line. The locomotives seem to be capable of the same performance as those for Count Zborowski and Capt. Howey. The safety valves (these are the J.R. Co.'s "Greenly" pop valves illustrated in the *Model Engineer* for March 12th, 1925) are very good. The superheater is the same as yours, and the little locomotives surpass my expectations. Sunday we carried 7,000 passengers."

In the cutting at the bottom of the 1 in 50 grade.

The accompanying photograph Mr. Martens sends us shows one of the trains standing in the "Süd" (South) station with a train of eight coaches. To advertise the line, Mr. Martens has lent one of his English-built half-inch scale locomotives rigged up with passengers, and scenery to a scale comparable to a 15-inch gauge railway, with one-sixth size models of the open coaches used for the Exhibition railway. It is interesting to note that the model locomotive is the first coal-fired half-inch scale engine built to the writer's designs for Mr. Martens' private use in 1913. It was one of three engines which were exhibited at the Manchester Model Engineer Society's show in the aforementioned year.

A train in the Süd station.

Full particulars of the Munich locomotives are on the way, and it is intended to publish all technical details in the *Model Engineer* in due course. In concluding these remarks I must congratulate Mr. Martens and his firm, Messrs. Krauss, on the success they have obtained. I know from the correspondence that has passed between us during the last six months that every item in the design of the engines has been carefully considered.

H. G.

Model L.S.W. (S.R.) Overbridge.

Following the design published in our March issue, Messrs. Bassett-Lowke, Ltd., have made up a model reinforced-concrete type overbridge for No. 0 gauge. As illustrated, this is placed on two pedestal bases. These would not be used where the bridge is arranged to rest on the station platform in the ordinary way.

A Canadian Model Railway.

By Gerald S. B. Rees.

MY road is a combination of Old Country and Canadian styles, blissfully intermingled without any regard to law and order, but none the less effective. Occupies practically entire basement of residence. Mounted on permanent trestle three feet high, three feet wide three sides, with mountain section fourth side; made up of built-up bridges of different styles with painted mountain scenery at back. Every inch of the space taken up with some kind of reproduction of life-size railway, all hand made and fitted, painted in contrasting colours and wall of basement backed with cut-out railway posters, blended into " blue sky " and blue - painted building paper cut scenery-stage style to hide the ceiling and lend realism. Lighting of room from behind scenery. Ballasted with fine sand throughout to depth of 1 in. Gauge 0 track bought, electric, with power supplied from the main through a transformer at 12/15 volts with switchboard and various controls, including voltmeter to show current supplied when operating and check upon short circuits. In use three years and not the slightest trouble with the power.

" Pour Encourager."– My main idea in writing this is to encourage would-be owners of railroads without practical experience or expensive tools. A simple knowledge of electricity, keen eye for observation and patience, main factors. My curves are sharp ordinary tin-plate gauge, but with care trains are handled round same without trouble. Trackage " all over the place," as the system has just " growed," but it constitutes an inner and outer " circle " with connecting links and spurs, as well as access to a six - stall round house. The turntable was made from " beaver-board " and rests on brass rounded headed nails at outer edge to provide smooth turning by friction wheel at side, and fitted with electric lamp connections that show light when turntable in line with any round-house pair of rails. Several lights in system connected with transformer at 4 volts. Short circuiting caused originally by painting all track except running edge; paint worked into joins of connecting rails. Most of rail joins now soldered, also where there are four tracks parallel. Wires are connected to them all across at the same point, as this ensures a safe circuit in case any " missing current " in any section.

Disastrous Salt.—Use of salt to imitate snow disastrous, as it dampened the sand and caused short circuit, a bursting water-pipe overhead for same reason put one section out of action for two weeks till sand dried. Track laid on battens. Flat-surface trestle work covered with building paper to prevent ballast falling through anywhere, and this paper laps over the front edge all round for a foot and makes neat appearance when painted brown. A strip of wood all round rising one inch above the level at end edges enables the ballast to be laid right up to edge of the lay-out; looks neat and finished. To take care of cars when not in use and relieve trackage, a " high - line " viaduct is built over one track, reached up-grade; cars hauled up by meccano electric engine geared to drum with thin string and hook as hauling cable, as grade too steep for engines. Here are few tips for some amateurs who have a mind to build.

Fencing.—Cut out of stiff cardboard, with narrow strips across to represent the longitudinal wood; paint white, fix at bottom on narrow strip of wood. Cost practically nil; very effective. Most of my track is railed; around some of the curves looks like " Tattenham Corner."

Signals.—Use cigar-box wood. Use rubber band for holding at horizontal. Use thin fishing cord (other kind rots) for leads to your signal levers; works splendidly, using small eyelets, and you can take the cord round curves almost any distance.

Elevator for loading sand, sugar, etc., into cars made from a Quaker-oats carton mounted on wood base with four round wood supports over track with built-up cardboard spout, controlled by valve made from sheet tin worked with thin string from central point; works well by running an open car underneath. Spout on centre line of track high enough to clear cars.

Crossing Gates.—Built up from wood and cardboard same as fencing, controlled by rubber bands and worked by thin twine to lever central point.

As stated earlier, curves are sharp, being 12 in. radius in some places, but by setting the car couplings low on cars and not putting on too many cars, trains can be operated safely.

Rolling stock, all home made except the trucks, are built up from wood and cardboard (music-sheet mending paper varnished makes excellent windows) as near scale as possible, mostly based on Canadian Pacific rolling stock, includes one complete train with baggage car, diner, two sleepers and observation, as well as "general manager's" private car. Engine of this train is German make, altered and built up to look like a C.P.R. main-line engine. Runs at great speed, wears out its pinions quickly, but I keep a stock on hand and replace same. I mention this to explain that the entire railway is not an expensive proposition, but such as any ordinary individual with a little money to spare can work at and get satisfactory results and have a hobby that gives pleasant hours, amusement to the younger members of the family (my young son is "general manager") and is of benefit otherwise. Railway was on exhibition at the Annual Fair and was considered one of the star attractions, as much possibly for its novelty as anything else. It could not be readily moved now, as it is all fixed and built into its permanent home. About 120 feet of running track. Electric bells, imitation "tickers" that one can operate as telegraph, mechanism from alarm clock for operating warning bell at drawbridge all add to the realism. Rolling stock also includes several other passenger cars, snow-plough, three flats, two "gondola" cars, two "caboose" cars, one made to scale with all details including miniature swinging lamps, so one is able to make up complete passenger and freight trains. Six locos, all electric, steam-type pattern. Use of small rocks and small twigs, branches of Christmas trees offer a most deceptive landscape, enabling one to build up cuttings, bluffs, and tunnels. Telegraph posts are meat skewers, painted with cardboard cross pieces and white thread as wires strung along the right of way all round; also dummy lamp standards where needed. The diagram showing outline is not to scale and only roughly prepared, but it will give you an idea. Pole yard, cordwood yard, real-estate office, Indian wigwams, etc., all contribute their share to the make up of the scenic part of the work. Railway can be controlled from any one of five points at different parts of the basement. This enables one to operate it where one happens to be at the moment, without returning to the original control.

One thing to note: avoid use of any grades, especially on electric roads, as the results are not worth the extra touch of realism. Imitation galvanized roofing can be made from corrugated paper, painted slate grey and varnished. All roofs of buildings and sheds are stuccoed with sand on glue and painted bright red. General colour scheme is brown. Locomotives, some black, some Midland red: rolling stock, brown or black.

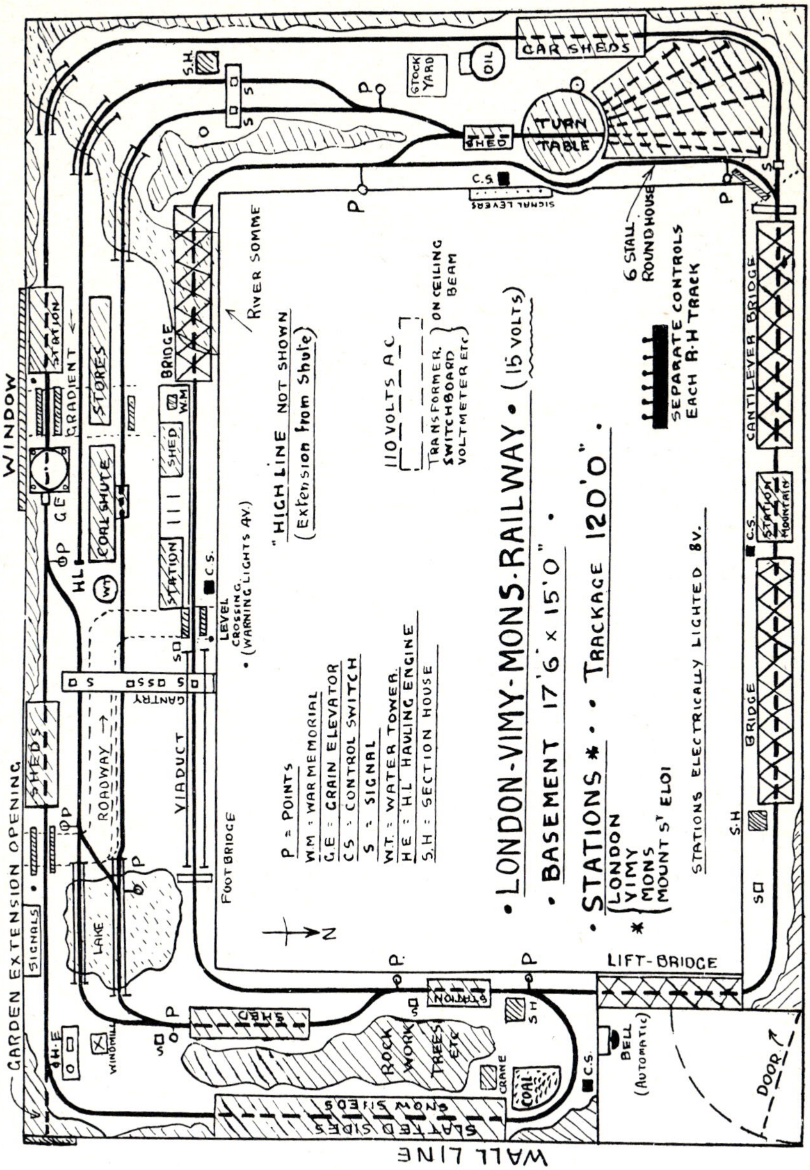

Lay-out of Mr. Rees' "O" Gauge Railway.

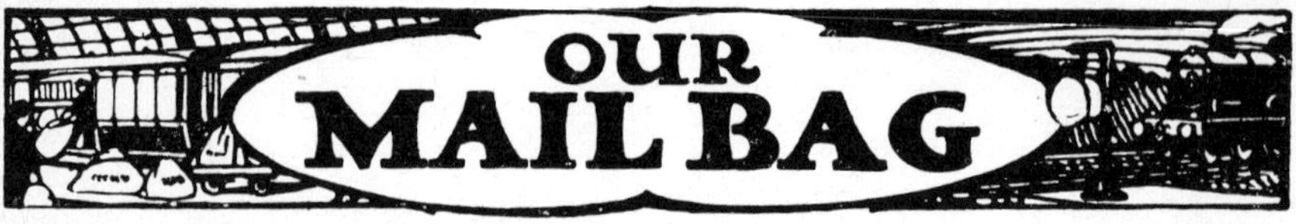

Canadian Locos.

To the Editor, MODEL RAILWAY NEWS.

DEAR SIR,

I am sending you some snaps of Canadian locos which, I think, may be of interest to readers of the M.R.N. They were taken in a small town in Saskatchewan, Glenavon, about 80 miles east of Regina.

The two of the C.N.R. 4—6—0, No. 1381, were taken in May, 1924. They were both taken from the same point, the first waiting at the platform and the next just after starting. In the second you notice that the bell is ringing. One thing that struck me as peculiar was that the second pair of wheels on the engine bogie were Mansell pattern. Can you explain this ?

The other two were taken in the middle of November, the same day as I left Glenavon on my way home. The engine this time is a 4—6—2 Pacific. I nearly froze my fingers taking these, as the temperature was about 20° below zero and there was about one foot of snow on the ground.

Yours truly,

Sutton. FRANCIS G. HAGBORG.

(We regret that we were only able to find room for one of Mr. Hagborg's photographs.)

A C.N.R. 4—6—0 Locomotive.

Model Railway Racing.

To the Editor, MODEL RAILWAY NEWS.

DEAR SIR,

The account you publish of Sir Berkeley Sheffield's splendid model railway has, I am sure, aroused the interest of a wide circle of readers, and prompts me to ask whether Sir Berkeley has done any racing with his locomotives. With a double track some hundreds of feet long and two engines of such similar dimensions and build as his Pacifics appear to be, some most exciting contests might be run. And while on the subject, may I express my surprise that so little is heard in the model railway world of the pitting of one loomotive against another, either for speed or for power. Handicapping could easily be arranged, either according to rail and loading gauges, or, more simply, to weight. Conjure up the fearful excitement as the small $2\frac{1}{2}$-in. gauge single-wheeler is seen tearing round Tattenham Corner—having been given a suitable start—and then in a few seconds a $\frac{3}{4}$-in. scale Atlantic comes roaring up on a parallel track, gaining yard by yard till the winning post is passed, perhaps at dead heat. And in the case of equal-sized locos we might have tugs-of-war ! Why not ? And perhaps win a silver cup ! Why really not ?

Yours seriously,

G. JAMES.

Westwood Park.

Mr. L. S. Monk's 2-in. Gauge Clockwork Loco.

A 2-in Gauge Clockwork Loco.

To the Editor, MODEL RAILWAY NEWS.

DEAR SIR,

I am sending you herewith a photograph and sketch of my 2-in. gauge clockwork locomotive.

You will notice that I have used a "Meccano" motor as the motive power, which, in spite of the fact that they are not constructed for this kind of work, answers the purpose very well.

The model is made up entirely of sheet brass wherever possible, the only castings being used were for the wheels, chimney, dome and safety valve. Small castings such as side rods, bogey frames, etc., I cast myself in white metal. The boiler, cab bunker and frames were cut from sheet and soft-soldered together, as unfortunately I have no appliances for hard soldering.

Needless to say, the model is not so powerful as most clockwork models of this gauge, but it puts in quite a good performance with a light load.

Having perforce to keep the cost as low as possible, I made the whole engine for 30*s*.

Yours truly,

L. S. MONK.

Saltley, Birmingham.

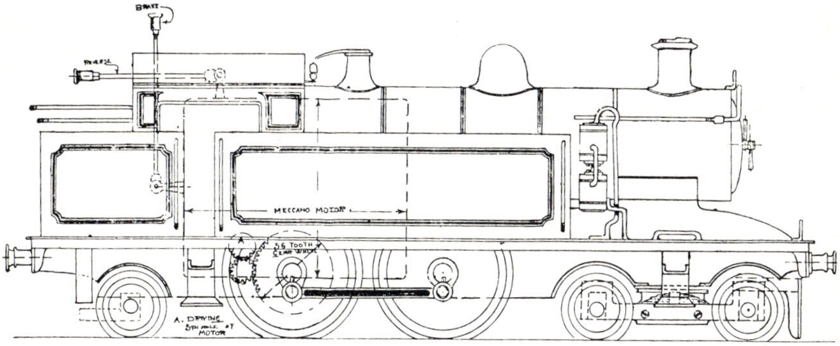

Side elevation of Mr. Monk's Loco.

Cleaning Rails of Model Electric Railways.

To the Editor, MODEL RAILWAY NEWS.

DEAR SIR,

One of the problems that beset the owners of model electric railways is the difficulty of keeping the conductor and running rails (if used as a return) sufficiently clean to enable the locomotives to get their full volts.

Mr. Henry Greenly, in his book, " Model Electric Railways," suggests that a small swab soaked in paraffin is useful in removing the greasy coatings which get rolled into both the conductor and running rails, and advocates the use of sand-paper in preference to emery. The writer finds that the rails do not keep clean very long if sand-paper is used, and has adopted the plan of using " Bluebell " metal polish, which keeps the rails clean and bright very much longer, even if the room is damp. Sand-paper is only used if the rails are very dirty and in such instances this is followed by a rub up with metal polish.

In the old *Model Railways* it was suggested that graphite might be used with advantage, especially in the case of steel rails. Graphite is classed among the conductors of electricity and is the base of one of the most modern rust-resisting paints for iron work (*Model Railways*, May, 1913). The writer has not used this method, as the few lengths of steel rails in use have been scrapped, as the dampness in the room where the railway is laid makes it inadvisable to use anything but brass or copper rails.

Perhaps other readers who are aced with this difficulty will say how they deal with it.

Yours faithfully,

GREAT WESTERN.

Converting Locomotives.

To the Editor, MODEL RAILWAY NEWS.

DEAR SIR,

I have got a gauge 00 and a gauge 1 railway. On the 00, I frequently run expresses, and I thought that the ordinary tank loco on an express did not look realistic. So I attempted to convert a tank into a tender engine, first experimenting on a broken engine. I took the rear bunker and back right off, leaving the open cab. Then I took a goods truck and cut the one end open and the sides to represent a tender, joining the two together with wire.

Yours faithfully,

O. JACOBSEN.

Birmingham.

Time-table Tips.

To the Editor, MODEL RAILWAY NEWS.

DEAR SIR,

I have an idea which I think may be new, and rather useful to owners of model railways who run time tables.

There appears to be a difficulty in obtaining lengthy runs between stations, and some trains probably have to be timed to split seconds at junctions.

If, for instance, a train takes 20 seconds, start to stop, from one station to another, and waits 10 seconds in the station, why not consider these times as two and one minute respectively ? This would appear more in line with a suburban time-table. Expresses would have longer timings.

To make this workable, a clock could be arranged to allow the minute-hand to make a complete revolution in 10 minutes or so. The ratio could be adopted to suit the individual or the system. If the clock is hung in a position visible to every operator, it would simplify matters by enabling them to time trains from one o'clock.

I have not tried this idea, as my interest in railways is confined to reading about them, but having hit on the notion, I am passing it on, in the hope that it will help many railway owners over a peculiar difficulty.

Yours faithfully,

W. O. BROWN.

Gipsy Hill, S.E.

Mr. T. J. Henry's Rolling Stock.

"O" Gauge Engines and Rolling Stock.

To the Editor, MODEL RAILWAY NEWS.

DEAR SIR,

Enclosed is photo of some rolling stock of my 0 gauge railway. There is nothing startling about them except that they show the type of guard's van used here, also double-deck sheep trucks and bogie freezing waggon used to take meat from the works to the boats. The engines I built myself, two steam ones being built from description in *Model Engineer*, February 10th, 1910. They are good engines, steam well and are great pullers. The other engine is clockwork driven, but will not pull near as much as the steam ones. The wagons I have are home made, of wood, rather on the heavy side; the clockwork engine will pull eight trucks and the steam engines pull 18. That's a train about 11 ft. long. Glad if above is any use to you.

Yours faithfully,

T. J. HENRY.

Wellington, N.Z.

Mountain Railways.

To the Editor, MODEL RAILWAY NEWS.

DEAR SIR,

In regard to the question of space, would not a miniature mountain railway, in the form of a spiral, solve the problem to a certain extent, where no room is available for an extensive level line?

If the track was made continuous, it seems to me the line might be worked by gravitation. A loaded train coming down could pull a light one up to the top.

If an outdoor line was constructed, the trains might be worked by wind-power, as suggested in "Windmills and Wind Motors."

I have not tried the ideas, but I think they are workable.

I am not an enthusiast, but find the MODEL RAILWAY NEWS very interesting from the artistic point of view.

Yours faithfully,

Maidstone. F. FARRANCE.

"OO" Gauge Possibilities.

To the Editor, MODEL RAILWAY NEWS.

DEAR SIR,

If any of your readers have given the 00 gauge Bavarian electrical locos a trial on tinplate rails (as supplied with the sets), I should be very interested to know results.

To my mind this gauge offers wonderful possibilities for a really good track lay-out in the small space most of us have at our disposal, and I am pleased to note one manufacturer is making several types of locos in gauge "00," but these, like the standard engines supplied with the Continental sets, have no connecting rods.

At present I am working a "0" gauge lay-out in a room 8 ft. × 9 ft. 6 in., which means sharp curves and little scope for realistic train running—four coaches and a hefty tank loco mean one side of the track filled!

My only loco is a 4—4—4 metropolitan tank (outside cylinders) which I converted from a "George V" 4—4—0 express.

Best wishes to our "M.R.N.," which fills a long-felt want.

Yours sincerely,

Aylesbury. "ENTHUSIAST."

"OO" Gauge Hints and Grouping.

To the Editor, MODEL RAILWAY NEWS.

DEAR SIR,

The drawing is of a type of signal resembling the G.N.R. somersault, suitable for 00 gauge. It is of very simple construction.

I have just discovered that a No. 0 clock key fits the table railway engines. This is a great advantage, as it is of stout construction.

A useful fence can be made for this gauge out of the wooden pegs supplied to the boot trade. They are just the right height and are pointed.

I shall be very interested to hear more about the new mechanism which was referred to in the January issue

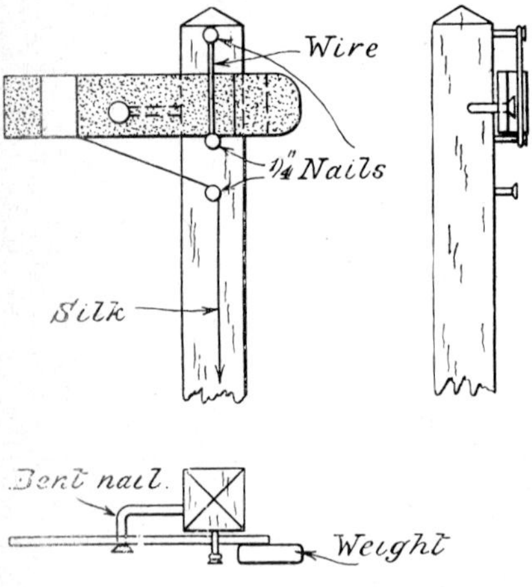

An "OO" Gauge Signal.

by Mr. Stewart-Reidpath, as a long run is very desirable. It is on account of the short run given by these little engines that a continuous railway is an advantage.

Concerning grouping, I heartily sympathize with those enthusiasts who have an interest in one railway, but there is another side to the problem. If one admires certain locomotives of different railways then grouping can be blamed for the incongruity of the loco stud.

Yours truly.

Belfast. G. A. MCCULLAGH.

Grades for Model Clockwork Locomotives.

To the Editor, MODEL RAILWAY NEWS.

SIR,

I regret not having replied to your New York correspondent, Mr. Tibor Singer's letter, referred to in your May issue. Clockwork locomotives are all "vim" at the start. There is usually no difficulty in accelerating the train; and the stored-up power would only be wasted in the internal-governor brakes if the engine were assisted by a down grade at the start. At the finish the power available is at a low ebb and the train may be assisted by a down gradient. Using an "up" gradient at the finish would only tend to shorten the run. Clockwork locomotives are, of course, only of very limited flexibility in their action.

Yours faithfully,

HENRY GREENLY.

A Protest.

To the Editor, MODEL RAILWAY NEWS.

DEAR SIR,

Just a line of gentle protest against the somewhat aggressive views of "Disgruntled" and Col. Hamilton. "Live and let live" should apply to model matters. Both correspondents make peculiar statements—why should a motor function badly in a steam-outline loco, "Disgruntled"?—and why does the Colonel class clockwork and steam against electric and freak?

Let us remain at liberty to choose the type of loco that best suits our individual requirements — without feeling we are "beyond the pale" by so doing.

Yours very truly,

A. R. WALKLEY.

Wimbledon.

Signals for 3½-in Gauge Outdoor Model Railway.

To the Editor, MODEL RAILWAY NEWS.

DEAR SIR,

I enclose a short description of some signals I am building for my line. I do not claim that the idea is original. Similar schemes have probably been worked out and described in the model engineering press. I worked out this idea myself, not having seen any similar arrangement.

I rather question whether it is advisable or possible to equip an outdoor model railway of the above scale with a complete installation of signals worked from frames and interlocked with points, etc. For one thing, changing climatic conditions are sure to cause trouble, and again, I venture to maintain that the chief interest in such a railway, if worked by steam, is the management of the locomotives. In any case, the necessity of working a complete set of signals would involve a corresponding increase in the operating staff.

A Bracket Signal.

On the other hand, I have badly felt the want of some means of indicating the state of points which would be visible from a distance. As described in the Model Railway News for April, my line is a continuous track, with two loops, besides sidings. Trains are run in either direction. I have, therefore, had the idea that a bracket signal at each set of points in the main line, connected to the point rod, so that one arm is "off" when the other is "on" and *vice versa*, according to the set of the points, would meet the case, being of real practical use, besides adding to the appearance of the line.

The posts are made of any handy wood, and all the metal parts of any scraps I had about. The arms and spectacle plates were cut out solid from some galvanized sheet iron. In the case of the ringed arm, this was also cut out solid with the arm. The bell cranks were made from odd pieces of brass plate from old door locks, etc. The pivots for the arms, short pieces of 3-32-in. brass wire. At one end a screw thread is cut for a short distance, allowing room for a nut (to go between post and arm), arm, and lock-nut outside. The hole in the arm was tapped for extra security. The end of the wire passing through post was furnished with a washer and simply bent over. A piece of the same wire was used between the lowest bell crank and centre straight lever. A smaller gauge will do for the shorter lengths.

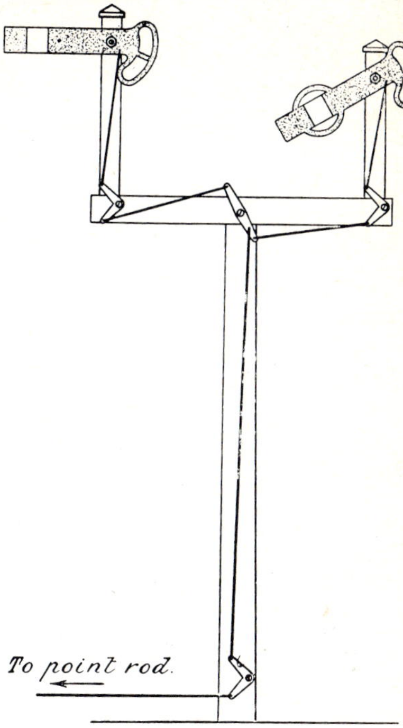

Wiring of Signal for 3½ in. Gauge.

The bell cranks are pivoted at the centre with small No. 4 wood screws, a washer being placed between crank and post. The wires are simply threaded through small holes at the ends. The finials, being of London and North-Western pattern, are easily made. The arms should, of course, be made of fairly stiff metal.

No great skill is required in the work, and only an ordinary set of tools. A die and wrench is required for screw-threading the arm pivots.

H. Simpson (Major).

Carlisle.

Designed by Col. Hamilton for very narrow curves, fitted with link motion reversing gear and Smithie's type water-tube boiler.

A Loco. for Sharp Curves.

To the Editor, MODEL RAILWAY NEWS.

DEAR SIR,

The "Vulcan" was designed by me as a tender engine which could take exceptionally sharp curves for its gauge. This should interest a lot of model engineers, as the great bugbear of most of them is the narrow curve. I see several writers telling us "Have curves of large radius." They might as well say "Be good and you will be happy." This loco shown in the photo above can take a 4-in. radius curve, with a outer rail elevation of $\frac{1}{8}$ in. easily, and can get into a siding of $3\frac{1}{2}$in. Gauge 2 in.! It was designed to be driven just like a real engine. To be started slowly, stopped, reversed, and to take its turn at shunting. Consequently I had the regulator and reversing lever made larger than scale. To go on strictly scale lines is an absurdity. Some things you can make to scale and some you certainly can not, particularly on the smaller gauges.

Yours sincerely,

W. HAMILTON.

Suggestion *re* Model Weigh Table, and a Lay-out.

To the Editor, MODEL RAILWAY NEWS.

DEAR SIR,

Please let me thank you for the little journal to hand. It is just the kind of publication I have been looking for. Several suggestions and hints have already been tried out and have proved successful.

I find it very difficult to do any model work here. I have not yet found any firm stocking parts for the model maker. It makes one long to walk into one of the well-known stores in London and have a good feast once again.

In regard to the reverse lever, p. 125 (April number), I have tried a similar arrangement but have found the trip jerked right back at contact and often failing to reverse. To remedy this I have drilled a small hole in that part of the trip which rests on the permanent way, and have a small weight suspended from it. This also automatically sets the trip for the next train. By coupling it up with the signals I find I have a good preventative for trains overrunning the signals. It is fixed with good results in front of "starters." On releasing the signal the trip is lifted out of action.

I have also tried out the "model weigh table," described in the same issue, but find there is a tendency to cant too much and fall off on the outside of the table. May I suggest instead of the lever suspension, as provided in the sketch on p. 112, something on the lines of the sketch herewith. A is a pivot, B a pivot to block C on base D, E are spiral springs of which there are six, two at each end and two in centre each side. Pins could be housed into plate F, passing through springs and also base D. I have not yet had time to try it out, but feel sure it will act all right.

My model, the "Edithville" Railway, is anything but pretentious.

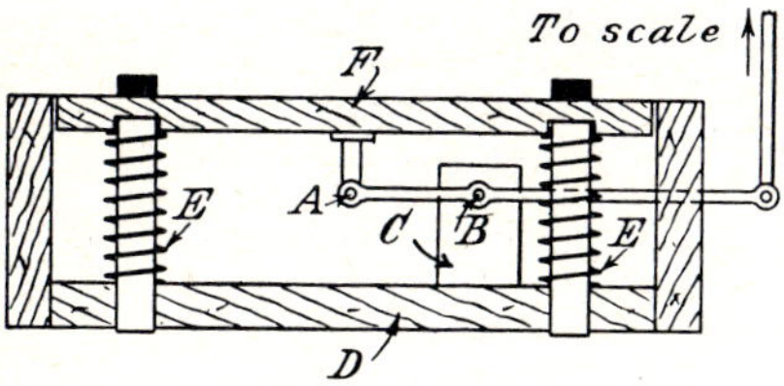

First of all I am cramped for room—the only available being a former chaff house, 16 ft. × 8 ft. Signals, loco shed, goods depot, and some of the rolling stock are home made. I only have one loco at present, but am at work on a free-lance tank 0—4—0.

Am enclosing a sketch of the "lay-out," which is built up on a shelf two feet above ground level. A and B are departure platforms—west and east respectively—C is arrival platform for all trains. I hope to work a turntable in soon and expect to have to shorten dead end D and run a road off the loco-shed road.

With the very best of wishes to the fraternity of model railway enthusiasts, and to you all of the MODEL RAILWAY NEWS.

Wishing our paper every success.

Yours very sincerely,

(REV.) JOSEPH W. BUDGE.

Western Australia.

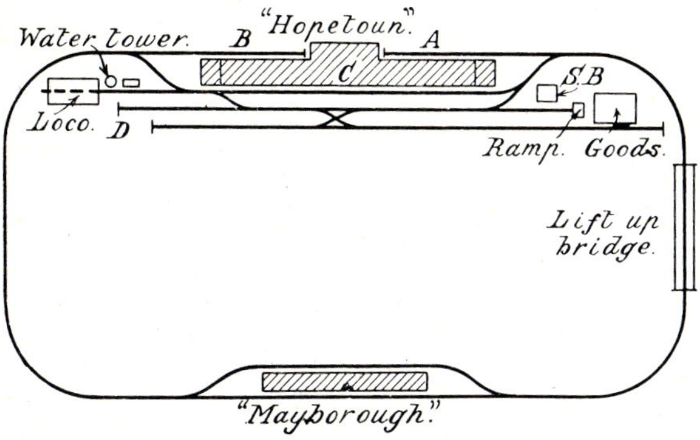

G.W. v. L.N.E.R.

To the Editor, MODEL RAILWAY NEWS.

DEAR SIR,

First of all, congratulations for the fine little paper. It is the very thing for us young enthusiasts who have little skill and scanty means, but the beginnings of a model railway, and the wish to make it a first-class concern.

In the last month's issue, I noted a letter (from Mr. J. Francis Parker) which is nicely calculated to annoy any L.N.E.R. enthusiast. I should have thought that if this gentleman had read all the available accounts of the trials, more especially Mr. C. J. Allen's articles in the *Railway Magazine*, he would have come to the conclusion that no opinion can be formed as to which of the two was the better, and that the only sensible thing to do is to keep an open mind, giving the locomotives equal honours.

A Great Eastern driver told a friend of mine that, given a "1500," a good fireman, and a month to get used to the whims of the engine, he would beat "Caerphilly Castle" on her own track. This serves to show the great faith the Great Eastern men have in their fine machines, and if some of your G.W. enthusiasts could see these "1500's" toddling up Brentwood Bank with 14 and even 16 bogie carriages, including kitchen and restaurant cars, they might think that other 4—6—0's besides their own can do some fine work when they choose.

Now this brings me to my real reason for writing to you. Can you, or any of your readers explain the lack of G.E. model locomotives? Only on three occasions have I heard of a G.E. model; (1) A "Claud" built by a G.E. employee, illustrated in the *G.E.R. Magazine* before the war; (2) "L.B.S.C." mentioned a little while ago in the *M.E.* that he had a "1500" awaiting repairs. (3) Mr. Howie mentions gauge 1 clockwork locos of L.N.W.R., G.E.R., M.R. and L.M.S.R. types.

No one can deny the prettiness of the "Clauds" and "Super Clauds," indeed, I think the latter may vie even with the G.C. "Directors" for appearance. The D 81 0—6—0's provide a boiler big enough for any model maker's requirements, and why "Decapod" was never modelled (except in paper weights) I cannot understand. Nothing could be more imposing than a ten-coupled tank on one's railway, although its long wheelbase might be some hindrance. If any reader has G.E. models, and has photographed them at any time, I am sure many of your readers would be glad if such photos were published in the M.R.N.

Yours faithfully,

ALAN C. SANDWELL.

Brentwood.

G.W.R. Model Rolling Stock.

To the Editor, MODEL RAILWAY NEWS.

DEAR SIR,

I have read with interest the various complaints against the model manufacturers in the way which the Great Western has been slighted with regard to models of this Company's rolling stock. I myself have been interested in small-scale models for many years, but never have I even seen a passable reproduction of a Great Western engine in the smaller scale. There are, true, one or two on the market, but they are very poor. Those awful flanges and bogies hanging by a bit of wire are not the type of loco we older hands are interested in. I am inclined to think that the trouble is due to the G.W. engines having a distinct appearance.

For instance, a standard 4—4—0 type on most railways will lend itself to another line by simply altering the cab and, say, splashers, but it cannot be done with the G.W. and call it a "County." I have my mind on a 4—4—2 tank now on the market. Some are painted black and lettered L.N.W.R.; others are green and marked G.N.R., another model, presumably a George V type, was standing in the same show case, but sported a beautiful coat of green paint. Whether this was intended to represent a Great Western loco, the makers did not say. This may be all very well for the casual who does not care if his locos are painted blue or green as long as they go round the track, but it will not do for us older hands.

It is up to the makers to cater for the thousands of Great Western admirers and let us have a "Castle" (perhaps the cylinders are in the way of the trailing bogie wheels), or a rebuilt "Saint," with its small wheels, would be an ideal type. But do let them put wheels with small flanges under it, as they utterly ruin all small models. Surely, there are enough L.N.E. "Flying Scotsmen" and L.M.S. "George V's" on the market to stock all lines. Why the most famous engines in the country should be ignored is hard to say.

A. P.

Oldbury.

Scale Tonnage.

To the Editor, MODEL RAILWAY NEWS.

DEAR SIR,

I beg to submit the following list for reference purposes.

Scale-model tonnages usually adopted in the various standard gauges:—

Gauge No. 0 ($1\frac{1}{4}$ in.)	1 lb. = 29 tons
Gauge No. 1 ($1\frac{3}{4}$ in.)	1 lb. = 13 tons.
Gauge No. 2 (2 in.)	1 lb. = 7 tons.
Gauge $2\frac{1}{2}$ in.	1 lb. = 5·41 tons
Gauge $3\frac{1}{4}$ in.	1 lb. = 2·4 tons.
Gauge $3\frac{1}{2}$ in.	1 lb. = 1·82 tons

Yours truly,

W. W. TASKER.

Argoed, Mon.

[We acknowledge the receipt of several other letters, which we have been obliged through lack of space to hold over till our next issue.]

Queries and Replies.

T. H. W. (Beccles) sends plan for criticism and signalling lay-out.

Where a single line loops out into two platform roads it is usual to arrange the main line signalling so that trains run into the left-hand roads only in each direction. In the "down" direction only, platform No. 2 at station B would be used and No. 1 for the "up" trains. This will considerably simplify the signalling arrangements. You will also do well to cut out the wall-side platform at station B. This procedure would allow you to increase the radius of the entering and exit curves by at least four inches. At station A, the platform numbered 6 would be the "down" and No. 5 the "up." No. 7 is, of course, available for trains in either direction. And for shunting purposes, all roads can be used. These operations, being within the control of station boxes, are similar in effect to the use of the wrong road for passing purposes, which is common to double-line railways where accommodation sidings do not exist.

Taking the "down" signals first from station B, the following may be used :—

"Down" Signals.

- Starter from No. 2 (B).
- Advance starter.
- Distant for A.
- Home for A.
- Starter and distant A 6.
- Starter and distant 6 7.
- Junction home.
- Distant for B on gantry.
- Outer home.
- Inner home with shunt signal for No. 1 road.

"Up" Signals.

- Starter and distant from No. 1.
- Home for B No. 7.
- Home and distant for No. 5.
- Shunt signal for No. 6.
- Main home signal for No. 5.
- Starter for No. 5.
- Siding starter for No. 4.
- Advance starter.
- Distant for No. A 1.
- Home for No. A 1.

Crossover disc signals as required.

(Note.—Distant signals may be omitted.)

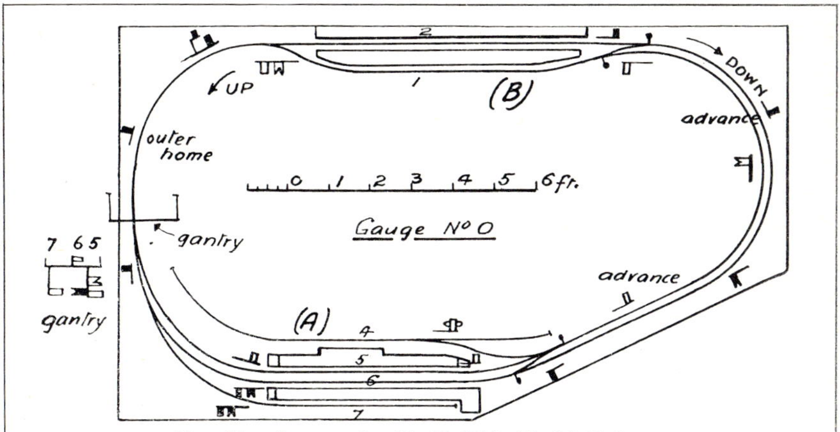

Signalling Lay-out for T. H. W.'s Model Railway.

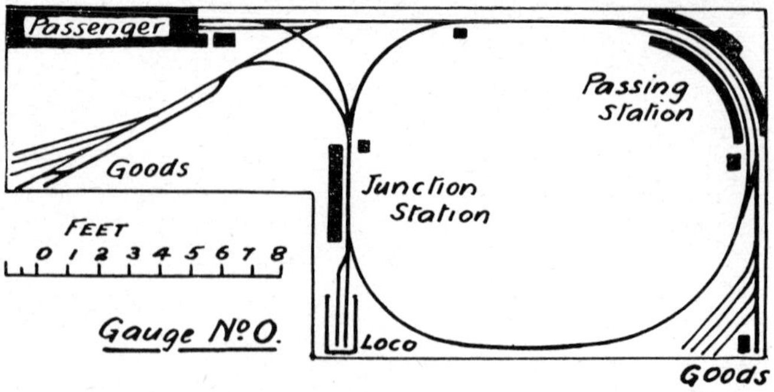

Plan for C. S.

C. S. (London, N. 10) writes, sending a plan of a room 24 ft. long, asking for an idea for a plan.

By this time our columns are containing the main characteristics of nearly all the types of plans we can think of. Therefore, readers must not expect us to be able to invent a new kind of plan for any and every conceivable shape of room that may be encountered.

The shape and size of the room referred to in this instance, however, suggests a modification of the single terminus, triangular junction type of plan in which there is also a continuous line. In the block plan sketch herewith—we must refer readers to other published plans and to the many requirements of practical railway working laid down in Mr. H. Greenly's book, "Model Railways," for the minor details—we have shown the passenger terminus station and the main goods yard in the annexe. The main portion of the space is occupied by the continuous line. This part of the line comprises a passing station with a minor goods yard and a junction station controlling one way into the terminus and principal goods yard. Near this station is arranged the locomotive depot. This scheme is not uncommon in real practice. Very often the loco department is situated some distance from a large town and the working in and out of light engines will certainly increase the interest of the line. Quite large-radius curves are possible in all parts of the main line. It is only necessary to reduce the radius to 2 ft. 6 in. in the smaller goods sidings. The line really requires several operators to get the best out of it.

H. M. P. (Golders Green).—We are interested in your appreciative letter and are sorry that you were not a prize winner. Yes, of course, you can apply elliptical entrances to curves, as transition curves are more particularly useful in the smaller-gauge railways. You are also correct in your surmise that if ordinary tangential curves are used (a straight line running direct into a circle of given radius) the superelevation of the outer rail must commence on the straight. Marking out track on a wooden substructure by centre lines is useful in that sleepers can be marked with a centre line and an equal overhand on each side of the rail obtained. The method of marking out is of small importance only, so long as the marking out, in some shape or form, is done with reasonable accuracy. Mr. H. Greenly, in introducing the popular variety of No. 00 gauge, used a scale of 4 mm. to the foot. Others prefer to use $3\frac{1}{2}$ mm. Everything depends on the degree of accuracy and quality of workmanship that is desired or that is possible.

WITH THE CLUBS

The Model Railway Club.

Mr. Fish's Lecture on the subject of "Models of Long Ago" on the 23rd July was well attended by an interested audience. The lecturer took us back nearly a hundred years, if not quite; but he had only to go back a few decades to show his audience models as far behind present-day developments as the most archaic machines recently on view at the Darlington Centenary. It was interesting and amusing to see the antics of a commercial model of the early Nineties under its own steam.

An innovation in the form of a "ramble" under the charge of Mr. W. R. S. Smart took place on the 25th July. A strong party assembled at King's Cross; taking the train to Potter's Bar, the party walked by the side of the line to Hatfield, where tea had been arranged, returning thence by train to London.

There is an equally suitable walk in the South of London, and it is proposed to organise another of these rambles.

Fixtures for September :—Saturday 5th, Shed Visit to Willesden, L M.S.R.; Thursday 10th, Track night; Saturday 19th, Old Oak Carriage Sidings, G.W.R.; Thursday 24th, Lecture; Saturday 26th, Shed Visit to Brick layer s Arms, S.R. Hon Secretary, R. Henvey, White Cottage, Shirley, near Croydon

The Wimbledon & District Model Railway Club.

September Time-Sheet :—7th, 7.30 p.m.—Red Cross Hall, Church Road. A lecture on "The Romance of the Railway Centenary." By Mr. J. F. Gains, Editor of the *Railway Magazine*. An interesting evening is assured, so invite all your friends who are interested in railway matters. On September 21st. at 7.30 p.m.—Test Track Night and Rummage Sale. These sales are always good fun and much useful material changes hands. All members are requested to take a part in the proceedings. Sept. 26th—A visit to Kentish Town L.M.S.R. Meet Kentish Town (Underground), 2.45 p.m.

The King's Cross visit on July 25th was essentially a locomotive day, several Pacifics, a N.E. section Atlantic, a G.C. "Lord Farringdon" and one of the original G.N. Atlantics being viewed at close range.

All active members are requested to take part in this year's "Shephard Cup" competition. We want a really good show this time. Full particulars of rules, etc., can be obtained from the Hon. Secretary.

Prospective members are notified that only half the yearly subscription is required from those joining during the remaining portion of the year. Hon. Secretary, R. Shephard, 27, Bernard Gardens, Wimbledon.

The Manchester & District Model Railway Club.

Since the last report the following events have taken place :—

18th July. A club visit to Crewe North Steam Sheds, L.M.S. (L. and N.W. Section), A number of excellent photographs were obtained, and members thoroughly enjoyed the visit.

11th August. A paper "Scales and Standards in the Smaller Gauges" was given by Mr. Theodore Horn, M.A.

Future Events :—8th September. Club meeting at Headquarters. Quarterly subscriptions due. This is the last of the Summer session monthly meetings. Winter session meetings will be held bi-monthly.

12th to 19th September. The Secretary will not be able to attend to any club business.

September visits to Loco Sheds not arranged at time of going to press, but the Secretary of the Stephenson

Locomotive Society (Lancashire branch) would allow any members to join his party on visits to Horwich and Preston sheds on 12th September, and Bank Hall and Aintree on September 26th. Any member desirous of attending is requested to let me have a postcard at least three days before the visit. This is imperative, in order to make arrangements. J. A. Dean, Hon. Secretary, 29, Gorse Lane, Gorse Hill, Stretford, Manchester.

Model Railway Planning Competition.—No. 1.

Mr. H. M. Pearson's Plan.

The following was among the plans commended in the recent competition. Mr. H. M. Pearson (London, N.W.), the designer, says:—

"The model railway is designed to serve four towns—A, a large city, the headquarters of the Railway Co., corresponding, say, to a London terminus; B, a market town like Banbury; C, a large commercial town such as Sheffield, and D, a city like Mânchester.

The railway is level throughout on the continuous main line, but from beyond the North junction at C, the branch to D rises at 1 in 35 to within five feet of the buffer stops.

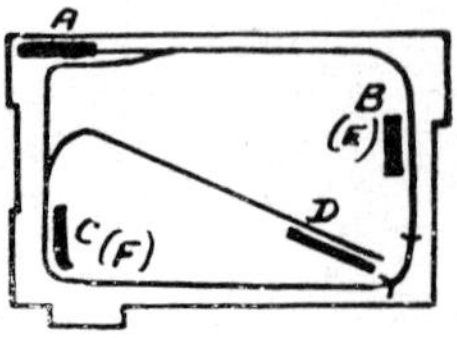

The line is single throughout, but between A and B two single lines are provided in view of local traffic. Nearly all the main line curves are of 3 ft. radius and 2 ft. 6 in. curves elsewhere, with a few 2 ft. radius curves in the yards at C and B. For convenience in working traffic to a time table the stations B and C are double-named, B becoming E for trains from C and station C being F for trains from E, as shown in the block diagram above."

A specimen time table was included but this is not reproduced herewith.

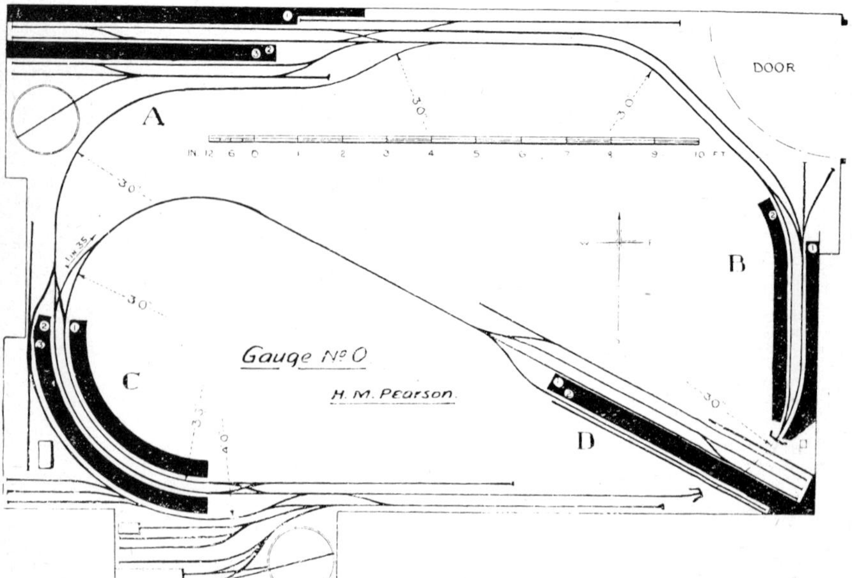

The New Model L.N.E.R. type loco.

The New Model 2-6-0 Locomotives.

WE are now able to publish a photograph of the new Bassett-Lowke model L.N.E.R. type loco and a drawing of the L.M.S. type, of which a photograph appeared last month.

The general specification given of the L.M.S. type applies to the other models. In the Great Western model the valves are operated by inside eccentrics, as in the prototype.

All the models will be obtainable in two styles of finish :—

(1). In the standard colour and lettering of the Company and

(2) In plain eggshell black with red lining as adopted as the standard in tank engines and goods locomotives.

The clockwork movement fitted to these three models is the best that it is possible to obtain, being built up with extra wide pinions and long bearing surfaces for the spindles, and constructed to give the maximum length of run that is possible with a spring motor mechanism that will go into the space available in the body.

We intend to deal next month with the new permanent magnet motor that has been designed specially for those locomotives fitted with electric propulsion. This motor will be found suitable for all model railway requirements where a permanent magnet motor is preferred. The magnet is a recently-discovered steel alloy and its outstanding features are its extraordinary power, combined with a practically everlasting permanency, both qualities being very valuable for model electric locomotives.

In addition to being supplied complete in the locomotives, these motors will be available, complete with wheels for those who wish to build their own models. The mechanism will be made up in two

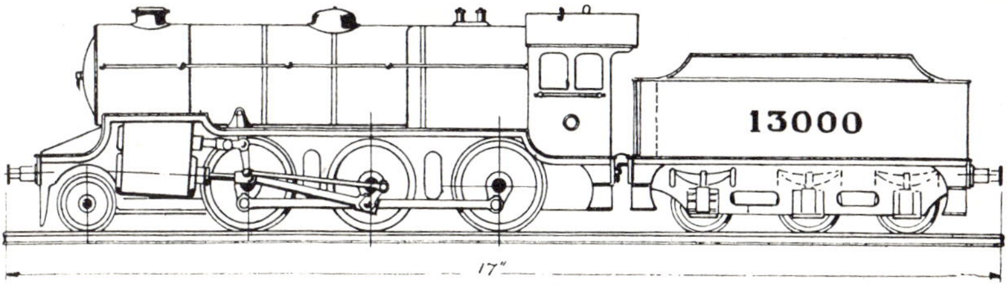

Quarter-scale elevation of the model L.M.S. 2-6-0 mixed traffic steam loco.

types, four-wheeled and six-wheeled, and will be supplied with wheels in cast iron and steel axles, also coupling rods, all finished in dull nickel plate. The motors are wound for a voltage of 6/8 d.c.

Messrs. Bassett-Lowke, Ltd., Northampton, will supply their leaflet dealing with these latest productions, or you may call at their London or Edinburgh branch to inspect the new models.

New 2½ in. Gauge Castings.

Messrs. Bond, Ltd., of Euston Road, London, N.W., are exhibiting new castings and finished parts in the "J.R." series. Some of these were referred to in their last month's advertisement, but castings are now available for the large Roscoe type lubricator designed for piston-valve type outside cylinders described in the *Model Engineer* (May 14th issue). This lubricator fits between the frames over the leading bogie wheel as shown in Fig. 1.

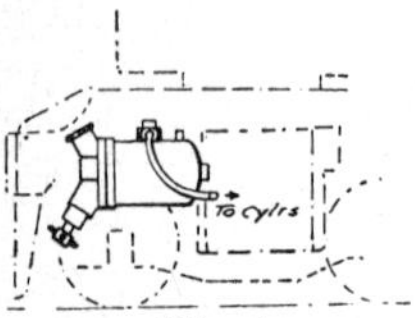

Fig. 1.

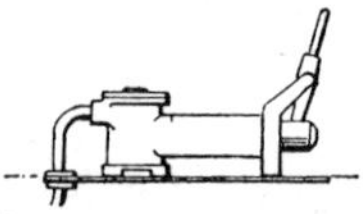
Fig. 2.

The efficiency of the submerged pump (Fig. 2) is well known, and castings for this are also listed. The reverse-lever standard and the internal petticoat pipe (Fig. 3), which renders chimney fixing so easy a matter, are also available in either the rough or finished state.

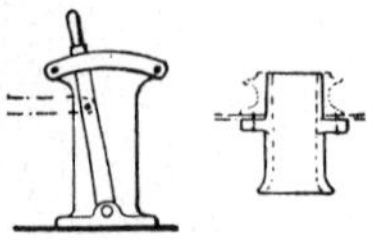
Fig. 3.

Small-Scale Steel Rails.

A correspondent, who asked us whether or no a small-scale steel rail with pressed metal chairs was available, said that he had received a sample of Bond's rail with the spring chairs, but that it seemed to be rather large for a No. 0 gauge line. We referred him to various other tracks. Messrs. Bond's, Ltd., of 254, Euston Road, have a steel rail smaller than the No. 1 gauge standard with a slide-on pressed steel chair of exceptional neatness. The base of the chair measures only 11 × 6 mm. and is roughly two-thirds the size of the larger chair which Messrs. Bond's, Ltd., have marketed for many years past. We hope to be able, in the near future, to lay down a sample length of this track and to recommend suitable check-rail dimensions. Although check-rail chairs are not yet available, it would appear possible to adopt the larger of the No. 0 gauge standard "between-tyre" dimensions, viz., 28·5 mm., by fitting the check rails up with ordinary chairs in the well-known staggered method. This arrangement reduces the gap at the frogs.

A New "O" Gauge Railway Wagon.

The illustration below is of a new lead-coloured wagon decorated with black metal work and white lettering. This wagon has been specially made by Messrs. Bassett- Lowke, Ltd., to the instructions of the publicity department of Messrs. Schweppes, Ltd., and can be obtained from their Head Office,

Marble Arch House, London, W.C. 2, or from their stand in the Schweppes pavilion, at Wembley, or from any of Messrs. Bassett-Lowke, Ltd. addresses.

As an advertisement, this wagon has been offered at a specially low price of 5s., 1s. 6d. less than the usual price for 1¼-in. gauge wood wagons.

The MODEL RAILWAY NEWS

Editorial and Publishing Offices :

66, FARRINGDON STREET, LONDON, E.C. 4.

Single Copies, post free, 7½d. Annual Subscription, 7s. 6d.

Vol. I. No. 10. OCTOBER, 1925. Price, 6d.

Notes of the Month.

FROM various signs and tokens which come our way, we anticipate that the coming Winter season is going to see a considerable addition to the ranks of model railway enthusiasts. Quite a number of correspondents have confessed in their letters to us that, although they have no model railway at the moment, they are desperately keen to start one, and mean to do so in the near future. We also hear that more and more shop-keepers are realizing the advantage of stocking model railway goods, and naturally, if the goods are shown, interest will be aroused and converts to the model railway hobby will be made. Another interesting sign is the growing number of model railway clubs. The latest proposal is that one should be established for Leicester and district. A very keen model railway enthusiast is taking the matter in hand, Mr. G. S. Anderson, " Bexcourt," Stoneygate Road, Leicester, and he will welcome enquiries from any local readers who are interested. There is no doubt about the advantage of joining a model railway club. You not only have the opportunity of seeing other members' model railways and gaining new knowledge and ideas, but you have a number of friends always available to help you with their advice and experience on any difficulties which arise in your own work.

The Model Railway Club scored a real success with their exhibit of models at the recent Railway Centenary at Darlington. It was very appropriate that the leading model railway organization of the country should take part in such an historic display, and their models added very much to the interest of the exhibition. Mr. Keen and Lieut-Col. Henvey were in attendance as the official representatives of the Club.

* * *

Is this going to be an " electric " season ? We breathe the question very softly because of the steam-lovers who will read these lines. We do not think the steam model is going to lose ground at all, but we think that quite a number of model railway enthusiasts are being recruited from the ranks of those who are slowing down on " wireless." They have their accumulators available, and they know a good deal about wiring, switches, contacts, and other electrical gear. The electrical possibilities of a model railway appeal to them, and if they are asked to choose between steam and electricity as their motive power, there is little doubt which way their vote will go. The " steam " man will always be with us ; the realism of steam propulsion is undoubtedly a fascinating thing, and it will be a sad day for the model railway world if the steam locomotive model ever declines in popularity.

A reproduction of the Southern Railway's "King Arthur" paperweight. This casting, which is an exact scale model and an excellent facsimile, is obtainable, price 5/-, from the Advertising Department, London Bridge Station, and all bookstalls.

The Wimbledon & District Model Railway Club.

Time sheet for October.—3rd, 7.45 p.m., Whist Drive at "Seymours," The Broadway, Wimbledon; tickets, 1s. 6d. each. 5th, 7.30 p.m., Lecture by Mr. Chas. Klapper, "London's Railway Traffic Problems," at Red Cross Hall, Church Road. 19th, 7.30 p.m., Test Track night, and practical demonstration on "Model Permanent Way," by Mr. Stewart-Reidpath, at Red Cross Hall. 24th, 2.45 p.m., Visit to Wimbledon Borough Sewage Farm. Meet Durnsford Road.

Judging from the amount of construction now under way, ranging from 1-in. scale to 00 gauge, there should be a good show on the Competition night in December. "Every member should enter at least one model" should be the slogan.

The Manchester & District Model Railway Club.

The meetings for the Winter session will be held on the second and fourth Tuesday, from October to March, inclusive, at 7.30 p.m., at Headquarters.

Since the last report the following events have taken place :—

5th September.—A visit was paid to the L.M.S. Loco sheds at Patricroft.

8th September.—The September meeting at Headquarters was well attended, doubtless due to a very interesting and instructive talk on "Locomotives of Forty Years Ago," by Mr. T. E. Irwin,

12th September.—A visit to the Buxton L.M.S. Loco sheds.

26th September.—A visit to Longsight Loco sheds will have taken place

FUTURE EVENTS, OCTOBER, 1925.

10th.—A visit to the Edgeley (Stockport) Loco sheds. Meet at Edgeley Station at 2.45 p.m.

13th.—Meeting at Headquarters, 7.30 p.m. A lecture on Signalling will be given by Mr. R. A. Mills.

27th.—Second October meeting at Headquarters.

Scale Drawings for Model Locomotives and Rolling Stock.

Mr. A. W. H. Pealling, 108, Forest Gate, Dalston, London, E. 8, has sent two specimen prints of scale drawings for model locomotives. They are very clear and defined and give the leading dimensions marked in figures. He also sends a list of prints for No. 00 gauge locomotives and rolling stock. It contains 58 different items. The prices of these prints range from 6*d*. to 9*d*. each; 2*d*. extra for prints of tenders for locomotives.

A Railway Centenary Souvenir.

As a commemorative supplement to the *Locomotive Railway Carriage and Wagon Review*, the Locomotive Publishing Co., Ltd., have issued a 124-page volume descriptive of the progress of British railways from 1825 to the present time, with a special reference to the more historical locomotives of that period.

Special reference is, of course, made to the Stockton and Darlington Railway. The volume, besides comprising photographs of notable locomotive and railway structures, includes six coloured illustrations and composite photographs of S.D.R., L.N.E.R., L.M.S.R., S.R., G.W.R., and Metropolitan locomotives. There is a chapter on signals also. The price of the book is 3s. 6d.

NOTABLE MODEL RAILWAYS

Mr. G. F. Vollmer's Electric System.

L.N.W. train leaving Toronto Station.

IT has always been my ambition since boyhood to have a model railway system sufficiently extensive for trains to be operated on a time-table, but until 1920 my ambition could not be realized, though various railway models, such as goods wagons, a double cross-over and a 12-lever interlocking signal cabin had been made previously.

As the object of the railway was operation of trains, I decided on the $1\frac{1}{4}$-in. gauge, as this would make the station sidings of reasonable length while keeping somewhere near scale length for cars.

The plan shows the general lay-out of the line, which is built as a single track on a trestle about 18 inches above the ground. It will be seen that it consists of a main line from Toronto through Hamilton to Windsor with a branch from Hamilton to Niagara Falls. Toronto Station being inside the garage. It is practically level throughout, though the three terminal stations will all be approached by short gradients of 1 in 100.

The rails are brass, flat-bottomed, the greater part being scale 100-lb. rail for $1\frac{3}{4}$-in. gauge which, though on the large side, look very well. The total length of track is about 300 feet. The two branches to Niagara Falls and Windsor are now in process of extension of about 36 feet each.

Power is supplied at 12 volts to a centre rail from an automobile storage battery, which is kept charged by a motor generator set, operated from the house-lighting system.

Each station is self-contained in that each has a separate control system, and they are connected one with the other by buzzers, allowing

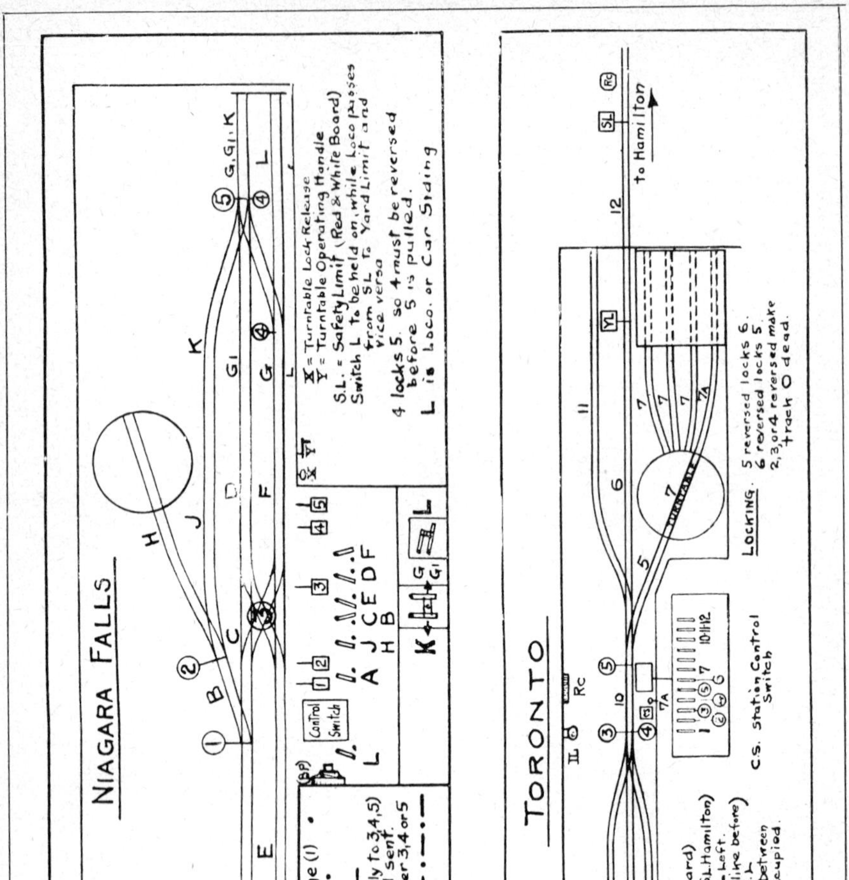
NIAGARA FALLS
to Hamilton
SL
Tree
YARD LIMIT
CALLS
(BP) Bell Push to Hamilton
1) Call up ——
2) Acknowledge (1) •
3) Passenger Train —— ——
4) Freight Train • —— •
5) Locomotive only ••• ——
6) Track not clear • (in reply to 3,4,5)
7) Track clear. Repeat call sent.
8) Loco. in reverse ••••• after 3,4 or 5
9) Repeat (if call not understood) • —— • —— •
Control Switch
X = Turntable Lock Release
Y = Turntable Operating Handle
S.L. = Safety Limit (Red & White Board)
Switch L to be held on, while loco passes from SL to Yard Limit and vice versa
4 locks 5. so 4 must be reversed before 5 is pulled.
L is Loco. or Car Siding
TORONTO
to Hamilton
TURNTABLE
YL Yard Limit Board
SL Safety Limit (Red & White Board)
RC Reversing Control (Section to SL Hamilton)
Rc Normal to Right. Reverse to Left.
Rc2 (Toronto & Hamilton) to be set alike before train allowed to pass S.L.
IL Light indicating that Section between Toronto SL & Hamilton SL is occupied.
C.S. Station Control Switch
LOCKING. 5 reversed locks 6.
6 reversed locks 5.
2, 3, or 4 reversed make track O dead.

the operation of the trains on a bell-call system. No attempt has been made to erect buildings or other station accessories, excepting as cover for operating apparatus.

The lay-outs of the four stations are shown on the plans herewith, the passing sidings being of sufficient length to take a four-car passenger train. At Toronto and Niagara Falls there are turntables, and at Windsor a Y for reversing the locomotives. The centre rail is divided into various sections, each controlled by an electric switch. All track switches are worked from the operating station and are interlocked, both mechanically and electrically, where necessary. The current goes to the centre-rail section switches through a reversing resistance controller. All locos are designed to reverse automatically on reversal of the main current, thus they can be run to any part of the station without being touched.

The passenger cars are 15 in number, 12 of English type bought in England, two of Canadian chair-car type built up from aluminium castings, and a dining car bought in England. All these cars are about 50-ft. scale length, the longest that can be obtained from makers on this side being under 40-ft. scale length.

Goods wagons are at present only six in number, including three coal wagons, one box and one flat wagon, and a guard's van, all on bogies and all built practically to scale by myself.

Bogie coal wagons, built by Mr. A. W. Line.

have 10 bogie coal wagons being built for me.

Locomotive power is very varied, and includes tender and tank locos, with steam lines of British make, some of which are awaiting 12-volt mechanisms from England. A 4—4—4 American reversing electric type is being converted into a 2—4—2 with automatic reverser. I have built

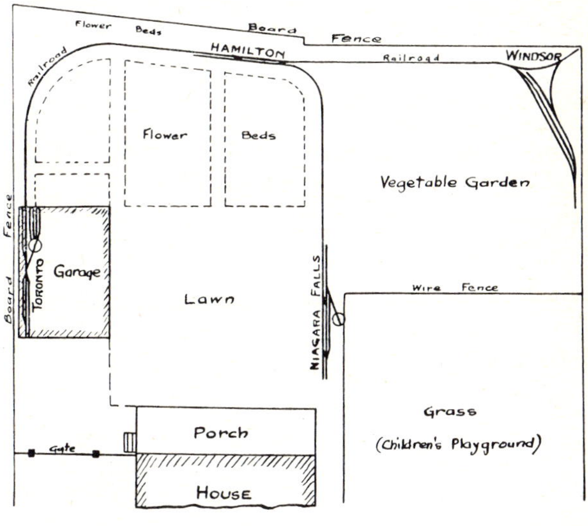

General layout of the line.

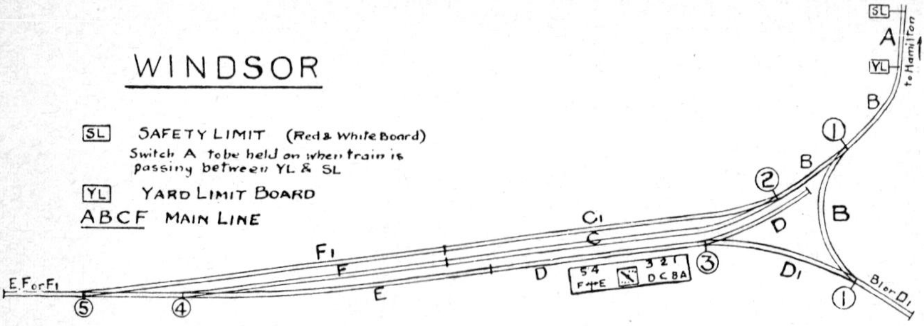

an 0—4—4—0 twin-motor loco with automatic reverser, using two six-volt American motors in series, English wheels, frame and cover of my own design. The scale weight is 120 tons and it has hauled 18 cars, or an equivalent of over 600 tons.

The station yards are made in sections, which can easily be removed by withdrawing a few brass screws, and are stored away in the house during the winter months. The trestle generally wants levelling up and aligning each Spring when the frost comes out of the ground, but otherwise stands up splendidly.

For outdoor work, I would recommend a higher voltage, say, about 25 volts for this scale, as with the present voltage, the surfaces of the rails have to be frequently cleaned.

The time-table is now in process of revision to allow for the extra length of track. As the main lines are single track, following common practice on this side of the water, it needs careful working out. I intend to make various speed and hauling-capacity tests, which may be of interest to fellow-modellers.

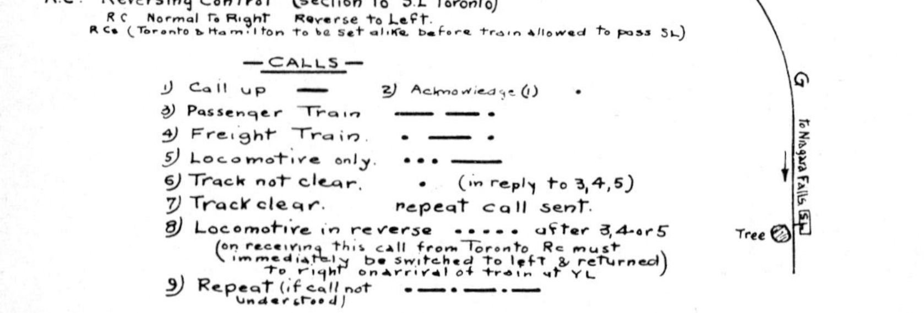

The Rail Planning Competition.

We reproduce herewith one of the plans sent in for the recent competition. This scheme also introduces gradients, and is a two-terminii non-continuous plan with a return line, which allows a train from the No. 1 terminus to double back to that station, instead of going to the second terminus. It is doubtful whether the gradient could be as easy as 1 in 60 as there appears to be only a length of about 23 feet in which to provide for the eastern part of the main line crossing the low-level station No. 2. The plan in such a small room also leaves very little space for the operators. By removing the door and hanging a curtain in its place, the whole area of the room could have been utilized, an arrangement which we think would much improve the whole lay-out. The run-round crossovers at A are, we think, very necessary. The competitor, Mr. H. D. Pinnington, of Aintree, Liverpool, in describing his plan, writes as follows :—

"The plan provides for either terminal-to-terminal running, or 'out and back,' returning to the main terminus.

"The main terminus allows trains to arrive at or depart from all four platforms. While it is true that any shunting on the goods lines may stop passenger trains entering platform No. 4, I contend that most model railway enthusiasts would not wish to run so much traffic that only this one platform was available. Engines coming out of the loco shed can run down on to any of the four platforms.

"Leaving this station, trains pass round an elliptical curve and cross over the second terminus by a girder bridge and immediately meet a falling gradient of 1 in 60. They can either diverge to the right, circle the loop and come round, or they can pass straight on, still on the down grade,

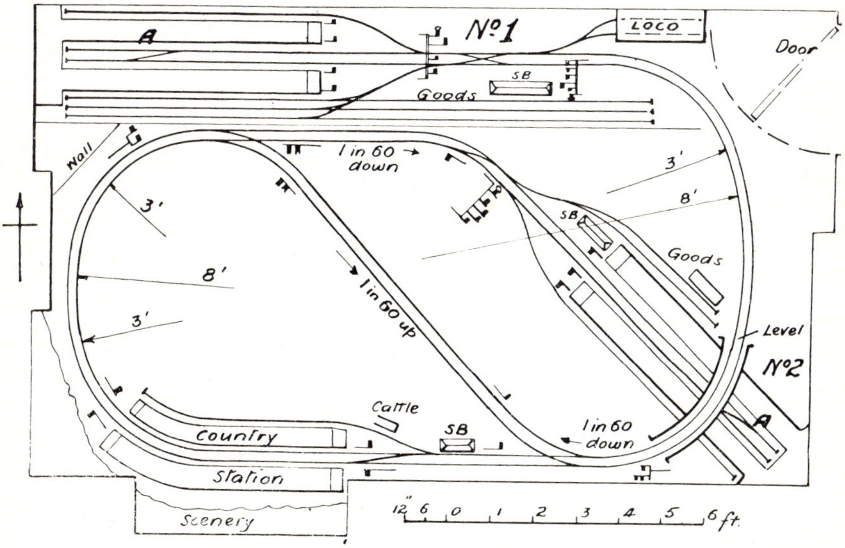

Mr. H. D. Pinnington's Competition Plan for Gauge "0" Indoor Railway.

through the country station and either climb back up the loop and return to the main terminus, or continue to drop into the second terminus, where they have the choice of three platform roads, and also a goods siding, all of which can be entered without shunting back.

"As regards time-table working, the following scheme may be taken as an example :—

"A train leaves the main terminus and proceeds to the country station, where it waits until the train that has left the second terminus has passed into the intermediate section. The first train then leaves and passes right round the loop and returns to the main terminus, entering platform No. 3. Meanwhile, the second train, after a stop at the country station, proceeds to the main (No. 1) terminus and enters platform No. 4. A third locomotive now comes out of the loco shed, backs down on the train in platform No. 3 and takes away its coaches on an express to terminus No. 2. The engine of this train now shunts into No. 4 platform. Provided a fourth locomotive is available at No. 2 terminus, the process can be repeated. This only needs four locomotives, but if only three are available (and I think this is the minimum number possible) crossover roads may be arranged in the stations as shown at A, so that engines may run round the trains."

"00" Gauge Couplings.

The sketches herewith may prove of some utility to those who are "fed up" with the very pitiful type of coupling fitted to the standard train sets. While the coupling here depicted cannot claim to be much of an advance upon the former, it certainly does possess two advantages: it may be operated from either end of a vehicle, and therefore excludes the necessity of having to lift up models and turn them round before coupling them; and, secondly, it certainly looks and *is* more realistic than its toy-shop predecessor. If it is found difficult to cut the slots in the coupler-eyes, the standard couplers may be used, the tongue from the one being soldered to the eye of the other. A is a perspective sketch of one coupler, B shows a pair in perspective coupled, C is a dimensioned drawing, and D gives a side elevation of one pair coupled. In the case of locomotives, there is no need to fit anything beyond the standard eye - coupler at each end. The couplers should be arranged to work quite loosely on their pivots.

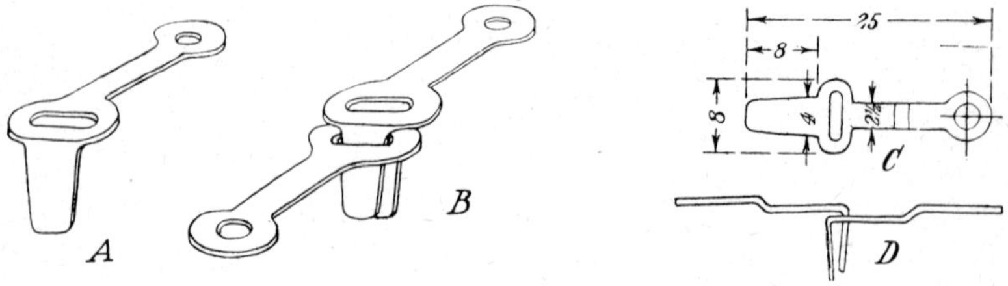

Not a house to let, but a fine example of Cardboard Model Making.

Cardboard Model Making.

By H. H. Hudson.

MOST model railway owners have, at times, experienced the desire to make their own station buildings for the better ornamentation of their systems, and those who have endeavoured to carry this desire into effect have, almost invariably, selected wood as a medium of construction. Others, who have not, as yet, tried their hand at building construction, deterred possibly by a lack of knowledge of the subject, have missed a fascinating branch of the model-maker's art. The former will find their labours considerably lightened, and the latter a material well within their capabilities of working, in the use of cardboard.

The Knack of Cutting.

Practically the whole of the art lies in the cutting, which must be clean and neat, otherwise the effect will be lost, as anything in the nature of "whiskers" round a cut edge will at once destroy the sharpness of outline. Some people are born to the use of the knife and to them cutting cleanly comes with ease, but these fortunate individuals are few in number, and for the most part the knack of cutting will only come with practice.

Tools.

In the first place, then, the knife, as the most important factor, requires to be considered. This, in common with all cutting tools, should possess a very keen edge, and should be made of the best steel. It should be let down in temper until there is a total absence of brittleness, but not so much so that the edge is likely to be easily turned in use. Ordinary pocket knives, if the steel is good, are quite suitable, or large machine hacksaw blades, broken into suitable pieces, are excellent, but whatever is used as a base, it should be ground so that in elevation it presents the appearance shown in Fig. 1

The point being fashioned in this manner enables the user to get right in the corner of a window opening, for instance, with a perfectly clean cut and with the mimimum amount of damage to the cardboard.

The knife should also be ground so that the inside edge of it is perfectly flat, while the outside edge is ground on an even angle from the thickness of the steel at the top to a razor edge at the bottom. In section we should have the effect shown in Fig. 2.

By this means we ensure that the most delicate part of the blade, *i.e.*, its cutting edge, is adequately supported and strengthened by the metal above, and also, when we place the knife against a straight-edge for the purpose of making a cut, providing we hold the knife upright, we can hardly avoid making a square cut, that is to say, a cut edge that is at right angles to the face of the cardboard. If a hacksaw blade is used, it should be mounted in a simple wooden handle, as, otherwise, if cutting through thick cardboard is to be done, corns and sore places on the fingers will certainly result.

The Straight-Edge.

We shall next require a straight-edge for cutting against, and for this purpose nothing better can be suggested than a steel rule, it is laid upon a piece of cardboard, and in perfect alignment with a line previously drawn and which it is proposed to cut. The knife is then drawn by the edge of the rule until the cardboard is cut through, thus ensuring that the cut will be perfectly straight.

There is one important point to always bear in mind, and that is, that the straight-edge should always be placed over that side of the line which, when cut, we wish to retain, for the following reason. As it is impossible to get a knife that is the same thickness all the way from the extreme cutting edge to the back. With the knife suggested, we shall find that the edge of the cut nearest the outside of the knife will be slightly bevelled to an angle corresponding to that to which the knife is ground, while the inside edge of the cut will, if the knife has not been canted in cutting, either to the right or left, be found to be at right angles to the face of the cardboard.

These are practically all the tools required for cardboard modelling, although small wood-working tools, such as chisels, gouges and a small plane will be found useful when we have to use wood for any purpose, which is sometimes the case. Scissors, however, should never be used, all cutting being done by a knife, and it is better not to include them in your kit, in order to avoid encouragement in their use.

Cardboard.

With regard to cardboard, only the very best should be used if you desire to get the best results. For the stouter cards, from 1-32nd of an inch in thickness upwards, use a built-up board made from layers of paper. Faced pulp-board is only possible, as a medium, in the hands of an expert.

Unless it is desired to make something that is a novelty on account of its adaptation from odds and ends, the saving in cost is so negligible as to be more than offset by the easier adaptability and working in a better material. It should be remembered that in this branch of model making, labour is the principal item, so little material, comparatively speaking, is used, and that of an inexpensive nature.

Below 1-32nd of an inch in thickness, the best material to use is undoubtedly Bristol Board, and Reeve's make is recommended, as it is not so liable to split as other makes.

Setting out the Design.

Before, however, we can commence cutting out, we must draw or set out the design we propose to work to, and for this purpose we shall require a drawing-board, T-square and set square. Both 30°—60° and 45° will be found useful and as the celluloid variety are not very expensive it would be as well to equip ourselves with one of each.

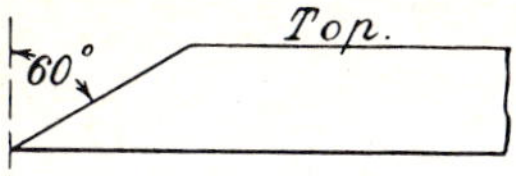

Fig 1

Photographing Prototypes.

Let us assume that we have decided upon the building we propose to make, say, a goods depot. It is not always easy to obtain architect's drawings of railway buildings, but the actual thing is nearly always to be seen within a reasonable distance of home. If we are equipped with a cheap kodak, it is a simple matter to visit the building we have chosen as our prototype and take a complete set of photographs of it. It should be borne in mind that if it is necessary to enter railway property for this purpose, permission should first be obtained from some responsible authority.

In taking our photographs, we should get as near as possible to the building in order to be able to distinguish the bricks on the finished photo. The reason for this will appear later. If it is not possible to get a complete view of one side of the building in one snap, take two in such a manner that when prints are made they overlap each other at some definitely recognizable point. We should then take each side of the building in turn, making sure that no part of it is missing from our series of snaps.

Fig 2

Measuring Buildings.

Having done this, we should next make a rough sketch of the ground plan, and provided the building is a brick one, we can get our measurements with a fair degree of accuracy without the use of a tape measure or any instrument. All that is necessary is to count the bricks lengthwise along the base line. Two half-bricks should be counted as one whole one. If, for instance, one end wall has 54 whole bricks and 26 half-bricks, the equivalent total would be 67 whole bricks. As the majority of bricks are nine inches in length, it will be seen that a simple multiplication of 67 by 9 will give us the length of the wall in inches—603 inches or 50 feet 3 inches. If we wish to be more precise in our calculation, we should add half an inch for the mortar division between each brick.

We should then note the depth of the reveals at window and door openings, that is to say, the distance from the face of the wall to the face of the window or door framing. In a building such as we are engaged upon the distance would normally be the width of a brick—4½ inches, but where metal frames are used, these may be almost flush with the wall face.

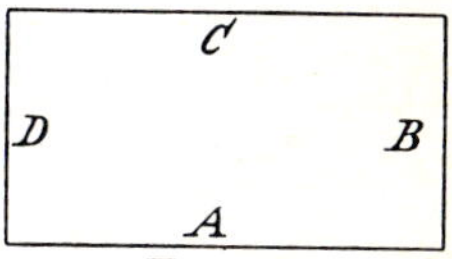

Front
Fig 3

Colour Details.

We should next make careful notes of all colour details, that is, if we are proposing to make an exact copy of the building.

We are now equipped with all the information we are likely to require, and our next move is to get the films developed and prints made. When these are ready, we can make a start.

Drawing Plans.

The first thing to do is to obtain a sheet of stout strawboard about 3-32nd of an inch in thickness, and which can be obtained from most picture-frame dealers for about 4d. per sheet. This we attach to our drawing-board, and upon it we set out a correct outline of the plan from the rough sketch we have already made, and to the scale we are making the model. This will ultimately form the base upon which to build up the walls, and during the setting out of the elevations we should take all our measurements for length from it.

This done, we can next proceed to set out the elevations and for the purpose of an illustration, we will suppose that the building is of a simple, box-like shape.

Reference Letters.

On the plan we should put a letter against each separate wall for reference. This is not so necessary in the present illustration, but if we are making a building with a complicated plan outline, such as jutting-out walls and recesses, we shall find this reference a great help in setting out and afterwards in building up. The reference letters should be in exact sequence round the building, starting from the front wall, so that "B" will fit next to "A" and so on. (Fig. 3.)

We now come to the setting out of the elevations, and we should remove the strawboard plan from the drawing-board and substitute a sheet of good cardboard, such as already described. The thickness is dependent upon the distance from the wall face to window frame, in this case 4½ inches, in 7-mm. scale. This would mean that we shall require something about 3-32nd of an inch in thickness. If this is not easily obtainable, we can either use 1-16th-inch cardboard by itself, or mount another piece on to it to make the required thickness. Care should be taken that the mounting is thoroughly done, otherwise when cutting out the window openings, we may strike an air-pocket, and the edges of the cut will gape open, a state of affairs it is impossible to neatly remedy.

Calculating Heights.

We can get our various heights from photos in the same way that we the calculated the length, that is, by counting the bricks. If, for instance, we wish to get the height of a door from the ground, we count the bricks from the base line to the corner of the arch over the door. This time, however, we multiply by three, as the height of a brick is invariably three inches.

If we take the first elevation shewn on the plan, that marked "A," and select all the photographs from our series which show this elevation, and range them in front of us in consecutive order, we can visualize the whole of the wall we are dealing with. We will suppose that the building has two floors, and has therefore, two rows of window. We can count the bricks to the top line of the sills, convert into feet and inches, and having previously, with the aid of the T-square, drawn a line on the cardboard to represent the ground line, scale off the distance up from this line, and draw lightly a parallel line. We proceed, in like manner, to get the heights of the windows from the ground ,and lightly mark this in, as in the previous case. The next measurement will be the sill line of the first-floor windows, and so on until all the horizontal lines have been put in, including the line to indicate the top of the wall. As the eaves of the roof project over the face of the wall, this line should be the thickness of a brick higher than is apparent from the photograph.

Vertical Lines.

We can next proceed with the vertical lines; we first put in a hard vertical line to represent the left side of the wall and from the strawboard plan we can get the distance the wall extends. At this point on our elevation we again put in a hard line. Starting from the right or left we count the bricks from the edge of the wall to the lines of the first opening, remembering in this case to multiply by nine. When all the vertical lines have been put in, we shall find that we have a large rectangle, representing the wall itself, with the inside space broken by a number of lightly drawn lines forming smaller rectangles, representing the window and door openings. These lines should be hardened by going over them with a pencil.

Lines should be indicated to show the positions of all projections, such as mouldings, etc., and where the end walls are set out these should show the angle of the roof, if it sho ld be gabled. The usual roof angle in 45.°

(To be continued.)

A No. 00 Gauge Wagon Bogie.

THE accompanying photograph and enlarged drawing illustrates an experimental wagon bogie made for a No. 00 gauge railway. The scale of the bogie is 4 mm. to the foot.

The bogie is a hand-made model, the side frames being of sheet brass with axle boxes soldered on, dummy bolster springs also being soldered on.

The completed bogie.

The general design is similar to Mr. A. W. Line's models of American car trucks.

The side frames are equalized, the bogie-pin transome being a block of brass which is to some extent lightened by drilled holes. To limit the frame movement a 1-16th in. peg is fitted in the centre of the side frames. This projects inwards and engages a larger (3-32nd in.) hole drilled in the transome.

The wheels, which, by the way, were turned out of white bronze rod, were made with a view of trying out how small the flanges could be made and yet work on the standard pressed-metal track and points—which at the moment the great majority of " Double O " gaugers are using. Owing to imperfections of manufacture the flanges, which are 1 mm. deep, would not prevent a derailment on points which, although new, were quite satisfactory with the ordinary purchased stock. It is proposed, therefore, to revert to a previous sample of wheels with flanges 1¼ mm. deep.

The treads are approximately 3 mm. wide over all, but these dimensions are not absolutely fixed, as for a proposed track with larger radius curves than the standard tin-plate curves, the design has not yet been settled. Many things have to be considered when " frogged " points are substituted for the " positive " hinged points.

As made, the bogie is heavy—a good fault in itself. It weighs about seven-eighths of an ounce—approximately nine tons instead of the scale equivalent of two or three tons. The writer thinks however, that the limits of tyre and wheel dimensions indicated on the drawing may form a workable standard. The use of the 4-mm. scale, it will be noticed, gives very nearly correct centres of journals and distance between outside frames, viz., 26 mm. (6 ft. 6 in.) and 24 mm. (6 ft.).

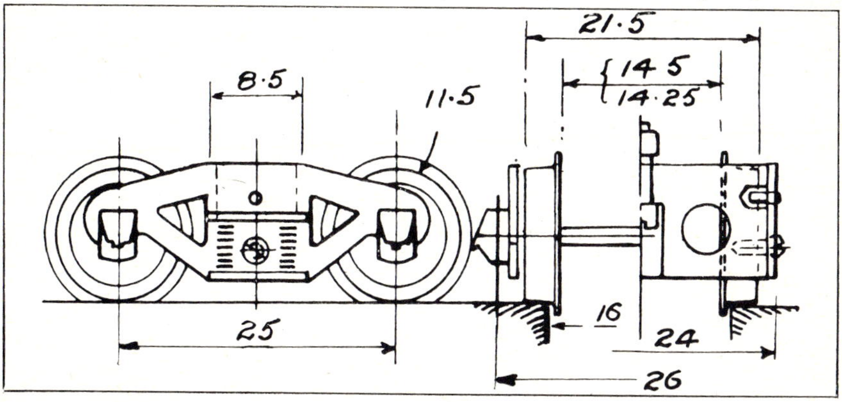

"O" Gauge Tips.

By H. A. Haylett.

DOUBTLESS many of your readers have in their possession foreign-made locos which, although possessing good mechanisms, unfortunately are hideous in design. For many years I had one such engine, an 0—4—0 outside cylinder, tender type, with the footplate far too high. The super-

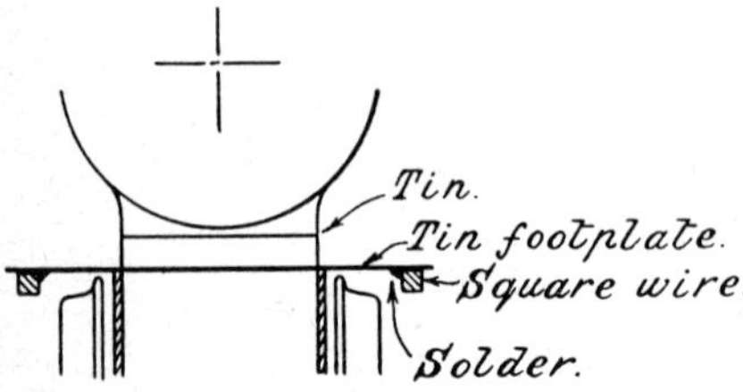

Fig. 1.

structure was fairly good, but it was impossible to move the clockwork backwards or forwards and add another pair of wheels. Not feeling disposed to build a new engine, I decided to rebuild it as a 4—4—0 inside cylinder. This proved quite simple and might be useful to others.

The front portion of the footplate, including dummy cylinders, was sawn off and a new one several inches longer made. This was cut from an ordinary tin, and strengthened by soldering No. 14 square, tinned copper wire (as used for wireless) along either side about 1-16th in. from the edge (Fig. 1.). I do not know if this has been suggested previously, but it certainly makes a strong job, overcomes any kink which invariably appears in re-used tin, and gives the footplate a very realistic appearance, often missing in quite expensive models. A cross-piece behind the buffer-plank also strengthens this. A step or bend in the footplate where it is soldered to the old one, helps to disguise the join and brings it to the correct level from the rail. The smoke-box saddle is also made from tin soldered together, while the smoke box itself is an ordinary tin, slightly larger than the original, to which it is soldered after the end had been burred over to make a tight fit. The funnel was then bolted on, the dome moved further forward, and a safety-valve added. Next buffers and draw-hook were refitted, lamps and brake pipe added and finally the bogie attached. Thus at very little cost, the appearance has been greatly enhanced.

Another inexpensive tip when building suburban coaches is the use of match-sticks for window frames. Panels A and B are made from thin deal (taken from old boxes) and joined together by panels C at either end. Lengths of match DD, Fig. 2,

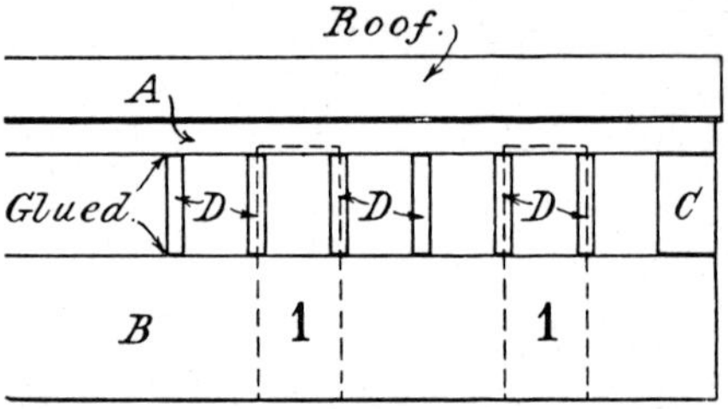

Fig. 2.

are then glued in to represent frames, and look quite good when complete. This, of course, is only applicable when the prototype has narrow frames such as the new L.N.E.R. (G.E. Section) coaches.

A Novel Fish Truck.

One of the exhibits at the Munich Transport Exhibition consists of a large bogie fish truck arranged for carrying its load alive. The inside of the truck is divided into separate tanks about three feet deep. Different kinds of fish can, therefore, be carried in one wagon. At the end of the truck is a compartment with several oxygen cylinders in it. These are used for aerating the water.

"OO" Gauge Electric Locos.

By Edward Beal.

THE writer always feels that he had a very lively part in the introduction of this small gauge into practical use. At any rate, as far back as 1916, he has distinct recollections of correspondence with more than one model engineering firm as to the practicability of such a small scale. In those days the problem of motive power was the only impediment, though one enterprising firm was willing to build an electric locomotive on the risk of its possible failure to work when complete. It was to have been a sort of "heads you win, tails we lose" affair, but, unfortunately, the matter never materialized. In these days things are much brighter for the model railway man, and, while the range of choice in model locomotives is not yet great, it is quite possible for the enthusiast to build up his own motive power, especially since the advent upon the market of the electric locomotives built on the Continent. It is something of a poser for the layman to understand how such an excellent piece of mechanism can be sold at such a low cost, and for one to dismantle one of the little machines and examine it, is to be all the more astonished.

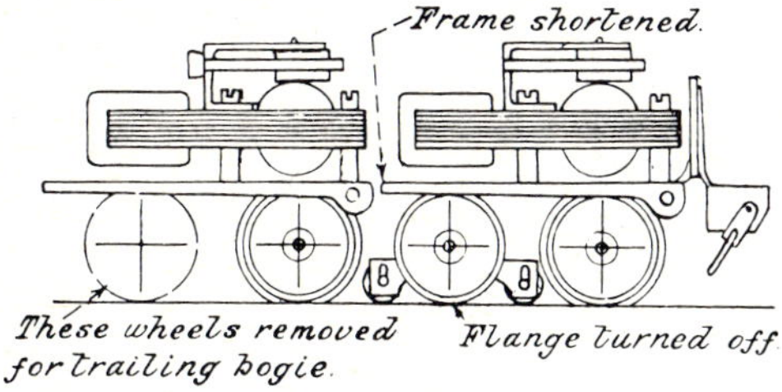

Fig. 1.

The difficulties in the way of satisfactory locomotive equipment appear to centre around the questions of rail-curvature and hauling-power. A four-coupled engine is the only type that will negotiate the standard radius track, unless some such scheme as turning off the wheel flanges or articulating the wheel-base be resorted to. From the standpoint of haulage, the electric mechanism seems to possess little advantage over the spring-motor type, and it is, therefore, necessary to duplicate the mechanisms if there is a desire to run trains consisting of anything like a realistic number of wagons or coaches. The position of the reversing switch on the standard motor makes it impossible to arrange the mechanisms in tandem, unless one of the switches be dispensed with altogether. This leads to the necessity of special wiring and other arrangements. A further point of great importance is that flanges cannot be turned off driving wheels. If this is done, it will be found that the wheels will slip when under power and will prove altogether inefficient.

Let us take, as an example, a possible 0—8—0 tank engine. On deciding which flanges shall be removed, it will at once be seen that those of the front coupled wheels are out of the question, owing to the ugly appearance of the engine when taking curves, and the difficulty of persuading it to avoid scraping the sides of station platforms in passing. In view of the larger overhang of the switch at the rear end, the same is true of

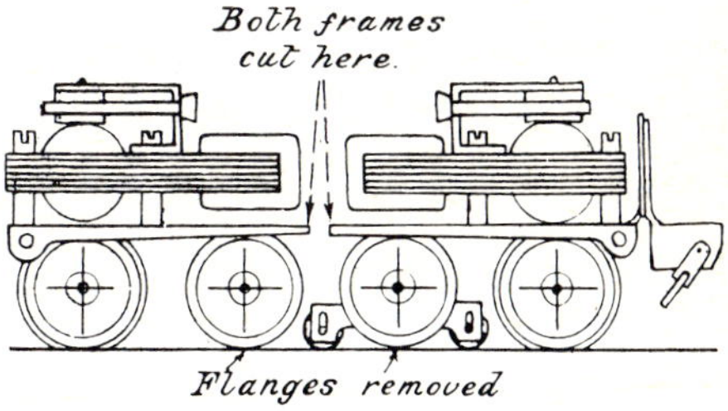

Fig. 2.

the rear coupled wheels. It, therefore, becomes a matter of making front and rear outside coupled wheels serve as the drivers, and of taking off the

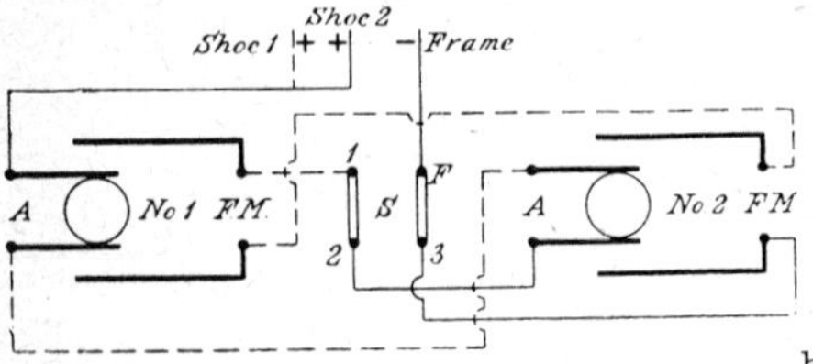

Fig. 3.

flanges from both pairs of inside wheels. This involves the reversing of one of the motors in its relation to the other; in other words, the mechanisms will require to be wired in opposition to each other. Fig. 2 will make this clear. In order that both pairs of driving wheels shall rotate together in one direction, the mechanisms, since they are back to back, must be wired in opposed relation. In the case of Fig. 1, where there are only six coupled wheels, there is no such necessity, and these motors are arranged in simple parallel or series.

The designing of the mechanisms has been carried out with the very

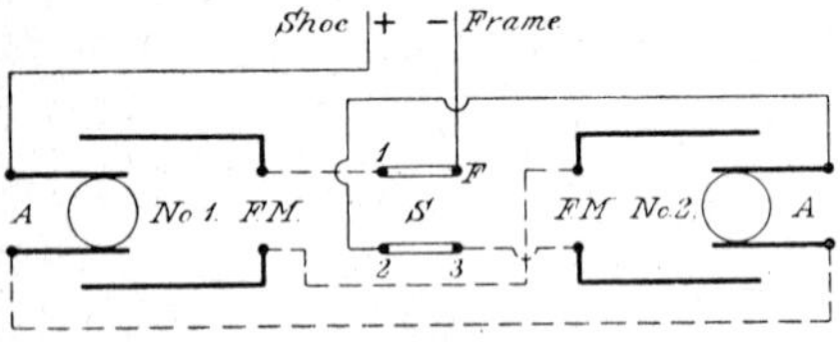

Fig. 4.

greatest forethought and care, and they lend themselves most conveniently to the various adaptations required by the different wheel arrangements. Thus (Fig. 1) one pair of wheels is easily dismantled altogether from the chassis, and a hole can easily be bored in the frame-centre to take the pivot-screw of the leading pony truck or the trailing bogie. The pivoting of the bogie is an improvement upon the former method employed with clockwork models, and leaves a much greater margin for the swing of the truck.

In arranging the two motors in tandem, it will be found necessary to cut a short length off the end of the chassis-frame with a fine metal saw, in order to bring the two pairs of inside wheels into the correctly spaced position. This is shown in Figs. 1 and 2. In the former case, where the natural arrangement of the motors is resorted to, it will only be necessary to treat one of the frames in this manner; but, in the second case, where the motors are arranged end to end, both plates must be cut. In all cases the length to be cut off amounts to five millimetres. In

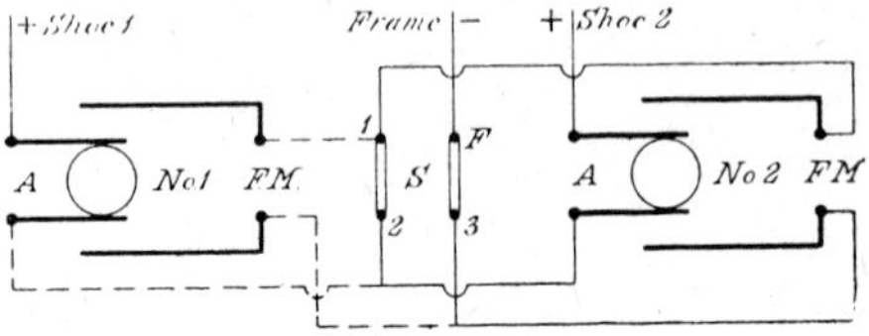

Fig. 5.

building up the superstructure of the locomotive it becomes necessary to provide drilled lugs on the sides of the footplate to take the screws which serve to hold the motors in position. One of the switches is, of course, removed by unscrewing the pair of screws just above the driving wheels. For the removal of the flanges any lathe-owner will have the necessary equipment, but in case the amateur is not so fortunate as to possess a lathe, it may be pointed out that any mechanic will remove the flanges from a dozen wheels for a few pence. The writer keeps a stock of these flangeless wheels on hand, and it is very useful to have them.

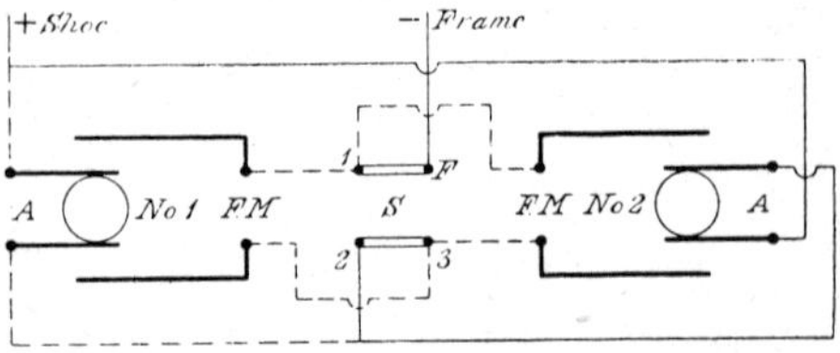

Fig. 6.

Now for the matter of wiring. It should first be pointed out that the switch supplied with the standard motors is really of the four-pole type, though there are only three contactors visible. The fourth, of course, is within the cylinder itself, and is fed directly from the locomotive frames. In the drawings (Figs. 3, 4, 5, 6) these four contacts are marked 1, 2, 3 and F, the latter signifying the stud fed from the frames as described. Fig. 3 shows the wiring scheme adapted to the arrangement of motors shown in Fig. 1, that is, the simple series arrangement. Nos. 1 and 2 are the respective motors, A the armature contacts, FM the field-magnet contacts, S the switch attached to motor No. 2. The motors as sold separately are already wired for individual use, and it is unnecessary to remove the whole of these wires. In the sketch, therefore, wires which may be allowed to remain are drawn plain, while new wires are shown dotted. One or two collecting shoes may be used, as occasion demands. The new wires necessary are as follows :—

Left-hand armature contact motor 1 toright-hand contact motor 2.

Switch contact 1 to right-hand FM motor 1.

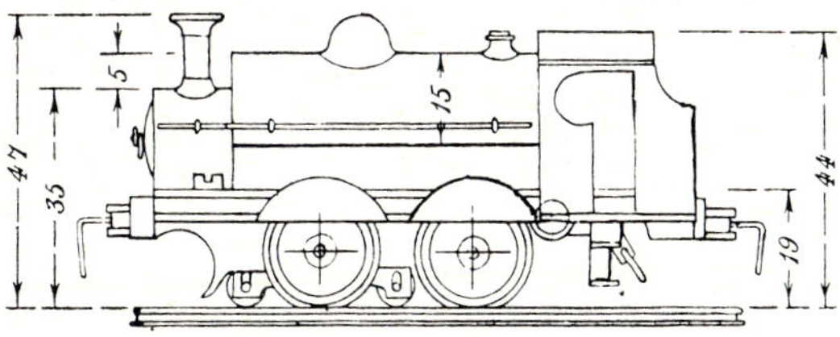

Fig. 8.—Design for a saddle tank shunting loco.

FM left-hand motor 1 to FM right-hand motor 2.

Shoe of motor 2 to shoe of motor 1, if two shoes are employed.

In Fig. 4, the same series system is followed, that is, the current passes *through* one motor to the other, but the one motor is opposed to the other. The wheels will thus run in opposite directions until the mechanisms are put in place, back to back, as required. In this case only one collecting shoe is possible, owing to the fact that the leading wheels of the original motors come together. In the parallel arrangement (Figs. 5 and 6) the current, instead of passing through one motor to the other, is fed to each motor separately. Whether the series or parallel wiring will be resorted to is a matter for the builder to decide. In the larger gauges it is often the custom to arrange for both methods to be applied, the one being used for starting the engine and the parallel system being switched in when the loco is under way. The reason for this lies in the fact that, while the series method consumes double the amperage required by the parallel system, it concentrates more power into the work of moving the load from a stationary position. In the 00 gauge, however, the parallel wiring is doubtless the preferable system, and it is slightly simpler than the series.

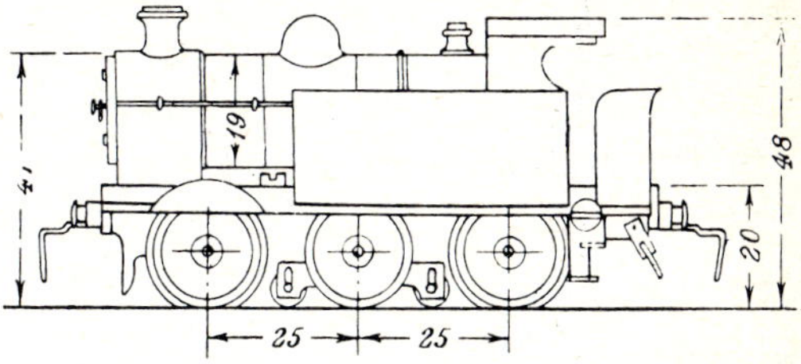

Fig 7.—Design for a six-coupled local service loco.

Great care should be taken to insulate thoroughly the various wires within the engine boiler. If this is not done, endless troubles will result. If possible, stout rubber tubing, as supplied with the standard mechanisms, should be used throughout.

We may now pass on to look at several typical locomotive designs. Here, one or two inescapable drawbacks in the standard design of the motors may be deplored. In the first place, it is a pity that the arrangement of the crown wheel on the gearing brings it so low down as to exclude the possibility of using wheels any smaller than those supplied. If smaller wheels are fitted, it will be found that the crown wheel will engage the tops of the sleepers of the standard track. Wheels $\frac{5}{8}$ in. in diameter on treads could be used, but the advantages of these over those supplied is so slight, that they are scarcely worth the trouble. Another unsatisfactory feature is the high foot-plate required by the chassis-frame. In the design for the shunting loco (Fig. 8) both these difficulties will be only too apparent, though an attempt has been made to overcome the second. Fig. 7 depicts a simple six-wheel tank engine for suburban trains, or for short-distance freight trains. The tank sides are brought down as low as possible, in order to conceal the necessary clumsiness of the foot-plate sides, which are required to be broad to cover the chassis-frames. The steps form an integral part of the foot-plate sides, and also serve as the "lug" through which passes the chassis-screws. The wheel-splashers may consist of either cardboard or tinplate discs glued or soldered on the surface of the foot-plate sides. The saddle-tank shunting engine (Fig. 8) is much the same and requires no description. Fig. 9 is a more ambitious and realistic attempt at a 2—6—2 tank engine, the motors being two in number and being arranged in simple sequence. Note the recess on the tank sides, which may be thus left for the purpose of permitting ready access to the chassis-screws. If undesirable, of course, these may be omitted, and the top cover of the side tanks may be made detachable so as to permit the insertion of a small screw-driver. An especially long slot should be cut in the front buffer-beam to allow plenty

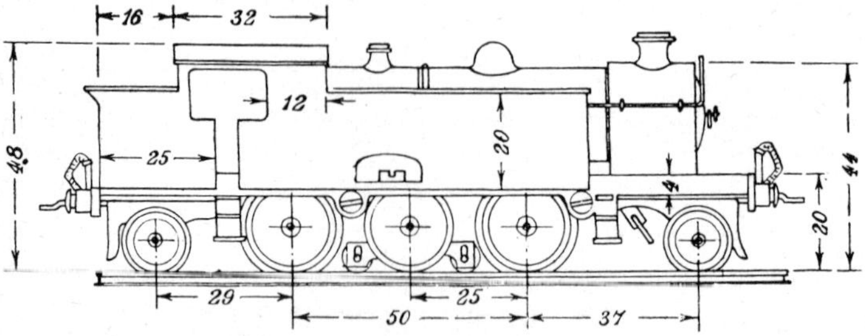

Fig. 9.—Design for a six-coupled loco.

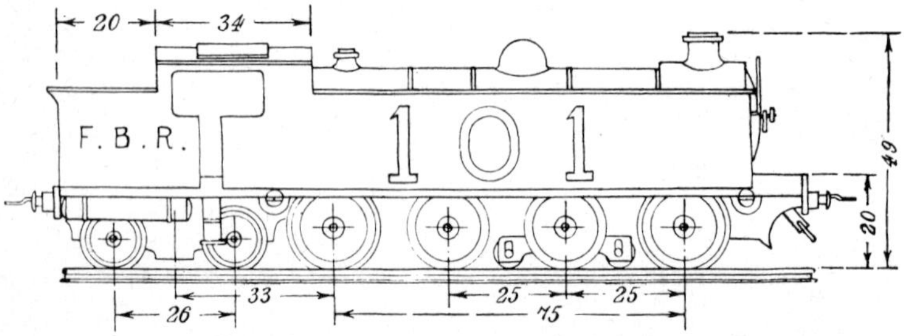

Fig. 10.—Design for 0–8–4 goods tank engine with two motors.

of side-play for the leading truck. Special truck frames are employed at both front and rear. In Fig. 10 it has been found necessary to produce the side tanks the full length of the boiler, a fact which detracts somewhat from the appearance of the model, but which in no way renders it unfaithful to actual practice. Here the motors are arranged in opposition. The trailing truck has four wheels and is arranged to slide laterally upon a pivot which passes through an arc-shaped slot in the bogie frame.

The scale adopted for the designs here given is that of 3½ mm., but the maximum loading gauge has been followed in the case of the larger engines. This is due to the fact that the standard electric mechanism is designed to suit the 4-mm. scale which Mr. Greenly has championed from the beginning. For practical purposes, however, in the writer's opinion, there is nothing to beat the "half 0 gauge" scale. There is much greater convenience in designing models from standard blue prints and so forth, and when it is remembered that a very larger number of designs are now published to a scale half that of 0 gauge, it will at once be apparent that, by following the 3½-mm. scale, full-size drawings are often accessible. There is also the important matter of space.

Answers to Correspondents.

W. G. B. Maitland. (The Gables, Southfields Road, Eastbourne).—The plan you send us is, generally speaking, quite feasible in a room of the dimensions you give, but we think that it should be improved by using four or five feet radius for all the main line curves. The terminus "B" certainly requires some method of getting the arriving engines round a train. Of course, if you have shunting engines at each terminus this is not a difficult matter. As designed, the goods department is all at one end of the system. This is more or less an impossible arrangement where the line is a non-continuous or "point to point" railway. We are publishing your address, as we note that you wish to meet other model railway enthusiasts living in your district.

G. M. (Banbury).—Messrs. Marshall, Stewart & Co., 209, Balham High Road, London, S.W. 17, specialize in No. 00 gauge accessories. Bassett-Lowke, Ltd., Northampton, and Messrs. Bond are among our advertisers who stock the original standard locomotives, rails and other parts. Some new designs are to be expected this coming season.

F. J. E. (Eastbourne).—You do not say whether in arranging the plan it is allowable to cut through the walls of the adjacent rooms. From a practicable point of view, this work offers no difficulties so long as it can be permitted.

L. W. (Stockwell).—We have no means of getting a plan otherwise than doing what you can accomplish yourself by a visit to the Exhibition. As far as we remember, the model railway has a detailed plan hanging alongside it.

E. M. (London, N.).—We cannot promise to publish drawings in a definite issue. You can get some idea of the proportions of the particular coach by visiting your nearest station. This is what we should have to do, as the official drawings are not available.

To Kew Readers.

Mr. F. E. Williams of Rosneath, Kew Gardens, wishes interested model railway enthusiasts residing in Kew Gardens or Richmond (Surrey) district to communicate with him at the above address, with a view of starting a local model railway club.

Queries and Replies.

J. V. (Sutton) wants a double-line, terminal to terminal plan for room, as sketch. The Northern projection can be tunnelled.

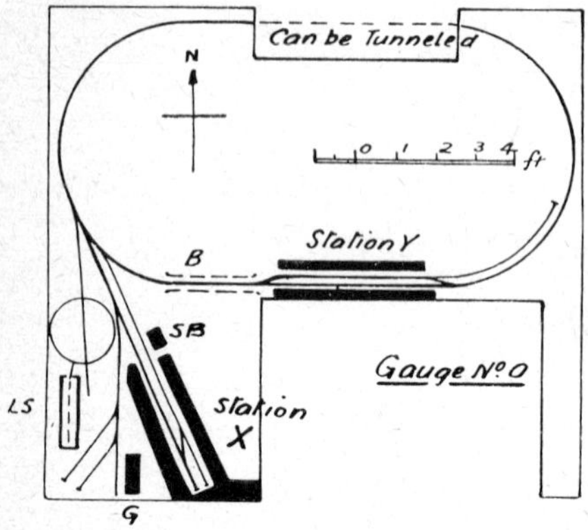

Rail Plan for room with protruding obstructions.

Your plan is not an easy one and it is not immediately obvious how your requirements could be met in every particular. We suggest a continuous line with a main terminus (station X) on a branch from the circle in the south-western alcove. A bridge at B would be useful to allow of easy access to the station operating space. It could be fixed, however, as long as the railway is about 3 ft. 3 in. from the ground and the bridge girders are mainly above the track. The station Y is a loop-road station at which trains could be reversed. It would then act as a terminal station. A double-line railway is hardly practicable. The station X includes a loco shed (L.S.) and accommodation for goods at G. The long narrow space at the S.E. corner of the room is more or less unusable.

D. Edie (Fife) requires a plan for a set of long attic rooms as shown in the accompanying sketch.

You are very lucky to have so much room at your disposal; though we cannot spare time to give you a detailed plan we have suggested the general lay-out. The line can be single throughout, but at the main station, at Y, it would be a double line giving up and down services. This scheme will simplify signalling and, at the same time, allow for all the minor goods sidings to be arranged without run-round loops. The main station would have a large goods yard and a loco depot in the North bay at Y. A run-round and reception loop is necessary at this yard, because trains in both directions have to be provided for. Main-line curves should be a three-foot radius minimum. The station, Q, can be made a mere halt or roadside station. At X and Z, stations with two roads to allow for the passing of trains. Only one road need be platformed.

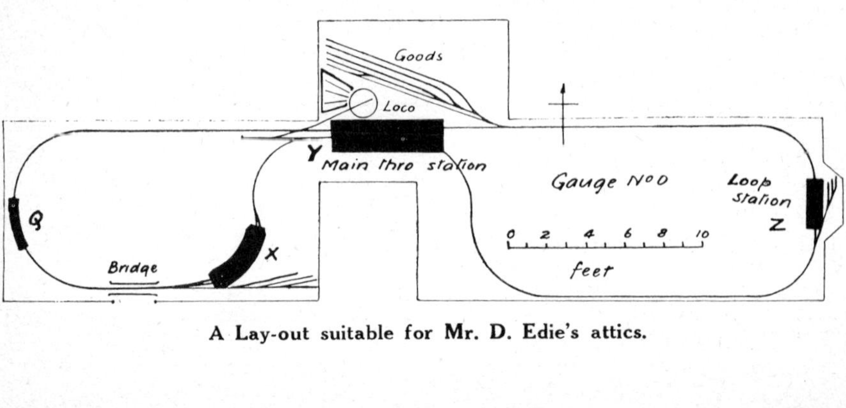

A Lay-out suitable for Mr. D. Edie's attics.

00 Gauge Post Office Van.

To the Editor, MODEL RAILWAY NEWS.

DEAR SIR,

In view of the interest now being taken in 00 gauge, I thought that perhaps a photo and short description of a L.N.W.R. six-wheeled Post Office Van might be of interest, which I recently constructed to the $3\frac{1}{2}$ mm. to the foot scale. Working corridor connections, three-link couplings, net lamps, etc., are fitted. The collecting net and mail-bag discharging arm are operated by usual ramp in track. The van works very well, and is painted in the old L.N.W.R. style, which is very effective in a model. Is it possible to have more photos and descriptions of locos and rolling stock in this gauge ? as I am sure they would be appreciated by 00 enthusiasts, being a change from the usual gauge 0 and 1 models.

Yours sincerely,

R. EVANS.

Manchester.

Mr. R. Evan's 00 Gauge Post Office Van.

"A personal Explanation."

To the Editor, MODEL RAILWAY NEWS.

DEAR SIR,

I note Mr. A. R. Walkley's letter in last issue of MODEL RAILWAY NEWS, and I hasten to explain that my remarks anent electricity and very tiny models were not intended in a derogatory sense, or that those who went in for either systems should be regarded as being " out of the pale." What I intended to convey was that I personally had no experience of these things, and consequently could give no advice.

No doubt, I expressed myself awkwardly. I may add that I quite agree with Mr. Walkley that " live and let live " should apply to model matters. We readers of the MODEL RAILWAY NEWS are men of all ages and of all classes, drawn together by a common enthusiasm. In fact, a sort of " Freemason Society," where every member is bound to help his fellow-member, with our guide, philosopher and friend (the Editor) as our Grand Master. Of course, we must advocate different views, but, without offending the susceptibility of our fellows, and, for fear I have myself done this, I send you this explanatory letter.

Yours sincerely,
WILLIAM HAMILTON (Col.).
Co. Donegal.

The Electric Explosion.

To the Editor, MODEL RAILWAY NEWS.

DEAR SIR,

I read with great interest the observations made by our friend, "Disgruntled," *re* electric and other locomotives, in the August issue of MODEL RAILWAY NEWS. I should like to make a few remarks on the subject.

Firstly, I will rule out of the discussion altogether, the "clockwork" loco, which I regard as merely a child's plaything (and very useful as such), but not worth the attentions of any real "model railwayist." This leaves steam and electricity available for our locomotives, just as in real practice. In real railway work, there are definite types of steam and electric locomotives respectively, but has anyone ever heard of a locomotive of the steam type being fitted with electric equipment instead of steam? The bare idea is grotesque, unthinkable. Then why is it not so in the model railway sphere, since we pride ourselves on being as "true to life" as possible? I am sure the logic of this is apparent to every thinking reader.

Please yourselves whether you have electric locomotives or steam, or even both, but, "for the love of Stephenson" (or Faraday), *don't* mix the two in one vehicle.

Personally, I think that much more realistic representations of railway working can be made by using electricity, either with locomotives or motor-coach trains (I myself prefer the latter, and there are certain added advantages). For instance, everything can be done without introducing such an extremely out-of-scale object as the human hand, except at the control panels and switchgear. One may run trains in either direction; couple coaches; uncouple them; operate points and signals; all without touching any of the actual railway gear, whereas, to do this with steam, one must often fly to the loco, clutch it violently, and handle some lever on it, to avoid a catastrophy.

In this wise, then, do I express my undoubted preference for the *Electric* Model Railway.

Yours sincerely,
"INTERLOCK."
Charlton.

An Electric System.

To the Editor, MODEL RAILWAY NEWS.

DEAR SIR,

I am pleased to note "Disgruntled's" article in the August number of the MODEL RAILWAY NEWS. I agree with him entirely. If some model firms were to produce locos and motor trains, I am sure there would be a market.

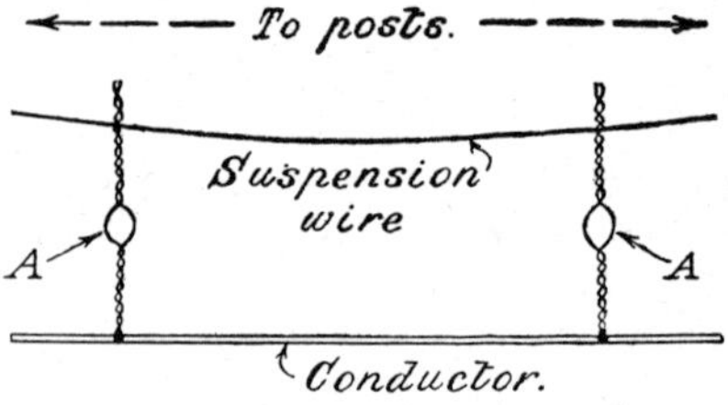

When I began my railway, I used the third-rail system, and it was most troublesome, owing to short circuits. With the overhead system, my troubles vanished.

"Disgruntled," unfortunately, does nor give us any constructional details. I have adopted a system similar to that described by Mr. Greenly in his book.

Short lengths of wire are wound round the conductor at intervals of six inches. These are then soldered and the underneath part filed away. This is then attached to the suspension wire in the manner shown. By means of the large loops, A, the conductor can be raised or lowered.

I have just finished the first of a set of tube trains. The body comes down nearly to the track, to hide the large wheels fitted to ordinary motor mechanisms. The over-all height is much less than the usual. Finished in varnish and white, they look very nice.

IAN F. MARSHALL.

Renfrewshire.

A Shunting Problem.

To the Editor, MODEL RAILWAY NEWS.

DEAR SIR,

Being an interested reader of your paper, I thought, perhaps, other readers might be interested in this little problem dealing with trains :—

Two trains, "A" and "B," going in opposite directions on a single line, say each train consists of engine and six trucks, there is a siding which accommodates the six trucks but not the whole train. In passing, the trucks must not be split up but the engine may be uncoupled and used for shunting purposes.

The trains have got to pass with the least possible delay and in as few moves as possible.

"A's" trucks are shown in the diagram herewith in solid black, and "B's" are shown shaded.

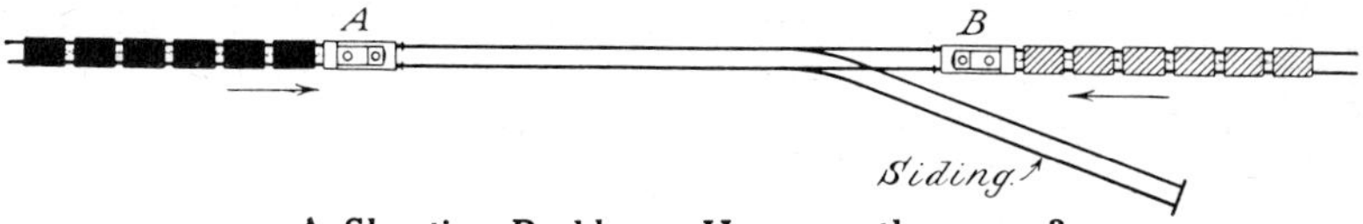

A Shunting Problem.—How can they pass?

Wishing your paper success.

Yours faithfully,

J. R. MILTON.

Leyton, E. 10.

[The solution to this problem will be published in our next issue.]

O Gauge G.N.R. "Atlantic."

To the Editor, MODEL RAILWAY NEWS.

DEAR SIR,

I am enclosing a decent photo of my engine, just made, gauge 0, and you can possibly reproduce it in connection with my article in the September issue. If possible, I should like the loan of the block for a short time when you have finished with it, so that I could have the picture reproduced in the local paper in

A Canadian Reader's model G.N.R. "Atlantic" loco.

connection with the fall fair here, where I will have it on exhibition and also boost the MODEL RAILWAY NEWS.

The beauty of this engine is that it is practically made from odds and ends around the house, and I have no lathe or tools beyond a few house tools. It is, of course, not quite true to prototype, but is a fair imitation.

Yours truly,

Nelson, B.C. G. S. REES.

Point Levers.

To the Editor, MODEL RAILWAY NEWS.

DEAR SIR,

I have been following Mr. G. Winteringham's articles on track and have made points, etc. They are quite satisfactory, and take trains going at about 140 m.p.h. scale speed.

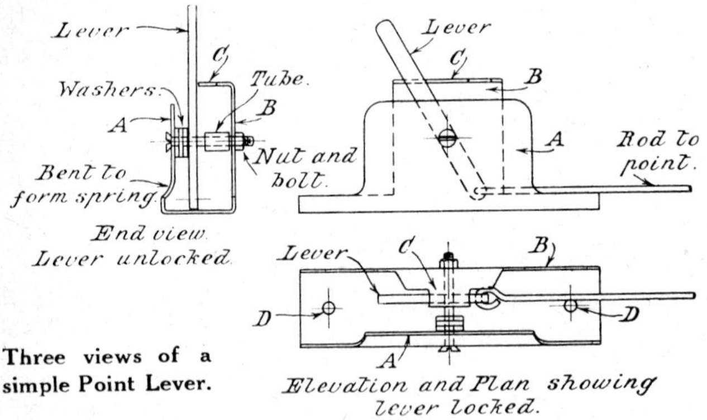

Three views of a simple Point Lever.

I have been experimenting with point levers for the above, and the one I have made works quite well. Thinking it may be useful to other readers, I give a description below.

It can be made of scrap tin, brass, copper, etc.

The idea is to work the lever like a double brake. The points, being made of brass, are naturally springy, so I made the lever thus:—Having cut the tin to required shape, I drilled through both sides to take the nut and bolt, and two holes DD in the base for holding down screws.

I next took a length of brass rail, and drilled it to take nut and bolt and point rodding.

Next, place enough washers between side A and lever to make the lever a tight sliding fit across the tongue C. (This should be left long until the lever is fixed.) Then place some more washers or a piece of tube, to prevent the lever sliding slantwise, and put the nut on loosely. Connect rod to lever and point and mark C at each end of the throw of the lever. Allow 1-24th in. each end. so that lever is a tight fit when locked, and cut away surplus.

This lever is cheap and efficient, and suits any type of point. I have left the exact size to the discretion of the future maker.

Yours truly,

R. H. K. WICKHAM.

West Bromwich.

More " Explosion."

To the Editor,
MODEL RAILWAY NEWS.

DEAR SIR,

Why should one feel morally obliged to run electric locos proper on our model railway? Let "Disgruntled" run them if it pleases him, and "L. B. S. C." his pukka miniature steam locos.

It pleases *me* to run electric steam-outline models. And why? Because, as a boy, I had a great affection for the steam-outline loco as I knew it then, and being a boy still at heart, I prefer to do as I do.

After all, happiness and contentment are the great objects of model railways; and true art is that which can be deceptive in its realism, thus pleasing the senses and so making for happiness.

Therefore, don't be discouraged, "steam outliners"; carry on and enjoy your model engineering in any way you please and you will be all the better for it.

Besides ('tween you and me), it

takes far more ingenuity and brains to fit a motor to a steam outline than to a box-like electric model such as the purist electric fans idolize.

Yours faithfully,

"OVIDIAN."

Mr. C. H. Roberts' Gauge 1 Model 2-4-2 Tank Loco.

An Argentine Model Railway.

To the Editor, MODEL RAILWAY NEWS.

DEAR SIR,

I herewith enclose some photographs of my brother, Mr. C. H. Roberts' Gauge 1 model railway, in San Martin, Argentina.

The two engines, with the exception of a few parts purchased at Messrs. Bassett-Lowke, Ltd., were built by the owner. The 0-4-0 tank, (not reproduced), has one slide valve cylinder, 7-16th × ¾-in., slip eccentric reversing. It has a tractive effort of 5½ oz., and works at a pressure of 40 to 60 lb. The 2—4—2 tank loco has two cylinders, 7-16th by ¾-in., Walschaert's gear, and a tractive effort of 16 oz., at 60 to 80 lb. pressure.

The Station, and the "Safety First" poster.

The rolling stock is entirely home made, the bogie frames being cast of white metal. The coaches are typical of those used on the Argentine railways, with seats on each side of a central corridor.

Above the station may be seen an actual Central Argentine Railway "safety first" poster, the wording of which, literally translated, means "It is better to lose the train than to lose your life."

The single-span bridge, shown in one of the photos, is also entirely made by the owner. It is 36 inches long, and is built up of 1-16th-inch steel plate, and ¼-in. angle, riveted together. In the same photograph may be seen a model of a railway engineer's rail-motor car.

I am, Yours truly,

Bournemouth. H. D. ROBERTS.

O Gauge G.W.R. Models.

To the Editor, MODEL RAILWAY NEWS.

DEAR SIR,

I see in your September issue a letter from "A. P," who seems very disconsolate at the lack of small-gauge scale G. W. R. models on the market. As I was the first in your excellent

The steel-plate Bridge.

Some of Mr. C. H. Roberts' guage 1 rolling-stock.

journal to raise this outcry, may I be permitted to enlighten him and others in the same frame of mind, where G.W.R. types may be bought or made at the same price as stock models? I only quote 0 gauge. I also hasten to add I have absolutely no interest in any firm or individual mentioned, other than that of a satisfied customer. The following are from 1924 — 1925 season's catalogues. I have no official intimation of other G.W.R. types to be stocked.

Locomotives.

Bassett-Lowke.—"County Class," clockwork, electric; "Moguls," steam, clockwork, electric.

Leeds Models.—"Castle Class," clockwork, electric; Other four-cylinder classes, clockwork, electric.

Kay Models.—"Castle Class," clockwork, electric. They also make to order practically at stock prices any type required.

F. W. E. Stevens, Cheddar.—Makes to order practically at stock prices any type required.

Rolling Stock.

Bassett-Lowke.—Tin-plate G.W.R. corridor coaches in the late red colour. I imagine, when this stock is exhausted, they will put on the new, or old original colours.

Leeds Models.—Do not at present stock G.W.R. coaches, but we live in hope.

Mills Bros.—Make a G.W.R. type of goods bogie, which can be filed to represent the pre-war type, or the one now fitted to "Macaw" and "Crocodile" bogie types.

Leeds and Kay.—Both make underslung American-type coach bogies as used on the G.W.R.

All firms stock various G.W.R. goods vehicles of many types.

Sets of Parts.

Leeds and Mills both stock these in goods types, and these can be easily altered and lettered to make actual G.W.R. models.

In answering "A.P.'s" letter, I am also prompted by the Editorial comments of the June issue, and previous to that, for information as to where things can be obtained.

In the near future, I hope to send along my own humble efforts, or rather description of them, with detail of difficulties and how overcome. I am a mere beginner, and it may be of use to those similarly situated.

I have concentrated on G.W.R. goods rolling stock to gain experience. I have made "Macaw B" and "Crocodile A" bogies, besides making up parts from Leeds and Mills Bros., both excellent to teach one how to make, and now hope to start on coaches.

One observation. So many people are content just to give a description of their model railway, complete, with suitable photos, but there are a lot of structural details, both in the railway, locomotives and rolling stock omitted, which, to my mind, can well be added. For instance, locomotives are shown which are quoted to be exceptionally powerful (clockwork).

Where were these made, and which firm's mechanism is fitted, etc.? All this is most important, I feel sure, to many besides myself. I hope that those who build their own rolling stock, both passenger and goods, will be kind enough to send articles to you, with *full* details of construction.

These will be of real value.

Yours faithfully,
"SPARKS."

Henley Station.

To the Editor, MODEL RAILWAY NEWS.

DEAR SIR,

I was greatly interested in the notes by "Lord of the Isles" in the August issue of the MODEL RAILWAY NEWS.

As an old resident of Henley I have pleasure in sending you the enclosed plan, showing the general arrangement of the station and tracks. It will be seen that there are three platforms, arranged in two lengths, each of which may be said to form an island. The two roads to the left of No. 3 platform used at one time to run right through the station on to the original turntable, the site of which is now occupied by the cab-rank. Beyond this is an engine shed, coal siding, and the present turntable, which is of the modern balanced type. To the right, at the back of No. 1 platform, is a bay road, goods depot and a long coal siding. The station signal box is of blue brick and contains a locking frame of 65 levers. Beyond this are several long carriage sidings running right back to Mill Lane bridge. This bridge replaces a level crossing which once stood here. The signals shown with crosses on the arms, together with the small box at Mill Lane, are only used during the regatta week, when traffic is exceptionally heavy. Your correspondent, however, was mistaken in thinking this branch to be a single line, as it has been double-tracked now for some years past.

The explanation of letters on diagram are :—S.B., signal box ; C.T., cottage ; G.D., ground disc ; W.C., water columns ; C., crane ; G.S., goods shed ; C.P., cattle pens ; W.T., water tank ; W.R., waiting rooms and offices ; C.S., coal stacks ; T.T., turntable ; P.H., platelayers' hut ; E.S., engine shed ; B., bookstall ; W.M., weighing machine ; B.O., booking office ; E.H., entrance hall ; P., platforms.

Hoping you will find this letter of interest and the plan of some use.

Yours sincerely,
Harlesden. F. C. ALLEWAY.

[We have to acknowledge a plan and photos of Henley Station from another reader, which we hope to find room for in our next issue.—Ed., M.R.N.]

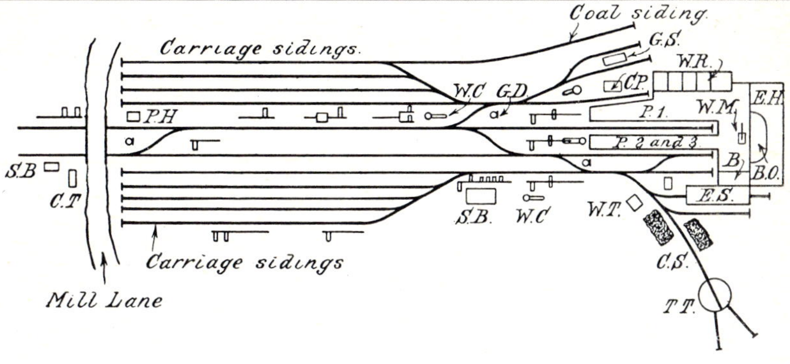

Rail plan at Henley Station (not to scale).

For Winnipeg readers.

To the Editor, MODEL RAILWAY NEWS.

DEAR SIR,

I beg to encroach upon a little of the valuable space of the MODEL RAILWAY NEWS in the hope that this letter will catch the eye of the model engineering enthusiasts of Winnipeg.

I have lived in this city now for the past 18 months and have only been able to find two other such enthusiasts.

Now I do not for a minute doubt but that there must be a few other fellows with this delightful hobby, and it is my earnest wish that we all get together and endeavour to form a local society of model engineers.

Having been a member of the Hull (England) society, I miss most acutely the delights and pleasures of such an organization.

Therefore, would any enthusiast, interested in such a proposition, communicate with the writer or Mr. J. Wood, 74, Lloyd Street, Norwood, Winnipeg.

I should very much like to get this established by the beginning of the winter.

Yours sincerely,

ERIC ABLE.

828, East Kildonan Road,
Winnipeg, Man., Canada.

Concrete Posts and the Electric Explosion.

To the Editor, MODEL RAILWAY NEWS.

DEAR SIR,

I have got dimensions of concrete telegraph posts, signal-wire posts, gradient-posts, mile-posts and fencing. If you think they will be of use to fellow "railwayists," I should be only too glad to send drawings. The first-mentioned I have seen no models of, and they are, in my opinion, an improvement on the usual posts. The article by "Disgruntled" in your August number is interesting, but he should remember that it is not everyone who *wants* to model electric locomotives. I agree with him that there is a great deal to be said for electric locomotives, but there are other views to take.

From the extreme "purist's" idea, it is, of course, against his will to utilize electricity for steam models, and if he is "true to his cause" he will be all-steam or all-electric. But the majority are not extreme "purists" and realize that the advantages to be gained by utilizing electricity for their steam models outweigh the disadvantage of camouflage that "Disgruntled" mentions. I must say a steam loco looks slightly out of place on electric track—but do we not see examples in everyday life on such railways as the Metropolitan and the S.R.? There are many most interesting electric locomotives to model, but there are as well so many fine steam locos, and if such a convenient form of power as electricity can be used, what harm in using it?

The fine points given in the article certainly show decided advantages for the all-electric loco. Can any steam enthusiast give five equally strong points in favour of the electric-steam model? In a limited space, there is the additional small advantage that no turntables are required for electric locos.

Yours faithfully,

K. H. S. MASSEY.

London, W.C. 1

Make-Believe Brick Wall.

To the Editor, MODEL RAILWAY NEWS.

DEAR SIR,

It may interest some of your readers to learn that model-makers are not the only ones reduced to make-believe. At a small station called Clocksbriggs, just out of Forfar, on the old Caledonian Railway, is a signal-box whose surface is flat, like plaster. But this plaster is painted red and has white lines drawn on it so that the result is a neat and, although conventional, realistic representation of a brick wall. It is the first time that I have seen anything of the sort and I would like to know if any other boxes are like that.

Yours sincerely,

J. MILNE.

Berkhamsted.

Lott's Bricks for Model Railways.

WE reproduce herewith photographs of a model of Watford Station, and a two-arch bridge made up from Lott's bricks. Although, in the prospectus, the bricks are described as toy building blocks, it will be seen that the results obtainable with them are very realistic, and that they are a practical proposition for the model railway owner. They are made of artificial stone, and when built up give a very satisfactory solidity of appearance. The blocks are made in 11 different shapes, all multiples of the inch, and they lend themselves to a great variety of constructions. Besides the station and the bridge, plans are given for building warehouses, schools, a masonic hall, a cathedral, a guildhall, and a beacon tower, as well as many kinds of small houses, goods sheds, barns, garages and bungalows, complete with trees, palings and fences. It is observed that with these models the blank spaces which so often detract from the realism of model railways, could be most appropriately filled. There is, however, one point to be noticed, and that is the size of the buildings relative to the gauge of the railway. The two models here illustrated are suitable for 0 gauge. There is just sufficient clearance under the bridge, which is four feet long over all, for locomotives and coaches, as each span is $4\frac{3}{4}$ inches high and $10\frac{1}{2}$ inches in width. The station buildings are 2 ft. 3 in. long, which is rather short, as it will barely accommodate three coaches with the locomotive outside. However, the platform, which is the correct scale height of $1\frac{1}{4}$ in. from the track level, could easily be extended. Therein lies the charm of these bricks, for it is quite unnecessary to follow definite plans, and modifications or alterations are easily made. Moreover, for any odd jobs, such as facing cuttings and tunnel mouths, they should be very useful. Particulars may be had from Lott's Bricks, Ltd., Watford.

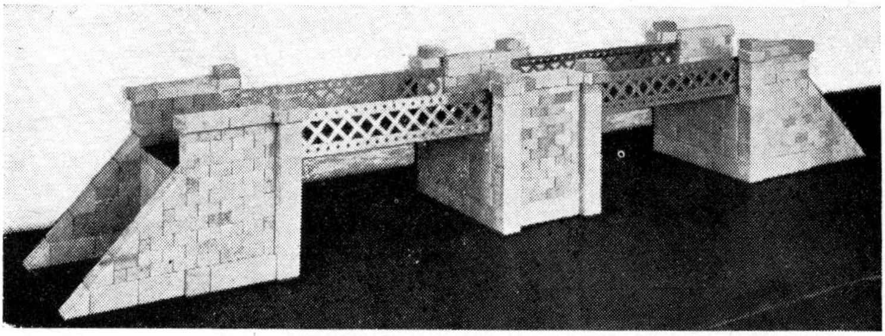

A realistic bridge made from Lott's bricks.

Platform view of a model of Watford station made from Lott's Bricks.

New Electro-Motor Mechanisms.

SOME time past the demand for a really well-made electro-motor mechanism had reached the acute stage. The traction type of motor, using both permanent magnet and wound fields, had already been accepted as the most satisfactory type of motor. In this design, the armature shaft is parallel to the longitudinal axis of the locomotive and therefore not bounded by the limitations of the rail gauge. The pre-war "Tracto" motor of this type supplied by Messrs. Bassett-Lowke, Ltd., was, as far as the motor was concerned, the best thing that had been done. The bevel gearing, used for the transmission was however not entirely efficient, and much of the extra power given out by the motor was lost in friction.

With the new mechanism, two outstanding improvements have been made (there are several other minor ones to recount), viz. :—The use of a newly invented steel-alloy of high magnetic value and permanency for the field magnets, and secondly, for the first time in the annals of model engineering, a worm gear of high efficiency which is reversible in its action. The latter term has nothing to do with the reversal in the direction of rotation—the motor is capable of being automatically reversed by changing over the direction of the current in the ordinary way—but refers to the gear ratio of the worm being such that the wheel will drive the worm as well as the worm driving the wheel. This desirable feature is obtained by using a four-threaded worm made in steel and a worm wheel of bronze which is "generated" by a milling cutter or "hob" on a special machine.

The shortcomings of the ordinary common worm and wheel, as used on constructional toys, are well known. The locomotive stops immediately the current supply falls below a certain value, and, further, the gear ratios are so large that only a snail's pace can be got out of the engine.

In the new motor mechanisms the ratio of gearing is about 7:1. This gives both an ample tractive effort and a fast speed. The permanent field magnet is short and does not take up much room. It fits on to soft cast-iron machined pole-pieces. The armature is of the tripolar type, made in cast-iron in two parts—an arrangement which is designed to reduce eddy current losses as much as possible. The poles are accurately machined so that a very small air gap is obtained.

New 2—6—0 G.W.R. Gauge "0" Loco.

The 4-coupled mechanism.

The diameter is no less than 1 in. for a No. 0 gauge locomotive, and also has a length of one inch. Silk-covered wire is used to allow the largest possible amount of windings to be crowded on to the armature. The brush gear and commutator are especially robust, yet the brush pressure is exceptionally light. The slots in the commutator are cut obliquely.

The motor is built up on to brass side frames, which carry the frame running wheels, brass being used both because it is non-magnetic and a better material than sheet steel for axle bearings. The parallel side-frames are pierced to allow access to the commutator and brushes. The mechanisms are made up to suit both four- and six-coupled wheels, and as shown by the diagrams and photographs, there is ample space between the duplex collector shoes, in the six-coupled mechanism more particularly. These collectors are of the "spoon" type and can be adjusted by bending to suit both the all-level and the raised-third rail systems. The rubbing action of the spoon collectors is to be preferred, on the whole, to the roller type of collectors previously used. The dirt is brushed off rather than rolled in.

The 6-coupled mechanisms.

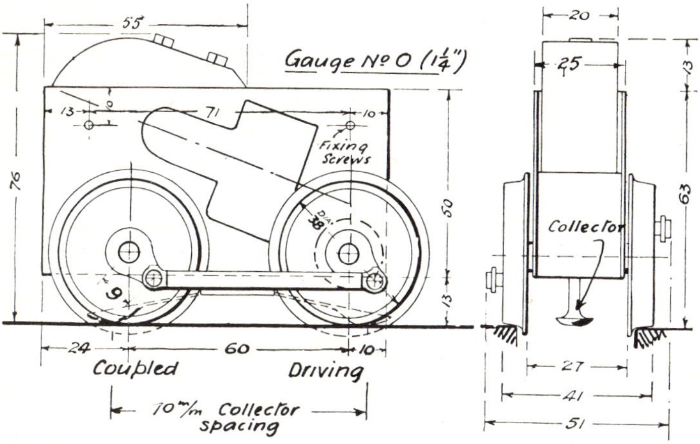

Dimensioned views of the 4-coupled mechanism.

It is in this particular motor the reversibility of the worm gear is only noticeable in the forward direction because of the large diameter of the thrust-bearing area of the commutator, but it *is* present, and the momentum

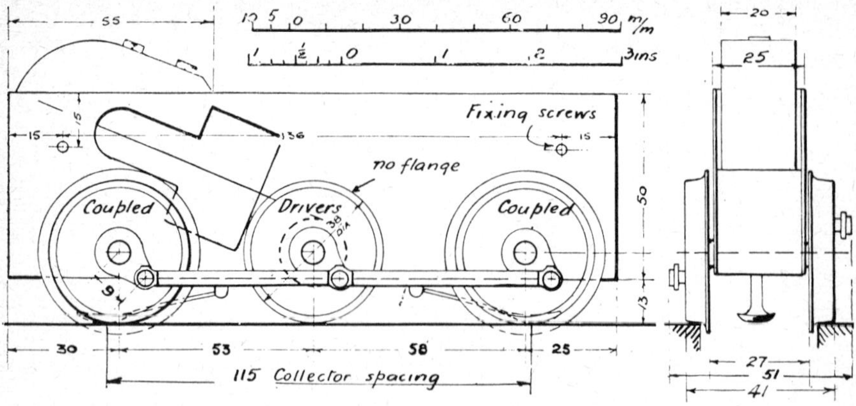

Dimensioned views of the 6-coupled mechanism.

of the armature shaft is sufficient to allow the locomotive to roll to an easy stop. With the worms previously supplied for models, the pitch and general efficiency was so bad as to lock the wheels directly the current flow stopped. To attain this non-locking feature because of the braking action of the permanent magnetism, it is necessary to put enough current through to take up the internal friction of the armature and destroy this magnetic braking action.

The voltage of the motors has been raised from the usual 4–6 volts to 6–8 volts. This scheme, coupled with the lower voltage consumption, should considerably reduce the amperage passing through the brushes. This alone is a noteworthy improvement.

Testing the Six-coupled Set.

We were able to run the six-coupled mechanism (without a body) and pull six coaches for a start on a grade of 1 in 30 to 1 in 28. The consumption was 2·7 amperes at 8 volts. Running fast (downhill) with the same load the amperage fell to 1. The standing amperage at 8 volts was 4·7. Testing it in comparison with a pre-war "Tracto" motor the current consumption was much lower, the latter (older) motor taking 5·5 to 6 amperes starting and 4 and 2 amperes running under the same conditions as above.

The motor was decidedly the more powerful of the two, as well as having a higher electrical efficiency. A regulating resistance was not available, the No. 0 gauge railway on which the motor was tested having voltage controllers (4 or 8 only) and no means of providing intermediate values.

Underside views of the two types, showing spoon collectors.

The MODEL RAILWAY NEWS

Editorial and Publishing Offices :
66, FARRINGDON STREET, LONDON, E.C.4.

Single Copies, post free, 7½d. Annual Subscription, 7s. 6d.

Vol. I. No. 11. NOVEMBER, 1925. Price, 6d.

Notes of the Month.

THE event of the past month in the world of model railways has been the opening of the new running track of the Society of Model and Experimental Engineers. Although this Society takes a broad outlook on model engineering and deals with every branch of that fascinating hobby, it has a very strong element of model locomotive enthusiasts in its membership. It has had a model railway track of some kind or another since its very earliest days, and locomotive testing and running has always been a feature of its winter programme. The new track is a very well-designed structure, much lower than its predecessor, and more suitable for passenger hauling. It is of a portable character, the various lengths being fitted together so that it can be erected or removed in a minimum amount of time. The opening ceremony took place on October 6th, when Mr. Percival Marshall drove the famous steam model, "Cosmo Bonsor," on the first official trip along the track, breaking a silk ribbon on the way. Three cheers for the new track and one for the builders, a vigorous blowing of "Cosmo Bonsor's" whistle, and the "chuff-chuff" of a healthy beat as this wonderful old warrior among locomotives chortled along the track, gave the ceremony an appropriate amount of noise and enthusiasm. "Cosmo Bonsor" has recently been in the shops for a complete overhaul, after celebrating her 21st year of active life. She is now in excellent trim, and is likely to add very considerably to the total of 70,000 passengers she has already hauled. The new track is certain to do much to stimulate model locomotive interest among the Society members.

* * *

On the same evening, Mr. Forward, of the Science Museum, gave a most interesting lantern lecture on the history of the locomotive. This is a subject which has often been dealt with before technical societies, but we can safely say we have never heard it more interestingly treated, nor have we seen a better set of slides than those Mr. Forward put upon the screen to illustrate his points. We understand that the history of the model locomotive is to be dealt with at a later date by a prominent member of the society. This should be even more interesting to model engineers.

* * *

In discussing the advantages of steam as compared with electric propulsion for model railways, a correspondent raises the interesting point of "realistic noise." We all know the characteristic noises of a real railway—the beat of the engines, the blowing-off of the steam, the screeching of the whistles, and the roar of the express as it speeds on its journey. The reproduction of these noises in miniature undoubtedly adds a very realistic note to a model railway, and there is much to be said for the steam model from this point of view. The question of whether steam, clockwork, or electric propulsion is best will never be settled to the satisfaction of everybody, for there is no one and only answer. There are so many different points of view, and individual preferences. Everybody will settle the question for himself to his own liking, and will be happy with his decision.

* * *

If we asked our readers the question "What interests you most about your model railway?" we are quite certain we should get a variety of answers. Some would say the general realism of the whole system, making the model as much like a real railway in miniature as possible. Others would say, the running, switching, and shunting of trains, with appropriate signalling. Others would reply that their interest centred in the locomotives, while still another section would undoubtedly vote for the pleasure they got in doing constructive work, in track-laying, and in building coaches, stations, signals, bridges, and scenic effects. It is a great testimony to the attractiveness of model railway work as a hobby that such a variety of interest should be possible, but this very diversity of interest precludes a definite answer being given as to the most suitable kind of power, unless the question is simplified by the attaching of certain conditions or limitations.

* * *

We are very appreciative of the many interesting letters we receive for our mail bag. This free exchange of knowledge and opinion amongst our readers is one of the most helpful features of the MODEL RAILWAY NEWS, and we hope readers will continue to make use of our pages in this way. We are naturally obliged to give preference in publication to letters having the greatest general interest, and if any correspondent finds that we have been unable to print his communication, we hope he will understand that it is due to the limitations of our space rather than to any lack of appreciation of his desire to help. We should like to comment once again on the poor quality of many of the photographs of model railways which are sent to us with a view to publication. Some readers seem to have a wonderful faith in our ability to make an A 1 picture out of a C 3 photograph. Under-exposed "snaps" of a midget size are really of very little use. They do not show detail either clearly enough, or large enough, to be of any real use to another reader, and frequently they do not do justice to what may be a very excellent model railway. If a model railway is worth illustrating at all, it is worth illustrating well, and we would, therefore, urge on our readers the desirability of a good camera, a competent operator, and a plate of sufficient size.

Romney, Hythe and Dymchurch Miniature Railway.

A NEW 15-inch gauge railway—a public line for passengers, mails and goods—has been planned to connect New Romney, Southern Railway, to Hythe, Kent, serving the seaside village of Dymchurch halfway. The length of the line is about nine miles, and Mr. Henry Greenly, who is the engineer and manager, has just completed the survey and is applying on behalf of Capt. J E. P. Howey for the necessary powers. The "Green Goddess" and its sister engine, "Northern Chief," will work the passenger services, and for goods work some 2—8—2 type locomotives are being considered. The "Northern Chief" Pacific underwent its bench brake-tests last month, developing 46 I.H.P. Mr. Henry Greenly's office is now at New Romney.

NOTABLE MODEL RAILWAYS

Dr. W. T. Dobson's "0" Gauge Electric.

DR. W. T. DOBSON, of "The Red House," Uxbridge, in the intervals of a busy practice, cultivates the art of model engineering, and particularly model railway engineering, to a marked degree. During an interview with him the writer saw and examined no less than four separate railway systems at the doctor's home. One of these is but a test track, or tracks, which are duly electrified and are in his sanctum, and apparently are used to test the going capacity of a loco. Another is a toy railway constructed for the doctor's boys. This, although but a simple affair, involves a point of practical interest. It is set up on a board, about 6½ ft. by 4 ft., which is hinged as a flap to a frame attached to the wall. When not in use, and with all stock put away, it can be shut up into the frame, and being duly papered to match the wall, conveniently disposes of what would ordinarily be an encumbrance and an eyesore. The third system is a garden railway, about 70 feet long, with terminals. This is multi-gauge and is principally used for longer test runs. The rails, which are of brass with bottom flanges attached to planking on piles, are arranged as in the diagram, Fig. 1. Four standard gauges are used, the three largest of which are provided with centre rails. Fig. 2 shows four of the models (all electric driven) standing on their respective gauges on this railway. A point of interest is that the planking is carried through a tunnel opening in the wall of an outhouse, the floor of which, being at a lower level than the garden, gives convenient headroom for operating the under-firing of steam models. In this building the planking and rails are carried some little distance to a dead end, the former being holed for convenience in getting to the underside of the models. The fourth railway, which concerns us most in this article, is of a particularly complete construction and detail. It is 0 gauge, electric, and is set up in a loft, 16 ft.

Fig 2.—Models on the garden track.

Fig. 4.—"Loftown" Station and Engine Shed.

by 13½ ft., above the doctor's consulting rooms, which are separate from his home.

Fig. 3 is a scale plan of the lay-out of the 0 gauge railway. In the corner of the room is a photographic dark room, 6 ft. by 5½ ft., partitioned off, which is duly equipped and is used for its legitimate purpose. Through this partitioned room, which, when not engaged, does duty as a main line tunnel, the double track passes upon a trestle which is fitted with a hinged "counter" flap. The actual bolt which secures the flap constitutes the junction of the electric circuit. The room is approached up a staircase giving access through a rectangular opening in floor. Over this opening the main line passes on a 2-ft. span lattice girder bridge. As viewed on the plan, to the left of this bridge is a level crossing, which virtually divides the system into town and country. That beyond the crossing contains the town station, engine sheds, etc., and that short of it the country station, open country and a country goods depot. Short of the crossing also, and near the main-line bridge, is a single-line junction which, passing townward, and up a bank of average gradient, 1 in 36, ultimately crosses the main line by a single-track girder bridge, by the tunnel, and, entering by its own tunnel facia, goes to a dead end in the dark room.

The town station is designated "Loftown" and the other "Bridgtown." A portion of the former, together with the road foot-bridge and level-crossing, are seen in Fig. 4, while some idea of the latter can be gleaned from Fig. 5. Fig. 6 shows the tunnel openings and single-track girder-bridge, which constitutes a difficult bit of railway engineering. The deck of the railway stands about 3 ft. 2 in. above the loft floor, and, on a projection of it, as seen in the

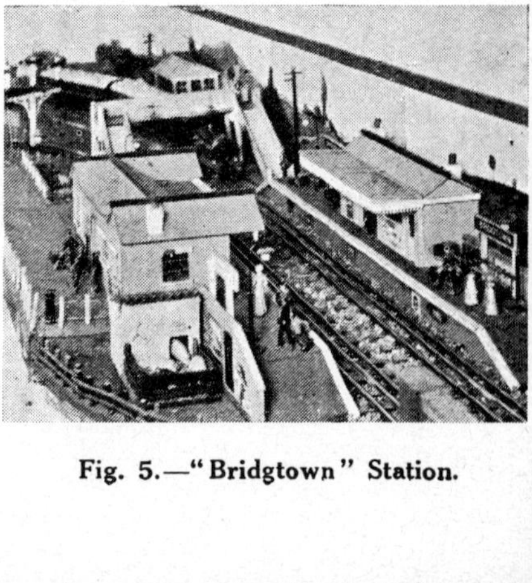

Fig. 5.—"Bridgtown" Station.

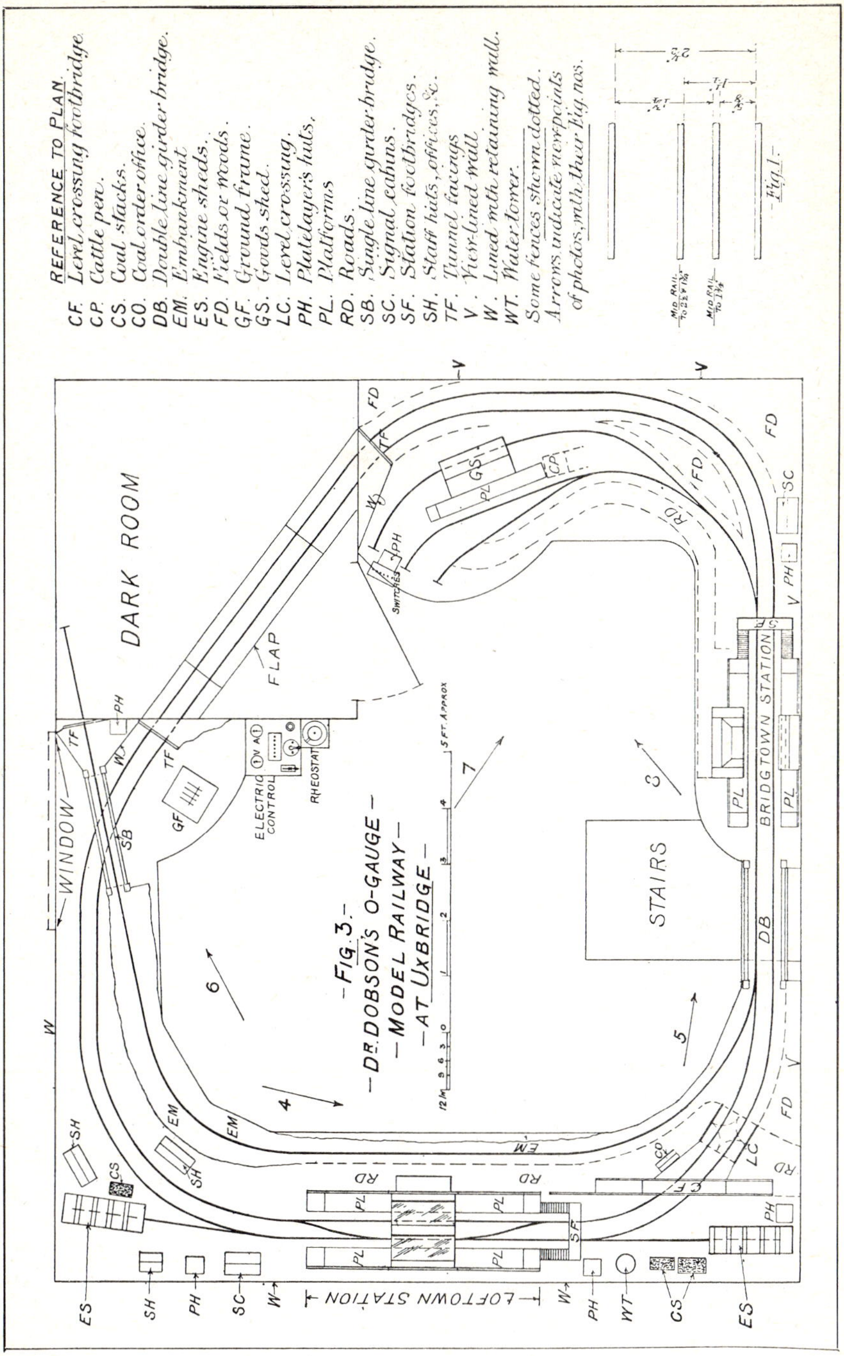
REFERENCE TO PLAN.
CF. Level crossing footbridge.
CP. Cattle pen.
CS. Coal stacks.
CO. Coal order office.
DB. Double line girder bridge.
EM. Embankment.
ES. Engine sheds.
FD. Fields or woods.
GF. Ground frame.
GS. Goods shed.
LC. Level crossing.
PH. Platelayer's huts.
PL. Platforms.
RD. Roads.
SB. Single line girder bridge.
SC. Signal cabins.
SF. Station footbridges.
SH. Staff huts, offices, &c.
TF. Tunnel facings.
V. View-lined wall.
W. Lined with retaining wall.
WT. Water tower.
Some fences shown dotted.
Arrows indicate view-points of photos, with their fig. nos.
Fig. 1.
DARK ROOM
FLAP
SWITCHES
ELECTRIC CONTROL
RHEOSTAT
WINDOW
STAIRS
BRIDGETOWN STATION
LOFTOWN STATION
5 FT. APPROX.
Fig. 3.
Dr. Dobson's O-Gauge
Model Railway
at Uxbridge

Fig. 6.—The tunnels at "dark room."

last-mentioned picture, is a four-lever ground frame, which operates the single-line junctions to engine sheds, and two crossover roads, all in the town-station area. Beyond this, all junctions and signals are locally operated. Near this ground-frame, as seen on plan, is the electric control board containing voltmeter and its push switch and ammeter, distributing switches to up and down main, bank, engine sheds, and goods yard, while the latter has its own distribution switches put locally. The main switchboard has also, beside a main switch, a reversing switch and a particularly effective circular rheostat, which enables the operator to draw up any combination or single vehicle in a most realistic manner.

The writer does not remember having seen such a diverse and numerous collection of model locos, steam, electric and clockwork, as has Dr. Dobson in his collection as a whole. Of these, belonging to the loft railway, there are three tender expresses, four main-line tanks and one shunting tank, and, in addition, a single-driven bogie motor coach, "Metropolitan" pattern, which the doctor constructed himself. The

Fig. 7.—A view across country.

rolling stock includes six main-line bogie coaches to different classes and 20 "goods" items, which, besides brake vans, open and closed waggons, comprise an oil tank, a motor-car waggon, a double-bogie large-capacity open waggon, a two-part timber truck, and a cattle truck with its load.

A strong feature of the railway is its realism in point of detail. Wheeled vehicles used in the furnishings line tunnel facia leading to dark room. There are three sidings in goods yard, all to dead ends, the lead to which, in one case, passes through goods shed and against an inside platform. Another siding passes an outer platform of goods station at the end of which is a pen for loading cattle full of sheep for entrainment.

The general equipment includes two signal cabins, besides various huts, coal stacks, sheds and shelters, and include a double-horse hay cart loaded, a single-horse milk cart, goods and milk-can trolleys and luggage trolleys and barrows. The figures are very complete in variety, and live stock includes horses, cattle, pigs, sheep, geese, ducks, and chickens, and there are deer in the woods, and passengers and their friends are accompanied by their dogs, and there is one station cat.

Fig. 8.—Goods yard and station.

A general idea of the animal accessories and their disposition can be gathered from Fig. 7, a view across country, showing the junctions of goods depot in foreground, and a hay-cart on the road. Fig. 8 is a view of the goods yard and station, showing, in the background, the main-loose articles such as general luggage. Rug rolls, golf sticks and the like, abound and there are the usual notices, advertisements, pillar posts, slot machines and their guardian policemen. An ordinary observer would need hours to take in the points of this railway, which is scale iron track on chairs and sleepers, with ballast, and Dr. Dobson has discovered that surgical lint stuck to cardboard and soaked with the right tint oil-colour makes the most realistic grass and undergrowth effect. He also uses a surgical instrument, known as crocodile-jaw forceps, which have very small jaws, long shank, and scissors handle, as a convenient form of coupling pole.

Model Railways Abroad.

DURING my recent visit to Switzerland and South Germany with a member of the London Society of Model Engineers who wishes to remain nameless, we were much impressed with the growth of interest in railways and model railways in particular. Years ago, when I put down a line in Geneva, the local boy took little or no notice of the miniature engines. At the Munich Exhibition there now is quite a different feeling. There was the usual rush of small boys for the front seat in the train to view more closely the working of the locomotive. The drivers are just as much in love with their locomotives as their English confreres.

In a village in Switzerland we were also much amused with a coterie of small boys building and operating a model railway in a garden which could be looked down on from the neighbouring road. So the interest in railways and locomotives, the absence of which Mr. Roland Martens deplored so much when I last saw him in Mannheim 13 years ago, is evidently developing.

At the Munich Transport Exhibition the Government have laid down quite the largest model railway that has been built. It measures at least 120 feet long by 70 feet wide, and is a No. 1 gauge line, electrically operated.

The railway is sunk in a well, so that the onlookers can see every part of the line. The main scheme is a double main line running lengthways across the centre and disappearing into tunnels at each side. In these tunnels under the onlookers' platform huge turntables are fitted, so that the trains can be returned on the " up " line after their down journey out of sight. This idea is, of course, an English one and was adopted by Mr. Winteringham for the White City Exhibition lay-out made for the L.N.W.R. Company some 14 or 15 years ago. On each side of the main line there are numerous sidings, goods depots, factory yards, shunting and marshalling yards, complete with buildings and other railway accessories, all served by representative locomotives, both steam and electric, from shunting types to huge Mallet banking engines. All the vehicles were fitted with working models of the Schaffenburg automatic coupling, a new invention which is likely to be adopted on the Continent before many years pass.

The whole line is sectionalized and controlled by a huge switch board. Several mechanics are employed to provide for maintenance, and performances which are explained, are made at stated intervals. We understood from Mr. Roland Martens that the model will most likely be preserved in the new Deutsches Museum, at Munich, after the Exhibition closes.

The miniature railway has been a great success, and up to the time of our visit has carried 400,000 passengers. Being in a permanent exhibition park and built under the paternal care of the Government, it will not be disbanded. It can always be re-opened when the grounds are employed for another show.

By the courtesy of the civil and mechanical engineers of the line, Herrn Flugel and Roland Martens, both of us visitors were allowed to take several trips on the locomotives.

The operators are all real railway men and, as is usual in things done in the Fatherland, the line is neat, thoroughly well done and orderly in the extreme. We also much appreciated the high compliments paid to the English-made vacuum brake designed by the writer. It is working quite successfully on 10 coach trains.

H. G.

2½ in. Gauge Model Rolling Stock.

By ERNEST BLACKBURN.

HAVING had many years' experience in the actual design and construction of almost every type of vehicle in use on home, colonial and foreign railways, I am familiar with the many features peculiar to them, both for use on narrow and broad gauge lines. Consequently when I commenced seriously on model railway work as a hobby, I decided that instead of copying the types of rolling stock in use on any one particular railway, I would use my own designs and ideas.

The first, and to my mind the most important point to which I devoted my attention, was the running gear, *i.e.*, springs and wheels. I was determined to use scale flanges. This was rather a difficult thing to accomplish, having regard to the general roughness and unevenness of my track, which is exposed to all weathers, and abounds with exceedingly sharp curves, varying from eight-feet radius to as small as six-feet radius. After many trials, I was successful and have adopted spiral springs over the axle-boxes. I have also succeeded in producing a spring which is "standard" for all my stock, bogie and non-bogie, as well as "standardizing" axle-guards and axle-boxes. I had great difficulty in preventing vehicles from buffer-locking with the usual type of side buffers. I am, therefore, replacing these with a central buffer coupling, and have all my passenger vehicles so fitted and most of the goods stock. This has got over the difficulty, and I am able to run trains at excessive speeds, and very seldom have a derailment; in fact, a derailment is so rare, that should one occur, it is quite an event.

The spiral spring over the axle-boxes in lieu of the conventional plate spring has caused comment amongst several of my model-making friends, but it might interest readers to learn that there are bogie carriages and ordinary wagons running to-day in England so fitted.

A 2½ in. gauge 1st and 3rd class corridor coach.

The underframes of my four-wheeled vehicles are quite simple, and Figs. 1 and 2 show the construction. They are interchangeable with all trucks of similar lengths. They are built up out of strip wood, glued together and pinned with "cigar-box" nails, the axle-guards and other fittings being screwed up before the frame is assembled. I generally give the first coat of paint during erection.

The bodies are cut with a fret saw out of mahogany, the joints of the boards being scribed by means of an awl. The strapping and hinges are cut from good quality card (old visiting cards are excellent), and glued in place. Ordinary household pins are then hammered in to represent the bolts, etc.

The bodies are attached to the underframes by means of fine screws through the frame into the floor.

Fig. 3 shows the various details, and needs no explanation.

Fig. 4 shows sections of one of my carriages. The sides and partitions are carefully cut from fret wood and thoroughly sandpapered. The outside of the body is then scribed or panelled, and the first coat of paint applied. This is then well pumiced down and all is covered with "filling." When dry, this is again "rubbed" down, and the first finishing colour applied. Then the interior is scribed, well sandpapered, and stained, thick white drawing paper glued over the cornices as a frieze. Pictures and mirrors and parcel racks are then fixed up and finally the seats, which are secured to the partition, the "padding" being glued over afterwards. The stained portion should now receive a wax polish. The floor should be covered with the lino, or tiles, and the position of the partitions marked. Then fix all partitions in place, together with the ends. The longitudinal corridor partition may now be fitted with windows, as shewn on the drawing, and blinds glued up. After the windows have been well cleaned, this partition can be secured to the cross partitions. The outsides may now have the glass fitted, together with blinds and doors, and after the glass has been thoroughly cleaned can be finally screwed up. The roof may be of thin zinc bent to the required shape over a wooden template. Ventilators and lamps should then be fitted, and finally painted dead white inside and out.

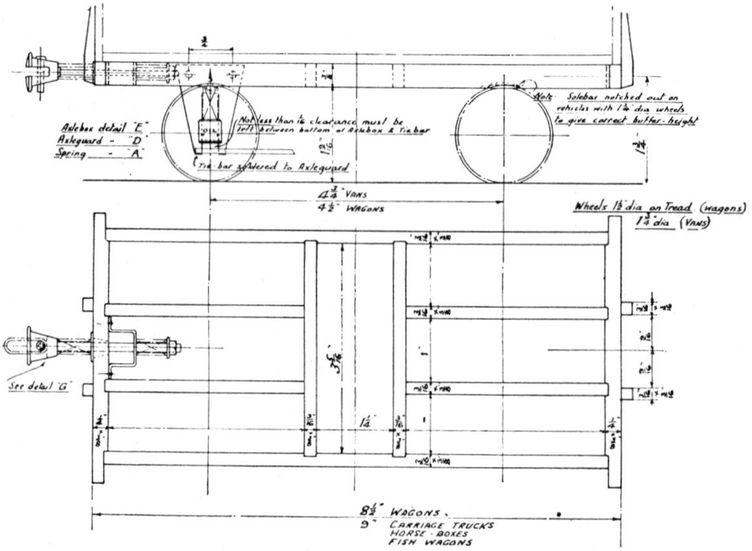

Fig. 1.—Underframes for 2½ in. gauge four-wheeled vehicles.

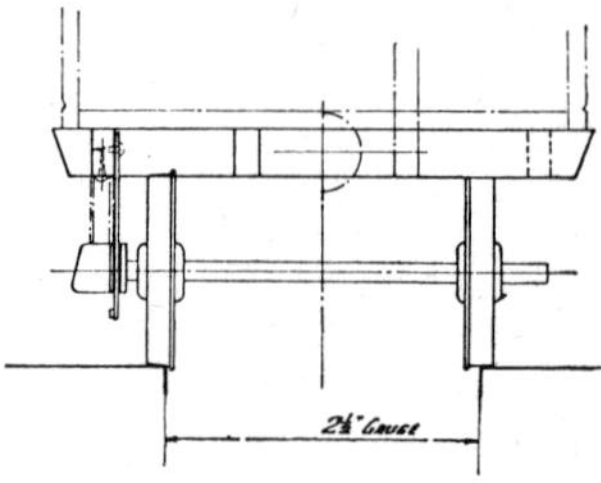

Fig. 2.—End view.

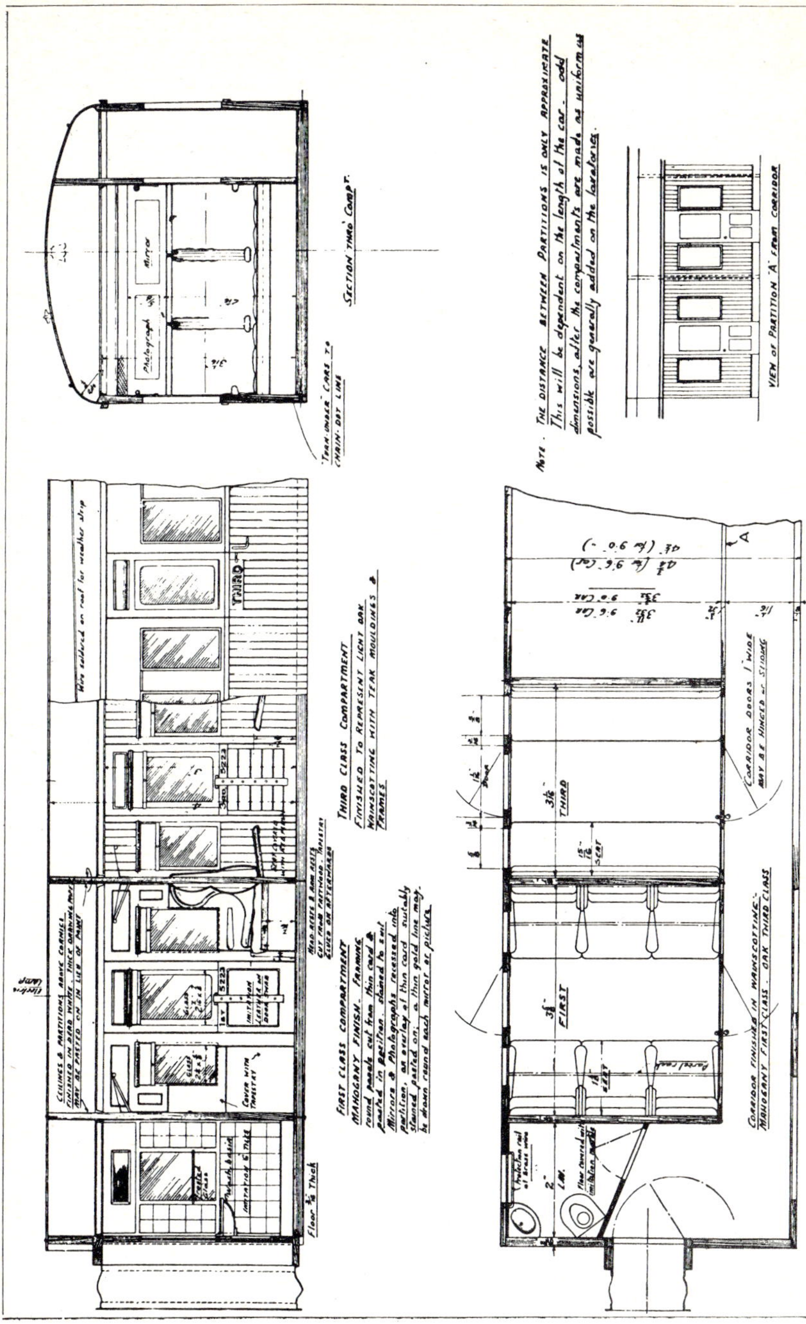

Fig. 4.—Sections and details of a $2\frac{1}{2}$ in. gauge carriage.

When thoroughly dry, screw in place through the ends and partitions.

The body is now ready to receive the final coats of paint. The lining and lettering can be effectively done with a drawing pen, the paint being well strained and *without* varnish. I do not varnish my vehicles, but give them a coat of good wax polish, which leaves a nice "egg-shell" gloss.

Four-wheeled open goods wagon and a tank car.

The blinds are made from *passe-partout* of the desired colour, rolled round a match stick, and then glued in place, a piece of card forming the bottom lath.

Parcel racks are made from brass-gauze soldered to small angle pieces of tin which are pinned to the partitions. The front is then soldered over a piece of brass wire, and brass wire supports fixed from front to back. The whole then receives a coat of gold paint.

Photographs can be cut from picture post cards, or cigarette cards, and mirrors from small looking glasses.

First-class seats are trimmed in heather-pattern silk rep, with cotton wool for padding. Antimacassars are made from the fancy lace paper round the edges of chocolate boxes.

Arm rests and head rest are cut out of fret wood, covered with rep and glued in place.

Third-class compartments are trimmed in red plush, parcel racks and blinds being similar to those used in the first-class cars.

Window glass can be cut from

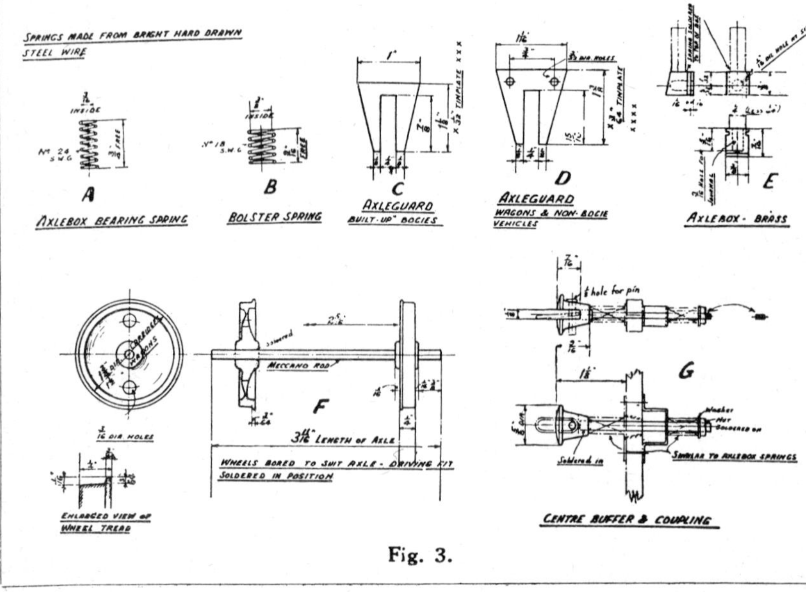

Fig. 3.

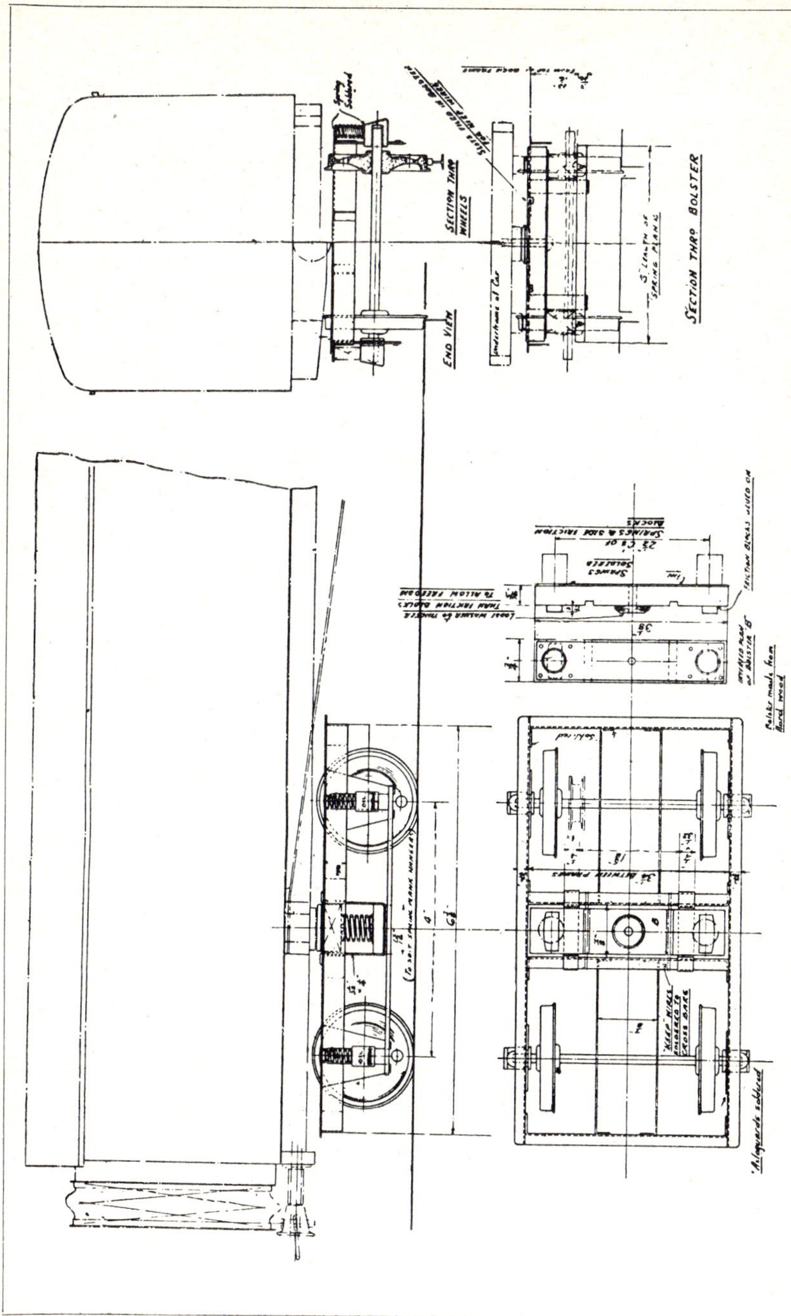

Details of the four-wheeled bogie for $2\frac{1}{2}$ in. gauge carriages.

photograph negative glasses, and for "frosted" glass in lavatories an undeveloped negative makes an excellent job. The imitation linoleum can be cut from the small reproductions of actual lino in the manufacturers' catalogues. Imitation embossed paper for tiles and panels

A $2\frac{1}{2}$ in. gauge loco. boiler wagon.

can be got from small reproductions of "cameoid" in some wall-paper pattern books. Rugs for first-class floors can be embroidered in silk, or small paper reproductions used similar to the lino.

Door-window straps are made from imitation leather paper. Door knobs, inside, from small brass-headed escutcheon pins. Door handles, outside, from brass wire. Window protection bars are also made from brass wire, bent to length, pointed each end, and pushed into the framing each side of the window.

Corridor-end gangways may be cut solid from wood, and covered with a piece from a roller bandage, then painted black; or they may be constructed of wood, with a small tin angle, similar to what is shown on the drawing.

Dynamo is made from hard wood turned to shape with a spindle running through, to which is attached at one end a pulley with a deep groove.

Accumulator boxes from cardboard suspended by means of tin straps.

Lighting is effected by means of flash-lamp bulbs. Batteries are carried in the luggage van, and the connections made from one vehicle to another by means of plugs in the gangways.

I think the drawings and photographs give any further information necessary.

Model American Pacific Loco.

The accompanying photograph is of a gauge No. 1 model American Pacific engine made up from a published drawing by Messrs. Bassett-Lowke, Ltd., Northampton. The model has the ordinary slide-valve cylinders arranged with the valve chests on top, and is spirit-fired.

A Reversing Clockwork Loco.

In Gauge "00." Scale 4 mm.

By H. G. Kerr.

THE prototype of this model is the G.E.R. T 19 class express engine, as rebuilt by the designer (J. Holden) in 1902.

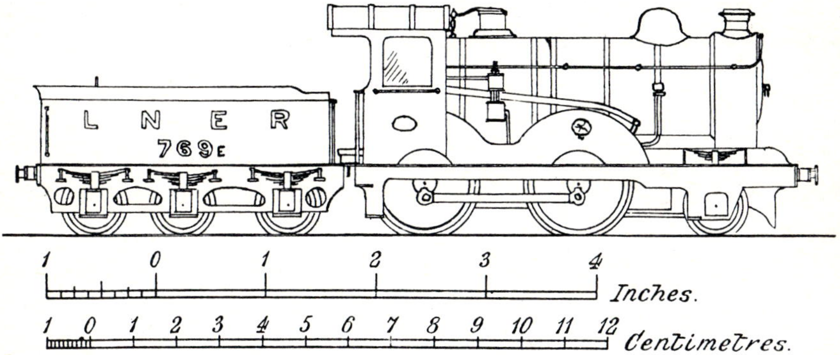

Model "00" gauge L.N.E.R. (G.E.R. section) locomotive.

The type offers the advantages of a short wheelbase combined with a fairly high-pitched boiler.

The construction of the superstructure presents little difficulty and follows the lines usually adopted in Gauge 0 practice, using thinner material.

The wheels used are those supplied by the Kay Model Co., the drivers being $\frac{7}{8}$-in. diameter, and standard wagon wheels being used for the tender. The leading wheels (on a pony truck) were cast solid, using a wheel from a German locomotive as a pattern, and were turned up by Col. Henvey.

The most important part of the locomotive is, of course, the mechanism, and this is the first reversing motion actually running on this gauge.

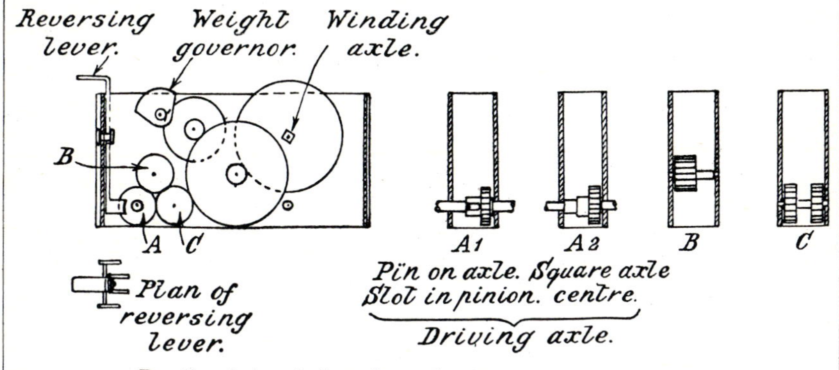

Details of the clockwork mechanism with reversing gear.

The diagram shews the main features of the design and is drawn to scale for this mechanism, but could be modified to suit the gears, etc., which might be available.

The sliding pinion wheel on the driving axle can be made in either way, as both have proved workable in practice, the easiest to make being the square centre to the axle and corresponding square hole in the pinion.

One important point is that the set of pinions A, B and C, must be of the same pitch and diameter to ensure the teeth meshing when sliding from one pinion to the other.

As there are no forces tending to push the pinions out of gear, as in the usual Gauge 0 reversing gear, there is no need for a spring or catch to hold the reversing lever in place.

The fork on the reversing rod (which is made out of a piece of tin-plate) should be a rather slack fit on the sides of the pinion, as it is only required to slide the pinion over at the moment of reversing and not to hold it in place.

A Milk-Tank Bogie Van.

By G. B. Denty.

In the issue of our contemporary, *The Locomotive*, for May 15th, 1925, appeared an article entitled "Railway Milk Transport in Bulk." This was accompanied by an illustration of a tank car suitable for use on British railways. Although the bulk method of milk transport has not yet been adopted by British railways, it is in fairly extensive use in parts of U.S.A. The accompanying drawing shows the general arrangement of a milk-tank car recently built by the writer for an 0 gauger who wanted something that nobody else had got.

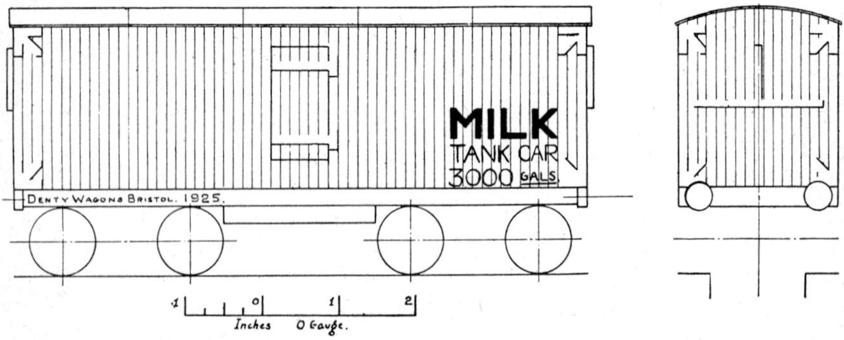

Elevation and end view for an "0" gauge milk-tank bogie van.

The construction of a box van is too well known to render a full description necessary. The whole of the work was carried out in ⅛-in. American whitewood, except the roof, which is of 1-16th-in. mahogany. The sides and ends are lined out to represent boards. The corner plates and hinges are of thin cardboard. The bogies are of the usual diamond-frame pattern, although bogies with inside bearings were suggested in the original drawings.

The vehicle is painted white, with red lettering. The underworks are black

A neat model factory made of cardboard.

Cardboard Model Making.

By H. H. Hudson.

(*Continued from* Page 300.)

INDICATING the brickwork should now be tackled, and for this purpose we shall require a kind of scriber. This can be easily made by mounting an ordinary wire nail in a round piece of wood for a handle, point outwards. This point should be sharpened on an oilstone, so that when held and used as one would a pencil (but using rather more pressure) one obtains an impressed line in the cardboard.

Having obtained the right effect, we can commence scribing a series of horizontal lines from the top downwards, at a distance, and at even intervals, of a scale three inches. Care should be taken not to scribe these lines across the immediate top of the window and door openings, the arches of which are usually made of bricks laid endwise, and on a slight camber, or else of a concrete block, and these ought to be indicated first by the same method.

Bonding Bricks.

After these are done, the vertical lines can be put in with the aid of a set square. There are various methods of bonding bricks, but the easiest way for our purpose, and one that looks quite well, is to follow the arrangement indicated in Fig. 4.

Each vertical line should be a scale nine inches apart from the preceding one.

Cutting Door and Window Openings.

We can now cut out the window and door openings, but no attempt should yet be made to trim the walls down to size. The cutting should be done in the way previously explained, and, when finished, the whole sheet or sheets of cardboard should be given a thin coat of shellac varnish, made from an ounce or two of shellac dissolved in methylated spirit. Treating the cardboard in this way will have the effect of hardening it, and also of waterproofing it to a limited extent. It will further, prepare the surface for its coat of flat oil paint to be applied later.

Window Frames.

We must now lay it aside to dry for a time, and when ready we can commence on the window frames. There are two methods of doing this part of the job. The first, and easier, is to have ready some pieces of glass cut about half an inch larger all round than the window opening they are intended to fit against. The window frames are then drawn on this by means of a ruling pen, and using a good quality enamel of a suitable colour, thinned down with turpentine to a consistency which will enable it to flow evenly, but not too quickly, from the pen.

The second, but undoubtedly more effective method, is to cut out roughly each wall, leaving a margin for trimming down, and putting one such wall over a piece of three-sheet Bristol board of about the same size, with a very sharply pointed pencil, carefully trace round the inside of each window opening. The framing should next be carefully drawn on to each space thus made, and then the card between the frames should be cut out.

Fig. 4.—Method of Bonding Bricks.

Enamelling.

When each wall has been treated in turn in the same fashion, the edges should be given a coat of thin shellac; afterwards, when dry, they can be painted with thin enamel. Maurice's Porcelain is to be recommended for this purpose. They should now be laid aside until the enamel is quite dry, and, meanwhile, the inside edges of the window openings in the thicker card should be painted with some of the brick colour, with which we propose to paint the completed model.

When the paint is thoroughly dry, we can take the thick cardboard and carefully and evenly coat the inner side with seccotine. This might, with advantage, be thinned a trifle with water and applied with a cheap water-colour brush. This piece of cardboard can then be laid over the Bristol board "frames," taking care that the framings are quite central in the appropriate openings in the thick card.

The two pieces should then be placed on a perfectly flat board, another flat board or piece of plate glass laid on top, and weights placed over all, to keep the cardboard flat while drying. This should be left thus for at least 12 hours, and each wall should be treated in the same manner.

Arranging the Walls.

We can now take our strawboard plan, and going round the outline, we draw parallel lines set back from the original lines a distance corresponding to the thickness of the combined pieces of cardboard forming the wall. This done, we can cut the base to the second or new lines, and if this has been done correctly, the walls, when butted against the edge, should occupy the same space as the original outline.

When the walls are quite dry, we take the one lettered "A" and cut it carefully to the base line and the line of the eaves. We shall find that if we cut the sides to the pencilled line, that each end will overhang the ends of the base by approximately the thickness of the walls, so we must cut these down until they are flush. The next wall "B" can then be fitted in the same way, and so on, until all the walls have been done. They should not, as yet, be fixed permanently, however.

Fixing the Windows.

We shall now want some pieces of ground glass cut to a size about half an inch larger all round than the window openings. The backs of the frames should next be evenly applied with seccotine, and the glass laid over, the whole again being put under pressure until dry.

While waiting for this, we can make some square pieces of wood, of as large a section as will conveniently fit in the corners of the walls. The size will depend upon the amount of space available from the edge of the nearest opening to the edge of the wall.

Joining the Corners.

If our cutting has been done aright, the two end walls will butt against the edges of the front and rear walls, and we should next take the square wood and cut four pieces to the exact height of the walls, less the thickness of the strawboard base. One of these can now be stuck on the inner side of wall "A," flush with the edge at the end. Another piece can be stuck at the opposite end, and the rear wall treated in exactly the same manner with the two remaining pieces, the thickness of the base being allowed for at the bottom when sticking on.

Strips of any kind of rough cardboard, but of the same thickness as the glass should now be filled in between the window glasses, and strips again laid across these, over the edge of the glass, to prevent the latter from falling or being pushed in. These should once more be allowed to dry under weights, to prevent any tendency to curl while so doing; once dry there will be very little or no tendency to do so.

Building Up.

Building up can now be started, and, commencing with wall "A," we seccotine the appropriate edge of the base, and push the wall against it. This operation is better done on a sheet of plate glass, to ensure a level base to build up on, and an ordinary carpenter's square should be used to get the wall perfectly upright. The rear wall can be put up in the same way, and the two end walls butted against them.

We should now have an oblong box, with the two ends rising above the level of the top of sides in the form of triangles, and inside each corner a square piece of wood. More of this square wood can now be used both in horizontal and vertical strips, whereever it is possible to put a piece in flat against the inside of the wall, providing it will serve a useful purpose by strengthening. In the case of a simple rectangular building, such as we are considering, it would be better to cut two or more pieces of three-eighths or half-an-inch thick wood to fit across the inside between the front and rear walls, shaped at the top to the same angles as the end walls. They should not, however, rise to the same height as the end walls, but should be a quarter of an inch shorter.

These should be placed in such a position that they will miss obscuring all windows, both back and front, and fixed firmly with seccotine.

Factory buildings made of cardboard.

Wood Supports.

Two pieces of quarter-inch wood can now be cut to fit in the space between both gable ends, of a width equal to the distance from the apex of the triangle forming the gable, to its base, the top edges being chamfered to an angle to enable them to fit closely together at the top, and the bottom edges being similarly bevelled to fit on the top of the front and back walls.

These, when fitted into place, should rest on the wooden supporting pieces previously referred to and should present a perfectly level stretch from one end of the building to the other, but, of course, peaked in the usual manner of such rooves.

The Roof.

We shall want a sheet of cardboard just under 1-16th of an inch in thickness, which should be mounted on the drawing board, and slates indicated in the same way that the brickwork was done. This finished, it should be given a thin coat of shellac, and when dry, pieces cut to fit back and front of the roof. They should overhang about 3-16ths of an inch all round, except at the top of the roof, where the two pieces should make a flush joint.

Ridge tiles can be made by bending a narrow strip of stout drawing paper in half and sticking this along the peak of the roof.

Chimneys.

Chimneys should be formed by planing a piece of smooth pine to the required size, and if brick, covered with card upon which we have previously scribed brick lines. The effect of capping can be obtained by mounting a piece of cardboard on the top with the edges overhanging the chimney column, and again mounting on this one or more pieces about 1-16th of an inch smaller. Chimney pots should be turned out of beech and stuck on the top of this.

Should the walls of the building be ornamented by mouldings, almost any section can be successfully imitated by building up in various thicknesses of cardboard.

Doors.

Doors should be made by setting out the design on card of scale thickness, cutting out the panels, and sticking on to another piece of stout cardboard. They should be painted before fixing in position behind the doorway.

Painting.

The last operation is that of painting, and this should not be undertaken, except in the cases previously referred to, until every part has been made and fixed in position. The secret of good painting is to apply evenly, thinly and, as nearly as possible, at one operation, without touching up.

The painting should be done in flat oil colours, and for this purpose "Ripolin" is to be recommended. The paint should be well stirred before using, and it is better to pour off a fair quantity of the oil that is usually to be found at the top of the tin when freshly opened, substituting the best quality turpentine as a thinning agent. Certain of the colours, notably those having a white content, have a pronounced tendency to dry "fatty" or glossy, but this can be counteracted by the method mentioned.

The greatest care should be taken in the painting, as an otherwise well-made model can be completely marred by scrappy and slovenly painting. On the other hand, careful painting can often pull together and make a creditable job of a model in which the workmanship is not of the best.

I have not touched upon every phase of this type of model-making, which must, of necessity, be left to the ingenuity of the reader, but it is hoped that the average craftsman may, at least, find sufficient information to start him on the right road.

Track Laying.

IN full-size practice it is possible to limits of a small percentage of error to place the chairs on the sleepers before commencing to lay down the rails. If means can be provided to obtain the same degree of accuracy, this procedure could be adopted with a small model railway

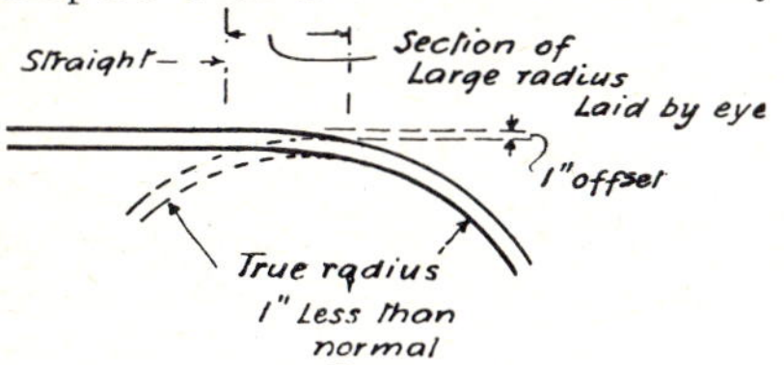

Fig. 1.

material, but as a rule it will be found better to fix the chairs to the rails first. With " slide-on " chairs this is necessary in any case, as it is impracticable to attempt to push a rail endways through a number of already fixed chairs.

I have also found that in model work, whether the line is of No. 0 gauge or 15-in. gauge, that success is only obtained where the formation level—*i.e.*, the bed on which the sleepers are laid—is good, and also where the rail on one side is fixed down and truly faired before attempting to deal with the opposite rail. This means that there must always be one length of single rail properly faired up in advance of the double track. As a matter of fact, if a long section of model railway which is unbroken by points or crossings—I am not referring to outdoor lines where walking from one point to another with heavy material has to be considered—has to be laid down. I would recommend finishing off the rail on one side completely before tackling the other. If curved sections are included in the length, it is better to choose the inner rail for this purpose, as this will not be affected by superelevation. Of course, the presence of an S curve would then be considered as dividing the length into two separate sections as far as the track-laying is concerned.

Tangential straights from curved sections should be avoided. As already mentioned in these columns, this method makes it necessary to start superelevating on the straight. If the maximum radius is, say, three feet, it is much better to arrange for it to be two feet eleven inches, and to offset the straight the other one inch as shown in the diagram Fig. 1 herewith. The straight can then be drawn over in the flattest curve obtainable in the length to lead into the curve.

Although I often show on diagrams of railways laid round the four walls of a room two corner curves joined by a short straight (*see* A, Fig. 2), I should never think of laying the straight line thus. In the actual job it would be laid as a very large radius curve as at B in the same diagram.

When one rail is laid and faired (*i.e.*, that is trued up by eye when viewed in a longitudinal direction) it is easy to make the other rail true to gauge and equally free from twists. This process of fairing must precede the laying of the opposite rail, otherwise it is difficult to obtain a perfect track.

H. G.

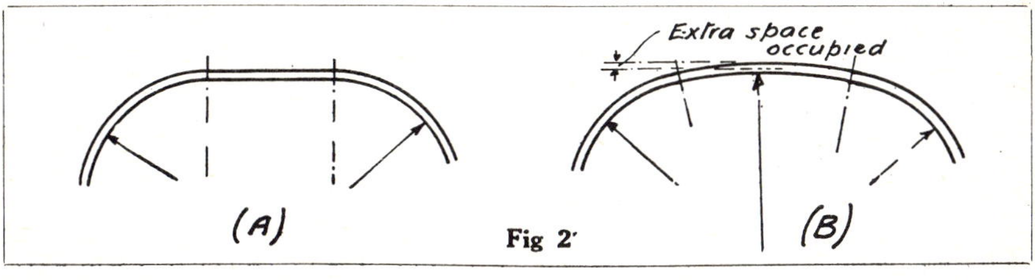

Fig 2

An "0" Gauge L.M.S. Line.

To the Editor, MODEL RAILWAY NEWS.

DEAR SIR,

I beg to enclose a photo of my Gauge 0 L.M.S. model line which, no doubt, will be of interest to your readers. I am trying to get together a few interested friends with a view to starting a club here in Limerick. I am afraid model railways are somewhat few and far between in Ireland nevertheless, I am somewhat proud of my humble efforts in this direction, and I shall not be afraid of an inspection by Mr. Henry Greenly.

Perhaps a short description would interest you. The railway runs round three sides of my garden and, when complete, will cover the four sides. The main terminus is in my workshop. The track is Bassett-Lowke's standard tinplate straights and the curves are Lowko, fitted with check rails. Contrary to report and expectations, the tinplate track has proved an undoubted success. I painted each section lead colour before laying, and I laid the sections with the aid of a spirit level and each sleeper is screwed to the platform with wood screws the whole being a firm and level job. I have found it extremely satisfactory, and derailments are unknown except perhaps when the ballast gets disturbed. I have incorporated with the line a colliery with three lines of sidings. This includes pit shaft, engine house, tall chimney stack and two sheds. The colliery is reached from the main up line by a right-hand set of points. The other station I have named Northampton, as a compliment to Messrs. Bassett-Lowke, Ltd., and this will be a double-line junction when the system is completed. The locos (I have two at present, a 4—4—0 express engine and a 4—4—0 T) I have made myself and are clockwork models.

A view of Mr. T. W. Marsden's Northampton Station on his model "0" gauge railway.

The goods wagons I constructed myself, but for passenger rolling stock I have relied on Messrs. Bassett-Lowke and the Clyde Model Dockyard up to the present.

I am also constructing a single-span cantilever bridge in $\frac{3}{8}$-in. × $\frac{1}{8}$-in. iron and, when completed, I will have great pleasure in forwarding you a photo of it.

In conclusion, I would add that I find the MODEL RAILWAY NEWS very interesting and an education in itself in the subject it embraces.

Yours faithfully,

THOS. W. MARSDEN.

Limerick.

Locomotive Sheds.

To the Editor, MODEL RAILWAY NEWS.

DEAR SIR,

In the August issue you publish two articles on the above subject and in one of them Mr. Greenly says that the "saw-tooth" roof is the most satisfactory for multi-road sheds. The enclosed sketch, however, shows a variation of the gable-ended variety which is in use at Crewe and Sandhills (Liverpool) sheds on the L.M.S.,

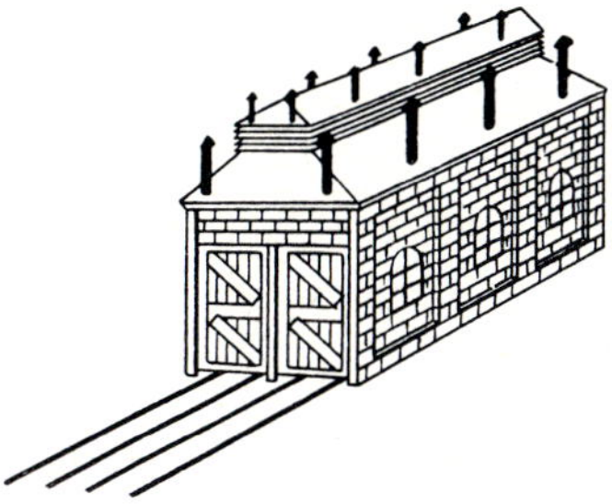

Type of loco. shed at Crewe.

which is capable of being made to span any number of tracks and which has decided architectural points. So far as I know, the model-maker has entirely neglected this type of loco-shed.

I was very pleased to see the result of the rail-planning competition in the July number and, although I, personally, was unsuccessful, I must thank you for your kind commendation and offer my sincere congratulations to Mr. Axford.

Yours faithfully,

H. D. PINNINGTON.

Liverpool.

Cleaning Model Electric Track.

To the Editor, MODEL RAILWAY NEWS.

DEAR SIR,

Re correspondence cleaning model electric rails on gauge 0 system. Dirtiness of track is a drawback but is very hard to avoid, especially if tinplate track with the usual push-in connections is in use. While liquid polish, such as Bluebell, is a good cleansing agent, a word of caution as to its use is necessary, as there will be every tendency for the liquid to work into the rail joins, and in this case, where current is conducted through the joins, it might short circuit, or rather, block the current, and you wonder where the loss of voltage is, with hard work to ascertain its position. The liquid may rust or cake and prevent a proper connection. Of course, where you have your rails soldered as well this would not matter.

Sandpaper is too hard on the track, also emery. So one is almost reduced to some liquid for the purpose. But use carefully and sparingly, and if one uses only a rag dampened with coal oil, and uses frequently, the trouble I mention may be avoided. Taking some sections apart of my system the other day, I found the joins in many cases quite rusty, and as basement is not damp enough to cause this, I put it down to too frequent use of liquid in cleansing the track. I have some rustless track for garden extension bought from a U.S.A. house, and wonder how it will stand up to the work. So far it is all right. A shower of rain leaves a few blue (mildewy-looking) spots which would indicate some copper in rail, but do not think the rails are copper for the price I paid for same.

Yours truly,

GERALD S. REES.

P.S.—I should like to get in touch with other owners of model railways in Canada. Will they please write to me.

Box 883, Nelson B.C., Canada.

Cab Fittings for Model Electric and Clockwork Locos.

To the Editor, MODEL RAILWAY NEWS.
DEAR SIR,

How is it that model electric and clockwork locomotives are never fitted with any controls or instruments in the cab, except to special order? Even the more expensive makes, replete with all external details, such as brake connections and lamp brackets, are absolutely void of any cab-fittings.

These should include firehole door, regulator, reversing quadrant, and "clocks," at least. They might be made in lead and touched up with paint, and would at any rate look better than a mere void in what is, perhaps, the most important part of the engine.

What have your other readers to say about it?

I remain,
G. H. SWANN.

Rotherham.

Indoor Scenic Effects.

To the Editor, MODEL RAILWAY NEWS,
DEAR SIR,

In the September issue an article appeared under the above title. I should like to give a few more points connected with this subject. A model railway which is quite flat is very monotonous. I myself have a 00 gauge line with an upper and lower level. This gives a slight rise and fall to begin with. On my own line there is not much more difference than six inches in the two levels. There is a line going under a higher level line. This gives plenty of opportunity for cuttings and embankments and a bridge. The question then arises as to how we are to make the embankment and cuttings. The answer is really very simple; sawdust can be got in large quantities, and this when dyed green makes very good grass. In 00 gauge, grey sawdust is very suitable for ballast, for use in stations and goods yards. Fences are very prominent things on a real railway, and consequently a fence is a great asset to a model railway. An easy way to make a fence (00 gauge) is to use up all old gramophone needles. When these are placed at an interval of about an inch or under and then wound round with two or three threads of cotton, a very realistic fence can be made.

Youis truly,
G. R. WHITCOMBE.

Herts.

"Grouping."

To the Editor, MODEL RAILWAY NEWS.
DEAR SIR,

I noticed in the May issue that Major Simpson referred to the late L.N.W. Railway as the premier line of England.

I travel daily, and have done so for a few years, on the L.M. & S. line and have never been able to understand the constant reference to this line as the premier. Premier in what? Surely not in comfort for the third-class passenger. The Midland or the North Eastern had it beaten hollow in this respect, in my opinion.

Again, Major Simpson lamented that the coach colours of chocolate and white were rapidly being replaced by the new colour.

Personally, I consider the latter a great improvement on the former. However smart the white of the L.N.W. might look when turned out new, how long would it retain its whiteness when in daily contact with the smoke and grime of a steam railway? Even on a model railway, coaches painted in L.N.W. colours need constant attention to keep them clean looking.

The new livery of the engines, too, is much more pleasing to my eye than the former despondent-looking black.

Apart from the points mentioned, I am in entire agreement with Major Simpson that no good word can be said for grouping.

Yours faithfully,
JOS. C. ROBINSON.

Rhyl.

Shunting Problem Solution.

To the Editor, MODEL RAILWAY NEWS.

DEAR SIR,

The solution to the shunting problem given in last month's issue is as follows :—

" B " shunts trucks in siding and goes back up line. (Fig. 1.)

" A " brings out " B's " trucks. " B " engine goes in siding. (Fig. 2.)

" A " takes " B's " trucks up line.

to say that, though having no experience of building locomotives in cardboard, practically all the permanent structures of a railway, which in a model are introduced for spectacular reasons only (such as tunnel-mouths, box-girder overbridges, etc.) can be realistically reproduced in this material. Where extra strength is necessary it can be reinforced by thin wooden strips.

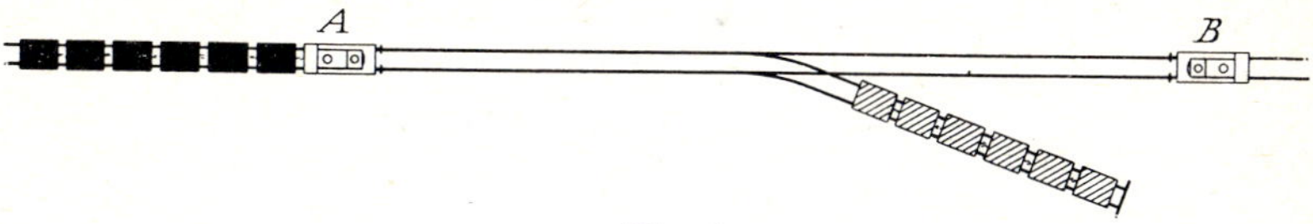

Fig. 1.

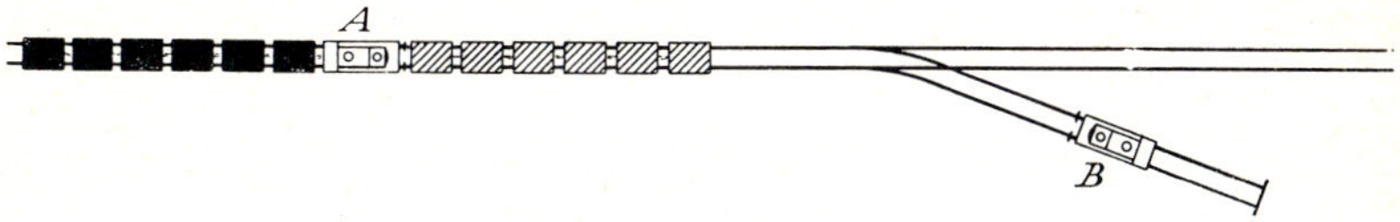

Fig. 2.

" B " engine comes out of siding and goes up line. (Fig. 3.)

" A " shunts " B's " trucks in siding and proceeds. (Fig. 4.) " B " engine then couples up and proceeds in the other direction.

Yours faithfully,

J. R. MILTON.

Leyton, E. 10.

On a small portable indoor railway (0 gauge) since dismantled, I commenced building two years ago, cardboard was extensively employed for station platforms and buildings, retaining walls, cattle pens, etc., finished off in most cases with brick paper, and a most realistic finish was obtained. Furthermore the cost was exceedingly

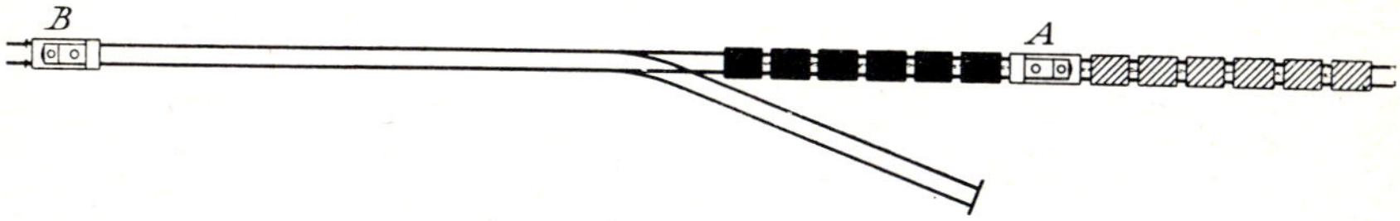

Fig. 3.

Fig. 4.

Cardboard and Model Railways.

To the Editor, MODEL RAILWAY NEWS.

DEAR SIR,

Regarding " E. J. L. B.'s " letter on page 219 of the July issue on model cardboard locomotives, I should like

small (this was an important point, as I was then still at school). I only made one attempt at cardboard rolling-stock, the M.R. 30-ton bogie wagon being chosen as the prototype.

The sides and solebars of this wagon

are flush, this simplifying the construction. The body and underframes were entirely of cardboard, with the bogies screwed to wooden cross-transomes glued to the cardboard underfloor. The buffers were soldered to ends of bogie frames, likewise coupling gear, thus taking all strain from the body. The wagon withstood quite hard knocks, and was not so flimsy as might be imagined.

Some time I will send some photos of some of the old cardboard models if thought to be of interest, with a description of their construction.

Wishing the " NEWS " every success.

Yours faithfully,

G. E. TENTON.

Gillingham, Kent.

More Explosion.

To the Editor, MODEL RAILWAY NEWS.

DEAR SIR,

Despite a very limited experience, I heartily endorse the remarks offered by " Disgruntled " against the steam model in small gauges. Besides the difficulty of efficient construction, there is the old trouble of realistic working. In fact, we are arrived at the old question of the real interest in model railways—the locomotive or the railway. For, with no convenient means of controlling a steam model when once it is " under way," anything which approaches realistic working becomes impracticable. (The writer had hopes that some electrical control of the steam locomotives might be perfected, for there were several experiments carried out in the days of *Models, Railways and Locomotives* and those conducted by Mr. T. W. Pitt seemed to promise permanent benefit to all.) Nevertheless, our hobby must claim adherents of all opinions, and if the locomotive is of paramount interest to some of them, we on the opposition benches have no authority to cry them down, even were that possible.

Now we may turn to the real object " Disgruntled's " notes — the advocacy of an " all-electric " model railway. And may the writer concede at the outset that for absolute realism his system cannot be challenged. Yet there are some of us with a love for the steam locomotive because of its appearance ; some of us who deplore the arrival of the electric locomotive on our British railways, who cannot see the character and differentiating features of electric locomotives. Number 500 would impress us no differently than would number 501 of identical type, whereas two such steam locomotives would have very different qualities in our eyes. We should find a flatness about the varied types of electric locomotives which is absent when comparing different types of steam locomotives. Now " Disgruntled " may say, and the writer admits that he may very well be right, that this is the result of long acquaintance with the steam, which has built up a prejudice in us against the electric locomotive. Yet this is not sufficient to overcome that prejudice and so he must still find it reflected in our model systems.

Let us consider that there are two main features in a model—the work it does and the way it does that work. Over the steam enthusiast we claim that, although our electric locomotives are all wrong in the way they do their work, the work that they do resembles to a marvellous degree, the work done by their prototypes. " Disgruntled," however, has claims over all of us. His locomotives imitate their prototypes in both respects, their income and expenditure of power are replicas of those of full-size electric systems. And yet we cannot support his ideas even when he offers us the practical advantages of ease of construction and increased power.

Logically, " Disgruntled," you must convince us. Sentimentally, we are bigots in our opinion.

Yours, etc.,

E. C. K.

Wigan.

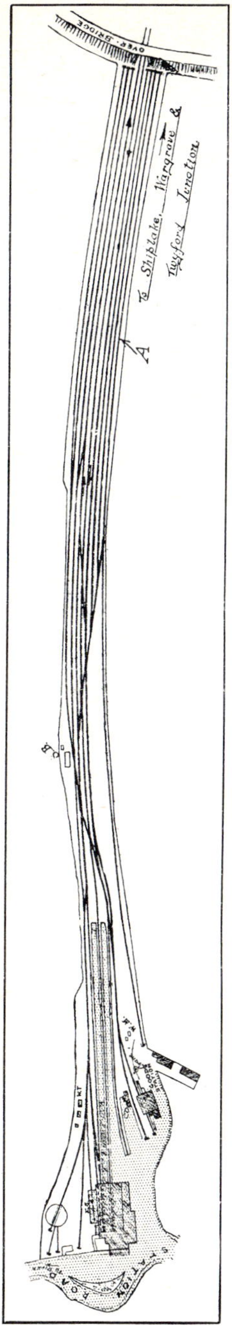

Plan of terminus station, Henley-on-Thames, branch line, G.W.R.

Henley as a Prototype.

To the Editor, MODEL RAILWAY NEWS,

DEAR SIR,

I have much pleasure in sending you a description of the terminus station at Henley-on-Thames. Also a few photographs and a tracing from ordnance sheets, as requested by your correspondent, "Lord of the Isles," in your August issue.

Fig. 1.

I would like to point out that the line is double right up to the junction (Twyford). Description of photographs are as follows :—

Fig. 1.—View of crane, and opposite end of goods depot.

Fig. 2.—View looking into station. Note span roof ; also engine shed, 2—4—0 T, and water tower on the right.

Fig. 2.

Fig. 3.—Turntable.

Fig. 4.—View from signal box, shewing a train backed out on the sidings. These sidings are capable of holding 15 to 20 of the large bogie

Fig. 3.

coaches each. They were originally intended for Regatta trains, but are used during the winter as a dump for surplus coaches, with the exception of the line marked "A," which is reserved for goods shunting.

Fig. 4.

Hoping my efforts will be of some use to readers, and wishing success to the MODEL RAILWAY NEWS.

I remain,

Yours faithfully,

R. A. HITCHMAN.

Henley-on-Thames.

Grouping and the Loco. Tests.

To the Editor, MODEL RAILWAY NEWS.

DEAR SIR,

So far, no one seems to have written a good word for grouping, so here are two reasons for my so doing so.

Number one is purely personal. I like the locomotives and rolling stock of the L.N.E.R. far better than those of any other company.

Number two is because grouping should enable manufacturers to satisfy all tastes, and this with a reduction in the quantity of stock to be carried, whereas, in my opinion, far too much attention has been paid hitherto to the so-called "premier line."

Still, if one does not favour the new arrangement, I can see no reason to change.

Here, three enthusiasts are very busy with a 0 gauge L.N.E. electric system and a 2½-in. gauge steam line, both of which are causing considerable interest — not always flattering — amongst our neighbours.

A correspondent remarks on the horrible difficulty of the L.N.E. to find locos which would haul its main expresses in a manner comparable to that of the G.W. loco featured in the recent loco exchanges. From Mr. Cecil J. Allen's remarks in the *Railway Magazine*, I see that the general work of the late G.N. Pacifics is equal to, if not better than that of "Pendennis Castle" during the tests, except in the matter of starting, where the higher tractive effort and steam pressure of the latter engine have undoubted advantages, and in the matter of coal consumption ; and even in this respect, the performance of Pacific No. 2545 in the tests is considered to be below the usual work done by these engines. No, even if the 5.45 p.m. out of King's Cross reaches 600 tons behind the engine, I do not think the L.N.E. will have to borrow engines from the G.W.R.—or from any other company for that matter—in order to haul this load with reasonable economy.

In conclusion, I would like to congratulate Mr. W. Pretty on the realism he has obtained on his line. I am hoping for the same effect and am finding the work quite as difficult as he says.

Wishing you continued success,

Faithfully yours,

F. N. RUSH.

Lagunitos, Peru.

"0" Gauge Steam Locomotives.

To the Editor, MODEL RAILWAY NEWS.

DEAR SIR,

In my opinion one can learn much more from a plan of somebody else's model railway (especially if a scale is attached and an account of how various difficulties were overcome) than from an account of how to build a banana van or other pieces of rolling stock.

By the way, could you introduce some articles on 0 gauge steam locomotives? The subject has been shamefully neglected. Writers on the subject always gloss it over by saying that, owing to limits in size, successful 0 gauge steam engines are impossible; yet compare the geared oscillating cylinder locomotive of 1920 with the latest Bassett-Lowke production. It should be borne in mind, however, that for successful working, the following points should be observed as strictly as possible:—

(1) The track should be as well laid and as level as possible.

(2) The boiler should be washed out periodically with petrol or benzine. Oil from the lubricator is liable to run back into the boiler and a film of oil over the water prevents good steaming.

(3) By Act of Parliament a quantity of paraffin is mixed with all methylated spirit. This causes an oily deposit to be left in the lamp. The "packing" in the vaporizing spirit lamp should, therefore, be washed in benzine or petrol from time to time: otherwise the lamp will not burn properly.

(4) Attention should be paid to the safety valve. As far as my experience goes, whenever the safety valve "blows off" the small rubber washer blows off too, and so allows the steam to escape easily. I, therefore, usually screw up the safety valve as tightly as possible. There is no danger in this, as the small rubber washer is very weak, and if the lamp actually burns well enough to generate steam at 45-lb. pressure per square inch, this same small washer blows off easily.

(5) Leaks of steam can be caused by the faulty screwing in of the safety valve or the lubricator plug. Sometimes, too, the lubricator plug becomes unscrewed while on the run, and so causes bad running due to a leakage of steam.

There are probably many other points which go towards the most efficient running of a 0 gauge steam locomotive, which could be pointed out by other readers, and perhaps one day an excellent and efficient range of such locomotives may be obtainable.

Yours faithfully,
KENNETH R. M. BIGGS.

Hampstead.

A Child's Plaything.

To the Editor, MODEL RAILWAY NEWS.

DEAR SIR,

Does "Interlock" forbid anyone being regarded as a real model railwayist because he uses that "child's plaything," a clockwork-driven steam-outline loco? There must be many who prefer to make their own locos and rolling stock, who have not the means to build steam models. I know several.—and I am one myself. But I can assure "Interlock" that even he might be found to reconsider his condemnation when he sees a spring-driven loco—scale size and weight—with great tractive effort, fulfilling all needs both for (scale) power and speed. I have two such locos and they give every satisfaction. Moreover, my line is capable of being worked almost entirely without the introduction of my out-of-scale hand! I confess I like the spirit of "Ovidian" better.

I have complete drawings of a gauge 1 dining car from which I have made one car. I will give these to any "modellist" who will write and ask for them.

Yours very truly,
(Rev.) H. FRYER.

Lymington.

Answers to Correspondents.

E. P. F. (London)—We do not think that parts for "Simpull" track are now supplied, even if it is made at all. You would be well advised to use either the parts of "Lowko" track or of Messrs. Bond's or "Millbro" solid steel rail, pressed steel chairs and wood sleepers. The solid steel rail has many advantages over a hollow rail.

Lt.-Col. P. N. G. R. (Devon.)—Rustless steel would be the only solution to the difficulty, but we understand that the cost is prohibitive at present. The trade is quite aware that coated rails do not offer absolutely perfect protection. The tinning, zincing, and the sherardizing processes are among the best. Electrically depositing the coating—the writer tried a lead covering—did not work out so satisfactory as others, due to the fact that the non-corrosive coating was deposited in molecules and the structure tended to be porous. The demand for special types of engines alone settles the supply, and you should register your desires with the various manufacturers. The G.W.R. types of engines should, of course, be well represented in new season's models, as there is little justification for the present preponderance of L.N.W.R. types, except that some of them are simple to make. Some of us think that even prior to the amalgamation, that the locos of this line were hopelessly out of date, considering the arduous nature of their duties.

W. V. H. (Ruislip).—The tonnage co-efficient for No 1 gauge is 13. This means that a model vehicle weighing 1 lb. represents 13 scale tons and every ton of the prototype is 1-13th of a lb. in the model. *See* "Model Railways," by H. Greenly, price 6*s*. 6*d*. post free from this office.

R. W. (Sheffield).—The particular example of the moving frog referred to in "Model Railways," by Greenly, was at Chester, at the Birkenhead end of the triangle junction there. The exact construction is not remembered, but possibly one of our readers may be acquainted with the scheme and be able to send details of this or any similar device. The moving part, of course, eliminates the gap at the frog and requires to be altered in position at the same time as the point rails. We also understand that some American railways use this fitting.

Revd. J. C. (Winchester). — Your question has been dealt with direct. We note that you use Bowden wire cable for working distant points. Various methods are in use, but your idea, as it works, is quite a sound one.

F. A. B. (Yorkshire). — The conductor rail in a model electric railway is raised so that the collector can cross running rails at points and crossings without short-circuiting on the latter. The "all-level" systems provide *other* means of preventing this "shorting," and therefore all rails can be level; *see* the book "Model Electric Locomotives and Railways," price 6s. net.

L. R. (Cornwall).—Copper is much better than brass for small boilers. It is somewhat difficult to get very thin (No. 26 S.W.G.) tube, and, therefore, it is usual to seam small "plain pot" low-pressure boilers.

C. R. M. (Manchester). and **K. H. S. M. (London).**—We are putting your request on record. Official drawings will have to be obtained at the outset, and this will take a little time.

Will **Mr. F. C. Alleway, of Harlesden,** whose letter on Henley Station appeared in the October issue, please let us have his full address, as a correspondent wishes to write to him.

WITH THE CLUBS

The Wimbledon & District Model Railway Club.

November 2nd, 7.30 p.m.—Lecture on "Austrian Railways," by Mr. A. Earley. November 16th, 7.30 p.m.—Test track and practical demonstrations by members (including test-load hauling by Mr. A. R. Walkley's electric-drive 00 gauge loco.). Both at Red Cross Hall, Church Road, Wimbledon.

As these notes are written before the Surrey Handicrafts Exhibition at Croydon (October 6th to 9th) takes place, we hope to include a short account of the club's exhibit there in next month's notes, with the Editor's permission. Passenger-carrying by members' locos and a good show of railway models in all gauges are a feature of our exhibit.

Copies of No. 2 of *Railway Pie*, the club's official journal, $4\frac{1}{2}$*d.* post free, can still be obtained from the Hon. Secretary, R. Shephard, 27, Bernard Gardens, Wimbledon, who will also be pleased to supply members with full particulars of the forthcoming "Shephard Cup" competition.

The Manchester & District Model Railway Club.

Now is the time to take note of the material or parts you require for that model you intend building, so send your order through the club. You will help the club and receive a discount off your order; also you are saved the trouble of postages, carriage, and cost of money or postal order charges. Select your goods from the firms below:—

These discounts can only be obtained through the club.

Bassett-Lowke, Ltd.—All Supplies, less 5 %.

Mr. Crookes.—Scale Track, less 5 %.

Henry Greenly. Blue Prints, less $12\frac{1}{2}$ %.

Leeds Model Co., Ltd.—All Supplies, less $3\frac{3}{4}$ %.

Pealling, A. W. K.—Blue Prints, less 25 %.

"Papers" are required for future meetings. Will members please offer to give one?

The Winter meetings for the 1925—1926 session will be held on the second and fourth Tuesday of each month (October to March inclusive), at 7.30 p.m., at Headquarters, the Clarion Café, Market Street, Manchester.

Archibald Dean, Hon. Secretary, 29, Gorse Lane, Gorse Hill, Stretford, Manchester.

The Smee Society, St. Paul's School.

Model Railway Section.

We are now firmly established on our feet, and the following is a précis of our doings since our formation.

The test track is now virtually completed and is to be opened with a gathering of model railway men in about the middle of this term, when an article describing the club and its work will be sent in. The club possesses an Atlantic locomotive (L.N.E. gauge 1), an L.N.E. 4—4—0, and weight cars, in addition to five bogie corridor coaches.

Last term a lecture was given on "Casting." This was, of course, of great use to many members of the society who had not previously made castings for themselves.

This term it was decided that, as several members had left the School at the end of the Summer term, the opportunity should be taken to limit the membership to 50.

We have had three railway visits so far, viz., Old Oak Common Sheds (G.W.R.), Lot's Road Power Station (Underground), and Willesden Sheds (L.M.S.). There was a rush for all these, and this term we are having, we hope, five visits. The two already fixed are Neasden Sheds and Power Station (Metropolitan) and Neasden (L.N.E.).

H. N. PERKINS, Hon. Sec.

The Latest "J.R." List.

Messrs. Jackson Rigby Engineering Co., Ltd., Station Road, Shalford, near Guildford, Surrey, have sent us a latest (October, 1925) list of their well-known parts and castings for 2½-in. gauge ½-in. scale steam locomotives. It is a neat list of nine sheets, holed ready for filing, and as this cancels all previous lists issued, builders and prospective builders in this gauge should secure a copy.

These standard parts, designed by Mr. H. Greenly, can be supplied either as castings, machined or finished complete. The list includes the prices of practically everything from the buffers of the engine to the similar portion of the tender; most of these are ready, and it is stated that new patterns are being added daily.

Drawings are also supplied at practically cost price for either the complete set or any part separately, independent of whether castings are purchased.

What should interest our U.S.A. readers is that these parts may be employed to build American models, for which special boiler castings are now being got out.

Readers in London can, if they wish, see this firm's products at their London agents, Messrs. Bond's, Ltd., 254, Euston Road, N.W. 1.

Messrs. Bassett-Lowke's Christmas Catalogue.

Messrs. Bassett-Lowke have made a bold move this season in reducing the price of their catalogue to 6d., although the book is larger than in previous years. It has the additional feature of a frontispiece printed in four colours of their new range of 2—6—0 "Mogul" type locomotives, in clockwork, steam and electric.

Garden railway locomotives are featured, the principal one being a 1½-in. to the foot scale model of the L.M.S. "George the Fifth."

Nearly all of the electric locomotives in Gauge 0 are fitted with their new permanent magnet motor, and are finished in the new Grouping colours.

In goods rolling stock in wood, several important new introductions have been made, viz. :—

L.M.S. loco coal wagon; L.M.S. 10-ton goods wagon; L.N.E.R. brake van; L.N.E.R. covered goods wagon; L.M.S. 10-ton brake van; L.N.E.R. open wagon.

To meet the demand for an inexpensive larger-radius track, Messrs. Bassett-Lowke have made special tools for producing what they call their new "Sixfut" track, which is standard tinplate rail, with five sleepers, in both ordinary and electric, a circle having a diameter of six feet and consisting of 20 pieces, so that it is divisible by four. Points have also been introduced.

Among the signals, we noticed the new G.N.R. somersault signal, both home and distant.

Another welcome feature this season is the further reduction in price of many of their leading locomotives, coaches, wagons, etc.

Erratum. — In Messrs. Bassett-Lowke's advertisement on page iv of the October issue, the price of their new Standard Model 2—6—0 locomotive was erroneously given as £5; this should have read £5 5s. Will readers kindly note, and accept our apologies?

The MODEL RAILWAY NEWS

Editorial and Publishing Offices:
66, FARRINGDON STREET, LONDON, E.C. 4.

Single Copies, post free, 7½d. Annual Subscription, 7s. 6d.

Vol. I. No. 12. DECEMBER, 1925. Price, 6d.

Notes of the Month.

ALTHOUGH this issue is published a little in advance of the festive season, we take this opportunity of wishing all our readers the best of good things for Christmas and the coming New Year. The Model Railway News has gathered together during the past year a very happy family of model railway enthusiasts, and we are quite sure our good wishes will be received and reciprocated in a very cordial spirit.

* * *

With this issue we present an index to our first volume. It only needs a brief glance at this index to see how thoroughly the field of model railway engineering has been covered during the past year. But, although the field has been so well covered, it by no means follows that everything possible has been said or done. The interest in model railway work is ever changing, and ever developing, and this constitutes one of its greatest charms. There are always new models to build, new ideas to try out, extensions to be made, and opinions to be expressed. For this reason we approach our second volume in the fullest confidence that the interest of our pages will be maintained. There are still dozens of new model railways to be described. Some are, doubtless, completed, and we shall be glad to have photographs, lay-outs and descriptions from the owners. Others are in progress, and in due course we shall hope to receive the story. We should like to express our grateful acknowledgments of the help so many correspondents have given us during the past year. The articles, photographs and letters which these friends have sent us have contributed much to the interest of our pages, and we hope that not only will they continue their helpful co-operation, but that many new friends will come along and send us something of interest for publication.

* * *

Another point to be noticed in connection with this issue is the growth in the number of our advertisements. We regard this feature of the Model Railway News as a very valuable one from the reader's point of view. It forms an excellent guide as to where his various requirements can be fulfilled, and the broader the range of goods offered the easier it becomes to satisfy individual needs. We hope our readers will make full use of the information given in our advertising pages, and that when replying to any advertisement they will always say "I saw it in the Model Railway News." This helps everybody concerned.

* * *

Now about your subscription. The very large number of readers who dated their subscriptions from No. 1

have their order completed with this issue. We shall be happy to receive their renewal subscriptions by an early post We ask for an early remittance because the Christmas holidays always congest office work, and we should like to get our subscribers' list for next year entered up as much in advance as possible. So fill in the form in this issue, send it along to us with your 7*s.* 6*d.*, and make sure of receiving your MODEL RAILWAY NEWS promptly at the beginning of every month.

* * *

We hear that the Model Railway Club at St. Paul's School, London, which is a section of the Smee Society, is looking forward to a good season. The opening meeting is to be held at 5.30 p.m. on December 11th, and we extend our very cordial wishes for a successful and interesting gathering. We should like to have some news from the other School Model Railway Clubs. Honorary Secretaries please note.

Treasure Island Railway.

AT the close of the Wembley Exhibition, the work of the 9½-in. gauge engines running under the superintendence of Mr. Terence Holder is worth recording. The "Peter Pan" G.N.R. 2-in. scale "Atlantic" engine, which was designed in 1909 (built in 1910) by H. Greenly for Capt. J. E. P. Howey, worked the whole of the time the exhibition was open. It was ably supplemented towards the end of July by Mr. J. A. Holder's 4—4—0 type Worsdell N.E. Railway loco, which pulled during August alone, 52,000 persons. Although not at all suited to such strenuous duties, the scale-model 0—4—4 tank engine "Alice," built by Mr. T. A. Common some 20 years ago, assisted in the work.

The total number of passengers hauled was 212,000 adults and children, and the total mileage by the three engines was, roughly, 3,000.

Couplings for Small Gauges.

By G. B. DENTY.

ALTHOUGH the central-buffer coupling cannot yet be regarded as a standard fitting for British rolling stock, this should not prevent a neat buffer coupling being fitted to model rolling stock, in place of some of the atrocities frequently used presumably with the "anti-buffer-locking" idea.

The writer recently conceived a notion that "patent snap dress fasteners" might be used for couplings. A short strip of metal, pivoted at one end to the underside of the floor of the vehicle, works through a slot in the buffer beam. The end is upturned at right angles, and the snap fitting is soldered on—the cupped portion one end, and the bossed portion the other end of the vehicle. To couple, it is merely necessary to bring two vehicles together, and a snap does the trick.

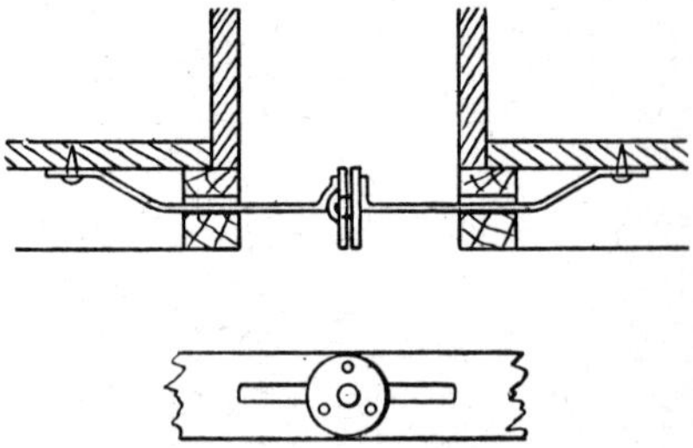

Section and end view of the "snap fastener" coupling.

The accompanying sketch is self-explanatory. Difficulties might accrue through the use of triangle junctions and turntables, but the scheme would appear to have possibilities, especially where vestibule connections are used, when the fasteners could be attached to the vestibules themselves.

"Millbro" Specialities.

Our readers in the Liverpool district will be interested to know that the Liverpool Tools and Castings Co., Ltd. are carrying a complete stock of the "Millbro" railway specialities, and a visit to 41, South Castle Street, Liverpool, will be well worth while.

NOTABLE MODEL RAILWAYS

Mr. G. N. Southerden's Gauge 1 Clockwork Line.

THIS railway was described in the *Model Engineer* for February 23rd, 1922, and in general form is much the same as it was then, but there have been several minor improvements.

The only lay-out change of importance is at "Plymouth," where a new line has been introduced (*see* Fig. 2). The new line allows shunting from the spur to Platform 2, while an up train is signalled from Platform 1, acts as a trap siding protecting the up main line from the spur, and obviates the necessity of the "George the Fifth" using the sharply curved slip road of the diamond crossing when running (from Platform 2 to the spur) round its train.

Small pieces of cardboard have been introduced to support the flanges of wheels when passing over the frogs of the diamond crossing (on the tramway principle), since, owing to the curved slip road mentioned, the wing rails could not be placed sufficiently near the "V" to avoid bumping.

The chief improvements, however, have been in the signalling at "Exeter" and "Plymouth." The hanging cotton-reels have given place to a very simple lever-frame. The rack was cut out of "cocoa tin" in the form of a comb, the ends of the teeth being secured between two pieces of strip-wood. The levers themselves were made from umbrella ribs, annealed by heating in the fire to red heat and allowing to cool, so that the upper part of the lever might be hammered flat. The holes for the connections to the signal wires were

A view of Exeter Station, showing up and down passenger trains.

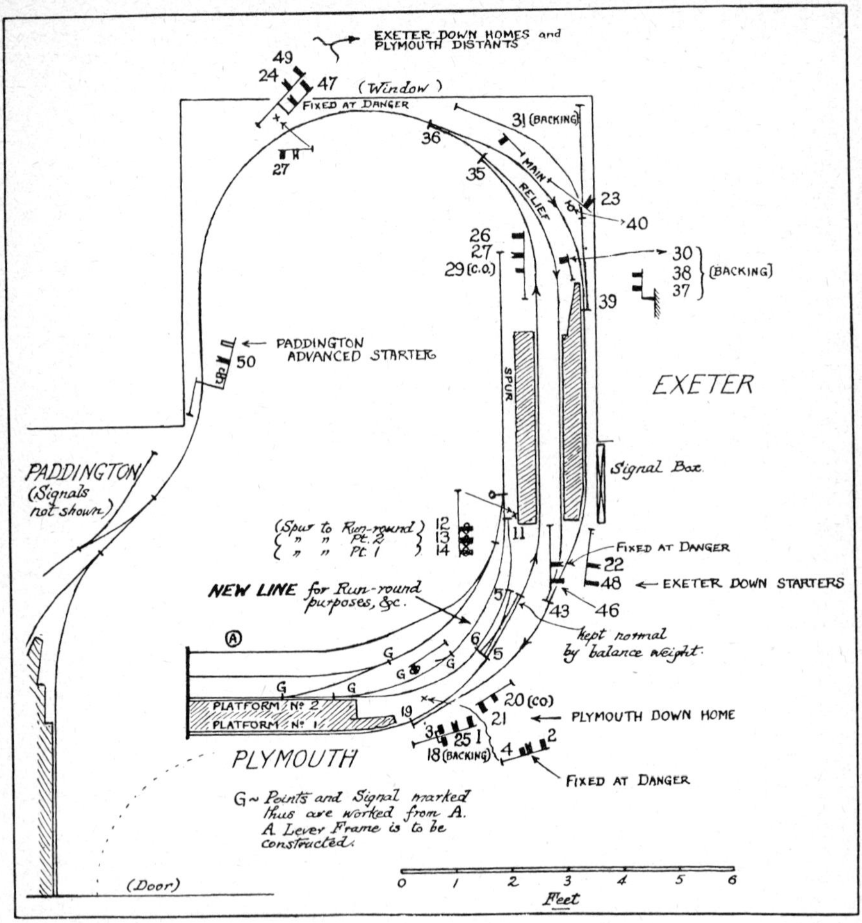

Fig 2.—The lay-out of Mr. G. N. Southerden's gauge 1 line.

made by a file. The diagram (Fig. 1) shows the general arrangement. The signals are still worked by thread, but owing to the long "travel" of the wire at the signal box and the considerable use of half-inch Meccano pulleys, adjustments do not have to be made frequently. Points are worked in a similar way, but a double thickness of thread or old violin E strings are used, sometimes with cranks cut out of tin.

The "Exeter" signal box consists of two frames independent of one another, levers Nos. 1–24 controlling "Plymouth" and 25–50 "Exeter." The "Plymouth" distant signals allow the down main "Exeter" Distant to be pulled off even when the line is not clear into "Plymouth," since they give adequate warning of the "Plymouth" home. Also the scheme is an example of signalling a very short section, since all the distant signals are correctly slotted (by a slightly modified form of the arrangement on the post described

Shunting operations at Exeter Station.

in the article in the *M.E.* mentioned above). The "Exeter" down main distant (No. 50 on the diagram) is slotted by the "Paddington" advanced starter and is pulled off after Nos. 48 and 49, but as yet has not been so interlocked. The down main "Plymouth" distant (No. 24)

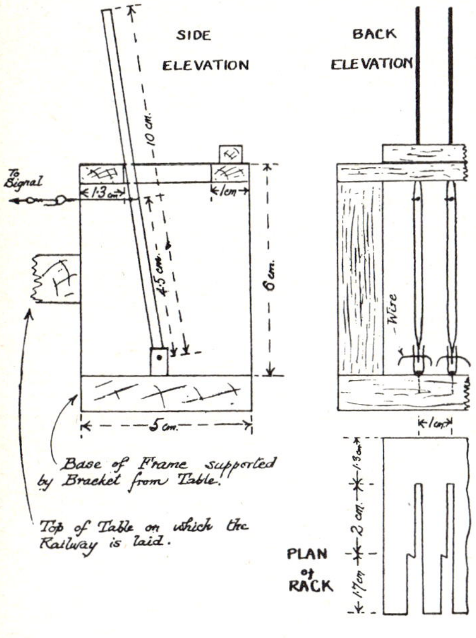

Fig. 1.—The Lever Frame.

is slotted by the "Exeter" down main home (No. 49) and backslotted by the "Exeter" down main starter (No. 48). The "Plymouth" down main intermediate distant (No. 23) is also backslotted by No. 48. The "Plymouth" down main inner distant (No. 22) is slotted by No. 48 only. The two "Plymouth" distant signals, applying to trains running through "Exeter" on the down relief line, are fixed at danger, as through trains are rarely on this line, which is mostly used for run-round purposes when up goods trains require to shunt in the "Exeter" siding. In the up direction there are the "Exeter" up main distant (No. 25), slotted by the "Plymouth" up main starter (No. 1); and the "Paddington" up main distant, slotted by the "Exeter" up main starter (No. 27). On account of the sharp curve at "Exeter," No. 27 is repeated on the post of the up main home (No. 26), by which signal it is slotted. The signal, although a repeater, is painted red (instead of yellow), since it also functions as an inner distant signal.

The semaphores are cut out of tin, the spectacles not being transparent. On the front of the spectacle, "glasses" are left white and are painted black on the back. The general effect is quite good, however.

An up goods train.

The calling-on arms are lettered "CO" when painted; the two holes in the backing signals are punched out with toy ticket punchers: the "O's" and "S's" are cut from the thin tin from the tops of cigarette tins and are glued to semaphores.

I have made a number of point-detectors out of "cocoa tin." They do not attempt to be to scale, but they are real safety devices and exactly illustrate the principle of the ordinary mechanical detector. Fig. 3 shows the four parts of the detector as cut out. The sides of "D" are bent along the dotted lines so as to form a box, and "B," "C" are placed in "bb," "cc." For strength, the top of "A" is bent through a right-angle. It is then placed in the slots "*aa*." "A," "B," "C" are connected to the points and two signals respectively, as in Fig. 4, which shows one signal detecting the point. Since none of the points are worked by rods, it is most satisfactory to

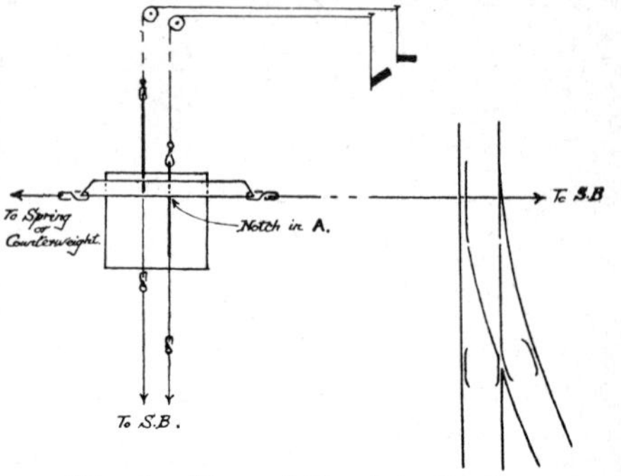

Fig. 4.—Plan of the detector in use (not to scale).

place the detector between the points and counterweight rather than between the points and signal box. When either signal is "off" the points are locked so that to some extent it may be a substitute for interlocking at the signal box.

The throw of the points "T" should be *over-* rather than under-estimated, since the former error may be easily remedied by widening the notch in "A."

NOTE.—If the point is required to be detected in one position only, "D" should be made symmetrical about "*bb*," and "A" modified accordingly.

The railway is worked to time-table by the two (clockwork) engines shown in the photos. A Bassett-Lowke G.W. corridor carriage now runs with the G.N. six-wheeler as one train.

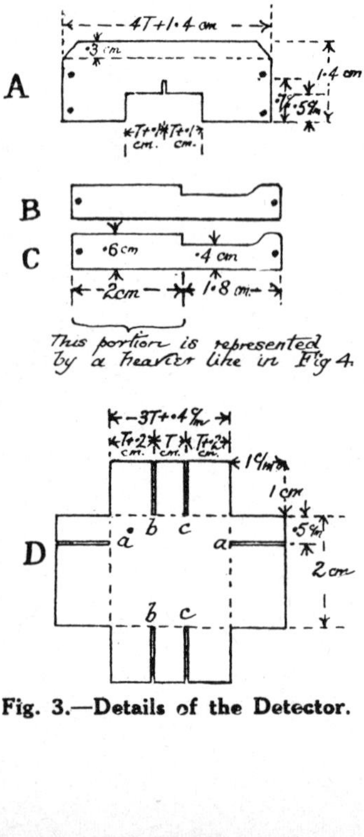

Fig. 3.—Details of the Detector.

Mr. C. L. Bennett's "O" Gauge Solid-Fuel Tank Engine.

I HOPE the latest photo of my 0 gauge solid-fuel tank engine (refer January issue) will be of interest to the readers of the MODEL RAILWAY NEWS. The background effect was obtained by placing a piece of track on a burnt-out bonfire.

The loco only awaits the tiny pressure gauge to complete it. A "displacement" lubricator has been fitted and looks after the cylinder lubrication in an excellent manner. It was a tight squeeze to get this in between firebox and crankshaft, there being only ¼-in. to spare. A hand pump ¼-in. bore by 9-16th-in. stroke has been fitted in the left-hand side tank and there was just room for it. The other tank is no longer a dummy, and is filled through the lid like its big sister. New steel wheels are now fitted and well repay the time spent on them. They have the correct number of spokes and are faithful copies of Stroudley's wheels, except depth of flange (1-16th in. bare), and thickness (3-16th in. bare). The trailing wheels are cut from solid steel blanks and run on sprung stud axles. The drivers are each built up of five parts and brazed together. While the loco was down for its additions, I decided to try springing the axle boxes, and the way they work also well repays the time spent on them. From actual running results, I would recommend all 0 gauge stock to be fitted with springs. The front coupled and trailing wheels have working laminated springs 1-16th in. bare wide and ⅛-in. deep by 1 in. and 15-16th in. long respectively, and main drivers have two coil springs to each axle box. The reason for fitting the trailing wheels on stud axles was to get a longer run on one stoking, but the loco has run just as well with fire-bars above the centre line of trailing axle. Of course, the fire required more attention, hence the fitting of a false firebox.

In conclusion, I would like to mention that I am indebted to Mr. H. E. Sandy for the excellent photograph. His L.N.W.R. truck is coupled to loco.

Reducing Rolling Friction.

By A. R. Walkley.

IN connection with a $3\frac{1}{2}$-mm. scale railway now in course of construction it was early realized, in view of the lightness of the rolling stock, friction between the axles and their boxes must be reduced to a minimum if anything like free running was to be obtained. As the type of bearing eventually adopted has proved very successful in service and is equally applicable to the larger gauges, it is thought that a short note on the subject may be of use to fellow-readers. It is quite easy to convert the standard 0 gauge vehicle with white-metal wheels on mild-steel axles running in die-cast boxes. On the railway in question, the matter is somewhat complicated by the necessity of each box and wheel being insulated, but as it is hoped to deal with the electrical details of the line later on, this point will be ignored in the present instance, and the conversion of a standard 0 gauge vehicle, as mentioned above, will be described.

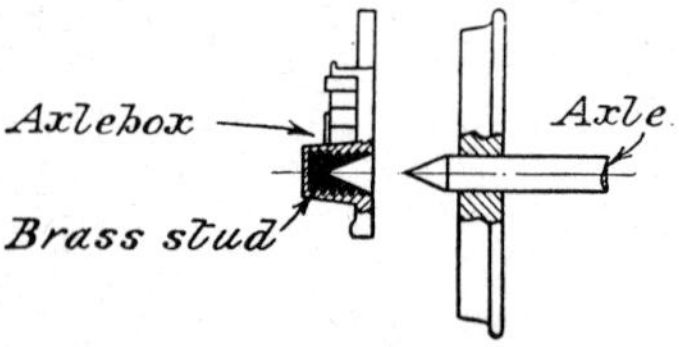

Section through axlebox of the suggested bearing for reducing rolling friction.

First remove the wheels and axleboxes. Force the wheels off the axles and turn the two ends of each axle to a point, a fairly blunt angle being best. Although a lathe is, of course, desirable, this can be done in the time-honoured way by mounting the axles in the hand-drill chuck and filing the points.

Then look through your stock of BA brass bolts (or visit the local wireless shop!) and select a bolt that will comfortably cut its own thread in the blind axlebox holes. Screw home and cut off flush with the inside of box, four being needed for a goods vehicle, of course. Then grind up a pin-drill to approximately the same angle as the pointed axles and, after carefully centre-popping the brass "studs" in the boxes, drill each one out (as shown in black section on the sketch herewith), being careful not to go through the further end of the "stud." Replace wheels on axles to gauge and erect the axleguards in the usual way, lubricate with *thin* oil and you will find the track will run at least twice as freely as it did before.

One ventures to assert that you will not rest until you have converted all your rolling-stock! Be careful to leave sufficient end-play between the bearings and there should be no need to stress the importance of the two axles being in line "all ways." Besides allowing your locos to pull more stock this type of bearing will enable you to do shunting in a much more realistic manner than is usually the case on a model line. The writer would be interested to hear of the results obtained by this method in 0, 1 or 2 gauges.

In 00 gauge the weight of a goods truck averages from about $1\frac{1}{4}$ to 2 oz., and as the writer has practically completed a 0—4—4 tank loco with a permanent-magnet motor that comfortably hauls 4 lb., it will be seen that a really long goods-train can be worked if required.

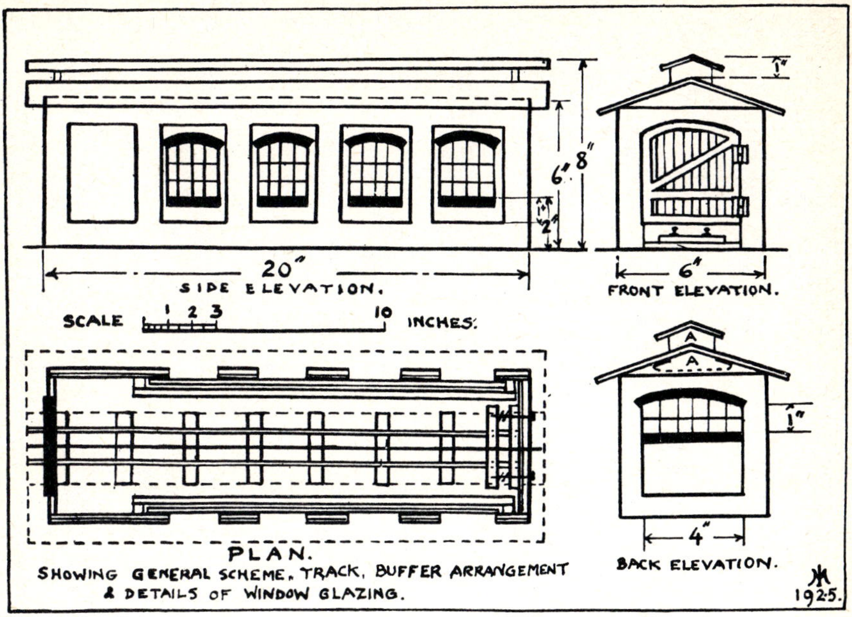

A Gauge "O" Engine Shed.

By Dr. J. Magri.

THE model described below can be easily made with very few tools, and though the result is most pleasing and effective, the cost is negligible.

Start by constructing the side walls. Cut a piece of stout cardboard 20 in. × 6 in. Draw on it the four windows in position and cut them out. Cut two pieces, of ¼-in. thick wood, 20 in. × 1 in. Glue and nail these to the top and to the base of the cardboard. The upper piece should have its edge planed obliquely to take the slope of the roof. Now cut six pieces of the same wood, 4 in. × 1 in. each, and glue and nail them to the cardboard, each reaching vertically from top to base. They divide the wall into five equal divisions as shown in the side elevation.

The window bars are represented by iron wire cut into suitable lengths, and fixed by passing the ends bent at right angles into holes in the cardboard and bending them over. Each window has at its top an arched piece of ¼ in. × ¼ in. wood, and these are best cut by fretsaw. At the base of each window is a straight piece cut from the same wood.

Having thus completed one of the two side walls, proceed to construct the other on similar lines.

For the front wall the same construction of cardboard and wood applies. The door is a solid piece of ¼ in. thick wood cut into shape and hinged to the wall. The design on the door is made by pieces of cardboard cut into shape and glued on to it.

The back wall is also constructed in a similar manner. It has a single high, large window. A simple buffer arrangement can be made by cutting two buffer beams from ¼-in. thick wood, and boring two holes near the ends of one of them into which nails

A rear view of the "0" gauge shed.

can run freely. Corresponding holes are cut into the cardboard wall at suitable level and the latter buffer beam is securely glued and nailed to it. Two nails, amply stout, are then passed through the holes, two small wire springs are inserted on them, and the nails are then driven into the other buffer beam.

Now the floor and the roof of the model remain to be made. The floor is a piece of $\frac{1}{4}$-in. thick wood, 20 in. × 6 in. The rails are laid and fixed to it, preferably after giving the floor two coats of grey paint.

The roof is constructed of the same stout cardboard. Cut one piece 22 in. × 8 in., and another piece, 22 in. × 3 in. Draw a line in the middle of each along its whole length and run your penknife lightly along this line. Now bend each piece along this line to the required angle, which corresponds to the angle at the top of the front and back walls. Two pieces of $\frac{1}{4}$-in. thick wood are cut as in AA in the back elevation. The top part of each of them is passed into a corresponding hole in the larger piece of cardboard, which is the roof proper. These holes are $19\frac{1}{2}$ in. apart. The roof proper is then glued and nailed to them. The smaller piece of cardboard is the roof of the ventilator and should be glued and nailed to the top of the AA pieces. For glazing the windows $\frac{1}{4}$ in. × $\frac{1}{4}$ in. wood, grooved to take the glass and cut in suitable lengths, is fixed below the windows' level, and running their whole length. Two similar pieces 3 in. each are fixed vertically on either side. The glass should not be dropped in until the painting of the model is over.

The floor and the four walls are now all securely fixed together by glue and nail. The roof is intended to be removable and simply lies down on top, the AA pieces being just inside the front and back walls, and keeping it in position.

The finishing of the model now receives consideration. The walls, and the under surface of the roof are all painted white. The outer side of the roof, and the design on the door are painted grey. The window arches and basements are painted brick red. The buffer beam is painted buffer-beam red. Advertisements fixed outside, fire buckets, lamps and loco pictures fixed inside, all greatly add to the detail. The door should be provided with a minute latch. Chimneys have been purposely omitted but can be added if required. Electric lighting can also be easily fitted.

A locomotive entering the model "0" gauge shed.

The model is now complete and the result will be very gratifying. Personally, I have very little spare time, but the model can be easily constructed in a short period.

Those taking model railways as their hobby in Egypt have to struggle against many difficulties. They have none of the facilities which exist in England. There is not a single store in the country which can supply their requirements. Still we always try to do our bit. I say " we " in the hope that there are many model railwaymen in Egypt, but, sorry to say, we are quite unknown to each other.

A view of Dwiggle Jct. and Swoshby Terminus.

Rev. H. A. Turner's Re-erected "OO" Gauge Line.

MY "00" gauge line, built and exhibited as a sideshow at a bazaar in Bath last January, and of which an account was given in the June issue, has now been re-erected and improved on my removal to a country vicarage. It is now erected in an attic, 20 ft. × 11 ft. 6 in. There is in this a staircase which is shut off by a glass door and glass-fitted partition. The line is now double to just beyond the first station, where at a scissors crossing it becomes two single lines, one climbing at 1 in 45, continuing round the room, passing through the partition, carried on a curved bridge over the staircase, along a window-sill, and again through the partition, is brought over the main terminus on a viaduct, passes, at a higher level, at the back of the main line, and on another curved viaduct over the main line, descends at 1 in 30 to the level again and terminates at a station alongside the above-mentioned first station out. Only thus could I

A view looking towards Tillywhympleton and Little Biffham Stations.

Another view of Tillywhympleton station.

get an end to end longish run. This gives me a run of 72 feet, with five stations.

The other line leaves the main at the scissor crossing, and enters a tunnel, marked "A" on lay-out, passing under the main and through the wall into a false roof, and thence into another attic. This is not completed and is not a success, as access to it means going down one flight of stairs, along a passage, a landing, and up another flight. Eventually it is proposed to bring this line back by a curve and another hole in the wall into the original room and terminate at a port with quay, harbour and steamer complete.

The only addition to the stock is a 68-ft. restaurant car, built of wood, and running on scale bogies, beautiful models, from Marshall, Stewart and Co. Next winter it is hoped to build a train to match the dining car, but lighter materials will be used, as the car is rather heavy. It is fitted with dummy vestibules, and two of the original bogie coaches have been fitted likewise, to run with it. The German clockwork engines will pull this car and three other bogie coaches on the level only. Every train has to be assisted up the bank, unless it is the close-coupled three 4-wheel coach train, which the engines will pull up unassisted.

Some of the stock is fitted with Marshall, Stewart & Co.'s scale wheels, but it is difficult to make them stay on my round-section rails. If I had known originally that scale wheels were procurable, I should have made the track of square section. It would be rather too big a job to relay the whole, as altogether there are several hundreds of feet of it. Perhaps some time in the future, the Editor may allow me to send some photos of the new stock, and also the harbour and quay-side lay out, when completed. In the meantime, oh, for a decent clockwork engine that will reverse and go a fair distance with one winding.

Answers to Correspondents.

T. A. (Todmorden).—There is no objection in having an accumulator of a slightly higher voltage than nominally required for any given model electric locomotive. A regulating resistance would be used to control the speed. For a six-volt locomotive, eight volts may be used without danger, although there is something wrong in the connections or the motor if the engine will not run on the rated voltage. The engines with the "sequence" type of automatic reverser should have a long space between the collecting brushes to guard against a break in the continuity of the current supply at points and crossings. The "sequence" type of reverser works by virtue of a stoppage and restarting of the current, and therefore this should not be allowed to happen uncontrolled.

F. W. H. (Chiswick)—We do not think you will be able to purchase moulds for casting axleguards in white-metal alloy. Such moulds are very expensive and you would have to make thousands of fittings to repay the cost of one mould. If you are a skilled mechanic you can, of course, make such moulds.

A train on viaduct passing over the main line. The train in foreground just leaving Tillywhympleton Station.

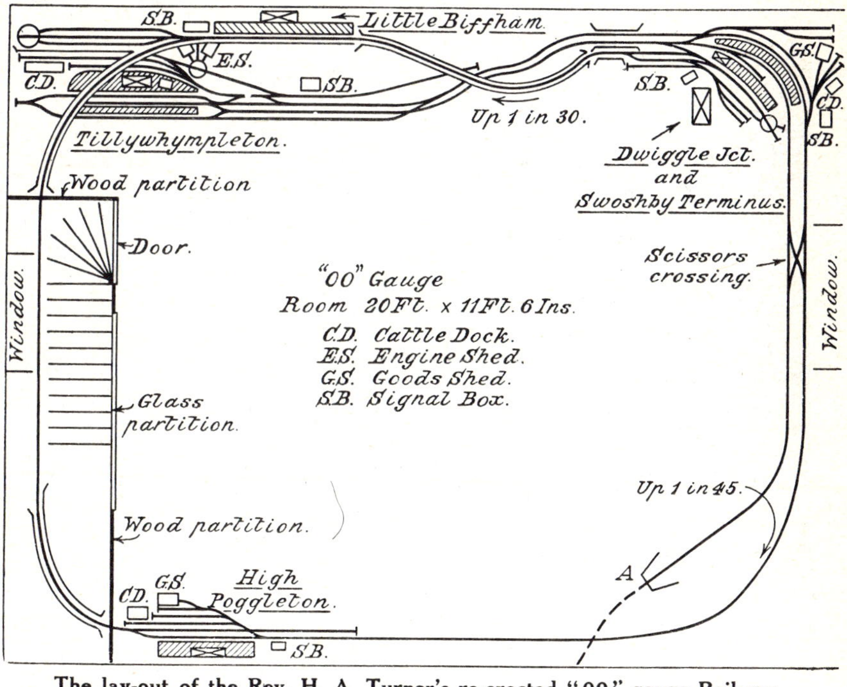

The lay-out of the Rev. H. A. Turner's re-erected "00" gauge Railway.

Ballasting Model Railways.

By H. P. Powell.

THE question of ballasting a model railway is not often raised, but the idea would be adopted by a great many if they only realized the advantages gained by it.

To deal with the question of the material to use first. Two substances which are practically alike may be employed—granite or flint chips. These are sold cheaply by almost any corn and poultry food dealer. The writer paid 1s. per stone of 14 lbs. for his flint chips, and found that it took three and a half stones to do completely his 0 gauge track which is laid double round a room 12 ft. × 11 ft., and with two longish sidings. The track used is "Lowko," and the ballast does not go as far, thus using it with rails on battens, than it might do otherwise.

There are two great advantages of using ballast. One is, the great reduction of any tinny noise made by the rolling stock, especially when tin-plate rolling stock is used, although with wood, the effect is the same.

The other is the touch of realism it gives. It improves the look of the line 100 %, and it is also nearly true to scale, at any rate on the larger gauges of 1, 2, 3 and upwards. Although the chips are rather too big to be scale for 0 gauge, they *look* all right, and after all it is looks that count.

In conclusion, may I add that if any difficulty is found in getting these chips, I shall be pleased to furnish the address of my dealer on application to the M.R.N. offices.

Model Railway at Munich Exhibition.

The accompanying photograph, for which we are indebted to Herr Roland Martens, gives some idea of the huge No. 1 gauge railway to which we referred in last month's issue.

The portion in the foreground of the picture is the docks with the travelling and transporter cranes. The main line of railway can also be seen running through the centre, the model town the railway is supposed to be serving being at the other end of the lay-out on the left. The detail work is excellent throughout.

Distant Control of the Larger Steam Locomotive Models.

By H. Greenly.

I HAVE been asked by Mr. C. Geo. Harrison, of Wakefield, to give more particulars of the scheme I proposed before the war for the control of model steam locomotives of a size which, although not suitable for riding on, are too powerful to be allowed to run alone. It will be remembered that some 20 odd years ago, the late Mr. Henry Lea, M.I.C.E., built a locomotive of 3½ in. gauge—a Midland single—which was fitted up with an electrical regulator controller and at the same time made it possible to work the injector from the signal box. He was not able within his lifetime to proceed any further with his experiments but as far as they went they were perfectly successful. Mr. Lea used two "third-conductor rails," one for each operation, and employed a high voltage current working solenoid magnets.

The scheme I proposed is quite different in principle. The regulator speed governing and the reversing are effected by one conductor rail which may be of any convenient low voltage—between, say 8 and 25 volts—and by using a permanent magnet motor or its equivalent by reversing the current supplied to the locomotive it is quite easy to couple the motor to a mechanism which will pull over the valve gear at the will of the distant operator. The extent of the opening of the regulator depends on the speed at which the electro motor is driven, which again is within control of the signalman - driver. The governing motor has to be sufficiently powerful to do this—not a very arduous task—and actuates a fly-ball governor of the stationary steam-engine type against the tension of a spring or springs. On shutting off the supply current the motor stops and the steam regulator closes. This is more or less obvious from the sketch herewith, but the action of the reversing gear perhaps needs further description. On the weigh shaft a section of a worm wheel is fitted. The length of the arc of teeth which engages the fine thread worm must be proportioned so that when the weigh-shaft is either in the full back or fore gear, the rotation of the worm has no further effect on it. Light springs should be fitted to the weigh shaft so that the last tooth still tends to remain in mesh with the worm. On a reversal of the motor the worm will then move the weigh shaft over to the other end of

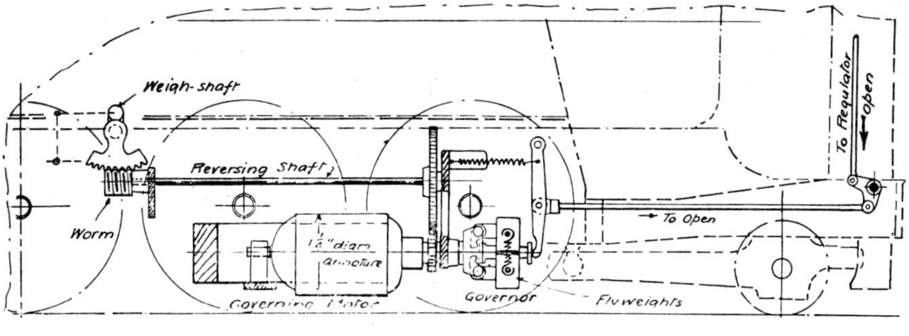

The proposed gear applied to a "Pacific" type loco for distant control.

its arc of movement and the same thing will happen. The governing motor may continue to be run but will not move the weight shaft past its proper full gear position.

The use of the worm gear—in addition to the three-to-one reduction gear introduced into the design herewith—should provide ample power to accomplish the act of reversing, and, by a suitable adjustment of the spring gear on the speed-regulation portion of the device, the revolutions of the motor during the reversing may not be sufficient to open the regulator either at all or to an extent which will matter.

I have shown the gear applied to a Pacific locomotive. It would, of course, be possible to rig the motor up in the tender above the footplate and to couple it with a flexible drive to mechanism situated on the footplate. Practically every locomotive will require special treatment, and where the experimenter wishes to utilize an existing or ready-made permanent motor, the tender-drive idea is perhaps to be preferred. The same remark applies to an arrangement in which a series motor, with a polarized auto-reversing switch is employed.

Electric Locomotive Types for Modelling.

By A. W. Line.

WHEN deciding upon the best type of electric locomotive to model, one of the most important things to consider is realism and action when in motion. The electrically operated steam-outline locomotive has, of course, the realistic action of the coupling and connecting rods and of the counterbalance blocks to attract the eye of the beholder, but many designs of electric-outline locomotives are geared throughout and, except for the revolving of the wheels, generally almost hidden, they have no external moving parts, and the machine merely seems to glide along in an uninteresting sort of way. Where coupling rods are used, the locomotive springs to life upon starting, and the revolving rods, when running, supply the action which is so attractive to the spectator.

To anyone interested, the following three designs of side-rod electric locomotives are recommended for modelling:—Norfolk and Western Railway, 2—4—4—2 locomotives, operated in pairs, of the first design; Pennsylvania Railroad System, Class FF–1 articulated 2—6—6—2 locomotive, also Class L–5 non-articulated 2—4—4—2 locomotive. Drawings and illustrations of these and other electric locomotives have been published in the railway engineering press from time to time, and American readers may also find them in the fifty odd pages of the electric locomotive section of the "Locomotive Cyclopedia," 1922 or 1925 editions, the latter being just off the press. British readers also may find drawings of the locomotives readily available in the files of the model press as follows:—Drawings of the Norfolk and Western Railway are to be found in *Everyday Science and Models* of January, 1922, and a side elevation of the P.R.R. 2—6—6—2 design was printed in the December, 1921, issue.

The latest and probably the best to model of the three above-mentioned designs is the P.R.R. Class L–5 2—4—4—2 type. Mr. Chas. S. Lake has given us a dimensioned outline drawing and a good photograph of this locomotive in his column "Locomotive News and Notes" in the *Model Engineer*. The drawing appeared in the issue of August 28th, 1924, and the illustration was printed in the February 19th, 1925, issue.

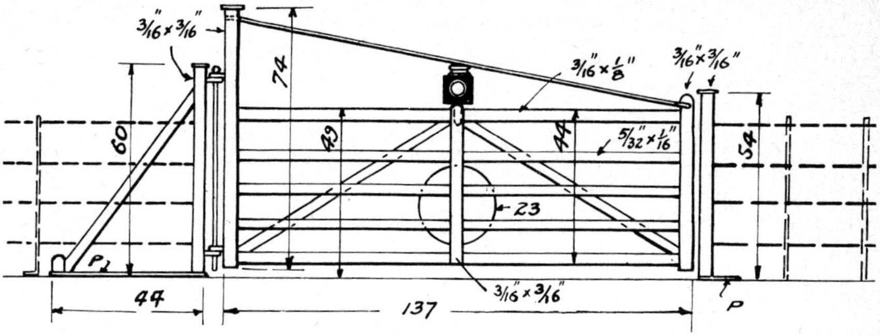

Fig. 3.—Design for No. 1 gauge single line pair of crossing gates.

Model Level Crossing Gates.

FOR a single line of railway, level crossing gates need not be in pairs on each side of the track. The total width between low uprights in No. 1 gauge is given on the well-known blue print (P 91) at 135 mm., and this would mean that the gates would span a roadway equal to about 13½ ft. wide. This is quite enough for the average model line, and unless a double

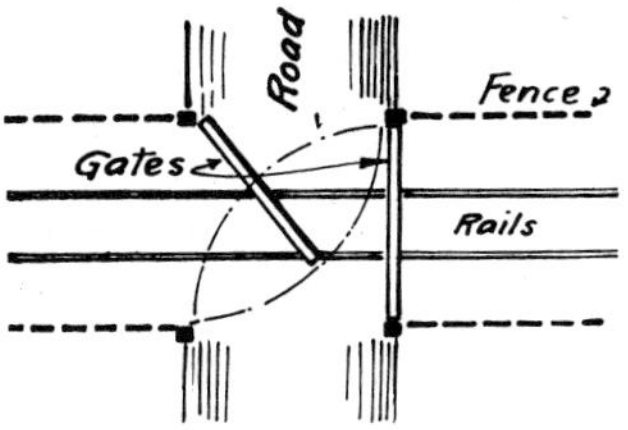

Fig. 1.—Crossing gates for a single line.

line of railway has to be dealt with there is no point in taking up any further space. For a double line the half of the total width of line would be about 132 mm. and it is, therefore, possible to use gates made on the same jigs but in duplicate, in either case. The roadway would, therefore, be approximately, 264 mm. wide at the gates.

For No. 0 gauge these dimensions are roughly seven-tenths of those employed in No. 1 gauge, but for more exact figures reference should be made to the standard dimensions, sheet No. P90. The sketches, Figs. 1 and 2, show the two methods of arranging gates.

It is always advisable to build up gates on jigs or formers made by fixing blocks of wood representing the spaces between the various members on a plank of sufficient size. The parts can then be cut to length and laid in place with an accuracy dependent on the setting out of the jig and with the knowledge that all models built up on the jig will be of the same size.

The gates can be made of strip wood, although a much neater and stronger result can be obtained by using rectangular brass sections, joining them together with a touch of the soldering iron. With wood,

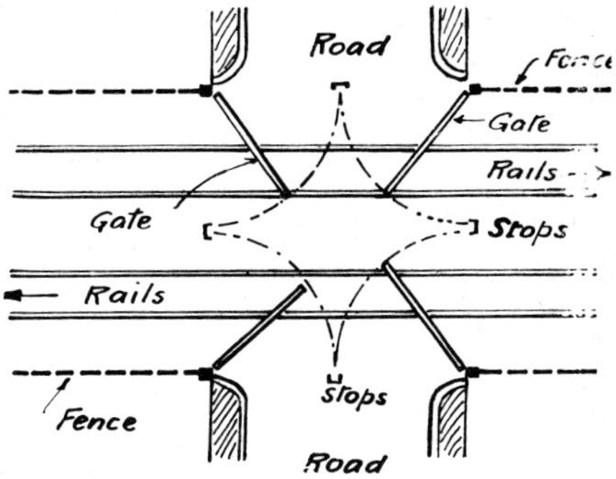

Fig. 2.—Gates for double line.

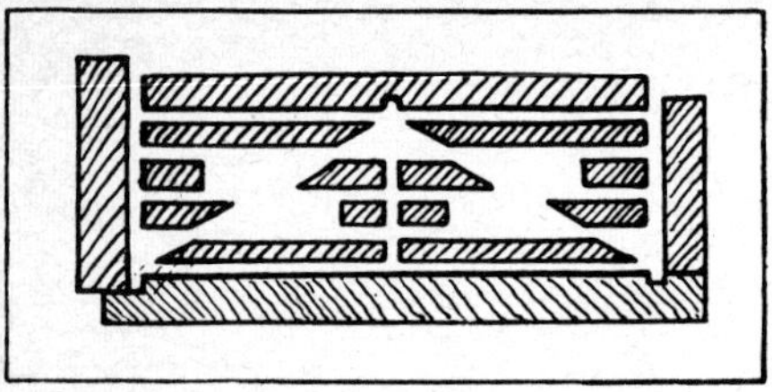

Fig. 4.—Jig for making gates.

reliance must be made on glue, as the parts, if they are made sufficiently large in cross section to stand nailing together with panel pins, are apt to look very clumsy. Those readers who "funk" soldering should practice on such models as gates and fencing. A little roughness in finish, which is bound to characterize "first attempts" does not matter so much in a model gate or fence.

Fig. 3 is a design for a single gate. The main post is extended to provide for a tension member made of wire. This is common practice. The frame of the gate itself is strutted by diagonals. All the main posts may be made of 3-16th in. square brass, notched for the horizontal members. These notchings may be arranged to

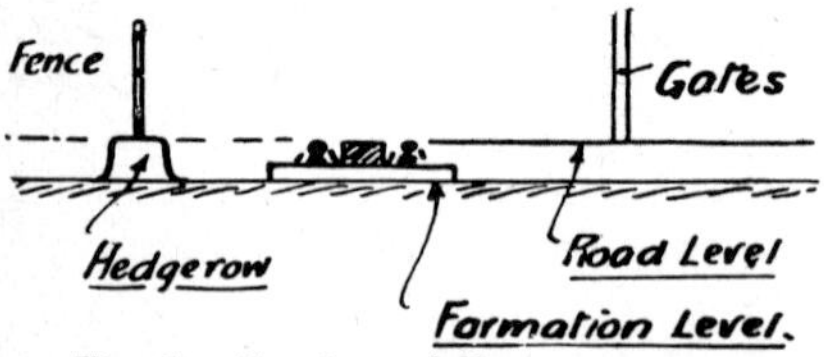

Fig. 5.—Section of line at gates.

provide a framework which is flush on one side. This method will simplify both the construction of the jig and the gate members, the flush side being placed on the inside, or railway side, when the gate is closing the road. The sketch, Fig. 4, illustrates the jig and shows how the blocks fixed to the baseboard will hold the job during the process of soldering. The greatest care should be taken to make the job symmetrical, as it may prove convenient to be able to turn the work over during the soldering operations. The red "danger" disc may be attached after the job is taken out of the jig, also the caps, lamp, and wire tension member. The hinge post should be mounted on a metal base so that a secure fixing to the baseboard of the railway may be obtained.

In placing the posts it will be noticed that the fixed members do not take up an exactly correct "four-square" position, but the proper places can be marked out on the job after the gates are made and are attached to the hinge posts.

The level of the lower part of the gates is another point to consider. As the rail level is above the formation to the extent of the depth of the metals and sleepers, the roadway will have to be built up to form a flat surface, with a piece of wood (or sleepers) laid between rails in the usual manner. To preserve this rail level throughout, the fences on each side of the line may be built up on a sort of hedgerow — a strip of wood actually— and the plates(P) at the bottom corner and hinge of the posts laid on this. These strips will serve to restrain the loose ballast to the railway. Outside the fencing the surface of the ground may be finished as desired, either to represent earth or grass.

Fig. 6.—Lamp for gates.

The gates should be painted white, with black fittings and the disc being finished vermillion or signal red. The lamp should be painted red or illuminated to show a red signal in both directions transversely to the gates.

———

FOR MANCHESTER READERS.

Mr. F. Howarth, of 40, Kirkmanshulme Lane, Longsight, Manchester, wishes to form a "Longsight Junior Model Railway Club." Would those readers between the ages of 15 to 17 years, who are interested in the above. communicate with him at the above address.

" OO " gauge L.N.E.R. "Pacific."

" OO " Gauge Developments.

By A. Wain.

THE accompanying photograph shows the possibilities of this new gauge for those model makers who wish to " get in " the maximum effects in the minimum of space. It has been my experience, in the past, in common with others, to find that any pretentions to realism, even in " 0 " gauge, roads, sidings, bays, sheds, etc., has required an amount of room which was not always available for a " permanent " lay-out inside a residence, and one fails to obtain any lasting satisfaction with a portable lay-out. Some model enthusiasts are fortunate enough to have an attic, spare room, or a room seldom used which they can avail themselves of for the purpose of installing a " permanent " lay-out. But what of the many who, having no suitable accommodation for " 0 " gauge, have necessarily to forego the pleasure of a " model railway "?

Where " OO " Wins.

This new gauge allows of a considerable loco " stud," rolling stock, sheds, sidings, etc., and also a large scope for ingenuity. The photograph shows a L.N.E.R. " Pacific " built to 4 mm. to the foot, which was built in my leisure hours as long ago as December, 1924, to prove beyond dispute that " 00 " gauge can be made representative of any type on any line and give complete satisfaction over the little tank locos now on the market, stamped " made in Bavaria." The only departure from the real " Pacifics " was the omission of the " gear " to cylinders, etc., as this was found rather too small in such a tiny model, the entire length over buffers being under 11 inches, and it was found not to detract from the general appearance. The engine was fitted with an electric motor, painted and lined in correct L.N.E.R. colours by Messrs. Kay Models, Ltd., of Acton, to my instructions, cab number was 1924 (year of build), no number on tender and maker's name over centre wheels, *i.e.*, " Arthur Wain."

An Appreciation.

I should like to record my appreciation of Messrs. Kay Models, Ltd., keen interest in the " Pacific " and the kindly assistance given in the matter of " mechanism " and wheels, etc. All wheels are correctly " spoked " and " flanged " and " five-eighters " need not go to the trouble of turning wheels out of brass, etc. Good die castings are available and obtainable in all sizes from bogie wheels to " drivers." I mention this for the benefit of those " loco " men who, perhaps, are unaware as to their being easily obtainable, and also can state that anything for this gauge is now obtainable, even " blue prints." When I built my " Pacific " no blue prints were obtainable and I built to half-size of a L.M.C. blue print of their " 0 " gauge " Pacific."

The L.N.E.R. on the Rhine.

LIEUT. H. AWDE, R.E., worked for some years with Messrs. Robert Stephenson & Co., of Darlington, the makers of the first passenger engine in the world, "Locomotion" No. 1, and it is perhaps fitting that he should employ his leisure hours, when not on duty with the British Army on the Rhine, in the construction of model engines of the types with which he is so familiar.

He has just completed the construction of a most interesting model express passenger locomotive 4—4—0 N.E.R. class R type, and operates this, for the benefit of the German children and the members of his regiment, on a track some 200 yards long with a gauge of 10¼ inches. He also has for railway stock three cars or trucks, giving "first-class," "second class," "third-class" and "no-class" accommodation in English, and the words "Raucher" and "Nachtr Raucher" in German.

The following particulars are of the locomotive, which is a surprising model, seeing that it has been constructed entirely from memory :—

The loco. during construction.

Cylinders: 2-in. bore, 4-in. stroke. Coupled wheels: 13¼ in. diameter. Heating space: 1,800 square inches. Grate area: 70 square inches. Length over buffers: 9 ft. 3½ in. Weight: 8 cwts. Tender capacity: water, 40 litres, coal, ½ cwt.

At the Royal Engineers' sports on July 27th last, the Commanding Officer of the British Army of the Rhine was much interested in the L.N.E.R. engine, and German railway officers, who were also present on that occasion, actually were persuaded to travel by L.N.E.R. on the Rhine.

Lieut. Awde gives a joy-ride to German children.

OUR MAIL BAG

Improvements in the "00" Gauge Electric Locos.

To the Editor, MODEL RAILWAY NEWS,

DEAR SIR,

I have read with great interest Mr. Edward Beal's excellent article on 00 gauge locomotives. May I suggest two improvements on his design. First, coupling rods. I have them on both my locomotives and would not build one without them, as it makes all the difference in hauling power, and looks, my six-coupled tank will take a three-foot train, which is more than I require. Second, the reversing switch under the cab, with the handle coming through the roof or through the cab windows. If the train is at a platform it is almost impossible to reverse the engine with the usual handle.

I would advise anyone taking up this gauge to have over-size flanges on all wheels if their track, like mine, is semi-portable. Scale flanges may be all right on a perfect track, on a dead smooth substructure, but not otherwise, and the flanges do not show unless you get your eye at rail level.

I have used brass strip track since the first days of this gauge and am not satisfied with it for electric working, for two reasons: if it is not used for several days, it must all be cleaned before use, or otherwise the engines will not pick up from the centre rail, and also the sharp inside edge of the rail causes bad wheel slip, even with coupled engines.

Yours faithfully,
G. C.

Shalford (Surrey).

Model Loco. Rebuild.

To the Editor, MODEL RAILWAY NEWS,

DEAR SIR,

Please find enclosed photo of mode loco rebuild. The loco was a Hornby 0—4—0 outside-cylinder driving on to back wheel. I took footplate off, lengthened same to form front of G.W.R. county loco, made front four-wheel truck (this does not fall away from model on being lifted up). I was able to use the old cylinder, added bars and cross-head and coupled wheel. Made a taper boiler and firebox, G.W.R. type. The loco will run fine, much steadier, and will take a 2-ft. radius curve with ease. I am rebuilding another of the same type into a G.W.R. 2—4—2 T 3601 type. Should any readers require similar loco rebuild, I should be

Mr. A. T. Daines's rebuilt Locomotive.

pleased to do them or supply particulars.

Yours truly,
A. T. DAINES.

Ealing, W. 5.

"00" Gauge Electric Locos.

To the Editor, MODEL RAILWAY NEWS,

DEAR SIR,

With regard to Mr. Edward Beal's article on "00 Gauge Electric Locos," in the October number of the MODEL RAILWAY NEWS on page 305 he makes the following statement :—

". . . The series method consumes double the amperage required by the parallel system." This is entirely incorrect and I assume that it is a misprint. Motors in series consume half the current of the same motors in parallel if the supply voltage remains the same.

Yours faithfully,
A. B. LOCKHART.
Commander, R.N.

Atlantic Fleet.

[We thank our correspondent for his letter: Mr. Beal, in his article may not have expressed the meaning he intended to convey. For a given amount of current per motor the series arrangement takes one-half the amount which would be taken by the parallel arrangement, because the same current will flow through each motor. The starting effort will be the same in each case but the consumption of energy will be approximately halved with the motors in series. The object of series-parallel control in full-size practice is to effect economy in starting with or without resistance control, the motors being connected first in series and then in parallel. With a fixed-line voltage the motors connected in series will take a certain amount of current and will rotate at half the speed which would obtain if they were connected in parallel. When connected in parallel the speed of rotation will tend to be double the series speed. If the motors are connected in parallel and allowed to take as much current as they can each will take approximately double the amount taken by the series arrangement, the total energy consumed and work done will be four times as great, and the starting effort will be doubled. Series-parallel control admits of various combinations of motors, field coils and armatures and may be used in conjunction with resistances. The matter depends upon circumstances and regulation of current by control

---

Getting Down to "00" Gauge.

To the Editor, MODEL RAILWAY NEWS,

DEAR SIR,

I was interested in Mr. R. Evans' article and remarks in the October issue of the M.R.N. concerning "00 gauge." Perhaps the following description and photo of a 0—4—2 type tank engine I have recently constructed to the 3·5-mm. scale may interest readers.

From the photo it will be seen the model represents one of William Stroudley's famous D1 class tanks, built in 1873, and of which a large number are still familiar little objects on the Southern Railway.

The usual comment is, does it go? Unfortunately, it does not, unless you push it. When I commenced to build the model I did not know of a mechanism, either clockwork or electric, small enough on the market. But have since heard that Marshall, Stewart & Co., of Balham, are experimenting with this type of mechanism. So we must wait and see. Perhaps my old friend Mr. C. L. Bennett would care to undertake the job of a coal-fired boiler, 3·5-mm. scale.

Anyhow, the question of a mechanism could easily be overcome by concealing it in a brake-van next to the engine, a very cowardly action for a Stroudley, I admit.

The model is rather a super detail, having polished cap on funnel, balanced safety valves on dome, handrails, feed pipes, Westinghouse pump, smokebox door, complete with hinges and fastenings, air brake and train-heating pipe connections, compressed air cylinder, tool box, tank fillers, etc.,

Mr. G. W. Markham's 3·5 mm "00" gauge 0—4—2 tank locomotive.

and the firebox can be seen between the driving and trailing wheels. On the tanks are to be found a fireman's shovel and bucket, also a tiny oil can, whilst real coal in the bunker adds a realistic appearance to the model. The only fittings purchased were the buffers and axles, which are Marshall, Stewart standards.

The model is constructed entirely of brass. The wheels, which are at present solid, have treads 1½ mm. wide and flanges 1 mm. deep. All wheel measurements, gauge, buffer centres and standard measurements are all taken from the 3·5-mm. sheet of "00 gauge" standard measurements as published by M. S. & Co., and general information was kindly given me by the same firm.

The livery is Southern green. I found Judson's art enamels very satisfactory, which can be obtained in a variety of colours, in 2½*d.* tins. For lining and lettering I used Windsor and Newton's artist colours, mixed with copal varnish and put on with a fine drawing pen. When dry the whole was copal varnished and hardened.

In conclusion, I should like to congratulate Mr. Evans on his post-office van, and I certainly agree that it would be a welcome change from the usual gauges to have more photos and descriptions of "00 locos" and rolling stock. So now "00" enthusiasts! keep the ball rolling.

For after having had the pleasure of inspecting Mr. A. Stewart Reidpath's "00" models, including his Southern Railway dining car, which is a very much super-detail model, I am firmly convinced that 3·5 mm. is the ideal scale for "00" gauge and it is certainly worth while getting down to.

Yours faithfully,
G. W. MARKHAM.

London, S.W. 17

The Shunting Problem Solution.

To the Editor, MODEL RAILWAY NEWS,

DEAR SIR,

With reference to the solution to the shunting problem by Mr. J. R. Milton in the November issue, I beg to suggest that it does not accomplish the task "with the least possible delay and in as few moves as possible." I submit the following as a quicker and easier method :—

"B" engine goes into siding—2 moves. "A" moves down where "B's" trucks are—1 move. "B" engine comes out of siding—1 move. "A" shunts "B's" trucks into siding and proceeds—4 moves. "B" engine fetches her trucks and proceeds—2 moves.

This method takes only 10 moves, 6 of which are with a load. Mr. Milton's method takes 16 moves, 9 of which are with a load.

Yours faithfully,

D. A. R. SMITH.

Liverpool.

Test Track, Buffer Stops and Automatic Signalling.

To the Editor, MODEL RAILWAY NEWS.

DEAR SIR,

I am sending you a short description of a piece of test track, in gauges 00 and 0. I started it about one year ago out of three yards of electric permanent way, which I constructed myself. The centre rail was so placed

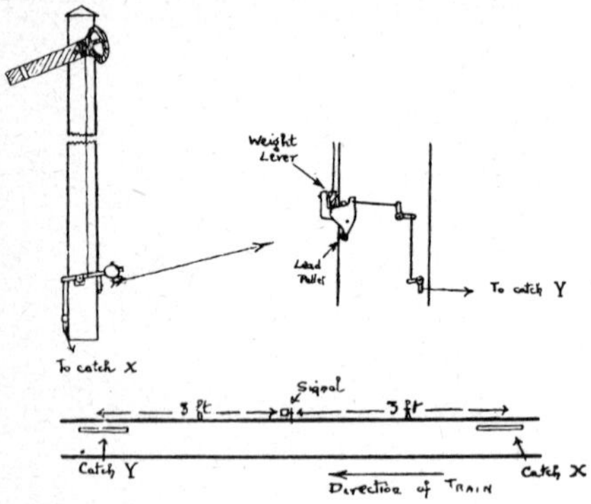

Details of the Automatic Signalling.

that rolling stock in gauge 00 could use it for running on, together with the outer rail. Between these two rails runs a thin copper strip for electric 00 gauge traction. The centre portion of track is fitted for electric signalling, and contains an electric switch for some small catch points in the same section. Spring buffer stops in both gauges were fitted at one end; those for the smaller gauge being as in the diagram. The flattened rails A and B are not rigidly fixed (except in PQ), but slide through the bar XY. S is the spring.

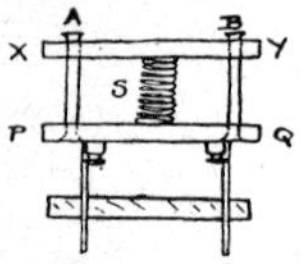

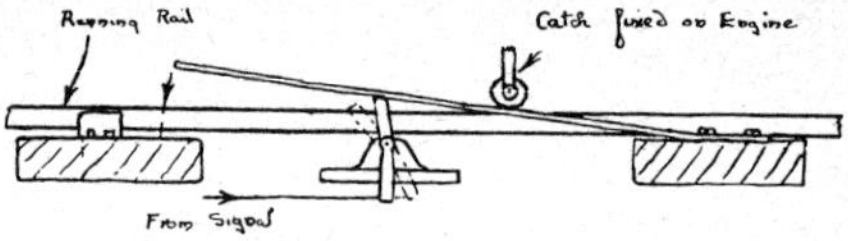

Side view of the catches.

Catches for automatic signals (also illustrated, but not to scale) are fitted to the track as well.

Yours truly,

Harpenden. J. F. SALZMAN.

"0" Gauge Scale Wagon Wheels.

To the Editor, MODEL RAILWAY NEWS,

DEAR SIR,

To give honour where such is due, may I recommend "Mills Bros." and "Kay Models" wagon wheels as by far the best I have yet been supplied with.

It seems strange that these two comparatively new and small firms are the only ones whom I have found supply *consistently accurate wheels,* both for finish and smooth running, and above all, for correct centering of axles, flange distances and for absence of wobble.

Further comment is unnecessary, but I advise model makers to give them a trial.

Yours faithfully,

Exeter. "SPARKS."

Steam *v.* Electric.

To the Editor, MODEL RAILWAY NEWS.

DEAR SIR,

I have always followed with interest the clashings of the "electric" and "steam" upholders in your magazine, and would like to point out something that is so obvious as to have so far been overlooked, that is, the noise accompanying a railway of any size. Even on 0 gauge the exhaust sounds quite realistic, and the "electricians" miss this entirely. One of the most fascinating things to me, on my 0 gauge railway, is to hear the engine's "tf—tf—tf" when I open the regulator wide after throttling down through a station.

Another item of noise is where you back a steam engine on to a train, in a

Loco No. 66. "Experiment" connected to the "Manchester" Corridor Express.

kind of small jerk, with a long "tffff" from the exhaust. An "electrician," true, can back slowly, but he misses the noise which sounds so like the real thing on a steam model.

Thank you for your excellent little paper, to which I hope to remain always a regular reader. Good luck to it!

Yours very truly,
H. P. Powell.

South Croydon.

A Gauge 1 Clockwork Line.

To the Editor, Model Railway News.

Dear Sir,

I have read with great interest your very interesting publication, and heartily congratulate you upon it. Seeing that it is customary for your readers to send for publication descriptions and photos of their own railways, I have ventured to send some photos and a short description of my own railway, which is a joint line, controlled by my brother, my cousin and myself. The photos were taken by a friend of mine and are, in my opinion, exceptionally good.

The Glover-Merriam railway is a gauge 1 line, worked throughout by clockwork locomotives, which have proved enormously successful and whose performances are a wonder and a joy to me. The three express engines are all L.N.W.R. models—to wit, a 4—6—0 "Experiment," a 4—4—0 "George the Fifth," and a 4—4—2 "Precursor Tank." There are also three 0—4—0 shunters of the "Gamage" type. The rolling stock consists of eight bogie coaches, one of

A general view of the Glover-Merriam Railway.

The 4—4—2 Tank No. 44 and 4—4—0 No. 2663 "George the Fifth" on the engine siding.

which is a twelve-wheeled dining saloon. This includes a complete model corridor set. The local stock are standard four-wheelers. The goods stock consists of coal trucks, oil carriers, wood trucks and closed vans of various patterns. There are some 150 feet of track, the great majority of which is of "Lowko" type.

I remain, Sir,
Yours truly,
J. G. GLOVER,
Director, G.M.R.

Oundle.

Advantages of the "Child's Plaything."

To the Editor, MODEL RAILWAY NEWS.

DEAR SIR,

May I be allowed to say a few words in reply to the letter of "Interlock" in the October issue on "The Electric Explosion."

He leads off by saying that the "clockwork" loco is a child's plaything, but not worth the attentions of the real "model railwayist." May I be allowed to suggest, from personal experience, that herein "Interlock" shows complete ignorance of certain circumstances?

To quote my own case: My model railway—in locos, rolling stock, size and equipment *anything* but a "child's plaything"—was instituted as a means for experimenting in all directions in the *signalling* section (which, incidentally, has not been without fruit on the full-size railway). I found that for certain experiments I needed moderately heavy trains (*i.e.*, ones that would not disappear after slipping a few coaches, etc.), and although making a point of keeping to scale appearance I did not feel inclined to buy the dearer steam or electric models, *which entail a continuous outlay*. Two or three years' experience convinced me that for a *given outlay*, a respectable clockwork "child's plaything" gave *greater power* than a steam or electric loco for the same money; also that once purchased the cost of maintenance of the two latter could be added to the funds of signalling.

I fully recognize "Interlock's" right to voice his own opinion (even as I now voice mine) and although heartily agreeing with his "hypocrit" "two-in-one" vehicle being cried down, I beg to express my warmest dissent to his ridiculously sweeping statement *re* clockwork locomotion.

I am,
Yours truly,

Swindon. THOS. WATSON.

The Electric Explosion Reaches Canada.

The Editor, MODEL RAILWAY NEWS.

DEAR SIR,

With reference to the article in the August issue by "Disgruntled" under the caption "An Electric Explosion," he is certainly a rabid fan (this is an American expression indicating super-enthusiasm) for the simon-pure electric type of loco and in some ways his arguments are incontrovertible, but he overlooks the fact that so long as the modern prototypes in use are steam-run engines, for the most part with the familiar steam outlines, then so long will the model maker, amateur and professional, conform to those standards in appearance even if not using the same motive force.

I fail to see that, if the electric system is used with the third rail and with steam outlines, electric-run locos, why there should be any unusual troubles with insulation and short circuits.

I have had my system in force (described in the September issue and since had a 50-feet garden extension put in on the same third-rail system) for several years, and a check up with a voltmeter the other day disclosed a 14-volt current at numerous points, including terminal sidings, etc., this being the exact voltage allowed to pass through the transformer 110v. A.C. house current. True, occasionally, at times there will be short circuits due to, perhaps, a derailed car on siding or a loose nail or metal particle dropping on track, but a little care will always disclose this. In the *outside* part the great thing is to keep the actual rails clear of any earthing circuit: *inside* I pack the sand and earthen roadbed right up to the sleepers, same as on real roadbeds. We have several feet of snow here in the winter, with zero weather, so I have built a snow plough for use and anticipate having a lively time keeping the track clear outside.

To my mind, to stick an electric-loco type engine on the head end of a made-up modern-type passenger model train spoils the illusion and I will have none of it. Some day the former kind will doubtless supplant the latter, and that will be time enough I think, for the enthusiast to remodel his locos to suit the then prevailing kind. I have travelled over some of the roads in the U.S.A. that are electrified, also in Europe. They are wonderful. They are the forrunners of the future motive power for all railroads.

Yours truly,

GERALD S. REES.

Nelson B.C. Canada.

P.S.—A great advantage of the electric is the easy natural control from one local point of reversing locos and automatic couplers cars—man handling is reduced to a minimum (and this is desirable). I can control my main circuit point from any one of any other six points, either starting, stopping or at speeds. In fact, the invisibility of controls adds to the naturalness of any model railroad.

Safety Hint for Stub Points.

To the Editor, MODEL RAILWAY NEWS,

DEAR SIR,

Herewith a suggestion for greater safety when trains are negotiating a "stub-point" turn-out. It consists of the running rails (R.R.) and pivoted point rails (P.R.), as per diagram on page 115 of Mr. Greenly's "Model Railways," with the addition of check rails (A) bolted to the pivoted points and check rails (A1 and A2) bolted to the running rails (R.R.) with, of course, the proper distance pieces to maintain the correct clearance between check and stock rails.

Yours faithfully,

J. C. WINGROVE.

Hammersmith.

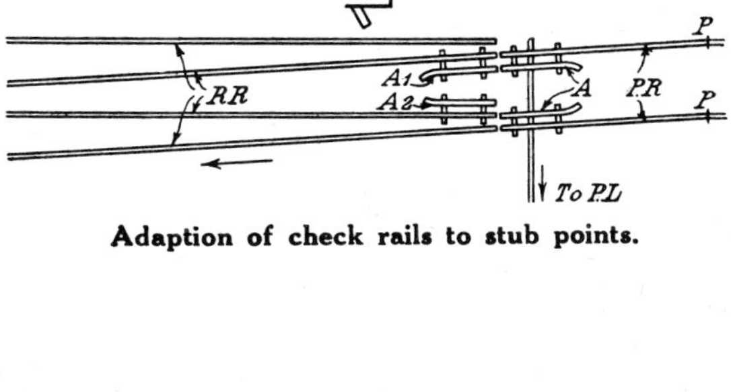

Adaption of check rails to stub points.

ANSWERS to CORRESPONDENTS

W. H. C. R. (London)—The keyed track is very good and key trouble is no more serious than it is on a full-size railway. As the manufacturers themselves will tell you, the only real drawback to the scale-model permanent way is the cost. We would prefer the spring steel chairs to cast white-metal chairs for the No. 1 gauge track proposed. Send to Mills Bros., 89, Ellesmere Road, Sheffield, and to Bond's, Ltd., Euston Road London, N.W., for samples of track, prices and particulars of point parts.

G. C. H. (Ealing, W.). — It is difficult for our trade supporters to make every type of accessory for every kind of vehicle. Therefore, amateurs will always have to make some minor details themselves. You should be able to make without much difficulty such fittings as G.W.R. type coach destination board brackets and G.W.R. door handles. With regard to scale speed there is a difference in opinion as to whether a speed should vary directly with the scale. We understand that our official model aeroplane experimenters use a square law function in comparing the model with the full-size article. Possibly Mr. Stevens, of Farnborough, who is a mathematician of distinction, as well as a model railway enthusiast, might be induced to explain the point in a scientific manner. Messrs. Mills Bros. of 89, Ellesmere Road, Sheffield, have made flexible vestibule connections in the past for their wooden coaches. For further details of "Scale Tonnage" *see* Greenly's "Model Railways."

H. R. N. (Brighton).—We have attempted several methods of dealing with your electric coloured-light signal problem, but with not much success. It is difficult to get at the basis of your scheme and why a semaphore signal system should be provided with a coloured light distant or whether you intend it to be a fully automatic series—operated system, such as Mr. H. L. Stevens (*see* Greenly's book, "Model Electric Railways"). It is not clear whether the semaphore is to be hand operated. However, as far as we see it there are many complications in the arrangement of a slotted signal working automatically and do not see the reason for introducing this when a straight auto-system with very short sections can be adopted. Another point arises in using Mr. Stevens' system and employing coloured-light signals. The signal current is the same as that passing through the locomotive in the section and will be of a fluctuating character, both voltage and amperage, which will not suit small lamps. You will, therefore, have to introduce relays of local batteries to work the lights.

J. C. W. (London, W.). — Your scheme is one method of arranging the cutting-in of separate sections and is quite good of its kind. The limitations are those which are inherent to any scheme which only has one controller. Personally, the writer likes to have a separate controller for the up and the down roads. When this is provided, all that is necessary is some safeguard against short-circuiting due to the accidental placing of controllers in opposite reverse position when the cross-over from an up to a down road is being used.

To Belfast Readers.

Mr. F. Keenan, of 5, Lothair Avenue, Antrim Road, Belfast, would like to get in touch with Model Railway enthusiasts in Belfast, and would be glad if they would write to him at the above address.

WITH THE CLUBS

The Model Railway Club.

At the meeting on October 22nd, another innovation was tried, with successful results, in the form of "Impromptu Talks." Members present were called upon to speak upon some specified subject, with the result that some really valuable "tips" were forthcoming. There is no doubt that much useful knowledge can be spread once the difficulty of getting members, unaccustomed to public speaking, on their legs is overcome.

Among the speakers were:—Mr. W. J. Bassett-Lowke on Present-day Continental Practice; Col. Henvey on Narrow-gauge Railways; Messrs. Fish and Straker on "0" Gauge Steam Locomotives; Mr. Lance on "0" Gauge Coaches; Mr. Hart on Spirit Burners and "Chicken Feed"; Mr. Lloyd Owen on the Economical Purchase of Track; and Mr. Keen on the Difficulties of the Trade.

Messrs. Thompson, Clarke, and other members also spoke. Fixtures for December:—December 10th: Track Night and Election of Hon. Auditors. December 31st: Annual Social.

Particulars of the Club may be obtained from the Hon. Secretary, R. Henvey, White Cottage, Shirley, near Croydon.

The Manchester & District Model Railway Club.

The first November meeting was held at Headquarters, the Clarion Café, Market Street, Manchester, on the 10th inst. There was a good attendance. Mr. R. A. Mills gave the second portion of his lecture on "Signalling." This was illustrated by means of a track, complete with junction, sidings, etc., marked on a long board and appropriately fitted with miniature signals fitted in slots. Mr. Mills, being a practical man in signalling, engaged the attention of his audience so thoroughly that a resolution was passed to have a special track in 00 gauge made. This will be similar to Mr. Mills's plan and will be equipped with 00 gauge passenger and goods trains, and correct signals.

Fixtures for December, 1925.

8th.—Club meeting at Headquarters, 7.30 p.m. A "Rummage" Sale will be held.

22nd.—Meeting at Headquarters, 7.30 p.m. Quarterly Subscriptions due.

It is expected that the 00 gauge "Signalling" track will be ready this month, and Mr. Mills has kindly consented to lecture on same.

All Manchester and local readers are strongly advised to join this club and be enabled to get the best out of their interest in railways, either model or full size. Full particulars from the Hon. Secretary, Archibald Dean, 29, Gorse Lane, Gorse Hill, Stretford, Manchester.

The Wimbledon & District Model Railway Club.

On October 19th, Mr. A. Stewart-Reidpath gave an informative lecture on "Model Track Laying," members gaining many valuable hints on this branch of the art. Mr. A. Earley's lecture "Austrian Railways," delivered on November 2nd, was also of great interest, the lecturer having first-hand knowledge of Central Europe railway practice.

Events for the month:—December 7th, 7.30 p.m. Red Cross Hall, Church Road. Lecture on "Railway Bridges," by Mr. H. Cook.

December 21st, 7.30 p.m. Welcome Hall, High Street, Wimbledon. Social Evening and Exhibition. Competition for the 1925 "Shephard" Cup and other prizes. Prize list. Club Cup, 1925, given by Mr. W. H. Shephard, for the best piece of work made during the year (junior or senior). 1st prize senior, One guinea, Sir Joseph Hood, Bart., J.P.; 1st prize junior, One guinea, Mr. C. F. Cook; 2nd prize senior, Half-guinea, and 2nd junior, Half-guinea, given by the Club; and 3rd junior, Five shillings, Mr. A. R. Walkley. Half-guinea prize by Mr. R. Shephard for best drawing of any railway appliance.

Rules:—(1) Models must be in the Hall by 7.15 p.m. Entries close at 7.45 p.m. (2) Only members who have paid their subscriptions eligible, but any may exhibit in the loan section. (3) Models must have been started after January 1st, 1925, and must be the work of amateur members of the Club. (4) A white card containing full particulars in block letters must accompany each entry. Competitor's name, whether senior or junior, and a list of parts not made by the entrant should be stated.

Members should see that exhibits are in the hall as early as possible after 6.30 p.m. Visitors are heartily welcomed, a small charge of 6*d*. admission being made to non-members. Refreshments will be obtainable. Doors open 7.30 p.m., proceedings will continue until 9.45 p.m.

Any further particulars can be obtained from the Hon. Secretary, R. Shephard, 27, Bernard Gardens, Wimbledon.

Wimbledon Model Railway Club Exhibit at Croydon.

In connection with the Surrey Handicrafts Exhibition held at the Public Hall, George Street, Croydon, on October 6th to 9th, there was a comprehensive show of models loaned by members of the Wimbledon Model Railway Club. The Club exhibit was staged in a separate hall from the main Exhibition, a small charge being made for admission, the proceeds, after deducting expenses, etc., being devoted to the same object as the Exhibition as a whole.

The smaller models were excellently arranged by Mr. A. Knock, on a series of tables down one side of the hall. In front were the small-scale club track and the large passenger-carrying track.

This latter served to form a barrier between the visitors and models and greatly added to the moral effect of the artistic "Do Not Touch" notices supplied by Messrs. Hudson and Dawkins, Balham, S.W. 12. Various club announcements, photos of the Kearney Railway and a really excellent show of S.R., L.M.S., G.W.R. and Underground posters, kindly loaned by these companies, formed an appropriate background. Mr. Temple's $\frac{3}{4}$-in. scale and Mr. Lamb's $\frac{1}{2}$-in. scale locos were frequently in steam on the large track and many 0 gauge trains were running on the smaller one and never failed to arouse interest. Although we have not space to describe all the models shown in detail, every member who exhibited should feel that his help in making the show a success is fully appreciated by the Club as a whole. Mr. Knock's 0-gauge set-piece, representing a country station, and a similar lay-out in 00 gauge by Mr. W. P. Ashdown, were very effective.

The members who worked so hard in setting up, arranging and dismantling the exhibits and those who placed motor transport at our disposal deserve special thanks; theirs was no light task at times. We should not forget those who kindly took charge during the time the exhibition was open; they had an interesting and sometimes amusing time, cheerfully answering the many questions, intelligent and otherwise, put to them by the interested visitors. A pleasing feature was the many congratulatory remarks made upon the standard of workmanship shown. Especially appreciated were the kind comments of Southern Railway officials.

Bond's o' Euston Road, Ltd.

Model Price List.

Messrs. Bond's, Ltd., 254, Euston Road, London, N.W. 1 have issued a new price list for 1926. It is of small size, suitable for carrying in a pocket, and contains a great variety of illustrations and particulars of model supplies and complete models. It not only caters for model railway builders and users, but for model engineers in general. The branches of model engineering, locomotive, marine and stationary, are dealt with, and items such as gear-wheels and gearing, chair and sprocket transmission, screws, bolts, nuts and rivets required by constructors of mechanisms are included. We specially mention solid and turned brass wheels on axles for 00 gauge rolling stock to replace pressed tin wheels. Messrs. Bond claim that rolling stock fitted with these will travel 25 per cent. greater distance and will not derail. Also standard types of solid fuel boilers for $\frac{1}{2}$-inch or gauge 1 scale locomotive and to suit the new J.R. $\frac{1}{2}$-inch scale locomotive, made in copper with riveted and silver-brazed joints, "Torrid" fuel burners and 00 gauge parts and accessories. In a letter to us, Messrs. Bond remark "the convenient size of the list allows it to be carried in the pocket by day or an excellent bed book before falling asleep, worth awakening early in the morning to read and, placed under the pillow, will induce restful, refreshing slumbers, so that there is no need to be parted from it during the wh dismal round." We are not sure whether reading in bed at night is a good thing or to be advocated, but v.e concede that the catalogue is usefi l reading for model engineers in general and quite worth the price, *4d.*, asked for it.

Earl Model Co., Bayley Lane,

Coventry, have sent a copy of their price list of model railway rolling stock and supplies. It contains illustrations and prices of a variety of waggons for $1\frac{1}{4}$-in. to $1\frac{3}{4}$-in. gauges and particulars of a series to suit the now popular 00 gauge. There are also prices and particulars of various model railway buildings and accessories, such as locomotive sheds, coal offices, field signs and level indicators, fittings for building waggons and coaches, model bricks made of granite chippings and cement, and blue prints of rolling stock for gauges 0, 1 and 00. The price of the catalogue is *4d.* The various items constitute quite a useful range, and we have no doubt will be interesting to owners and builders of model railways.

Miniature Supplies for Model Railways.

Messrs. Miniature Reproductions Company, 21, Industry Road, Darnall, Sheffield, have sent a loose-leaf list with prices and particulars of their present range of goods. The firm are makers of models of all kinds for all purposes and specialize in material and supplies for 0 gauge railways. The list comprises station fittings, such as window frames, curving brackets and cranks, forked ends, point rods and reversing levers for 0 gauge track, waggons and waggon fittings of various kinds, and wheels. The prices are very moderate. We consider that this firm should be a useful source of supplies for builders of model railways. Repairs and rebuilding of all kinds of 0 gauge models, stationary engines and boilers is also undertaken, as example, converting a standard 0—6—0 engine into an outside cylindered 2—6—0 engine, and so on. Enquiries are welcomed and quotations given for locomotive, carriage and wagon stock to be built to uncommon or free-lance design. This list will be sent to any reader on receipt of fourpence to cover cost of postage.

News from Leeds.

We hear from the Leeds Model Co., Ltd., that an important reduction has been made in the price of their No. EA/26 L.M.C. controller for electric railways. This controller provides for six speeds in each direction and is now reduced from £3 15s. to £2 2s.

We have also received particulars of some recent tests of the L.M.C. standard four-coupled electric mechanism gauge 0.

These tests were carried out on the L.M.C. test track at Balm Road works, this track being 63 feet in circumference, having curves of 4-feet radius, and one turnout for a siding on which stand the coaches used for test loads. Tabulated below are the results.

MECHANISM ALONE.—First run. Current 8 volts. Consumption 2 amps. After a few laps, a load of 11 coaches was attached, and a weight of 3½ lb. fixed to the mechanism to give better wheel adhesion. Total weight of train hauled, 11¾ lb. Mechanism and weight, 4 lb. 13 oz. Current 8 volts 4 amps. After several laps there was no overheating whatever. The above runs had worn the initial stiffness off the gears and bearings, and, on being run light, the consumption had fallen to 1 amp.

MECHANISM IN STANDARD 4—4—0 TANK BODY.—A weight of 13 oz. was fitted in the bunker to give extra adhesion. A duration test was then given, hauling a bogie brake-van and a three-coach articulated train. The loco was running for 27 minutes non-stop, during which time it covered 1 mile 2 furlongs 26 yards, at an average speed of 15¼ secs. per lap of 63 feet.

The current consumption at the commencement of the run was 2 amps. but by the 80th lap it was reduced to 1·5 amps. which remained steady till the train was stopped.

Subsequent tests were carried out on, 6, 4 and 2 volts. Loads of 11 coaches were hauled on 6 and 4 volts, while on 2 volts a three-coach articulated set was successfully hauled at a speed of 19·5 secs. per lap. The loco was then weighted with ingots of white-metal, 5 lb. in all, and a train consisting of 20 coaches, 1 flat bogie truck and 15 goods wagons was started and hauled for 12 laps non-stop, a distance of 756 feet. The consumption was 3·5 amps. with 6 volts. The total weight of the train was 21 lb. and the loco 6½ lb., the drawbar pull being about 8 oz.

Hamley's New List.

An excellent new model railway catalogue of 48 pages, post free on request, has just been issued by Messrs. Hamley's, 200–202, Regent Street, London, W. 1. The main feature of the list is a complete new range of 0 gauge locomotives. These are 2—6—0 type with outside cylinders. They are produced in the colours of the L.M. & S., G.W.R. and L.N.E.R., and, though of similar size and type, have certain modifications in external details to a close representation to their prototypes. The list also gives particulars of a new form of extra large radius tinplate track, called "Sixfut," specially produced to meet the requirements of these new six-coupled engines. An attractive range of rolling-stock, track and accessories, and a section on boats, hulls, launch engines, steam fittings and tools complete a very interesting catalogue.

French Award for Messrs. Bassett-Lowke.

Messrs. Bassett-Lowke, Ltd., have been awarded a Diplome d'Honneur for artistic craftsmanship displayed in the models they exhibited at the recent Exhibition of Decorative Arts and Crafts at Paris.